Walter John Sedgefield

King Alfred's Old English Version of Boethius De Consolatione Philosophiae

Walter John Sedgefield

King Alfred's Old English Version of Boethius De Consolatione Philosophiae

ISBN/EAN: 9783337068752

Printed in Europe, USA, Canada, Australia, Japan

Cover: Foto ©ninafisch / pixelio.de

More available books at **www.hansebooks.com**

KING ALFRED'S
OLD ENGLISH VERSION OF
BOETHIUS

SEDGEFIELD

KING ALFRED'S
OLD ENGLISH VERSION OF
BOETHIUS
DE CONSOLATIONE PHILOSOPHIAE

EDITED FROM THE MSS., WITH INTRODUCTION
CRITICAL NOTES AND GLOSSARY

BY

WALTER JOHN SEDGEFIELD

M.A. MELB., B.A. CANTAB.
LATE SCHOLAR OF TRINITY COLLEGE, MELBOURNE

Oxford
AT THE CLARENDON PRESS
1899

TO

PROFESSOR EDWARD ELLIS MORRIS

M.A., LITT. D.

THIS BOOK IS GRATEFULLY DEDICATED

BY HIS OLD PUPIL

PREFACE

THIS edition of King Alfred's most personal and therefore most important work, may be regarded as a compromise, aiming as it does at meeting the wants of the scientific investigator of Old English on the one hand, and of the student of our literature on the other. The former has long been calling for a text which should faithfully reproduce the Cotton MS., and in offering him such a text I ask him to bear in mind the difficulty of the task. Even when MSS. are in perfect condition it is almost impossible to avoid errors in copying, as will be readily granted by those who have had experience of this kind of work; but when, as in the case of the chief MS. of the Old English *Boethius*, fire and water have played havoc with almost every page, the labour of deciphering and the liability to error are immensely increased. Individual pages of this MS. have received as much as an hour's scrutiny, and this scrutiny was repeated three or even four times in a few instances. By taking advantage of the rare intervals of London sunshine during the winter and spring months, I found much decipherable which in ordinary light would have remained hidden.

A fresh examination of this MS. by better eyes than mine may show that a few more letters and words can be made out, but I have made it a rule throughout only to print as clear what I could see really distinctly.

It may be remarked here that as Professor Bright in his *Anglo-Saxon Reader* gives some passages from King Alfred's *Boethius* based on a fresh collation with the Cotton MS., I have made a special re-collation of his text with that MS.

A complete edition of the Old English *Boethius* would include not only the text of both the English MSS., but also the Latin text, and perhaps a full collection of marginal scholia and passages from Latin Commentaries, to illustrate in detail King Alfred's obligations to the work of others. In default of such completeness it is hoped that the analysis by chapters and sections given in the Introduction will be useful in showing how far the King departs from his original. The copious extracts from the article by the late Dr. Schepss, whose untimely death removed one of the chief authorities on the textual criticism of *Boethius*, require but slight apology, as they throw what must to many be a new light on King Alfred considered as a maker of books. The facts known about this work are not many, and such as they are will be found collected in the Introduction, varied with a discussion of theories in the case of the Cotton *Metra*. These *Metra*, though included in the complete glossary forming part of Grein's *Bibliothek der angelsächsischen Poesie*, are also indexed in the Glossary of the present work, for the sake of completeness, especially as a number of new readings of the Cotton MS. are now given for the first time.

The Glossary, too, I have tried to make useful to the student of Old English who requires help in his reading, as well as to the phonologist, for whom it is primarily meant.

The interesting question of the dialect of the *Boethius* has not received more than a short notice, as it requires for its proper elucidation more room and time than I have been able to give.

My best thanks are due to Professor York Powell for kind assistance in collating parts of the Bodleian MS., and much sound advice ; to Professor A. S. Napier for supplying me with some valuable notes on several points ; to Professor Eduard Sievers for a communication on the subject of dialect ; to Ernst Krämer of Bonn for the loan of his collation of the Cotton *Metra* ; to Frau Professor Schepss of Speyer for kindly sending me some notes by her late husband ; to Sir Edward Maunde Thompson, and to Dr. Henry Sweet. Valuable help was given in verifying the references in the Glossary by two ladies whose names I am asked not to mention. Finally, I heartily thank the Rev. Dr. W. W. Skeat, whose kindly criticism and encouragement have been invaluable to a junior worker in his own field, who esteems himself fortunate to belong to the University and College so long adorned by the Elrington and Bosworth Professor of Anglo-Saxon.

CHRIST'S COLLEGE, CAMBRIDGE.
November 5, 1898.

INTRODUCTION

—◆—

§ i. *MSS.*

THE Old English version of Boethius' treatise *De Consolatione Philosophiae* is preserved, as far as is known, in three MSS., one of which is but a small fragment, and in one paper transcript.

1. The Cotton MS. (C) Otho A. vi (Wanley, p. 217) in the British Museum, bound up with a Latin life of Edward the Confessor, '*per Ailredum, Abb. Rievallis,*' contains a prose version of the Latin prose, and an alliterating version of the Latin carmina. It was injured in the fire which proved so disastrous to the Cotton library in 1731, but the loose leaves were rather more than a century later collected and carefully mounted in an album. Wanley thus describes this MS. as it was before the fire: '*Codex membr. in octavo grandiori, ex duobus simul compactis, confectum* (sic), *in quo continetur I fol.* 1 *Boethius de Consolatione Philosophiae, Saxonice per Ælfredum*

Regem versus, quo vivente, aut saltem paullo post obitum eius, hunc codicem scriptum credo.'

At the present time about three-quarters of the whole remain, mostly legible, though some leaves can only be properly read in a good light, and for a few even direct sunlight is necessary. The leaves vary in size from charred fragments a square inch or so in area to almost perfect specimens; but not one has quite escaped the action of fire or water. It seems that the latter element is responsible for most of the obliteration, for parts merely charred are generally easy to read by a strong transmitted light. There are now 129 leaves in C, the size of the most perfect being, on the average, about $7\frac{1}{4}$ by $4\frac{1}{2}$ inches. The first three leaves are missing, as well as one between fols. 79 *b* and 80 *a*, and two between fols. 127 *b* and 128 *a*. The usual number of lines to the page is 26 or 27, but occasionally 28; and about 7 words go to the line. The MS. is in one distinct and neat handwriting, generally written with a fine pen. The writing varies considerably in size, perhaps in part owing to the unequal shrinking of the vellum under the influence of intense heat, as it is frequently small at the top of a page, and grows larger towards the bottom. There is no formal division into chapters, but each of the Metra begins a fresh line, with a large space left for the initial capital, which has, however, not been written. Illumination is entirely absent. Paragraphs are generally marked by the use of small or medium capitals, but these, like the marks of punctuation, are not always logically used. Words are not run together, but letters are frequently combined, especially certain groups with the letter *e*, which has two forms, the short and the tall. A few prefixes, especially *ge-* and *be-*, are often separated from the main word ; and some common proclitics, such as *ne*, are merged in the following word, thus : *nemæg*.

Contractions are on the whole infrequent, especially at the beginning of the book, though they increase in number towards the end. The principal ones are *cwð=cwæð* (once or twice *cw̄ð*), *æft=æfter*, and now and then *þonn̄=þonne*. The letter *m* is not seldom replaced by a stroke over the preceding vowel, especially in dative forms. Punctuation, represented only by the dot or full stop, is fairly frequent in the prose, marking paragraphs rather than sentences ; but is rarer in the verse, which is externally in no way distinguished from prose. Of individual letters it may be noticed that *y* has a short tail curved to the left, and there is no dot above it ; *s* is either ſ or ꞅ, the form S only occurring as a capital. As a final, ð is used with few exceptions ; medially and initially *h* probably predominates, except in pronominal forms. Accents are rare, and occur chiefly on the adverb *a*, the verbal prefix *a-*, and on *god*, good, which however is generally written *good*.

Sir Edward Maunde Thompson believes C to have been written shortly after the middle of the tenth century, about 960–970 A.D. Dr. Henry Sweet, in his Anglo-Saxon Reader, ascribes it to the beginning of the tenth century, agreeing with Wanley, who saw it before it was injured, and referred it, as we have seen, to King Alfred's lifetime, or the period immediately following his death.

2. The Bodleian MS. (B), (Wanley, p. 64), formerly lettered on the back NE. C. 3. 11, now numbered 180

(2079), contains 94 leaves of vellum. The 12 fragments of another work formerly bound up with this MS. were in 1884 taken out of the binding, and are now numbered Bodl. Add. D. 98. The vellum pages, which have been much pared in parts, measure about $11\frac{1}{4}$ by $7\frac{1}{2}$ inches, and the written page fills a rectangle of about 9 by $6\frac{1}{2}$ inches. With few exceptions there are 24 lines of writing to the page, though as many as 27 lines have been frequently ruled, and about 11 or 12 is the average number of words to the line. The gatherings are of five or six plies each, and are generally numbered for the binder, the numerals i, ii, iiii, v, vii being marked on fols. 10*b*, 11*a*, 31*a*, 41*a*, 61*a* respectively. B is written and corrected in a bold English hand hardly earlier than the beginning of the twelfth century. The text has initials in red, blue, purple and green, at the beginning of chapters, and occasionally of sections, but these colours have not lasted as well as the ordinary ink, which is of a very legible dark brown. The writing grows rougher, and the vellum worse towards the end of the book. The text-writer has occasionally left small initials in the margin as guides to the rubricator.

The text is divided into forty-two chapters by Roman numerals written after the last word of the preceding chapter on the same line, while sections and paragraphs are marked by initial capitals of medium size. Punctuation, represented by the dot, is frequent, but not always logical. The mark of interrogation occurs once or twice, closely resembling the modern form (?). Accents are rare, except on one or two pages, where they have been sprinkled in profusion in an undecided manner, perhaps by a later hand. The chief contractions are a stroke over vowels denoting an omitted *m*, and the form *þōn* for *þonne*, both being very common. A curly mark above the line represents *-us* in the words *Papinianus* and *Apollinus* (p. 66, l. 30 and p. 116, l. 1). *Wæter* (p. 80, l. 18) is written *wæt* with a mark over the *t* denoting *-er*. The proper names *Caucaseas* (p. 43, l. 9), *Boetius* (p. 58, l. 29), and *Orfeus* (p. 101, l. 25), are written with initial capitals.

The original spelling is fairly well preserved in B for so late a MS., but a number of errors have crept in, letters and words being often omitted. In its text B agrees on the whole pretty closely with C, of which however it seems independent, and has moreover a table of contents at the beginning. A prayer is added at the end, written in a hand resembling that of the main text, of which it may have been an imitation[1]. A close examination decides against the identity of the two hands, which however may belong to the same school of handwriting. This prayer seems hastily written with a hard pen. One example of the continental *g* occurs.

It may be here noticed that the fragments (Bodl. MSS. Add. D. 98), formerly in the binding of MS. 180, are part of a folio double-column digest, apparently written in England in the beginning of the fourteenth century, with glosses. The writing on one of them in a sixteenth-century hand runs—'*Boetius de consolatiōe philosophiae translated into the Saxonic tūg by King Aelfred.*'

3. A fragment (N) of a third MS. was discovered

---

[1] This prayer is entered by Wanley in his Catalogue as a separate work distinct from B, under the heading *Oratio ad Deum*.

in 1886 by Professor A. S. Napier, of Oxford, whose transcript is printed with some words of introduction (in German) in the *Zeitschrift für deutsches Alterthum*, vol. xxxi. pp. 52–54 (vol. xix. part I, new series, 1887). Professor Napier says—'The following fragment of the Alfredian translation of Boethius in a hand of the first half of the tenth century forms the last leaf of MS. Bodl. 86. This leaf, which evidently has been used previously in the binding, was placed in its present position by the binder, and originally belonged to a small folio Boethius MS. The fragment formed the lower half of a leaf, and judging by the part missing between the two sides each page must have contained about thirty-eight lines. The writing is in parts very indistinct, as the letters are frequently blurred; the parchment is also perforated here and there, so that some letters are quite gone.'

Some years ago N was taken out and bound separately, but it has since been temporarily mislaid, so that the present editor has not been able to see it. The words in Professor Napier's transcript, which accurately represents the MS., are much run together, and no capitals are used. Contractions and accents are relatively frequent. The vowels *a* and *o*, following *h*, *m*, and *n*, are in some cases formed by a looped prolongation of the last stroke of these consonants below the line, a characteristic of the age of the fragment.

The relations of the MSS. are conjecturally represented in the following diagram, where A represents the archetype of B, C, and perhaps of N, and A_1 stands for the archetype of the Cotton Metra.

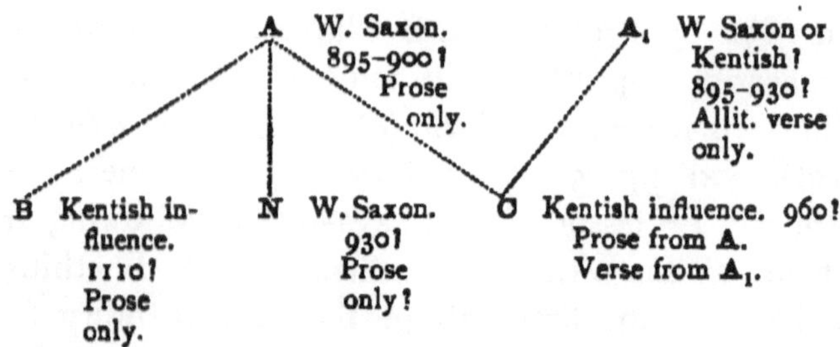

4. In the Bodleian library there is also a transcript (Jun. 12) of B, made by Franciscus Junius, with his selection of the more notable C variants in the margin ; also a good copy which he made of the Cott. Metra. As Junius made these excerpts and copy of C before the latter MS. was injured by fire, his readings are often our only authority for it. The whole of the transcript with the printed Latin text pasted in, and occasional notes by Junius, are bound up in one large folio volume. Wanley (Catalogue, p. 80) states that among the MSS. presented to the chapter of Exeter Cathedral by Bishop Leofric in the eleventh century was an Old English version of the *De Consolatione*, known as *Boeties boc on englisc*. Of its subsequent history we know nothing, unless perchance it was one of the MSS. just described. It is probable that such a popular work as the *De Consolatione* would have been frequently copied in its English dress during the tenth and eleventh centuries, so that it is somewhat surprising that only two perfect MSS. have reached modern times.

§ ii. *Present Edition.*

The present edition contains the three parts of the extant Old English version of the *De Consolatione*, viz. :

b

1. The prose version of the Latin prose original, common to B and C.

2. The prose version of the Latin *carmina*, only found in B.

3. The alliterating metrical version of the Latin *carmina*, only found in C.

As regards (1), the text adopted is that of C. Where C is uninjured and legible, the chief variants of B are given in footnotes, but variations constantly recurring, such as B's *mihte* for C's *meahte*, B's *ðam* for C's *ðæm*, &c., are not reproduced. Where C is injured or at all illegible, the text of B is printed, and the C readings preserved by Junius are given in footnotes marked J. If part of a word is visible in C the word is completed from B, or from J where available; for this the footnotes should be consulted. All words in the text not in C, or illegible in C, are in italics; all parts now missing from C are in square brackets, while words and letters not in C from the first are in round brackets. Words and letters in italics, but not in brackets, do occur in C but are not legible. In short, it may be assumed that *all words in italics are from B, unless otherwise stated in the footnotes.*

As regards (2) the text of B is printed, and these prose Metra are printed (in italics) just where they occur in B.

For (3), the Metra are printed together after the prose, though they occupy in C the places filled by (2) in B. The text is that of C, supplemented (in italics) where deficient from the transcript of the C Metra made by Junius, and also referred to as J in the footnotes. The numbering of these Metra was first made by Fox, and is here retained. Grein's arrangement of the lines is generally followed.

C is in parts much injured with holes in the parchment, which is also creased to such an extent that it is often impossible to indicate in a printed text exactly what is missing and what illegible. In such cases the passage is enclosed in square brackets, and a note is added to the effect that part is gone, part illegible in C.

Contractions are not expanded, but given as they occur. except in two or three instances noted above in the description of B. The wavy mark (~) over the *t* in *æft* (= *æfter*) and one or two other words is intended to stand for exactly the same sign as the straight mark printed in other cases, such as *ðōn, ðā,* &c., which in the MSS. is generally straight but occasionally somewhat wavy. The letters of the MSS. are not specially reproduced as to form, except that *ð* and *þ* are given as they occur in B, C, and J. The abbreviation 7 (= *and*) is after a full stop printed as a capital, but does not occur as such in the MSS. When a bracket bisects the digraph *æ* the latter is written *ae*.

Accents are marked where they occur in the MSS.

The particles corresponding to the German separable particles, and used in Old English either as adverbs or prepositions, such as *fram, of, on,* &c., are generally treated as prepositions when following their cases, if there is a regimen ; and as adverbs, where there is no regimen. In either case they are printed separately. Occasionally, however, they form true compounds with verbs, and are then printed as such both in the text and the glossary.

Emendations and conjectures, which occur chiefly

in the text of B, are mostly self-evident corrections of errors made by the scribe in copying. Many of these had already been made by Junius, and reproduced by later editors. In this edition only the more important emendations and conjectures suggested by Junius, and Grein (in the verse), and one by Professor Napier, are specially acknowledged. In addition to these, however, a considerable number have been made by the present editor, where they seemed necessary to an intelligible text. *All emendations and conjectures are marked as such in the footnotes.* The division of the prose text into sections was first made by Junius, who also supplied the references to the Latin original. A few corrections and alterations have been made in the former, and the latter have been carefully verified from Peiper's text (Leipzig 1871, Teubner). Where the beginning of a section does not coincide with a Latin section, the corresponding page and line in Peiper are given in a footnote. For the punctuation of the text the editor is responsible. That of the prose part is modernized for the first time, for convenience in reading. In the Metra, Grein's punctuation is followed on the whole, but with numerous exceptions. In Old English writings it is not always easy to clearly mark by punctuation the correlation of words and sentences, and the MSS. are frequently unsatisfactory and even misleading in this respect.

The fragment N is printed from Professor Napier's text as an appendix on pp. 205–206, but with modern punctuation and words separated ; contractions are left unexpanded except in the case of the looped *h*, *m*, and *n*, where the vowels are printed in italics (*v. supra*).

The Glossary is intended to give every word occurring in the text, and every instance, except of constantly recurring words. In these cases the first instance of the word's occurrence is given from the prose, and generally from the verse, and an *&c.* added. As the Glossary aims at being phonological rather than syntactical or lexicographical, a full record of forms is given, rather than of shades of meaning, though these latter have not been neglected. The prepositions indeed have been treated with some fullness, in view of their high syntactical importance and the interesting light they throw on the ways of thought of the early users of our language. It should be remembered that as the B text is here not printed in full, *the Glossary is incomplete as a register of B forms.*

§ iii. *Bibliography.*

1. *Previous Editions.* (*a*) By Christopher Rawlinson, Oxford, 1698, containing the whole text of B, the C variants, and the Cotton Metra; printed, with no additions (except a Latin preface and a number of quotations from early writers concerning King Alfred's authorship of the Old English *Boethius*), directly from the transcript by Junius above described. There is a full-page engraved portrait of Junius facing the title-page, after the picture by Van Dyck. The *imprimatur* of John Meare, Vice-Chancellor of the University of Oxford, is dated April 2, 1698. There are further a small copper engraving representing Boethius in his dungeon, with a female figure at his side, crowned with a halo and pointing upwards, and also a portrait of King Alfred, with the legend *Aluredus R. ex Lapide in Coll. Aenei Nasi.*

(*b*) By J. S. Cardale, London, 1829. The B text is

given, embodying emendations and conjectures, with English translation and explanatory notes, and a specimen of the Cotton Metra.

(*c*) King Alfred's Anglo-Saxon version of the Metra of Boethius, with an English prose translation and explanatory notes, by the Rev. Samuel Fox, M.A., of Pembroke College, Oxford.   William Pickering, London, 1835.

(*d*) Complete edition by the Rev. Samuel Fox, Bohn, London, 1864.   The text of the prose is that of B, apparently copied from Rawlinson's edition without collation with B itself.   Up to Chapter xxix, only the readings from C excerpted by Junius and printed in Rawlinson's edition are given in footnotes; afterwards these latter are supplemented by some more variants taken directly from C.   A literal English translation faces each page of the original.   The Metra of C are collected at the end of the book, apparently copied from the Junius transcript, or from Rawlinson, without fresh collation with C.   An English rhymed translation of the Metra, by Martin F. Tupper, is printed side by side with the text; there are some explanatory notes and a word-list at the end.

(*e*) The Cotton Metra are printed with critical notes and emendations in C. W. M. Grein's *Bibliothek der angelsächsischen Poesie*.

Hickes in his *Thesaurus* had printed some extracts from these Metra, using Rawlinson's edition.

Extracts from the prose and verse parts of the Old English Boethius are given in various Readers and Analecta, a list of which will be found in Wülker's *Grundriss zur Geschichte der angelsächsischen Literatur*.   Professor Bright in his Anglo-Saxon Reader has printed portions of the prose, embodying a fresh collation of C; in the other Readers the text of the editions is followed.

A facsimile of a page of Cott. MS. Otho A 6 is given in the Jubilee edition of the *Works of King Alfred the Great*, p. 515.

2. *Translations.* In addition to the translations given in the editions of Cardale and Fox, the latter's version of the Old English prose and Tupper's rhyming paraphrase of the verse are printed in the Jubilee edition of the *Whole Works of King Alfred the Great.* Tupper also published his version separately in 1850. A good deal of Alfred's Boethius is translated in Sharon Turner's *History of the Anglo-Saxons* (vol. ii. ch. ii, seventh edition, 1852), accompanying a full analysis of the work and a commentary, with a literal translation of the corresponding passages in the original Latin added in the footnotes.

In his *Proeve eener geschiedenis der dichtkunst en fraaje letteren onder de Angel-Saksen* (Amsterdam, 1842) J. P. Arend has some notes on Alfred's Boethius, followed by a Dutch translation of some passages (pp. 130–180). A part of the fable of Orpheus and Eurydice is translated into French in H. Taine's *Histoire de la littérature anglaise* (vol. i. pp. 59–63, eighth edition, 1892); and Grein gives an alliterating German version in his *Dichtungen der Angelsachsen.*

3. *Literature.* The question of the authorship of the Cotton Metra has been fully discussed by A. Leicht in *Anglia*, vi. 126–170; by M. Hartmann in *Anglia*, v. 411–450; and by O. Zimmermann in a dissertation published at Greifswald in 1882. Wülker in his *Grundriss* gives a *précis* of the researches and argu-

ments of these writers, and his own summing up. Leicht also wrote an article in *Anglia*, vii. 178–202, supplementing his first one, and containing notes on the MSS. (as represented in Fox's edition) and their phonology, and a comparison of the Old English version with the original Latin. In *Boethius, an Essay*, by H. F. Stewart (pp. 170–178), there is an interesting appreciation of Alfred's translation.

In a very suggestive article in the *Archiv für das Studium der neueren Sprachen* 94 (2 and 3), pp. 149–160, the late Dr. Georg Schepss showed that many illustrations and amplifications found in the Old English version of the *De Consolatione* and hitherto credited to King Alfred, especially those of a marked Christian tendency, are undoubtedly derived from Old Latin commentaries, belonging to two types, now represented by (1) a complete separate commentary bound up with the Boethius MS. written by Froumund in the tenth century and now belonging to the Öttingen-Wallerstein library at Maihingen ; and (2) the marginal Scholia of the Munich MS. no. 19452, written in the tenth or the eleventh century.

J. W. Tupper, in a dissertation published in Baltimore, U.S.A., in 1897, investigates the tropes and figures in the prose of the Boethius.

In *Modern Language Notes* for 1894 (no. 6), pp. 321–342, there is an article on the close connexion between the Alfredian Boethius and the Alfredian Soliloquies or 'Blooms.'

Max Rieger gives an analysis of the metre of the Cott. verses in his *Die alt- und angelsächsische Verskunst* (Halle, 1876), first published as an article in Zacher's *Zeitschrift für deutsche Philologie*.

A Latin MS. of the *De Consolatione* with Old English glosses (Corp. 214, Camb.) is described by Professor W. W. Skeat in the *American Journal of Philology*, v. (4) p. 488; but, as Dr. Skeat remarks, these glosses are in no way connected with Alfred's Boethius.

In Richard Wülker's *Grundriss zur Geschichte der angelsächsischen Literatur* will be found further information about the literature of the *Boethius*.

§ iv. *Relation to Latin Original.*

The following analysis by chapters and sections will serve to show the degree of correspondence between the Old English version and its Latin original, as represented in R. Peiper's text. It may be premised that the words 'close' or 'literal' have a looser sense than usual, as here applied to our version. Even in his most faithful translation, that of the *Cura Pastoralis*, King Alfred is by no means what would in these days be called literal; while in his *Boethius* it is the exception to find a passage of even a few lines rendered word for word.

ABBREVIATIONS.

ab.	= abridged.	*nL.*	= not in the Latin original.
add.	= addition(s), added.	*ps.*	= passage(s).
ch.	= chapter.	*r.*	= rather, fairly.
cl.	= close, literal.	*ref.*	= refers, referring.
ex.	= expanded, expansion.	*st.*	= sentence.
f.	= free.	*trs.*	= transposed.
l.	= line, lines.	*v.*	= very, greatly.
L.	= the Latin original.	*vv.*	= very greatly.

i *nL.* ii *r. cl.* iii = i, ii, iii, iv *of L. trs. and vv. ab. Ch.* . iv *of L. om. Metr.* iii *and* iv *om.* iv *r. cl. In* v § 1 ðære

heofoncundan Ierusalem *nL.* § 2 *r. cl., but simpler than L.*
v, vi *r. cl.* **vii** §§ 1, 2 *r. f. Metr.* ii 1 *om.* § 3 *v. f. and ex.
especially at end. After* smyltra yða (*p.* 17 *l.* 26) *is om.* nunc
procellis ac fluctibus inhorrescere. *After the allusion to
Croesus and Cyrus, a ref. to Paulus and the Persian King
is om.* § 5 *nL.* **viii** *vv. f.* **ix** *gives the sense.* **x** *Beginning
and end ex. The ps. ref. to Symmachus and the wife and
sons of Boethius is cl.* **xi** *gives sense, but is loose and full.
The last words,* þ wæron ealle þa halgan martiras, *are nL.*
xii *is more detailed than L. The application of the moral is
nL; no mention in L. of Christ and God.* **xiii** *r. cl. on the
whole.* **xiv** *First part r. cl., the latter half of* § 1 (*p.* 30 *l.* 3
to end) *is v. ex. In* § 3 *the passage* Gif ðu nu wære
wegferend *etc.* (*p.* 33 *l.* 8)=Tu igitur qui nunc contum
gladiumque sollicitus pertimescis, si uitae huius callem uacuus
uiator intrasses, coram latrone cantares. **xv** *r. cl. The
words* ac nu . . . forbaernð (*p.* 34 *l.* 7–10)=Sed saeuior
ignibus Aetnae Feruens amor ardet habendi. **xvi** *vv. ex.
The ref. in* § 1 *to Theodoric is nL. The explanation* se is
on Sicilia ðæm ealonde . . . wæs (*p.* 34 *l.* 28–30) *is nL.
Tarquin* (*l.* 31) *is not named in L. In* § 2 *the allusions
to gnats and the flea are nL.* (*p.* 36 *l.* 8 *and* 11). *The Latin
words* liberum quemdam *are mistranslated* romaniscum
æðelinge, se wæs haten Liberius (*p.* 36 *l.* 17). *The story of
Busiris* (*l.* 29 *et seq.*) *rests on* Busiridem accipimus necare
hospites solitum ab Hercule hospite fuisse mactatum. *That
of Regulus*=Regulus plures Poenorum bello captos in
uincla coniecerat, sed mox ipse uictorum catenis manus
praebuit. *The division between Books* i *and* ii *is wrong*
(*p.* 38 *l.* 6). § 3 *is vv. ex.; the latter half* (*p.* 38 *l.* 14 *to end*)
is ex. from 13 *l. of L.* § 4 *is more detailed than L., where
there is no mention of the heavenly power.* **xvii** *is nL. except
the first* 5 *lines.* **xviii** *In* § 1 *the words* (*p.* 41 *l.* 23) on
ðære bec ðe Astralogium hatte=astrologicis demonstra-
tionibus, *and* se towrat . . . anre bec (*l.* 27) *is nL. The rest*

of this § *is r. cl., as also are the remaining* §§ *of the ch. except the words* þ ge næfre ... manega ðioda (*p.* 42 *l.* 25), *the ref. to the Scythians* (*p.* 43 *l.* 10), *the blame cast on careless historians* (*p.* 44 *l.* 1–8) *and the concluding sentence of* § 3, *none of which are in L.*   **xix** *r. cl.* 'The bones of Weland' *is suggested by* ossa Fabricii. *The error* oðre naman Cassius (*p.* 46 *l.* 22) *should be noted.*   Cato *in L. is* rigidus Cato. **xx** *r. cl.;* frontem *is mistaken for* fontem (*p.* 47 *l.* 9). *The words* Ac seo orsorhnes ... windes pyf = illam uideas uentosam fluentem suique semper ignaram.   **xxi** *v. ex.* God = caelo imperitans amor.   **xxii** *ex. Last st.* § 1 = talia sunt quippe quae restant, ut degustata quidem mordeant, interius autem recepta dulcescant.   **xxiii** *r. cl.*   **xxiv** § 1 *is f. after the first few l.;* God (*p.* 52 *l.* 20) = bonum. *The last st. about the brooks and the sea is nL.*   § 2 *is r. cl.*   § 3 *has add. of slight importance; the words* buton ðæs getreowan freondes ... cræftas (*p.* 54 *l.* 15–22) *are nL. The latter part of* § 4, wenst ðu *etc.* (*p.* 55 *l.* 31), *is f. and ex.   The ps. on p.* 55 *l.* 28–31 *is nL.*   **xxv** *r. cl., except the last part,* seo ræst *etc.* (*p.* 57 *l.* 31 *to end), which is nL.* englum (*l.* 8) *is also nL.*   **xxvi** § 1 *r. cl., but* þ is God (*p.* 58 *l.* 8) *is nL.*   § 2 *r. cl. except last part* (*p.* 60 *l.* 15 *to end*).   § 3 *r. cl., but the words* 7 ðeah he erige his land mid ðusend sula = oneret bacis colla rubri litoris.   **xxvii** § 1 *r. ex.   The ps. about* Catulus (*p.* 61 *l.* 16 *to end*) = unde Catullus licet in curuli Nonium sedentem strumam tamen appellat. (*One Latin MS. has here* Catulus.)   § 2 *has add. The words* ðæs unrihtwisan cyninges Ðiodrices = Decorato. *The ps. on p.* 62 *l.* 24–31 *is nL.   In* § 3 *the last part* (*p.* 63 *l.* 27 *to end) is nL.*   § 4 *f.*   Hit wæs gio ... ænig is (*p.* 64 *l.* 11–16) = atqui praefectura magna olim potestas nunc inane nomen et senatorii census grauis sarcina: si quis populi quondam curasset annonam, magnus habebatur, nunc ea praefectura quid abiectius?   **xxviii** *f. but not ex.*   **xxix** *The first* 15 *l. of* § 1 *are an ex. of* 4 *in L.   The sent.* forðam cwæð gio *etc.* (*p.* 65 *l.* 27) = expertus sortis suae periculorum tyrannus regni metus pendentis supra uerticem gladii terrore simulauit. *The last part, beginning* Ac ic wat (*p.* 66 *l.* 4 *to end*), *is v. ex. In* § 2 *the allusion to Seneca in L. is simply* Nero Senecam familiarem praeceptoremque suum ad eligendae mortis coegit arbitrium (*cf. p.* 66 *l.* 23–29); *and the sent. relating to Papinianus* = Papinianum diu inter aulicos potentem militum gladiis Antonius obiecit. *The rest of the* § *is ex.* § 3 *r. cl., but the* Ultima Thyle *of L. is ex.* (*p.* 67 *l.* 32 *etc.*). **xxx** *In* § 1 sum sceop . . . nane eart = tragicus exclamat ὦ δόξα δόξα μυρίοισι δὴ βροτῶν οὐδὲν γεγῶσιν ὄγκον ὤγκωσας μέγαν. (*The Latin MSS. vary here.*) *The ps.* ealle men . . . meder (*p.* 68 *l.* 30) = uidetur namque esse nobilitas quaedam de meritis ueniens laus parentum. *The rest of the* § *is r. ex. In* § 2 forðam hi ealle comon of anum fæder 7 of anre meder (*p.* 69 *l.* 18) *is r. f., and the word* God *is nL.* **xxxi** *The chief add. in* § 1 *are,* 7 hu micele . . . ðurhteah (*p.* 70 *l.* 10–13), Gif nu hwa cwið . . . wrænnesse (*l.* 14–18), *and* forðæmðe manig wif . . . dæd wæs (*l.* 21–27). § 2 *r. cl.* **xxxii** § 1 *mostly r. cl.; but the last part,* 7 ðeah ðu *etc.* (*p.* 72 *l.* 8 *to end of* §) *is add. In* § 2 swa swa Aristotelis . . . lox (*p.* 73 *l.* 1–3) = Quod si, ut Aristoteles ait, lynceis oculis homines uterentur. § 3 *r. cl.;* se weg is God (*p.* 73 *l.* 24) *is nL.* **xxxiii** § 1 *is r. cl.* §§ 2 *and* 3 *f. and v. ex.* § 4 *f.* § 5 *vv. ex. from* 28 *l. in L.* **xxxiv** *The first half of* § 1 *is f., and last part ex.* swa swa sum micel æwelm . . . riða of (*p.* 82 *l.* 27) = quidam omnium fons bonorum. § 2 *r. cl. The middle part of* § 3 (*p.* 84 *l.* 18—*p.* 85 *l.* 2) *is nL. except the st.* ac we sculon . . . betst. § 4 *r. cl. except that the last few lines* (*p.* 85 *l.* 22 *to end*) = ueluti geometrae solent demonstratis propositis aliquid inferre quae porismata ipsi uocant. *The middle part of* § 5, se is stemn . . . áfæred (*p.* 86 *l.* 2–10) *is nL.* § 6 *v. ex. The chief add. are,* swa swa of ðære sæ . . . eft to sæ (*p.* 86 *l.* 18–22), swa swa nu saul . . . cræftas (*p.* 86 *l.* 29—*p.* 87 *l.* 9). § 7 *r. cl.* § 8 *f.*

*The allusions in L. to Tagus, Hermus, and Indus are not
rendered.* § 9 *f.* § 10 *r. cl.* Hwa mæg . . . anwald (*p.* 92
l. 7–10) *is nL. In* § 11 *the ps.* gif ðu ðonne . . . ær wæs
(*p.* 92 *l.* 25), *and* ðu meaht witan . . . asyndred (*p.* 92 *l.* 32—
p. 93 *l.* 6) *are nL. In* § 12 *there are considerable but
unimportant add.* **xxxv** § 1 *gives the sense fairly.* § 2 *f.
but not v. ex. The last sent.* ðone god *etc.* (*p.* 96 *l.* 22) =
Hoc quidquid est quo condita manent atque agitantur usitato
cunctis uocabulo deum nomino. *In* § 3 *the last part,* Nu ic
ðe andette *etc.* (*p.* 97 *l.* 13 *to end*) *is nL. In* § 4 *the first
half is r. cl., except the allusion to* ða wiðerweardan englas
(*p.* 98 *l.* 13), *which is nL. But the latter half, beginning*
Hwæt, ic wæt . . . (*p.* 98 *l.* 26 *to end*) *is an ex. of* Accepisti,
inquit, in fabulis lacessentes caelum gigantas: sed illos
quoque, uti condignum fuit, benigna fortitudo deposuit. § 5.
r. cl. In § 6 *the quotation from Parmenides is* πάντοθεν
εὐκύκλου σφαίρης ἐναλίγκιον ὄγκῳ (*cf. p.* 101 *l.* 3 *et seq.*). *In*
§ 7 *the story of Orpheus has numerous add. explanations, the
chief of which are:* Sio wæs on Creca rice . . . Orfeus
(*p.* 101 *l.* 24); Sio . . . Eurudice (*l.* 26); 7 ða stanas . . .
swege (*l.* 27); Ða sædon hi . . . dæges 7 nihtes (*p.* 102
l. 1–5); Ða ðohte he . . . swiðe oreald (*l.* 10–18). *These
last* 2 *ps.* = Infernas adiit domos, *and* stupet tergeminus
ianitor. *Next follow* ðe folcisce men hata ð Parcas (*l.* 22);
Ða hi secgað . . . wyrde (*l.* 24); Ða eode he . . . ðe he bæd
(*l.* 26–29); wæs to gebunden . . . scylde (*l.* 30); ðe hine
ær . . . hearpode (*p.* 103 *l.* 1–4); Ða eode . . . ðæs wifes
(*l.* 11–13). **xxxvi** §§ 1–5 *r. cl. In* § 3 *the words* ðe we
hata ð Saturnus . . . tungol *are nL.* (*p.* 105 *l.* 12–14). *In*
§ 6 hwæt, ða cild . . . ealdum monnum *is nL.* (*p.* 108
l. 8–12); *also* þ is God . . . to lufianne (*l.* 19–21), *and* þ ilce
. . . Gode (*l.* 24) *are nL.* § 7 *ex.* § 8 *v. f.* Swa swa
ælces . . . hrof ge flor (*p.* 110 *l.* 22–25) *is nL.* **xxxvii**
§ *v. f. and ex.* § 2 *r. f. The ps.* Nis þ eac . . . gebyreð
(*p.* 112 *l.* 20–27) *is an ex. of* uti currendi (*al.* currenti) in

stadio propter quam curritur iacet praemium corona. § 3
r. cl. Swa swa an mon . . . ær wæs (*p.* 114 *l.* 4–9) *is nL.*
§ 4 *r. cl. The ps.* ðe symle . . . ðæron (*p.* 115 *l.* 6–10) *is
nL.* **xxxviii** § 1 *is much more detailed than L. The first
part, as far as the mention of Circe (to p.* 116 *l.* 2) *is in L.*
'Vela neritii ducis Et uagas pelago rates Eurus appulit insulae.
§ 2 *f.*; swa swa great beam . . . swiðe earme (*p.* 117 *l.* 29–31)
is nL. The first part of § 3 *is r. cl. (to p.* 119 *l.* 9); *the rest
is ex.* § 4 *ex.* § 5 *f.*; unhale eagan (*p.* 121 *l.* 9) = oculos
tenebris assuetos, *and* ne magon . . . willan (*l.* 9–13) *is nL.;
also* forðæm hi ne lyst . . . lichoman (*l.* 19–29) *is nL. The
last part is v. ex.* § 6 *r. cl.* § 7 *not ex., but f. in parts.*
xxxix § 1 *r. cl. but the st.* lufie . . . mæg (*p.* 124 *l.* 16) *is
nL.* § 2 *r. cl.* Se ælmchtega God (*p.* 125 *l.* 14) = deus
rector. § 3 *ex. in the astronomical part at the beginning;
Saturn is not mentioned in L. In* § 4 *the ps.* ða race . . . fyre
(*p.* 127 *l.* 4–14) *is an ex. of* talis namque materia est, ut una
dubitatione succisa innumerabiles aliae uelut hydrae capita
succrescant. *The ps.* Forðæm hit . . . langan spell (*p.* 127
l. 26–29) *is nL. The last part of* § 5 *is f.;* deus *does not
occur in L. but only* diuina ratio *and* diuinae mentis. § 6 *r. cl.*
§ 7 *v. ex. from about* 10 *l. in L. In* § 8 *the ps.* sume
uðwiotan . . . heora scylda (*p.* 131 *l.* 8–15) *with the allusion
to* cristene men *is nL.* § 9 *r. cl.* § 10 *f.; a quotation from
Lucan is om.* Se godcunda . . . eagan (*p.* 133 *l.* 11–13) =
ἀνδρὸς δὴ ἱεροῦ δέμας αἰθέρες ᾠκοδόμησαν. § 11 *r. cl.* Ac hwæt
. . . goodan willan (*p.* 134 *l.* 9–13) *nL.; also* se gooda læce
þ is God (*l.* 16) *is nL.* § 12 *f. A quotation from the Iliad
(in Greek) is om.* § 13 *r. cl.;* oð domes dæg (*p.* 136 *l.* 8) *is
nL.* **xl** § 1 *r. ex.* § 2 *r. cl.* § 3 *f. In* § 4 *nearly all L.
om.; here there are a number of mythological allusions in
L.* § 5 *r. cl.; last part condensed. The last part of* § 6
condensed. Lib. v *carm.* 1 *om. In* § 7 englas (*p.* 140 *l.* 28)
= supernis diuinisque substantiis, *and the further ref. (l.* 31)
is nL. An ælmihtig God (*p.* 141 *l.* 7) = ille ab aeterno

cuncta prospiciens. ,**xli** *In* § 1 se gooda sceop ... selest
(*p.* 141 *l.* 11–13) *is nL., otherwise the* § *is r. cl.* § 2
condensed and feebler than L. Lib. v *carm.* 3 *and* 4 *are om.*
§ 3 *v. f. The account of Cicero* (*p.* 143 *l.* 5) *and what follows*
(*to l.* 15) *is nL. There is no ref. to God in L. The simile of
the steersman at the end is nL.* § 4 *gives the sense.* Sio
gesihð (*p.* 145 *l.* 24) = ratio *or* intelligentiae celsior oculus.
In § 5 *only the first* 5 *l. correspond to L. The rest is nL.
Lib.* v *carm.* 4 *and* 5 *om.* § 6 *gives the bare sense.* **xlii**
Here the L. is laid aside, except in God ece is (*p.* 147 *l.* 19),
and Hwæt is ecnes (*l.* 22); *all the rest to the end of the book
is nL.*

It may here be convenient to supply some notable
instances of the use, in the Old English version, of
early Latin commentaries. They are taken from the
article by Dr. Schepss, mentioned above.

The mention of 'the heavenly Jerusalem' (p. 11,
l. 17), which is not in the Latin text, is taken from
the commentary, which runs: (*hoc*) *tam ad Romae
civitatem quam ad ecclesiam seu ad caelestem Hieru-
salem referri potest* (Lib. i. prosa 5, Peiper, p. 19, l. 14).

The allusion to 'the holy martyrs' (p. 26, l. 21)
comes from the Froumund MS. commentaries (F),
which have *hic sanctos martires vult intellegi, qui, ut
beatitudinem perennem acciperent, diversa potius tor-
menta quam simplicem mortem desiderabant* (Lib. ii.
prosa 4, P. 35. 91).

The words *perennis sedes* and *humili saxo* (Lib. ii.
metr. 4, l. 1 and l. 15) are in the Munich commentary
MS. (M), explained in a Christian sense, and *in deo*
is written over *saxo*. F has *saxo id est in Christo*.
The Old English has *Crist* (p. 27, l. 7).

In the account of Nero's crimes (Lib. ii. metr. 6,

P. 43, *v.* 1 ff.) F and M explain *urbe flammata*
with the remark that Nero set Rome on fire, *volens
videre quantum fuerit incendium Troiae.* The Old
English has *æfter ðære bisene ðe gio Trogia burg barn.
Hine lyste eac geseon hu seo burne, hu lange, 7 hu
leohte be ðære oðerre* (p. 39, l. 20).

The passage on the elements and seasons (*p.* 49, *l.* 5
et seq.) does not occur in Boethius, but F and M give
explanatory notes to which the Old English version
closely corresponds.

In Lib. iii. met. 9 (Peiper 70, *v.* 1 *et seq.*) the word
numeris is annotated at some length, and here too the
Old English version closely follows the commentary
(*p.* 80, *l.* 5 *et seq.*).   In the commentary to the same
poem (*v.* 13 *et seq.*), we find a note explaining that by
the words *triplicis mediam naturae animam* we are to
understand *anima rationabilis*, together with *anima
irascibilis* and *anima concupiscibilis.*   The Old English
runs (*p.* 81, *l.* 17–19) *An ðara gecynda is þ heo bið
wilnigende, oðer þ hio bið irsiende, ðridde þ hio bið
gesceadwis.*

At the end of this poem the commentaries add the
words *per quem (per)veniamus ad te*; the Old English
has *ðe ealle men to fundiað.*

To the words of Boethius (Lib. iii. prosa 12, P. 83.
52) *nihil est quod naturam seruans deo contraire
conetur*, Alfred adds *buton dysig mon, oððe eft ða
wiðerweardan englas* (p. 98, l. 12, 13).   This seems
to be taken from the commentary, which, in speaking
of the devil, mentions that he was good *in sui natura*
but that he *voluntate deo resistit.*

In Lib. iii. prosa 12 (P. 84. 65) occur the words
lacessentes caelum gigantas.   In M. we find *loquitur*

secundum fidem gentilium vel veritatem tangit, quando divisio linguarum facta est.   This biblical allusion is not lost on King Alfred (p. 99, l. 6).

In Lib. iv. prosa 1 (P. 89. 33) M. annotates *domum* thus: *ad apicem pristinae intelligentiae mentisque secretum seu ad paradysum, ubi domus est naturalis.* The Old English version has (p. 104, l. 27) *to đære heofonlican byrig đe đu ær of come.*

The *gelidi senis* of Boethius in Lib. iv. metr. 1 (P. 90. 11) is explained as *Saturnus* in the commentaries.

In Lib. iv. metr. 5 (P. v. 1–3 ff.) *Arcturi . . . Bootes*, the commentaries explain *Bootes stella est in temone plaustri quae graece arctofilax vocatur, id est, custos plaustri . . . sidera quanto viciniora sunt cardini, tanto tardiores habent occasus et celeriores ortus, quoniam diu videntur, parvum autem occultantur.   Unde Bootes quia primus (proximus?) est cardini, parvo tempore occultatur, ergo semper tardius ad occasum quam ad ortum venit . . . Rursus, quanto longius fuerint sidera a cardine, celerius occidunt et tardius oriuntur.*   Compare with this the Old English (p. 126, l. 1 ff.).

The elaborate simile of the wheel contained in Chapter xxxix. § 7 of the Old English version (p. 129, l. 19) seems also to owe something to the words of the commentary.

Finally, the simile of the egg (Metr. xx. 169), which has generally been ascribed to King Alfred, is to be found indicated in the marginal scholia of the Froumund Codex in the words *Caelum et terram mareque in modum ovi figurari.*

Dr. Schepss further shows that Alfred might have avoided certain errors if he had been able to make consistent use of the commentaries above described. Thus Alfred speaks of *sumum romaniscum æðelinge, se wæs haten Liberius* (*p.* 36, *l.* 17), where the Latin text has *liber quidam;* but the commentaries refer the allusion to Anaxagoras, Zeno, or Anaxarchus.

Alfred's error *se wisa Catulus* for *Catullus* (p. 61, l. 17) may have been due to a faulty reading in his MS., or perhaps to the mention of Catulus in Orosius, but the commentary M has a note *nobilis et veronensis poeta*. The identification of Brutus with Cassius (*p.* 46, *l.* 22) seems to show carelessness or ignorance on Alfred's part, but at the same time he avoids some blunders which we find in the commentaries. For example, he does not regard *Alcibiades* as *nomen mulieris famosae pulchritudinis*, as is gravely set forth in the commentary F. The curious mistake which makes Ulysses a prince of Rhaetia (p. 115, l. 16 and Metr. xxvi. 8) is due to the reading *velani retii* for *vela neritii.*

Alfred seems to have left unused a mass of material contained in the commentaries regarding matters metrical, grammatical, and etymological, but eagerly availed himself of any hints and information he could get on Biblical, mythological, and historical questions, and all that related to what we now call natural science.

Dr. Schepss has undoubtedly made out a strong case, and has indicated a new field of inquiry which may lead to still further interesting discoveries of the same nature, as he has only dealt with the more notable of the explanations and expansions of the Latin text which have been generally ascribed to King Alfred. In this connexion William of Malmesbury's statement that Asser *sensum librorum Boetii de consolatione planioribus verbis enodavit* is of interest, as it almost looks as if Asser were the author of the above-mentioned commentaries F and M ; but, as Dr. Schepss points out, it is safer to believe that in the written and oral explanations which he gave the king, Asser made use of commentaries already in existence.

§ v.   *Dialect of text.*

The following short note kindly communicated to the Editor by Professor Eduard Sievers will be of interest. '' The dialect question (of the O. E. Boethius) is rather puzzling. The Bodl. MS. contains a good many Kenticisms, and so does Cott. The latter is evidently copied from an Early W. Saxon source, but the scribe has introduced Kentish forms here and there, especially his Kentish *e* for E. W. S. *ie*, and, what is perhaps of greater weight, Kentish *io* for E. W. S. (or O. E.) *eo*, as in *swior, ðiof ;* also *weoruld* for W. S. *woruld* (on the latter see *Beitr.* xxii. 255). It is only the *ĕo* which represents W. Germ. *eu* or *e* that is replaced by Kent. *io*, not the *ĕo* which stands for W. Germ. *iu* or *i*, and written *io* in E. W. S. too, as far as it exists. Then the Metra are so full of Kentish forms that I cannot but believe that they were done in Kent, and probably the versifier worked from a Kentish copy of the prose text. I have a short note on this question in *Beitr.* x. 197, but without amounting to proof I consider the following observation rather convincing. The prose text (*p.* 136, *l.* 23) reads thus : *þanon he welt ðam gewealdleðerum ealle gesceaftu.* The versifier makes *ðam gewealdleðerum* (Metr. xxix. 76) a regular half line ; consequently he

had to alter the words immediately preceding, and
I believe he did it this way:

> /.   /·*walded*|
> *ðanon he welt* | *ðam gewealdleðerum.*

Then he, or some scribe, copied out what he found
before him, but his eye was caught by the *welt*, and
so he wrote what we find in the Metra: *he ðonan
walded*[1] *ðam geweltleðrum.*   So the Kentish *welt* evidently was in the (original) prose text from which the
man worked.'   There are numerous other Kenticisms in
the text of both B and C, and this question of dialect
is one that calls for detailed investigation, as it may
throw light on the source of these two MSS.   An
examination of the Cott. Metra from this point of view
would probably lead to results regarding their authorship of greater value than those hitherto obtained by
other methods (*v. infra*).   The fragment N, which is
older than the other two MSS., is West Saxon, with
no important admixture of Kentish or other dialect.

§ vi.   *Authorship and date of the Work.*

That King Alfred translated into English the *De
Consolatione* of Boethius is testified by several early
writers of varying authority.   Æthelweard in his
Chronicle (Lib. iv. cap. 3 ad 901 A. D.) has this
passage: *Divinis quippe super omnia documentis im-
butus, nam ex Latino rhetorico fasmate in propriam
verterat linguam volumina, numero ignoto, ita varie,
ita praeopime, ut non tantum expertioribus sed et
audientibus liber (librum ?) Boetii lachrymosus quodam-
modo suscitaretur motus.*

William of Malmesbury says (*De Gestis Regum*

---

[1] Cott. MS. has *he ðone anwald deð*.   Ed.

Angliae, Lib. ii. cap. 4, § 122), *Hic* (i. e. Asser) *sensum librorum Boetii de Consolatione Philosophiae planioribus verbis enodavit, quos ipse rex in anglicam linguam convertit;* and a little further on he again speaks of Alfred's translation of the work. In his *Gesta Pontificum Angliae*, ii. 248 (page 177 of Hamilton's edition), occurs this passage, *Asserus...non usquequaque contempnendae scientiae fuit, qui librum Boetii de consolatione philosophiae planioribus elucidavit, labore illis diebus necessario, nostris ridiculo. Sed enim iussu regis factum est, ut levius ab eodem in anglicum transferretur sermonem.*

Robert Plot in his *Historia Naturalis Comitatus Oxon.* (cap. x, § 118) remarks that there seems to have formerly existed at Woodstock (Wudestoc) a Royal residence, dating from King Alfred's time, as it appears from a Cotton MS. (sub Othone A) that that King translated at Woodstock the *De Consolatione* of Boethius into 'Saxon.' Plot probably refers to MS. Cott. Otho A x, now destroyed except for a few charred fragments. Wanley in his Catalogue makes no mention of this statement alleged to be contained in the MS.

In the *Liber monasterii de Hyda* (edited by Edwards 1866) it is stated that Alfred caused the *De Consolatione* of Boethius as well as Gregory's *Dialogues* to be translated into the Saxon tongue by Bishop Wirefrith (i. e. Werfrith of Worcester). Several other early writers from whose works extracts are printed in the preface to Rawlinson's edition, such as Bromton, Polydorus Vergilius, Leland, and Bale, refer to Alfred's translation of the *De Consolatione* in nearly the same words as those just quoted.

Most modern critics have seen no reason to doubt

the tradition of antiquity and the express statement in the prefaces to the Old English version of Boethius, that King Alfred was its author. At least there has been no doubt as to his authorship of the prose rendering of the prose and verse of the original. The whole of this version bears the strong personal impress of its author, and in the views of life expressed, especially of a king's life, with its manifold cares and duties, we can hardly fail to recognize the great king's voice. Often groping darkly after the sense of his original and failing to find it, he is always earnestly trying his utmost to utter in his simple speech the high thoughts that surge within him.

But with regard to the authorship of the *Cotton Metra* there is not this unanimity. This question has been exhaustively treated in the articles already referred to, by Leicht, Hartmann, and Zimmermann, and nothing has since been contributed to its discussion. Ingenious arguments for and against Alfred's authorship have been brought forward, but it cannot be said that the question is settled. However, certain facts and conclusions have emerged from the discussion, and may be here shortly stated.

It is established beyond doubt that the Cotton Metra are based directly on the corresponding prose version found in B, without further reference to the Latin original. They reproduce in metrical dress the prose version, omitting little, and adding few thoughts of any importance; and they seem to have been composed by rearranging the words of the prose version, and inserting poetical commonplaces or 'tags,' to bring the lines into an alliterating form, much as a schoolboy might use a Gradus in making Latin verses.

It has been remarked that certain of the Latin Metra are translated in B, but omitted in C (Metra i. 6, ii. 2, iv. 7), and that it is precisely these Metra that in B lack the formulae which generally introduce and dismiss a metrum. This fact is used as an argument against the King's authorship of the Cotton Metra. But, on the other hand, it is pointed out that the prose version of Metr. i. 7 has also no formulae, but is nevertheless versified in C.

Leicht, who has investigated the question most thoroughly, shows that none of the usual arguments against the King's authorship amount to proof, whether those of an *a priori* nature, or those drawn from certain discrepancies observed in the correspondence between the B and C versions of the Metra. He himself, however, after carefully comparing one version with the other, finds that the alliterating Metra of C 'offer nothing fresh, such as we should expect of Alfred, but only a weak dilution of the terse and vigorous prose'; and accordingly he decides against the King's authorship. The consensus of critical opinion seems to be against Alfred's authorship of the prose and metrical prefaces, on the authority of which the authorship of the Cotton Metra is often ascribed to him; but nothing has been clearly proved one way or the other. The prose preface which is found in both B and C closely resembles certain passages in Alfred's preface to his translation of Gregory's *Cura Pastoralis.* It clearly states that King Alfred *'translated this book from Latin into English prose, and afterwards into verse (leoðe).'* The metrical preface makes the same assertion in more words.

Leicht shows that the prose preface could not have

been prefixed to the original version containing the prose translation of the Metra, but must have accompanied C only, or its archetype, and was afterwards added to later copies of the first edition, such as B. The Cotton Metra have been compared with the verses in the preface to Alfred's *Cura Pastoralis*, which Dr. H. Sweet in his edition of the latter work with some justice styles 'doggerel,' but they seem to stand on a rather higher level than these latter. They share certain characteristics with the West Saxon verse of the tenth century, and clearly belong to a period when the rules of Old English prosody, observed so carefully in the golden age of Cynewulf and in the Beowulf, were neglected, and perhaps almost forgotten. Thus the laws of alliteration of the classic poetry are often transgressed. Provided he has one or two words in the first half line alliterating with one in the second, or *vice versa*, the versifier does not much care what words bear the stress, while proclitics are at times divorced from their main words in a most inelegant manner.

In conclusion we may say that it lies with the opponents of the King's authorship of the Cotton Metra to prove their case, and this they have not done. An investigation of the language of these Metra may, however, throw some further light on the question. The King, we are told by Asser, was fond of the poetry of his native land, and learned much of it by heart, and we can well believe that he would please both himself and his people by adding a metrical version. His hearers, for readers were few in those days, would find even a rude rhythm more impressive and more easily remembered than the terser prose ;

and Alfred himself might perhaps, as an unpoetical, practical West Saxon, have regarded these Metra with considerable satisfaction. On the other hand, he may perhaps have commissioned some skilled *leoðwyrhta*, possibly a Kentish clerk, to undertake the versification, and the latter's version when incorporated into Alfred's prose may conceivably have passed from the first under the name of the King [1].

As regards the date when Alfred translated the *De Consolatione* no certain conclusion is possible. Critics vary greatly in their chronological arrangement of the King's literary works, arguing chiefly from *a priori* grounds, unfortunately almost the only grounds available. Wülker's view, that Alfred translated Boethius' treatise after the *Handboc*, the *Cura Pastoralis*, and the *Orosius*, about the year 897, seems reasonable, as our work does not look like the production of a novice in composition, but bears the stamp of a mature mind wielding the language with the ease that could only come from practice.

§ vii.

The references to B are given here in order not to further burden the margin of the text. Page and line of this edition are printed opposite each folio number.

7*a* = 12. 30	8*b* = 15. 16	10*a* = 17. 31
7*b* = 13. 24	9*a* = 16. 14	10*b* = 18. 26
8*a* = 14. 18	9*b* = 17. 7	11*a* = 19. 20

[1] Professor E. Sievers, in *Beiträge* (Paul and Braune), x. 197 *note*, declares against Alfred's authorship of these Metra, and says that he believes they were originally written in the Kentish dialect by a Kentishman, and based on a Kentish version of the prose text. Our MSS., B and C, according to Prof. Sievers, represent this Kentish text partially re-converted into W. Saxon.

$11b = 20.\ 15$	$32b = 53.\ 10$	$53b = 85.\ 8$
$12a = 21.\ 10$	$33a = 54.\ 2$	$54a = 86.\ 3$
$12b = 22.\ 8$	$33b = 54.\ 27$	$54b = 86.\ 28$
$13a = 23.\ 2$	$34a = 55.\ 22$	$55a = 87.\ 23$
$13b = 23.\ 27$	$34b = 56.\ 17$	$55b = 88.\ 17$
$14a = 24.\ 21$	$35a = 57.\ 10$	$56a = 89.\ 10$
$14b = 25.\ 15$	$35b = 58.\ 1$	$56b = 90.\ 3$
$15a = 26.\ 7$	$36a = 58.\ 27$	$57a = 90.\ 30$
$15b = 26.\ 31$	$36b = 59.\ 24$	$57b = 91.\ 24$
$16a = 27.\ 23$	$37a = 60.\ 15$	$58a = 92.\ 21$
$16b = 28.\ 21$	$37b = 61.\ 10$	$58b = 93.\ 16$
$17a = 29.\ 15$	$38a = 62.\ 11$	$59a = 94.\ 10$
$17b = 30.\ 11$	$38b = 63.\ 4$	$59b = 95.\ 4$
$18a = 31.\ 5$	$39a = 63.\ 30$	$60a = 95.\ 27$
$18b = 31.\ 31$	$39b = 64.\ 24$	$60b = 96.\ 19$
$19a = 32.\ 23$	$40a = 65.\ 16$	$61a = 97.\ 12$
$19b = 33.\ 17$	$40b = 66.\ 12$	$61b = 98.\ 6$
$20a = 34.\ 8$	$41a = 67.\ 3$	$62a = 98.\ 31$
$20b = 35.\ 2$	$41b = 67.\ 26$	$62b = 99.\ 26$
$21a = 35.\ 26$	$42a = 68.\ 16$	$63a = 100.\ 21$
$21b = 36.\ 20$	$42b = 69.\ 10$	$63b = 101.\ 16$
$22a = 37.\ 12$	$43a = 70.\ 1$	$64a = 102.\ 12$
$22b = 38.\ 3$	$43b = 70.\ 24$	$64b = 103.\ 5$
$23a = 38.\ 28$	$44a = 71.\ 19$	$65a = 103.\ 29$
$23b = 39.\ 18$	$44b = 72.\ 15$	$65b = 104.\ 25$
$24a = 40.\ 9$	$45a = 73.\ 8$	$66a = 105.\ 18$
$24b = 41.\ 6$	$45b = 73.\ 32$	$66b = 106.\ 15$
$25a = 41.\ 28$	$46a = 74.\ 24$	$67a = 107.\ 6$
$25b = 42.\ 25$	$46b = 75.\ 18$	$67b = 108.\ 3$
$26a = 43.\ 18$	$47a = 76.\ 5$	$68a = 108.\ 30$
$26b = 44.\ 10$	$47b = 76.\ 27$	$68b = 109.\ 25$
$27a = 45.\ 3$	$48a = 77.\ 17$	$69a = 110.\ 19$
$27b = 45.\ 27$	$48b = 78.\ 10$	$69b = 111.\ 8$
$28a = 46.\ 18$	$49a = 79.\ 2$	$70a = 112.\ 2$
$28b = 47.\ 7$	$49b = 79.\ 23$	$70b = 112.\ 26$
$29a = 48.\ 4$	$50a = 80.\ 9$	$71a = 113.\ 22$
$29b = 48.\ 27$	$50b = 80.\ 32$	$71b = 114.\ 14$
$30a = 49.\ 19$	$51a = 81.\ 19$	$72a = 115.\ 8$
$30b = 50.\ 7$	$51b = 82.\ 7$	$72b = 116.\ 4$
$31a = 50.\ 28$	$52a = 82.\ 30$	$73a = 116.\ 26$
$31b = 51.\ 22$	$52b = 83.\ 24$	$73b = 117.\ 17$
$32a = 52.\ 16$	$53a = 84.\ 16$	$74a = 118.\ 11$

$74b = 119.\ 4$	$81b = 129.\ 24$	$88a = 139.\ 25$
$75a = 119.\ 27$	$82a = 130.\ 18$	$88b = 140.\ 20$
$75b = 120.\ 18$	$82b = 131.\ 13$	$89a = 141.\ 11$
$76a = 121.\ 11$	$83a = 132.\ 6$	$89b = 142.\ 3$
$76b = 122.\ 4$	$83b = 132.\ 29$	$90a = 142.\ 30$
$77a = 122.\ 30$	$84a = 133.\ 21$	$90b = 143.\ 27$
$77b = 123.\ 21$	$84b = 134.\ 13$	$91a = 144.\ 20$
$78a = 124.\ 12$	$85a = 135.\ 7$	$91b = 145.\ 12$
$78b = 125.\ 7$	$85b = 135.\ 30$	$92a = 146.\ 6$
$79a = 125.\ 31$	$86a = 136.\ 19$	$92b = 146.\ 29$
$79b = 126.\ 21$	$86b = 137.\ 10$	$93a = 147.\ 18$
$80a = 127.\ 14$	$87a = 138.\ 6$	$93b = 148.\ 14$
$80b = 128.\ 5$	$87b = 138.\ 30$	$94a = 149.\ 5$
$81a = 128.\ 31$		

ADDITIONS AND CORRECTIONS

On p. 32, l. 16, read *dierran ðonne.*   MSS. omit *ðonne.*

On p. 89, l. 22, the em. *ðæsternes* was suggested by E. Thomson; see Fox, p. 358, n. 44.

On p. 94, l. 7, B has *ealle gesceafte 7 ealle wuhta*; l. 22, B has *ic wite* with *ic* erased.

On p. 190, *n.* 3, for *wyrst* read *wyrst.*

Metr. xxix, l. 7, read *fyrene ne mot*; C om. *ne*; l. 8, read *monan* for C's *monna*, as Leicht suggests (*Anglia*, vi. 151).

GLOSSARY.—Diminish by one each line-number of p. 91 and of p. 112 after l. 11.

Several references to p. 50 are a line out.

s.v. ābcdecian, for 71. 12 read 71. 17.

s.v. āscierpan, the *pp. ascerped*, p. 47, l. 27, had better perhaps be taken as connected with *sceorp*, and = equipped, prepared; the Latin has *succinctam.*

s.v. āstīeran, dele *astyrest* and *astyrast* which belong to *āstyrian.*

s.v. dōm, add *domes dæg* 120. 31.

s.v. dysilic, dele 42. 10.

s.v. fær, for *aspect?* read *motion.*

s.v. forbūgan, dele *prevent.*

s.v. gierwan, add *pp.* gegyrewod 32. 27.

s.v. hwelc, for *us* read *usual.*

For *locian* read *lōcian*, and for *lucude* 11. 1 read *locude* 11. 1.

s.v. gemyndwierðe, supply ' *worthy of mention.*'

s.v. sæstrēam, for *seaman* read *water of the sea.*

PROEM

ÆLFRED KUNING wæs wealhstod ðisse bec, 7 hie of boclædene[1] on englisc wende, swa hio nu is gedon. Hwilum he sette word be worde, hwilum andgit of andgite, swa swa he hit þa sweotolost 7 andgitfullicast gereccan mihte for þam mistlicū[2] 7 manigfealdum weoruldbisgum[3] þe hine oft ægðer ge on mode ge on lichoman bisgodan. Ða bisgu us sint swiþe earfoþrime[4] þe on his dagum on þa ricu becoman þe he underfangen hæfde, 7 þeah ða þas boc hæfde[5] geleornode 7 of lædene to engliscū spelle gewende, 7 geworhte[6] hi eft to leoðe[6], swa swa heo nu gedon is; 7 nu bit 7 for Godes naman he halsað[7] ælcne þara þe þas boc rædan lyste, þ he for hine gebidde, 7 him ne wite gif he hit rihtlicor ongite þonne he mihte[8]; forþampe ælc mon sceal be his andgites mæðe 7 be his æmettan sprecan þ he sprecð, 7 don þ þæt he deþ.

15

---

[1] So also J, where the first vowel is apparently *e* turned into *o.*
[2] *mislicum* J.　　[3] So J, *wordū 7 bisgum* B.　　[4] *earfoðrimu* J.
[5] em. *hæfe* B.　　[6] *þa geworhte he hi efter to leoðe* J.　　[7] *healsað* J.
[8] *meahte* J.

HEADINGS OF CHAPTERS

I. Ærest hu Gotan gewunnon Romana rice, 7 hu Boetius hi wolde eft[1] berædan, 7 Ðeodric þa þ anfunde, 7 hine het on carcerne gebringan.

II. Hu Boetius on þam carcerne his sar seofiende wæs.

III. Hu se Wisdom com to Boetie ærest inne on þā carcerne, 7 hine ongan frefrian.

IV. Hu Boetius hine singende gebæd, 7 his earfoðu to Gode mænde.

V. Hu se Wisdom hine eft rete 7 rihte mid his andsworum.

VI. Hu he him rehte bispell bi þære sunnan 7 bi oðrum tunglum 7 be wolcnum.

VII. Hu se Wisdom sæde þā Mode þ him naht swiðor nære þonne hit forloren hæfde þa woruldsælða þe hit ær to gewunod hæfde ; 7 sæde him bispell hu he hit macian sceolde gif he heora þegen beon sceolde ; 7 be þæs scipes segele, 7 hu his gódena weorca ealra wolde her on worulde habban lean.

VIII. Hu þ Mod andsworede þære Gesceadwisnesse, 7 sæde þ hit hit æghwonan ongeate scyldig ; eac sæde þ hit wære ofseten mid ðæs laþes sare, þ hit ne mihte him geandsworian. Þa cwæð se Wisdom: þ is nu git þinre[2] unrihtwisnesse þ ðu eart fulneah forþoht[3]; tele nu þa gesælþa wið þam sorgum.

IX: Ða ongan se Wisdom eft secgan bispell be þærę sunnan, hu heo oferliht ealle oþre steoran, 7 geþiostraþ mid hire leohte ; 7 hu þone smyltan sæ þæs windes yst. . .

[1] *eft* above line. [2] *þiře* B. [3] em. *foþoht* B.

B 2

X. Hu Boetius sæde hu swytole ongiten hæfde þ hit eall soð wære þæt se Wisdom sæde; 7 seo orsorhnes, 7 þa sælða þe he ær wende þæt gesælða beon sceoldan, nauhtas næran; 7 hu se Wisdom sæde þ he ne mihte gereccan þ he ungesælig 5 *wære; sæde þ his ancor wære þa git fæst on eorþan.*

XI. Hu seo Gesceadwisnes him andsworede 7 cwæþ þ heo wende þæt heo hine hwæthwegnunges ûp ahafen hæfde 7 fulneah gebroht æt þam ilcan weorþscipe[1] þe he ær hæfde; 7 acsode hine hwa hafde eall þ he wolde on þisse worulde; sume habbað 10 *æþelo 7 nabbaþ are.*

XII. Hu se Wisdom hine lærde, gif he fæst hus timbrian wolde, þ he hit ne sette up on þone hehstan cnoll.

XIII. Hu se Wisdom sæde þ hie meahtan[2] ða smealicor sprecan, forþamþe seo lar hwæthwegnunges eode on his 15 *andgit.*

XIV. Hu þ Mod cwæð hwi him ne[3] sceolde lician fæger land; 7 hu se Wisdom ahsode hwæt him belûpe to hira fægernesse.

XV. Hu seo Gesceadwisnes sæde hu gesælig seo forme 20 *eld wæs.*

XVI. Hu se Wisdom sæde þ hi hi woldon ahebban for þam anweald oð ðone heofen; 7 be Ðeodrices anwealde[4] 7 Nerones.

XVII. Hu þ Mod sæde þ him næfre seo mægþ 7 seo 25 *gitsung forwel ne licode, buton to laþe he tilade.*

XVIII, XIX. Be hlisan. Be hlisan.

XX. Be þære wiðerweardan wyrde, 7 be þære orsorgan.

XXI. Be þæs ælmihtigan Godes anwealde; hu he well eallū his gesceaftū.

30 *XXII. Hu se Wisdom 7 seo Gesceadwisnes hæfdon þ Mod aret ægþer ge mid smealicre spræce ge mid wynsuman sange.*

XXIII. Hu se Wisdom lærde þone þe he wolde wæstmbære land sawan, þ he atuhge of ærest þa þornas, 7 þa fyrsas, 7 þa 35 *unnyttan weod; 7 hu he sæde gif hwa biteres hwes onberede, þ him þuhte beobread þi swetre.*

---

[1] *weoþscipe* B.   [2] em. *mealtan* B.   [3] *ne* above line.   [4] *anweald* B.

XXIV. Hu menn willniað þurh[1] *ungelice gearnunga cuman to anre eadignesse.*

XXV. Hu God welt ealra gesceafta mid þam bridlũ his anwealdes, 7 hu ælc gesceaft wrigað wið hire gecyndes, 7 wilnað þ hit cume þider ðonan þe hit ær com.

XXVI. Hu se Wisdom sæde þ men mihton be Gode swelce hi mæte; 7 hwæþer se wela mihte þone mon gedon swa weline þ he maran ne þorfte; 7 hwæþer Boetie eall his woruld licode þa he gesælgost wæs[2].

XXVII. Hu se weorðscipe mæg gedon tu[3] *ðing: ðone dysegan þam oðrũ dysegũ weorþne; 7 hu Nonius wæs forcweden for þam gyldenan scridwæne; 7 hu ælces monnes yfel bið þy openre gif he anwald hæfð*[4].

XXVIII. Be Nerone ðam casere.

XXIX. Hwæðer[5] *þæs cyninges neawest 7 his freondscipe mæge ænigne mon weligne 7 waldendne gedon; 7 hu þa oðre friend cumað mid þā welan, 7 eft mid þam welan gewitað.*

XXX. Hu se scop sang þ ma manna fægnodon dysiges folces gedwolan þonne hie fægnedon soþra spella, þ is þ hi wendon his beteran þonne he wære; þonne fægniað hi þæs þe hi sceamian sceolde.

XXXI. Hu se sceal fela nearanessa geþolian þe þæs lichoman lustas forlætan nele[6]; *7 hu mon mæg ðy ilcan weorce cweþan þ netenu send gesælige, gif man cwið þ þa men sen gesælige þa heora lichoman lustum fulgað*[7].

XXXII. Hu þes anwearda wela merð þa men þe beoþ atihte to þā soðum gesælðum; 7 hu se wisdom is an anlipe cræft[8] *þære sawle, 7 is þeah betera ðonne ealle þæs lichoman cræftas; 7 þeah hwa gegaderie ealle þas andweardan god, þonne ne mæg he no þe raðor beon swa welig swa he wolde, ne he eft him næfð þ þæt he ær wende.*

XXXIII. Hu se Wisdom hæfde getæht þā Mode þa anlicnessa þara soðena sælþa; wolde hi þa selfe getæcan, 7 be bam fif gesælðum[9]: *þ is wela 7 anweald*[10] *7 weorðscipe 7 foremærnes 7 willa.*

---

[1] *þũh* B.   [2] *wæs* above line in B.   [3] *tũ* (twa) B.   [4] em. *hæf* B.
[5] em. *Hwðer* B.   [6] *sceal* (nele) B.   [7] *fyligað* (fulgað) B.   [8] em. *cræf* B.
[9] em. *gesæðum* B.   [10] em. *andweald* B.

*XXXIV. Hu se Wisdom hæfde gereht hwæt þ hehste god
wæs; wolde him þa gereccan hwær hit wæs, 7 hu of þam
mycelan gode cumað[1] þa læssan.*

*XXXV. Hu se Wisdom lærde þæt Mod þ hit sohte oninnan
him þ hit ær ymbutan hit sohte, 7 forlæte unnytte ymbhogan
swa he swiðost mihte; 7 hu God wealt ealra gesceafta 7 eallra
goda mid þā steorroðre his godnesse.*

*XXXVI. Hu þ Mod sæde þā Wisdome þ hit ongeate þ him
God reahte þurh hine þæt þ he rehte; 7 forhwy se goda God
læte ænig yfel beon; 7 hu seo Gesceadwisnes bæd þ Mod þ
hit sæte on hire scridwæne, 7 heo sceolde beon his ladteaw;
7 hu heo sæde þ tu[2] ðing wæren, willa 7 anweald; gif hwam
þara auþres wana wære, þ heora ne mihte naðer buton oþrum
nauht don.*

*XXXVII. Be þam ofermodan rican 7 unryhtwisan, 7 hu
mon hehþ þone heafodbeah æt þæs ærneweges ende, 7 hu mon
sceolde ælcne mon hatan be þam deore þe he gelicost wære.*

*XXXVIII. Be Troia gewinne; hu Eulixes se cyning
hæfde[3] twa ðeoda under þam casere, 7 hu his þegnas wurdan
forsceapene to wildeorū.*

*XXXIX. Be ryhtre[4] fiounge 7 be unrihtre, 7 be ryhtum
eadleane, 7 hu mistlicu witu[5] 7 manigfeald earfoðu[6] oft cumað
to þam godū swa hi to þam yfelū sceoldan; 7 be þære foreteo-
hunga Godes 7 be þære wyrde.*

*XL. Hu ælc wyrd beoð god, sam heo mannū god þince,
sam heo him yfel þince.*

*XLI. Hu Omerus se goda sceop herede þa sunnan, 7 be
þā freodome.*

*XLII. Hu we sceoldan eallon mægne spyrian æfter Gode,
ælc be his andgites mæþe.*

---

[1] em. *camað* B.   [2] *tū̆* B.   [3] *hæf* B.   [4] em. *ryhre* B.
[5] em. *mistlicum witū* B.   [6] em. *earfoðum* B.

ON ðære tide ðe Gotan of Sciððiu mægðe wið Romana rice
gewin up ahofon, 7 mid[1] heora cyningū, Rædgota 7 Eallerica
wæron hatne, Romane burig abrǣcon, 7 eall Italia rice þ is
betwux þam muntū 7 Sicilia þam ealonde in anwald[2] gerehton,
5 7 þa æfter þā foresprecenan cyningū Þeodric feng to þam ilcan
rice. Se Ðeodric wæs Amulinga ; he was cristen, þeah he on
þā arrianiscan gedwolan þurhwunode. He gehet Romanū his
freondscipe, swa þ hi mostan heora ealdrihta wyrðe beon. Ac
he þa gehat swiðe yfele gelæste[3], 7 swiðe wraðe geendode mia
10 manegū mane. Þ wæs to eacan oðrū unarimedū yflū þ hę[4]
Iohannes þone papan het ofslean. Þa wæs sum consul, þ we
heretoha hata ð, Boetius wæs gehaten[5] ; se wæs in boccrǣflū 7
on woruldþeawum se rihtwisesta. Se þa ongeat þa manig-
fealdan yfel þe se cyning Ðeodric wið þā cristenandome 7 wið
15 þā romaniscū witum dyde. He þa gemunde þara eðnessa 7
þara ealdrihta þe hi under þā caserū hæfdon heora ealdhlafordū.
Þa ongan he smeagan 7 leornigan on him selfū hu he þ rice þā
unrihtwisan cyninge aferran mihte, 7 on ryhtgeleaffulra 7 on
rihtwisra anwealde[6] gebringan. Sende þa digellice[7] ærend-
20 gewritu to þā kasere to Constentinopolim, þær is Creca heahburg
7 heora cynestol, forþā se kasere wæs heora ealdhlafordcynnes ;
bædon hine þæt he him to heora cristendome 7 to heora ealdrihtū
gefultumede. Þa þ ongeat se wælhreowa cyning Ðeodric, þa
het he hine * gebringan[8] on carcerne 7 þærinne belucan. Þa * 4a B.
25 hit ða gelomp þ se arwyrða wæs on swa micelre nearanesse

^a Cott. Metr. i.

[1] em. *mið* B.   [2] *anwal*ᵈ B.   [3] em. *gelæst* B.   [4] *he* above line B.
[5] ᵍᵉ*haten* B.   [6] *anweald* B.   [7] *digelice* B.   [8] *gebingan* B.

becom, þa wæs he swa micle swiðor on his mode gedrefed swa
his mod ær swiðor to þā woruldsælþū gewunod wæs ; 7 he þa
nanre frofre beinnan þā carcerne ne gemunde ; ac he gefeoll
niwol ofdune on þa flor, 7 hine astrehte swiðe unrot, 7 ormod
hine selfne ongan wepan 7 þus singend cwæð :   5

II ^a.

ÐA lioð þe ic wrecca geo lustbærlice song ic sceal nu heofiende
singan, 7 mid swiþe[1] ungeradū wordū gesettan, þeah ic geo
hwilū gecoplice funde ; ac ic nu wepende 7 gisciende ofgeradra
worda misfo. Me ablendan þas ungetreowan woruldsælþa, 7
me þa forletan swa blindne on þis dimme hol 7 me[2] þa bereafodon 10
ælcere lustbærnesse þa ða ic hī æfre betst truwode ; þa wendon
hi me heora bæc to, 7 me mid ealle from gewitan. To hwon
sceoldan la mine friend seggan ꝥ ic gesælig mon wære ?   Hu
mæg se beon gesælig se þe on þā gesælþū þurhwunian[3] ne mot ?

III ^b.

§ i. ÞA ic þa þis leoð, cwæð Boetius, geomriende asungen 15
hæfde, þa com þær gan in to me heofencund Wisdom, 7 ꝥ min
murnende mod mid his wordū gegrette, 7 þus cwæð : Hu ne
eart ðu se mon þe on minre scole wære afed[4] 7 gelæred ?   Ac
hwonon wurde þu mid þissū woruldsorgū þus swiðe geswenced ?
buton ic wat ꝥ þu hæfst þara wæpna to hraðe forgiten þe ic þe 20
ær sealde. Ða clipode[5] se Wisdom 7 cwæð : Gewitaþ nu
awirgede woruldsorga of mines þegenes mode, forþā ge sind þa
mæstan sceaþan.   *Lætaþ hine eft hweorfan to minū larū.

* 4b B.

Ða eode se Wisdō near, cwæð Boetius, minū hreowsiendū
geþohte, 7 hit swa niowul[6] þa hwæthwega[7] up arærde; adrigde 25
þa mines[8] modes eagan, 7 hit fran bliþū[9] wordū hwæðer hit
oncneowe his fostermodor[10]. Mid þā þe ða ꝥ Mod wið his[11]

---

^a Boeth. i. met. i. ' Carmina qui quondam,' &c. Cott. Metr. ii.
^b Boeth. i. pr. i. ' Haec dum mecum,' &c.

[1] em. *swi* B.   [2] *7 me* ab. l.   [3] em. *þuhwunian* B.   [4] *afeded* J.
[5] *cleopode* J.   [6] From J, *niowoul* B, written over *niwoll*.   [7] *hwæthwugu* J.   [8] From J, *minenes* B.   [9] *frægn liþū* J.   [10] *fæstermodor* J.   [11] *his* from J, om. B.

*bewende, þa gecneow hit swiðe sweotele his agne[1] modor ;
þ wæs se Wisdom ðe hit lange ær tyde 7 lærde.   Ac hit ongeat
his lare swiðe totorenne[2] 7 swiðe tobrocene[3] mid dysigra hondū,
7 hine þa fran[4] hu þ gewurde.   Ða andwyrde[5] se Wisdom hī
7 sæde þ his gingran hæfdon hine swa totorenne, þær þær hi
teohhodon þ hi hine eallne habban sceoldon ; ac hi gegaderiað
monifeald[6] dysig on ðære fortruwunga 7 on þā gilpe, butan
heora hwelc eft to hyre[7] bote gecirre.*

§ ii[c]. *Ða ongan se Wisdom hreowsian for þæs Modes tydernesse, 7 ongan þa giddian 7 þus cwæð : Eala on hu grundleasum
seaðe þ mod drigð, þōn hit bestyrmað þisse worulde ungeþwær-
nessa[8].   Gif hit þōn forget his ahgen[9] leoht, þ is ece gefea, 7
ðringð on þa frēdan þistro, þ sind woruldsorga, swa swa ðis
Mod nu deð, nu hit nauht elles nat butan gnornunga.*

§ iii. *Þa se Wisdō þa 7 seo Gesceadwisnes þis leoð asungen
hæfdō, þa ongan he eft sprecan 7 cwæð to þan Mode : Ic geseo
þ þe is nu frofres mare þearf þōn unrotnesse.*

§ iv. *Forþā gif þu þe ofsceamian[10] wilt þines gedwolan, þōn
onginne ic þe sona beran 7 bringe mid me to heofonū.   Þa
andsworode him þ unrote Mod 7 cwæð : Hwæt la hwæt, sint
þis *nu þa gōd[11] 7 þa edlean þe þu ealne weg gehete þā monnū   * 5a B.
þe þe heorsumian woldan ?   Is þis nu se cwide þe þu me geo
sædest þ se wisa Plato cwæde, þ was þ nan anweald nære riht
butan rihtū þeawū ?   Gesihst þu nu þ þa rihtwisan sint laðe 7
forþrycte, forþā hi þinū willan woldan fulgān, 7 þa unryhtwisan seondan[12] up ahafene þurh heora won dæda 7 þurh heora
selflice ?   Þ hi ðy eð mægen heora unriht gewill forðbringan hi
sind mid gifū 7 mid gestreonū[13] gefyrðrode.   Forþā ic nu wille
geornlice to Gode cleopian.   Ongan ða giddien, 7 þus singende
cwæð :*

---

[c] Boeth. i. met. 2. ‘ Heu, quam praecipiti,’ &c.   Cott. Metr. iii.

[1] *agene* J.   [2] *totorene* J.   [3] 7 *s. t.* ab. 1. B, *tobrogdene* J.   [4] *frægn* J.
[5] *7wyrde* B.   [6] em. *monifeal* B.   [7] *rihtre* J.   [8] em. *un-
geþhærnessa* B.   [9] So B.   [10] *onsceamian* J.   [11] *good* J.
[12] *siendon* J.   [13] *gestrodum* J.

IV d.

*EALA þu scippend heofones 7 eorþan; þu þe on þā ecan
setle ricsast, þu þe on hrædū færelde þone heofon ymbhweorfest,
7 þa tunglu þu gedest þe gehyrsume, 7 þa sunnan þu gedest þ
heo mid heore beorhtan sciman þa þeostro adwæscð þære
sweartan nihte.   Swa deð eac se mona mid his blacan leohte* 5
þ þa beorhtan steorran dunniað on þā heofone, ge eac hwilum
þa sunnan heore leohtes bereafaþ, þonne he betwux us 7 hire
wyrð; ge eac hwilū þone beorhtan steorran þe we hatað
morgensteorra, þone ilcan we hatað oðre naman æfensteorra*[1].
Þu þe ðam winterdagū selest scorte tida 7 þæs sumeres dahū* 10
langran; þu þe þa treowu*[2] þurh þone stearcan wind norþan
7 eastan on hærfesttid heora leafa bereafast, 7 eft on lencten
oþru leaf sellest þurh þone smyltan suðanwesternan wind.*

 *Hwæt, þe * ealle gesceafta heorsumiað, 7 þa gesetnessa þinra
beboda healdað, butan men anū; se þe oferheorð.   Eala þu* 15
*ælmihtiga scippend 7 rihtend eallra gesceafta, help nu þinū
earmum moncynne.   Hwy þu la Drihten æfre woldest þ seo
wyrd swa hwyrfan sceolde? heo þreat þa unscildigan 7 nauht
ne ðreaþ þam scildigū.   Sittað manfulle on heahsetlū, 7 halige
under heora fotū þrycað; stīciað gehydde beorhte*[3] cræftas, 7* 20
*þa unrihtwisan tælað þa rihtwisan.   Nauht ne deregað monnū
mane aþas, ne þ lease lot þe beoð mid þā wrencū bewrigen*[4].
*Forþā went nu fulneah eall moncyn on tweonunga, gif seo wyrd
swa hweorfan mot on yfelra manna gewill, 7 þu heore nelt
stiran.   Eala min Drihten, þu þe ealle gesceafta ofersihst*[5], 25
hawa nu mildelice[6] *on þas earman eorþan, 7 eac on eall moncyn,
forþā hit nu eall winð on þā yðum þisse worulde.*

V e.

§ i. *ÞA þ Mod þa þillic sar cweðende wæs, 7 þis leoð singende wæs, se Wisdom þa 7 seo Gesceadwisnes him bliðum*

---

d Boeth. i. met. 5. 'O stelliferi conditor,' &c. Cott. Metr. iv.
e Boeth. i. pr. 5. 'Haec ubi continuato dolore delatraui,' &c.

[1] em. *æfenþeorra* B.   [2] em. *treowa* B.   [3] em. *beorte* B.
[4] *beᵂrigen* B.   [5] em. *ofersiht* B.   [6] em. *midelice* B.

eahum on locodon[1] *; 7 he for þæs Modes geomerunge*[2] *næs
nauht gedrefed, ac cwæð to þā Mode : Sona swa ic þe ærest
on þisse unrotnesse geseah þus murciende*[3] *ic ongeat þ þu wære
ut afaren*[4] *of þines fæder eðele, þ is for*[5] *minum larum. Þær
5 ðu him fore of*[6] *þa þu*[7] *þine fæstrædnesse*[8] *forlete, 7 wendest
þ seo weord*[9] *þas woruld wende heore agenes ðonces buton
Godes geþeahte 7 his þafunge*[10] *7 monna gewyrhtū. Ic wiste*[11]
*þ þu ut afaren wære, ac ic nysste hu feor, ær ðu þe self hit me
gerehtest mid *þinū sarcwidū. Ac þeah þu nu fyr seo*[12] *ðon* * 6a B.
10 *þu wære, ne eart þu þeah ealles of þā earde adrifen, ðeah þu
þæron gedwolode. Ne gebrohte þe eac nan oðer man on þā
gedwolan butan þe sylfum þurh þine agene gemeleste*[13]*. Ne
sceolde þe eac nan man swelces to gelefan þær þu gemunan
woldest hwylcra gebyrda þu wære 7 hwylcra burgwara for
15 worulde ; oððe eft gastlice hwilces geferscipes þu wære on þinū
mode, 7 on ðinre*[14] *gesceadwisnesse ; þ is þ þu eart an þara
rihtwisena 7 þara ryhtwillendra ; þa beoð þære heofencundan
Ierusalem burgware. Of ðære næfre nan, buta*[15] *he self
wolde, ne wearð adrifen, þ is of his godan willan*[16] *; wære þer
20 he wære, simle he hæfde þone mid him ; þōn he ðone*[17] *mid him
hæfde, wære þær he wære, þōn wære*[18] *he mid his agnū cynne
7 mid his agnū burgwarū on his agnū earde þōn he wæs on
ðara ryhtwisena gemanan. Swa hwa þōn swa þæs wyrðe bið
þ he on heora þeowdome*[19] *beon mot, þōn bið he on ðam hehstan*[20]
25 freodome. Ne onscunige ic no þæs neoþeran 7 þæs* *unclænan * Here be-
stowe gif ic þe geradne gemete; ne me [*na*]*[21] ne lyst mid glase gins C.
[*geworht*]ra waga ne*[22] [*hea*]hsetla mid golde [7] mid gimmū
gerenodra, ne boca mid golde awritenra me swa swiðe ne lyst
swa me lyst on þe rihtes willan. [9]Ne *sece* ic no her þa bec, ac
30 þ ðæt þa bec *f*orstent, ðæt is, [*þin*] gewit. Swiðe ri[*h*]te þu
seofodes[*t þ*]a wóon wyrd ægþer ge on ða[*ra unr*]ihtwisra

---

[1] *eagum onlocude* J.   [2] *geomrunga* J.   [3] *murcniende* J.
[4] *utadrifen* J.   [5] *of* J.   [6] em. *hof* B.   [7] *þu* from J, om. B.
[8] em. *fætrædnesse* B.   [9] *sio wyrd* J.   [10] *geðafunga* J.   [11] *wisse* B.
[12] *fier sie* J.   [13] *giemelieste* J.   [14] From J, *winne* B, orig. *ðinne* B.
[15] *buton* J.   [16] em. *willa* B.   [17] em. *ðon* B.   [18] *wæs* J.
[19] *þeawdome*   [20] em. *hehtan* B.   [21] *no* J.   [22] *ne* om. B.

anwald[a] heanesse [*ge on m*]inre unweo[*rþ*]nesse 7 for-
se[*wenne*]sse ge on þara manfulra forðforlætnesse on ðas
weoruldspeda. Ac forþon þe þe is swa[1] micel unrotnes
nu get[2] getenge ge of þinum irre ge of þinre gnornunga, ic
þe ne mæg nu giet geandwyrdan ærþon ðæs tiid wyrð; foiðon 5
eall þ mon untiidlice ongynð næfð hit no æltæwne ende.

§ ii [f]. Þonne ðære sunnan scima on Agustes[3] monðe
hatost scinð ðonne dysegað se ðe þonne wile hwelc sæd
oðfæstan þæm drygū furum. Swa deð eac se ðe wintregum
wedcru[*m*] wile blostman [*se*]can. Ne meaht þu win wringan 10
* 1b C. on [*mide*[4]]winter, þeah *[*ðe wel lyste wearmes mustes*.

§ iii [g]. *Ða clipode se Wisdo*]m 7 cwæð: Mot ic nu cunnian
[*h*]won[5] þinre fæstræd[*nes*]se, þ ic þonan ongietan mæge
hwonon ic þin tilian scyle 7 hu? Ða andwyrde þ Mod 7
cwæð: Cunna swa þu wille. Ða cwæð seo Sceadwisnes[6]: 15
Gelefst ðu[7] þ sio wyrd wealde [*þi*]sse worulde, [*oð*]ðe auht
godes s[*wa*] geweorðan mæge [*but*]an þæm wyrhtan[8]? Ða
andwyrde [*þ Mod 7 cw*]æð: Ne gelyfe[9] ic no þ hit ge[*weorþan*]
meahte swa endebyrdlice, [*ac t*]o soðum ic wat ðætte God[10]
rihtere is his agenes weorces, 7 ic no ne wearð of þam soðan 20
gelea(*fan*)[11]. Ða andwyrde se Wisdom eft 7 cwæð: Ymb þ
ilce þu giddodest nu hwene ær 7 cwæde þ ælc wuht from
Gode wisse his rihttiman 7 his rihtgesetnesse fuleode, butan
men anum. Forðæ ic wundrige swiðe ungemetlice hwæt þe
sy oððe hwæt þu mæne nu þu ðone geleafan hæfst. Ac wit 25
sculon þeah giet dioplicor ymb ðæt bion. Ic nat ful geare
ymb hwæt þu giet tweos*t*; ges*ege* me, nu þu cwist þ ðu noht
ne tweoge þte God [*þi*]sse worul*de* rihtwisige[12], hu h[*e*]
* 2a C. *þon*]ne wolde þ heo wære. *[*Ða andwyrde þ Mod 7 cwæþ:
Uneaþe*] ic mæg forstandan[13] þine a*csunga*, 7 cwyst þe[*ah*] þ ic 30
þe andwyrdan scyle. Se Wisdom þa cwæð: Wenstu þ ic nyte

[f] Boeth. i. met. 6. 'Cum Phoebi radiis grave,' &c.
[g] Boeth. i. pr. 6. 'Primum igitur paterisne me,' &c.

[1] *swiþe* B.   [2] *get* om. B.   [3] *augustus* B.   [4] *midne* J.
[5] *hwŏn* B.   [6] *gesceaðwisnes* B.   [7] *ne lefs þu* B.   [8] *wyrhtum* B.
[9] *gelifde* B.   [10] *Gŏd* above line C.   [11] *gelea* occurs at end of line
in C; *fan* omitted.   [12] *rihtere sie* B.   [13] The *s* above line in C.

[*þone*] dem[1] þinre gedræfednesse þe þu [*mid*] ymbfangen
eart? ac sæge me hw[*elces*] endes ælc angin wilnige. Ða
andwirde ðæt Mod 7 cwæð: Ic hit[2] gemunde gio, ac me
hæfð þios gnornung ðære [*ge*]mynde benumen. Ða cwæð
5 se Wisdo[*m*] : Wast þu hwonan ælc wuht cume? Ð[*a*] andwyrde ꝥ Mod 7 cwæð: Ic wat ꝥ ælc wuht from Gode com.
Ða cwæð se Wisdom : Hu mæg þæt bion, nu þu ðæ[*t*] angin
wast, þæt ðu eac ðone ende nyte; forðæm sio gedrefednes
mæg ꝥ mod[3] *onstyrian*[4], ac hio hit ne mæg his *gewilles*
10 *bereafian*. Ac ic wolde þæt þu me sædes*t* hwæþer ðu wisse
hwæt þu self wære. Hit þa andwyrde 7 cwæð: [*Ic wat*] ꝥ
ic on libbendum men 7 on gescead[*wi*]sum eom 7 þeah on
deadlicum. Ða andwyrde se Wisdom 7 cwæð: Wastu
[*auht*[5]] oþres bi þe selfum to secganne buton ꝥ þu nu sædest?
15 Ða cwæð ꝥ Mod: Nat ic nauht oðres. Ða cwæð se Wisdom :
Nu [*ic*] hæbbe ongiten þine ormodnesse, *[*nu ðu self nast* * 2b C.
hwæt þu self eart, ac ic wat hu þin man tilian[6] *sceal. Forþam
þu sæd*]est ꝥ þu wræccea wære 7 berea[*fod*] ælces godes
forðon þu [*ne*]stes hwæt [*þu*] wære. Þa þu cyddest ꝥ ðu
20 nystes hwe[*lc*]es endes ælc angin wilnode, þa ðu wen[*d*]est
ðætte stiorlease men 7 recelea[*s*]e wæren gesælie 7 wealdendas
þisse [*w*]orulde ; 7[7] ðær þu cyddest[8] eac ꝥ þu nys[*t*]es mid
hwelcere[9] gerece God wilt ðisse [*w*]orulde, oðþe hu he wolde
ꝥ hio wære, [*þ*]a ðu sædest ꝥ ðu wende ꝥ þios sliðne [*w*]yrd
25 ðas worul(*d*)[10] wende buton Godes ge[*þ*]eahte. Eac ꝥ wæs
swiðe micel pleoh ꝥ [*ð*]u swa wenan sceoldes ; næs hit no
ꝥ an [*ꝥ*] þu on ungemetlicum ungesælðum wære, ac eac ꝥ þu
fulneah mid ealle forwurde. Ðonca nu Gode ꝥ he ðe gesul-
tumade ꝥ ic þin gewit mid ealle ne forlet. We habbað nu
30 giet þone mæstan dæl þære tyndran þinre hæl*e*, nu ðu
geliefæst ꝥ sio wyrd þurh [*hi*]e selfe *butan* Godes geþeahte
þas [*w*]eoruld wendan ne mæge. Nu ðu ne þe[*a*]rft þe nauht
ondrædan, forðæm[*þ*]e of ðæm lytlan spearcan þe þu mid

---

[1] *wol* B.   [2] *hit* om. B.   [3] From B, *mode* C.   [4] *astyrigan* J.
[5] From J, *aht* B.   [6] *getilian* B.   [7] 7 om. B.   [8] *cyðdest* B.
[9] *hwilcan* B.   [10] From B, *worul* C.

ðære tyndran gefenge lifes leoht þe onlyhte[1]. Ac hit nis
* 3ª C. giet se tima * þ ic þe [*healicor mæge onbryrdan, for*]ðæm hit
[*i*]s[2] ælces modes wis*e* þte [*sona*] swa hit forlæt soðcwidas,
swa folga[þ] hit leasspellunga. Of ðæm ðonne onginnað
weaxan þa mistas ðe þ mod gedrefað, 7 mid ealle fordwilmað 5
ða soðan gesihðe swelce mistas swe[*l*]ce nu on þinum mode
sindon. Ac [*ic*] hi sceal æræst geþinnian, þ ic siðð[*an*] ðy
eð mæge þ s[*oþe*] leoht on þe gebringan.

VI [h].

(Loca nu be þære sunnan 7 eac be oðru tunglu; þōn sweartan
wolcnu him beforan gað ne mahon hi þōn heora leoht sellan. 10
Swa eac se suðerna wind hwilu mid[3] miclum storme gedrefeð þa
sæ þe ær wæs smylte wedere glæshlutru on to seonne. Þōn heo
þōn swa gemenged wyrð mid ðan ypum, þōn wyrð heo swiðe
hraðe ungladu, þeah heo ær gladu wære on to locienne. Hwæt,
eac se broc[4], þeah he swife[5] of his rihtryne, ðōn þær micel stan 15
wealwiende of þā heohan munte oninnan feald 7 hine todæld
7 hī his rihtrynes wiðstent. Swa doð nu ða þeostro þinre
gedrefed nesse wiðstandan minū leohtū larū. Ac gif ðu wilnige
on rihtū geleafan þ soðe leoht oncnawan, afyr frā þe ða yfelan
sælþa 7 þa unnettan, 7 eac ða unnettan ungesælþa 7 þone yflan 20
ege þisse worulde, þ is þæt þu þe ne anhebbe on ofermetto on
þinre gesundfulnesse 7 on ðinre orsorgnesse, ne eft þe ne
geortrywe nanes godes on nanre wiðerweardnesse. Forðam
þ mod siemle bið gebunden mid gedrefednesse, þær þissa twega
yfela auðer[6] ricsað.)   25

VII [i].

§ i. Ða geswigode se Wisdom ane lytle hwile oð þ he
ongeat þæs Modes ingeþoncas. Ða he hi þ[*a*] ongiet*en*
hæ[*fde*], þa cwæð he: Gif ic þine unrotn[*esse on*] riht

---

[h] Boeth. i. met. 7. ' Nubibus atris,' &c. Cott. Metr. v.
[i] Boeth. ii. pr. 1. ' Post haec paulisper opticuit,' &c.

[1] *onliehte* B.   [2] *is* conj. om. B.   [3] *mid* above line.   [4] Some
words appar. omitted here, vid. Metr.   [5] em. *swiðe* B.   [6] em. *auðes* B.

ongieten hæbbe, þonn[*e nis þe n*]oh[*t*][1] swiðor þonne ðæt þ
þu fo[*rloren hæfst þ*]a woruldsælða þe þu [*ær hæfdest*, 7
geo]mrast nu forðæm þe hio [*o*]nhwyrfed is.   Ic ongiete
genoh sweot*u*le þ þa woruldsælða mid swiðe monigre swetnesse
5 swiðe lytelice olleccað þæm modū ða[2] hie on last willað swi-
þost beswican; 7 þonne æt nihstan, þonn[*e hy*] læs[*t*] wenað[3],
hi on ormodnesse[4] forlætað on þæm mæstan sare.   Gif þu
[*n*]u witan wilt hwonan hi[5] cumað, þonne meaht þu ongietan
þ hi cumað of woruldgidsunga.   Gif þu þonne heora þeawas
10 witan wilt, þonne meaht þu ongietan þ hie ne beoð nanū
men getreowe[6].   Be þæm þu meaht ongietan ðæt þu þær
nane myrhðe on næfdest *[*ða þa þu hie hæfdest, ne eft nane* * 4b C.
ne forlure þa] ða þu hi forlur[*e.   Ic wende þ ic þe*] geo
gelæred hæfde [*þ þu hi oncnawa*]n cuðe[7], 7 ic wisse þ [*þu hi*
15 *onscune*]dest ða ða þu. hi hæfdest, ðeah þu hiora bruce.   Ic
wisse þæt ðu mine cw[*id*]as wið hiora willan oft sædest,
ac [*ic*] wat þ nan gew[*una*] ne m[*æg*] nanum men[8] bion
onwend[*ed þ*] þ mod ne sy *be* sumū [*dæle onstyred*].   Forðæm þu [*e*]art eac [*nu of þinre s*]tilnesse ahworfen.

20   § ii[k]. Eala [*Mod, hwæt be*]wearp þe on ðas[9] care 7 on
þas g[*no*]rnunga?   Wenst[10] þu þ hit hwæt niwes sie oþþe
hwæthwugu *ungewunelices*[11] þ þe[12] on becumen is, swelce
oþrum *monn*ū ær þ ilce ne eglede?   Gif *þu* þonne wenst þ hit
on þe gelong sie[13] [*þ*] ða woruldsælða on ðe swa onwenda
25 sint, þonne eart ðu on gedwolan, ac swylce[14] hiora þea[*w*]as
sint;   hi beheoldon on ðe hiora agen gecynd, 7 on hiora
wandlunga hy gecyðdon hiora unfæstrædnesse[15].   Swylce
hi wæron rihte ða hi ðe mæst geolectan[16] swilce hi nu sindon,
þeah ðe hi ðe liolcen[17] on þa leasan sælða[18].   Nu ðu hæfst[19]
30 ongiten ða wanclan *[truwa*[20] *þæs blindan lustes.   Þa triowa* * 5a C.

[k] Boeth. ii. pr. 1. l. 24 P.   'Quid est igitur, o homo,' &c.

[1] *nauht* B.   [2] *þe* B.   [3] *wænað* B.   [4] *ofermodnesse* B.
[5] *hy* B.   [6] *ne treowe* B, for *getreowe*.   [7] *cuðest* B.   [8] *man* B.
[9] *þa* B.   [10] Instead of *Wenst . . . ungewislices* B has only *hwæt hwega
ungewunelices*.   [11] *ungewislices* J.   [12] *ðe* from B, *te* C.   [13] *se* B.
[14] In B *swelce* follows *sint*.   [15] *un* above line C, *fæstrædnesse* B.
[16] *geolettan* B.   [17] *oleccan* B.   [18] *leasū sælðu* B.   [19] From B,
hæft C.   [20] *treowa* J.

þe þe nu sindon opene hi sindon git mid manegū oðrū behelede.
Nu þu wast hwelce þeawas þa woruldsælða habbað 7 hu hi
hwearfiað.   Gif þu þōn heora þegen beon wilt 7 þe heora
þeawas liciað, to hwon myrnst þu swa swiðe ?   Hwi ne
hwearfost þu] eac m[*id him ?   Gif þu þonne heora*] untrio[*wa* 5
onscunige, oferhoga [1] *hi*] þonne [*7 adrif hi frā þe*] ; hi[2] spanað
[*þe to þinre unðearefe.   Ða*] ilcan þe þe [*gedydon nu þas*
gnornunga] forðæm þe þu hi [*hæfdest, þa ilcan þe*] wæren on
stilness[*e gif þu hi na ne*] underfenge.   Ða [*ilcan þe habbað*
nu heo]ra agnes ðonces [*forlæten* [3], *nales ðines*], ða ðe næfre 10
nan[*ne mon buton sor*]ge ne forlætað.   [*Þync*]að þe nu swiðe
diore [4] 7 swiðe le[*o*]fe ða ðing ða ðe nawðer [5] ne sint ne
getr*ewe* to habbanne, ne eac ieðe to forlætanne?   ac ðonne
hi hwæm frō hweorfende bioð he hi sceal mid ðæm mæstan
sare his modes forlætan?   Nu ðu hi ðonne æfter þinum 15
willan þe getrewe hab*ban* ne meaht, 7 *hy þe* willað *[on*
murcunga [6] *gebringan þōn hie þe fram hweorfað, to hwæm*
cumað hi þōn elles butan to tacnunge sorges 7 anfealdes sares ?
Ne sindon þa woruldsælþa ana ymb to þencenne þe mon þōn
hæfð, ac ælc gleaw mod beheält hwelcne [7] *ende hi habbað, 7 hit* 20
gewarenað ægðer ge wið heora þreaunga ge wið olecunga.   Ac
gif] þu wil[*t beon heora þegn*] [8] þon[*ne scealt þu georne geðolian*
ge]hwæt [*þæs þe to heora þenungū*] 7 to hiora [*þeawū 7 to*
heora willan] belipet.   Gif [*þu þōn wilnast þ*] hi for
þinū ðin[*gū oþre ðeawas*] nimen oðer hiora [*willa 7 heora* 25
gewun]a is, hu ne un[*weorþast þu þōn*] ðe selfne, þ ðu [*winsð* [9]
wið þā hlaf]ordscipe þe ðu [*self gecure, 7 swa*]ðeah ne [10]
meaht hiora [*si*]du 7 hio[*ra*] gecynd onwendan.   Hwæt, þu
[*wast*] gif þu þines scipes segl ongean þone wind tobrædest,
þ þu þonne lætæst eall eower færeld to ðæs windes dome.   Swa 30
eac [11] gif þu þe selfne to anwalde þæm woruldsælðum gesealdest
hit is riht þæt þu eac hiora þeawū fulgonge.   Wenst þu *þ
ðu þ [hwerfende] hweol þonne [hit on] ryne [wyrð mæge]*

---

[1] *oferhige* J.   [2] *forðæm hi* B.   [3] em. *forletan* B.   [4] *dyre* B.
[5] *nauðer* B.   [6] From J, *murnuga* B.   [7] em. *hwelne* B.   [8] *þegn 7
hiora hiera* J.   [9] So J, *wilt* B.   [10] *ne* om. B.   [11] *geac* B.

oncerran? Ne mih[*t þ*]u þon ma þara woruldsælða hwe[*ar*]-
funga onwendan.

§ iii[1]. Ic wolde nu giet ðæt wit ma[1] spræcen emb[2] ða
woruldsælða. To hwæm ætwit(*e*) ðu me ær þ þu hi for
minum *ðingū* forlure[3]? Hwi murc[*nast*[4]] ðu *wið min*, swelce þu
for min[*ū ðingū*] sie *ðines agnes* [*benumen, ægþer ge þin*]ra[5]
welona ge [*þines weorþscipes? ægþer*] þara þe com [*ær*[6] *from
me þa hi þe onlænde*[7] *wæron. Ute nu tellan beforan swilcum
deman swilce þu wille; gif ðu geseþan miht þ ænig deaðlic
man swelces hwæt agnes ahte, ic hit þe eft eal agife þ þu
gereccan miht þ þines agnes wære. Dysine 7 ungelæredne*[8]
*ic þe underfeng þa þu ærest to monnū become, 7 þa þe getydde
7 gelærde, 7 þe þa snyttro on gebroh*]te, *þe þu þa woruld*[*are
mid begeate, þe þu nu*] sorg[*iende anforlete*]. Þu meaht þæs
habban [*þanc þæt þu*] minra gifa *wel* bruc[*e. Ne miht*] þu no
gereccan þ þu [*þines auht for*]lure. Hwæt siofast þu [*wið
me? Habbe*] ic þe awer benumen þinr[*a gifena þara *ðe from
me comon? Ælc soþ wela 7*] soþ weorþscip[*e sindan*] minc
[*ag*]ne þeowas, 7 swa hwær swa ic beo hie bioð mid me.
Wite þu for soð, gif þ þine agne welan wæron þe þu mændest
þ þu forlure, ne meahtes[*t þu*] hi na forleosan. Eala, [*h*]u
yfele [*me do*]ð mænige weoruldmenn mid þæ [*þ ic ne mot
wealdan min*]ra agenra þea[*wa. Se heofen mot bre*]ngan
leohte [*dagas 7 eft þ leoht mid*] þeostrum [*behelian; þ gear
mot*] brengan blost[*man 7 þy ilcan gear*]e eft geniman; [*seo
sæ mot brucan*] smyltra yþa, [*7 ealle gesceafta*] motan hiora
ge[*wunan 7 heora will*]an bewitigan, [*butan me anum*]. Ic
ana eom benu[*men minra þeawa 7*] eom getogen to [*fremdū
þeawū þurh þ*]a ungefylledan [*gitsunge*[9] *woruldmon*]na.
Þurh ða gid[*sunga hi me*[10] *habbað*] benumen mines [*naman
þe ic mid*] rihte habban sceolde. [*Þone naman ic*] scolde

* 6b C
about here.

---

[1] Boeth. ii. pr. 2. 'Vellem autem pauca tecum,' &c.

[1] *mare* B.   [2] *ymbe* B.   [3] In B *forlure* follows *hi*.   [4] So J,
murcas B.   [5] em. *þira* B.   [6] From here to next square bracket
more than half gone from Cott., rest illegible.   [7] em.
onlande B.   [8] *Dysigne 7 unlæredne* J.   [9] *gitsunga* J.   [10] *me*
conject. om. B.

mid rihte hab[*ban þ ic wære wela*] 7 weorðscipe, ac hy [*hine habbað*] on me genumen, 7 hi [*me habbað ge*]sealdne [1] hiora wlencū [*7 getehhod*] to heora leasū welū, þ ic *ne mot [*mid*] minum ðeo[*wum*] min[*ra þe*]nunga f[*ulgan*]gan swa ealla oþra [*ge*]sceafta moton.   Ða mine þeowas si[*nd*]on wisdomas 5 7 cræftas 7 soðe welan; mid þæm þeowum wæs on symbel min plega; mid þæm þeowū ic eom ealne þone hefon ymbhweorfende, 7 þa niðemystan ic gebringe æt þæm hehstan, 7 þa hehstan æt ðæm niðemæstan; ðæt is þ ic gebringe eadmodness[*e*] on heofonum, 7 ða hefonlican god æt þæm 10 eaðmodū.   Ac þonne ic up gefere mid minum þeowū [*þo*]nne forseo we þas styrmendan woruld swa se earn ðonne he up gew*it* bufan ða wolcnu styrmendū wedrū, þ *him* þa stormas derigan ne mægen [2].   Swa ic wolde, la [*Mod*], þ þu þe fore up *to us* gif þe lyste, on þa gerad [3] þ þu *eft* mid us þa eorðan 15 secan wille for godra *man*na þearfe.   Hu ne wastu mine þeawas, hu georne ic symle wæs *y*mbe godra *man*na þearfe? Wast þu hu ic gew*and* ymb Croeses [4] þearfe Creca cyninges, þa þa hine Cirus *Pærsa cyning* gefangen hæfde 7 hine forbær*nan* wolde?   Ða hine mon on þæt fyr wearp þa alysde 20 ic *[hine mid heofonlicon rene.   Ac þu ðe fortruwu*]dest for þinre r[*ihtwis*]nesse 7 [*fo*]r þinum godan willan; wendest þæt þe nanwuht unrihtlices on becuman ne meahte, swelce þu wolde [5] þa lean eal þinra godena weorca on þisse weoruld habban.   Hu meahtest þu sittan on middū gemænū rice 25 þ ðu ne sceolde [6] þ ilce geþolian þ oðre men?   Hu meahtes þu bion on midre þisse hwearfunga þ [7] ðu eac mid ne hwearfode [7]?   Hwæt singað þa leoðwyrhtan oðres be ðisse woruld buton mislica hwearfunga þisse worulde?   Hwæt is þe ðonne þ þu þærmid ne hwearfie?   Hwæt recstu hu ge 30 hwearfigen nu ic [*siemle mid þe beo*]? ðe wæs þios hwe[*a*]rfung [8] *bet*ere forðæm þ ðe ðissa woruldsælða to wel ne lyste, 7 þæt ðu þe eac betre *na* gelefde [8].

---

[1] *geheldene* B.   [2] *mahan* B.   [3] From B, *geard* C.   [4] *Croesos* B.
[5] *woldest* B.   [6] *sceoldest* B.   [7] *þ þu eac mid earefoðe sū eofel ne gefeldest* B.   [8] *hwearfung sælþa to wel gelyste. 7 þ þu eac betera ne gelefdest* B.   *na* in text is from J.

§ iv [m]. Ðeah þæ[1] feohgitsere cume swa fela welena swa
þara sondcorna bið be þisum sæclifum oþþe þara steorrena
ðe þiostrū nihtum scinað, ne forlæt he þeah no ða seofunga
þ he ne seofige his ermða. Þeah nu God gefylle þara weligra
5 monna willan *[*ge mid golde ge mid seolfre ge mid eallū* * 8a C.
deorwy]rōnessum, swaðeah [*him*[2] *ne beoð se*] ðurst gefylled
hiora git[*sunga, ac s*]io grundlease swelgend hæfð [*swi*]ðe
mænegu westu holu[3] on to gadrianne. Hwa mæg þæm
wedendan gietsere geno[*h*] forgifan? Swa him mon mare
10 selð, swa hine ma lyst.

    § v [n]. Hu wilt þu nu andwyrdan þæm woruldsælðū gif hi
cweðað[4] to þe: Hwæt witst þu, la Mod, us? Hwi yrsast
þu wið us? On hwæm abulgon we þe? Hwæt, þe ongan
lystan ure, nales us þin; *þu* settest us on þ setl ðines sc[*eop*]-
15 pendes þa ðu [*w*]ilnodest to us þæs godes ðe ðu to hi[*m*]
sceoldes. Þu cwist[5] ðæt we hæbban þe beswicen*ne*, ac we
*magan cwe*þan ma þæt þu hæbbe us be[*swicene*], nu us ðurh
þine lust 7 þur[*h þin*]e gitsunga[6] onscunian sceal ea[*lra
ge*]sceafta sceppend. Nu [*þu eart scyldig*]ra þonne we, ægþer
20 [*ge for þinū ag*]nū unrihtlustum ge eac forðæmþe we ne
moton for ðe fulgan ures sceppendes willan; forðæmðe he
ure ðe onlænde æfter his bebodū to brucanne, *[nallas*[7] *þinre* * 8b C.
unrihtgitsunga gewill to ful]fremmanne. [*Andwyrde unc nu*],
cwæð se Wisdom, swa swa þu [*wille*]; wit geanbidiað þinre
25 o[*ndswore*].

VIII.

Ða cwæð þ Mod: Ic me ongite [*æghwo*]nan s[*cy*]ldigne,
ac ic eom *mid þæs* laðes sare swa swiðe ofðrycced þæt [*ic*]
inc geandwyrdan ne mæg. Þa cwæð se Wisdom eft: þ is
nu giet þinre unrihtwisnesse þ ðu *eart ful*neah forþoht. Ac
30 ic nolde þ þu þe forþohte, ac ic wolde þ ðe sceamode *swelces*
gedwolan; forðæm se se ðe hine forþencð se bið *or*mod, ac

[m] Boeth. ii. met. 2. 'Si quantas rapidis flatibus incitus,' &c.
[n] Boeth. ii. pr. 3. 'His igitur,' &c.

[1] *þæm* om. B.   [2] em. *hi* B.   [3] *manega weste hola* B.   [4] *cwðan* B.
[5] *wilt* B.   [6] *lustgitsunga* B.   [7] *nales* J.

se se ðe hine sce*amað* se bið on hreowsunga. Gif ⁰ þu nu
ge*mun*an wilt ealra ðara arw*yr*ðnessa þe ðu for þisse weoruld[*e
hæfdest*] siððan ðu ærest [*geboren wære oð*] *ð*isne *dæg : gif*
þu nu [*atelan* ¹] *wilt ealle* þa bliþnessa wið [*þā*] *unrotnessū*, ne
meaht ðu ſu[*leaþe cweðan*] ꝥ þu earm sie 7 unges[*ælig ;* 5
forþam ic] ðe geongne ² underſeng *unlydne* 7 unlæredne, 7
me to bearne genom, 7 to minum tyhtū getyde. Hwa mæg
þonne auht oðres cweðan but*an* ꝥ þu wære se ge*sælgesta,

* 9ª C.

þa þu me wær[*e ær leof þōn*]ne cuþ, 7 ær þon þa ³ ðu cuðe
min[*ne*] tyht 7 mine þeawas, 7 ic þe giongne gelærde swylce 10
snytro swelc m*an*egum oðrum eldran gewittum oſtogen is, 7
ic þe geſyrðrede mid minum larum to ðon ꝥ þe ⁴ mon to
domere geceas? Gif þu nu ſorðæm cw*ist* ꝥ þu gesælig ne
sie þe þu nu næſst ða hwilendlican awyrðnessa 7 ða
bliþn*essa* ⁵ þe þu ær hæſdest, þonne neart ðu þeah ungesælig, 15
forðæmðe ⁶ þa unrotnessa þe þu nu on eart swa ilce ⁷ oſergað
swa ðu cwist ðæt þa blissa ær dydon. Wenstu nu ꝥ þe
anum þellecu hwearſung 7 þillecu unrotn*es on* becume 7 nan*ū*
oðr[*ū*] mode swelc [*ne on*] become, ne ær þe [*ne æfter*] þe?
[*O*]þþe wenst þu ꝥte on *ænegū menni*ſcū mode mæge auht 20
fæstrædlices bion buton hwearſu[*nga? Oð*]ðc gif hit on
ænegum [*ænige hwile*] fæstlice wunað, [*se deaþ hit*] huru
aferreð ꝥ hit bion *ne mæg* þær hit ær *wæs*. Hwæt ſyndon ða
woruldsælða oðr*es* buton deaðes tacnung? *Forþam* se deað

* 9b C.

ne cymð to nanū *oðrū ðingu butan ꝥ he ꝥ lif afyrre* ⁸ *; swa* 25
*eac þa woruldsælða cumað to ð*æ *mode to þā* ꝥ hi hit ben[*im*]en
þæs ðe him leofaſt bið ðisse weorulde; þæt bið þonne þonne
hie him *fram* gewitað. Gesege, *la* Mod, hwæðer þe betere
þince, nu nanwuht woruldlices ⁹ fæstes 7 un[*h*]wearfiendes
bion ne mæg? Hwæðer ðe ðu *hi forsco,* 7 þines *agnes þonces* 30
hi forlete buton sare, þe þu *gebide* hwonne *hi* ðe sorgiendne
forlæten ?

⁰ Boeth. ii. pr. 3. l. 13 P. ‘ Verumtamen ne te,’ &c.

¹ *atellan* J.   ² C has either *geoncne* or *geonene, giungne* B.   ³ *þe* B.
⁴ From B, *þte* C. ⁵ *7 ða bliþn.* ab. l. in C. ⁶ *ðe* ab. l. in C. ⁷ *ælce* B.
⁸ *aferre* J.   ⁹ *nauht woruldrices* B.

IX p.

Ða ongan se Wisdom *singan 7 giddode þus:* ÞŌN *seo
sunne on hadrū heofone beorhtost*[1] *scineð, þon apeostriað ealle
steorran*[2]*, forþaþe heora beorhtnes ne beoð nan beorhtnes*[3] *for
hire. Þōn smylte blaweð suþanwestan wind, þōn weaxað*
5 *swiðe hraðe feldes blosman; ac þōn se stearca wind cymð
norðaneastan, þōn toweorpð he swiðe hraþe þære*[4] *rosan wlite;
swa oft þone to smylton sæ þæs norðāwindes yst onstyreð.
Eala þ nanwuht nis fæste stondendes weorces a wuniende on
worulde.*

X q.

10   *Þa** cwæð Boetius[5]: *Eala,* Wisdom, *þu þe eart* modor[6] *eallra*   * 10a C.
mægena, ne mæg ic na wiðcweðan ne andsac*igan þ þe*[7] *þu me
ær sædest, forþonþe hit is eall soð ; forþa ic nu hæbbe ongiten
þ ða mine sælða 7* sio *orsorgnes, þe ic ær wende þ gesælða beon
sceoldan, nane sælða ne sint, forðam hi swa rædlice* gewitaþ. Ac
15 *þ me hæfð eallra swiðost gedrefed þōn ic ymbe swelc* smealicost
þence, þ ic nu sweotole ongiten hæbbe *þ þæt is seo mæste*
unsælð on þys *andweardan life þ mon ærest weorðe*[8] *gesælig,
7 æfter þā ungesælig.* Þa andsworede *se* Wisdom *7* sio
Gesceadwisnes, *7 cwæð: Ne meaht þu* no mid soðe *getælan*
20 *þine wyrd 7 þine gesælða, swa swa þu wenst, for þā leasū
ungesælþū*[9] *þe þu ðrowast. Hit is* leasung *þ þu wenst ðæt
ðu sie* ungesælig. Ac gif þe *nu þ swa swiðe* gedref*ed 7*
geunrotsad hæfð (*þte þu forlure þa leasan gesælþa*), þonn̄ mæg
ic *þe openlice gereccan þ ðu swutole ongitsð þte þu* giet
25 hæfst * [*ðone mæstan dæl*] þara[10] gesælða þe [*þu ær*] hæfdest. * 10b C.
Saga me nu hwæ[ðer] þu mid rihte mæge siofian [þin]a
unsælða, swelce ðu eallunga [h]æbbe forloren þina gesælða ;

p Boeth. ii. met. 3. 'Cum polo Phoebus,' &c. Cott. Metr. vi.
q Boeth. ii. pr. 4. 'Tum ego, Vera, inquam,' &c.

[1] em. *beohtost* B.   [2] em. *þeorran* B.   [3] em. *beohtnes* B.   [4] em.
þær B.   [5] *beotius* B.   [6] *modur* B.   [7] *andsacigian þæs þe* J.
[8] *sy* J.   [9] *unsælðum* J.   [10] *þinra* B. (*þara*)

ac ðu hæfst get gesund gehealden eall þ *d*eorwyrðoste ðætte
þu ðe b*e*sorgost hæfdes.   Hu meaht þu þonne mænan þ
wyrse 7 þ laðre nu ðu ðæt leofre hæfst gehealden ?   Hwæt,
þu wast þ sio duguð ealles moncynnes 7 ðe se [*mæ*]sta
weorðscipe get leofað, þ is [*Si*]machus ðin swior.   Hwæt, he 5
is giet [*ha*]l 7 gesund, 7 hæfð ælces godes ge[*n*]og; forðon
ðe ic wat þ ðu auht[1] ne forslawode þte þu þin agen feorh
for hine *ne* sealde*st*[2] *gif* þu hine ge*sawe on* hwelcum earfoðū,
forðæm [*se*] wer is domes[3] 7 cræfta full, 7 geno[*g*] orsorg
nu get ælces eorðlices eges.   Se is swiðe sarig for ðinū 10
earfoðum 7 for ðinū wræcsiðe.   Hu ne liofað þin [*wif eac,*
þæs ilcan] Simaches dohtor ? 7 sio is swiðe [*wel*] gerad 7
swiðe gemetfæst; sio hæfð eall oþru wif oferðungen[4] mid
clænnesse.   Eall hire god ic þe mæg mid feam wordum

areccan ; *þæt is ðæt hio is on *ealū* [*þeawū hiere*] fæder gelic. 15
Sio liofað [*nu þe, þe anum, for*]ðæmðe hio nanwuht ell[*es ne*
lufað] buton þe.   Ælces godes hio hæ[*fþ*[5] *genoh on*] ðys
andweardan life, [*ac heo hit hæfð*] eall forsawen ofer ðe
[*anne*[6] *; eall heo hit*] onscunað, forðæmþe [*heo þe ænne*]
næfð; þæs anes hire is [*nu wana.   For*] þinre æfweardnesse 20
hire þincð [*eall*] noht þ hio hæfð, forðæm hio is [*for*] þinum
lufum ormod 7 fulneah [*dead*] for tearum 7 for unrotnesse.
[*Hwæt*] wille we cweðan be *þinum twam*[7] [*sunū*]?   ða *sint*
ealdormen 7 gcðeahtera[*s ; on*] þæm is *swiotol sio* gi*fu* 7 ealla[8]
ða[9] d[*ugu*]þa heora fæder 7 heora eldran *fæder*, swa swa 25
geonge[10] men magon gelicoste [*beon*] ealdum monnum.   Þy
ic wundrige h*wi* ðu ne mæge ongietan þ ðu eart nu git
swiðe gesælig, nu ðu *git liofost* 7 eart hal.   Hwæt, þ is sio
meste *ar deað*licra monna (þ *hie libban*) 7 sien hale; 7 þu
hæfst nu giet to eacan eall þ ic ðe ær tealde.   Hwæt, ic wat 30
þ þ is giet diorwyrþre þonne mon[*nes li*]f, forðæm mænegum
men is leo[*fre þæt*] he ær self swelte ær he gesio his wif 7

---

[1] *naht* B.   [2] Between *sealdest* and *gif* B has inserted ab. l. 7 *hu*
ne leofoð þin wif eac þæs ilcan Simaches dohter 7 sio is swiðe (repeated
below).   [3] *wisdomes* B.   [4] A letter appar. erased, between the ð
and *u* of *oferðungen*, in C; *oferðungen* B.   [5] em. *hæft* B.   [6] *anne* J.
[7] *twæm* J.   [8] *ealá* C.   [9] *ða* C.   [10] *giunge* J.

his beaŕh swelt[*en*]de. Ac hwi **[tilast[1] þu þōn]* to wepann*e* * 11b C.
buto[*n andweorce? Ne*] meaht ðu nu giet þinre [*wyrde
nauht*] oðwitan ne þin lif no [*getælan, n*]e eart þu no eallunga
to [*nauhte ge*]don swa swa þu wenst. [*Nis þe nu git*] nan
5 *un*aberendlic [*broc gelenge*], forðon (*ðin*) ancer is giet [*on
eorðan fæ*]st ; þ sint ða ealdor[*men*] þe we ær ymb spræcon.
þa ðe ne [*la*]etað geortrewan[2] be þys and[*wear*]dan life ; 7
eft þin agna treow*a* [*7 seo*] godcunde lufu 7 se tohopa, [*þa
ðr*]eo þe ne lætað geortr*ewan* be þam ecan life. ða and-
10 sworode *þæt unrote Mod* 7 *cwæð :* Eala, wær*an þa ancras
swa trume*[3] 7 swa ðurh*wuniende*, ge for Gode ge for *worulde,
swa swa þu segst ; þonne mihte we micle þy eð*[4] *geþolian swa
hwæt* earfoþnessa *swa us on* become. *Eall hie* us þyncað þy
leohtran ða h*wile þe* þa oncras *fæste* bioð. Ac þu *miht* þeah
15 ongitan hu þa mina sælða 7 se min weorðscipe (*her for
worulde*) is oncerred.

XI ^r.

§ i. Ða andswarode se Wisdom 7 seo Gescead[*wisnes*], 7
cwæð: Ic wene þeah þ ic hwæthwugununges **[þe up ahofe of* * 11b ends,
þære unrotnesse 7 fulneah gebrohte æt þam ilcan weorðscipe þe next fol.
20 *þu ær hæfdes, buton þu git to ful sy þæs þe þe læfed*[5] *is, þ þe* missing in
forðy wlatige. Ac ic ne mæg adreohan[6] *þine seofunga for* C.
*þam lytlan þe þu forlure ; forþā þu simle mid wope 7 mid
unrotnesse mænst gif þe ænies willan wana bið, þeah hit lytles
hwæt sie. Hwa wæs æfre on þis andweardan life, oððe hwa*
25 *wyrð get æfter us on þisse worulde, þ him nanwuht wið his
willan ne sie, ne lytles ne miceles ? Swiðe nearewe sent*[7] *7 swiðe
heanlice*[8] *þa menniscan gesælþa, forþam oþer twega oððe hie
næfre to nanū men ne becumaþ, oððe hi ðær næfre fæstlice*[9] *ne
ðurhwuniað swelca swelce hi ær to coman. Þæt ic wille her*

---

^r Boeth. ii. pr. 4. l. 34 P. 'Et illa, Promonimus, inquit,' &c.

[1] *tiolast* J. [2] *geortreowan* B. [3] em. *rume* B. [4] *ieð* J. [5] *alyfed* J.
[6] *adreogan* J. [7] *nearwa sint* J. [8] *heanlica* J. [9] em. *fætlice* B.

beæftan sweotolor gereccan.   We witon *þ*[1] *monige* habbað
ælces woruldwelan genog[1], ac hi habbað sceame þæs welan gif
hi ne beoð swa æþele on gebyrdū swa hi woldon.   Sume beoð
swiðe æþele 7 widcuðe on heora gebyrdū, ac hi beoþ mid wædle
7 mid henðe[2] ofþrycte 7 geunrotsode, þ hī wære leofre þæt hie 5
wæran unæþele þon swa earme, gif hit on heora anwealde wære.
Manege beoð þeah ægðer ge full æðele ge full welige, 7 beoð þeah
full unrote, þon hi oðer twega oððe wif habbað[3] him gemæc, oððe
him gemede nabbað[3].   Manige[8] habbað genog gesælilice[4] gewifod,
ac for bearnleste eallne þone welan þe hi gegaderigað hi lætað[5] 10
fræmdū to brucanne, 7 hi beoþ forþam unrote.   Sume habbað
bearn genoge, ac þa beoþ hwilū unhale oððe yfele 7 unweorþe[6],
oððe hraðe gefarað, þ þa eldran forðam gnorniað ealle heora
woruld.   Forþā ne mæg nan man on þys andweardan[7] life
eallunga gerad beon wið his wyrd.   Þeah he nu nanwuht elles 15
nabbe ymbe to sorgienne, þ him mæg to sorge þæt he nat hwæt
him toweard bið, hwæðer þe god þe yfel, ðon ma þe þu wistest;
7 eac þæt þ he þon gesællice brycð he ondræt þ he scyle forlætan.
Getæc me nu sumne mann þara ðe þe gesælegost þince] * 7 on
his se[lfwille sy swiðost gewiten]; ic þe gerecce swiðe hraþe 20
þ ðu ongitst þ he bið for swiðe lytlum þingū oft swiðe
ungemetlice gedrefed, gif him ænig wuht bið wið his willan
oððe wið his gewunan, þeah hit nu lytles hwæt sie, buton he
to [æl]cum men mæge gebecnan þ he irne[8] on his willan.
Wundrum lytel mæg gedon þone ealra gesælgostan mon her 25
on[9] worulde þ he wenð ðæt his gesælða sien oððe swiðe
gewanode oððe mid ealle forlorena.   Þu wensð (nu) þ þu [seo]
swiðe ungesælig, 7 ic wat ðæt monegū men þuhte þ he wære
to hefonum ahæfen gif he ænigne dæl hæfde þara þinra
gesælða[10] þe þu nu giet hæfst.   Ge furðum sio stow þe ðu nu 30
on gehæft[11] e[a]rt[12] 7 þu cwist ðæt þin wræcstow sie[13], hio is

* 12a C.

---

[8] Boeth. ii. pr. 4.   l. 45 P.   'Ille nuptiis felix,' &c.

[1] *monige habbað ælces woroldwillan genog* J, *þ mæg habbað æles
woruldwelan genog* B.   [2] *hænðe* J.   [3] *nabbað oððe him gemæc
oððe gemede nabbað* J.   [4] *gesællice* J.   [5] *læfað* J.   [6] *unweorð* J.
[7] em. *anweardan* B.   [8] *ierne* J.   [9] *for* B.   [10] *ungesælða* B.
[11] *hæft* B.   [12] *eard* B.   [13] Conject. C has *si[]*, B *sy*.

þæm monnum eþel þe ðæron gebor*ene* wæron, 7 *eac* þam þe
hiora willum þæron eardiað.   Ne nanwuht ne bið *y*fel ær
mon wene ꝥ hit yfel sie, 7 þeah hit nu hefig sie 7 wiðerweard,
þeah hit bið gesælð gif hit mon lustlic*e* [*de*]ð 7 geþyldelice
5 aræfneð. Feawe sint [1] to *þ*æm gesceadwise, *[gif he wyrð on*   * 12b C.
ungeðylde, ꝥ he ne wilnige [2] *ꝥ his*] sælð[*a*] weorðen onwen[*de*].
Wið swiðe monige biternesse is gemenged sio swetnes þisse
worulde; ðeah hio hwæm wynsumu ðynce, ne mæg he hi
no gehabban [3] gif hio hine flion onginð.   Hu ne is hit þær
10 swiðe swiotol hu werelica [4] þas woruldsælða sint, nu hi ne
magon þone earman gefyllan, for[þ]æm he [5] symle wilnað
hwæshwugu [þ]æs ðe he þonne næfð; ne hi þæm [*g*]eþyld-
egum 7 þæm gemetfæstum [*s*]ymle ne wuniað.

§ ii [t]. Hwy sece ge þonñ *y*mbutan eow þa gesælða þe ge
15 [*o*]ninnan iow habbað þurh þa godcundan mieht geset ?   Ac
ge nyton hwæt ge *doð* ; ge sint *on* gedwolan.   Ac ic eow mæg
m*id fe*a*wum* wordum gereccan *hwæt se* hrof is ealra gesælða ;
wið *þas ic* wat þu wilt higian þon ær þe ðu *hine* ongitest; ꝥ [6]
is þonne good.   Meaht þu nu ongitan hwæðer þu auht þe [7]
20 deorwyrðre hæbbe þonne þe selfne ?   Ic wene þeah ꝥ ðu
wille cw[*eþ*]an ꝥ þu nauht deorwyrðre næbbe.   Ic wat, gif þu
nu *hæfde [8] fulne [*anweald þines selfes, þōn*] hæfde þu hwæt-   * 13a C.
hwugu on ðe sel*fum* þæs ðe þu næfre þinum willū alætan
noldes [9], ne sio wyrd þe on geniman ne meahte.   Forðæm
25 ic ðe mindgige ꝥ þu ongite ꝥte nan gesælð nis on þis andweardan life [10] ðonne *seo* gesceadwisnes, forðæm hio þur*h* nan
þing *ne mæg þæm men losi*an; forðy *is betere þæt* feoh ꝥte
næfre losian ne *mæg* ðonne ꝥte *mæg* 7 sceal.   Hu ne is þe
nu geno*h sweo*tole gesæd ꝥ sio wyrd þe *ne mæg nane*
30 *gesælða sellan ?* forþæm*þe ægþer is unfæst, ge seo wyrd ge seo*
gesælð ; forþam sint swiðe tedre 7 swiðre hreosende þas gesælþa.

[t] Boeth. ii. pr. 4.   1. 67 P.   ‘ Quid igitur, o mortales,’ &c.

[1] *sient* B.   [2] em. *he wilnige* B.   [3] *habban* B.   [4] *hwerflice* B.
[5] From B. *hy* C.   [6] *ðe* B.   [7] *þe* om. B.   [8] *næfdest* B.   [9] *woldest* B.
[10] In B between *life* and *ðonne* are the words *ac onget þæt nauht nis*
betere on þis andweardum life.

Hwæt, ælc þara þe þas woruldgesælþa *hæfð oþer twega oððe
he wat þ hi*[1] *him fromwearde beoð, oððe he hit þōn nat. Gif he
hit þōn nat, hwelce gesælþa* hæfð *he æt þā welan gif he bið swa
dysig 7 swa ungewiss*[2] *þ he þæt witan ne mæg? Gif he hit
þōn wat,* þonne ondræt *he him þ hi losien, 7 eac geara wat þ* 5
he hi alætan sceal.   **[Se singala ege ne læt nonne mon gesæ-
lin]*ne bion. Gif þonne hwa ne recð hwæðer he þa gesælþa
hæbbe þe[3] næbbe þe he þonne hæfð, hwæt, þ þonne *beoð* for
lytla sælða oþþe nane, *þæt mon* swa eaðe forlætan mæg. *Ic
wene nu þ ic* þe[4] hæfde ær geno*g sweotole ger*eaht be monegum 10
tac*num þte monna* sawla[5] sint *undead*lica 7 *ece*[6], 7 *þ*is is
genog sweotol þte nænne mon þæs [*t*]weogan ne *þear*f þte ealle
men geendiað[7] on þam deaðe, 7 eac heora welan. *Þi* [*ic*]
wundrige hw*i* men sien swa [*ungescea*]dwise þ hi wenen þæt
te þis [*andwear*]de lif [*ma*]ege þone mon[*nan d*]on[8] gesæligne 15
þa hwile þe he [*leofað*], þonne hit hine ne mæg [*æfter*] þys
life earmne gedon. [*Hwæt*], *we* gewislice witon unrim [*ða*]ra
monna [*þe*] þa ecan gesælða sohton nalles þurh þ an þ hi
wilnodon ðæs [*lich*]omlican deaðes, ac eac *managra* sarlicra
wita hi gewil[*nodon wið*] þæm [*ec*]an life; þæt wæron ealle[9] 20
þa h[*a*]lgan martiras.

XII [u].

   **[Þa ongan se Wisdom gliowian 7 geoddode þus; ecte þæt
spell mid leoðe þ he ær sæde, 7 cwæð:]* (*Se þe wille fæst hus
timbrian ne sceal he hit no settan up on ðone hehstan cnoll, 7 se
ðe wille godcundne wisdom secan ne mæg he hine wið ofermetta;* 25
*7 eft se þe wille fæst hus timbrian ne sette he hit on sondbeorhas.
Swa eac gif þu wisdom timbrian wille, ne sete þu hine on uppan
þa gitsunga, forþā swa swa sigende sond þone ren swylgð, swa
swylgð seo gitsung þa dreosendan welan þisses middangeardes,
forþā hio hiora simle bið þurstegu. Ne mæg hus naht lange* 30
standan on þā hean munte gif hit full ungemetlic[10] *wind*

---

[u] Boeth. ii. met. 4. 'Quisquis uolet,' &c. Cott. Metr. vii.

[1] em. *he* B.   [2] *unwis* J.   [3] *þe he* B.   [4] *þe* om. B.   [5] *sawula* B.
[6] *eca* J.   [7] *geendi að* C, with space between *i* and *a*.   [8] *monn andon* B.
[9] *ealle* om. B.   [10] em. *ungametlic* B.

gestent ; næfð[1] *þæt þte on ðam sigendā sonde stent for*
swiðlicū rene. Swa eac þ mennisce mod bið undereten 7 aweged
of his stede þōn hit se wind strongra geswinca astyroð oððe se
ren ungemetlices ymbhogan. Ac se þe wille habban þa ecan
5 *gesælða he sceal fleon þone frecnan wlite þises middaneardes*
7 timbrian þ hus his[2] *modes on þam fæstā stane eaðmetta,*
forþāðe Crist eardað on þære dene eadmodnesse 7 on þā
gemynde wisdomes. Forþam simle se wisa mon eall his lif læt
on gefean unonwendendlice 7 orsorg, þōn he forsihþ ægðer ge
10 *þas eorðlican gôd ge eac þa yflu, 7 hopað to þā toweardā ; þ*
sint þa ecan. Forþāþe God hine gehelt æghwonan singallice
wuniendne on his modes gesælðum, ðeah þe se wind þara earfoþa
7 seo singale gemen þissa woruldsælða him on blawe.)

XIII [v].

Ða se Wisdom þa 7 *seo* Gesceadwisnes þis leoð a[s]ungen
15 hæfde[3], *þa* ongon he e[*ft*] secgean spel 7 þu[*s cwæ*]ð: *Me þincð*
[*nu*] þ wit mægen [*smealicor sprecan 7 diogolran*] wordum,
for[*þam ic ongite þ min*] lar hwæthwu[*gu in gæð on þin*
ondgit] 7 þu genoh *wel* [*understenst þ ic þe to*] sprece. Geþenc [*nu hwæt þines agnes*] sie ealra ðissa [*woruldæhta*[4] 7
20 *welena, oððe hwæt þu þæron age unandergildes, gif þu him*
sceadwislice[5] *æfter spy*]rest. Hwæt *hæfst þu* [*æt þam gifū*]
þe þu cwyst þ *seo* wyrd eow [*gife, 7 æt*] ðæm welan, þeah hy
nu ece *wæ*[*ron*]? Sæge me nu *hwæðer* se þin wela [*þines*]
ðances swa diore *seo, þe for his agen*re gecynde. *Hwæðer ic*
25 *þe secge þeah* ðæt hit is of his *agenre gecynde,* næs of þinre.
Gif hit þōn his agenre gecynde *is, nas of þinre, hwi eart þu*
þonne *a þy betera for his gode*[6]? *Sege* me [*nu hwæt his þe*
deorast[7]] þince, hwæ[*ðer þe gold þe hwæt*]. Ic wat þeah gold.
[*Ac þeah hit nu god*[8]] sie 7 diore, ðeah [*bið hliseadigra*] 7
30 *leofwend*ra se ðe hit *[*selð þon se ðe hit gaderað 7 on oðrū* * 15b C.

▼ Boeth. ii. pr. 5. 'Sed quoniam rationum,' &c.

[1] em. *næft* B.   [2] *his* above line B.   [3] *hæfdon* B.   [4] In C the words in square brackets are partly gone; rest illegible.   [5] *gesceadwislice* J.
[6] *goode* J.   [7] *diorust* J.   [8] From J, *gold* B.

reafað.   Ge eac þa welan] bioð hlisead[*igran*] 7 leoftæ*l*ran
þonne þonne[1] hi mon selð þonne hi bion ðonne hi mon
gadr[*að*] 7 hilt[2].   Hwæt, sio gitsung gedeð [*heore git*]*seras*
[*laðe*] ægþer ge [*Gode ge monnū, 7 þa cysta*] gedoð [*þa simle
leoftæle 7*] *hliseadige 7* we[*orðe ægþer ge Gode ge*] monnum ðe 5
[*hie lufiað.   Nu þ feoh þōn*] *ægþer* ne [*mæg beon ge mid þā
þe*] *hit* selð ge [*mid þam þe hit mon s*]elð[3], nu is for[*þā ælc
feoh betere*] 7 deorwyrðre [*geseald þōn gehe*]alden.   Gif nu eall
[*þises middanea*]rdes wela come to [*anū men*], *hu* ne wæren
þonne ealle [*oþre men*] *wædlan* buton him[4] anum ?   [*Genoh*] 10
*sweo*tol þ is þætte god word 7 [*god hlisa*] ælces *monnes* bið
betra 7 [*deorra*[5] *þōn ænig*] wela ; hwæt, þæt [*w*]ord gefylð
[*ælces*[6] *þ*]ara earan þe hit geherð, 7 ne bi[*ð þe*]ah na þy
læsse mid þæm þe hit spr[*icð.   H*]]is heortan diegelnesse hit
geopen[*að*[7], 7 þæs o]ðres [*heort*]an belocena hit [*þurhfærð, 7* 15
on þā] færelde þærbetwyx [*ne bið hit no*] gewanod ; n[*e mæg
hit mon mid sweorde* o]fslean ne *mid* rape gebindan, [*ne hit
n*]æfre ne[8] acwylð.   Ac þa eowre welan, [*þeah hi*] ealne weg
mid eow sien[9], ne þincð *eow* no þy hraðor hiora genoh ; 7
ðeah ge hi þonne oþrum monnum sellen[10], ne magon ge *no* 20
þe ma mid þæm hiora wædle 7 *heora gitsunge* gefyllan.   Þeah
ðu hi *smale*[11] *todæle* swa dust, ne *miht þu ðeah ea*lle men
emn*lice mid gehealdan ; 7 þōn* þu ealle ged*ælde hæfst þōn bist*
þu ðe *self* wædla.   Sint *þ werilice*[12] *welan* þisses middangeardes,
þōn hi nan mon fullice habban *ne mæg, ne hie nanne* mon 25
gewelegian *ne magon, buton hie* oðerne gedon to *wædlan.*
Hwæþer[13] *nu* gimma wlite eowre eagan to him [*ge*]tio hiora
to wundriganne ?   Swa ic w[*at*] þ hi doð.   Hwæt, sio duguð
þonne þæs wlites þe on þæm gimmum bið, bið heora, næs
eower.   Þy ic eom swiðe ungemetlice ofwundrod hwi eow 30
þince þære ungesceadwisan *gesceafte* godweb b[*ete*]re þonne
eower [*agen*] god ; hwi ge swa ungemetlice wu[*ndrigen*] *þara*

[1] *þonne* once B.   [2] *healt* B.   [3] em. *þe hit nimð* B, *mon selð* J.
[4] *him* om. B.   [5] *diorra* J.   [6] From J, *eallra* B.   [7] *idelnesse hit openað* B.
[8] *ne* above line.   [9] *eowre sin* B.   [10] *sellan* B.   [11] *smale* B, *swa
smealice* J.   [12] *werelice* J.   [13] J, *hwær* B.

gimm[*a*] oþþ[*e æniges*] þara [*deadlice*]na ðinga þe [*gescead-*
wisnesse næfð]; forðæm hi *[*mid nanū ryhte ne magon*] ∗ 16b C.
gearni[*gan þ ge he*]ora wundrien. Þeah hi Godes [*gescea*]ftes
sien, ne sint hi no wið eo[*w t*]o metanne [1], forðæm [2] þe oþer
5 twega oððe hit nán gód nis for *eow* selfe, oððe þeah forlytel god wið *eow* to metane [3]. [*T*]o swiðe we herwað [*us*
selfe þon]ne we [*þ* [4]] ma lufiað þte [*under*] us is on us[*sum*] [5]
anwalde, þonne *us* selfe oððe [*þon*]e drihten þe us [*ge*]sceop,
7 us eall [*ða*] god forgeaf. Hw[*æ*]þer þe nu licien [*f*]ægru [6]
10 lond ?

XIV [w].

§ i. Ða andsworode þ Mod [*þa*]ere Gesceadwisnesse 7
cwæð : Hwi ne [*sc*]eolde me lician fæger lond ? Hu ne is
[*þæ*]t se fægeresta dæl Godes gesceaf[*ta ? Ge*], ful oft we
fageniað smyltre sæ, [*7 e*]ac wundriað þæs wlites þære sunnan
15 [*7*] þæs monan 7 ealra þara steorrena. [*ð*]a andswarode se
Wisdom 7 seo Gesceadwisnes þæm Mode 7 þus cwæð :
Hwæt belimpð þe to hiora fægernes[*s*]a ? Hwæðer [7] þu
dyrre gilpan þæt [*h*]iora fægern[*es þ*]in sie ? Nese, nese.
[*H*]u ne was[*t*] þu [*þ ðu*] hiora nan ne worhtest [8] ? [*Ac gif*
20 *þu*] gilpan wille, gilp [9] Godes. Hwæðer þu n[*u fægerra*]
blos[*tmæna*] fægnige on eas[*tran, swelce þu hie gescope ?*
∗Hwæðer ðu nu swelces auht wyrcan mæge, oððe geworhtes* ∗ 17a C.
habbe ? Nese, nese. Ne do þu swa [10]. *Hwæþer hit nu þines*
gewealdes se [11] *þ se hærfest sie swa welig*] on wæ[*stmū ? Hu*
25 *ne wat ic þ hit*] nis no [*þines gewealdes ? Hwi eart þu*]
þonne [*onæled mid swa idele gefean*], oððe hwi [*lufast þu ða*
fremdan god] swa unge[*metlice, swelce hi sen þine get nu* [12]] ?
Wenst þu mæge [*seo wyrd þe gedon þ*] þa þing þin agnu [13]
[*sen þa ðe heora agene* [14]] gecynd þe ged[*on* [15] *fremde ? Nese,*

---

[w] Boeth. ii. pr. 5. l. 30 P. 'Quidni ? Est enim pulcherrimi,' &c.

[1] Second *n* above line. [2] *of þā* B. [3] *metanne* B. [4] *þ* from J, *mare þ
lufiað* B. [5] *ussum* J, *urum* B. [6] *fægrĕ* C, *fægeru* B. [7] *Hwær* B.
[8] *nanne ne geworhtest* B. [9] *gilp* above line. [10] *no swa* J. [11] So B.
[12] *agnu* for *get nu* J. [13] *agnu agnu* C. [14] *agnu* J. [15] *gedydon* J.

nese].   *Nis* hit[1] no þe gecynde [*þte þu hi age*]; ne him *nis*
gebyrde [*þ hi ðe folgien*].   Ac þa hefoncu[*ndan þing ðe sint*[2]]
gecynde, næs þæs [*eorðlican. Pas eorð*lican wæstmas sin[*t*
gesceapene nete]num[3] to andlifene; [7 *þa woruldwelan*] sin*t*
gesceapene to bi[*swice*] *þā* mon[*nū*] þe bioð neatum[4] gelic[*e, þ* 5
beoð un]rih[*t*]wise 7 ungemetfæs[*te. To*] þæm hi ea[*c*] becumað
oftost.   *Gif* [*þu*] þonne þæ[*t*] gemet habban *wille*, 7[5] *þa*
*nyd*þearf[*e*] witan wille, *þōn is þæt* mete and [*dry*]nc 7
claðas [7 *tōl to*] *swelcū* cræfte [*swelce þu cunne þ þe is*]

* 17b C. gecynde 7 þ [*þe is riht to habbenne*].   Hwilc fremu i[*s** þe þ 10
þæt þu wilnige þissa andweardena gesælþa ofer gemet, þōn hie
naþer[6] *ne magon ne þin gehelpan, ne heora selfra?   On swiðe*
lytlon hiera hæfð seo gecynd genog; on swa micl]ū hio [*hæfð*
genog swa we ær spræco]n.   Gif ðu [*heore mare selest, oþer*
twe]ga oððe [*hit þe derað, oððe hit ðe þ*]eah[7] unwyn[*sū bið,* 15
oððe unget]æse, oððe fre[*cenlic, eall þ þu nu o*]fer gemet dest.
[*Gif ðu nu ofer gemet*] itst, oððe drin[*cst, oððe claða þe*[8] *ma*
on]hehst[9] þonne [*þu þurfe, seo*[10]] oferinc[11] þe wyrð oððe [*to*
sare, oððe to] wlættan, oþþe to un[*gerisenū, oððe*] to plio.   Gif
þu nu wenst þte [*wundorlice*] gegerela[12] hwelc weo[*r*]ðmy*nd* 20
sie, þon]ne telle ic þa weorð[*m*]ynde *þā wy*]rhtan þe hi worhte,
nealles[13] *þe*.   Se *wyrhta* is God[14]; þæs cræft ic þær [*h*]erige
on.   Wenst þu þ sio menigo [*ðinra*] monna þe mæge don
gesælig[*ne*]?   Nese nese.   Ac gif hi yfele sint [7 *lytige*[15]]
þonne sint hi þe pliolicran [7 *geswi*]ncfulran hæ*fd*[16] ðonne 25
næfd[17]; [*forþ*]æm yfele þ[*egnas*] bioð simle [*heora*] hlafo[*rdes*

* 18a C. *fiend*].   Gif hi þonne [*gode beoð 7 hlaford** holde 7 untwifealde,*
about here. *hu ne beoð þ þōn heora godes, næs þines?   Hu miht þu þōn þe*
agnian heora god?   Gif þu nu þæs gilpst, hu ne gilpst þu
þōn heora godes, næs þines?   30
   § ii[x]. *Nu þe is genoh openlice gecyþed þæt*]te na[*n þara*

---

[x] Boeth. ii. pr. 5. l. 51 P. 'Ex quibus omnibus,' &c.

[1] *hit* om. B.   [2] *sendan* J.   [3] *nytenum* J.   [4] *neatenum* B.
[5] 7 conj. om. B.   [6] *nawðer* J.   [7] Conj. *þeah* om. B.   [8] *claðe ma* J.
[9] *hæfst* B.   [10] *sio* J.   [11] *ofering* B.   [12] *gérela* B.   [13] *næs na* B.
[14] *g od* C, an *o* appar. erased, *gód* B.   [15] 7 *lytige* from J, om. B.   [16] *gehæfd*
B.   [17] *genæfd* B.

goda þin nis, þe we ær] ymb[1] spræcon, 7 [*þu teohhodest*[2] *þ̄ hi*
ðine] bion sceolden.   Gif [*ðonne*[3] *þisse wo*]rulde wlites 7 wela
[*to wilnienne nis*], hwæt murcnast[4] þ[*u þōn æfter þā*] þe þu
forlure, oð[*ðe to hwon fag*]nast þu þæs þe ðu [*ær hæfdest*[5] *?*
5 *Gif hit*] fæger is, þ̄ is of hio[*ra agnū gecynde*], næs of þinum;
hior[*a fæger hit is, nas*] þin.   Hwæt fægnast [*þu þōn heora*]
fægres?   Hwæt belimpð[6] [*his to þe ? Ne þu hit*] ne[7]
gesceope, ne hi þ[*ine agene ne sent*].   Gif hi nu *gode* sint
[7 *fægere, þōn*] wæron hi swa gesceap[*ene ; 7 swælce hi*
10 *wo*]ldan bion, þeah þu h[*i næfre nahtest*].   Wenst þu þ̄ hi a
ðy deo[*rwyrðran seon*[8] *þe hi*] to þinre note gelæ[*nde wæran ?*
Ac f]orþæmþe heora d[*ysige men wafiað 7 hi*] him þincað
de[*ore, forþā þu hi gaderast 7*] helst[9] * o[*n þinū horde. Hwæt*
wilnast þu þōn þ̄ þu hæbbe æt swelcere gelicnesse[10] *?   Gelef*[11]
15 *me, nu ic hit þe secge : næfst þu þær nauht æt, buton þ̄ þu tilast*[12]
wædle to flionne, 7 forþy gæderast mare þōn þu ðurfe[13].   *Ac*
ic wat þeah swiðe geara þ̄te eall þ̄ ic her sprece is wið þinū
willan.   Ac eowra gesælða ne sint no þ̄ ge wenað þæt] hi [*sen,*
forþā se þe micel] *innierfe*[14] 7 mislic [*agan wile, he beðea*]rf *
20 eac miceles ful[*tumes.   Se ealda cwi*]de is swiðe soð þe [*mon*
gefyrn cwæð], þætte þa micles be[*ðurfon þe micel a*]gan
willað, 7 þa þur[*fon swiþe lytles þe*] maran ne wilniað [*þōn*
genoges.   But]an hi wilnien mid ofer[*inge hiora gitsu*]nga
gefyllan, þ̄ hi næ[*fre ne gedoð.   I*]c[15] wat þ̄ ge wenað þæt
25 ge [*nan gecundlic*[16]] god ne gesælþa onin[*nan eow selfū*]
næbben[17], forðæm ge hi [*secað butan eow*] to fremdū gesceaftū.
[*Swa hit is mis*]hweorfed þ̄ þæm men þincð, [*þeah he se god*]-
cundlice gescead*wis*, [*þ̄ he on him sel*]fū næbbe sælþa ge[*noge,*
buton he] mare gegader*ige* þara [*ungesceadwisene*[18]] gesceafta
30 þonne [*he beþurfe oððe him*] gemetlicre[19] sie ; [7 *þa ungescead-*
wisan neotena[20]] ne wil[*niað nanes oðres feos*[21], ac þincð him
genog on þā þe hi binnan heora ægenre hyde habbað to eacan

** 18a C ends here, rest gone.*

** 18b C begins, first part gone.*

---

[1] *b* ab. l.   [2] *tiohhodes* J.   [3] *ðone* B.   [4] *murñast* C.   [5] *þær hæfst* J.
[6] *be* above line C.   [7] *ne* om. B.   [8] *deorran sien* J.   [9] *heltst* B.
[10] So B, *gesælignesse* J.   [11] *gelief* J.   [12] *tiolast* J.   [13] *ðyrfe* J.
[14] From J, *inerfe* B.   [15] cm. *Ac* B.   [16] *gecyndelic* J.   [17] *nabbað* B.
[18] So B.   [19] *gemetlic* B.   [20] *neat* J.   [21] *fios* J.

** 19a C about here.* *þā fodre þe him gecyndelic bið. *Hwæt, ge þōn þeah hwæthwega godcundlices on eowerre saule habbað, þ is andgit 7 gemynd, 7 se gesceadwislica willa þ hine þara twega l]yste. [Se þe þōn þas ðreo hæfð]*, þonne hæfð *[he his sceoppendes onlic]*nesse swa forð *[swa swa ænegu gesceaft]* fyrmest [1] mæg *[hiere sceppendes* 5 *on]licnesse* habban. *[Ac ge secað þære]* hean gecynde *[gesælþa 7 heore weorð]scipe* to ðæm niþ*[erlicum* [2] *7 to þā]* hreosendlicum [3] *[þingū. Ac ge ne]* ongitað hu micel*[ne leonan ge doð]* Gode eowrū scippe*[nde, forþāþe]* he wolde þte ealle *[men wæran eal]ra* oþerra gescea*[fta* 10 *wealdendas]*; ac ge underþeodað *[eowre hehstan]* medemnesse under *[þa eallra nyðe]mestan* gesceafta ; *[mid þā ge]* habbað gecyðed *[þ æfter eowrū]* agnum dome ge *[doð eow selfe wyr]san* þonne eowra *[agne* [4] *æhta, nu ge w]*enað þ eowre ** 19a C ends, rest gone.* n*[auht welan* [5] *send eowre gesæ]*lþa,* *[7 leohhiað þæt eall eowre* 15 *woruldgod sien dierran* [6] *ge selfe. Swa hit eac wyrð þōn ge swa willað.*

§ iii [7]. *Þæs menniscan lifes gecynd is þ hi þy anan seon* [7] *beforan eallū oðrū gesceaftum þy hi hie selfe ongiton hwæt hie send* [8] *7 hwonan hi send* [8] *; 7 þi hi send* [9] *wyrsan þōn nytenu* [10]*, 20 þy hi nellað witan hwæt hi sint, oððe hwonan hi sint. Þā ** 19b C begins, first part gone.* neatū]* *is gecynde *[þ hi nyton hwæt hie]* send [8]; ac þ is þa*[ra monna unðeaw]* þæt hi niton *[hwæt hie sen. Nu þe]* is swiþe sweotol *[þæt ge beoþ on gedwolan]*, þonne ge wenað *[þ ænig]* mæg mid frem*[dū welū beon geweorþod. Gif hwa nu* 25 *bið mid hwelcū]* welū geweorþod *[7 mid hwelcū]* deorwyrþū *æhtū [gegyrewod* [11]*, hu ne b]*elimpð se weorðscipe *[þōn to þā]* þe hine geweorðað? *[Þæt is to heriann]e* hwene rihtlicor. *[Ne þæt ne beoþ]* no ðy fægerre þ mid *[elleshwā gere]nod* bið, þeah þa ge*[renu fægru]* sien þe hit mid gerenod *[bið. Gif* 30 *hit]* ær scandlic wæs, *ne [bið hit no ðy fa]*egerre. Wite þu fo*[r soð þ nan god n]e* dereð þæm *[þe hit ah. Hwæt, þu*

---

[7] Boeth. ii. pr. 5. l. 81 P. ' Humanae quippe naturae,' &c.

[1] *furemest* B.   [2] em. *niþerlicam* B.   [3] *hreorendū* B.   [4] *agna* J.
[5] *noht welan* J.   [6] *diorran* J.   [7] *sie* J.   [8] *sien* J.   [9] *sint* J.
[10] em. *nytena* B.   [11] *gearod* J.

wast nu] ꝥ ic [*þe ne leoge, 7 eac wast þæt þa welan oft deriað
þam*]* þe hi agon on man*e*gum þingū, [*7 on*] ðæm swiðost ꝥ * 20a C.
te men weorðað [*swa up*]ahæfene for ðæm welan [1] þæt oft [*se*]
ealra wyrresta 7 se ealra unw[*eor*]ðesta mon wenð ꝥ he sie
5 ealles [*þæs*] welan wyrðe þe on þisse [2] worul[*de*] is, gif he
wisse hu he him to cuman meahte. Se ðe micelne we[*lan*]
hæfð, he him ondræt monige [3] [*feond* [4]] ; gif he nan*e* æhta
næfde, ne þ[*or*]fte he him nænne ondræda[*n*]. Gif þu nu
wære wegferend 7 hæfd[*est*] micel gold on ðe, [*7*] þu þonne
10 beco[*me*] on þiofscole, þonne ne wendes þu þe þines feor*es*,
þonne [5] gif ðu þ[*onne*] swelces nanwuht næfde, þonne n[*e*]
ðorftes þu ðe nanwuht ondræd[*an*], ac meahtes þe gan
singende þo[*ne*] ealdan cwide þe mon gefyrn sa[*ng*], ꝥ se
nacoda wegferend him nanw[*uht*] ne ondrede. Þonne þ[*u*]
15 þonne orsorg wære, 7 þa þeofas þe from gewiten wær*on*,
þonne meahtes þu *bi*smrian þæs andweardan welan, [*7 mea*]htes
cweþan : Eala ꝥ hit is god [*7 wynsum*] ꝥ mon micelne
welan hæ[*bbe, nu*] se næfre ne wyrð orsorg þe hine
underfehð.

XV [z].

20 [*Þa seo Gesceadwisnes þa þis spell asæd hæfde, þa ongan
heo singan 7 þus cwæð :*] (*Eala, hu gesælig seo forme eld was
þises midangeardes, ða ælcum men þuhte genog on þære
eorþan wæstmū. Næron þa welige hamas, ne mistlice swotmettas, ne drincas, ne diorwyrðra hrægla hi ne girndan,
25 forþam hi þa git næran, ne hio nanwuht ne gesawon, ne ne
geherdon. Ne gemdon hie nanes fyrenlustes, buton swiðe
gemetlice þa gecynd beeodan ; ealne weg hi æton æne on dæg,
7 ꝥ was to æfennes. Treowa wæstmas hi æton 7 wyrta, nalles
scir win hi ne druncan, ne nanne wætan hi ne cuþon wið hunige
30 mengan ; ne seolocenra hrægla mid mistlicū bleowū hi ne
gimdon. Ealne weg hi slepon ute on triowa sceadū ; hluterra*

---

* Boeth. ii. met. 5. ' Felix nimium,' &c. Cott. Metr. viii.

[1] *welan* from B, C has simply *la*. [2] *þisse* om. B. [3] *monigne* B.
[4] *fynd* J. [5] *þonne* om. B.

D

wella wæter hi druncon. Ne geseah nan cepa ealand ne weroð, ne geherde non mon þa get nanne sciphere, ne furþon ymbe nan gefeoht sprecan. Ne seo eorðe þa get besmiten mid ofslægenes monnes blode, ne mon furðum gewundod; ne monn ne geseah þa git yfelwillende men; nænne weorðscipe næfdon, ne hi non 5 *mon ne lufude. Eala þ ure tida nu ne mihtan weorþan swilce. Ac nu manna gitsung is swa byrnende swa þ fyr on þære helle, seo is on þā munte þe Ætne hatte, on þam ieglande þe Sicilia hatte; se munt bið simle swefte birnende, 7 ealla þa neahstowa þærymbutan forbærnð. Æala, hwæt se forma* 10 *gitsere wære, þe ærest þa eorþan ongan delfan æfter golde, 7 æfter gimmū, 7 þa frecnan deorwyrðnesse* [1] *funde þe ær behyd wæs 7 behelod mid ðære eorþan.*)

XVI[a].

§ i. Þa se Wisdom þa þis leoð asungen hæfde, þa ongan he eft spellian 7 þus cwæþ : Hwæt mæg ic þy [2] mare secgan 15 be þæm weorðscipe 7 be *þæm anwe*alde þisse *w*orulde? For ðæm anwealde ge eow [*w*]oldon áhebban up oð ðone heo*f*en, gif ge [3] meahten. Þ is forðæm*þe ge ne* gemunon ne *eac* ne ongi*taðþ*one heofoncundan anwe*ald* 7 þone weorðscipe; se is *eower* agen, 7 *þ*onan ge comon [4]. *Hwæt*, se eower wela 20 þonne 7 s*e eower* a*n*weald, þe ge nu weorðsci*p*e hat*að*, gif he becymð to þā eallra wyrrestan men, 7 to þā þe his eallra unweorðost bið, swa he nu dyde to þis ilcan *Þeodrice, 7 iu [5] ær to Nerone þæm [c]asere, 7 oft eac to mænegum hiora gelicum, hu ne wile he ðonn̄ don swa hi dydon 7 get doð, ealle ða 25 *ricu* þe him under bioð oððe *awer on* neaweste, forslean 7 forheregian, swæ swa fyres leg deð drigne hæðfeld, oððe eft se byrnenda swefel ðone munt bærnð þe we hatað Etne [6], se is on Sicilia ðæm ealonde; swiðe onlic ðæm miclan flode ðe *giu on Noes* dagum wæs. Ic wene ðæt þu mæge gemunan 30 ðætte eowre eldran gio Roman*a* witan on Torcwines

* 22a C.

---

* Boeth. ii. pr. 6. ‘Quid autem de dignitatibus,’ &c.

[1] em. *deorwyrðnessa* B.   [2] *ic þe nu* B.   [3] *hi* B.   [4] *noman* B.   [5] *eac* B.   [6] *ætna* B.

dagum þæs ofermodan cyninges for his ofermettum þone
cynelican naman of Romebyr*ig* æresð adydon. Ond eft
swa ilce þa heretogan ðe hine[1] ær ut adrifon hi wolden eft
ut adrifan for hiora ofermettū ; ac hi ne meahton, forðæmþe
5 se æftera anweald þara heretogena þæm *ro*maniscum
*wit*um get wyrs li[*code þōn se*] ærra þara cyn[*inga. Gif hit*]
þonne æfre gewirð, [*swa hit swiðe*] seldon gewyrð, þæt [*se
anwea*]ld 7 se weorðscipe becu*me* **to godum men* 7 to wisum, * 22b C.
hwæt [*bið þ*]ær þonne licwyrðes but*on his* god 7 his weorð-
10 scipe, þæs *godan cyninges*, næs þæs an*wealdes ? Forþāþe*
se anwald *næfre ne bið* good but*on* se *god* sie þe *hine hæ*bbe ;
ðy[2] hit bið *þæs monnes god*[3] næs *þæs anwealdes*, gif se anweald
god *bið. Forþā* hi*t* bið *þæt*te nan *man* for his rice *ne*
cymð *to cræft*um 7 to me*demnesse, ac for his* cræftum 7 *for*
15 his med*ū*nesse *he cymð to* rice 7 *to*[4] *anwealde. Þi ne bið nan*
man for *his anwealde na þe* betera, ac for *his cræftū he beoð*
good, gif he *god*[5] *bið*, 7 *for his* cræftum he *bið anwealdes*
weorðe, gif he his weor*ð*e *bið. Leorniað* forðæm wisdom, 7
þonne ge hine geleornod hæbben, ne *forhycga*ð[6] *hine* þonne.
20 * Þonne secge ic* eow but*on* ælcum tweon *þ ge magon þurh* hine
becuma*n to anwealde, þeah ge no þæs anwealdes ne wilnigan.*
Ne þurfon ge no hogian[7] *on þam anwealde, ne him æfter*
þringan. **Gif ge wise* beoð 7 gode, he wile fol*gian eow*, * 23a C.
þeah ge his no ne wilnigen. Ac [*sege me*] nu hwæt eower
25 deor*wyrðesta* wela 7 anwald sie, þe ge *swiðost girnaþ.* Ic
wat þeah þ hit *is þis andwearde*[8] lif 7 ðes brosnienda w*ela* ðe
we ær ymbe spræcon.

§ ii [b]. Eala, hwæðer ge netenlican[9] men ongiten hwilc s*e*
*w*ela sie, 7 *se* anwald, 7 ða *woruld*sælða? *Þa* sint eowere
30 *hlafordas* 7 eowere waldendas, næs *ge heora.* Gif ge nu
*gesawan hwelce mus þ wæ*re hla*ford ofer oð*re *mys*, 7 *setle*
him *domas*, 7 nedde *hie æfter* gafole, hu *wunderlic* wolde *eow*

---

[b] Boeth. ii. pr. 6. l. 14 P. ' Nonne o terrena animalia,' &c.

[1] *hi* B.   [2] *þe* B.   [3] *good* J.   [4] *to* from J, om. B.   [5] *good* J.
[6] From J, *forhogiað* B.   [7] *hongian* J.   [8] em. *anwearda* B.
[9] *netelican* B.

ðæt þincan; hwelce *ceh*hettung*e* ge wol*dan* þæs *habban*, 7
mid hwelce hleahtr*e* ge woldon bion astered.   Hu micle
mar*e* is ðonne þæs *mon*nes lichom*a* to met*enne* wi*ð* þ mod
þon*ne seo mus* wi*ð* ðone mon.   Hwæt, [*ge þonne*] magon
ea*ð*e ge*þ*encan, [*gif ge hit georne*] *ymbe smeag*an willa*ð* 7 [*æfter* 5
spyrigan, þ [1] *nanre wuhte lichoma ne beoð þōn tederra þōn þæs*
*mon*nes.   *Þ*æm *magon derian þa* **læ*]s*t*an fleogan, ge *ð*a
gnættas mid swy*ð*e lytlum sticelum hi[*m*] deria*ð*, 7 eac *ð*a
smalan w[*yrmas*] *ð*e *ð*one mon æg*ð*er ge *innan ge* utan
wyrda*ð*, 7 hwilum fu*ln*eah deadne gedo*ð*; ge fur*ð*um þios 10
lytle loppe hine deadne [2] gede*ð*.   Swilca wuhta him deriga*ð*
æg*ð*er [*g*]e innan ge utan.   On hwæm mæg [*æ*]nig mon
o*ð*rum derian buton on his licho*m*an, o*ðð*e eft on hiora
welum, *þe ge hata*ð gesæl*ð*a?   Ne nan *mon* ne mæg *ð*æm
gesceadwisan *m*ode *ge*derian, ne hi*m* gedon þ hit sie [3] *ð*æt 15
*ð*æt hit ne [4] bi*ð*.   *Ð*æt is swi*ð*e sweotol *to ongitan*ne be
sumum roman*iscum* æþelinge, se wæs *haten* Liberius [5]; se
wæs to man*egum witū geworht, forð*æmþe he nolde *meldian*
on his geferan þe mid [*him*] siredon ymb *ð*one *cyning* [*þe*
hie ær] mid unrihte gewun*nen* [*hæfdon* [6].   *Þ*]a he *ð*a beforan 20
*ð*one [*graman*] cyning gelæd wæs, [7 *he hine het*] secgan
hwæt hi[*s geferan wæron*] *ð*e mid him [*ymbe sieredon* [7], *þa*]
*forc*eaw he [*his tungan* 7] **wearp* hine mid *ð*ære tung[*an* [8] *on*
þæt n]eb foran.   For*ð*æm hit ge[*wearð þ ð*]æm wisan men
com to lofe [7 *to wyrð*]scipe þ se unrihtwisa [*cyning him*] 25
tiohhode to wite.   [*Hwæt is þ*] *dem*ma [9] *ð*æt ænig mon mæge
o*ð*rum do[*n*], þ he ne mæge him don *ð*æt ilce?   Gif he ne
mæg, o*ð*er mon mæg.   We leornodon eac be *ð*æm wælreowan Bosiridem, se wæs on Egyptum.   *Ð*æs leodhatan
gewuna wæs þ he wolde ælcne cuman swi*ð*e arlice underfoon 30
7 swi*ð*e swæslice wi*ð* gebæran, *ð*onne he æres*ð* him to com.
Ac eft, ær he him from cerde, *he* sceolde bion ofslægen.
Ond *ð*a geberede [10] hit *ð*æt Erculus [*I*]obes *s*unu co[*m*] to

him. þa wolde he do[n] *ymbe* hine swa swa he ymbe
m[*anigne*] cuman ær dyde ; wolde hine [*a*]drencan on þære
ea ðe Nilus [*hat*]te. ða wearð he strengra, [7 *adre*]ncte
hine swiðe rihte [*be Godes dome*], swa swa he manign[*e*
5 *oðerne ær dy*]de. Hwæt, eac Regul*us*, [*se*] foremæra [*heret*]og[*a,*
þa he feaht] wið Africanas [1], [*he hæf*]de [*fulneah*] **unasec-* * 24b C about here.
gendlicne sige of[*er þa Afric*]anas [2] ; þa he (*hi*) þa swiðost
[*forslagen*] hæfde, ða het he hi bind[*an 7 on ba*]lcan lecgan.
ða *gebyrede* [*hit swiðe*] hraðe ꝥ (*he*) wearð *gebunden* [*mid*
10 *hira*] racentum. *Hwæt wenst* [*þu þon*] hwæt godes se [3]
anweald [*sie, þon*] he [4] on nane *wisan* his agenes cræftes ne
mæg forbugan ꝥ he ðæt *ilce* yfel ne geðafige oðrum *monnū*
ꝥ he ær *oðrū* dyde ? Hu ne *is* se anw*eald þon þær* nauht ?

    § iii [c]. Hwæt *wenst þu ? gif se* weorðscipe 7 se *anweald* [5] *his*
15 *agnes þonces god wære 7 his selfes anweald hæfde, hwæ*ðer he
wolde *þā forcuðestū monnū* folgian *swa he nu* hwilum [6] *deð* ?
Hu *ne wast þu ꝥ hit nis nauht gecynde ne nauht gewunelic*
ꝥ ænig wiðerweard þing bion gemenged wið oðrū wiðerweardū,
oððe ænige geferrædenne wið habban ? Ac seo gecynd hit
20 *onscunað* þæt hi *ne magon weor*ðan togædere gemeng*ed,* [*þe* [7]]
ma ðe ꝥ good 7 ðæt *y*fel *magon ætgædere* bion. Nu þe is
*swiðe openlice gecy*ðed ꝥ þi[*s andwearde rice*] 7 *þas* weoruld-
gesælþa 7 þes anweald of heora [8] agnū gec[*ynde 7 heora agnes*
ge]wealdes nauht **[gode ne sie*]nt, ne heora selfr[*a nanne* * 25a C.
25 *a*]nwald *n*abbað, nu hi willað cl[*ifian*] [9] *on þam* wyrrestan
monnum, 7 *him geþafiað þæt hi* bioð hiora hla*fordas. Nis*
ðæs nu nan tweo ðæt *oft þa* [10] *eallra forcuþestan men cumað* to
þam anwealde 7 *to þam* weorðscipe. *Gif se* anw*eald* ðonne of
his ag*enre gecyn*de 7 his agnes *gewealdes god ware, ne*
30 underfenge *he næfre þa y*felan *ac þa* godan. Þæs ilcan is to
wenanne to eallū ðæm gesælþum þe *seo* wyrd brengð þisses

---

[c] Boeth. ii. pr. 6. l. 38 P. ‘ Ad haec, si ipsis dignitatibus,’ &c.

[1] em. *Affricanus* C, *Affricanas* B.   [2] em.]*anus* C, *Africas* B.
[3] *se godes* B.   [4] *he* from B, *hio* C.   [5] em. *anweal* B.   [6] *hwilcū* B.
[7] *þon* J.   [8] *þæs anwealdes hiora* J.   [9] *cliofian* J.   [10] *oft þa* from
J, *of þam* B.

andweardan *lifes* ge on cræftum *ge on æhtū ; forþæm*þe hi
hwilum *becumað to þā* forcuðestum. Hwæt, we [1] *gen[og georne]*
witon ðæt nanne mon *þæs ne tweoð* ꝥ se sie strong on his
mægene þe mon gesihð ꝥ stronglic we*orc* wyrcð ; ne *þōn ma,* gif
he *hwæt* bið, ne tweoð nænne mon ꝥ *he* hwæt ne sie.   Her [2] 5

* 25b C. endað *sio for*me boc Boetius 7 ong*inne*ð *sio æftere* [2].   *Swa
mæg [3] eac se dr*eamcræft* ðæt se mon bið dreame[*re*], 7 se
læce*cræft* ꝥ he *bið* læce, 7 *seo racu deð* [4] þæt he bið *reccere.*
Swa deð *eac* se *gecynda cræft* ælcum *men* ðæt ꝥ *god ne mæg*
*be*on wið ðæ*t* yfel *gemenged, ne* ꝥ yfel wið ꝥ god ; *þeah hie* 10
buta on anum men sien, þeah bið ægðer him onsundran.   ꝥ
gecynd *nyle* næfre *nanwuht wi*ðerweardes lætan *gemengan,*
forðæm heora ægðer *onscunað* oðer, 7 ægðer wile bion ꝥ ðæt
hit bið.   Ne mæg se wela *gedon* ꝥ se gitsere ne sie *gitsere, ne*
ða grundleasan *gitsunga* gefyllan ; ne se an[*weald*] ne mæg 15
gedon his waldend *wealden*dne.   Nu þonne nu ælc [*gesc*]eaft
onscunað ðæt ðæt *hi*re wiðerweard bið, 7 swiðe georne
tiolað ꝥ hit him ꝥ from as*c*ufe, hwylce twa sint þonne
wiðerweardran b[*etwuh him*] þonne god 7 yfel?   Ne
[*weorþað hi*] næfre tosomne ge[*feged.   Be*] þæm þu meaht 20

* 26a C. ong[*itan, gif þa* *gesælþa ðises andweardan lifes þurh hie selfe*
heora selfra geweald ahton, 7 of heora agnū gecynde gode
wæron, þōn woldon hi simle on þā clifian [5] *þe him god]* mid
wo[*rhte, nalæs* [6] *yfel.   Ac*] ðær ðær [*hi gode beoð, þōn be*]oð
hi þurh [*þæs godan monnes*] god gode þe [*him god mid wyrcð*], 25
7 se bið þurh God go[*d.   Gif hine*] þonne yfel mon [*hæfð,*
þōn] bið he yfel þurh [*þæs monnes*] yfel þe him yfel [*mid deð,*
7 þurh] dioful [7].   Hwæt godes is [*se wela*] ðonne, ðonne he ne
*mæg þa gr*undleasan gitsunga *afyllan* þæs gitseres ;   oððe
se anweald, ðonne he ne mæg *his* waldend waldendne gedon ? 30
Ac hine *ge*bindað þa won welnunga m*id* hiora unabindendlicum racentum. ðeah mon nu yfelū men anwald selle, ne gedeð
se anwald hine godne ne m*e*[*do*]mne [8], gif he ær næs, ac

---

[1] *we* om. B.   [2] This sentence, omitted by B, is completed from J.
[3] *gedeð* B.   [4] *gedeð* J.   [5] *cleofian* J.   [6] *nalles* J.   [7] *deofel* B.
[8] From J, *meodumne* B.

ge[*op*]enað his yfel, gif he ær yfel [*w*]æs, 7 gede*ð* hit ðonne
sweo[*t*]ol, gif hit ær næs. Forðæm **þeah* [1] *he ær yfel wolde,* * 26b C.
þōn nysste he hu he hit swa fullice acyðde [2]*, ær he fullne
anweald hæfde. Þæt gewyrð for þam dysige þe ge fægniað*
5 *þæt ge moton sceppan þone* [3] *naman, hatan þ sælþa þ nane ne
beoð, 7 þæt medumnes þ nan medomnes* [4] *ne beoð ; forþā hi
gecyðað on heora endunge, þōn hie endiað, þ hie nauðcr ne* [5] *bioð,
forþæm nawðer* [5] *ne se wela ne se anweald ne se weorðscipe ne
beoð to wenanne þ hit seo soþe gesælð sie. Swa hit is nu hraðost* [6]
10 *to secganne* [7] *be eallum þā* woruldgesælðum [8] *þe seo wyrd brengð,
þ nan wuht on nis ðæs þær to wilnianne seo, forþāðe þær
nan* wuht gecyndelices *godes on nis þæs ðe of* him *cume. Þ* is
on ðæm sweotol *þ* hi hi symle to ðæm godū ne ðcodað [9],
ne ða yfelan gode ne *gedoð* þe *hi hie* oftosð to geþiodað.

15   § iv [d]. *Đa* se Wisdom ða þis [*spell*] ðus areaht hæfde, ða
ong[*an he*] [10] *eft* giddian 7 þus cwæð : *(*Hwæt, we witon* * 27a C.
*hwelce wælriownessa 7 hwilce hryras 7 unryhthæmedu 7 hwilc
man 7 hwilce arleasnesse se unrihtwisa* [11] *kasere Neron weorhte.
Se het æt sumum cyrre forbærnan ealle Romeburg on anne sið*
20 *æfter þære bisene þe gio Trogiaburg barn. Hine lyste eac
geseon hu seo burne, hu lange, 7 hu leohte be þære oðerre ; 7 eft
he het ofslean ealle þa wisestan witan Romana, ge furðon his
agene modor, 7 his agene broðor ; ge furðō his agen wif he
ofslog mid sweorde ; 7 for ðyllecū næs he nanwuht geunrotsod,*
25 *ac wæs þy bliþra 7 fagenode þæs. Ond þeah betwuh þyllecum
unrihtū wæs* [12] *him no þy læs underþeod eall þes middangeard
from easteweardū oþ westeweardne, 7 eft from suðeweardū oð
norðeweardne ; eall he was on his anwealde. Wenst ðu þ se
godcunda anweald ne mihte afyrran þone ānweald þā unrihtwīsan*
30 *kāsere, 7 him þære wūhhunge gestēoran, gif he wolde ? Gise,
la, gese ; īc wat þæt he mihte, gif he wolde. Eala, eaw, hu*

---

[d] Boeth. ii. met. 6. 'Nouimus quantas,' &c. Cott. Metr. ix.

[1] Only a few words legible on fol. 26b.   [2] *gecyþde* J.   [3] *wone* J.
[4] *þ nan medomnes* from J, om. B.   [5] *ne . . . nawðer* from J, om. B.
[6] em. *hradost* B.   [7] em. *secgange* B.   [8] *sælðum* J.   [9] *geðeodað* B.
[10] *he* conject. om. B.   [11] em. *unrihwisa* B.   [12] *næs* (was) B.

hefig géoc hē beslēpte[1] *on*[2] *eallæ þā þæ on his tidū libbende
wæron on eorðan; 7 hu oft his sweord wæron besyled on
unscyldegū blode.   Hu ne was þær genog sweotol þ se anweald
his agenes ðonces god næs, þa se god næs þe he to cō?*)

XVII [e].

*Ð*a se Wisdom *ða þis leoð* asungen hæfde, ða gesugode[3]
he; 7 þa andswarode[4] þæt Mod 7 þus cwæð: Eala, Gesceadwisnes, hwæt, þu [*wa*]st þ *[me næfre seo gitsung 7 seo gemægð
þisses eorðlican anwealdes forwel ne licode, ne ic ealles for-
swiðe ne girnde þisses eorðlican rices, buton tola*[5] *ic wilnode þeah
7 andweorces to þā weorce þe me beboden was to wyrcanne; þ
was þ ic unfracodlice*[6] *7 gerisenlice mihte steoran 7 reccan
þone]* anwald þe me be[*fæst wæs. Hwæt, þu*] wast þ nan
[*mon ne mæg*] nænne cræft cyðan [*ne nænne an*]weald reccan
ne stio[*ran butū*[7]] *tolū* 7 andweorce. [*Þ bið ælces*] cræftes
andweorc [*þ mon*] þone cræft *buton*[8] wyrcan [*ne*[9] *mæg. Þ*]
bið þonne cyninges [*andweorc*[10] *7*] *his* tol mid to ric*sianne, þ
he h*æbbe his lond fullmonn*ad*; he sceal habb*an* gebed*men* 7
fyrdmen[11] 7 weorcmen.   Hwæt, þu *wast þæt*te butan þissan
tolan[12] *nan cyning his cræft* ne *mæg cyðan. Þ* is eac his
ondweorc, *þ he habban* sceal to ðæm *tolū þā þrim* geferscipū
biw*iste. Þ is þon heora biwist:* land *to bugianne, 7 gifta*[13], 7
wæpnu, 7 mete, 7 *ealo*[14], *7 claþas, 7 gehwæt þæs ðe þa þre
geferscipas behofiað*[15]. *Ne mæg he butan þisū þas tol gehealdan,
ne buton þisū tolū nan þara þinga wyrcan þe him beboden is to
wyrcenne. Forþy ic wilnode andweorces* þone anweald mid to
reccenne, *þ mine cræftas 7 anweald ne wurden*[16] *forgitene 7
forholene*[16]. *Forþā ælc cræft 7 ælc* anweald bið *sona forealdod
7 for*sugod[17], gif he bið *buton* [*wisdome*]; forðæm ne mæg

[e] Boeth. ii. pr. 7. 'Tum ego, Scis, inquam,' &c.

[1] The second *e* of *beslēpte* is altered to *y*.   [2] *7 on* B.   [3] *geswigode* B.
[4] *andsworede* B.   [5] From J, *la* B.   [6] *unfracoðlice* J.   [7] *butan* J.
[8] *butan* J.   [9] *ne ne* B.   [10] From J, *weorc 7 weorc* B.   [11] *ferdmen* J.
[12] *ðisum tolum* B.   [13] *gifa* J.   [14] *ealu* J.   The greater part of fol.
29a illeg.   [15] *behofigen* J.   [16] From J; *wurde forgifen 7 forholen* B.
[17] *forswugod* B.

[*non mon nænne*] cræft bringan[1] *buton* [*wisdome*]; forðæmþe
swa *hwæt* [*swa þurh dy*]sig[2] gedon bið, *e* mæg [*hit mon*]
næfre to *cræfte* [*gerecan*[3]. *þ is nu*] hraðost to *secganne*, [*þ ic
wilnode*] weorðfullice to libb[*anne þa hwi*]le þe ic lifde, 7
5 [*æfter minū*] life þæm monnum [*to læfanne*] þe[4] æfter me
wæren min[5] *gemyn*dig[6] on godum weorcum.

XVIII [f].

§ i. *Ða* ðis þa gesprecen *was*, *þa* gesugode[7] *þ* Mod, 7 *seo
Gesceadwi*snes ongon sprecan 7 *þus cwæþ :* Eala, Mod, *eala*[8];
an[9] *yfel is* swiðe[10] to *a*nscunianne ; *þ is þ þte* swiðe singallice
10 7 swiðe hefiglice be*swicð* ealra *[þara monna mod þe beoð*[11] * 29b C.
on heora gecynde gecorene, 7 þeah ne beoð to þū hrofe þōn git
cumen fulfremedra mægena ; þ is þōn wilnung leases gilpes
7 unryhtes anwealdes 7 ungemetlices hlisan godra weorca ofer
eall folc. Forþam*[12] *wilnigað monige men*[13] *anwealdes þe hie
15 woldon habban godne hlisan, þeah*] hi his[14] unwyr[*ðe sien ; ge
furð*]um se ealra [*forcuþesta wil*]nað þæs ilcan. Ac [*se þe
wile wisli*]ce 7 geornlice [*æfter þam*] hlisan spyrian, [*þōn*]
*ongi*t he swiðe hræðe [*hu lytel*] he bið, 7 hu læne, 7 hu [*ledre,
7 h*]u bedæled ælces godes. [*Gif þu nu*] geornlice smeagan
20 wilt [*7 witan will*] ymb ealræ þisse eorðan ym[*b*]hwyrft from
easteweard*an ðisses*[15] middangeard(*es*) oð westewear[*d*]ne, 7
from suðeweardum oð norðeweardne[16], swa (*swa*) þu
liornodest on þære bec þe Astralogium hatte, ðonne meaht
þu ongetan *þ* he *is* eal wið þone heofon to metanne[17]
25 swilce an lytlu price[18] on bradum brede[19], oðþe rondbeag
on scelde, *æfter* *[wisra monna*[20] *dome. Hu ne wast þu þ ðu* * 30a C.
*leornodest on Ptolomeus bocū, se towrat ealles þises middangeardes
gemēt on anre bēc ? Þær þu miht on geseon þ eall moncynn 7 ealle*

---

[f] Boeth. ii. pr. 7. l. 4 P. ' Et illa : Atqui hoc unum est,' &c.

[1] *forðbringan* B.   [2] *dysige* B.   [3] *gereccan* J.   [4] *þe* om. B.   [5] *min* from
J, om. B.   [6] From J, *gemynd* B.   [7] *geswigode* B.   [8] *ea* J.   [9] *an* om. B.
[10] *swiðe swiðe* J.   [11] em. *þeoð* B.   [12] *forþon* J.   [13] *woruldmen* J.
[14] *his* om. B.   [15] Conject. *þis* B.   [16] From B, *norðeweardum* C.
[17] *metāne* C.   [18] *lytel pricu* B.   [19] *brādan brēde* B.   [20] From J,
mona B.

netenu ne notigað nawer neah [1]] feorðan [2] [*dæles þisse eorðan*]
ðæs þe men ge[*faran* [3] *magan, for*]þæmþe hy hit ne
[*magon eall ge*]bugian, sum [*for hǽto, sum for*] cile [4]; 7 þone
mæsta*n* [*dæl his*] hæfð sæ oferseten [5]. [*Do nu of ðam*]
feorðan dæle an þinū [*mode*] eall þ seo sæ *h*is [*ofseten hæfð*], 7 5
eal þa sceard þe hio [*him on ge*]numen hæfð, 7 eall þ his fennas
7 moras genumen *habbað*, 7 eall þ on eallum þiodum westes
ligeð, þonne meaht þu o[*ngita*]n þte þæs ealles nis monnum
*þon*ne mare læfed to bugianne, [*b*]uton swelce on [6] lytel
cauertun [7].   Is þ þonne fordyslic geswinc þ ge winnað 10
[*eow*]re woruld to ðon þæt ge wil[*n*]iað eowerne hlisan
ungemet[*li*]ce to brædanne [8] ofer swelcne cauertun [7]; swelce
þ is ðætte men *[*bugiað þisse worulde fulneah swilce an*
prica [9] *for þæt oðer.   Ac hwæt rumedlices oððe micellices oððe*
weorðfullices hæfð se cower gilp þe ge þær bogiað [10] *on þā* 15
fiftan dæle healfū londes 7 unlondes, mid sæ, mid fænne,
mid ealle, swa hit is [11] *gene*]rwed.   [*To hwon wilnige ge*]
þonne to un[*gemetlice þ ge*] eowerne naman [*tobrædan ofer*]
þone teoðan dæl, [*nu his mare nis*] mid sæ, mid [*fænne,*
mid eal]le ?   20

§ ii [s]. Geðencað eac [*þ on ði*]sum lytlan pear[*roce þe*] *we*
ær ymb spræcon [*bugiað*] swiðe manega þeoda 7 swiðe *mis-*
*li*ca [12], 7 swiðe ungelica ægþer ge on spræce ge on þeawum
ge on eallum sidum, ealra þara þeoda þe ge nu wilniað swiðe
ungemetlice [*þ ge scylon*] eowerne naman ofer tobrædan.   þ 25
ge næfre gedon ne magon, forðon [13] hiora spræc is todæled
on twa 7 (*on*) hundseofontig, 7 ælc þara spræca is todæled on
manega þioda [14], 7 þ[*a* [15] *sint*] tolegena 7 todælda mid sæ 7 [16] [*mid*]
wudum 7 mid muntum 7 (*mid*) *f*ennum [17], 7 mid manegum 7
(*mid*) mislicum weste[*num*] *7 ungeferum [18] londum, þ hit 30
furð[*ū*] cepemen *ne gefa*rað.   Ac hu mag ð[*ær*] þonne [19]

<hr>

[s] Boeth. ii. pr. 7.   l. 23 P.   'Adde quod hoc ipsum,' &c.

[1] *notiað furðum nawer* J.   [2] *fĕorðan* B.   [3] *geferan* J.   [4] *cýle* B.
[5] *sǽ ofersĕten* B.   [6] *an* B.   [7] *cafertun* B.   [8] *to gebrædanne* B.
[9] *price* J.   [10] *bugiað* J.   [11] *hit is* from J, *his* B.   [12] *mislica* from
J, *mistlice* B.   [13] *forðam* B.   [14] em. *þiod* C, *þeoda* B.   [15] *þa* conject.
om. B.   [16] 7 om. B.   [17] *fænnum* B.   [18] *ungefærum* B.   [19] *þōn* B.

synderlice anes rices monnes nama *cuman*, þonne þær mon
furðum *þære burge nam*an ne geherð ne þære *þeode þe he* on
hãfæst bið? Ðy *ic nat for hwilcon* [1] dysige ge girnað [2] þ ge
*woldon eowe*rne naman tobrædan geond ealle eorþan; þ ge
5 næfre gedon ne magon, ne furðum nawer *neah*. Hwæt, þu
wast hu micel *Romana* [*rice*] wæs on Marcuses *dagū þæs he*retogan; se wæs oðre *naman* haten 'Tullius, 7 þriddan Cicero.
Hwæt, he cyðde on sumre his boca ðætte [3] þa get Romana
(*nama ne*) come ofer þa muntas, þa [4] we hatað Caucaseas, ne
10 ða Sciððeas þe on oðre healfe þara munt[*a bugi*]að furðum
þære burge naman ne þæs folces ne geherd[*o*]n, ac þa he
com ærest to Parð*um* [5], 7 wæs (*þær*) swiðe niwe; ac he wæs
þeah *þærymbu*tan manegum folce swiðe egeful. Hu ne
ongite ge nu hu nearo se eower hlisa bion wile þe ge þær
15 ymb swincað *[7 *unr*]ihtlice tioliað *to* gebrædanne? [*Hwa*]et [*] 31b C.
wenstu hu *micelne hlisan* 7 hu micelne weorðscipe *an* [6]
romanisc man mæge habban *on þā* lande þær mon *furðum*
ðære burge naman ne *geherde*, ne ealles ðæs *folces* hlisa *ne*
com? Þeah nu hwelc mon unge*metlice* 7 ungedafenlice
20 wilnige *þ* he scyle his hlisan tobrædan ofer ealle eorþan, *he ne*
mæg þ forðbringan, forþ[*ampe*] þara ðeoda þeawas sint
[*swiðe*] ungelice, 7 hiora geseten[*essa*] *swiðe mislica* [7], swa
ðætte [*þ*] on oð[*rum*] *lande betst licað* [8] þte þ bið hwilum on
ðæm oðrum tælwyrðlicosð, 7 eac micles wites wyrðe.
25 Forðæm ne mæg nan mon habb*an gelic* lof on ælcum londe,
[*forþonðe on*] ælcum londe ne licað þ on oðrum licað.

§ iii [b]. Forðy sceolde ælc m*on* bion on [9] ðæm wel gehealden þ he *on his* agnum earde licode. Þeah he nu maran
wilnig*e*, he ne mæg furðum þ forð*bri*ngan, forþæmþe
30 seldhwonne bið þte auht monegum monnum anes hwæt
licige [10]; *forþy wyrð oft* *[*godes monnes lof alegen inne on* [11] [*] 32a C.
þære ilcan þeode þe he on hamfæst bið, 7 eac forþāþe hit oft

---

[b] Boeth. ii. pr. 7. l. 40 P. 'Erit igitur peruagata,' &c.

[1] *nat hwelce* J.   [2] *geornað* B.   [3] *þ* B.   [4] *þe* B.   [5] *parððum* B.
[6] *on* B.   [7] From J, *mistle* B.   [8] *licode* J.   [9] *on* above line in C.
[10] *licige . . . oft* concealed under the paper mounting.   [11] *in* J.

swiðe sarlice gebyrede þurh þa] heard[*sælþa þara writera*]
ðæt hi for [*heora slæwðe 7 for gi*]meleste 7 eac[1] [*for recceleste
for*]leton unwriten [*þara monna ðeawas*] 7 hiora dæda, þe o[*n
hiora dagum*] formæroste [*7 weorðgeornuste*] wæron.   7 þeah
hi [*nu eall hiora*] lif 7 hira dæda awr[*iten hæfdon*], swa swa 5
hi sceold*on* [*gif hi dohton*], hu ne forealdodon þa g[*ewritu*]
þeah 7 losodon þonec*an* [*þe hit wære*], swa some swa þa
wri[*teras dydon, 7*] eac þa ðe[2] hi ymb wri[*ton.   7 eow þincð*]
þeah þ ge hæbben ece [*are gif ge mæ*]gen on ealre eowerre
[*worulde ge*]earnigan þ ge hæbben [*godne hlisan*] æfter 10
eowrum *d*agum.   [*Gif þu nu*] getelest þa hwila þisses
[*andweardan*] lifes 7 þisses hwile*ndlican*[3] [*wið þæs*] ungeendodan lifes hwi*l*a, [*hwæt bið*] hit þonne?   Tele nu þa lengu[4]
þ[*ære hwile*] þe þu þin eage on bepre*wan*[5] mæge wið ten[6]
ðusend wintra ; þon*ne* habbað þa hwila hwæthwugu *[*onlices*, 15
*þeah hit lytel sie ; þ is þōn þ heora ægþer hæfð ende. Tele nu þon
þ ten þusend geara, ge þeah þu ma wille, wið þ ece 7 þæt
ungeendode lif ; þōn ne finst þu þær nauht angelices*[7], *forðam*]
þ ten[6] ðusend [*geara, þeah hit lan*]g ðince, ascor[*taþ, 7 þæs
oðres*] næfre[8] ne cymð [*nan ende.   Forþæ*]m[9] hit nis no to 20
[*metanne þ gee*]ndodlice wið ðæt [*ungeendodlice.   Þe*]ah þu nu
telle [*from þises m*]iddangeardes fru[*man oð ðone*] ende,
7 mete þonne [*þa gear wið*] þ ðe nænne ende næfð, [*þonne*]
ne bið þær nauht anlices.   [*Swa bið*] eac se hlisa þara
for[*emærena*[10] *monn*]a ; þeah he hwilum [*lang sie, 7 fe*]la geara 25
þurhwu[*nige, he bið þ*]eah swiðe scort to [*metanne wi*]ð ðone
þe næfre [*ne geendað.*

§ iv[i]. 7] ge ne reccað ðeah [*hweðer ge a*]uht to gode don
wið [*ænegū oþrū*] þingum buton [*wið þam lytlan*] lofe þæs
folces, [*7 wið*] þæm scortan hlisan þe we ær *y*mb spræcon. 30
Earniað þæs, 7 *f*orsioð þa cræftas eoweres ingeðonces 7

---

[1] Boeth. ii. pr. 7.   l. 60 P.   'Vos autem, nisi ad populares auras,' &c.

[1] *eac* om. B.   [2] *ðe* om. B.   [3] *þises hwilwendlican* B.   [4] *lenge* B.
[5] So J ; B. has *beprenan* with the first *n* altered to *w*.   [6] *tin* B.
[7] *anlices* J.   [8] *næfre* follows *cymþ* in B.   [9] em. *foþam* B.
[10] *formæra* J.

eowres andgietes 7 eowre gescead *wisnesse, [7 *wold*]on * 33ª C.
habban eowerra godena *weorca* mede æt fremdra mo*nna*
cwiddunge. Wilnigað[1] þærto þære *mede þe ge to Gode* sceolden.
*Hwæt, þu gehyrdest þæt*te gio dagū *gelomp þ an swiðe wis*
5 mon 7 swiðe *rice* ongan *fandigan*[2] *anes* uðwitan 7 hine
bismrode, *forð*æm he hine swa orgellice *up ahof*, 7 *bodo*de þæs
þ he uðwita wære ; *ne cyð*de he hit mid nænum *cræftū*, ac
mid leasum 7 ofer*modlicū* gelpe[3]. Þa wolde se wisa *mon his*
*f*andian, hwæðer he swa wis *wære* swa he self wende þ he
10 wære.   Ongon hine þa hyspan, 7 hearmcwidian[4].   Þa
geherde se uðwita swiðe geþyldelice þæs wisan monnes word
sume hwile ; ac siððan he his hispinge gehered hæfde, þa
sc*y*lde[5] he ongean swiðe ungeþyldelice[6], þeah he ær lic*e*tte þ
he uðwita wære. (*Ahsode hine þa eft hwæðer him þuhte þ he*
15 *upwita wære*) þe nære. Ða andswarode se wisa mon him 7
cwæð: Ic wolde cweþ[*an*] þ þu uðwita wære, gif þu
ge[*ðyldig wæ*]re 7 gesugian meahte[7]. [*Hu lang*]sum wæs
him se hlisa, þa [*he*] ær mid leasungum wilnode. *[Hu ne * 33ᵇ C.
for]bærst [*he þa þærri*]hte for ðæm anum and*w*yrde. Hwæt
20 forstod þ[*onn*]e þæm betstum monnum *þe ær us wæron þ hi*
swa swiðe wilnodon *þæs idelan gilpes*[8] 7 þæs hlisan æfte*r*
heora deaþe ? oððe hw*æt forstent* hit þæm þe nu sindo*n* ? *Þy*
wære ælcum [*men*] mare þe[*arf þ he*] wilnode godr*a* cræfta
þōn leases hlisan. Hwæ*t* hæfð he *æt þā* hlisan æfter þæs
25 li*choman* ge*d*ale 7 þære sawle ? [*Hu ne*] witon we þ ealle
me[*n*] lichom*lice* sweltað, 7 þeah sio sawl bið libb[*ende*] ? *Ac*
sio sawl færð swiðe friolice to hefonum, siððan hio ontiged
bið, 7 for[9] þæm carcern*e þæs* lichoman onlesed bið. *Heo*
forsihð[10] þonne eall [*ðas eorðli*]can þing, 7 fægnað[11] þæs þ
30 hio *mot* brucan þæs heofonlican, siððan[12] hio bið abrogden
from ðæm eorðlican. Þonne þ mod him selfum gewita bið
God*es* willan.

---

[1] *wilniað* J.   [2] *fandian* J.   [3] *gilpe* B.   [4] *hearmcwiddigan* B.
[5] From J, *sealde* B.   [6] *ðyldelice* B.   [7] *mihtest* B.   [8] *gelpes* J.
[9] *of* B.   [10] *forseohð* B.   [11] *fagenað* B.   [12] *siðæs* B.

XIX [k].

Ða se Wisdom þa [*þis*] spel areaht hæfde, ða o[*ngan he*]
gyddian 7 ðus singende [*cwæð:*] *(Swa hwa swa wilnige to
habbenne þone idelan hlisan 7 þone unnyttan gilp, behealde he on
feower healfe his hu widgille þæs heofones hwealfa bið, 7 hu
neara þære eorðan stede is, þeah heo us rum þince. Þōn mæg* 5
hine scamigan[1] *þære brædinge his hlisan, forþam he hine ne
mæg furðum tobrædan ofer þa nearwan eorðan ane. Æala,
ofermodan, hwi ge wilnigen þ ge underlutan mid eowrū swiran
þ deaðlice geoc? oððe hwi ge seon on swa idelan geswince þ ge
woldon eowerne hlisan tobrædan ofer swa manega þeoda? Þeah* 10
*hit nu gebyrige þ ða utemestan ðioda eowerne naman up ahebban,
7 on manig þeodisc eow herigen, 7 þeah hwa wexe mid micelre
æþelcundnesse his gebyrda, 7 þeo on eallū welū 7 on eallū
wlencū, ne se deaþ þeah swelces ne recð. Ac he forsiehð þa
æþelo, 7 þone rican gelice 7 þone heanan ofswelgð*[2], *7 swa* 15
geemnet þa rican 7 þa heanan. <u>Hwæt synt nu þæs foremeran</u>
7 þæs wisan goldsmiðes ban Welondes? Forþi ic cwæð þæs
wisan forþy þā cræftegan ne mæg næfre his cræft losigan, ne
hine mon ne mæg þon eð on him geniman ðe mon mæg þa sunnan
awendan of hiere stede.* <u>Hwær synt nu þæs Welondes ban, oððe</u> 20
<u>hwa wat nu hwær hi wæron?</u> Oððe hwær is nu se foremæra
7 se aræda Romwara heretoga, se wæs haten Brutus, oðre
naman Cassius? Oððe se wisa 7 fæstræda Cato, se wæs eac
Romana heretoga; se wæs openlice uðwita. Hu ne wæran
þas gefyrn forðgewitene? 7 nan mon nat hwær hi nu sint.* 25
*Hwæt is heora nu to lafe, butan se lytla hlisa 7 se nama mid
feaum stafū awriten? 7 þæt git wyrse is, þ we witon manige
foremære 7 gemyndwyrþe weras forðgewitene þe swiðe feawa
manna a ongit. Ac manige licggað deade mid ealle forgitene,
þ se hlisa hie furðū cuþe ne gedeð. Þeah ge nu wenen 7 wilnian* 30
*þ ge lange libban scylan her on worulde, hwæt bið eow þōn þy
bet? Hu ne cymð se deað þeah, þeah he*[3] *late cume, 7 adeð eow*

---

[k] Boeth. ii. met. 7. 'Quicumque solam,' &c. Cott. Metr. x.

[1] *scamian* B.   [2] em. *ofswelfð* B.   [3] *deað* ab. l., over *he* erased.

*of ðisse worulde ?   7 hwæt forstent eow þon se gilp, huru þā þe
se æfterra deað gegripð 7 on ecnesse gehæfð ?*)

XXI.

Ða se Wisdom þa [*þis leoð*] asungen hæfde, ða [*ongan*] *he*
spillian 7 ðus cwæð : Ne wen ðu no ꝥ ic to *an*willice winne
5 wið ða wyrd; *forðæm* ic hit no self nauht ne ondræde,
for[*þā hit oft*] gebyreð ꝥ sio lease [*wyrd nauþ*]er ne *mæg*
þæm men [*don*] ne fultum ne eac nænne dē. [*Forþā*] hio
nis naues lofes wyrðe, *[*forþā*] hio *hire* se[*lf g*]ecyð ꝥ *heo*   * 35b C.
nan*wuht* ne bi*ð* ; ac heo onwrihð hire æwelm þon[*ne* [1] *heo geop-*
10 *enað*] *hiore* þeawas.   Ic [*we*]ne ðe[*ah ꝥ ðu*] *ne forstande* nu get
hwæt *ic þe to cweðe; forþam* hit is wund*orlic þæt ic secgan*
wille, 7 *ic* hit *mæg uneaðe* mid wordum areccan [2] swa swa *ic*
wolde ; ꝥ is ðæt (*ic* [3]) wa*t* [4] ðætte [5] sio wið*erwearde wyrd*
*bi*ð ælcum men nytw*yrðre þon* sio orsorge.   Forðæm *seo*
15 *orsorge simle* lihð 7 licet *ꝥ mon scyle wenan* ꝥ hio is [6] sio so*ð*e
gesælð ; ac sio wiðerwearde is sio *soðe gesælþ,* þeah hwæm
swa ne *þynce,* forðæm *heo is fæst*ræd 7 *gehæt* simle ꝥte soð
bið.   Sio oðru [*is leas*] 7 beswicð *ealle* hire [*geferan, for*]ðæm
hio hit [7] gecyð se*lf* [*mid hire hwu*]*rf*ulnesse ꝥ hio bið [*swiðe*
20 *wancol*] ; ac sio wiðerwearde ge[*bet 7*] gelæreð ælcne þara þe
hio hi *to* geþiet.   Sio oðru gebinð ælc ðara moda ðe hire
bryc ð mid ðære hiwunga þe (*hio*) licet ꝥ hio sie god ; sio
wiðerwearde [*þōn*] onbinð [8] 7 ge*f*reoð ælc [*þara þe*] hio to
geðiet, mid ðæm þe [*hio him*] geopenað *hu tiedre* [9] *[ꝥæs*   * 36a C
25 *andweardan gesælða sint.   Ac seo orsorhnes* [10] *gæð scyrmælū*   about here.
swæðer [11] *windes þyf* [12]; *sio wiðerweardnes þōn bið simle*
untælu 7 wæru [13], *ascirped* [14] *mid þære styringe hire agenre*

[1] Boeth. ii. pr. 8.   'Sed ne me inexorabile,' &c.

[1] Conj. ðōn B.   [2] *gereccan* B.   [3] Conject. om. C and B.   [4] Apparently
wa C.   [5] *te* om. B.   [6] *seo* B.   [7] *hit* om. B.   [8] *anbint* B.   [9] *tedra* J.
[10] em. *orsohnes* B.   [11] *swa þær* J.   [12] em. suggested by Prof.
Napier ; *ðyf* B; no reading in J.   [13] From J, *wracu* B.   [14] Orig.
ascirred in B, but the second *r* changed to *þ*; J has *ascerped.*

*frecennesse.   Ac sio lease gesæld hio tihð on last neadinga þa þe
hiere to geðeodað f*]rom þæm soð[*ū* [1] *gesælðum mid hiere* [2]]
oliccunge [3] ; sio wið[*erweardnes* [4] *þōn ful*] oft ealle ða ðe
[*hiere underþeodde bioð neadi*]nga getyhð to ð[*am soðum
gesælðum*], swa swa mid angl[*e fisc gefangen bið*].   Ðincð ðe 5
nu þ [*lytel gestreon 7 lytel*] eaca þinra gesæl[*ða þætte ðeos
reðe 7*] þios egeslice wiðerweardnes [*þe bringð*]?   þ is þ hio
swiðe hraðe ða [*mod þe geope*]nað þinra getreowra f[*r*]eonda
[*7 eac*] þinra fionda, þ þu hi mı̄ht swiðe sweotole [5] tocnawan?
Ac þæ[*s leasan ge*]sælða, þonne hi ðe from gewitað, þonne 10
nimað hi hiora *men* mid him, 7 lætað [6] þine feawan getreowan
mid ðe.   Hu woldes ðu nu gebyc[*ggan þa*] þu gesælegost
wære 7 þ[*e þuhte þ se*]o wyrd swiðost [*on þinne willan wode*]?
mid hu m[*icelan* [7] *feo woldest þu þa habban geboht þ ðu switole*

* 36b C   *mihtest tocnawan þine frind* [8] *7 ðine fynd* [9] *?   *Ic wat ðeah þ* 15
about here. *ðu hit woldest habban mid miclan feo* [10] *geboht þ ðu hi cuðest
wel toscadan.   Þeah þe nu þince þ ðu deorwyrðe feoh* [11] *forloren
habbe, þu hæfst þeah micle diorwyrðre mid geboht ; þ sint
getreowe friend ; þa ðu miht nu tocnawan, 7 wast hwæt þu hiora
hæfst*].   Hwæt, þ [*is þ eallra deorweo*]rðoste fioh.   20

XXI [m].

[*Ða se Wisdom þa ðis*] spell asæd hæfde, [*þa ongan he
giddigan* [12]] 7 þus singende [*cwæð*]: (*An sceppend is buton
ælcum tweon, 7 se is eac wealdend heofones 7 eorðan 7 ealra
gesceafta, gesewenlicra 7 eac ungesewenlicra ; þ is God ælmihtig.   Þā ðeowiað ealle þa þe ðeowiað, ge ða þe cunnon ge þa* 25
*þe ne cunnon, ge þa ðe hit witon þ hie him ðeowiað ge þa ðe hit
nyton.   Se ilca gesette unawendendlicne sido 7 þeawas 7 eac
gecyndelice sibbe eallū 'his gesceaftū, ða þa he wolde, 7 swa swa
he wolde, 7 swa lange swa he wolde ; þa nu sculon standan to
worulde.   Ðara unstillena gesceafta styring ne mæg no* 30

[m] Boeth. ii. met. 8. 'Quod mundus,' &c.   Cott. Metr. xi.

[1] *soþan* J.   [2] *þære* J.   [3] *olecunge* B.   [4] em. *wiðerwerdnes* B.
[5] From J, *swutele* B.   [6] From B, *lædað* C.   [7] *micle* J.   [8] *frend* J.
[9] *fiend* J.   [10] *micle fio* J.   [11] *fioh* J.   [12] *giddian* J.

*weorðan gestilled, ne eac onwend of þam ryne 7 of þære
endebyrdnesse þe him geset is; ac se anwealda hæfð ealle his
gesceafta swa mid his bridle befangene 7 getogene 7 gemanode
swa þ hi nauþer ne gestillan ne moton, ne eac swiðor styrian*
5 *þōn he him þæt gerū his wealdleðeres to forlæt. Swa hæfð se
ælmihtiga God geheaðorade ealle his gescefta mid his anwealde
þæt heora ælc winð wið oðer, 7 þeah wræðeð oðer, þ hie ne moton
toslupan, ac bioð*[1] *gehwerfde eft to þā ilcan ryne þe hie ær urnon,
7 swa weorðað eft geedniwade. Swa hi hit fagiað þ þa wiðer-*
10 *weardan gesceafta ægðer ge hie betwux hī winnað, ge eac fæste
sibbe betwux*[2] *him healdað. Swa nu fyr deð, 7 wæter 7 sæ 7
eorðe, 7 manega oðra gesceafta þe beoð a swa ungeðwæra
betwux him swa swa hi beoð; 7 þeah hi beoð swa geþwæra
þætte no þ an þæt hi magon geferan beon, ac þy furðor þ heora*
15 *furðum nan buton oðrū beon ne mæg. Ac a sceal þ wiðerwearde
þ oðer wiðerwearde gemetgian. Swa nu hæfð se ælmihtega
God swiðe gesceadwislice 7 swiðe limplice geset þ gewrixle eallū
his gesceaftū. Swa nu lencten 7 hærfest: on lencten hit
grewð, 7 on hærfest hit wealwað. 7 eft sumer 7 winter: on*
20 *sumera hit bið wearm, 7 on wintra ceald. Swa eac sio sunne
bringð leohte dagas, 7 se mona liht on niht, þurh þæs ilcan
Godes miht. Se ilca forwyrnð þæræ sæ þ heo ne mot þone
þeorscwold oferstæppan þære eorþan*[3]. *Ac he hæfð heora
mearce swa gesette þ hie ne*[4] *mot heore mearce gebrædan ofer*
25 *þa stillan eorþan. Mid þā ilcan gerece is gereaht swiðe anlic
gewrixle þæs flodes 7 þæs ebban. Þa gesetennesse*[5] *þa he læt
standan þa hwile þe he wile. Ac þonne ær þe he þ gewealdleðer
forlæt þara bridla þe he ða gesceafta nu mid gebridlode hæfð: þ
is*[6] *seo wiðerweardnes þe we ær ymbe spræcon: gif he þa læt*
30 *toslupan, þōn forlætað hi þa sibbe ðe hi nu healdað, 7 winð
heora ælc on oðer æfter his agenū willan, 7 forlætað heora
geferrædenne, 7 fordoð ealne ðysne middaneard, 7 weorðað him
selfe to nauhte. Se ilca God gefegð mid freondrædenne folc*

---

[1] *bið* B.   [2] em. *betwx* B.   [3] *mæru* follows *eorðan* above line.
[4] *ne* conj. om. B.   [5] em. *gesetennes* B.   [6] *is* conj. om. B.

*togædere, 7 sinhigscipas gesamnað mid clænlicre lufe.   He
gegaderað frind 7 geferan þ hie getreowlice heora sibbe 7 heora
freondrædenne healdað.   Eala þte þis moncyn wære gesælig, gif
heora mod wære swa riht 7 swa gestaðelod 7 swa geendebyrd
swa swa þa oðre gesceafta sindon.)   Her endað nu seo æftre* 5
*frofer*boc[1] Boeties, 7 onginð *sio* þridde.   Se Boetius wæs
oðre naman haten[2] S*euerinus;* se wæs heretoga Romana.

XXII [n].

§ i. *Ða* se Wisdom þa ðis lioð asungen hæfde, þa hæfde
he me gebundenne mid *þære* wynsumnesse his san[*ges, þ ic
his*] wæs swiðe wafiende 7 swi[*ðe lu*]stbære (*hine*) to geheranne 10
mid [*inne*]wearde mode, 7 þa fulhræðe [*ðæs ic*] cleopode to
him 7 þus cwæð: [*Eala, Wis*]dom, þu ðe eart sio heh[*ste
fro*]fer ealra werigra moda[3]; hu þu me hæfst afrefredne ægþer ge mid þinre smealican spræce, ge mid þinre wynsumnesse þines sanges.   To þæm þu me hæfst n[*u*] aretne[4] 15
7 ofercumene mid þin[*re*] gesceadwisnesse, þ me nu ðincð
ð[*æt*]te no þ an þ ic [*ðas*] unwyrd aræf[*nan *mæg ðe me on
becumen is, ac þeah me*] giet mare frecenes[5] on becume, ne *cwi*ðe
ic *næfre* ma þ hit butan g[*ewyrhtū sie*]; forðæm ic wat þ ic
[*maran 7 hefigran*] wyrðe wære. [*Ac ic wolde ymbe þone*] 20
læcedom [*þara þinra lara hwene mare*] geheran. Þ[*eah þu
nu hwene ær sæ*]de þ þu wende þ *hi woldon me swi*ðe bitere
þincan, *ne ondræde*[6] ic hi me nu nauht[7], *ac ic heora eom* swiðe
gifre æg ðer g[*e*] to geheranne ge eac to gehealdenne, 7 þe
swiðe georne bidde þ þu hi me gelæste, s[*wa swa ðu me*] nu 25
lytle ær gehete. Þ[*a cwæð se*] *Wisdom:* Ic onge*at* sona [*þa
ðu swa wel*] geswugodes 7 swa lustlic[*e geher*]dest mina lara,
þ þu woldest [*mid*] innewearde mode hi ong[*iton*] 7 smeagean. Forðæm *ic* gean*bid*ode swiðe wel oþ ic wisse hwæt
[*þu woldest*] 7 hu þu hit understandan *woldest*, 7 eac þy 30
furður ic tiolode swiðe geornfullice þ þu hit forstandan

---

[n] Boeth. iii. pr. 1. 'Iam cantum illa finiuerat,' &c.
[1] *æfterre frofrboc* J.   [2] *gehaten* B.   [3] *doma* B.   [4] *geretne* B.
[5] *frecennes* B.   [6] em. *ondrade* B.   [7] *me nauht nu* B.

meah[*te*] [1].   Ac ic þe nu wille secgan hwilc se [*læ*]cecræft is
minre lare þe þu *me nu* bitst.   He is swiðe biter on *muðe*, 7
he þe tirð on ða þrotan *[*þōn ðu his ærast fandast ; ac he*] * 39b C.
weredað [2] siððan he innan bið 7 [3] *swiðe* [4] *li*ðe on ðæm *i*nnoðe,
5 7 [*swi*]ðe swiðe [*swete*] to bealcetenne [5].

§ ii. [n*] Ac [*þær ðu ongeate h*]wider ic ðe [*nu*] tiohige [*to
lædenne* [6], *ic wat*] ðæt þu wold*est* [*swiðe georne þider fundian
7 swiðe swiðlice beon onæled mid þ*]ære *gitsunge*, *forþā ic
geherde þ ðu ær sædest þ þu swiðe* geornfull *wære hit to
10 gehyranne.*   Da cwæð þ Mod :   Hwid*er* wilt ðu me (*nu
swiðost*) lædan ?   Da   andwyrde   sio   Gesceadw[*is*]nes 7
cwæð :   To [*þ*]æm soðum gesælðum ic tiohige ðæt [*ic þe
læde*], þær [7] þin mod oft ymb [*ræsweð 7 eac*] mæt [8] ; 7 þu ne
meahtes *gyt ful rihtn*]e weg aredian to ðæm [*soðum
15 gesa*]elðum, forðon [9] þin mod [*wæs abis*]god mid ðære
ansene [10] þissa [*leasena*] gesælða.   Da cwæð þ Mod : Ic [*þ*]e
*hea*lsige þ þu me oðewe butan [*ælcū tw*]eon hwæt sio soðe
gesælð sie.   Da *c*wæð sio Gesceadwisnes :   Ic wille forlustlice
for ðinum lufum ; [*ac*] ic *sceal* be sumre bysene sume
20 anlicnesse þære wisan (*ðe*) getæcan, [*oð*] ðe þæt þing cuðre
sie, to ðæm þ þu þa bisne sweotole [11] gesceaw[*ige, 7 þon*]ne
be þære anlicnesse þara [*soðena *gesælþa ðu mæge ongitan þa * 40a C.
soðan gesælða, 7 forlætan* [12] *þætte him wiðer*]weard bið ; þ sint
þa leasan gesa[*elða ; 7 þonne mid ealles modes geornfulla*[n]
25 ingeðonce *higie* [13] þ þu mæge becuman *to þā* gesælðum þe ece
þurh*uniað.*

XXIII [o].

ÐA se Wisdom ða ðis spell aræd [14] *hæfde, þa ongan he eft
giddian, 7 ðus* [15] *cwæð : (Swa hwa swa wille sawan westmbære
land, atio ærest of ða þornas 7 þa fyrsas 7 þ fearn 7 ealle þa*

[n*] Boeth. iii. pr. 1.   l. 14 P.   ' Sed quod tu te audiendi,' &c.
[o] Boeth. iii. met. 1.   ' Qui serere,' &c.   Cott. Metr. xii.

[1] From J, *mihtest* B.   [2] *ðe weredað* J, *werodað* B.   [3] *innað 7
hið* B.   [4] em. *swðe* B.   [5] *belcentan* B.   [6] *lædanne* J.   [7] *þe* B.
[8] *hræswæð 7 eac mæt* J, *ræsweð 7 eaðmet* B.   [9] *forþam* B.   [10] *ansine* B.
[11] *swëole* C.   [12] From J, *forlæt* B.   [13] *higige* J.   [14] From J, *areht* B.
[15] *ðus ðus* B.

*weod þe he gesio þ þā æcerū derigen, þ se hwǣte mæge þy bet
weaxan.   Eac is ðeos bisen to geðencenne, þ is þ ælcū men
þincð huniges biobread þy weorodra gif he hwene ær biteres
onbirigð.   7 eft smylte weder bið þy þancwyrðre gif hit hwene
ær bið stearce stormas 7 norðanwindas 7 micle renas 7 snawas. 5
7 þancwyrðre bið eac þas dæges leoht for þære egeslican þiostro
þære nihte, þōn hit wære gif nan niht nære.   Swa bið eac
micle þe winsumre sio soðe gesælð to habbenne efter þā eormðum
þisses andweardan lifes.   7 eac micle ði eð þu miht þa soðan
gesælða gecnawan 7 to hiora cyðði becuman, gif ðu ærest 10
awyrtwalast of þinū mode ða leasan gesælða, 7 hi of aliht oð
ðone grund.   Siððan þu hi þōn gecnawan miht, ðonne wat ic þ
ðu ne wilnast nanes oðres þinges ofer þa.)*

XXIV ^p.

§ i. [*Þa he þa*] þis leoð asungen h[*æfde, þ*]a forlet he
þone sang, [*7 gesw*]ugode ane hwile, 7 *on*[*gann*] smealice 15
þencan *on his modes ingeþance*, 7 ða[1] cwæð: Ælc deaðlic
man swencð hine *selfne* [*mid mistli*]cum[2] 7 mænigfealdum
ymb[*ho*]gum, 7 þeah wilniað ea*lle* [*ðurh mist*]lice[3] paðas
cuman to anū ende ; [*þ is*] þ hi wilniað þurh ungelic*e*
earnunga cuman to anre *eadig*nesse; þ is þonne God; [*se*] 20
is fruma 7 ende ælces goodes, 7 *he* is sio hehste gesælð.   Ða
cwæð *ðæt Mod: [4] Ðæt me ðincð sie þ hehste good[4], [*þæt*]te
mon[5] ne [*ðurfe nanes oðres godes*], ne eac [*ne recce ofer þ,
siððan*] he þ hæbbe [*þ is hrof*[6] *eallra oðerra*] good[*a ; forþā
hit eall oðru god*[7]] utan be*fehð*, [*7 eall oninnan him*] hæfð. 25
Nære *hit* [*no þ hehste god*[7]] gif him ænig [*butan wære, for*]-
þæm hit þonn[*e*] hæfde[8] t[*o wilnian*]ne sumes goodes þe hit
[*self*] næfde.   þa andswarode *sio* [*Gesce*]adwisnes 7 cwæð:
Ðæt is[9] swið[*e sweotol*] þ ðæt is sio hehste ges[*ælð, for*]ðæm
hit is ægðer ge hrof [*ge flor*] ealles goodes.   Hwæt is ðæt 30
[*þōn*] buton sio seleste ges[*ælð, þe ða*] oðra gesælða ealla on-

^p Boeth. iii. pr. 2.   'Tum defixo paululum uisu,' &c.
[1] *ðus* B.   [2] *mislicum* J.   [3] *mislice* J.   [4] *ðæt . . . good* gone from
top of fol. 41a, but written at bottom of fol. 40b in a modern hand.
[5] *þ se man* B.   [6] *frofr* J.   [7] *good* J.   [8] *hæfde þōn* B.   [9] *is* om. B.

[*innan him*] gegaderað, 7 hi utan ymb[*hæfð*[1], 7] oninnan
him gehelt, 7 him *n*anes ne bið wana, ne he nanes nedþearfe
næfð, ac hi cumað eall of him, 7 eft eall to him, swa swa
eall wætru cumað of ðære sæ, [7] eft cumað ealle[2] to ðære
sæ? Nis nan to ðæs lytel æwylm[3] þ he þa sæ ne [*ge*]sece ;
7 eft of ðære sæ *he gelent in on þa eorð*an, [7 *sw*]a he bið
smugende geond þa eorð[*an oð he*] eft cymð to ðæm *ilcan[4] * 41b C.
æwe[*lme þe he ær ut fleow, 7 swa eft to þære sæ.*

  § ii [q]. *Ðis is n*]u bysen *þara* [*soþena gesælða ; þara*] wilniað
[*ealle deaðlice men to begitanne, þeah hi ðurh mislice wegas
ðencan to cumanne. Forþā ægh*]welc man hæfð [*gecyndelic god
on him*] selfum, for[*þā ælc mod wilnað so*]ðes godes to [*begitanne ; ac hit bið*] amerred mid [*þā lænum*] godum[5], forðæm
hit [*bið*] ofdælre[6] ðærto. Forð[*ā sume menn wenað þæt þ se
seo seleste gesælð þ mon seo swa welig þ he nanes ðinges maran
ne ðurfe, 7 wilniað hiora*] woruld æfter [*þā. Sume men wenað
þ þ sie þæt hehte god þ he sie his geferū his geferena weorðost,
7 eallon ma*]egene ðæs tiolað. *Sume wenað þ ðæt hehste
good sie on þā* hehs*t*an anwalde; þa wil*niað oðer* twega, oððe
him selfe *ricsian*, oððe hi to ðæra ricena freondscipe geþiod[*an*].
Sume þonne tiohiað þ ðæt betst sie þ mon sie foremære 7
widmære, 7 hæbbe godne[7] hlisan ; tiliað þonne þæs ægðer ge
on sibbe ge on gewinne. [*Manege tella*]ð þ t[*o*] mæst[*u*]m
goode [7 *to mæstere g*]esælðe *[*þ mon sie simle bliðe on þis* * 42a C.
*andweardan life, 7 fulga eallum his lustū. Sume þonne þa þe
ðas welan wilniað, hi his wilniað forþā þæt hi*[8] *woldean ðy
maran anweald habban, þ he mihte*[9] *þy orsorglicor ðissa
woruldlusta brucan, 7 eac þas welan. Mane*]ga[10] sint þ[*ara þe
forþi wilniað an*]waldes þe *hie* [*woldon ormæte feoh*[11] *gega*]-
derian ; oððe [*eft þone hlisan heo*]ra naman hi [*wilniað þ hi
gebrædan*].

---

[q] Boeth. iii. pr. 2. l. 13 P. 'Est enim mentibus hominum,' &c.

[1] *ymbfehð* J.   [2] *ealle cumað* B.   [3] *æwelm* B.   [4] *ilcan æwe*[
written at bottom of fol. 41a in a modern hand, cf. p. 52, note 4.
[5] *goodum* J.   [6] em. by Junius, *oftðælre* J, *ofðælre* B.   [7] *heah be gone* B.
[8] em. *he* B.   [9] *meahte* J.   [10] *manegæ* B.   [11] *fioh* J.

§ iii [r]. On swilcum 7 [*on oðrum swelcū læ*]num 7 hreo*sendū* [1]
[*weorðscipū*] ælces mennisces [*modes ingeþanc bið*] *ges*wenced
mid ðære geor[*nfulnesse 7*] *mid* ðære tilun*c*ga [2]; wenð [*þōn*]
þ hit hæbbe sum healic [*god* [3] *gestryned*] þonne hit hæfð
genumen [4] [*þæs folces*] ole*c*unga; 7 [5] me þincð *þ* hit [*hæbbe* 5
ge]*boht* sume swiðe leaslice [*mærðe*].   *Sume* filiað mid
micelre [*geo*]rnfulnesse wifa, forðæm *þ* he þurh ðæt mæge
mæst bearna be[*gil*]an, 7 eac wynsumlice libban.   Ð[*a*
getr]iewan friend þonne ic secgge sie ðæt *deorwyr*ðeste ðing
ealra þissa wco[*ruldgesæl*]ða; þa ne sint furðum [6] [*to woruld-* 10

godū to te]llanne, ac to godcundum; *[*forþā seo lease wyrd hi*
. na forð ne bringð, ac se God þe hi gecyndelice gesceop to gemagū.
Forþamðe ælces oðres þinges on þisse worulde mon wilnað,
oððe forþāþe he mæg þurh þ to anwealde cuman, oððe to sumū
woruldluste, butan þæs getreowan freondes; þone] mon lu[*fað* 15
hwilū for lufū 7] for trio[*wum, þeah he him*] nanra oðerra
[*læna* [7] *ne wene. Þ*] gecynd gefægð [8] [*7 gelimð þa friend*]
togadre mid [*swiðe untodeledlicre l*]ufe.   Ac [*mid þissū*
wo]ruldgesælðum 7 [*mid þis andwe*]ardan welan mon
[*wyrcð of*]tor fiond ðonne freond. [*Be ðisan* [9] *7 be*] mænegum 20
þillicum mæg [*beon eal*]lū monnum cuð ðætte [*ealle þa*
lic]umlican [10] good bioð for[*cuðran*] ðonne ðære sawle cræftas.
[*Hwæt, we*] wenað ðæt mon bio *þy* stren*c*ra [11] þe he bið
micel on his lic*homan.*   *Seo* fægernes ðonne 7 sio hwæt*nes*
þa[*es*] lichoman geblissað ðone mon 7 ar[*e*]t, 7 sio hælo hine 25
gedeð lusðbærne.   On eallum ðissum lic[*um*]licū [12] ge-
sæli[*g*]nessū men s[*ecað anfealde*] eadignesse ðæs ð[*e him*

ðincð, forþā **þe* [13] *æghwelc man swa hwæt swa he ofer ealle*
oðre þing swiðost lufað, þ he teohhað [14] *þ him sie betst, 7 þæt*
bið his hehste god [15]; *þōn he þæt ðōn begiten hæfð, þōn* 30
tihhað [16] *he þ he mæge beon swiðe gesælig*].   Ne [17] onsac[*e*

---

[r] Boeth. iii. pr. 2. l. 28 P. 'In his igitur ceterisque,' &c.

[1] *hi reosendū* B.   [2] From J, *tiolunga* B.   [3] *good* J.   [4] *gewunnen* B.
[5] *ond* B.   [6] *furðon* B.   [7] *leana* J.   [8] *gefehð* B.   [9] *ðis* J.
[10] From J, *lichamlican* B.   [11] From J, *strængra* B.   [12] From
J, *licamlicum* B.   [13] Top of fol. 43a C partly gone, partly illegible.
[14] *tiohhað* J.   [15] *good* J.   [16] *tiohhað* J.   [17] *ħ* C.

ic nauht þ ða gesælða] 7 *(seo)*[1] eadignes [*sie þæt hehste*[2]
god[3] *þises*] andweard[*an lifes ; forþā ðe*[4] *æg*]hwilc mon[5]
tiohh[*að*[6] *þ þ ðing betst*] sie þ he swiðust [*ofer oðre þing
lu*]fað; 7 þonne he [*tiohhað þ he sie*] swiðe gesælig gif [*he
5 þæt begitan mæg*] ðæt he þonne swiþus[*t willnað. Hu ne*] is
þ[7] nu genoh openlice g[*eeowad*] þara leasena gesælða *anlic-*
[*nes,*] þ is þonne æhta 7 weorðscip[*e 7 an*]weald 7 gielp 7
woruldlust? [*Be þā*] woruldluste Epeccurus[8] [*se uðwi*]ta
sæde, þa he ymb ealle [*þas oð*]ra gesælða smeade þe we
10 [*ær nem*]don; þa sæde he þ se lust [*wære*] þ hehste good,
forðæm eall[*e þa oðru*] good þe we ær nemdon olec[*cað þā*]
mode 7 hit retað[9]; se lust ðo[*nne*[10] *ana olec*]ð ðæm lichoman
an[*ū swiðost.*]

§ iv[8]. *Ac we w*]ill[*að*] *nu* giet sprec[*an ymbe manna gecynd*
15 *7 ymbe heora tilunga.* **Þa nu þeah heora mod 7 heora gecynd*   * 43b C
sie adimmad, 7 hi sien on þ ofdæle asigen to yfele 7 þider healde,   about here.
þeah hi wilniað þæs ðe hi cunnon 7 magon þæs hehstan[11] *godes*[12].
Swa swa oferdruncen man wat þ he sceolde] to his huse [*7 to
his ræste, 7 ne mæg þea*]h ðider [*aredian, swa bið eac þā*]
20 mode [*þōn hit bið ahefigad*] mid ðæm [*ymhogū þisse*] worulde;
hit bið [*mid þā hwilū ofer*]drenced 7 gedwe[*lod to þā*[13] *þ hit
ne mæg*]e full rihte[14] [*aredian to gode*]. Ne þincð þeah þǣ
[*monnū þ hi*] auht mearrigen þe [*þæs*[15] *wilniað*] to begitanne,
þ hi maran [*ne ðurfon*] tilian; ac wenað þ hi *mæ*[*gen*[16] *ealle*[17]]
25 þas good gegadrian *togædere,* [*þætte nan*] butan þære gesomnunga [*ne sie*]. *Ny*ton þonne nan herre[18] good [*þōn*] eallra
þara deorwyrðesten*a* [*ðin*]ga gegadrunga to hiora [*anwealde*]
ðæt he nanes ðinges buton [*þæm*[19] *ne*] þyrfe. Ac ðæt nis
nan [*man þt*]e sumes eacan ne ðyrfe, [*buton Go*]de anum;
30 he hæfð on his [*agenū gen*]og, ne ðearf he nane[*s þinges
buton*] ðæs þe [*he on him selfū hæfð*]. We[*nst þu nu þ ða*

---

[8] Boeth. iii. pr. 2. l. 49 P. 'Sed ad hominum studia reuertor,' &c.

[1] em. *þeo* B.　[2] em. *hehte* B.　[3] *good* J.　[4] *þy* J.　[5] *mann* B.
[6] *tehhað* B.　[7] *ðe* B.　[8] *epiccurus* B.　[9] em. *ret* C, *setað* B.
[10] Conj. *ðōn* B.　[11] em. *hehtan* B.　[12] *goodes* J.　[13] *gedweuld to ðon* J.
[14] *ryht* B.　[15] *mearrigende þæs* B.　[16] em. *him agen* B.　[17] *eall* J.
[18] em. *here* C, *heora* B.　[19] conj. *butam* for *buton þæm*. B.

dysegian þe[1] **wenað þte ꝥ ðing sie ælces weorðscipes*[2] *betst wyrðe þte hi*[3] *medemast ongiton magon ?   Nese, nese.   Ic wat ꝥ hit
nis no to forseone.   Hu mæg ꝥ yfel beon þte ælces monnes
ingeþanc wend ꝥ*]te good s[*ie, 7 æfter higað, 7 wilnað to
be*]gitanne ?   *Nese,* [*nis hit na yfel ; ꝥ is ꝥ*] hehste good. 5
[*Hwi nis nu anweald to*] tellanne to [*sumū þara hehstena*]
goda þisses [*andweardan lifes ?   Hwæðer*] ꝥ nu sie to
talia[*nne waclic 7 unnyt*] ðætte nytwyrðos[*t is eallra þissa*]
woruldþinga, ꝥ is a[*nweald ?   Hwæðer*[4] *nu*] good hlisa 7
forema[*ernes seo*[5] *for*] nauht to tellenne ?   Nese, nes[*e ; nis* 10
hit nan[6]] cyn ꝥ mon ðæt for nau[*ht telle*], forðæmðe ælc
mon wenð [*ꝥ ꝥ betst*] sie ꝥ he swiðost lufað.   Hu ne [*witon*]
we ꝥ nan nearones[7] ne nan e[*arforðu*] ne nan unrotnes ne
nan sar ne [*nan*] hefignes nis nan gesælð ?   Hwæt þurfon[8]
we nu ma ymbe þa gesælða sprecan ?   Hu ne wat ælc mon 15
hwæt ða bioð, 7 eac wat ꝥ hi[9] bioð ꝥ hehste good *?   7 þeah
secð* (*fulneah*) ælc mon on swiðe lytlum þingum [*ða s*]elestan
gesælða ; forþæm he [*wend ꝥ he*] hi þonne ealle hæbbe, gif he

[*hæfð ꝥ ꝥ he þōn swi*]ðost wilnað *[*to begitanne.   Ꝥ is ðon ꝥ
hi swiðost wilniað to begitanne : wela 7 weorðscipe 7 rice 7* 20
*þisse worulde wuldor 7 gilp 7 woruldlust.   Ðisses ealles hi
wilniað, forþōþe hi wenað ꝥ hie þurh þa þing scylon begitan ꝥ
him ne seo*[10] *nanes willan wana, naðer*[11] *ne weorð*]scipes ne[12]
[*anwealdes ne foremærne*]sse ne blisse.   Ðæs ealles hi wilniað,
7 wel doþ ꝥ hi þæs [*wilniað*], þeah hi mis[*tlice*[13] *his wilnigen.* 25
Be þā] þingum [*mon mæg sweotole ongitan*] ꝥ ælc mon [*þæs
wilnað ꝥ he mæge*] ꝥ hehste god[14] [*begitan þær hi hit*]
gecnawan mea[*htan, oððe on riht*] secan cuðen ; ac [*hi
hit ne secað on*] þone rihtestan weg ; [*hit nis on*] *þisse*
worulde. 30

[1] *dysiende* J.   [2] em. *weorscipes* B.   [3] *te hi* from J, om. B.
[4] em. *hwæder* B.   [5] *sie* J.   [6] *nan* om. J.   [7] *nearanes* B.   [8] *þurfe* B.
[9] *ða* B.   [10] *sie* J.   [11] *nauðer* J.   [12] *ne* om. B.   [13] *mislice* J.
[14] Appar. *gōd*, but accent not clear.

XXV t.

Ða se Wis[*dom þa ðis*] spel asæd hæfde, þa on[*gan he eft*]
singan 7 þus cwæð: (*Ic wille nu mid giddū gecyðan hu wundor-*
lice Drihten welt eallra gesceafta mid þā bridlū his anwealdes,
7 mid hwilcere endebyrdnesse he gestaðolað 7 gemetgað ealle
5 *gesceafta; 7 hu he hi hæfð geheaðorade 7 gehæfte mid his*
unanbindendlicū racentū, þ ælc gesceaft bið healdon locen wið
hire gecynde, þære gecynde þe heo to gesceapen wes, buton monnū
7 sumū englū; þa weorðað hwilū of hiora gecynde. Hwæt,
seo leo, þeah hio wel tam se, 7 fæste racentan habbe 7 hire
10 *magister swiðe lufige 7 eac ondræde, gif hit æfre gebyreð þæt*
heo blodes onbirigð, heo forgit sona hire niwan taman, 7
gemonð þæs wildan gewunan hire eldrana. Onginð þōn ryn
7 hire racentan brecan, 7 abit ærest hire ladteow, 7 siððan
æghwæt þæs þe heo gefon mæg, ge monna ge neata. Swa doð
15 *eac wudufuglas*[1]*; þeah hi beon wel atemede, gif hi on þam*
wuda weorðað, hi forseoð heora lareowas 7 wuniað on heora
gecynde. Þeah heora lareowas him þōn biodan þa ilcan mettas
þe hi ær tame mid gewenedon, ðōn ne reccað hi þara metta, gif
hi þæs wuda benugon; ac þincð him wynsūre þ him se weald
20 *oncweðe 7 hi gehiran oðerra fugla stemne. Swa bið eac þā*
treowū þe him gecynde bið up heah to standanne. Þeah þu teo
hwelcne boh ofdune to þære eorðan swelce þu began mæge,
swa þu hine alætst, swa sprincð he up 7 wrigað wið his
gecyndes. Swa deð eac seo sunne; þeah heo ofer midne dæg
25 *onsige 7 lute to þære eorþan, eft heo secð hire gecynde 7 stigð on*
þa dæglan wegas wið hire uprynæs, 7 swa hie ufor 7 ufor
oððe hio cymð swa up swa hire yfemest gecynde bið. Swa deð
ælc gesceaft; wrigað wið his gecyndes, 7 gefagen bið gif hit
æfre to cuman mæg. Nis nan gesceaft gesceapen ðara þe ne wil-
30 *nige þ hit þider cuman mæge þonan þe hit ær com, þ is to ræste*
7 to orsorgnesse. Seo ræst is mid Gode, 7 þæt is God. Ac ælc
gesceaft hwearfað on hire selfre swa swa hweol; 7 to þā heo swa

---

t Boeth. iii. met. 2.   'Quantas rerum,' &c.   Cott. Metr. xiii.
[1] em. *wudu fugas* B.

*hwearfað þ heo eft cume þær heo ær wæs, 7 beo þ ilce þ heo ær
wæs, ðonecan ðe heo utan behwerfed sie þ þ hio ær wæs, 7 do
þ þ heo ær dyde.)*

XXVI [u].

§ i. Ða se Wisdom ða [*ðis leoð asun*]gen [1] hæfde, þa on[*gan
he eft*] spellian 7 þus cwæð : [*Eala, h*]wæt, ge eorðlican [5]
men [2], ðeah g[*e eo*]w selfe nu don neatum gelice ſ[*or eow*]re
dysige, hwæt, ge þeah magon hwæthwugu ongitan swelce
eow m[*æt*]e be eowrum frumsceafte, þ is God ; ðone soðan
fruman 7 þone soðan [*en*]de [*ælc*]re gesælðe ge ongitað,
þeah ge [*hine fullice*] ne oncnawen [3] ; 7 swaðeah [*sio ge-* 10]
cynd eow tihð] to ðæm andgite, *[ac eow teohð [4] swiðe manigfeald gedwola of þā andgite. Geðencað nu hwæðer men mægen
cuman to þā soþum gesælðum þurh þa [5] andweardan gesælða ;
forþāðe fullneah ealle men cweðað þ se seo [6] se gesælgosta se þe
þas eorðlican gesælða] ealla hæfð. [*Hwæðer nu micel*] feoh [15]
oððe weorð[*scipe oððe eall*] þes andwearda wela [*mæge ænigne
mon*] don swa gesæligne [*þ he nanes þinges m*]aran ne þyrfe ?
[*Nese, nese ; ic wat þæt þ*] hi ne magon. Hwy [*nis hit
þōn on*] þy swiðe sweotol [*þ þas andwea*]rdan good ne sint
no [*þa soðan go*]d [7], forðæmþe hi ne [*magon sell*]an þæt [20]
hi gehatað ? (*Ac licettað þ hi gelæstan ne magon, þōn hi
gehatað*) þǣ [*þe hi lufian*] willað ða soðan gesæl[*þa ; 7
aleogaþ*] him þeah ma ðonne [*hi him ge*]læsten, forðæmðe
hi heo[*ra nabbaþ*] ma þōn hi heora hæbben. [*Geþenc þu*]
nu be ðe selfum, la, Boetius, *hwæðer þu æfre auht unrot* [25]
wære þa þa þu gesælegost wære, oððe hwæðer þe æfre
æniges welan [8] *wana wære þa ðu mæstn[e welan hæfdest,
oððe hwæðer þin woruld *þa eall wære æfter þinū willan ?
Þa andsworode Boetius 7 cwæð : Nese, la, nese ; næs ic
næfre git nane hwile swa emnes modes, þæs þe ic gemunan mæge,* [30]

---

[u] Boeth. iii. pr. 3. ‘ Vos quoque o terrena animalia,’ &c.

[1] *asuncgen* J.   [2] *hwæ þæs weorðlican men* B.   [3] *gecnawan* B.
[4] *tihð* J.   [5] *þas* J.   [6] *sie* J.   [7] *good* J.   [8] *willan* B.

*þ ic eallunga wære orsorg, þ ic swa orsorg wære þ ic nane
gedrefednesse næfde; ne me næfre gil ne licode eall þ ic wisste*[1]*, ne
me næfre næs ealles swa ic wolde, þeah ic his miðe].* Đa and-
swo[*rode se Wisdom 7 cwæð: Hwi*] nære ðu ðo[*nne*[2] *genog earm*
5 *7 genog*] unhydig[3], þ[*eah þe ðuhte þ ðu welig wæ*]re, þonne
[*ðu oðer twega, oððe hæfdest*] þ ðu noldes oððe [*næfdest þ ðu
woldest*]? Đa andswarode Boet[*ius 7 cwæð: Eall me*] wæs
swa swa ðu sæd[*est*]. (*Đa cwæð se Wisdom: hu ne bið ælc
mon genog earm þæs ðe he næfð, þon hit hine lyst habban ?*
10 *Þ· is soð, cwæð Boetius. Þa cwæð se Wisdom: Gif he þon
earm bið, ne he þon ne bið eadig; forði he eac wilnað þ he habbe
þ he næfð, þy he wolde genog habban. Þa cwæð Boetius: þ
is eall soð þ ðu segst.*) [*Đa cwæð se Wis*]dom : Hu ne
hæfdest [*þu þon þa yr*]mðe[4], ða ða ðu welgost [*wære ?*
15 *Đa and*]swarode *ic 7 cwæð:* Ic wat þ þu [*soð segst*], þ ic hi
hæfde. Đa cwæð se Wis[*dō : Hu*] ne þincð me ðonne *nu
þ* [*ealle þa w*]elan *þisses middaneardes* [*ne mægon*] gedon
ænne mon *weligne,* [*swa weligne*] þ he genog hæbbe 7 *no*
[*maran ne*] ðyrfe ? 7 swaðeah *hi* [*hit gehalað ælcu*]m ðara
20 þe hi hæ[*fð.** *Þa cwæð ic: Nis nan þing*[5] *soðre þon þ ðu
segst.*

    § ii [v]. *Þa cwæð se Wisdō: Ac hwi ne eart þu þon his
geðafa ? Hu ne miht þu geseon ælce dæg þ ða strengran
nimað þa welan of*[6] *þā unstrengū*[7] *? Hwi bið elles ælce dæg
25 swelc seofung 7 swelce geflitu 7 gemot 7 domas, buton þ ælc
bit þæs reaflaces þe him on genumen bið, oððe eft oðres gitsað ?
Þa andswarode*[8] *ic 7 cwæð: Genoh ryhte þu spyrast; swa
hit is swa þu segst. Þa cwæð he: For ðisū þingū beðearf ælc
mon fultume*]s *[*to eacan him selfū, þæt he*] mæge gehea[*ldan
30 his welan. Đa cwæ*]ð ic : Hwa oð[*sæcð þæs ? Đa cwæð he :
Gif he nau*]ht næfde [*þæs ðe he ondrede þ*] he forleosan [*þorfte,
þon ne*[9]] ðorfte he no maran [*fultomes þon*] his selfes. Đa cwæð
[*ic : Soð þu segst*]. Đa onsac se Wisdom [*sarlice 7 cwa*]eð :

* 47a C
ends, rest
gone.

* 47b C
begins,
first part
gone.

[v] Boeth. iii. pr. 3. l. 32 P. 'Quidni fateare,' &c.

[1] *wisse* J. [2] Conj. *ðōn* B. [3] *unhiðy* B. [4] From J, *earmðe* B.
[5] *þara* J. [6] *on* J. [7] em. *unþstrengum* B. [8] *andwyrde* J.
[9] *þōn he ne* B.

Eala, þ me þyncð wið[*erweard þing*] ælces monnes gewunan
7 æl[*ces monnes*] willan, þe[1] ic nu secgan wille; [*þ is þte*]
þonan þe hi tiohhiað þ h[*i scylan ead*]igran weorðan, þ hi
weorð[*að þonan ea*]rmran 7 eargran. Forðæm [*gif hi lytles*]
hwæt habbað, þonne be[*þurfon hi þ hi*] oleccen þæm æfter 5
[*friðe*[2] *þe ænigr*]e wuhte mare h[*abbað; sam hi þyrf*]en,
sa[*m hi ne þurfon, hi willað þeah*]. *Hwær is þōn seo gemetgung,*
*oððe hwa hæfð hi, oððe hwonne cymð heo, þ heo mæge *adri*]*fan
þa yrmða from ðæ[*m*[3] *welegum*] eall[*un*]ga? Swa he mare
h[*æfð, swa*] he ma monna[4] oleccan sceal. [*Hwæ*]ðer þa 10
welegan nu næfre ne [*hingrige*[5]], ne ne þyrste, ne ne [*cale*[6] ?
Ic wene] þeah þ þu wille nu [*cweðan þ ða wel*]gan hæbben
mid h[*wā hi mægen þæl*] call gebetan. [*Ac þeah ðu nu swa*]
cwæde, hit ne *mago*[*n ða welan ellun*]ga gebetan, þeah [*hi*
sume hwile] mægen. Forðæmþ[*e hi sculon ælce dæg*] ycan þ 15
mon ælce *dæg* [*wanað; forþam*]þe sio mennisce wædl [*ðe*
næfre ge]fylled ne bið wilnað ælce [*dæg hwæs*]hwugu[7] þysses
woruldwelan, [*ægðer*] ge hrægles ge metes ge dr[*ynces ge*]
monegra þinga to eacan [*þā. For*]ðæm nis nan mon swa
welig [*þ he*] maran ne þyrfe. Ac sio [*gitsung*] ne con 20
gemet[8], ne næfre ne bið g[*e*]healden on ðære nedðcarfe, ac
wilnað symle maran þon*n*e he þurfe. Ic nat hwi *ge*
fultruwiað ðæm hreo[*s*]endan welan, nu hy ne magon eowre
[*w*]ædle *eow* from ad[*o*]n; ac [*ge ecað eowre*] wædle[9] mid
ðæm ðe hi eow [*to cumað.* 25

§ iii[w]. *Đa s*]e Wisdom ða þis spel *[*asæd hæfde, þa ongan*
he eft giddian[10], *7 þus*] singende cwæð: (*Hwelc fremu byð*
þā welgan gitsere þ he gegaderige ungeri þissa welena 7 ælces
gimcynnes genog begite? 7 þeah he erige his land mid þusend
sula, 7 þeah eall ðes middaneard sie his anwealde underðeoded, 30
ne læt he his nanwuht of þis middanearde mid him mare þōn
he brohte hider.)

[w] Boeth. iii. met. 3. 'Quamuis fluente,' &c. Cott. Metr. xiv.

[1] þ B. [2] em. *frðe* B. [3] ðæm conj. om. B. [4] *maran* (*manna*) B. [5] *hingre* J.
[6] *kale* J. [7] So J, *hwæthweg* B. [8] *gemet* (*nan*) B. [9] *ermðe* B. [10] *giddigan* J.

XXVII [x].

§ i. [*Ða* [1]] se Wisdom ða ðis lioð â[*sun*]gen hæfde, ða
ongan he [*eft*] spellian 7 cwæð: Tu [2] þing [*mæg se*] weorðscipe 7 se anwald [*gedon*], gif he becymð to þæm dy[*sgan;*
h]e mæg hine gedon weorðne [7] andrysne oðrum dysegum.
5 Ac þonecan þe (*he*) ðone anwald forlæt, (*oððe* [3] *se anweald*
hine, þōn ne bið he nauðer þā dysegan ne weorð ne andrysne [4]).
Hwæðer nu se anwald hæbbe þone þeaw ðæt he astificige [5]
unðeawas 7 awyr[*t*]walige [6] of ricra monna [*m*]ode, [7]
plantige ðær cræft[*as on? Ic wat*] ðeah þ se eorðlica
10 [*anweald næfre* *ne sæwð þa cræftas, ac* [7] *lisð 7 gadrað* * 49a C.
unðeawas; 7 þonne hi gegadrad hæfð [7], *þōn* [8] *eowað he hi,*
nallas ne hilð; forþā ðara ricra monna unðeawas manige men
geseoð, forþāðe hi manige cunnon, 7 manege him mid beoð].
Forðæm we sy[*mle seofiað ymbe*] ðone anwald [7 *hine eac*
15 *forscoð, þon*]ne we ges[*eoð þ he cymð to þā wy*]rrestum 7 to
þ[*ā þe us unweorþoste*] bioð.   For ðæm [*þingū wæs gio þæt*
se] wisa Catulus hine [*gebealg 7 swa un*]gefræglice forcwæð
N[*oniū*] þone rican, forðæm he hine gemette sittan on gerenedum scridwæne; forðæm [9] hit wæs ða swiðe [9] micel sido
20 mid Romwarum þ [10] þær nane oðre *an* [11] ne sæton buton þa
weorðestan.   *Þa* forseah se Catulus hine, *forðy* he þæran
sittan sceolde; forðæm he hine wiste swiðe ungesce[*adw*]isne
7 swiðe ungemetfæstne.   Þa *ong*an se Catulus him spigettan
on; *se* Catulus wæs heretoga on Ro*me*, swiðe [*ge*]sceadwis
25 mon.   Ne forsawe he [*no þon*]e oðerne swa swiðe gif he nan
[*rice ne næ*]nne anwald [*na*]efde.

§ ii [y]. Hwæ[*þer þu nu mæge ongitan*] hu micelne [12] *[un-* * 49b C.
weorðscipe se] anwald brengð [*þā unmedeman*] gif he hine

---

[x] Boeth. iii. pr. 4. 'Sed dignitates,' &c.
[y] Boeth. iii. pr. 4. l. 7 P. 'Videsne quantum malis,' &c.

[1] *Da* . . . *cwæð* supplemented from J, om. B.   [2] *twa* B.   [3] Between
forlæt and *hwæðer* a line erased in C.   [4] em. *anðysne* B.
[5] *astyfecige* B.   [6] *wyrtwalige* B.   [7] *ac* . . . *hæfð* from J, om. B.
[8] *7 þōn* B.   [9] *forðæm* . . . *swiðe* om. B.   [10] *wæs þ* B.   [11] From
J, *on* B.   [12] *miclē* C.   Top of fol. 49b left blank.

under[*se*]hð? forðæm ælces monnes yfel bið þy openre gif
he anwald hæfð.   Ac gesege me nu, ic ascige ðe, þu Boetius,
hw*i* þu swa *manig*feald yfel hæfde 7 swa micele une[*ðn*]esse
on þam rice, þa hwile þe ðu [*hit h*]æfdest, oððe forhwy þu
hit [*eft*] þinum unwillum forlete?   Hu ne wasð þu ꝥ hit næs 5
for nanū oðrum ðingum buton forðæmþe þu nolde[*st*] on
eallum ðingum bion geþwære þæs unrihtwisan cyn[*in*]ges [1]
willan Þiodrices?   forðæmðe ð[*u*] hine ong[*eat*]e on eallum
[*þingū*] unwyrð[*ne*] þæs * an[*wealdes, swiðe sceamleasne 7
ungeþwærne* [2], *buton ælcū godū* [3] *þeawe.   Forþā we ne magon* 10
nauht eaðe secgan ꝥ þa yfelan sien gode [4], *þeah hi anweald
habban.   Ne wurde þu ðeah na adrifen from Ðeodrice, ne he
ðe na ne forsawe, gif*] þe [*licode his dysig 7 his un*]rihtwisnes
sw[*a wel swa his dysegū*] deorlingum *dyde.   [Gif þu nu
gesa*]we sumne swiðe [*wisne man þe hæf*]de swiðe gooda 15
[*oferhyda, 7 wære*] þeah swiðe earm 7 s[*wiðe ungesælig*],
hwæðer ðu wolde cweðan [*ꝥ he wære*] unwyrðe anwealdes
7 weo[*rðscipes*]?   Ða andswarode Boetius [*7 cwæð: Nese,
la,*] nese; gif ic hine swilcne [*gemete* [5] *ne*] cwæðe ic næfre
ðæt he sie un[*weorðe*] anwaldes 7 weorðscipes, *ac* [*ælces*] me 20
ðincð ꝥ he sie wyrð[*e þe on*] þisse worulde is.   Ða [*cwæð se*]
Wisdom: Ælc cræft hæfð his [*sun*]dorgife, 7 þa [6] gife 7
þone [6] weo[*rðsci*]pe þe he hæfð he forgifð [*swiðe*] hræðe
þæm [7] þe hine lufað.   *Sw*[*a swa wi*]sdom is se hehsta cræft,
[*7 se* [8] *hæf ð on hi*]m feower oðre cræftas; ð[*ara is an wærscipe*], 25
oðer gemetgung [9], ð[*ridde* * *is ellen, feorðe rihtwisnes.   Se
Wisdom gedeð his lufiendas wise 7 weorðe* [10] *7 gemetfæste 7
geþyldige 7 rihtwise, 7 ælces godes* [11] *þeawes* [12] *he gefyllð þone* [13]
*þe hine lufað.   Þæt ne magon don þa ðe þone anweald habbað
þisse worulde ; ne magon hi nanne cræft forgifan þā ðe hine* [14] 30
lufiað of hiora welan, gif hi hine] on [*heora*] ge[*cynde nabbað.
Be þ*]æm is swiðe sweo[*tol ꝥ ða rican on þ*]æm woruldwelan
[*nabbað nænne sun*]dorcræft; ac [*him bið* [15] *se wela ut*]ane

---

[1] *þines* B.   [2] em. *ungewærne* B; the *w* was orig. *þ*.   [3] *goodum* J.
[4] *goode* J.   [5] *mette* J.   [6] *þafige þone* B.   [7] *ælcū þara* B.   ' *he* J.
[9] *metgung* B.   [10] *wære* J.   [11] *goodes* J.   [12] em. *þeawas* B.
[13] em. *ðōn* B.   [14] *hi* J.   [15] *bið* from J, om. B.

cumen, 7 he [*ne mæg utan*]e nauht agnes habban. [*Geðenc
nu hw*]æðer ænig mon bio a ðe [1] [*unweorðra*] þe hine manige
men [*forseon* [2] *; gi*]f þonne ænig mon â [*þe unweor*]ðra bið,
þonne bið ælc [*dysig* [3]] man [4] þy unweorðra þe he [*mare*]
5 *rice hæfð* ælcum wisū [*men.   Be þ*]æm is genoh sweotol
[*þ se*] *anweald* 7 se wela ne mæg his [*wealde*]nd [5] gedon no
ðy weorðran, [*ac he*] hine gedeð ðy unweorðran [6] [*þe he*]
him to cymð, gif he ær ne [*dohte.   Swa bi*]ð eac se wela 7
se anwal[*d þi*] *wyrsa*, gif *se* ne deah þe hi[*ne ah ; æg*]ðer
10 hiora bið þy [*forcuðra gif hi hi gemetað.* *   * 51a C
about here.

§ iii [2]. *Ac ic þe mæg eaþe gereccan be sumere bisne, þ ðu
miht genoh sweotole ongiton þ ðis andwearde lif is swiðe anlic
sceade, 7* [7] *on þære sceade nan mon* [7] *ne mæg begitan þa soðan
gesælða.   Hu wenst ðu nu ? gif hwelc swiðe rice mon wyrð*
15 *adrifen of his earde oððe on his hlafordes ærende færð, cym*]ð
þo[*nne* [8] *on ælðeodig folc þær þær*] hine [*nan man ne can ne he
ne ænn*]e [9] mon, ne [*furðū þ geðeode ne*] can, wenstu mæge
[*his rice* [10]] hine þær on lond[*e wyrðne gedon ?   Ac*] ic wat þ
he ne mæg.   Gif [*þōn se weorð*]scipe þæm welan gecy[*nde
20 wære, 7*] he his agen wære, oððe eft [*se wela ðæs*] welegan
agen wære, þon[*ne ne me*]ahte [11] he hine no forlæt[*an.   Wære*]
se mon on swelcum lande sw[*elce he*] wære þe hi ahte, ðonne
wæ[*re his*] wela 7 his weorðscipe mid hi[*m.   Ac for*]]þæmþe
se wela 7 se anwald his [*agene ne*] bioð, forðy hi hine
25 forlætað ; [*7 forðyþe*] hi nan gecyndelic good on hi[*m
sel*]fum nabbað, forðy hi losi[*að swa swa*] sceadu oððe
smec. Þeah s[*e leasa wena*] 7 sio rædelse þaia dysi[*gena
monn*]a tiohhige þ se anwald [*7 se wela* [12]] sie þ hehs*te* good,
ac [*hit bið *eall oðer.   Þōn þa rican beoð oðer twega, oððe on* *51b C
30 ælðeode* [13] *oððe on hiora agenre gecyððe* [14] *mid gesceadwisū monnū,* about here.
þōn bið ægðer ge þā wisan ge þā ælðeodegan his wela for

---

[*] Boeth. iii. pr. 4.   l. 27 P.   'Atque ut agnoscas,' &c.

[1] ðy B.   [2] *forsioð* J.   [3] *dyſi* B, *dysig* J.   [4] *mon* J.
[5] From J, *anweald* B.   [6] ð above line in C, *wyrsan* B.   [7] *forþæm
on ðæm nan mon* J.   [8] Conject. *þōn* B.   [9] *nænne* J.   [10] *his wela 7
his rice* J.   [11] Conject. *mihte* B.   [12] *7 se wela* from J, om. B.
[13] *ellende* J.   [14] *cyððe* J.

nauht, siððan hi ongitað þ hi næron for nanū cræfte gecorene [1],
buton for dysges folces heringe.   Ac þær hi ænige wuht]
ag[*nes oððe gecyndelices godes an* [2] *heo*]ra [*anwealde hæfdon, þōn
hæfden*] hi þ mid h[*im, þeah hi þæt rice forle*]ten ; ne forlet[*on
hi no þ gecyndelice go*]od [3], ac simle him [*wolde þ fylgean*] 7 hi 5
symle weorðe [*gedon, wæron hi o*]n swelcum lande swylce [*hi
wæron*].

§ iv [a]. Nu ðu meaht ongitan þ se [*wela 7 se a*]nwald nænne
mon ne magon [*on ellende*] weorðne gedon.   Ic nat þeah
ðu [*wene þæt hi*] on hiora agenre cyððe ealne[*weg mægen*] ; 10
ac ðeah þu his wene, ic wat [*þ hi ne ma*]gon.   Hit wæs gio
giond ealle Ro[*mana m*]earce þ heretogan 7 domeras, [*7 þa
mað*]mhirdas þe þ fioh hioldon þe [*mon þa*]m ferdmonnum
on geare sella[*n sceolde, 7*] þa wisestan [4] witan, hæfdon mæst[*ne
weorð*]scipe ; nu þonne oðer twe[*ga, oððe*] þara nan nis, oððe 15
hi nænn[*e weorþscipe*] nabbað, gif hiora ænig [*is.   Swa hit
bið be*] ælcum þara þinga ðe ag[*en god* [3] 7 **gecyndelic* nabbað
on him selfū ; oðre hwile hit bið to tælenne, oðre hwile hit bið
to heriganne.   Ac hwæt þincð þe þōn on þā welan 7 on anwealde
wynsumes oððe nytwyrþes, nu hi nanes ðinges genog nabbaþ, ne* 20
hi nauht agnes] goodes nabbað, [*ne nauht þurhwunigend*]es
hiora weald[*endū sellan na magon*]?

* 52a C.

XXVIII [b].

Ða se Wisdom þa [*ðis spell asæd hæfde*], ða ongan he eft
giddigan [5] *7 þus cwæð :*] (*Ðeah nu se unrihtwisa cynig* [6] *Neron
hine gescyrpte mid eallū þam wlitegestū wædū 7 mid ælces cynnes* 25
*gimmū geglengde, hu ne wes he þeah ælcū witū lað 7 unweorð,
7 ælces unðeawes 7 firenlustes full ?   Hwæt, he þeah weorðode
his deorlingas mid miclū welū ; ac hwæt was him ðy bet ?
Hwelc gesceadwis mon mihte cweþan þ he a ðy weorðra wære
þeah he hine weorðode ?*) 30

---

[a] Boeth. iii. pr. 4. l. 37 P. ' Sed hoc apud exteras nationes,' &c.
[b] Boeth. iii. met. 4. ' Quamuis se tyrio,' &c. Cott. Metr. xv.

[1] *gecorenne* J.   [2] *goodes on* J.   [3] *good* J.   [4] *westan* B.
[5] *gieddian* J.   [6] So B.

XXIX [c].

§ 1. *Đa se* W[*is*]dom [*þa*] þis leoð a[*sun*]gen hæſ[*de, þa*] ongan he eſ[*t *spelligan* [1] *7 þus cwæð: Hweðer þu nu wene* * 52b C. *þ þæs cyninges geſerræden 7 se wela 7 se anweald þe he giſð his deorlingū mæge ænigne mon gedon weligne oððe wealdendne?* 5 *Đa andsworede ic 7 cwæt: Forhwi ne magon hi?   Hwæt is on ðis andwea*]rdan *liſ*[*e wynsūre 7 betere*] þonne þæs [*cyninges folgað 7 his*] neawest, 7 siðða[*n wela 7 anweald? Đa*] andswarode se [*Wisdō 7 cwæð: Sege*] me nu hwæðer [*þu æfre gehyrdeſt*] þ he ængum ða[*ra þe ær us w*]ære 10 eallunga þurh[*wunode; oððe*] wenstu hwæðer hine [*ænig þar*]a [*e*]alne weg habban mæge [*þe hine*] nu hæſð?   Hu ne wasð ðu þ[*te ealle b*]ec sind fulla þara biesena [*þara*] monna þe ær us wæren? 7 ælc [*mon wat*] þara þe nu leoſað ðætte [*manegū*] cyninge onhwearf se an[*weald*] 7 se wela [*o*]ð ðæt [2] 15 he eft wearð [*wædla*].   Eala ea, is þ [3] þonne forweorð[*ſullic*] wela þ [4] nauþer ne mæg ne hin[*e selfne g*]ehealdan ne his hlaſord, [*to þon*] þ he ne þyrſe maran ſul[*tu*]mes, oððe hi bioð begen ſorheal[*den*]?   Hu ne is þæt þeah sio eowru [*hehſt*]e gesælð [*þara*] cyninga anweald? *7 þe[*ah giſ þā* * 53a C. 20 *cyninge æniges willan*] wana bið, þonne lytlað ðæt his an[*weald*], 7 ecð his ermða; ſorðy bioð simle þa [*e*]ow[*r*]a gesælða on sumum þingum unsælða [5].   Hwæt, þa cyningas, þeah hi mænig ger [6] þioda wealden, ne wealdað hi þeah ealr[*a*] þara þe hi weald*an* woldan, ac [7] bioð ſorðæm swiðe [8] 25 earme on hiora mode ſorðy hi nabbað sume þara þe hi habban wolden [7]; ſorðæm ic wat þ se [*cy*]ning þe gitsere bið, þ he hæfð mar[*a*]n [9] ermðe þonne anwald.   Forðam cwæð gio *sum* cyning þe unrihtlice feng to rice : Eala, hwæt ðæt bið gesælig mon þe him ealne weg ne hangað nacod 30 sweor[*d o*]ſer ðæ heaſde be smale [10] þræde, [*swa sw*]a me [11]

---

[c] Boeth. iii. pr. 5. 'An uero regna,' &c.

[1] *spellian* J.   [2] *oððe þ* B.   [3] *þ* ab. l. in C.   [4] *þe* B.   [5] *ungesælða* B. [6] *manegra* for *mænig ger* B.   [7] *ac . . . wolden* erased and written afresh in C, but not on the erased portion, where the writing is still faintly visible.   [8] *swa* B.   [9] *maron* J.   [10] *smalan* B.   [11] *næ* B.

git symle[1] dyde? Hu þincð [*þe nu*], hu þe se wela 7 se
anwald licige, [*nu hi*][2] næfre ne bioð buton ege [7] earfoðū 7
sorgum?   Hwæt, þu wæst[3] þ æ[*lc cy*]ninc wolde bion butan
þissum, [7 *habb*]an þeah anwald gif he meahte; ac ic wat þ
he ne mæg; þy ic wundrige forhwy hi gilpen swelces an- 5
waldes.   Hwæðer þe nu þince þ se mon[4] m[*icelne a*]nwald

* 53b C.   **hæbbe 7 sie swiðe gesælig þe simle willnað þæ*]s þe he begitan
ne mæg?   Oððe [*we*]nstu þ se sie swiðe gesælig þe symle
mid micle[5] werede færð, oððe eft s[*e*] ð[*e*] ægðer ondræd ge
þone þe hine ondræ[*t*] ge þone þe hine no ne ondræt? 10
Hwæðe[*r*] þe nu þi[*n*]ce þ se mon micelne anwald hæbbe
þe him selfum ðincð þ he nænne næbbe, (*swa swa nu manegū
men ðincð, þ he nænne næbbe*) buton he hæbbe mænigne man
þe him here?   Hwæt wille we ma nu[6] sprecan be ðæm
cininge 7 be his folgerum, butan þ ælc gesceadwis man mæg 15
witan þ [*hi*] bioð full earme 7 ful unm*i*htig*e*?   Hu magon
þa[7] cyningas oðsa[*c*]an oððe forhelan heora unmeahte,
þ[*o*]nne hi ne magon nænne weorðscipe forðbrengan buton
hiora [*þeg*]na fultume?

   § ii [d]. Hwæt wille we (*nu*) e[*lles*[8] *sec*]ggean be ðæm þegnum 20
but[*on þ*] þ ðær oft gebyreð þ hi weo[*rðað*] bereafode ælcre
are, ge furðum þæs feores, from hiora leasan cyni[*nge*]?
Hwæt, we witon þ se unrihtwisa [*cyning*] Neron wolde hatan
his agenne magister 7 his fostorfæder ácwellan, þæs nama
wæs Seneca; se wæs uðwita.   Þa he þa onfunde þ he dead 25

* 54a C. bion [*sceolde*], þa bead *he* ealla his æhta *[*wið his feore ; þa
nolde se cyning þæs on*]fon, ne him his feores geunnan.   Ða
[*he þa*] þ ongeat, þa geceas he (*hī*) þone deað ðæt *hi*ne[9] mon
oflete blodes on ðæm earme; 7 ða dyde mon swa.   Hwæt,
we eac geherdon [*þæt*] Pap(*in*)ianus wæs Antoniose[10] ðæm 30
casere[11] eal[*ra*] his dyrlinga[12] besorgost, 7 ealles his folces
[*mæstne*] anwald hæfde; ac he hine het gebindan [7 *siððan*

---

[d] Boeth. iii. pr. 5. l. 23 P. 'Nam quid ego de regum familiaribus,' &c.

   [1] *simle git* B.   [2] em. *he* B.   [3] So C, *wast* B.   [4] *mon* om. B.
[5] *micelon* B.   [6] *nu mare* B.   [7] *þa* om. B.   [8] *elles* from J, om. B.
[9] From J, *hī* B.   [10] *ontoniose* B.   [11] *kasere* B.   [12] *deorlinga* B.

ofslean].   Hwæt, ealle men witan þæt se Seneca wæ[s
N]erone 7 Papinianus Antonie þa weorð[*est*]an 7 þa leofostan,
7 [*mæstne*] anwald hæfdon ge on hiora hirede ge buton, 7
þeah buton ælcre scylde wurdon fordo[*ne. Hwæt*], hi wil-
5 nedon begen (*eallon mægene*) þ ða hlafordas n[*a*]man swa
hwæt swa hi hæfden, 7 leten hi libban; ac hi ne meahten
þ begitan, forðæm þara cyninga wælhreownes wæs t[*o*] ðæm
heard þ hiora eaðmetto ne meaht[*o*]n nauht forstandan, ne
huru heora of[*ermet*]to dydon; swa hwæðer swa hi dydon
10 [*ne do*]hte him ða nawðer, þeah hi scold[*on*] þ feorh ælætan[1].
Forðæm se ðe his [*ær tid*]e ne tiolað, þonne bið his on tid
untilad[2].   Hu licað þe nu se anwald 7 se wela, nu ðu gehered
hæfst þ hine mon nawðer ne[3] butan ege *hab*ban ne mæg ne
forlætan ne mot, þeah he w[*ille*]?   Oððe hwæt forstod *[*seo* * 54b C.
15 *menigu þara freonda þā deorlingū*[4] *þara*] cyninga? oððe
hwæt forstent hio ænegū men?   Forðon[5] þa frend cumað
[*mid*] þæm welum 7 eft mid ðæm welan [*gewitað*] buton
swiðe feawa.   Ac ða frend [*þe hi*]ne ær for ðæm welan
lufiað þa ge[*witað*] eft mid þæm welan, 7 weorðað [*ðon*]ne
20 to feondum, buton þa [*feawan*] ðe hine ær for lufum 7 fo[*r*]
treowum lufedon; þa hine woldo*n* þeah lufian ðeah he earm
wære; þ[*a h*]im wuniað.   Hwylc is wirsa wol oððe ænegum
men mare daru þonne (*he*) hæbbe on his geferrædenne [7 *o*]n
h[*i*]s neaweste feond 7[6] freondes anl*i*cnesse?
25   § iii[e]. Ða se Wisdom ða[7] ðis spell areaht hæfde, þa ongan
he eft singan 7 þus cwæð: (*Se*[8] *þe wille fullice anweald agan,
he sceal tiligan*[9] *ærest þ he hæbbe anweald his agenes modes*, 7
ne sie to ungerisenlice underðeod his unþeawū, 7 *ado of his
mode ungerisenlice ymbhogan*, 7 *forlæte þa seofunga his eormþa.*
30 *Þeah he nu ricsige ofer eallne middangeard from eastewardū
oð westeweardne, frō Indeū, þ is se suðeastende þisses middaneardes, oð ðæt iland þe we hatað Tyle, þ is on þā norðwest-*

---

* Boeth. iii. met. 5. ' Qui se uolet,' &c.   Cott. Metr. xvi.

[1] So C, *alætan* B.   [2] *unlod* B.   [3] *ne* om. B.   [4] *diorlingum* J.
[5] *forðam* B.   [6] So B and C.   [7] *ða* om. B.   [8] em. *ðe* B.   [9] *tiliän* B.

ende þisses middaneardes, þær ne bið nawþer ne on sumera
niht, ne on wintra dæg: þeah he nu þæs ealles wealde, næfð
he no þe maran anweald gif he his ingeþances anweald næfð
7 gif he hine ne warenað wið þa unþeawas þe we ær ymb
spræcon.)   5

XXX f.

§ i. Ða se Wisdom þa þas fitte asungen hæfde, þa ongon
he eft seggan spell 7 cwæð :   Is þ ungerisenlic wuldor þisse
worulde 7 swiðe leas ; be ðæm wæs gio singende sum sceop.
Þa he forseah þis andwearde lif, ða cwæð he :   Eala, wuldur
þisse weorulde, ea, forhwy þe haten dys*i*ge men mid leasre 10
stemne wuldor, nu ðu n*ane* neart ?   Forðæmðe ma manna
hæfð micelne gielp 7 micel[1] wuldor 7 micelne weorðscipe
for dysiges folces wenan, þonne [*he ha*]ebbe for his gewyrhtum.   Ac sege[2] me nu hwæt ungerisenlicre sie ðonn[*e*]
þ, oððe forhwy hi (*ne*) mægen hiora [*ma*] scamian þonne 15
fægnian, þonne h[*i ge*]herað þ him man on lihð ?   Þeah mon
nu *[hwone godra[3] mid rihte herige]* 7 [4] soð an segge[5], ne
sceal he n*a* [*þe*][6] hræþor to ungemetlice fægnian ð[*æs*] folces
worda ; ac þæs he sceal fægn[*ian*][7] ðæt hi him soð an[8] seggað.
Þeah he nu [*þæs*] fægnige þ hi his naman bræden. ne [*bið*] 20
he no þy hræðor swa brad (*swa*) hi tihhað, [*f*]orðæm (*hi*)
hine ne magon tobrædan g*e*ond ealle eorðan, þeah hi on
sumū lande mægen ; forðæm þeah he sie anum gehered[9],
þonne bið *he* oðrum unhered[10] ; þeah he on þam land*e* sie
mære, þonne bið he on oðr[*um un*]mære[11].   Forðæm is þæs 25
folces h[*li*]sa ælcum men for nauht to habbanne forðæm he
to ælcum (*men*) ne cymð be his gewyrhtum, ne huru nanum
ealne weg ne wunað.   Geþenc nu ærest be þæm gebyrdum,
gif hwa þæs gilpð, hu idel 7 hu unnet (*se*) gylp bið ; forð[*a*]
þe ælc mon wat þ ealle men of[12] anum fæder comon 7 of anre 30
meder.   Oððe eft be þæs folces hlisan 7 be hiora heringe[13];

---

f Boeth. iii. pr. 6. 'Gloria uero,' &c.

[1] *micelne* B.   [2] *gesege* B.   [3] *goodra* J.   [4] 7 conject. om. B and C.
[5] *soð an segge* om. B.   [6] *þy* J.   [7] From J.   [8] *on* B.   [9] *geherod* B.
[10] *unherod* B.   [11] From J, *læsse* B.   [12] Appar. *ðf* C.   [13] *herige* B.

ic nat hwæs [1] we þær ſ[*ægn*]iað. Þeah ða [2] nu foremære sien
þe [*folcisce men h*]eriað, þeah bioð þa foremærran 7
rihtlicran to heriann[*e þa*] þe bioð mid cræftum ge-
weorð[*ode*]; forðæmþe nan mon ne bið mid r[*ihte* [3] **for oðres*** 56a C.
5 *gode ne for his cræftū no þy mærra ne no þy geheredra* [4], *gif
he hine self næfð. Hwæðer þu beo a þy fægerra for oðres
mannes fægere ? Bið men ful lytle þy bet þeah he godne
fæder hæbbe, gif he self to nauhte ne mæg. Forþā ic lære þ ðu
fægenige oðerra*] monna good[*es* [5] *7 heora æðelo to þon*] swiðe
10 *þ* þu ne [*tilige ðe selfum agnes*], forðæmþe æl[*ces monnes god* [6]
7 his] æþelo bioð [7] ma o[*n þā mode þōn*] on þæm flæs[*ce. Þ
an ic wat þeah godes* [8]] on þa æðelo, *þ* mænig[*ne mon sceamaþ*]
þ he wiorðe wyrsa þon[*nė his eldran*] wæron, 7 forðæm
higað eall[*on* [9] *mægne*] ðæt he wolde þara betst[*ena sumes*]
15 þeawas 7 his cræftas gefon [10].

§ ii [a]. [*Þa se*] Wisdom ða þis spell areah[*t* [11] *hæfde*], þa
ongan he singan ymb *þ* i[*lce* [12] *7 cwæð :*] (*Hwæt, ealle men
hæfdon gelicne fruman, forþā hi ealle coman of anū fæder 7 of
anre meder, 7 ealle hi beoð git gelice acennede. Nis þ nan*
20 *wundor, forþāþe an God is fæder eallra gesceafta forþā he hi
ealle gesceop 7 ealra welt. Se selð þære sunnan leoht, 7 þā
monan, 7 ealle tungl a geset. He gesceop men on eorþan;
gegaderode ļa saula 7 þone lichoman mid his þā anwealde, 7
ealle menn gesceop emnæþele on þære fruman gecynde. Hwi*
25 *ofermodige ge þōn ofer oðre men for eowrū gebyrdū buton
anweorce, nu ge nanne ne magon metan unæþelne ? ac ealle sint
emnæþele, gif ge willað þone fruman sceaft geþencan, 7 þone
scippend, 7 siððan eoweres ælces acennednesse. Ac þa ryht-
æþelo bið on þā mode, næs on þam flæsce, swa swa we ær*
30 *sædon. Ac ælc mon þe allunga underļeoded bið unþeawū
forlæt his sceppend 7 his fruman sceaft 7 his æðelo, 7 þonan
wyrð anæþelad oð ðæt he wyrð unæþele.*)

[a] Boeth. iii. met. 6. ' Omne hominum,' &c. Cott. Metr. xvii.

[1] *wat hwæt* B.   [2] From B, *ðu* C.   [3] *mid rihte for rihte* B.
[4] *heredra* J.   [5] So J, *godes* B.   [6] *good* J.   [7] *bioð* om. B.   [8] *goodes* J.
[9] *ealle* J.   [10] *geþeon* B.   [11] So J, *areht* B.   [12] em. *illce* B ab. l.

XXXI [h].

§ i. [*Ða s*]e Wisdom þa þis lioð á[*su*]ngen hæfde, þa ongan he [*eft s*]eggan spell 7 þus cwæð: [*Hwæt g*]odes magon we seggan [*on þa flæscli*]can unþeawas? For[*þā swa hwa s*]wa hi forlætan wile, [*he sceal geþolian*] micle nearanesse [7 **manige gearfoðu; forþā seo oferfyll simle fet* 5 *unþeawas, 7 þa unþeawas habbað oferðearfe hreowsunga, 7 seo hreowsung ne beoð na butan sorge 7 butan nearonesse. Eala, eaw, hu manega adla 7 hu micel sar 7 hu micele*[1] *wæccan 7 hu micle unrotnesse se hæfð þe ðo*]ne w[*on willan hæfð on þisse worul*]de.   7 hu micele m[*a wenst ðu þ hi scylon*] habban 10 æfter þi[*sse worulde edlean*] hiora earnun[*ga*[2]*; swa swa bearneacen*[3]] wif (acenð bearn 7) ðrowað [*micel earfoðu, æfter þā*] þe hio (*ær*) micel*ne* [*lust þurhteah. For*]þy ic nat[4] hwæt þa wor[*uldlustas*] myrges bringað hiora luf[*igendū*].   Gif nu (*hwa*) cwið þ se sie ges[*ælig se þe*] his woruldlustum eallu[15 *fulgæð*], hwi nele he cweðan eac (*þ ða*) ne[*tenu seon*] gesælegu, forðæm(*ðe*) hior[*a willa to*] nanum oðrum ðingum n[*is aþenod*] buton to gifernesse 7 to wr[*ænnesse*]? Swiðe gewynsum[5] hit bið þæt [*mon wif*] hæbbe 7 bearn; ac ðeah m[*anige*[6] *bear*]n bioð gestrined to hiora [*eldrena*] forwirde, 20 forðæmþe manig [*wif*] forswilt[7] for hire bearne ær [*heo hit*] brengan[8] mæge. 7 we leorno[*don*] eac þæt h[*wil*]um geberede swiðe *[*ungewunelic 7 ungecyndelic yfel, þ ða bearn getreowedon betwuh him 7 sieredon ymbe þone fæder ; ge furðon*[9] *þ wyrse wæs, we geheordon*[10] *geo geara on ealdū spellū þ sū sunu ofsloge* 25 *his fæder; ic nat humela, buton we witon þ hit unmennisclic*[11] *dæd wæs. Hwæt, ælc mon mæg witan hu hef*]ig so[*rg men beoð seo gem*]en his bearna ; ne [*þearf ic þe þeah þ s*]ecgan, forðæm [*þu hit hæfst afunden*[12]] be þe selfum. [*Be þære hæfegan*[13] *gemenne his*] bearna cwæð [*min mægister Eurupides*] 30

---

[h] Boeth. iii. pr. 7. 'Quid autem de corporis uoluptatibus,' &c.

[1] *micla* J.   [2] From J, *geearnunga* B.   [3] *bearneacen* from J, om. B.
[4] *wat* B.   [5] *wȳnsum* C, *gewunsū* B.   [6] *þeah mon manige* B.   [7] *swelt* B.
[8] *forðbringan* B.   [9] *furþum* J.   [10] *herdon* J.   [11] *umennisclicu* J.
[12] *afandad* J.   [13] *hefegan* J.

ꝥ hwilū ge[*byrede þā*] heardsælgan ꝥ him wæ[*re betere*] ꝥ he bearn næfde [*þōn he hæfde*].

§ ii [i]. Þa se Wisdom ða þis spel [*areht hæf*]de, þa ongan he eft giddian ·[7 *þus sing*]ende cwæð: (*Hwæt, se yfela*
5 *willa unrihthæmedes gedrefð fulneah ælces libbendes monnes mod. Swa swa seo beo sceal losian þōn heo hwæt irringa stingð, swa sceal ælc sawl forweorðan æfter þā unrihthæmede, buton se mon hweorfe to gode.*)

XXXII [k].

§ i. Ða se Wisdom þa þis leoð asungen [*hæf*]de, þa
10 ongan he eft spellian 7 þus cwæð: Forðæm nis nan tweo ꝥ þes andwearda wela myrð 7 let þa men þe bioð [*a*]tehte to þam soðum gesælðum; 7 he [*n*]ænne ne mæg *gebringan*[1] þær he him gehet, ꝥ is æt þæm he*hst*an goode.   Ac ic þe mæg mid feaum word[*ū ge*]secgan hu manegra yfela þa
15 [*welan sint*] gefylde.   Hwæt þu þonn[*e*[2] *mæne mid þa*]ere gidsunge þæs [*feos, nu þu hit nahu elles begitan ne miht buton þu hit*] forstele oððe gereafige oððe abeþecige, 7 þær (*þær*) hit þe wexð, þonne wanað hit *oþ*rum?   Ðu woldest nu bion foremære on weorðscipe; ac gif þu ꝥ habban wilt,
20 þonne scealt ðu oleccan swiðe earmlice 7 (*swiþe*) eadmodlice þæm ðe (*þe*) to þæm gefulteman[3] mæge.   Gif þu þe wilt don manegra beteran 7 weorðran, þonne scealt þu þe lætan anes wyrsan.   Hu ne is ꝥ þonne sum dæl yrmða ꝥ mon swa [*wereli*]ce[4] scyle culpian to þæm þe him gifan [*s*]cyle?
25 Anwaldes[5] ðu wilnast?   Ac þu *hi*ne næfre orsorgne ne begitst[6] for [*æ*]lðeodegum 7 git ma for ðinum agnum monnum 7 mægum.   Gilpes þu girnst?   [*Ac*] þu *hi*ne ne *me*aht habban orsorgne, *[forþā ðu scealt habban simle
hwæthweg*[7] *wið*]erweardes 7 ungetæses.   Þu woldest nu
30 brucan ungemetlicre wrænnesse?   Ac ðe willað þonne for-

* 58b C.

---

[1] Boeth. iii. met. 7.   'Habet omnis,' &c.   Cott. Metr. xviii.
[k] Boeth. iii. pr. 8.   'Nihil igitur dubium est,' &c.

[1] *mæge bringan* J.   [2] Conj. *þōn* B.   [3] *gefultumĭan* B.   [4] From J, *wærelice* B.   [5] *anwealdes* B.   [6] *begist* C.   [7] *hwæthwugu* J.

sion goode[1] Godes þeowas, forðæmþe þin werie[2] ˥flæsc
hafað þin anwald, [n]ales þu his. Hu mæg mon earmlicor
gebæron[3] þo[n]ne mon hine underðiede[4] his were[*gan*
flæsce, 7 *nel*]le his gesceadwisan [*saule? Hwæþer ge n*]u
sien maran on [*eowrū lichoman*] þonne elpend, oððe *strengran* 5
[*þōn*] leo oððe fear, oððe swiftra[n] þonne tigris? Þeah[5] ðu
nu wære mara þonne elpend 7 strengra þonne leo oððe fear
and[6] swiftra ðonne tigris þ deor[5], 7 þeah *þu wære eallra*
manna fægrost on wlite, 7 *þōn* (*woldest*) geornlice æfter
wisdome spyrian oððæt þu fullice riht on*geate*, þonne 10
meahtes ðu sweotole ongi*ton* ðæt ealle þa mægno 7 þa
[*cræftas*] þe we ær ymb spræcon ne sint to metanne[7] wið
þære sawle cræ*fta* ænne. Hwæt nu, wisdom is an an*lepe*
cræft þære sawle, 7 þea[h] *we witon* ealle þ he is betera
ðo[*nne*][8] ealle þa[9] oðre cræftas þe we ær [*ymbe*] spræcon.   15

    § ii[1]. Behealdað nu þa widgielne[*sse* *7 *fæstnesse 7 þa*
hrædfernesse þisses heofen]es; ðonne magon ge on*gitan* þ he
[*is ealles na*]uht wið his sceppend to metanne [7 *wið his*
we]aldend. Ac hwi ne læ*te* ge eow [*þōn*] aþreotan þ ge *ne*
wundrigen 7 ne [*herigen*] þte un[*nyttre is, þ is þes*] eorð*lica* 20
[*wela? Swa*] swa se heofon [*is betera*] 7 *hea*licra 7 *fægerra*
þonne eal*l his innung* buton monnum anum, [*swa is*] þæs[10]
monnes lichoma betera 7 deor[*wyrðra*] þonne ealle his æhta.
Ac [*hu micele þin*]cð[11] þe þonne sio sawl[12] bet[*ere 7 deorwyrðre*[13]]
þonne se lichoma? Æ[*lc*] gesceaft is to arianne be hire 25
andefn[*e,* 7 *sym*]le[14] sio hehste swiðost; forðæm[14] is *se*
[*godc*]unda anwald to arianne 7 to wyndrianne 7 to weorðianne ofer ealla[15] oðra gesceafta. Se wlite þæs lichoman is
swiðe flionde[16] 7 swiðe tedre 7 swiðe anlic eorðan blostmum.
Ðeah nu hwa sie [*swa*] fæger swa swa Alcibiadis se æþelincg 30
wæs; [*gif h*]wa *bið* swa scearpsiene þ he mæge [*hine*] þurhsion,

---

[1] Boeth. iii. pr. 8.   l. 16 P.   'Respicite caeli spatium,' &c.

[1] *gode* above line B.   [2] *werige* B.   [3] So also B.   [4] *underðeode*
hine B.   [5] *þeah . . . deor* om. B.   [6] So C.   [7] *wiðmetanne* B.
[8] Conj. ðōn B.   [9] *ealle þa* om. B.   [10] *þæs* from J, om. B.   [11] From B,
]nð C.   [12] *sawl* om. B.   [13] em. *deorwyrre* B.   [14] *symle* from J,
symle . . . forðæm om. B.   [15] From J, *ealle* B.   [16] *flowende* B.

swa swa Aristotelis[1] se uðwita sæde þ an[2] dior wære ðe[3]
meahte ælc wuht [þ]urhsion (*ge treowu*[4] *ge furðum stanas*) : þ
dior we hatað lox : gif þon[ne] hwa wære swa scearpsiene
þ he m[*ihte þone cni*]ht þurhsion þe we ær ym[*be spræcon*],
5 þonne ne ðuhte he him *[*no innon*[5] *swa fæger swa he utan*   * 59b C.
þuhte. Þeah] þu (*nu*) hwæm fæger ðince, ne *bið* [*hit no*] þy
hræðor swa ; ac sio *ungescead*[*wisnes*] hiora *eagena* hi myrð[6]
þ *hi ne* [*magon on*]giton þ hi ðe sceawiað utan, [*næs innan*].
Ac geþen[*cað nu swiðe georn*]lice, [7 *gescead*]wislice [*smeagð*[7]
10 *hwe*]lc þæs flæsli[*can*] good sie[*n*, 7 *þa ge*]sælða þe ge nu
ungemetlice [*wilniað*] ; þonne mag*an* ge sweotole o[*ngeotan*]
þ þæs lichoman fæger 7 his *strengo*[8] [*þa magon beon*[9]]
afyrred mid þreora [*daga fesfre*[10]]. Forðæm ic þe recce *eall* þ
ic þe ær r[*eahte*][11] forðæm ic ðe wolde[12] openl[*ice ge*]reccan on
15 ðæm ende þisses capit[*ulan*] þte eall þas andweardan good
ne magon gelæstan hiora lufiendum þ *hi* him gehatað ; þ is
þ hehste good þ hi him gehatað. Þeah hi nu gegaderien
eal[*le*] þas andweardan good, nabbað hi no ðy hra[*þor*[13]]
fulfremed good on ðæm, ne hi ne [*magon*] gedon hiora
20 lufiendas swa welige [*swa sw*]a hi woldon.

§ iii[m]. Ða se Wisdom ða þis sp[*ell*] areaht hæfde, þa
ongon he ef[*t*] gieddigan 7 þus singinde cwæð : (*Eala wa,
hu hefig 7 hu frecendlic þ dysig is þe ða earman men gedwelað
7 alæt of þā rihtan wege. Se weg is God. Hwæðer ge nu
25 secan gold on treowū ? ic wat þeah þ ge hit þær ne secað, ne
finde ge hit no, forþāðe ealle men witon þæt hit þær ne weaxð
þe ma ðe gimmas weaxað on wingeardū. Hwæðer ge nu
settan eower nett on þa hehstan dune, þōn ge fiscian willað ? Ic
wat þeah þ ge hit þær ne settað. Hwæðer ge nu eower hundas
30 7 eower net ut on þa sæ lædon, þōn ge huntian willað ? Ic
wene þeah þ ge hi þōn setton up on dunū 7 innon wudum.
Hwæt, þ is wundorlic þ geornfulle men witon þ hi sculon*

---

[m] Boeth. iii. met. 8. 'Eheu, quae miseros,' &c. Cott. Metr. xix.
[1] *aristodelis* B.   [2] *an* om. B.   [3] *þ* B.   [4] em. *treowa* B.
[5] *innan* J.   [6] *eagan hi amerrað* B.   [7] *smeageað* J.   [8] *streon* B.
[9] *bion* J.   [10] Second *f* erased, B.   [11] From J, *rehte* B.   [12] *wolde be* B.
[13] *raþor* B.

*secan be sæwaroðe 7 be æaofrū ægðer ge hwile gimmas ge
reade 7 ælces cynnes gimcyn ; 7 hi witon eac on hwelcū wæterū
7 on æghwelcra ea muþū hi sculon secan fiscas ; 7 ealne þisne
andweardan welan hi witon hwær hi secan sculon, 7 þone swiðe
unaðrotenlice secað. Ac hit is swiðe earmlic þing þ ða dysegan 5
men sint ælces domes swa blinde þ hi nyton hwær þa soðan
gesælþa sint gehydde, ne furðū nane lustbærnesse nabbað hi to
secanne ; ac wenað þ hi mægon on þissū lænan 7 on ðisū deadlicū
þingū findan þa soðan gesælða, þ is God. Ic nat nu hu ic
mæge heora dysig eall swa sweotole areccan 7 swa swiðe getælan 10
swa ic wolde, forþā hi sint earmran 7 dysigran 7 ungesæligran
þōn ic hit arecan mæge. Welan 7 weorðscipes hi willniað, 7
þōn hi hine habbað þōn wenað hi swa ungewitfulle þ hi habban
þa soðan gesælða.)*

XXXIII [n].

§ i. [*Þa*][1] se Wisdom þa þis leoð asun[*gen*] hæfde, ða 15
ongan he eft spellian 7 þus cwæð[1] : Genog ic þe hæbbe nu
gereaht ymb ða anlicnessa 7 emb ða sceaduwa[2] þære soðan
gesælðe. Ac gif þu nu sweotole gecnawan meaht þa anlicnesse þære soðan ges[*ælðe*] þonne is siððan[3] ðearf þ ic þe
[*hi sel*]fe getæce. Þa andwyrde ic 7 [*cwæð: Nu*] ic ongite 20
genog[4] *openlice* ðæt[*te ælces*] goodes genog nis *on* ðissum
[*woruld*]welum, ne æltæwe anwald nis [*on nanū*] weoruldrice,
ne se soða [*weorðscipe*] nis on þisse weoruld[*e, ne þa mæstan*]
mærða ne s[*int on ðysse woruldgylpe, ne*] sio heh[*ste blis nis*]
on þā flæsclicū lustū. Ða and]*sw*orede se Wisdom 7 [*cw*]æð: 25
Hwæþer *þu* nu fullice ongite forhwy hit þonne swa sie ? Ða
andswarede ic 7 cwæð: Þe[*ah*] ic his nu hwæthwugu ongite,
ic *wolde* hit þeah fullicor 7 openlicor of ðe ongitan. Ða
andsworode se Wis[*dom*] 7 cwæð : Genog sweotol hit is þte
God is anfeald 7 untodæ*l*endlic, þeah hine dysige men on 30
mænig todælen[5], [*þ*]onne hi dwoliende[6] secað þ hehste

---

[n] Boeth. iii. pr. 9. ' Hactenus mendacis formam,' &c.

[1] *þa se Wisdom . . . cwæð* om. B. [*þa*] and [*gen*] conject.
[2] Conject. letter between *d* and *w* in C, *sceadwa* B.   [3] *siððan is* B.
[4] *genog* om. B.   [5] *dælan* B.   [6] *dweligende* B.

god on ða sæmran[1] gesceafta. Hwæþer þu [*nu*] wene þ se
nauhtes maran ne þyr*ſe* se þe mæstne anwald hæfð þisse
*wor*ulde? Þa andsworede ic eft 7 cwæð: Ne secge ic no þ
he nauhtes maran ne ðyrſe, forðæm ic wat þ nan nis þæs[2]
5 welig þ he sumes eacan ne þyrſe. Ða andswarode se Wisdom
7 cwæð: [*Genog*] ri[*h*]te þu sægst; þeah hwa anwal[*d hæbbe*],
gif oðer hæfð maran, þonne b[*eþearf*] *se* unstrengra þæs
strengr[*a*]n fultumes. Ða cwæð ic: Eall hit is swa þu
sægst. Ða cwæð se Wisdom: Þeah mon nu [*anwe*]ald
10 7 genyht to twæm þingū *ne*mne, [*þea*]h hit is an. Þa cwæð
ic: Swa me þincð. [*Ða he cwæð*]: Wenstu nu [*þ*] se
anwald 7 [*þ geniht s*]ie to ſo[*rseonne*] oððe eft *[*swiðor*   * 61b C.
to weorðianne þon oðre[3]] good? Þa cwæð ic: Ne m[*æ*]g
nænne mon þæs tweogan þte anwald 7 genyht is to weorði-
15 anne.   Ða cwæð he: Uton *nu*, gif ðe swa þince, ecan[4]
þone anwald 7 þ ge*niht*, don *þær* weorðscipe to, 7 gereccan
þonne þa þreo to anum. Ða andswarode ic 7 *cwæð: Uton*
þæs, forðæm hit is soð. Ða *cwæð he: Hweþer* þe[5] þonne
þince unweorð 7 unmærlic sio gegaderunc þara ðriora þinga
20 þonne þa þrio bioð to anum gedon, oððe hwæðer hit þe eft
þince eallra þinga weorþlicosð 7 mærlicost? Gi[*ſ*] þu nu[6]
ænigne mon cuðe þara þe hæ*ſde* ælces þinces[7] anwald
7 ælcne weorðscipe hæfde, swa ſorð þ he na maran ne ðorfte,
geþenc *nu* hu weorðlic 7 hu fore*mær*lic þe wolde se man
25 þincan; 7 þeah he *nu* þa þ[*reo h*]æfde, gif he nære hliseadig,
[*þōn w*]ære him þeah sumes weorðscipe[*s wana*]. Þa cwæð
ic: Ne mæg ic þæs oðsa*[an*]. Þa cwæð he: Hu ne is þ
ðonne[8] *genog swe*otol þ we sculon don þa hlise*adig*nesse to
[*þ*]æm þrim, 7 don þa feower *to* anum? Ða cwæð *ic:* þ is
30 cyn. Þa cwæð he: Hwæþer þu n[*u*] wene þ se auht bliðe
sie ðe ealle þas ſ*e*[*ower*] hæfð? Fifte bið *seo* blis, 7 *mæg*
[*don eall þæt*] he wile, 7 nane[*s þing*]es mara[*n ne beþearf*
[þōn] he [*hæfð. Ða cwæð ic: Ne mæg ic næfre ge*]þencan,   * 62a C
gif he swylc wære 7 þ [*eall hæfde*], hwonan him ænig unrotnes ᵃᵇᵒᵘᵗ ʰᵉʳᵉ

[1] *samran* B.   [2] *swa* B.   [3] *oðru* J.   [4] *geecan* B.   [5] *þe* from
B, *þu* C.   [6] *nu* om. B.   [7] *þinges* B.   [8] *ðonne* from J, om. B.

cuman sceolde. Ða cwæð he : Swaþeah is[1] to geþencanne þ
ða fíf þing þe we ær ymb spr[*æ*]con, þeah hi tonemde sien
mid wordum, þ hit is eall an þing, þonne hi gegaderede bioð ;
þ is anwald 7 genyht 7 foremærnes 7 weorðscipe 7 blis.   Þa
fíf (*ðing*), þonne hi ealle gegaderade bioð, þonne bið þ God ; 5
forðæm þa fíf eall nan mennisc man fullice habban ne mæg
ða hwile þe he on þisse worulde bið.   Ac þonne þa fíf þing,
swa we ær cwædon, eall gegadorede bioð, þonne bið hit eall
an þing, 7 þ an ðing bið God ; 7 he bið anfeald untodæled,
þeah he ær [*o*]n mænig tonemned wære.   Ða andsworede ic 10
7 cwæð : Þisses ic eom ealles geþafa.

   § ii°. Þa cwæð he : Þeah nu God *anfeald* sie 7 untodæled,
swa swa he is, se mennisca gedwola hine todæleð on mænig
mid heora unnyttum wordum.   Ælc mon tiohhað him þ to
selestum goode[2] ðæt þ he swiðust lufað ; þonne *lufað* su*m* 15
ðæt, sum elles hwæt.   Þ bið þonne his god þ he þær swiðost
lufað.   Þonne hi þonne *heo*ra God on swa monige dælas
to*[*dælað, þŏn metað hi nauþe*]r ne God selfne ne þone dæl
gódes ðe hi swiðor lufiað.   Þonne hi hine selfne don ealne
ætgædere, nabbað þonne nauðer ne hine ealne ne þone dæl 20
þe hi þæróf dydon.   Forðy ne fint ælc mon þ he secð forðy
he hit on riht ne secð.   Ge secað þ[3] ge findan ne magon,
þonne ge secað eal good on anum go[*o*]de[4].   [*Ða cwæð*] ic :
Þ is soð.   Ða cwæð he : Þonne se mon wædla bið ne wilnað
he nanes anwealdes, ac he[5] wilnað[6] welan 7 flihð þa wædle ; 25
ne swin[*c*]ð he nauht æfter þæm hu he foremærost sie, ne
nan man eac ne begit þ he æft ne swincð.   He þonne winð[7]
ealle his weoruld æfter þæm welan, 7 forlæt mænigne weoruldlust wið þæm þe he þone welan begete 7 gehealde, forþæm
þe his hine lyst ofer eal oðru þing.   Gif he hine þonne beget, 30
þonne þincð him þ he næbbe genog buton he hæbbe (*eac*)
anwald þærto, forþæmþe him þincð þ he ne mæge þone
welan buton anwalde gehealdan.   Ne him eac næfre genog

° Boeth. iii. pr. 9. l. 43 P. ‘ Hoc igitur, quod est unum,’ &c.

[1] *is* above line.   [2] *gesælestū* B, om. *goode*.   [3] *þæ* B.   [4] From J,
gode B.   [5] *he* om. B.   [6] *willað* B.   [7] *swincð* B.

ne þincð ær he hæbbe eal ꝥ hine lyst, forðon[1] þe þone welan[2]
lyst anwaldes, 7 þone anwald lyst weorðscipes, 7 þone weorðscipe lyst mærða. *Siððan [he þæs welan full bið, þon þincð]*   * 63a C.
him ꝥ he hæbbe ælcne willan gif he hæ[b]be anwald; 7
5 gesælþ[3] ealne þone welan æft þæm anwalde, buton he hine
mid læssan begitan mæge; 7 forlæt ælcne oðerne [w]eorðscipe
wið ðæm þe he mæge to ðæm [anweal]de cuman. 7 þonne
gebyreð[4] oft, þonn[e] he eall wið anwalde geseald hæfð (ꝥ ꝥ
he hæfde), ꝥ he næfð nauðer ne þone anwald ne eac ꝥ (þæt)
10 he wið sealde, ac [w]yrð þonne swa earm ꝥ he næfð furþum[5]
þa nedþearfe ane; ꝥ is wist 7 wæda. Wilnað þeah þonne
þære nedðearfe, næs þæs anwaldes.

§ iii P. We spræcon ær be þæm fif gesælþum; ꝥ is wela
7 anwald 7 weorðscipe 7 formærnes 7 willa. Nu hæbbe
15 we gereaht be welan 7 be anwalde, 7 ꝥ ilce we m[agon] reccan
be þæm þrim ðe we u[nareht[6]] habbað; ꝥ is weorðscipe
7 foremærnes 7 willa. Þa[7] þrio þincg, 7 þa tu þe we ær
nēdon, þeah hwa wene ꝥ he on hiora anra hwylcum mæge
habban fulla gesælða, ne bið hit no ðy hræþor swa, ðeah
20 hi his wilnigen, buton hi þa fif ealle habben[8]. Ða andsworede
ic 7 cwæð: Hwæt sculon we þonne don, nu þu cwist ꝥ we
ne mægen on ðara anra hwylcum ꝥ hehste good habban 7 þa
fullan gesælða, ne we huru *[ne wenað ꝥ ure anra hwelc þa fi]*[* 63b C.
eall ætgædre begite? Ða andsworede he 7 cwð: Gif hwa
25 wilnað ꝥ he þa fif eall hæbbe, þonne wilnað he þara hehstena
gesælð[a]; ac he ne mæg ða fullice begitan on ðisse weorulde,
forðæm þeah he ealle þ[a] fif gesælða begite, þonne ne bið
[hit] þeah ꝥ hehste good ne þa selesta[n] gesæ[l]ða; forðæm
hi ne bioð ece. Þa andswarode ic (7 cwæð: Nu) ic ongite
30 genog sweotole ꝥ ða selestan gesælða ne sint on þisse
weorulde. Þa cwæð he: Ne þearf nan mon on ðys andweardan life spyrian æft þæm soðum gesælðum, ne þæs

---

P Boeth. iii. pr. 9. l. 59 P. 'Similiter ratiocinari,' &c.

[1] *forþam* B. [2] *welegan* B. [3] *geselð* B. [4] *getideð* B. [5] *furðon* B.
[6] *unreht* J. [7] *þas* B. [8] So C.

wenan ðæt he ær [1] mæge good genog findan. Đa cwæð ic:
Soð þu sægst.

§ iv [q]. Þa cwæð he: [*Ic w*]ene (*nu*) þ ic þe hæbbe genog
gesæd [*ym*]b ða leasan gesælða, ac ic wolde nu þ ðu wende
þin ingeþonc frō þæm leasum gesælðum; þonne ongitst þu 5
swiðe hræðe þa soðan gesælða þe ic ðe ær gehet þ ic þe
eowian wolde. Þa cwæþ ic: Ge furðum þa [2] dysegan [3] men
ongitað þte fulla gesælða sint, þeah hi þær ne sien þær hi
heora wenað. Þu me gehete nu lytle ær þ ðu hi wolde me
getæcan; ac þæs [4] me þincð ðæt þ bio sio soðe 7 sio ful- 10
* 64a C.   fremede gesælð *ðe mæg [ælcū hire folgera sellan ðurh*]wuni-
gendne welan [5] 7 ecne anwald 7 singalne weorðscipe 7 ece
mærða 7 fulle geniht. Ge furðum þ ic cweðe sie sio soðe
gesælð þe an [6] ðissa fifa mæg fullice forgifan, forðæmþe on
ælcum anum hi sint eall. Forðæm ic secge þas word ðe 15
forþy ic wille þ ðu wite ðæt se cwide [*sw*]iðe fæst is on minum
mode, swa fæst þ his me nan mon gedwellan [7] ne mæg. Þa
cwæð he: Eala, cniht, þy [8] þu eart gesælig þ þu hit swa
ongiten hæfst; ac ic wolde þ wyt spyredon get æft þæm þe
þe wana is. Đa cwæþ ic: Hwæt is þ ðonne? Þa cwæð 20
he: Wenst ðu hwæðer ænig þissa andweardana [9] gooda þe [10]
mæge sellan fulle gesælða? Đa andswarode ic 7 [*cw*]æð:
Nat ic nan wuht [10] on ðys andweard[*an*] life þe swilc gifan
mæge. Đa cwæð [*he: Þas*] andweardan good sint an-
licn[*essa þæs*] ecan goodes, næs ful goode, [*forþā*] hi ne 25
magon soð good 7 ful good forgifan hiora folgerum. Þa
cwæð ic: Ic eom genog wel geþafa þæs þe þu sægst. Đa
cwæð he: Nu ðu þonne wast hwæt ða leasan gesælða sint
7 hwæt þa so[*þ*]an ges[*æ*]lða sint, nu ic wolde þæt þu
* 64b C.   *[leornodest hu þu mihtest becuman to þā so*]þum gesælðum. 30
Đa cwæð ic: Hu ne gehete [11] þu me gefyrn ær þ ðu hit [12]
wolde me getæcan, 7 me lyste nu þ swiðe georne geheran.

[q] Boeth. iii. pr. 9.   l. 70 P.   ‘ Habes igitur, inquit,’ &c.

[1] *her* B.   [2] *þa* om. B.   [3] *dysige* B.   [4] So B, *þæs þe* C.   [5] *ðurhwunigendne welan* om. B, *ðurh-* from J.   [6] From B, *on* C.   [7] *gedweli-
gan* B.   [8] *hwæt* B.   [9] *andwearda* B.   [10] *þe . . . wuht* om. B.
[11] From B, *gehet* C.   [12] *hit* om. B.

Ða cwæð he: Hwæt sculon we nu don to þon [1] þ we mægen
cuman to þæm (*soðum*) gesælðum? Hwæþer we scylen
biddan þone gódcundan fultum ægðer ge on læssan ge on
ma[*ran*], swa swa ure uðwita sæde, Plato? Þa cwæð
5 ic: Ic wene þ we scylen biddan þone fæder ealra þinga;
forðæm se ðe hine biddan nyle þonne ne gemet he hine,
ne furþum [2] ryhtne weg wið his ne aredað. Ða cwæð
he: Swiðe rihte [3] þu sægst; 7 ongan ða s[*in*]gan 7 þus
cwæð:

10 § v [r]. (*Eala, Dryhten, hu micel 7 hu wúderlic þu earl, þu
ðe ealle þine gesceafta gesewenlice 7 eac ungesewenlice wunderlice gesceope 7 gesceadwislice heora weltst; ðu ðe tida frã
middaneardes fruman oð ðone ende endebyrdlice gesettest, swa
þte hi ægþer ge forð farað ge eft cumað; þu ðe ealle þa*
15 *unstillan gesceafta to þinũ willan astyrast, 7 þu self simle stille
7 unawendedlic þurhwunast; forþã ðe nan mihtigra þe nis,
ne nan þin gelica, ne þe nan neodþearf ne lærde to wyrcanne þ
þ ðu worhtest; ac mid þinũ agenũ willan 7 mid þinũ agenũ
anwealde þu ealle þing geworhtest, ðeah ðu heora nanes ne*
20 *beþorfte. Swiðe wunderlic is þ gecynd þines godes, forþãðe
hit is eall an, þu 7 þin godnes; þ god na uton cumen to þe,
ac hit is ðin agen. Ac eall þ we godes habbað on þisse
worulde, þ us is uton cumen; þ is from þe. Næfst þu nanne
andan to nanum þinge, forþãþe nan cræftigra nis þonne þu,*
25 *ne nan þin gelica; forþam ðu ealle god mid ðines anes geþeahte
geþohtest 7 geworhtest. Ne bisnode þe nan man, forþãþe nan
ær þe næs þara þe auht oððe nauht worhte. Ac þu ealle þing
geworhtest swiðe gode 7 swiðe fægere, 7 þu self eart þ hehste [4] god
7 þ fægereste. Swa swa þu self geþohtest þu geworhtest þisne*
30 *middangeard, 7 his weltst swa swa þu wilt, 7 þu self dælst
eall god swa swa þu wilt. 7 ealle gesceafta þu gesceope him
gelice, 7 eac on sumũ ðingũ ungelice. Þeah þu þa ealle
gesceafta ane naman genēde, elle þu nemdest togedere 7 hete
woruld; 7 þeah þone anne noman þu todældest on feower*

[r] Boeth. iii. met. 9. 'O qui perpetua mundum,' &c. Cott. Metr. xx.

[1] *þam* B.   [2] *furðon* B.   [3] *ryht* B.   [4] em. *hehte* B.

*gesceafta ; an þæra is eorðe, oðer wæter, ðridde lyft, feorþe fyr.
Ælcū þara þu gesettest his agene sunderstowe, 7 þeah ælc is
wið oðre genēned 7 sibsūlice gebunden mid þinū bebode, swa þ
heora nan oðres mearce ne ofereode, 7 se cile geþrowode wið ða
hæto, 7 þ wæt wið þā drygū. Eorðan gecynd 7 wæteres is* 5
*ceald ; sie eorðe is dryge 7 ceald, 7 þ wæter wæt 7 ceald. Sie
lyft*[1] *þonne is genemned þ hio is ægþer ge ceald ge wæt ge
wearm. Nis hit nan wunder, forþā ðe hio is gesceapen on þā
midle betwux*[2] *þære drygan 7 þære cealdan eorþan 7 þā hatā
fyre. Þ fyr is yfemest ofer ellū þissū woruldgesceaftū.* 10
*Þundorlic is þ þin geðeaht, þ ðu hæfst ægþer gedon: ge þa
gesceafta gemærsode betwux him, ge eac gemengde þa drigan
eorðan 7 þa cealdan under þā cealdan wætere 7 þā*[3] *wætan,
þ þæt hnesce 7 flowende wæter hæbbe flor on þære fæstan eorðan ; forþāþe hit ne mæg on him selfū gestandan. Ac seo* 15
eorðe hit helt 7[4] *be sumū dæle swilgð, 7 for þā sype heo bið
geleht þ hio grewð 7 blewð 7 westmas bringð ; forþā gif þ
wæt hi ne geðwænde, þon drugode hio 7 wurde todrifen mid
þam winde swa swa dust oððe axe. Ne mihte nanwuht
libbendes þære eorþan brucan ne þæs wæteres, ne on nauðrū* 20
*eardigan for cile, gif þu hi hwæthwegununga wið fir ne
gemengdest. Wundorlice cræfte þu hit hæfst gesceapen þæt þ
fyr ne forbærnð þ wæter 7 þa eorþan, nu hit gemenged is wið
ægðer ; ne eft wæter 7 seo eorðe eallunga ne adwæsceð þ fyr.
Þæs wæteres agnu cyð is on eorþan, 7 eac on lyfte, 7 eft bufan* 25
*þā rodore. Ac þæs fyres agen stede is ofer eallū woruld-
gesceaftū gesewenlicū, 7 þeah hit is gemenged wið ealle
gesceafta ; 7 þeah ne mæg nane þara gesceafta eallunga forcuman*[5]*,
forþampe hit næfð leafe þæs ælmihtigan. Sio eorþe þon
is hefigre 7 þiccre þon oðra gesceafta, forþā hio is nioðor* 30
*þon ænig oðru gesceaft buton þā rodore ; forþā se rodor hine
hæfð ælce dæg utane, þeah he hire nawer ne genealæce; on
ælcere stowe he is hire emnneah, ge ufan ge neoðon. Ælc þara
gesceafta þe we gefyrn ær ymbe spræcon hæfð his agenne
eard onsundron ; 7 þeah is ælc wið oðer gemenged, forðampe* 35

[1] em. *lyf* B. [2] em. *betwx* B. [3] em. *þ* B. [4] 7 Conject. om. B. [5] em. *orcuman* B.

nan ðara gesceafta ne mæg bion buton oðerre, ðeah hio unsweotol
sie on þære oðerre.   Swa swa nu eorðe is 7 wæter sint swiðe
earfoðe to geseonne oððe to ongitonne dysgū monnū on fyre, 7
swaþeah hi sint ðærwið gemengde.   Swa is eac þær fyr on
5 ðam stanū 7 on ðā wætere, swiðe earfoðhawe[1], ac hit is þeah
þara.   Þu gebunde þ fyr mid swiðe unanbindendlicū racentū,
þ hit ne mæg cuman to his agenū earde, þ is to þā mæstan
fyre ðe ofer us is, þylæs hit forlæte þa eorðan; 7 ealle oðre
gesceafta aswindað for ungemetlicū cile, gif hit eallunga
10 from gewite.   Ðu gestaðoladest eorðan swiðe wundorlice 7
fæstlice, þ heo ne helt on nane healfe ne on nanum eorðlicū
þinge ne stent; ne nanwuht eorðlices hi ne healt þ hio ne sige,
7 nis hire þeah þōn eðre to feallanne ofdune þōn up.   Þu eac
þa ðriefealdan sawla on geðwærū limū styrest, swa þ ðære
15 sawle þy læsse ne bið on ðam læstan fingre ðe on eallū þā
lichoman.   Forþi ic cwæð þæt sio sawul wære þreofeald,
forþāþe uðwitan secgað þ hio hæbbe þrio gecynd.   An ðara
gecynda is þ heo bið wilnigende, oðer þ hio bið irsiende,
þridde þ hio bið gesceadwis.   Twa þara gecynda[2] habbað netenu
20 swa same swa men; oðer þara is wilnung, oðer is irsung.
Ac se mon ana hæfð gesceadwisnesse, nalles nan oðru gesceaft;
forði he hæfð oferþungen ealle þa eorðlican gesceafta mid
geðeahte 7 mid andgite.   Forþā seo gesceadwisnes sceal wealdan
ægðer ge þære wilnunga ge þæs yrres, forþā hio is synderlic
25 cræft þære saule.   Swa ðu gesceope þa saule þæt hio sceolde
ealne weg hwearfian on hire selfre, swa swa eall þes rodor
hwerfð, oððe swa swa hweol onhwerfð, smeagende ymb hire
sceoppend, oððe ymbe hi selfe, oððe ymbe þas eorðlican gesceafta.   Þōn hio þōn ymbe hire scippend smeað, þōn bið hio
30 ofer hire selfre; ac þōn hio ymbe hi selfe smeað, þōn bið
hio on hire selfre; 7 under hire selfre hio bið þōn ðōn hio
lufað þas eorðlican þing, 7 þara wundrað.   Hwæt þu,
Drihten, forgeafe þā sawlum eard on hiofonū, 7 him þær
gifst weorðlice gifa, ælcere be hire geearnunge; 7 gedest þ
35 hi scinað swiðe beorhte, 7 þeah swiðe mistlice birhtu, sume

¹ em. *earðhawe* B.   ² em. *gecyndu* B.

beorhtor sume unbyrhtor, swa swa steorran, ælc be his geear-
nunga.   Hwæt þu, Drihten, gegæderast þa hiofonlican sawla
7 þa eorðlican lichoman, 7 hi on ðisse worulde gemengest.
Swa swa hi from þe hider comon, swa hi eac to þe hionan
fundiað. Þu fyldest ðas eorðan mid mistlicū cynrenū netena, 5
7 hi siððan aseowe mistlicū sæde treowa 7 wyrta.   Forgif nu,
Drihten, urū modū ꝥ hi moton to þe ạstigan þurh þas earfoðu
þisse worulde, 7 of þissū bisegū to þe cuman, 7 openū eagum
ures modes we moten geseon þone æþelan æwelm ealra goda ; ꝥ
eart ðu. Forgif us þōn hale eagan ures modes, ꝥ we hi þōn 10
moton afæstnian on þe ; 7 todrif ðone mist þe nu hangað
beforan ures modes eagū, 7 onliht þa eagan mid ðinū leohte ;
forþā ðu eart sio birhtu ðæs soðan leohtes, 7 þu eart sio sefte
ræst soðfæstra, 7 ðu gedest þæt hi ðe gesioð. Þu eart ealra
þinga fruma 7 ende. Ðu brist ealle þing buton geswince. Þu 15
eart ægðer ge weg, ge ladþeow, ge sio stow ðe se weg to ligð ;
ðe ealle men to fundiað.)

XXXIV [a].

§ i. Ða se Wisdom þa ðis leoð 7 þis gebed asungen hæfde,
þa ongan he eft spellian 7 þus cwæð: Ic wene ꝥ hit sie nu
ærest þearf ꝥ ic ðe gere[*cc*]e hwær ꝥ hehste good is, nu ic ðe 20
ær [*hæfde g*]ereaht hwæt hit wæs, oððe h[*wylc ꝥ medeme*]
good wæs, [1] hwylc ꝥ [*unmedeme. *Ac anes þinges ic þe wolde*
ærest acsian [2] : *H*]wæðer þu wene ꝥ ænig þing on þisse
worulde swa good sie ꝥ hit ðe mæge forgifa[*n*] fulla gesælða ?
Ðe [3] ic ðe ascige þ[*y ic*] nolde ꝥ unc beswice ænegu leas 25
a[*nli*]cnes for soða gesælða. Forðy [*n*]an [*mon*] ne mæg
oðsacan ꝥ sum good ne sie ꝥ hehste, swa swa sum micel
æwelm 7 diop, 7 irnen mænege [4] brocas 7 riða of. Forðy
mon cwið be sumū goode ꝥ hit ne sie ful good, forðæ *him*
bið hwæshwugu wana ; 7 þeah ne bið ealles butan, forðæm 30
þe ælc þing wyrð to nauhte gif hit nauht goodes on him

[a] Boeth. iii. pr. 10. 'Quoniam igitur,' &c.

[1] *hwylc . . . ac* om. B, *unmedeme ac* from J.   [2] *ascian* J.   [3] *þi* B.
[4] em. *mægene* C, *manige* B.

* 69b C.

næfð. Be þy ðu meaht ongit*an þ* of þam mæstan goode
cumað (*ða*) læss*an* god, næs of ðæm *læssan* þ mæste, þon[1]
[*ma*] þe sio ea *mæg* weorðan to æwelme. Ac se æwelm
mæg weorðan to *ea*, 7 *þea*h sio ea cymð eft to ðæm æwelme;
5 swa cymð ælc good of Gode 7 eft to him, 7 he is þ fulle
gód[2] 7 þ fullfremede, þ nanes willan wana ne bið. Nu þu
meaht sweotole ongitan þ þ is good[3] self. Hw*i* ne meaht
ðu geþencan, gi[*f nan*]wuht full nære, 'þonne [*nære nan
wuht*] wana, 7 gif nan wuh[*t wana nære*], *þon[ne nære * 70a C
10 nan wuht full?   Forþy bið*] ænig þing full[4] þe sum bið about here.
wana, (7) forðy bið ænig þing wana ðe sum bið full; ælc
þing bið fullost on his agnum earda[5]. Hwy ne meaht þu
þonne geðencan, gif on ænegum þissa eorðlicena gooda
æniges willan 7 æniges goodes wana is, þonne is sum good
15 full ælces willan, 7 nis nanes goodes wana? Ða andsworede
ic 7 cwæð: Swiðe rihtlice 7 (*swiðe*) *gesce*adwislice þu hæfst
me ofercumen 7 gefangen, þ ic ne mæg no wiðcweðan ne
furðum[6] ongean ðæt þencan[7], buton þ hit is eall swa swa
þu sægst.

20   § ii[t]. Þa cwæð se Wisdom: Nu ic wolde þ ðu ðohte
geornlice oð þ ðu ongeate hwær sio fulle gesælð sie. Hu
ne wast þu nu ðætte eall moncyn is anmodlice geþafa þ God
is fruma ealra gooda 7 waldend ealra gesceafta? He is þ
hehste good, ne nænne mon nu þæs ne tweoð; forðæ þe hi
25 nauht niton betere, ne furðū nauht emngoodes. Forðæm
us sægð ælc gesceadwisnes 7 ealle men þ ilce andettað[8] þ
God[9] sie þ hehste good, forþæmþe hi tacniað þte eall good
on him sien[10]; forðæm gif hit swa nære, þonne *[nære he þ * 70b C.
þ he gehalen is ; oððe æni*]g þing ær wære oððe æltæwre, þonne
30 wære þ betere þonne he. Ac forðæmþe nan þing næs ær
þonne he ne æltæwre þonne he ne diorwyrðre þonne he,
forðæm he is fruma 7 æwelm 7 hrof eallra gooda. Genog

---

[t] Boeth. iii. pr. 10. l. 21 P. 'Quo uero, inquit, habitet,' &c.

[1] From J, *þe* B. [2] Accent not quite clear. [3] *god* B. [4] *full þing* B.
[5] *earde* B.   [6] *furð* B.   [7] *geþencan* B.   [8] From B, *andette*) C.
[9] From B, *good* C.   [10] *sy* B.

sweotol hit is ðæt þ fulle good wæs ærðæm þe þ wana[1]. Þ
is to gelefanne þ se hehsta God[2] sie[3] ælces godes fullast,
þylæs we leng[4] sprecen ymb þonne we ne þyrfen. Se ilca
God is, swa swa we ær sædon, þ hehste good 7 þa selestan
gesælða, nu hit is openlice cuð, þ ða selestan gesælða on 5
nanum oðrum gesceaftum ne sint buton on Gode. Þa cwæð
ic : Ic eom geþafa.

§ iii [u]. Da cwæð he : Ic þe healsige þ ðu gesceadwislice
þ *ongi*te þte God is full ælcere fullfremednesse 7 ælces go*d*es
7 ælcere gesælðe. Ða cwæþ ic : Ic ne mæg fullice ongitan 10
forhwy ðu eft sægst þ ilce þ ðu ær sædest. Þa cwæð he :
Forðy ic (*hit*) þe secge eft, þy ic nolde þ ðu wende þ se
God[4] þe fæder is and fruma eallra gesceafta, þ him âhwonan
utan come his[5] sio hea goodnes þe he full is. Ne ic eac
nolde þ ðu wende *þte [oðer wære his god 7 his gesælð, oðer]* 15
he self ; forðæm gif ðu wenst þ him ahwonan ut*an* come þa
good þe he hæfð, þonne wære þ ðing betre þe hit him frō
come þonne he, gif hit swa wære. Ac þ is swiðe dy*s*lic 7
swiðe micel syn þ mon þæs wenan *scyl*e be Gode, oððe eft
wenan þæt ænig þing ær him wære oððe betre ðonne he 20
oððe him gelic. Ac we sculon bion geþafan þte se[6] God
sie ealra þinga betst. Gif þu nu gelyfst þte an[7] God sie,
swa swa on monnum við : oðer bið se mon, þ bið saul 7
lichoma, oðer bið his godnes ; þa gegaderað[8] God 7 (*efl*),
ætg*æ*dre gehelt 7 gemetgað : gif þu þonne gelefst þ hit swa 25
sie on Gode[9], þonne scealt þu nede gelefan þ sum anwald
sie mara þonne his, þ þonne his swa gesomnige swa he þone
urne deð. Hwæt, ælc þing þe tosceaden bið from oðrum
bið oðer, (*oþer*) þæt þing, þeah hi *ætgædre* sien ; gif þonne
hwylc þing tosceaden bið from þæm hehstan goode, þonne 30
ne bið þ no þ hehste good. Þ is (*þeah*) micel syn to geðencanne be Gode, þte ænig go*d sie* buton on him, oððe ænig

[u] Boeth. iii. pr. 10. l. 37 P. 'Sed quaeso, inquit, te,' &c.

[1] For *wana* B has *ne wene*.   [2] From B, *good* C.   [3] *is* B.
[4] *leng* om. B.   [5] *his is* B.   [6] *se* om. B.   [7] *an* above line in B.
[8] *gegadrað* C.   [9] From B, *goode* C.

from him adæled, forðæmþe nan wuht nis be*tere* *[*þōn he, ne* * 71b C.
emngod him. Hwilc þing mæg be]on betre þonne his sceppend?
Forðǣ ic secge mid ryhtre gesceadwisnesse ꝥ ꝥ sie ꝥ hehste
good on his agenre gecynde ꝥte fruma is eallra þinga. Ða
5 cwæð ic: (*Nu*) þu hæfst me nu swiðe rihte oferreahtne.
Þa cwæð *he: H*wæt, ic þonne ær sæde ꝥ ꝥ hehste good 7
sio hehste gesælð an wære. Ða cwæð ic: Swa hit is. Þa
cwæð he: Hwæt, wille we þonne secgan hwæt ꝥ sie elles
buton God? Ða cw̄ ic: Ne mæg ic ðæs oðsacan, forðæm
10 þe ic his wæs ær geþafa.

§ iv ᵛ. Ða cwæð he: Hwæðer þu hit a sweotolor ongitan
mæge gif ic þe sume bisne g*et* ma secge? Gif nu tu good
wæren þe ne meahton ætsomne bion, 7 wæren þeah buto
goode, hu ne *wære* hit þonne genog sweotol ꝥ hiora[1] nære
15 nauðer ꝥ oðer? forðy ne mæg ꝥ fulle *god* bion *no* tod*æ*led.
Hu mæg hit bion [*ægþer g*]e full ge wana? Forðæm we
cweðað ꝥ *sio f*ulle gesælð 7 god ꝥ hi sien an good, 7 ꝥ sie
ꝥ hehste; þa ne magon næfre weorðan todælede[2]. Hu ne
sculon we þonne nede bion geþafan ꝥte sio *hehste* gesælð
20 7 sio hea godcundnes a[*n*] sie? Þa cwæð ic: Nis nan þing
soðre þonne þæt; *ne ma[*gon we nanwuht findan betere*[3]] * 72a C.
þonne God. (*Ða cwæð he*[4]): Ac ic wolde giet (*mid*) sumre
*bi*sne þe behwerfan utan ꝥ þu ne *mihtst* nænne weg findan
ofer; swa swa uðwit*ena* gewuna *is ꝥ* hi willað simle hwæt-
25 hwugu niwes 7 *seld*cuþes eowian, ꝥ hi mægen mid *þy a*we*ccan
ꝥ mod þara geherendra.

§ v ᵂ. Hu ne hæf*don* we ær gereaht ꝥ ða gesælþa 7 sio
*godcund*nes an wære? Se þe þonne þa *gesælð*a hæfð, þonne
hæfð he ægþer, *se* þe þone ægþer hæfð. Hu ne bið *se* þonne
30 full eadig? Hu ne wast þu nu ꝥ we cweðað ꝥ *se* bio w*is* þe
wis*dom* hæfð, 7 rihtwis þe riht*wis*nesse hæfð? Swa *we*
cweðað eac ꝥ ꝥ sie God þe þa godcundnesse[5] hæfð 7 ða

ᵛ Boeth. iii. pr. 10. l. 63 P. 'Respice, inquit, an hinc,' &c.
ᵂ Boeth. iii. pr. 10. l. 79 P. 'Nam quoniam beatitudinis,' &c.

[1] *ꝥ hiora* om. B.   [2] *todælede* (*lædde*) B.   [3] *medemre* J.   [4] *Ða cwæð
he* conject. by Junius, om. C and B.   [5] *godnesse* B.

gesælða, 7 ælc gesæ*lig* (*mon*) bið God; 7 *þ*eah is an God[1],
se is stemn 7 staðol eallra goda[2]; *of* þæm cumað eall
good, 7 eft hi fundiað to him, 7 he welt ealra. Þeah *he* nu
sie se fruma 7 se staðol [3] ealra goodra 7 ealra gooda, þeah
is mænig good þe of him cymð[n]; swa swa ealle steorr*an* 5
weorðað onlihte 7 gebirhte of þære sunnan, sume þeah
beorhtor, sume unbeorhtor. Swa eac se mona, swa micl($\bar{u}$)

** 72b C.* he lyht swa sio sunne hine gescinð; **[þōn hio hine ealne
geondscinð, þōn]* bið he eall beorht. Ða ic þa þis spell
ongeat, þa wearð ic[4] agælwed 7 swiðe áfæred, 7 cwæð: Is 10
þis la wundorlic 7 wynsum 7 gesceadwislic[5] spell þ ðu nu
sægst. Ða cwæð he: Nis nan wuht wynsūre ne gewisre
þonne þ ðing þ þis[6] spell ymbe is 7 we nu embe sprecan
willað; forðæm me þincð good þ we hit gemengen to ðæm
*æ*rran. Ða cwæð ic: Hwæt is þ, la?   15

§ vi [x]. Ða cwæð he: Hwæt, þu wast ðæt ic þe *ær* sæde þ
sio soðe[7] gesælð wære good, 7 *of* þære soðan gesælðe cumað
eall ða oðru good þe we ær[8] embe spræcon, 7 eft to; swa
swa of þære sæ cymð þ wæter *inn*on ða eorðan, 7 þær
áfer(*s*)cað; cymð þonne up[9] æt þæm æwelme, wyrð þonne 20
to broce, þonne to ea, þonne *andlang*[10] *ea*, oð hit wyrð eft to
sæ. Ac *ic wolde* þe nu ascian hu þu þis spell *understand*en
hæfd*est*; hwæþer þu wene *þ þa fíf god* þe we oft ær ymbe
spr*æcc*an, *þ* is anwald 7 weorðscipe 7 foremærnes 7 geny*h*t
7 blis, ic wolde witan *hwæðer þu* wende þ þas[11] good wæren 25
limu *þære soþan* gesælþe, swa swa monegu *limu*[12] beoð on

** 73a C.* anum men, 7 weorðað þeah **[ealle to anū lichoman ; oððe þu
wendest]* þ hwylc an þara fíf god(*a*) worhte þa soðan gesælðe,
7 siþþan ða feower good wæren hire good; swa swa nu saul
7 lichoma wyrcað anne mon, 7 se an mon hæfð mænig[13] lim, 30

---

[x] Boeth. iii. pr. 10. l. 89 P. 'Cum multa, inquit, beatitudo,' &c.

[1] *7 se þeah is god* B.   [2] *godā* B.   [3] Instead of *ealra . . . cymð*
B has simply *eallra goda ðe of him cumað.*   [4] *he* B.   [5] *gesceadlic* B.
[6] *ðin* B.   [7] B has *þe* for *soðe.*   [8] *ær* om. B.   [9] From B, *ub* C.
[10] From B, which has *7 lang.*   [11] *þas* from B, *þæs* C.   [12] For
monegu limu B has *man hund lima*; *limu* from J.   [13] Orig. *manige*
B, but the *e* erased.

7 þeah to þæm twæm, þ is to þære saule 7 to þæm lichoman,
belimpað ealle þas[1] þæs monnes good ge gastlicu ge
lichomlicu. Þ is nu þæs lichoman good þ mon [*s*]ie fæger
[7 *str*]ang 7 lang 7 brad, 7 m[*ane*]gu [*oþ*]ru good (*to*)[2] eac
5 þæm ; 7 ne bið hit þeah se lichoma self, forðæm þeah he
þara gooda hwylc forleose, þeah he bið þ he æror wæs.
Þonne is ðære saule good wærscipe 7 gemetgung 7 geþyld 7
rihtwisnes 7 wisdom, 7 manege[3] swelce cræftas ; 7 swaþeah
bið oþer sio saul, oðer bioð hir*e craftas*. Ða cwæð ic : Ic
10 wolde þ ðu me *sædest get* sweotolor ymb þa oðru good þe *to*
ðære soðan gesælðe belimpað. *Ða* cwæð he : Ne sæde ic
þe ær þ sio *gesælð* good wære? *Gyse*[4], cwæð ic, ge þu þ
sædest þ hio þ hehste good wære. *Ða cwæð he :* Eart þu
nu[5] get geþafa þte *anweald* 7 weorðscipe 7 foremærnes 7
15 *genyht* 7 blis 7 sio eadignes 7 þ hehste *god*, *[þ ða sien eall*[6] * 73b C.
an, 7 þ an þon sie god? *Ða c*]wæð *ic :* *Hu* wille ic *nu*
þæs oðsacan? *Þa* cwæð he : Hwæþer þincð þe þonne þ
þa þincg sien, ðe ðara soðena gesælða limu, þe sio gesælð
self? Ða cwæð ic : Ic wat nu hwæt þu woldest witan ; ac
20 me lyste bet þ ðu me sæde sume hwile ymb þ, þonne þu me
ascode. Þa cwæð he : Hu ne meaht þu geðencan? gif þa
good wæ[*ron þa*]ere soþa[*n*] gesælðe limu, þonne *wæron hi*
hwæthwegu[7] *todæled ; swa swa* monnes lichoman limu[8] bioð
hwæthwugu todæled. Ac þara *lima* gecynd is þ hi gewercað
25 ænne lichoman, 7 þeah ne bioð eallunga gelice. Þa cwæð ic :
Ne þearft þu ma[9] swincan ymbe þ ; genog sweotole ðu hæfst
me gesæd þ ða good ne sint nanw[*u*]ht todæled from ðære
soðan gesælðe. Þa cwæð he : Genog rihte þu hit on[*gitst,*
nu] þu ongitst þ þa good ealle sint [*þ*] ilce þ gesælð is, 7
30 sio gesælð is ðæt [*he*]hste good, 7 þ hehste good is God[10],
7 se [*God*] is semle on anum untodæled. Ða [*cwæð ic :*
Nis] þæs[11] nan tweo ; ac ic wolde nu [*þ ðu*] me *sædest*
hwæthwugu uncuðes.

---

[1] *þas* om. B.   [2] *to* above line in B.   [3] From B, *manega* C.
[4] From B ; the letter foll. *g* very faint in C, but apparently not *y*.
[5] *nu* om. B.   [6] *ealle* J.   [7] *hwæthwugu* J.   [8] From B, C has *licu*.
[9] *mare* B.   [10] From B, *good* C.   [11] *þ* B.

§ vii [7]. Ða [*cwæð he : ꝥ*] *is*[1] nu sweotol ꝥte eall þa good
[*þe we æ*]r ymbe spræcon belimpað to ðæ *hehstan goode,
[*7 þi men secaþ god ge*]nog þe hi wenað ꝥ ðæt sie ꝥ hehste
good.   Þy[2] hi secað anwald 7 eac eall[3] *oðru* good þe we ær
ymb spræcon, ðy hi *wenaþ* ꝥ hit sie ꝥ hehste good.   Be þy [5]
þu meaht witan ꝥ ꝥ hehste good is hrof eallra ðara oðra
gooda þe men wilniað 7 hi lyst, forðæmþe nænne mon ne
lyst nanes þinges buton goode[*s oð*]ðe hwæshwugu þæs ðe
(*goode gelic bið.   Maniges þinges hi wilniaþ þæs ðe*) full good
ne bið, ac hit hæfð þeah hwæthwugu gelices goode.   Forðæm [10]
we cweðað ꝥ ꝥ hehste good sie se hehsta hrof eallra gooda
7 sio hior ðe[4] eall[5] good on hwearfað, [*7 eac*] ðæt þing þe
mon eall good fore deð; for ðæm þinge men lyst ælces þara
gooda þe hi lyst.   Ꝥ þu meaht swiðe sweotole ongitan be
þæm þe nænne mon ne lyst þæs þinges þe hine[6] lyst ne [15]
þæs þe he deð, ac þæs þe he mid ðæm carnað; forðæmðe
he wenð, gif he þonne lust begite 7 ꝥ þurhtio ꝥ he þonne
*ge*tiohhad hæfð, ꝥ he þonne hæ[*bbe ful*]le gesælða.   Hu ne
wast þu ꝥ *nan* mon forðy ne rit þe hine ridan lyst, ac rit for
ðy þe he mid ðære rade [*ear*]nað sume carnunga?   Sume[7] [20]
mid þære *[rade earnað sume ꝥ hie sien þy halran, sume
earniað ꝥ*] *hie* sien ðy cafran, s[*u*]me ꝥ hy woldon *cuman*
to sumre þara stowa þe hi *ðonne* to [*fu*]ndiað.   Hu ne is ðe
þonne[8] genog sweotol ꝥte men nanwuht swiðor ne lufiað
þonne hi doð ꝥ hehste god? forðæmþe ælc wuht þæs ðe hi [25]
wilniað oð*ðe doð hi doð forþyþe* hi woldon habban ꝥ hehste
good on ðæm.   Ac hi dwoliað sume on ðæm þe hi wenað
ðæt hi mægen habban full god 7 fulla [*gesælða*] on þisum
andweardum godū ; [*ac þ*]a fullan gesælða 7 ꝥ hehste good
[*is*] God self, swa swa we oft ær sædon.   Ða cwæð ic : Ne [30]
mæg ic no geþencan hu ic *þæs oðsacan* mæge.   Ða cwæð
he : Uton *lætan* þonne bion þa[9] spræce, 7 bion *unc ðæs*
orsorge, nu ðu swa fullice *ongit*en hæfst ꝥte God simle bið

---

[7] Boeth. iii. pr. 10. l. 112 P. 'Ad bonum uero cetera referri,' &c.

[1] *is* conj. om. B.   [2] *ꝥ* B.   [3] *eall* om. B.   [4] *hior ðe* fr. B, *eorðe* C.
[5] From B, *ealla* C.   [6] *hire* B.   [7] *earn. sume* om. B.   [8] *nu* B.   [9] *þas* B.

un*todæledlic* 7 full good, 7 þ his good 7 sio [*his gesælð*] him nahwonan utane ne com, ac wæs symle on him selfum, 7 *nu is*, 7 a bið.

§ viii [z]. Ða se Wisdom þa ðis *spell* asæd hæfde, þa ongan
5 he eft *singan* 7 þus cwæð : * (*Wella, men, wel ; ælc þara ðe freo*[1] *sie fundige to þā goode 7 to þā gesælðū ; 7 se ðe nu gehæft sie mid þære unnyttan lufe þisses*[2] *middaneardes sece him freodom hu he mæge becuman to þā gesælðum, forþam þ is sio an ræst eallra urra geswinca ; sio an hyð bið simle*
10 *smyltu*[3] *æfter eallū þā ystū 7 þā yðum urra geswinca. Þ is seo an friðstow 7 sio an frofer erminga æfter þā ermðū ðisses andweardan lifes. Ac þa gyldenan stanas, 7 þa seolfrenan, 7 ælces cynnes gimmas, 7 eall þes andwearda wela, ne onlihta ƀ hi nauht þæs modes eagan, ne heora scearpnesse nauht gebetað*
15 *to þære sceawunga þære soðan gesælðe ; ac get swiðor hi ablendað þæs modes eagan þōn hi hi ascirpan. Forþā ealle þa ðing þe her liciað on þisum andweardum life sint eorðlice, forþy hi sint fleonde*[4]*. Ac sio wundorlice beorhtnes þe ealle ðing gebirht 7 eallū welt, nyle þ ða sawla forweorðan, ac wile*
20 *hi onlihtan. Gif þōn hwelc mon mæge gesion þa birhtu þæs heofenlican leohtes mid hluttrū eagū · his modes, þōn wile he cweðan þ sio beorhtnes*[5] *þære*[6] *sunnan sciman sie þesternes*[7] *to metanne wið ða ecan birhtu Godes.*)

§ ix [a]. Ða se Wisdom ða ðis leoð asungen hæfde, þa
25 cwæð ic : Ic eom geþafa þæs þe þu sægst, forðæmþe þu hit hæfst geseðed mid ge*scead*wislicere race. Ða cwæð he : Mid *hu mi*cle feo woldest þu nu habban *geboht* þ þu meahte ongitan hwæt [*þ soðe*] god wære, 7 hwylc hit wære. [*Ða cwæð ic*] : Ic wolde fægnian mid swiðe [*ungemetlic*]e
30 gesean, 7 ic wolde mid [*unarime*]dū *feo*[8] gebycgan þ ic hit *moste gesion. Ða cwæð he : Ic hit þe þonne wille * 76a C. getæcan ; ac þ an ic þe bebiode, þ þu þeah for ðære

*74b C ends.

---

[z] Boeth. iii. met. 10. 'Huç omnes pariter,' &c. Cott. Metr. xxi.
[a] Boeth. iii. pr. 11. 'Assentior, inquam,' &c.

[1] em. *feor* B.   [2] em. *þisse* B.   [3] *smiltu* B.   [4] em. *flewonde* B.
[5] em. *beortnes* B.   [6] em. *wære* B.   [7] em. *þæs ær nes* B.   [8] *fio* J.

tæcinge[1] ne forgite þ þ ic ðe[2] ær tæhte. Da cwæð ic:
Nese, ne forgite ic hit no. Da cwæð he: Hu ne *sæ*don
we þe ær þ þis andwearde lif þe we her wilniað nære no
þ hehste good, forðæm hit wære mislic 7 *on* swa manigfeald
todæled[3], þ hit[4] nan mon ne mæg eall habban þ him ne sie 5
sumes þinges wana? *Ic ðe* tæhte þa þ þær wære ðæt
hehstæ go*d* þær þær þa good (*ealle*) gegadrade bioð, swe*l*ce
hi sien to anum wegge[5] gegoten. Þonne þ*ær* bið full good
þonne þa good eall*e* þe we ær ymb spræcon b*eoð* to anum
go*de ge*gadrad; þonne ne bi*þ* [*ðær*] nanes goodes wana; 10
þonne þa good *ealle* on annesse bioð, 7 sio annes bið on
ec*n*esse.   Gif hi ón ecnesse næren[6], þonne nære hiora swa
swiðe to girnanne. Da cwæð ic: Þ is gesæd; ne mæg
ic no þæs[7] twiogean. Þa cwæð he: Ær ic þe hæfde gesæd þ þ
nære full good þ eall *ætgædere næ*re, forðæm is þ fulle[8] good 15
þ eall ætgædre is untodæled. Da cwæð ic: Swæ me ðincð.

 Da *c*wæð he: Wenstu nu þ eall *[ða þing ðe gode sint
on þisse w*]eorulde forðy goode sien[9] þe[10] hi *hæ*bben[11] hwæthwugu goodes on him? Da cw̄ð ic: Hwæs mæg ic elles
wenan? hu ne is hit swa? Da cwæð he: Þu scealt þeah 20
gelyfan ðæt sio annes 7 sio good[*ne*]s an ðing sie. Da cwæð
ic: Ne mæg ic þæs oðsacan. Þa cwæð he: Hu ne meaht
þu geþencan þ ælc þing mæg bion, ge on þisse weorulde
ge on þære toweardan, þa hwile þe hit untodæled bið? þonne
ne bið hit eallunga swa swa *hit* ær wæs. Þa cwæð ic: Sege 25
me þ sweo*tolor*; ne mæg [*ic*] fullice ongitan æfter *hwā* þu
spy*rast*. *Da cwæð he: Wast þu hwæt m*on sie? Da cwæð
ic: Ic wat þ hi*t* bið[12] sawl 7 *lichoma*. [*Da cwæ*]ð he:
[*Hw*]æt, þu wast þ hi*t* bið mon, þa hwile þe sio saul 7 se
lichoma untodælde[13] bioð; ne bið hit nan mon siððan hi 30
todælde bioð. Swa eac se *li*choma bið lichoma þa hwile
þe *he* his limu ealle hæfð; *gif* he þonne hwilc lim forlyst,
[*þōn ne*] bið he eall swa he ær wæs. *Þ ilce* þu meaht

---

[1] *tæcninge* B.　　[2] *ðe* om. B.　　[3] *gedæled* B.　　[4] *hit* om. B.
[5] *wecge* B.　　[6] *ne sien* B.　　[7] *þæs no* B.　　[8] *full* B.　　[9] *sint* B.
[10] *þy* B.　[11] From J, *habbað* B.　　[12] *is* B.　　[13] *undælde* B.

geþencan be ælcum *þinge*, ꝥ *nan* þing ne bið swilce hit
wæs s*i*ððan hit wanian onginð.   Ða cw̄ð *ic :* Nu ic (*hit*) * 77ᵃ C.
wat.   Ða cwæð he : Wenst þu hwæðer ænig gesceaft sie þe
hire willum nylle ealne weg bion, ac will[*e*] hire agnū willum
5 for[*weor*]ðan ?

   § x ᵇ. Ða cwæð ic : Ne mæg ic nane cwuce [*w*]uht
ongitan þara þe wite hwæt [*h*]it wille, oððe [*h*]wæt hit nylle,
þe ungened lyste ¹ forweorðan ; forðæmþe ælc wuht wolde
bion hal 7 libban, þara þe me cwuco ðincð ; bute ic nat be
10 treowum 7 (*be*) wyrtum, 7 be swelcum gesceaftum swelce
nane sawle nabbað.   Ða smearcode he 7 cwæð : Ne þearft
þu no be þæm gesceaftum tweogan þon ² ma þe be ðæm
oðrum.   Hu ne meaht þu gesion ꝥ ælc wyrt 7 ælc wudu
wile weaxan on þæm lande selest þe him betst gerist 7 him
15 gecynde bið 7 gewunlic, 7 þær *þær* hit gefret ꝥ hit hraðost
weax[*an*] mæg 7 latost wealowian ? Sumra wyrta oððe
sumes wuda eard bið on dunū, sumra on merscum, sumra
on morum, sumra on cludum, sumra ³ on [*bar*]um sondum.
Nim ðonne [*swa wuda* ⁴] swa wyrt, swa˙hwæðer [*swa þu
20 wille, of þare stowe þe*] his eard [*7 æþelo bið*] *on* to wexanne, * 77ᵇ C.
7 sete ⁵ on ungecynde ⁶ stowe him ; þonne ne g[*egr*]ewð hit
þær nauht, ac forsearað ; fo[*r*]ðæm ælces landes ge[*cy*]nd is ⁷
ꝥ hit [*him g*]elica ⁸ wyrta 7 gelicne wudu tydr[*e* ⁹, *7 hit*] swa
deð.   Friðað 7 fyrðrað swið[*e geo*]rne, swa lange swa hiora
25 gecynd [*bið ꝥ*] hi growan ¹⁰ moton. Hwæt wenst þu, forhwy
ælc sæd creope ¹¹ inon ¹² þa eorðan, 7 to ciðū 7 to wyrtrumum weorðe (*on þære eorðan*), buton forðy ¹³ þe hi tiohhiað
ꝥ se stemn 7 se helm ¹⁴ mote þy fæstor 7 þe leng stondan ?
Hwy ne meaht þu ongitan, þeah þu hit gesion ne mæge, ꝥ
30 eall se dæl se ðe ¹⁵ þæs treowes on twelf monðum gewexð ¹⁶,
þæt he onginð of þæm wyrtrumum 7 swa upweardes grewð
oð ðone stemn, 7 siððan andlang þæs piðan, 7 andlang

<hr>

ᵇ Boeth. iii. pr. 11. l. 43 P.   'Si animalia, inquam, considerem,' &c.
¹ *lust* B.   ² *þe* B.   ³ *sume* B.   ⁴ *wudu* J.   ⁵ *sette* B.
⁶ *uncynde* B.   ⁷ *is* om. B.   ⁸ Conject., *gelica* om. B.   ⁹ From J,
tydrige B.   ¹⁰ From B, *growen* C.   ¹¹ *greowe* B.
¹² *innon* B.   ¹³ *þy* B.   ¹⁴ *welm* B.   ¹⁵ *ðe* om. B.   ¹⁶ *geweaxð* B.

þære rinde oð ðone helm, 7 siððan æſ t̃ þæm bogu[*m*], oððæt
hit ut aspringeð on leaſum 7 cn blostmum 7 on bledum?
Hwi ne meaht þu ongitan þte ælc wuht cwuces bið innanweard hnescost 7 unbroc[*h*]eardost? Hwæt, þu meht
gesion h[*u þ t*]reow bið utan gescerped[1] 7 be[*wæfed*[2] *mid*] 5
þære rinde wið ðone w[*inter* 7 *wið ða stea*]rcan sto[*rmas*
* 78a C.   7 *eac wið þære*] *sunnan hæto on sumera. Hwa mæg þ he
ne wundrie swel[*cr*]a gesceaſta ures scyppendes, 7 huru þæs
scyppendes? 7 þeah we his nu wundrigen, hwilc ure mæg
areccan medemlice ures scyppendes willan 7 anwald, hu his 10
gescea[*ſta*] wexað 7 eſt [*wania*]ð, þonne þæs tim[*a*] cymð,
7 oſ hiora sæde wiorðað eſ[*t ge*]edniwode, swylce hi þonne
weorð[*en*[3] *to*] edsceaſte? Hwæt, hi þonne eſt bioð, 7 eac
hwæthwugu anlice bioð swilce hi â bion, forðæm hi ælce
geare weorðað to edsceaſte.   15

§ xi[c]. Hwæþer þu giet ongite þ ða uncweðendan gesceaſta
wilnodon to bionne on ecnesse swa ilce swa mē, giſ hi
mealten? Hwæðer þu nu ongite forhwy þ ſyr ſundige up, 7
sio eorðe oſdune? Forhwy is þ buton forþyðe God gesceop
his eard *up* 7 hire oſdune; forðy fundiað[4] ælc gesceaſt þider 20
swiðost þider his eard 7 his *hælo*[5] swiðost bioð, 7 flihð þte
him wiðerweard bið 7 ungebyrde 7 ungelic. Hwæt, þa
stanas, forðæm [*hi*] sint stillre gecynde 7 heardre, [*bioð*]
earſoðe to tedælenne[6]; 7 eac un[*eaðe tosomne cuma*]ð, giſ hi
* 78b C.   todælde[7] *weorþað. Giſ þu þonne ænne stan toclifst, ne wyr[*ð* 25
h]e næfre gegadrod swa he ær wæs; ac þ wæter 7 sio lyſt
bioð hw[*ene*] hnescran gecynde; hi [*b*]ioð swiðe eðe[8] to
tedælenne[9], ac hi bioð [*eſt*] sona ætgædre. þ ſyr þonne ne
[*mæg*] næfre weorðan [*todæl*]ed. Ic sæde [*þeah*] nu hwene
ær þte nanwuht his [*agen*]um willum nolde forweorðan; *ac* 30
ic eom nu ma ymb [*þ*] gecynd þonne yb̃ þone willan, forðæm
hi hwilum willað on tu[10]. þu meaht witan[11] be manegum

---

[c] Boeth. iii. pr. 11. l. 69 P. ' Ea etiam quae inanimata esse,' &c.

[1] *gescyrped* B.   [2] From J, *beweroð* B.   [8] em. *weord*[C,
weordon B. [4] *fundað* B. [5] Appar. *æðelu* in C. [6] From B, *tedælende* C.
[7] *gedælede* B. [8] *eaðe* B. [9] So also B. [10] *twa* B. [11] *witan* om. B.

þingum ꝥ ꝥ gecynd is swiðe micel; is ꝥ formicel gecynd ðæt
urum lichoman cymð eall his mægen of ðæm mete þe we
þiggað, (7) þeah færð se mete ut þurh þone lichoman; ac his
swæc[1] ðeah 7 his cræft gecymð on[2] ælcre ædre, swa swa mon
5 meolo seft; ðæt meolo ðurgcrypð ælc ðyrel, 7 þa syfeða[3]
weorðað asyndred. Swa eac ure gast bið swiðe wide
farende[4] urum unwillum 7 ures ungewealdes for his ge-
c[y]nde, nalles for his willan; ꝥ bið þonne þonne we
slapað. Hwæt, [*þa*] nytenu ðonne 7 eac þa oðra
10 ges[*ceafta*] ma wilniað þ[*æs þe hi wilniað for gecynde*]
*ðonne for willan. Ungecyndelic is[5] *ælcre* wuhte ꝥ hit * 79a C.
wilnige frecennesse oððe deaðes, ac þeah mænig þing bið to
þæm gened ꝥ hit wilnað þara ægðres; forðæm se willa bið
þonne *strengra* þonne ꝥ gecynd. Hwilum bið *se* wil*la*
15 swiðra þonne ꝥ gecynd, hwilum *þæt* gecynd ofercymð þone
willan. Swa nu wrænnes deð; sio bið ælcu*m* men gecynde,
7 hwilum[6] *þeah hire* bið forwerned hi[*re gecyndes þurh*] þæs
monnes willan. Eall sio lufu [*þæs*] hæmedþinges bið for
gecynde, [*nallas*[7]] for willan.

20   § xii[d]. Be þæm þu meaht [*open*]lice witan ꝥ se sceppend[8]
ealra [*ge*]sceafta hæfð forgifen *ænne* [*lust*] 7 an gecynd
eallum his gesceaftū; þæt is ꝥ hi woldon â[9] bion. Ælcre
wuhte is gecynde ꝥ hit wilnige ꝥ hit â sie be þæm dæle [*þe
hit*[10]] his gecynde healdan mo*t* [7 *mæg*]. Ne þearft ðu no
25 tweogan [*ymbe ꝥ*] þe þu ær tweodest, ꝥ is be [*þā
ge*]sceaftum þe nane sawle n[*abbað*]; ælc þara gesceafta þe
[*sawle hæfð, ge*] eac þa þe nabbað, [*willniað simle to bionne.
Đa cwæð ic: Nu ic*] *ongite ꝥ ðæt ic ær ymbe tweode; ꝥ is * 79b C.
ðæt ælc gesceaft wilnað symle to bionne; ꝥ is swiðe sweo-
30 tol on ðære tidringe. Þa cwæð he: Hwæþer þu þonne
[*o*]ngite ꝥ ælc þara wuhta þe him[11] beon þenc[ð], ꝥ hit
þencð ætgædere bion, gehal, untodæled[12]? forðæm gif hit

---

[d] Boeth. iii. pr. 11. l. 92 P. 'Dedit enim providentia,' &c.

[1] *spræc* B. [2] *on* om. B. [3] *siofoða* B. [4] From B, *færende* C. [5] *bið*
B. [6] *gehwilcū* B. [7] *nales* J. [8] em. *seppend* C. [9] *a* om. B.
[10] *hit* from J, om. B. [11] *him* om. B. [12] *undæled* B.

[1] todæled bið, þonne ne bið hit no hal [1].   Ða cwð ic : ꝥ is
soð.   Ða cwæð he : (ꝥ *is*), eall þing hab*baþ* [*þeah*] ænne
willan, ðæt is ðæt hi *wold*on [*a bion ; þur*]h þone ænne
wil[*lan*] hi wilniað ðæs anes goodes þe â *bið*, ꝥ is God [2].
Ða cwæð ic : Swa hit is [*swa ð*]u sægst [3].   Ða cwæð he : 5
Hwæt, þu m[*iht*] openlice ongitan ꝥ ðæt is for[*inlice*] good
þing þe ealra [4] wuhta 7 eall*e* gesceafta wilniað to habban*ne*.
Ða cwæð ic : Ne mæg nan mon soðre secgan, forðæm ic
ongite ꝥ ealla ge[*sceafta*] toflowen [5] swa swa wæter, 7 [*nanne*]
sibbe ne nane endebyrd[*nesse*] ne heolden, ac swiðe unge- 10
rec[*lice* [6] *to*]slupen [7] 7 to nauhte wurden, [*swa swa*] we
lange ær sædon on ðisse [*ilcan bec*], gif hi næfdon ænne
God [8] [*þe him e*]allum stiorde 7 racode *[7 *rædde.   Ac nu*
forþæðe we witon ꝥ an wealdend is eallra þinga, we sceolon [9]
beon nede geþafan, sam we willan sã we nyllan, ꝥ he sie se 15
hehsta hrof eallra goda.   Ða smercode [10] *he wið min 7 cwæð :*
Eala [11]*, min cild, ea* [12]*; hwæt, þu eart swiðe gesælig, 7 ic*
swiðe bliðe, for minũ [13] *andgite.   Swiðe neah þu ongeate þa ꝥ*
riht, 7 ꝥ ilce ꝥ þu ær sædest ꝥ ðu ongiton ne mihtest, þæs þu
wære nu geþafa.   Ða cwæð ic : Hwæt wæs ꝥ ꝥ ic ær sæde 20
ꝥ ic nysste [14]*? Ða cwæð he : Nu þu sædest ꝥ ðu nystest* [11]
ælcre gesceafte ende ; ac wite nu ꝥ ꝥ is ælcre gesceafte ende
ꝥ ðu self ær nemdest, ꝥ is God [15]*; to þam fundiað ealle* [16]
gesceafta.   Nabbað hi nan god ofer ꝥ to secanne, ne hi nanwuht
ne magon ne ufor ne utor findan.   25

* 79b C
ends, next
2 fols.
missing.

XXXV [e].

§ i. *Ða he þa þis spell asæd hæfde, þa ongan he eft singan*
7 þus cwæð :] (*Swa hwa swa wille dioplice spirigan mid*
inneweardan mode æfter ryhte, 7 nylle ꝥ hine ænig mon oððe
ænig þing mage amerran, onginne þõn secan oninnan him

---

[e] Boeth. iii. met. 11. 'Quisquis profunda mente,' &c. Cott. Metr. xxii.

[1] *untodæled bið, þõn bið hit gehal* B.   [2] From B, *good* C.   [3] *swa*
ðu sægst J, om. B.   [4] *ealle* B.   [5] *tofleowon* B.   [6] From J, *ungelice* B.
[7] *7 . . . wurden* om. B.   [8] From B, *good* C.   [9] *sculon* J.   [10] *smear-*
code J.   [11] *ea* J.   [12] Orig. *eall* in B, but *ll* erased.   [13] *ðinum* J.
[14] *nesse* J.   [15] *ꝥ is god* from J, om. B.   [16] *ealla* J.

*selfū, þ he ær ymbuton hine sohte, 7 forlæte unnytte ymbhogan
swa he swiðost mæge ; 7 gegæderige to þam anum, 7 gesecge
þōn his anū mode þ hit mæg findan oninnan him selfum ealle
þa god þe hit ute secð. Þōn mæg he swiðe raþe ongitan eall[1] þ*
5 *yfel 7 þ unnet þ he ær on his mode hæfde ; swa sweotole swa ðu
miht þa sunnan geseon, 7 þu ongitst þin agen ingeþanc, þ hit
bið micele beorhtre[2] 7 leohtre þōn seo sunne. Forþā nan hæfignes
þæs lichoman ne nan unðeaw ne mæg eallunga ation of his
mode þa rihtwisnesse[3], swa þ he hire hwæthwegu nabbe on his*
10 *mode ; þeah sio swærnes ðæs lichoman 7 þa unþeawas oft
abisegien þ mod mid ofergiotulnesse, 7 mid þā gedwolmiste hit[4]
fortio þ hit ne mæge swa beorhte scinan swa hit wolde.
7 þeah bið simle corn þære soðfæstnesse sæd on þære sawle
wunigende, þa hwile þe sio sawl 7 se lichoma gederode bioð.*
15 *Þ corn sceal bion aweht mid ascunga 7 mid lare, gif hit
growan sceal. Hu mæg þōn ænig man ryhtwislice 7 gesceadwislice acsigan[5], gif he nan grot rihtwisnesse on him næfð ?
Nis nan swa swiðe bedæled ryhtwisnesse þ he nan ryht andwyrde nyte, gif mon acsað. Forþā hit is swiðe ryht spell*
20 *þ Plato se uðwita sæde ; he cwæð: swa hwa swa ungemyndig
sie rihtwisnesse[6], gecerre hine to his gemynde ; þōn fint he þær
þa ryhtwisnesse gehydde mid þæs lichoman hæfignesse 7 mid
his modes gedrefednesse 7 bisgunga.)*

§ ii[f]. [*Ða cwæð ic : Ic eom geðafa þ þ was soð spell þ*
25 *Plato sæde. Hu ne mynegodest[7] þu me eac nu tuwa þære
ilcan spræce ? ærest þu cwæde þ ic hæfde forgiten þ gecyndelice[8]
god þ ic oninnan me selfū hæfde, for ðæs lichoman hefignesse. Æt oðrū cerre þu me sædest þ ðu hæfdest ongiten þ me
selfū þuhte þ ic hæfde eallunga forloren þ gecyndelice god þ ic*
30 *oninnan me selfū sceolde habban, for þære ungemetlican unrotnesse þe ic hæfde for ðā forlætenan welan. Ða cwæð he :
Þær þu gemyndest þa word þe ic þe sæde on þære forman bec,*

<hr>

[f] Boeth. iii. pr. 12. 'Tum ego, Platoni, inquam,' &c.

[1] Orig. *ealle*, but *e* erased. [2] em. *beortre* B. [3] em. *unrihtwisnesse* B.
[4] Orig. *hig* B, *g* turned into *t*. [5] em. *acsigen* B. [6] em. *rihtwissesse* B.
[7] *myndgodest* J. [8] em. *gecyndelic* B.

þōn miht[1] þu be þā wordū genog sweotole ongitan þ þ ðu ær
sædest þ ðu nysstest[2]. Ða cwæð ic : Hwæt was þ, hwæt sæde
ic þ ic nyste[3]? Ða cwæð he : Ðu sædest on þære ilcan bec þ
ðu ongeate þte God weolde þisses middangeardes, ac þu sædest
þ þu[4] ne mihte witan humeta he his weolde, oððe hu he his 5
weold. Ða cwæð ic : Ic geman genog geara[5] min agen dysig,
7 ic his wæs ær þe geþafa.]   *ðeah ic hit ða be sumum

dæle ongeate, ic wolde giet his mare æt þe geheran. Ða
cwæð he : Ne ðe nauht ær ne tweode ðætte God rædde
7 wiolde ealles middangeardes. Ða cwæð ic : Ne me giet 10
nauht ne tweoð, ne nu næfre ne twioð ; ic ðe wille eac sona
sec[*gan*] be hwæm ic hit[6] ærest ongeat. Ic on[*geat*] þ ðes
middangeard wæs of swiðe [*maneg*]um 7 mislicum þingum
gega[*derod, 7 sw*]iðe fæste tosomne gelim[*ed 7 gef*]angod.
Nære(n)[7] ðe (hi) gegaderode 7 geradod[*e*], swa wiðerwearda 15
gesceafta, þon[*ne*][8] ne wurdon hi næfre ne geworht[*e*] ne eac
gegaderod ; 7 gif he hi ne gebunde mid his unanbindendlicum[9] racen[*tū*], ðonne toslupen hi ealla ; 7 næ[*re* [10] *no*] swa
gewislice ne swa endebyr[*dlice*] ne swa gemetlice hiora
stede 7 hiora ryne funden on hiora stowū 7 on hiora 20
tidum, gif an unanwendendlic God (*nære þe heora*[11] *weolde.*
Þone God), ðæt þ he is, þ ic hate God, swa swa ealle
gesceafta hatað.

§ iii[s]. Ða cwæð he : Nu ðu þ swa openlice ongiten
hæfst, ne ðearfe ic nu nauht swiðe ymb ðæt swincan þ ic ðe 25

ma be Gode *recce* ; forþ[*ā þu ea*]rt nu fulneah *cumen in on*[12]
ða ceastre þære soðan gesælðe, þe þu lange[13] ær ne meahtest
aredian. Ac wit sculon swaþeah secan þ þ wit ær mynton.
Þa cwæð ic : Hwæt is ðæt? Ða cwæð he : Hu ne tealdon
wit ær þte genyht wæren[14] gesælða, 7 þa gesælða [*wær*]en 30
God? Ða cwæð ic : Swa hit is [*swa þ*]u sægst. Ða (*cwæð*)
he : God ne beþearf [*nan*]es oðres fultomes buton h*is* [*selfes*]

---

[s] Boeth. iii. pr. 12. l. 25 P. ‘Tum illa, cum haec, inquit,’ &c.

[1] *meahte* J.   [2] *nesse* J.   [3] *nysse* J.   [4] Conject. om. B.
[5] *geare* J.   [6] *hit* om. B.   [7] Last *n* erased in B.   [8] Conj. *þōn* B.
[9] *unabindendlicū* B.   [10] *næron no* J.   [11] *þe heora* conj. om. B.
[12] *innon* B.   [13] *lang* C.   [14] *wære* B.

. his gesceafta mid to weald*anne*, [*þe*][1] ma þe he ær þorfte
to[2] [*þā*] weorce; forðæm gif he æniges [*fu*]ltomes on
ænegum þingum beðorf[*te*], þonne næfde he (*no*) self geno[*g*].
Đa cwæð ic: Swa hit is swa ðu [*segst*]. Đa cwæð he:
5 Þurg hine self[*ne he*] gesceop eall ðing 7 ealra wylt. Đa
[*cwæ*]ð ic: Ne mæg ic þæs oðsacan. Đa cwa[*e*]ð he: Ær
we þe hæfdon þ gereaht þ God wære þurh hine selfne good.
Đa cwæð ic: Ic geman þ ðu swa[3] sædest. Đa cwæð he:
Þurg good God gesceop eal[4] ðing, forðæm he wilt þurh hine
10 self[*ne*] ealles þæs þe we ær cwædon ðæt good wære; 7 he
is ana staðolfæst wealdend 7 stiora 7 steorroðer 7 helma[5],
forðæm he riht 7 [*ræt eallū*] gesceaft[*um*], *swa swa good   * 81a C.
stiora anum scipe. [*Đa*] cwæð ic: Nu ic ðe[6] andette þ ic
h[*æbbe*] funden duru þær þær ic ær ge[*seah ane*] lytle cinan,
15 swa ðæt ic uneað[*e*[7] *mihte*] gesion swiðe lytelne scima[*n*
leohtes] of þissum þiostrum; 7 þeah [*þu me*] tæhtest ær þa
duru, ac ic [*hire ne*] meahte mare aredian, b[*uton þ ic hire*]
grapode ymbutan [*þ þe ic þæt lyt*]le leoht geseah tw[*inclian.*
Ic þe sæde] gefyrn ær on þiss[*e ilcan bec þ ic*] nysse (*hwæt*
20 *se*) fruma wære ealra [*gesceafta*]; þa gerehtest þu me þ[8] hit
[*wæs God*]. Đa nysse ic eft ymb þone [*ende, ær*] þu me eft
gereahtes þ ðæt [*wære eac God*]. Đa sæde ic þe þ ic nysse
hu he [*ealra þara*] gesceafta wiolde; ac þu hit [*me*] hæfst nu
swiðe sweotole ge[*reht*][9], swylce þu hæbbe þa duru a[*broden*][10]
25 þe ic ær sohte. Đa andswarode [*he me*] 7 cwæð: Ic wat þ
ic ðe ær myndg[*ode*] ðære ilcan spræce, 7 nu me ði[*ncþ þ*]
þu ongite swa swa[11] leng swa bet [*ymbe*] þa soðfæstnesse;
ac (*ic*) wolde [*git þe*] eowian sume bysne, (*ac*) swa sweo[*tole*]
swa sio wæs þe ic (*þe*) ær sæde. Đ[*a cwæð ic*]: Hwæt [*is sio?*
30 § iv[h]. *Đa*] cwæð he: Ne *[*mæg nænne mon þæ*]s twiogean   * 81b C.
þte ealra gesceafta [*agnū*] willum God ricsað ofer hi,
7 eað[*modlice*] hiora willan wendað to his willan. [*Be þam*

---

[h] Boeth. iii. pr. 12. L. 44 P. 'Cum deus, inquit, omnia,' &c.

[1] *þon* J.   [2] *to* B.   [3] *swa* om. B.   [4] *ælc* B.   [5] *7 helma*
om. B.   [6] *ðe* om. B.   [7] *ungeaðe* B.   [8] *hwæt* B.   [9] *gereaht* J.
[10] *anbroden* B.   [11] *swa* only once B.

is] swiðe sweotol ðætte God æghwæs [*wealt mid þ*]æm
helman 7 mid ðæm stior[*roðre his*] goodnesse ; forðæmþe
ealla [*gesceafta*] gecyndelice hiora agnū [*willum fundiað*]
to cumanne to Gode, [*swa swa we*[1] *oft ær*] sædon on ðisse
ilcan [*bec. Ða cwæð ic: Hwi ne*[2]] mæg (*ic*) þæs twiogan ; 5
[*forþā Godes anwe*]ald nære full eadig[*lic gif þa ge*]sceafta
hiora unwillū him [*herden*[3] ; 7 *eft*] þa gesceafta næren nanes
[*þonces ne n*]anes weorðscipes wyrðe gif [*hi hiora un*]willum
hlaforde herden. Ða [*cwæð he*]: Nis nan gesceaft þe[4] tiohhie
[*þ hio*] scyle winnan wið hire scippen[*des willa*]n gif hio hire 10
cynd[5] healdan wille[6]. [*Ða cwæð*] ic : Nis nan gecynd[7] þe
wið hire [*scippen*]des willan winne buton dys[*ig mon, o*]ððe eft
þa wiðerweardan engl*as*. [*Ða cwæð*] he : Hwæt wenst ðu ?
gif ænegu [*gesceaft*[8]] tiohhode þ hio wið his willan [*sceolde*]
*win*nan, hwæt hio meahte wið [*swa mih*]tigne swa we hine 15
gereahtne [*habbað*]? Ða cwæð ic : Ne magon hi nauht,
[*þeah hi willon. Ða wundrode he* 7 *cwæð : Nis*] *nanwuht
þe mæge oððe wille swa heaum Gode[9] wiðcweðan. Ða
cwæð ic : Ne wene ic þ ænig wuht sie ðe wið winne, buton
ðæt wit ær spræcon. Ða smearcade he 7 cwæð : Wite geare 20
ðæt ðæt is þ hehste gód, ðæt hit eall swa mihtiglice macað
7 eall ðing gesceop 7 eallū swa [*ge*]reclice racað 7 swa
eðelice buton a[*elcū*] geswince hit eall set. Ða cwæð [*ic :
Wel*] me licode ðæt þu ær sædes, 7 þ[*ises me lyst nu*] giet
bet ; ac me sceamað nu ð[*æt*[10] *ic hit ær*] ne ongeat. Ða 25
cwæð he : (*Hwæt*), ic wat [*þ ðu ge*]herdest oft reccan on
ealdum [*leasū*] spellum þte Iob Saturnes[11] [*sunu sceo*]lde
bion se hehsta god of[*er ealle oðre*[12]] godu[13], 7 he sceolde bion
þæs heo[*fenes*] sunu, 7 sceolde ricsian on heo[*fenū*] ; 7
sceolden[14] gigantes[15] bion eorðan [*suna*], 7 ða sceolden ricsian 30
ofer eor[*þan* ; 7 *þa*] sceolden hi bion swelce hi wæren
[*geswys*]terna[16] bearn, forðæmþe he sce[*olde beon*] heofones
sunu, 7 hi eorðan.   7 þa [*sceolde*] þæm gigantum ofþincan

---

[1] *we* from J, om. B.   [2] *hwone* J.   [3] From J, *herdest* B.
[4] *þe he* B.   [5] *gecynd* B.   [6] *wile* C.   [7] *gesceaft* B.   [8] em. *gesceaf* B.
[9] *goode* B.   [10] *ðæt* conject., *þ* B.   [11] *saturnús* C.   [12] *oðru* J.
[13] *godas* B. [14] em. *sceolde* C, *scoldon* B. [15] *gigantas* B. [16] *geswystrena* B.

þ he hæfde hiera rice ; woldon þa tobrecan þo[*ne*] heofon
under him; þa sceolde he sendan þunras 7 ligeta [1] 7 windas,
7 toweorpan [*eall*] *hira* geweor[*c*] mid, 7 hi selfe ofslean.
*[*Đyl*]lica leasunga hi worhton, 7 meahton eaðe seggan   * 82b C.
5 soðspell, gif [2] him þa leasunga næren swetran, 7 þeah swiðe
gelic ðisum. Hi meahton seggan hwylc dysig Nefrod se
gigant worhte ; se Nefrod wæs Chuses sunu ; Chus wæs
Chames [3] sunu, Cham [4] Noes. Se Nefrod het w[*yrca*]n
ænne tor on ðæm felda ðe Nen[*sar*] [5] hatte, 7 on ðære þiode
10 ðe De*ira* [6] [*hatte, swi*]ðe neah þære byrig [*þe mon nu hæt*
Bab]ilonia. Þ hi dydon [*for þā ði*]ngum þe [7] hi woldon
witan hu heah [*hit wære*] to ðæm heofone, 7 hu ðicce se
[*hefon w*]ære 7 hu fæst, oððe hwæt þær[*ofer wære*]. Ac hit
gebyrede, swa hit [*cynn* [8] *was*], þ se godcunda wald [9] hi
15 tostenc[*te* [10] *ær hi*] hit fullwyrcan mosten, 7 to[*wearp*] ðone
tor, 7 hiora monigne of[*slog, 7 hiora s*]præce todælde ón tu
7 hund [*seofonti*]g geþioda. Swa gebyreð ælcū [*þara þ*]e
winð wið ðæm godcundan anwal[*de ; ne*] gewyxð him
nan weorðscipe on [*ðæm, a*]c wyrð se gewanod þe hi ær
20 hæfdon.

§ v [1]. Ac loca nu hwæðer þu wille ðæt [*wit*] giet spyrigen [11]
æft̃ ænigre gescead*wisnesse furð*ur, nu wit ðæt funden [12]
habbað þ wit ær *soht*on. Ic wene þeah, gif wit giet uncru
word *tosom*ne sleað, þ ðær *ásprunge sum spearca up soð-   * 83a C.
25 fæstnesse þara þe wit ær ne gesawon. Da cwæð ic: Do
(*swa*) swa ðu wille. Da cwæð he : Hwæt, nænne mon nu
ne tweoð þ God sie swa mihtig þ he mæge wyrcan þ þ he
wille. Da cwæð ic : Ne tweoð ðæs nænne [13] mon ðe auht
wat. Da cwæð he : Hwæðer ænig mon wene [14] þ [*auht sie*
þæs] þe God don ne mæge [15]. Da cw[*æð i*]c : Ic hit [16] wat
30 ðæt nauht nis þæs þe he [*don*] ne mæge. Da cwæð he :

---

[1] Boeth. iii. pr. 12. l. 66 P. ‘Sed uisne rationes,’ &c.

[1] *lygetu* B.   [2] *gif* above line C.   [3] From J, *chaames* B.
[4] *chaā* B.   [5] From J, *sennar* B.   [6] Looks like *dera* in C.   [7] þ B.
[8] *cyn* J.   [9] *anweald* B.   [10] *tostente* B.   [11] *gespyrigen* B.
[12] *afunden* B.   [13] *nan* B.   [14] *wære* B.   [15] *mæg* B.   [16] *hit* om. B.

Wenstu hwæðer [*he m*]æge ænig[1] yfel don? Ða cwæð ic:
Ic wa[*t þ*] he ne mæg. Ða cwæð he: Soð þu sægst,
forðæm hit is nauht; þær yfel auht wære, þonne meahte hit
God wyrcan; forðy hit is nauht. Ða cwæð ic: Me þincð
þ ðu me dwelle 7 dydre[2], swa mon cild deð; lædst me hidres 5
7 ðidres[3] on swa þicne wudu ðæt ic ne mæg ut aredian.
Forðæm ðu a ymbe sticce fehst (*eft*) on ða ilcan [*sp*]ræce þe
þu ær spræce, 7 forlætst eft ða ær ðu hi geendod hæbbe, 7
fehst on uncuðe; *þy* ic nat (*nu*) hwæt þu wilt. Me þincð
þ ðu *hwerfe* ymbeutan sume wundorlice 7 seldcuþe spræce 10
ymbe ða anfealdnesse[4] þære *godcundnesse*. Ic geman þ ðu me
ær reahtes *sū* wundor*lic spell* be ðā þa ðu me reahtes þ hit[5]

*wære eall an gesælða 7 þ hehste god, 7 cwæde þ ða gesælða
wæren on ðæm hehste goode fæste, 7 þ hehste good wære
God self, 7 he wære full ælcre gesælðe; 7 þu cwæde þ ælc 15
gesælig mon wære God.   7 eft þu sædes þ Godes goodnes[6]
7 his gesælignes [7] he self ðæt ðæt wære[7] eall an, 7 þ
ðon[*ne*][8] wære se hehsta God; 7 to ðæm god[*e eal*]la (*þa*)
gesceafta fundiað ðe hiora [*ge*]cynd healdað, 7 wilniað þ hy
to c[*umon*][9]. 7 eac þu sædes ðætte God wiolde ea[*ll*]ra (*his*) 20
gesceafta mid ðæm stiorroðre his goodnesse; 7 eac sædes þ
ealla gesceafta hiora agnum willum ungenedde him wæren
underðiodde. 7 nu on last þu sædes þ yfel nære nauht.
7 eal[*l*] þis þu gereahtes to soðe swiðe gesceadwi[*sli*]ce,
buton ælcre leasre rædelsan.   25

    § vi [k]. [*Ða*] cwæð he: Þu sædes ær þ ic[10] ðe dwealde[11];
ac me ðincð selfum þ ic þe nauht ne dwelle[11], ac ðe sæde[12]
swiðe lang spell 7 wundorlic, 7[13] swiðe gesceadlice be ðæm
Gode ðe wit unc gefyrn to gebædon; 7 nu giet ic tiohhie þ ic
ðe hwæthwugu uncuðes gerecce be ðæm ilcan Gode.   Hit is 30
g[*ec*]ynd þære godcundnesse þ hio mæg bion ungemenged

[k] Boeth. iii. pr. 12. l. 93 P. 'Tum illa, Minime, inquit,' &c.

[1] *ænig* om. B.   [2] *dwelige 7 dyderie* B.   [3] *lætst me hider 7 þider* B.
[4] *andfealdnesse* B.   [5] *hit* om. B.   [6] em. *goodes* C, *godness* B.
[7] *he wære* B.   [8] Conject. *þōn* B.   [9] *tocumen* J.   [10] *ic* om. B.
[11] *dwelode* B.   [12] *sæde ðe* B.   [13] 7 om. B.

wið oðr[*e*][1] gesceafta *buton oðerra gesceafta fultome, * 84a C.
swa swa nan oðer gesceaft ne mæg. Ne mæg nan oðru
gesceaft be him selfum bion, swa swa (*gio*) Parmenides se sciop
giddode 7 cwð : Se ælmihtega God[2] is eallra þinga reccend,
5 7 he ana unanwendendlic[3] wunað, 7 ealra ðara anwendendlicra welt. Forðæm ðu ne þearft nauht sw*iþe* w*und*rian ðeah we
spyrien æfter ðæm ðe *we ongun*non, swa mid læs worda swa
m[*id ma*], swæðer we hit gereccan magon. Ðeah [*we*] nu scylen
manega 7 mislica bisna 7 bispell reccan, ðeah hangað ure mod
10 ealne weg on þæm þe we æfterspyriað. Ne fo we no on[4] ða bisna
7 on ða[5] bispel for ðara leasena spella lufan, ac forðæmðe
we woldon mid gebecnan[6] þa soðfæstnesse, 7 woldon ðæt hit
wurde to nytte ðam geherendum. Ic gemunde nu ryhte þæs
wisan Platones lara suma, hu he cwæð ðæt te[7] se mon se ðe
15 bispell secgan wolde, ne sceolde fon on to ungelic bispell ðære
spræce þe he ðonne sprecan wolde. Ac geher nu geðylde-
lice hwæt ic nu sprecan wille, ðeah hit *þe*[8] gefyrn ær *unnyt*
þuhte, hwæðer *þe*[8] *se* ende a b*el* lician wille.

§ vii[1]. Ongon ða *singan 7 cwæð[9]: (*Gesælig bi'l se mon* * 84b C.
20 *þe mæg geseon þone hluttran æwellm þæs hehstan*[10] *godes, 7
of him selfū aweorpan mæg þa þiostro his modes. We sculon
get of ealdū leasū spellū ðe sū bispell reccan.*) *H*it gelamp
gio ðætte an hearpere wæs on ðære ðiode ðe Ðracia[11] hatte,
sio wæs on Creca rice; se hearpere wæs swiðe ungefræglice
25 good, ðæs nama wæs Orfeus; he hæfde an swiðe ænlic wif,
sio wæs haten Eurudice[12]. Ða ongon mon secgan be ðam
hearpere þ he meahte hearpian þ se wudu wagode, 7 þa
stanas hi styredon[13] for ðy[14] swege, 7 wildu dior ðær woldon
to irnan 7 stondan swilce hi tamu wæren, swa stille, ðeah him
30 men oððe hundas wið eoden, ðæt hi hi[15] na ne onscunedon.

---

[1] Boeth. iii. met. 12. 'Felix qui potuit boni,' &c. Cott. Metr. xxiii.

[1] *oðra* J.   [2] *God* om. B.   [3] *unawendenlic* B.   [4] From B, 7 C.
[5] *ða* om. B.   [6] *gebeacnian* B.   [7] *te* om. B.   [8] *þe* both from J,
om. B.   [9] After *cwæð* (in C) there is a letter (apparently *g*), then a
blank space of about two-thirds of the line. The allit. verse begins next
line.   [10] em. *hehtan* B.   [11] *racia* B.   [12] *eurudice* B also.
[13] *hirgedon* B.   [14] *þā* B.   [15] *hi* once B.

Ða sædon hi ꝥ ðæs hearperes [*wif*] sceolde acwelan, 7 hi*re*

saule mon sceolde *lædan to helle. Ða sceolde se *hearpere*
weorðan swa sarig ꝥ he ne meahte ongemong oðrum
monnum bion, ac teah to wuda, 7 sæt on ðæm muntum
ægðer ge dæges ge nihtes; weop 7 hearpode ðæt ða wudas 5
bifcdo[*n*][1] 7 þa *ea stodon*, 7 nan heort ne onscun*ode nanne*
leon, ne nan hara nænne hund, *ne nan* neat nyste nænne
andan ne nænne ege to oðrum for ðære mergðe [2] ðæs sones.
Ða ðæm hearpere ða ðuhte ðæt hine (*þa*) nanes ðinges ne
lyste on ðisse worulde, ða ðohte he ðæt he wolde gesecan 10
helle godu [3], 7 onginnan him oleccan mid his hearpan, 7
biddan ꝥ hi him ageafan [4] eft his wif. Þa he ða ðider com, ða
sceolde cuman ðære helle hund ongean hine, þæs nama wæs
Ceruerus [5], se [6] sceolde habban þrio heafdu; 7 (*ongan*)
onfægnian [7] mid his steorte, 7 plegian wið hine for his 15
hearpunga. Ða wæs ðær eac swiðe egeslic geatweard, ðæs
nama sceolde bion Caron; se hæfde eac þrio heafdu, 7 (*se*)
wæs swiðe oreald. Ða ongon se hearpere hine biddan ꝥ he
hine gemundbyrde ða hwile þe he ðær wære, 7 hine

gesundne eft ðonan *brohte. Ða gehet he him ðæt, forðæ 20
he wæs oflyst ðæs seldcuðan sones. Ða eode he furður, oð
he (*ge*)mette ða graman metena [8] ðe folcisce men hatað
Parcas, ða hi secgað ðæt on nanum men nyt[*on na*]ne are,
ac ælcū men wrecen [*be his*] gewyrhtū; þa hi secgað ðæt
walden [*a*]elces mannes wyrde. Ða ongon he biddan heora 25
blisse [9]; ða ongunnon hi wepan mid him. Ða eode he
furður, 7 him urnon ealle hellwaran ongean, 7 læddon hine
to hiora cininge, 7 ongunnon ealle sprecan mid him 7 biddan
þæs ðe [10] he bæd. 7 ꝥ unstille hweol ðe Ixion wæs [11] to
gebunden Leuita [12] cyning for his scylde, ðæt oðstod for his 30
hearpunga. 7 Tantulus se cyning ðe on ðisse worulde ungemetlice gifre wæs, 7 him ðær ðæt ilce yfel filgde [13] ðære [14] gifernesse, he gestilde. 7 se ultor [15] sceolde forlætan ðæt he ne [16]

---

[1] *bifodon* B.   [2] *mirhþe* B.   [3] *gatu* B.   [4] From B, *agefan* C.
[5] em. *cerueruerus* C, *aruerus* B.   [6] *se* om. B.   [7] *fægenian* B.
[8] *gydena* B.   [9] *miltse* B.   [10] *ðe* om. B.   [11] *wæs* om. B.   [12] *lauita* B.
[13] *fyligde* B.   [14] em. *ðæs* C and B.   [15] So B also.   [16] *ne* om. B.

slat ða lifre Sticces[1] þæs cyninges ðe hine ær mid ðy
witnode. 7 eall hellwara witu ges*t*ildon ða hwile þe he
beforan ðam cyninge h[e]arpode. Ða he ða *longe 7 longe * 86a C.
hearpode, ða cleopode se hellwara cyning 7 cwæð: Wutun
5 agifan ðæm esne his wif, forðæm he hi hæfð geearnad mid
his hearpunga. Ƀebead him ða þ he geare wisse [þ h]e[2]
hine næfre underbæc ne besawe, [si]ððan[3] he ðonanweard
wære; 7 sæd[e] gif he hine underbæc besawe þ he sceolde
forlætan ðæt wif. Ac ða lufe mon mæg swiðe uneaðe oððe
10 na[4] forbeodan; weilawei, hwæt, Orpheus ða lædde his wif
mid him oð[5] he com on þ gemære leohtes 7 ðiostro. Þa eode
þ wif æſt him. Ða he furðum[6] on ðæt leoht com, ða beseah
he hine underbæc wið ðæs wifes; ða losade hio him sona.
Ðas leasan (*spell*) lærað gehwylcne mon ðara ðe wilnað helle
15 ðiostro to flionne 7 to ðæs soðan godes liohte to cumanne,
þ he hine ne besio to[7] his ealdan[8] yflum, swa ðæt he hi eft
swa fullice fullfremme swa he hi ær dyde. Forðæm swa hwa
swa mid fulle willan his mod went to ðǽ yflum ðe he ær
forlet, 7 hi ðonne fullfremeð, 7 hi him þonne fullice liciað, 7
20 he hi næfre forlætan ne þenceð, ðonne forlyst he eall his
ærr*an* good, buton he hit eft gebete. H*er* endað nu sio
*þridde boc Boeties, 7 onginneð[9] sio fiorðe. * 86b C.

XXXVI[m].

§ i. Ða se Wisdom ða ðis leoð swiðe lustbærlice 7 gesceadwislice âsungen hæfde, ða hæfde ic ða giet hwylchwugu[10]
25 [gem]ynd on minum mode ðære unrotnes[se] þe ic (ær) hæfde,
7 cwæð: Eala Wisdom, ðu [þe] eart boda 7 forerynel ðæs
soðan leohtes, hu wundorlic me ðincð þ ðæt þu me recst;
forðæm ic ongite þte eall ðæt þu me ær reahtes me reahte[11]
God þurh ðe, 7 ic hit wisse eac ær be sumum dæle; ac me hæfde
30 þios unrotnes amerredne, þ ic hit hæfde mid ealle forgiten. 7 þ

---

[m] Boeth. iv. pr. 1. 'Haec cum Philosophia,' &c.

[1] *ſiccies* B.   [2] *he* conject. om. B.   [3] From J, *forþā* B.   [4] *oððe na*
om. B.   [5] *oðe* B.   [6] *forþ* B.   [7] *to* om. B.   [8] *ealdū* B.
[9] *onginð* C.   [10] *hwæthwega* B.   [11] For *me reahte* B has *mihte*.

is eac minre unrotnesse se mæsta dæl, ꝥ ic wundrige forhwy
se gooda God lǣte ænig yfel bion, oððe gif hit þeah bion [1]
scyle, 7 he hit geþafian wille, forhwy he hit (þōn) sona ne
wrece. Hwæt, þu meaht ðe self ongitan ꝥ ðæt is to wundrianne, 7 eac oðer ðincg me ðincð giet mare wundor ; ꝥ is ꝥte 5
dysig 7 unrihtwisnes nu rixsað ofer eallne middangeard, 7 se
wisdom 7 eac oðre cræftas nabbað nan lof ne nænne weorðscipe on ðisse worulde, ac licgað forsewe[ne] swa (swa) miox
under feltune ; 7 yfele men o[n a]elcum l[an]de sindon nu
*87a C. *weorþe 7 þa goodan habbað manigfeald witu. Hwa mæg 10
forberan ꝥ he ꝥ ne siofige 7 swelcre wæfðe ne wundrige, ðæt
te æfre swylc yfel geweorðan sceolde under ðæs ælmihtgan
Godes anwalde, nu we witon ꝥ he hit wat 7 ælc good wile?

§ ii [n]. [Ð]a cwæð he : Gif hit swa is swa ðu sægst,
ðonne is ꝥ egeslicre ðonne ænig oðer broga, 7 is endeleas 15
wundor, ðæm gelicost ðe on sumes cyninges hirede sien
gyldenu fatu 7 selfrenu [2] forsewen, 7 treowenu mon weorðige.
Nis hit [3] no swa swa ðu wenst ; ac gif ðu eall ðæt gemunan
wilt ꝥ we ær spræcon, mid ðæs Godes fultume ðe we nu
embe sprecað, ðonne meaht ðu ongitan ꝥ ða gódan beoð [4] 20
symle waldende, 7 þa yfelan nabbað nænne anwald ; 7 ðæt
þa cræftas ne bioð næfre buton heringe ne buton edleane,
[ne] þa unðeawas næfre ne bioð unwitnode, ac ða goodan
bioð symle gesælie, (7 þa yfelan ungesælige). Ic ðe mæg
eowian ðæs swiðe manega bisena, ða ðe magon getrymian 25
to ðon [5] ðæt þu nast hwæt þu leng siofige. Ac (ic) þe wille
nu giet getæcan ðone weg ðe ðe gelæt to þære heofonlican
*87b C. byrig þe ðu [ær] of come, siððan ðu ongitst *[þ]urh mine
lare hwæt sio soðe gesælð bið, 7 hwær hio bið. Ac ic sceal
ærest ðin mod gefeðeran [6], ðæt hit mæge hit ðe yð up 30
ahebban ær ðon hit fleogan onginne on ða heanesse, ꝥ hit
mæge hal 7 orsorh fleogan to his earde, 7 forlætan ælce
ðara gedrefednessa ðe hit nu ðrowað. Sitte him on minū

---

[n] Boeth. iv. pr. 1. l. 19 P. ‘Tum illa, Et esset, inquit,’ &c.

[1] *bion* om. B.   [2] *sylfrenu* B.   [3] *hit nis* B.   [4] *bioð* B.
[5] *þā* B.   [6] *gefiðerian* B.

hrædwæne; ðocrige him on minne weg; ic bio his ladðeow.

§ iii °. Da se Wisdom ða þis spell areaht hæfde, ða ongon
he singan 7 cwæð : (*Ic hæbbe swiðe swifte feþera, þ ic mæg*
5 *fliogan ofer þone hean hrof þæs heofones. Ac þær ic nu*
moste þin mod gefiðerigan mid þā fiðerū, þ ðu mihtest mid me
fliogan, þōn miht þu ofersion ealle þas eorðlican þing. Gif
þu mihtest þe fligon ofer þā rodore, þōn mihtest þu gesion þa
wolcnu under þe, 7 mihtest þe fliogan ofer þā fyre þe is
10 *betwux þā rodore 7 þære lyfte ; 7 mihtest þe feran mid þære*
sunnan betwyx þā tunglū, 7 þonon weorþan on þā rodore, 7
siððan to þā cealdan stiorran þe we hata ð Saturnes steorra. Se
is eall isig ; se wandra ð ofer oðrū steorrū ufor þōn ænig oðer
tungol. Siððon þu þōn forð ofer þone bist aferod [1], þōn bist þu
15 *bufan þā swiftan rodore, 7 lætst þōn behindan þe þone hehstan*
heofon. Siððan þu miht habban þinne dæl þæs soðan leohtes.
Þær ricsa ð an cyning ; se hæf ð anweald eallra oðra cyninga ;
se gemetga ð þone bridel 7 þ gewealdleþer ealles ymbhweorftes
hiofenes 7 eorþan ; se an dema is, gestæ ðdig 7 beorht ; se stiorð
20 *þā hrædwæne eallra gesceafta. Ac gif þu æfre cymst on þone*
weg 7 to þære stowe þe ðu nu geot forgiten hafst, þōn will ðu
cweþan : Þis is min riht eðel ; hionan ic was ær cumen, 7
hionan ic was acenned ; her ic wille nu standan fæste ; nelle ic
nu næfre hionon. Ic wat þeah, gif þe æfre gewyr ð þ ðu will
25 *oððe most eft fandian [2] þara þiostra þisse worulde, þōn gesihst*
þu nu [3] þa unrihtwisan cyningas [4] 7 ealle þa ofermodan rican
bion swiðe unmihtige 7 swiðe earme wreccan, þa ilcan þe þis
earme folc nu heardost ondræt.)

§ iv ᴾ. Ða cwæð (*ic*): Eala, Wisdom, micel is ðæt 7
30 wundorlic þ ðu gehætst, 7 ic eac nauht ne tweoge ðæt ðu
hit mæge gelæstan. Ac ic þe halsige ðæt ðu me no leng ne
lette [5], ac getæc me þone weg; forðæm þu meaht ongitan

° Boeth. iv. met. 1. ‘ Sunt etenim pennae,’ &c. Cott. Metr. xxiv.
ᴾ Boeth. iv. pr. 2. ‘ Tum ego, Papae, inquam,’ &c.

[1] *aferod* written over an erased word. [2] *fundian* B. [3] *nu* partly
erased. [4] em. B has *cyning*, with an indistinct letter following.
[5] *læde* B, with *t* written above the *d*.

þ me lyst ðæs weges. Ða cwæð he : þu sceal[*t*] ærest
ongitan þ ða goodan [*hab*]bað sy[*m*]le anw*eald*, 7 *þa yfelan*
næfre nanne, *ne nænne cræft; forðæm hiora nan ne ongit
þte good 7 yfel bioð symle gewinnan. Gif ða goodan
ðonne sȳle habbað anwald, þonne nabbað þa yflan næfre 5
nænne ; forðæm þ good 7 þ yfel sint swiðe unsamwræde.
Ac ic (*ðe*) wolde giet be ægðrū ðara hwæthwugu sweotolor
ger*æ*ccan, þ ðu mæge ðy bet gelefan ðe ic ðe oðre hwile
recce be ðæm oðrum, oðre hwile [*be*] ðæm oðrū. Twa
ðing sindon ðe ælce[*s*] monnes ingeðonc to fundað, þ is 10
ðonne willa 7 anwald ; gif ðonne hwæm ðara twega
hwæðres wana bið, þonne ne mæg he mid ðæm oðrū
nanwuht fullfremman[1]. Forðæm nan nyle onginnan þ þ
he nyle, buton he nede[2] scyle ; 7 ðeah he eall wille, he ne
mæg, gif he ðæs ðinges anwald næfð. Be ðæm ðu meaht 15
sweotole ongitan, gif ðu ænigne mon gesihst wilnian ðæs ðe
he næfð, ðæt (*þā biↄ*) anwaldes wana. Ða cwæð ic : þ is
soð ; ne mæg ic þæs oðsacan. Ða cwæð he : Gif ðu ðonne
hwone[3] gesihst ðe mæg don þ þ he don wile, ne ðe ðonne
nauht ne tweoð þ se hæbbe anwald. Ða cwæð ic : Ne tweoð 20
me ðæs nauht. Ða cwæð he : *Ælc mon bið waldend
ðæs ðe he[4] welt; (næfð he nanne anweald þæs ðe he ne welt).*
Ða cwæð ic : þæs ic eom geðafa. Ða cwæð he : Hwæðer
þu nu giet mæge gemunan þ ic ðe ær reahte ; þ wæs þte
ælces monnes ingeðanc wilnað to þære soðan gesælðe to 25
cumanne, ðeah hi[5] ungelice hiora earnien[6]. Ða cwæð ic :
þ ic geman ; genog sweotole me is ðæt gesæd. Ða cwæð
he : Gemunst ðu þ ic ðe (*ær*) sæde þ [*hit*] wære eall an good
7 gesælða ; se *þe* gesælða secð, he secð good. Ða cwæð ic :
þ ic hæbbe genog fæste on gemynde. Ða cwæð he : Ealle 30
men ge goode ge yfele wilniað to cumanne to goode, þeah
hi his mislice wilnien. Ða cwæð ic : þ is soð þ þu sægst.
Ða cwæð he : Genog sweotol þ is ðæt te[7] forðy sint gōde
men goode, ðe hi gód gemetað. Ða cwæð ic : Genog open

---

[1] *fremman* B. [2] *ne* B. [3] *hwæne* B. [4] *he* om. B. [5] *he* B.
[6] *earnige* B. [7] *te* om. B.

hit is. Ða cwæð he : Þa goodan begitað þ good þ hi
wilniað. Ða cwæð ic : Swa me ðyncð. Ða cwæð he : Þa
yfelan næron [*na*[1] *yfele g*]if hi gemetten ðæt good ðæt hi
wilniað; ac forðy hi sint yfle þe[2] hi hit ne metað[3], 7 forðy
5 hi hit ne metað[3] ðe hi hit on riht ne secað. Ða cwæð ic :
Swa hit is swa ðu sægst. Ða cwæð he : Forðæm *hit is[4] * 90a C.
nan tweo þ ta[5] goodan beoð sȳle waldende, 7 þa yflan
nabbað nænne anwald; forðy ða goodan ðæt gód on riht
secað, 7 (*ða*) yflan on woh. Ða cwæð ic : Se ðe ne[6] wenð
10 þ ðis soð sie[7], ðonne ne gelyfð he nanes soðes.

§ v[q]. Ða cwæð he : Hwæðer wenstu nu? *gif* twegen
men fundiað to anre stowe, 7 habbað emnmicelne willan to
to cu[*me*]nne, 7 oðer hæfð his fota[8] anweald þ he mæg gan
ðær he wile[9], swa swa eallum monnum gecynde wære þ hi
15 meahten, oðer næfð his fota geweald þ he mæge gan, 7
wilnað ðeah to feranne[10], (7) onginð creopan on þone ilcan
weg; hwæðer ðara twega[11] þincð[12] ðe mehtigra? Ða cwæð
ic : Nis þ gelic; se bið mehtigra se ðe gæð þonne se ðe criepð,
forðæm he mæg cuman eð ðider ðe he wile þonne se oðer;
20 sagá elles þ ðu wille, ðæt wat ælc mon. Ða cwæð he : Swa
ilce[13] bið ðæm goodum 7 ðæm yflum; ægþer heora wilnað
for gecynde þ he cume to ðæm hehstan goode. Ac se
gooda mæg cuman ðider he wilnað, forðæm he his on riht
wilnað, 7 se yfla ne mæg cuman to ðæm þe he wilnað,
25 *forðæm hi[14] hit on wog secað[15]. Ic nat ðeah þe elles hwæt * 90b C.
ðince[16]. Ða cwæð ic : Ne ðincð me nauht oðres of ðinum
spellū. Þa cwæð he : Genog rihte ðu hit ongitst, 7 þ is eac
tacn þinre hælo; swa swa læca gewuna is þ hi cweðað ðonne
hi siocne mon ge[*si*]oð, gif hi hwilc ungefæglic[17] tacn on
30 him[18] gesioð. Me ðincð nu þ þin gecynd [7] ðin gewuna
flite swiðe swiðlice wið ðæm dysige.

§ vi[r]. Ic hæbbe nu ongiten þ ðu eart gearo to ongitanne

[q] Boeth. iv. pr. 2. l. 42 P. 'Rursus, inquit, si duo sint,' &c.
[r] Boeth. iv. pr. 2. l. 69 P. 'Sed quoniam te ad intellegendum,' &c.
[1] *no* J.   [2] *þ* B.   [3] *gemetað* B.   [4] *nis* B.   [5] *ða* B.
[6] *ne* om. B.   [7] *ne sie* B.   [8] *foda* C.   [9] *þær he wile* om. B.
[10] *farenne* B.   [11] *twegra* B.   [12] *þinð* C.   [13] *gelice* B.   [14] *he* B.
[15] *secð* B.   [16] From B, *ðence* C.   [17] *unfæglic* B.   [18] *him on* B.

mina lara; forðy ic ðe wolde gegaderian man*i*gu spell 7
manega bisna be ðæm ꝥ ðu meahte ðy eð ongitan hwæt
ic *secg*an wille.   Ongit nu hu unmehtige þa yflan men bioð,
nu hi ne magon cuman ðider ðider ða ungewittigan ge-
*sce*afta wilniað to to[1] cumanne; 7 hu micle unmihtegran[2] hi 5
wæren gif hi his nan gecynde næfden.   Beheald nu mid hu
hefigre racentan dysiges 7 unges*æl*ða hi sint gebundene.
Hwæt, þa cild, ðonne hi furðum gan magon, 7 eac ða
ealdan ceorlas, þa hwile þe hi *gan* magon, wilni[*a*]ð sumes
weorðscipes 7 sum*re* mærðe.   Ða   cild   ridað   on hiora 10

* 91a C.

stafu*m* 7 ma*ni*gfealde plegan plegiað[3] *ðær hi hyriað[4] ealdum
monnū.   7 ða dy*s*egan nanwuht nellað onginnan ðæs ðe hi[5]
him awðer[6] mægen to wenan oððe lofes oððe leana, ac doð ꝥ
wyrse is;   irnað hidres ðidres[7] dwoligende under þæm hrofe
eallra ges*c*eafta;   7 ꝥte ða *ungewitte*[*gan*][8] *gesce*afta witon, ꝥ 15
niton ða *dysegan* men.   Forðy sint þa *cræftas* betera*n* ðonne
þa unðeawas, forðæmþe ælc mon sceal bion geþafa, sam *he*
wille sam he nylle, ꝥ se sie anwaldegost[9] ðe mæg becu*man to*
þā hehs*tā* hrofe eallra gesc*eafta*, ꝥ *is God;* þā nis nanwuht
beu*fan*[10] *ne nanwuht benyþan ne ymb*utan, ac ealle þing sint 20
binnan him on his anwalde.   Se God is swiðe to *lu*fianne.
Hu ne cwæde *þu ær* ꝥ se wære an feðe *mihtigost se þe* meahte
gan (*þeah he wolde*)· oð ðisse *eorþan ende*, swa ꝥte nan[11] dæl
þisse eorþan ofer ꝥ *næ*re? ꝥ ilce þu meaht geðencan *be* God*e*,
swa swa we ær cwædon, ꝥ se bið meahtegost þe to him 25
cuman mæg, forðæm he nohwider ofer ꝥ cuman ne mæg.

§ vii[s].   Be eallū ðissū racū *þu* meaht ongitan ꝥ ða goodan

* 91b C.

bioð *simle* *mi*h*tige, 7 ða yflan beoð ælces mægnes 7 ælces
cræftes bedælde.   Hwy wenstu ðonne ꝥ hi forlæten ða
cræftas 7 folgien ðæm unðeawum?   Ic wene ðeah ꝥ ðu 30
wille secgan ꝥ hit sie for dysige ꝥ hi hi ne cunnen tocnawan.

---

[s] Boeth. iv. pr. 2.   l. 86 P.   'Ex quo fit, quod huic obiacet,' &c.

[1] *to* once B.   [2] *ungemihran* B.   [3] *plegan plegiað* in small
characters beneath last line of page.   [4] Orig. *onhyriað* B, *on* crossed
out and *ofer* written above.   [5] From B, *hit* C.   [6] *ægþer* B.
[7] *hider 7 þider* B.   [8] *gewittigan* J.   [9] From J, *anwealde hegost* B.
[10] Conject. *bufan* B.   [11] *ǟn* C.

Ac hwæt sægst ðu þ[*onne*] þ sie forcuðre þonne sio un-
g[*esc*]eadwisnes? hwy geðafiað hi ðæt hi bioð dysige?
hwy nyllað hy spyrian æfͬ cræftum 7 æfͬ wisdome? Ic wat
þeah ðæt swongornes hi ofsit 7 hi mid slæwðe ofercymð, 7
5 gitsung hi ablent. Wit cwædon þeah ær þ nanwuht nære
wyrse þonne ungesceadwisnes. Ac hwæt willað wit nu
cweðan [1], gif þa gesceadwisan habbað unðeawas 7 nyllað
spyrian æfͬ wisdome 7 æfͬ cræftum? Ic wat þeah þ ðu wilt
cweðan þ wrænnes 7 ungemetfæstnes hi ofsitte; ac hwæt is
10 þonne unstrengra ðonne se mon þe bið to ungemetl*ice*
oferswiðed mid ðæm tedran flæsce, buton he eft geswice 7
winne wið þa unðeawas swa he swiðost mæge? Ac hwæt
wilt ðu þonne cweða[*n*], gif hwa nanwuht nyle wið winnan,
ac mid fulle willan forlæt ælc good *7 fulgæð ðæm yfle, 7 * 92a C.
15 bið ðeah gesce*adwi*s [2]? Ic secge sie unmehtig 7 eac ealles
nauht; forðæm swa hwa swa ðone *gemænan* God [3] eallra
goda [4] forlæt, buton tweonne ne bið se nauht. Ac hwa
swa [5] willnað þ he cræftig sie, he wilnað þ he wis sie; swa
hwa swa ðonne cræftig bið, he bið wis, 7 se ðe wis bið, he
20 bið good; se þe þonne good bið, se bið gesælig, 7 se ðe
gesælig bið, se bið eadig, 7 se þe eadig bið, se bið god, be
ðæm dæle ðe we ær reahton on ðisse ilcan bec. Ac ic wene
nu hwonne þ dysige men willen wundrian þæs ðe ic ær
sæde; ðæt wæs ðætte yfle men næren nauhtas, forðæm
25 (*þe*) ðara is ma þonne þara oðra. Ac ðeah hi his nu næfre
ne gelefen, ðeah hit is swa; ne magon we næfre gereccan
ðone yflan mon clænne 7 untwifealdne, ðon [6] ma ðe we
m*a*gon hatan oððe habban deadn*e* mon for cwucone [7]; ne
bið se [8] cwuca ðonne *nyttra* ðe *se* deada, gif him his yfel
30 *ne hreowð;* ac se *þe* ungereclice l*io*fað 7 his gecynd nyle
healdan, ne bið se nauht.

§ viii ͭ. Ic wene þeah þ ðu wille cweðan þ hit ne sie **ealles* * 92b C.
swa gelic, ðæt se yfla mæge don yfel ðeah he good [9] ne

---

* Boeth. iv. pr. 2. l. 106 P. 'Sed possunt, inquies, mali,' &c.

[1] From B, *wit nu wit cwæðan* C.   [2] em. *gesceadwise* C and B.
[3] From B. *gód* C.   [4] From B, *gooda* C.   [5] *swa hwa swa* B.
[6] *þe* B.   [7] Half the *u* of *cwucone* gone.   [8] *se* om. B.   [9] *good* above line in C.

mæge, 7 se deada ne mæge nauðer don ; ac ic ðe secge þ se
anwald ðara yflena ne cymð of nanum cræfte, ac of unðeawum ; ac gif ða yflan symle goode wæren, þonne ne *dy*den
hi nan yfel.   Ne bioð[1] ðæt nane mehta þ mon mæge yfel
don, ac bioð unmeahta ; gif (þ) soð is þ we ær gefyrn 5
reahton, þ þ yfel nauht ne sie, ðonne ne wyrcð se nauht,
(*se*) ðe yfel wyrcð.   Da cwæð ic: Genog soð þ is þ ðu
sægst.   Da cwæð he : Hu ne reahton we ær þ nanwuht
nære mehtigra ðonne þ hehste good?   Da cwð ic : Swa
hit is swa ðu sægst.   Da cwæð he : Ne hit þeah ne mæg 10
nan yfel don.   Da cwæð ic : Dæt is soð.   Da cwð he :
Hwæðer æni mon[2] wene þ ænig mon sie swa meahtig
þ he mæge don eall ðæt ðæt he wille?   Da cwæð ic : Ne
wenð *ða*es nan mon þe his gewit hæfð.   Da cwæð he :
Hwæt, yfle men magon ðeah yfel don.   Da cwæð ic : Eala, 15
ðær hi ne meahton.   Da cwæð he : Hit is sweotol þ hi
magon don yfel, 7 ne magon nan good ; þ is forðæmþe
þ yfel nis nauht ; *ac þa goodan, gif hi fulne anwald *hab*bað,
hi magon don to goode þ þ hi willað.   Forðy is se fulla
anwald to tellanne to ðæm hehstum goodum, forðæm ægþer 20
ge se anwald ge þa oðru good 7 ða cræftas ðe we longe ær
nemdon sindon fæste on ðæm hehstan goode.   Swa swa
ælces huses wah *bi*ð fæst ægðer ge on ðære flore ge on ðæm
hrofe, swa bið ælc good on Gode fæst ; forðæm he is ælces
gódes ægðer ge hrof ge flor.   Dy is â to wilnianne þæs 25
anwaldes þ mon mæge good don ; forðæm ðæt is se betsta
anwald þ mon mæge 7 wille wel don, swa læssan spedum
swa maran, swæðer he hæbbe.   Forðæm swa hwa swa[3]
wilnað[4] good to donne, he wilnað good to habbanne 7 mid
goode to bionne.   Forðy[5] is se Platones cwide genog soð (*þe*) 30
he cwæð: Da wisan ane magon don to goode þ hi wilniað ;
ða yflan magon onginnan þ hi willað[6].   Ic nat nu ðeah ðu[7]
wille cweð[*an þ*] þa goodan onginnen hwilū þ hi ne magon
forðbrengan ; ac ic cweðe þ[8] hi hit bringað symle forð;

---

[1] *bið* B.   [2] *ænimon* C.   [3] *swa* above line C.   [4] *willað* B.
[5] *for bis* B.   [6] *wilniað* B, apparently *willað* orig.   [7] *ðu* om. B.   [8] *þeah* B.

ðeah hi ðæt weorc ne mægen fullfremman, *hi habbað* ðeah * 93b C.
fullne[1] willan, 7 se untw*eo*fealda willa bið to tellanne[2] for
fullfremed weorc.   Forðæm he næfre ne forlist[3] ðæm
leanum oððe her oððe ðær oððe ægðer[4].   Þeah willað ða

5 yflan wircan ꝥ ꝥ hi lyst, ðeah hit nyt ne sie[5]; ne *for*leosað hi
eac ðone willan, ac hab*baþ* his wite oððe her oððe elleshwær
oððe ægðer; se yfla willa to donne[6] hiora welt.   Forðy hi ne
magon begitan ꝥ good ꝥ hi wilniað, forðy hi hit ðurg ðone
willan secað, nales þurg rihtne[7] weg.   Se yfla willa næfð

10 nænne geferscipe wið þa gesælða.   Ða se Wisdom ða ðis
spell areaht hæfde, ða ongan he eft singan 7 þus cwæð:

XXXVII [n].

§ i. (*Geher nu an spell be þā ofermodū 7 þam unrihtwisū*
cyningū. Þa we gesioð sittan on þā hehstan heahsetlū; þa scinað
on managra cynna hræglū, 7 beoð uton ymbstandene[8] mid

15 *miclon geferscipe hiora þegna ; 7 þa bioð mid fellum 7 mid*
gyldenū hyltsweordū 7 mid manigfealdū heregeatwū gehyrste,
7 þreatiað eal moncynn mid hiora þrymme. 7 se þe hiora welt
ne myrnð[9] nauþer ne friend ne fiend þe ma þe wedende hund, ac
bioð swiðe ungefræglice up ahafen on his mode for þā unge-

20 *mettican anwealde. Ac gif him mon þōn awint of þa claþas, 7*
him oftihð þara þenunga 7 þæs anwealdes, þōn miht þu geseon
ꝥ he bioð swiðe anlic þara his þegna sumū þe hī þar þeniað,
buton he forcuðra[10] sie. 7 gif him nu weas[11] gebyreð ꝥ him
wyrð sume hwile þara þenunga oftohen, 7 þara claþa, 7 þas

25 *anwealdes[12], þōn þincð him ꝥ he sie on carcerne gebroht, oððe on*
racentū. Forþā of þā unmætan[13] 7 þam ungemettican gegerelan,
of þā swetmettū 7 of mistlicū dryncū þæs liþes onwæcnað sio
wode þrag þære wrænnesse, 7 gedrefð hiora mod swiðe swið-
lice. Þōn weaxað eac þa ofermetta 7 ungeþwærnes ; 7 þōn hi

30 *weorðað gebolgen, þonne wyrð ꝥ mod beswungen mid þā welme*

---

[n] Boeth. iv. met. 2. 'Quos uides sedere,' &c. Cott. Metr. xxv.

[1] *fullͤ* C.   [2] em. *dællanne* C, *tellenne* B.   [3] So also B.   [4] *ægðer* B.
[5] *þeah hit nu ne sie nyt* B.   [6] From B, *ðonne* C.   [7] B has *þurhtne* for
þurg rihtne.   [8] em. *ymbstandende* B.   [9] orig. *murnð* in B, *u* altered to *y*.
[10] em. *forðra* B.   [11] em. *hwes* B.   [12] em. *anweades* B.   [13] em. *unmętta* B.

þære hatheortnesse, oððæt hi weorþað geræpte mid þære un-
rotnesse, 7 swa gehæfte. Siððan þ þon gedon bið, ðonne
onginð him leogan se tohopa þære wræce, 7 swa hwæs swa his
irsung wilnað[1]*, þon gehet him þæs his reccelest. Ic þe sæde gefyrn*
ær on þisse ilcan bec þ ealle gesceafta willnodon sumes godes 5
for gecynde ; ac þa unrihtwisan cyngas ne magon nan god don,
forþā ic þe nu sæde. Nis þ nan wundor, forþā hi hi underþiodað
eallū þā unþeawum þe ic þe ær nemde. Sceal ðonne nede to þara
hlaforda dome þe he hine ær underþeodde, 7 þte wyrse is, þ he hī
nyle furðū wið winnan. Þær he hit a anginnan wolde, 7 þon on 10
þam gewinne þurhwunian ne mihte, þon næfde he his nane scylde.)

§ ii[v]. Ða se Wisdom ða ðis leoð asungen hæfde, þa
ongon he eft spellian 7 þus cwæð : Gesihst þu nu on hu
miclum 7 on hu diopum 7 on hu þiostrum horoseaðe þara
unðeawa ða yfelwillendan sticiað, 7 hu ða goodan scinað 15
beorhtor þonne sunne ? Forðæm þa goodan næfre ne beoð
bedælde þara edleana hiora goodes, ne ða yflan næfre þara
wita ðe hi geearnigað. Ælc ðing ðe on þisse worulde gedon
bið hæfð edlean ; wyrce hwa þ ðæt he wyrce, oððe do þ[2] he
do, a he hæfð þ þ he geearnað[3]. Nis þ eac nauht unriht ; 20
swa swa gio[4] Romana þeaw wæs[5], 7 giet is on manegum
þiodum, þ mon hehð ænne heafodbeag gyldenne[6] æt sumes
ærneweges ende ; færð ðonne micel folc to, 7 yrnað ealle endemes[7], ða ðe hiora ærninge trewað. 7 swa hwelc swa ærest
to þæm beage cymð, þonne mot se hine habban him. Ælc 25
wilnað þ he scyle *[æ]rest to cuman 7 hine habban, ac anum
he þeah gebyreð. Swa deð eall moncyn on ðis andweardan
life ; irnað 7 onettað 7 wilniað ealle[8] þæs hehstan goodes ;
ac hit nis nanum anum men getiohhod, ac is eallum monnū.
Forðæm is ælcū ðearf þ he higie ealle mægene æft ðære 30
mede ; ðære mede ne wyrð (*næfre*) nan good man bedæled.
[9] Ne mæg hine mon no mid rihte hatan se gooda, gif he bið

[v] Boeth. iv. pr. 3. 'Videsne igitur,' &c.

[1] em. *willað* B.   [2] *þ þ* B.   [3] *earnað* B.   [4] *gio* om. B.
[5] *þeawas* for *þeaw wæs* B.   [6] *gyldeñe* C.   [7] *endemest* C.   [8] *ealles* B.
[9] *N . . . bedæled* om. B.

ðæs hehstan goodes bedæled, forðæm nan good ðeaw ne
bið buton goodū edleanū. Dón þa yflan ꝥ ꝥ hi don, sȳle
bið se beag goodes edleanes ðæm godū gehealden on
ecnesse. Ne mæg .þara yflena yfel þa[1] goodan beniman
5 heora goodes[2] 7 hiora wlites; ac gif hi ðæt good[2] buton
h*i*m selfum hæfden[3], ðonne meahte hi mon his[4] beniman,
oðer twega, oððe se þe hit ær sealde, oððe oðer mon[5]. Ac
ðonne forlyst good man his leanū ðonne he his good forlæt.   .
Ongit nu ꝥte ælcum men his agen good gifð good edlean,
10 ꝥ good ꝥte oninnan him selfū ·bið. Hwa wisra manna wile
cweðan ꝥ *æ*nig god m*a*n sie bedæled þæs hehstan goodes,
forðæm he sȳle æf͠t þæm swincð? Ac gemun ðu sȳle þæ[s]
miclan 7 þæs fægran *edleanes, forðæm ꝥ edlean is ofer eal *96a C.
oðr[u][6] lean to lufianne ; 7 do ðæs lean to ðæm for-
15 sprecenan[7] goodū þe ic þe ær tealde on þære þriddan bec.
Þonne hi þon(n)e gegaderudu bioð, ðonne meaht þu (þōn)
ongitan ꝥ ða gesælða 7 ꝥ hehste good [*bið*] eall an, 7 ꝥ bið
God.   7 þonne þu meaht eac ongitan ꝥ ælc good man bið
eadig, 7 ꝥ ealle gesælige men bioð godas, 7 habbað ecu
20 edlean heora goodes.

§ iii [w]. Forðæm ne þearf nænne wisne mon tweogan ꝥ ða
yflan næbben eac ecu edlean hiora yfles ; ꝥ bið ece wite. Þeah
ðu nu wene ꝥ hiora hwylc[8] gesælig[9] sie her for weorulde, he
hæfð þeah symle his yfel mid him, 7 eac þæs yfles edlean ða
25 hwile þe hit hī licað[10]. Nis nu nan wis mon ꝥ nyte ꝥte good
7 yfel bioð sȳle ungeþwære betweox him, 7 sȳle on tu willað;
7 swa swa ðæs gódan gódnes bið his agen good, 7 his agen
edlean, swa bið eac ðæs yfelan yfel his agen yfel 7 his edlean 7
his agen wite.   Ne tweoð nænne mon, gif he wite hæfð, ꝥ he
30 næbbe (*yfel*). Hwæt wenað þa yfelan ꝥ hi bion bedælde ðara
wita, 7 sint fulle ælces yfles ? Nalles no ꝥ an ꝥ hi bioð afylde,
ac forneah *[*to*] nauhte gedone. Ongit nu be ðæm gódū hu * 96b C.

[w] Boeth. iv. pr. 3. l. 30 P. 'Quae cum ita sint,' &c.

[1] From B, *þā* C.   [2] *god* B, 7 *hiora . . . good* om. B.   [3] *næfden* B.
[4] *hi* B.   [5] *ma* B.   [6] *oðru* J, *oðre* B.   [7] *foresprecenan* B.
[8] *hwylc* om. B.   [9] *gesælþe* B.   [10] *ne licað* B.

I

micel wite þa yfelan sȳle habbaðˈ; 7 gehere[1] get sum bispell,
7 geheald þa wel þe ic ðe ær sæde. Eall ꝥ ꝥte annesse
hæfð, ꝥ we secgað ꝥte[2] sie þa hwile þe hit æt[s]omne bið;
7 þa samwrædnesse we hataðˈ good. Swa swa an mon bið
man þa hwile ðe sio saul 7 se lichama ætsomne bioð, þonne 5
hi[3] ðonne gesindrede bioð, þonne[3] ne bið (*he*) ðæt ꝥ he ær
wæs. ꝥ ilce þu meaht geþencan be þæm lichoman 7 be his
limū; gif þara lima[4] hwylc of bið, þonne ne bið hit no full
man swa hit ær wæs. Gif eac hwylc good man from gode
gewit, þonne ne bið he þon[5] ma fullice good, gif he eallunga 10
frō gewit[6]; þonan hit gebereð ꝥ ða yflan forlætað ꝥ ꝥ hi
ær[7] ða dydon, 7[8] ne beoð ꝥ ꝥ hi ær wæron. Ac þonne hi ꝥ
good forlætað 7 weorðað yfle, þonne ne bioð hi nauhtas
butan anlicnes; ꝥ mon mæg gesion ꝥ hi gio men wæren,
ac hi habbað þæs mennisces þonne þone betstan dæl for- 15
loren, 7 þone forcuþestan[9] gehealden. Hi forlætað ꝥ
gecyndelice good, ꝥ sint mennisclice þeawas; *7 habbað
þeah mannes anlicnesse ða hwile þe hi libbað.

§ iv[x]. Ac swa swa manna goodnes hi āhefð ofer ða
menniscan gecynd to ðon[10] ꝥ hi bioð godas genemde[11], swa 20
eac hiora yfelnes awirpð (*hi*)[12] under þa mennis[*can gec*]ynd
to þon[13] ꝥ hio bioð yfle gehatene; ꝥ we cweðað sie nauht.
Forðæm gif ðu swa gewlætne mon metst ꝥ he bið ahwerfed
from goode to yfle, ne meaht þu hine na mid ryhte nemnan
man ac neat. Gif þu on hwilcum men ongitst ꝥ he bið 25
gitsere 7 reafere, ne scealt þu hine na[14] hatan mon, ac wulf;
7 þone reðan þe bið þweorteme ðu scealt hatan hund, nalles
mon; 7 þone leasan lytegan þu scealt hatan fox, næs man;
7 þone ungemetlice modgan 7 yrsiendan þe to micelne
andan hæfð þu scealt hatan leo[15], næs *man*; 7 þone sænan 30
þe bið swa[16] slaw [*þu s*]cealt hatan assa ma þonne man; 7

---

[x] Boeth. iv. pr. 3. l. 50 P. 'Sed cum ultra homines,' &c.

[1] *gehēr* B.　　[2] *te* om. B.　　[3] *hi . . . þonne* om. B.　　[4] *lima* om. B.
[5] *þe* B.　　[6] *from gode gewite* B.　　[7] *ær* om. B.　　[8] *7 om.* B.
[9] Orig. *forcuðesan* in B, the *s* altered to *r*.　　[10] *þā* B.　　[11] *genemnede*
B.　　[12] Conject. om. B and C.　　[13] *þā* B.　　[14] *na* om. B.　　[15] *lio* B.
[16] *to* B.

þone ungemetlice eargan þe him ondræt ma [1] þonne he
þyrfe ðu meaht hatan hara ma þonne mon; 7 þæm un-
gestæððegan 7 þæm galan [2] þu meaht [3] secgan ðæt he bið
winde gelicra [4] oððe *unstillū fugelum* þonne gemetfæstū * 97b C.
5 monnum; 7 þæm þe ðu ongitst þte [5] ligð on his lichoman
lustum, þ he bið anlicost fettum swinū þe sȳle willað licgan
on fulum ,[*sol*]um, 7 hy næfre [6] nellað aspy[*ligan* [7] *on*]
hluttru[*m*] wætrū; ac þeah hi seldū hw[*o*]nne beswemde
weorðen, þonne sleað hi eft on ða solu 7 bewealwiað hi [8]
10 þæron [9]. Ða se Wisdom þa ðis spe*ll* areaht hæfde, þa
ongon he eft [10] s*ingan* 7 *þ*us cwæð:

XXXVIII ꝩ.

§ i. (*IC ðe* [11] *mæg reccan of ealdū leasū spellū sum swiðe
anlic spell þære spræcè þe wit nu ymbe spræcon. Hit gebyrede gio on Troiana gewinne þ þær wæs an cyning þæs nama*
15 *Aulixes; se hæfde twa þioda under þā kasere. Þa ðioda
wæron hatene Iþacige 7 Retie, 7 þæs kaseres nama wæs
Agamenon. Ða se Aulixes mid þam kasere to þā gefiohte
for, þa hæfde he sume hundred scipa; þa wæron hi sume ten
gear on þā gewinne. Þa se cyning eft hā cerde frō þā kasere,*
20 *7 hi þ land hæfdon gewunnen, þa næfde he na* [12] *ma scipa þon
an; þ wæs þeah þereðre. Ða gestod hine heah weder 7
stormsæ. Wearð þa fordrifen on an iglond ut on ðære Wendelsæ. Þa wæs þær Apollines dohtor Iobes suna; se Iob was
hiora cyning, 7 licette þ he sceolde bion se hehsta god; 7 þ*
25 *dysige folc him gelyfde, forþaðe he was cynecynnes; 7 hi nyston
nænne oðerne god on þæne timan, buton hiora cyningas hi
weorþodon for godas. Þa sceolde þæs Iobes fæder bion eac
god; þæs nama wæs Saturnus; 7 his suna swa ilce ælcne* [13] *hi*

---

[7] Boeth. iv. met. 3. ‘ Vela Neritii ducis,’ &c. Cott. Metr. xxvi.

[1] *mare* B.   [2] *hælgan* B.   [3] em. *meah* C.   [4] From B, *gelicran* C.
[5] B has *he* for *te*.   [6] *næfre* om. B.   [7] *aspylian* J.   [8] *hi* om. B.
[9] Looks like *þæran* in C.   [10] *eft* om. B.   [11] Conject. the vowel in
B is a mixture of *a* and *e*.   [12] *he na* above line.   [13] em. *ælcine* B.

hæfdon for god. Þa was hiora an se Apollinus[1] *þe we ær
ymb spræcon. Þæs Apollines dohtor*[2] *sceolde bion gydene,
þære nama wæs Kirke. Sio hi sædon sceolde bion swiðe drycræftigu, 7 sio wunode on þā iglande þe se cyning on fordrifen
wearð, þe we ær ymbe spræcon. Hio hæfde þær swiðe micle* 5
*werode hire ðegna, 7 eac oðerra mædena. Sona swa hio
geseah þone fordrifenan cyning ðe we ær ymb spræcon, þæs
nama wæs Aulixes, þa ongan hio hine lufian, 7 hiora
ægþer oðerne swiðe ungemetlice, swa þte he for hire lufan
forlet his rice eall 7 his cynren, 7 wunode mid hire oð* 10
*ðone first þ his ðegnas him ne mihton leng mid gewunian, ac
for hiora eardes lufan 7 for þære wræce tihodon hine to
forlætenne. Ða ongunnon lease men wyrcan spell, 7 sædon þ
hio sceolde mid hire drycræft þa men forbredan, 7*[3] *weorpan hi
an wildedeora lic, 7 siððan slean on þa racentan 7 on cospas.* 15
*Sume hi sædon þ hio sceolde forsccoppan to leon, 7 þon seo
sceolde sprecan, þōn ryde hio. Sume sceoldan bion eforas,
7 bōn hi sceoldan hiora sar siofian, þōn grymetodan hi. Sume
wurdon to wulfan ; þa ðuton, þōn hi sprecan sceoldon. Sume
wurdon to þā deorcynne þe mon hat tigris. Swa wearð*[4] *eall* 20
*se geferscipe forhwerfed to mistlicum deorcynnū, ælc to sumū
diore, buton þā cyninge anū. Ælcne mete hi onscunedon þe
men etað, 7 wilnodon þara þe deor etaþ. Næfdon hi nane
anlicnesse manna ne on lichoman ne on stemne, 7 ælc wisste
þeah his gewit swa swa he ær wisste. Þ gewit was swiðe* 25
*sorgiende for þā ermðum ðe hi drogan. Hwæt, þa menn þe
ðisū leasungū gelefdon, þeah wisston þ hio mid þā drycræfte ne
mihte þara monna mod onwendan, þeah hio þa lichoman
onwende. Eala þ hit is micel cræft*[5] *þæs modes for þone
lichoman. Be swilcū 7 be swylcū þu miht ongitan þ se cræft* 30
*þæs lichoman bið on þā mode, 7 þte ælcū men ma deriað his
modes unþeawas. Ðæs modes unþeawas*[6] *tioð eallne þone
lichoman to hī, 7 þæs lichoman mettrumnes*[7] *ne mæg þ mod
eallunga to him getion.*)

---

[1] em. *þollin'* B. [2] em. *dohdor* B. [3] em. B has ð. [4] em. *weorcð* B.
[5] em. *cræf* B. [6] *unþeawas* conject. om. B. [7] *mettrumnes* B.

§ ii [z]. Ða cwæð ic : Ic eom geþafa þ þ is soð þ ðu ær
sædest; þ wæs ðæt hit nauht unriht nære þ mon þa yfelwillendan men hete ne[*l*]enu oððe wildior, þeah hi mannes
[*o*]nlicnesse hæbben ; ac gif ic hæfde [*swi*]lcne anwald swilce
5 se ælmihtiga [1] [*God hæ*]fð, þonne ne lete ic no ða [*yfela*]n
derigan þæm goodum swa swiðe swa hi nu doð. Ða cwæð
he : Nis hit him no swa longe alefed swa ðe ðincð; ac ðu
meaht ongitan ðæt him bið swiðe hrædlice gestiored [*hiora*]
orsorgnesse, swa ic *þe nu rihte [2] secgan wille, þeah ic get * 100a C.
10 æmettan næbbe for oðre spræce. Þær hi þone unnettan
anwald næfden ðe hi wenað þ hi hæbben, þonne næfden hi
swa micel wite swa hi habban sculon. Ða yflan bioð symle [3]
ungesæligran þonne þonne hi magon ðurgtion þ yfel þ hi
lyst, ðonne hi þonne [4] bion ðonne hi hit dón ne magon, þeah
15 his dysige men ne gelefen. Hit is swiðe yfel þ mon [5] yfel
wille [6], 7 hit is þeah micle wyrse þ hit mon mæge (*don*) [7];
forðæm se yfla willa bið tostenced swaþær rec [8] beforan
fyre, gif mon ðæt weorc þurgtion ne [9] mæg. Ac ða yflan
habbað hwilum ðrio unsælða [10]; an is þ hi yfel willað, oðer
20 þ þ hi magon, þridde þ hi hit þurgtioð; forðæmðe God
hæfð ge[*tio*]hhod to sellanne witu 7 ermða [*þā y*]flum
monnū for [11] hiora yflu*m* *weorcum*. Ða cwæð ic : Hit is
swa [12] [*swa*] ðu sægst ; 7 þeah ic wolde gewyˌscan, gif ic
meahte, þ hi næfden ða heardsælða þ hi meahten *yfel* dón.
25 Ða cwæð he : Ic wene ðeah þ *him losige se anwald ær * 100b C
þonne þu wolde oððe hi wenen ; forðæm nanwuht (*nis*) long-
færes on ðys andweardan life, þeah monnum ðynce þ hit
long sie. Ac swiðe oft se micla anwald ðara yflena gehrist
swiðe færlice, swa (*swa*) great beam on wuda wyrcð hludne
30 dynt þonne men læst wenað; 7 for ðæm ege hi beoð simle
swiðe earme. Gif hi þonne hiora yfel earme gedeð, hu ne
bið ðonne semle þ lange yfel wyrse þonne ðæt scorte ?

[z] Boeth. iv. pr. 4. 'Tum ego, Fateor, inquam,' &c.

[1] *ælmihĭga* C, *ælmihtega* B. [2] From B, *ruhte* C. [3] *micle* B. [4] *þōn
þōn hi* B.   [5] From B, C has *mon þ* instead of *þ mon*.   [6] *wile* C.
[7] *don* above line in B. [8] *swa þe recels* B. [9] *ne* om. B. [10] *ungesælþa*
B.   [11] *for* om. B.   [12] *swa hit is* B.

þeah nu ða yflan næfre ne wurden deade, þeah (*ic*) wolde
cweðan ꝥ hi wæren earmoste 7 ungesælgoste[1]. Gif þa
yrmða ealla soða sint þe we longe ær ymbe reahton ꝥ ða
yflan her on weorulde habban scolden, þonne is ðæ[*t*]
sweotol ꝥ ða yrmða bioð [*endele*]ase þe ece[2] bioð. Da cwæð 5
[*ic : Þæt is*] wundorlic ꝥ ðu sægst, 7 swið[*e*] earfoðlic
dysegum monnū to ongitanne; ac ic ongite þeah ꝥ hit
belimpð genog wel to ðære spræce ðe wit ær ymbe spræcon.

* 101a C. Da cwæð he: Ic ne sprece nu[3] no to *dysegum monnum,
ac sprece to ðam þe we[*l*] wilniað wisdom ongitan; 10
forðæm ꝥ bið tacn wisdomes ꝥ hine mon welnige geheran 7
ongitan.   Ac gif dysegra hwone tweoge æniges þara spella þe
we ær ymb spræcon on þisse ilcan bec, ðonne gerecce he gif
he mæge oðer twega, oððe þara spella sum leas, oððe ungelic
þære spræce þe wit æfterspyriað; oððe þridde wend, ongite 15
7 gelefe þæt wit on riht spyrigen. Gif he þara nan nyte[4],
þonne nat he hwæt[5] he mænð.

§ iii[a]. Ac ic þe mæg giet tæcan oðer þing ðe dysegum
monnum wile ðincan giet ungelefedlicre[6], 7 is þeah genog
gelic þam spelle ðe wit æfterspyriað. Da[7] cwæð ic: Hwæt 20
is ðæt la ðinga[7]? Da cwæð he: (*Hit*) is ꝥ ðæt þa yflan
bioð[8] micle gesæligran þe on ðisse weorulde habbað micelne
wean 7 manigfeald witu for hiora (*yfelū*), ðonne þa sien ðe
nane wræce nabbað ne nan wite on ðisse worulde for hiora
yfle. Ne wene þeah nan mon ꝥ ic for ðæm anum ðyllic 25

* 101b C. sprece ðe ic wolde unðeawas tælan *7 goode herian 7 mid
ðære bysne men ðreatigan 7 tyhtan to gódū þeawū for þæm
ege þæs wites; ac for oðrū ðincgum ic hit spræc[9] get[10] swiðor.
Da cwæð ic: For hwylcum oðrum ðingum woldes þu ꝥ sprecan
buton for ðæm þe þu nu sædes? Da cwæð he: Gemanst 30
þu hwæt[11] wit ær spræcon? ꝥ wæs þæt ða goodan hæfdon[12]
sȳle anwald 7 gesælða, 7 þa yflan næfden næfre nauðer.

* Boeth. iv. pr. 4. l. 37 P. ' Nam hoc quoque quod dicam,' &c.

[1] *7 ungesælgoste* om. B.   [2] From B, *eac* C.   [3] *nu* above line C.
[4] *ne deð* B.   [5] *naṇ ðarạ* between *he* and *hwæt* C.   [6] *ungelefendlicre*
B.   [7] *Da . . . ðinga* om. B.   [8] From B, *biod* C.   [9] *sprece* B.   [10] *get*
above line.   [11] *ꝥ* B.   [12] *hæfden* B.

Ða cwæð ic : þ ic geman.   Ða cwæð he : Hwæt wenst ðu
nu? gif þu gesihst hwylcne swiðe ungesæligne mon, 7
ongitst ðeah hwæthwugu goodes on him, hwæðer he sie swa
ungesælig swa se ðe nanwuht goodes næfð? Ða cwæð ic :
5 Se me ðincð gesæligra þe hwæthwugu hæfð.   Ða cwæð he :
Ac hu þincð þe ðonne be ðæm þe nanwuht goodes næfð,[1]
gif he hæfð[1] sumne eacan yfeles? se þu wilt secgan þonne
giet sie ungesæligra þonne se oðer, for ðæs yfles eacan.
Ða cwæð ic : Hwy ne sceolde me swa þyncan? (*Ða cwæð*
10 *he*[b]: *Telo þonne þ ðe swa þincð*); ongit[2] þonne mid
innewearde[3] mode þ þ ða yflan habbað sȳle hwæthwugu
gódes on gemong *hiora yfle[4]; þ is hiora wite; þ mon mæg   * 102a C.
swiðe eaðe gereccan mid rihte him to goode.   Ac þa þe him
bið (*unwitnode*) eall hiora yfel on þisse worulde habbað sū
15 yfel hefigre 7 frecenlicre þonne ænig wite swa[5] on þisse
worulde; þ þ is þ him bið unwitnod[6] hiora yfel on þisse
weorulde, ðæt is þ sweotoloste tacen þæs mæstan yfeles on
þisse weorulde, 7 þæs wyrrestan edleanes æfter þisse worulde.
Ða cwæð ic : Ne[7] mæg ic þæs oðsacan.   Ða cwð he :
20 Forðæm sint ungesæligran ða yflan forðæm him bið buton
gewyrhtū forgifen hiora yfel þonne ða sien ðe him bið hiora
yfel geleanod be hiora gewyrhtum.   Forðæm hit is riht
þ mon (*þa*) yflige ða yflan, 7 hit is wog þ hi mon læte
unwitnode.   Ða cwð ic : Hwa oðsæcð þæs?   Ða cwæð
25 he : Ne mæg nan mon oðsacan þ hit ne sie eall good þte
riht (*bið*), 7 eall yfel þte woh bið.   Ða cwæð ic : Ic eom
swiðe gedrefed mid ðisse spræce, 7 wundrie forhwy swa
rihtwis dema ænige unrihte gife wille forgifan.   Ða cwð he :
Be hwæm (*cwest þu þæt? Ða cwæð ic : Forþā*)ðe ðu ær
30 cwæde ðæt he unriht dyde þ he lete unwitnod ða *yflan.   * 102b C.
Ða cwæð he : Þ is his weorðscipe þ he swa giful is, 7 swa
rumedlice gifð; ðæt is micel gifo þ he gebit oðþ ða yflan
ongitað hiora yfel 7 gecierrað to goode.   Ða cwæð ic : Nu

<hr>

[b] Boeth. iv. pr. 4.   l. 58 P.   'Habent igitur improbi,' &c.

[1] *næfð* B.   [2] From B, *nu git* C.   [3] *inneweardan* B.
[4] *yfel* B.   [5] *sie* B.   [6] *ungewitnode* B.   [7] *ne* om. B.

ic (*on*)gite þ hit (*n*)is ecu gifu þ he gifð þæm yflum, ac is[1]
hwilchwugu[2] eldcung[3] 7 andbid[4] þæs hehstan deman. For
ðæm andbide 7 for ðæm geþylde me ðincð þ he sie ðe
swiðor forsewen; 7 þeah me licað þis spell genog wel, 7
ðincð me genog gelic ðæm ðe ðu ær sædes.   5

§ iv[c]. Ac ic ðe healsige giet ðæt þu me secge hwæðer ðu
wenc þ þa yflan habban[5] ænig wite æfter þisse weorulde;
oððe þa (*godan*) ænig edlean hiora goodes. Ða cwæð he:
Hu ne sæde ic ðe ær þ ða goodan habbað edlean heora
goodes ægþer ge her[6] ge on ecnesse, 7 ða yflan eac habbað 10
edlean hiora yfles, ægþer ge her ge eft on ecnesse. Ac ic
wille dælan þa yflan (*þā yfelū*) nu on twua[7]; forðǣþe oðer
dæl þara yflena hæfð ece wite, forðǣ hi nane mildheortnesse
ne geearnodon; oðer dæl sceal beon geclæsnod[8], 7 (*þa*)
amered on ðæm *heofonlican fyre, swa her bið seolfor, 15
forðæm he hæfð sume geearnungæ sumre mildheortnesse;
forðæm he mot cuman æft ðæm earfoðum to ecre are. Giet
ic (*þe*) meahte mare reccan ægðer ge be ðæm goodum ge
be þæm yflum, þær[9] ic nu æmettan hæfde. Ac ic ondræde
þ ic forlæte[10] þ wyt ær æfîspyredon; þ wæs þ wit woldon 20
gereccan þ þu ongeate ðæt ða yflan næfden nænne anwald
ne nænne weorðscipe ne on þisse weorulde ne on þære
toweardan. Forðæm þe þuhte ær þ eallra ðinga wyrrest þ
ðu wendes þ hi hæfden to micelne; 7 ðæt eallneg[11] siofodes
þ hi eallneg[11] næron on wite; 7 ic ðe sæde eallne weg þ hi 25
næfre ne bioð buton wite, ðeah þe swa ne þince. Ac ic wat
þeah þ ðu wilt siofian ðæt hi swa longne fyrst habbað leafe[12]
yfel to donne; 7 ic ðe sæde ealne weg þ se (*fyrst*) bið
swiðe lytle hwile; 7 ic þe secge giet, swa swa[13] he lengra
bið swa hi bioð ungesæligran; þ him wære eallra mæst 30
unsælð[14] (*þ*) þ se *fyrst wære oð domes dæg. 7 ic þe sæde
eac þ ða wæren ungesæligran þe him unrihtlice hiora yfel

* 103a C. (margin)
* 103b C. (margin)

---

[c] Boeth. iv. pr. 4. l. 70 P. 'Sed quaeso, inquam, te,' &c.

[1] From B, *ic* C. [2] *hwæthwegu* B. [3] *eldung* B. [4] *anbid* B. [5] So
C and B. [6] *ge her* om. B. [7] *twa* B. [8] *geclænsod* B. [9] *gif* B.
[10] *forlete* B. [11] *ealne weg* B. [12] *leaf* B. [13] *swa* once B. [14] *"nsælð* C.

forboren wære þonne þa wæren þe him [1] heora yfel rihtlice
on gewrecen wære. Git hit gebyreð ꝥ ðe ðincð ðæt þa
orsorgan bioð ungesæligran þonne þonne þa gewitnodan.

§ v[d]. Đa cwæð ic: Ne þincð me næfre nanwuht swa
5 soðlic swa me þincað þine spell ðæm tidum [2] ðe ic ða
gehere. Ac gif ic me wende to þises folces dome, þonne nis
hit no ðæt an ꝥ hi nyllað þisse þinre race gelefan, ac hi hit
nyllað furðum geheran. Đa cwæð he : Ni(s) ꝥ nan wundor;
hwæt, þu wast ꝥ þa men þe habbað unhale eagan ne magon
10 full eaðe locian ongean þa sunnan þonne hio beortost [3]
scinð, ne furðum on [4] fyr ne on nanwuht beortes [5] hi ne lyst
locian, gif se æppel lef bið. Swa beoð ða synfullan mod
ablend mid heora yflan willan ꝥ hi ne magon gesion ꝥ leoht
þære beorhtan soðfæstnesse, ꝥ is se hehsta wisdom. Ac him
15 bið swa þæm fug[*lu*]m 7 þæm dioru * ðe magon bet locian * 104ª C.
on niht þonne on [6] dæg; se dæg blent 7 þiostrað heora
eagan, 7 þære nihte ðiostro hi onlyhtað. Forðy wenað ða
ablendan mod ꝥ þæt sie sio mæste gesælð ꝥ men sie alefed
yfel to donne, 7 sio dæ*d* hī mote bion unwitnod. Forðæm
20 hi ne lyst spyrian æf̃t ælcre spræce swa longe oð hi ꝥ riht
witen, ac wenað [7] on hiora unnettan [8] willan 7 spyriað æf̃t
ðæm. Þe [9] ic nat hu nyt þu me tæhst to ðæm dysegū
monnum, þa [10] næfre æf̃t me ne spyriað; ic ne sprece næfre
to ðæm, ac ic sprece to þe, forðæm þu tiohhast ꝥ þu spyrie
25 æf̃t me, 7 swiðor swincst [11] on ðæm spore þonne hi don. Ne
recce ic hwæt hi demen; ic læte nu to þinū dome ma þonne
to hiora, forðæm hi eall [12] lociað mid bæm eagum on þas
eorðlican ðincg, 7 hi him liciað eallunga þær [13], ge (*on þæs
modes eagum ge*) on þæs lichoman. Ac þu ana hwilum
30 bescylst mid oðre eagan on þa heofonlican þincg, mid oðre
þu locast nu giet on þas eorðlican. Forðæm wenað þa
dysegan ꝥ ælc mon sie blind swa hi sint, 7 ꝥ nan mon ne

---

[d] Boeth. iv. pr. 4. l. 85 P. 'Tum ego, Cum tuas,' &c.

[1] *þe him* om. B.   [2] *timum* B.   [3] So C, *berrhtost* B.   [4] *on* from
B, *ofyr* C.   [5] *beorhtes* B.   [6] *on* om. B.   [7] *wendað* B.   [8] *unrihtan* B. (*nyttan*)
[9] *ðy* B.   [10] *þe* B.   [11] From B, *swincð* C.   [12] *ealle* B.   [13] *ægþer* B.

* 104b C. mæge *gesion[1] þ hi gesion ne magon. þ dysi is anlicost
þe sum cild sie full hal 7 ful æltæwe geboren, 7 swa fullice
ðionde on eallum cystum 7 cræftū þa hwile þe hit on cnihthade bið; 7 swa forð eallne giogoðhad[2], oð[3] he wyrð ælces
cræftes medeme, 7 ðonn lytle ær his midferhðe weorðe[4] bæm 5
eagum blind, 7 eac þæs modes eagan weorðan swa ablende
þ he[5] nanwuht ne gemune þæs ðe (*he*) æfre ær geseah
oððe geherde, 7 wene þeah ðæt he sie ælces þinges swa
medeme swa he æfre medomest[6] wære, 7 wenð þ ælcum men
(*sie swa swa hī si*, 7 *ælcum men*) ðince swa swa him þincð. 10
þeah ðe[7] he þonne swa dysig sie þ he þæs wene, hwæðer
we ðonne willen ealle wenan þæs ðe he wenð? Ic wene ðeah
þ we nyllen ; ac ic[8] wolde witan hu þe þuhte be þæm monnum
ðe wit ær cwædon þ unc ðuhte þ wæren wildiorum gelicran
þonne monnū, hu micelne wisdom þa hæfden ; me þincð 15
þeah ð hi næbben nænne.

§ vi[e]. Ic ðe wolde giet reccan sume swiðe[9] rihte raca[10] ; ac
* 105a C. ic wat þ þis folc his nele gelyfan ; þ is þ ða bioð gesælig*ran
þe mon witnað, þonne þa bion þe hi[11] witniað. Đa wundrode
ic ðæs 7 cwæð: Ic wolde þ þu me gereahte hu hit swa bion[12] 20
meahte. Đa cwæð he: Hwæðer þu ongite þ ælc yfelwillende mon 7 yfelwyrcende sie wites wyrðe? Đa cwæð
ic: Genog sweotole ic þ ongite. Đa cwæð he: Hu ne is se
ðonne yfelwillende 7 yfelwyrcende ðe þone unscyldigan
witnað? Đa cwð ic: Swa hit is swa ðu sægst. Đa cwæð 25
he: Hwæðer þu wene þ ða sien earme 7 ungesælige þe
wites wyrðe bioð? Đa cwæð ic: Ne wene ic his no, ac wat
geare. Đa cwæð he: Gif þu nu deman moste, hwæðerne
woldes þu deman wites wyrðran, þe ðone þe ðone[13] unscyldgan witnode, ðe ðone þe þ wite þolade? Đa cwæð 30
ic: Nis þ gelic; ic wolde helpan þæs ðe ðær unscyldig
wære, 7 henan þone þe hine yflode. Đa cwæð he: Þonne

[e] Boeth. iv. pr. 4. l. 107 P. ' Nam ne illud quidem adquiescent,' &c.

[1] *seon* B.   [2] *eallne þonne giogoðhad* B.   [3] *oðe* B.   [4] *weorðe*
om. B.   [5] From B, *hie* C.   [6] *medemast* B.   [7] *þeah ðe* om. B.
[8] *ic* om. B.   [9] *swiðe* om. B.   [10] *race* B.   [11] From B, *hit* C.
[12] *bion* om. B.   [13] *þe none* for *þ. ð. þ. ð.* B.

þe ðincð se earmra se ꝥ yfel deð ðonne se þe hit þafað.
Ða cwæð ic : Þæs ic gelefe ꝥte ælc unriht witnung sie þæs [1]
yfel þe hit deð, næs þæs ðe hit ðafæð, forðæm *his yfel hine * 105b C.
gedeð earmne ; 7 ic ongite ðæt þis is swiðe [2] riht racu ꝥ þu nu
5 recst, 7 swiðe anlic þæm þe þu ær reahtes ; ac ic wat þeah ꝥ
þis folce swa ne þincð.

§ vii [f]. Ða cwæð he : Wel þu hit ongitst ; ac ða þingeras
þingiað nu hwilum þæm þe læssan þearfe ahton ; þingiað þæm
(*þe*) þær man yflað, 7 ne þingiað þæm þe ꝥ yfel doð [3]. Þǣ
10 wære mare ðearf þe þa oðre unscyidige yflað ꝥ him mon
þingode to þæm ricum, 7 bæde ꝥ him mon dyde swa micel
wite swa hi þæm oðrū unscyldgum dydon. Swa swa se
sioca ah þearfe ꝥ hine mon læde to þæm læce, ꝥ he his tilige,
swa ah se (*þe*) ðæt yfel deð ꝥ hine mon læde to þæm ricum,
15 ꝥ mon þær mæge sniðan 7 bærnan his unþeawas. Ne cweðe ic na ꝥ ꝥ yfel sie ꝥ mon helpe þæs unscyldgan 7 him
foreþingie ; ac ic [4] cweðe ꝥ hit is betere ꝥ mon wrege þone
scyldgan ; 7 ic secge ꝥ sio forespræc ne dyge nauðer ne þǣ
scyldgan ne ðæm þe him foreþingað, gif hi þæs wilniað ꝥ
20 him heora yfel unwrecen sie be ðæs gyltes andefne.   *Ac ic * 106a C.
wat gif ða scyldgan ænigne spearcan wisdomes hæfden 7 be
ænegum dæle ongeaten ꝥ hi meahten heora scylda þurg ꝥ [5]
wite gebetan, þe him her on weorulde on become, þonne
noldon hi na cweðan ꝥ hit wære wite, ac woldan cweðan ꝥ
25 hit wære heora clænsung, 7 heora betrung ; 7 noldon nænne
þingere gesecan [6], ac lustlice hi woldon lætan þa rican hi
tucian æft̄ hiora agnum willan. Forðæm ne scyle nan wis
man nænne mannan hatian ; ne hatað nan mon þone gódan,
butan se eallra dysgosta ; ne ꝥ nis nan riht ꝥ mon
30 þone yflan hatige, ac hit is rihtre ꝥ him mon miltsige.
Ꝥ is þonne hiora [7] mildsung ꝥ mon wrece hiora unðeawas be
hiora gewyrhtum [8]. Ne scyle [9] nan mon siocne monnan 7 [10]
gesargodne swencan, ac hine mon scel [11] lædan to þæm læce

---

[f] Boeth. iv. pr. 4. l. 123 P. ‘ Atqui nunc, ait, contra faciunt,’ &c.

[1] *þæs* om. B.   [2] *swa* B.   [3] *dēð* C.   [4] *ic* om. B.   [5] *ꝥ* om. B.
[6] *secan* B.   [7] *hôra* C.   [8] From B, *unwyrhtum* C.   [9] *sceal* B.
[10] *7* om. B.   [11] *sceolde* B.

þ he his tilige.   Ða se Wisdom þa þis spell areaht hæfde, ða
ongan he eft[1] singan 7 þus cwð:

XXXIX [g].

§ i. (*Forhwi drefe ge eowru mod mid unrihtre fiounge, swa
swa yða for winde þa sæ hrerað? oððe[2] forhwy ælwile ge
eowerre wyrde þ hio nan geweald nah? oððe hwy ne[3] magon* 5
*ge gebidan gecyndelices deaðes[4], nu he eow ælce dæg toweardes
onet?   Hwi ne magon ge gesion þ he spyrað ælce dæg æfter
fuglum[5] 7 æfter dioru 7 æfter monnu, 7 ne forlæt nan
swæð ær he gefehð þ þ he æfterspyreð.   Walawa þ ða ungesæligan menn ne[6] magon gebidon hwonne he him to cume, ac* 10
*forsceotað hine foran, swa swa wilde deor willnað oðer to ac-
wellenne.   Ac hit nære no manna ryht þ hiora ænig oðerne
fiode; ac þ wære ryht þ hiora ælc gulde oðru edlean ælces
weorces æfter his gewyrhtu, þ is þ mon lufode þone godan,
swa swa riht is þ mon do, 7 mildsige þam yfelum, swa we ær* 15
*cwædon; lufie[7] þone man, 7 hatige his unþeawas; ceorfe him
of swa he swiðost mæg.*)

§ ii [h]. Ða he þa þis lioð asungen hæfde, þa geswugode he
ane hwile.   Ða cwæð ic: Nu ic ongite openlice ðæt sio
soðe gesælð stent on godra monna gecarnunga, 7 sio 20
unsælð stent on yfelra monna geearnunga [e].   Ac ic secge
get þ me ne[9] þyncð nauht lytel good þisses andweardan
lifes gesælða, ne[9] eac nauht lytel yfel his ungesælða[10];
forðæm ic næfre ne geseah ne geherde nænne wisne mon þe
ma wolde bion wrecca 7 earm 7 elðiodig 7 forsewen, þonne 25
welig 7 weorð 7 rice 7 foremære on his agnu earde.
Forðæm hi secgað þ hi mægen[11] þe[12] yð[13] hiora wisdome
fulgan 7 hine gehealdan[14], gif hiora anwald bið fullice ofer

---

[g] Boeth. iv. met. 4. 'Quid tantos,' &c.   Cott. Metr. xxvii.
[h] Boeth. iv. pr. 5. 'Hic ego: Video, inquam,' &c.

[1] *eft* om. B.   [2] em. *oðð* B.   [3] em. *ne ne* B.   [4] em. by J,
þeawes B.   [5] em. *fugum* B.   [6] *ne* conject. om. B.   [7] em. *lufien* B.
[8] B has *geearnungum*, the second last letter of which is a blend of *a*
and *u*.   [9] *ne* om. B.   [10] From B, *ungesalða* C.   [11] *hi mægen* om. B.
[12] *þy* B.   [13] *eð* B.   [14] *fullgehealdan* C.

þ folc þe him under bið; 7 eac be sumum dæle ofer ða þe
him on neaweste bioð ymbutan, forðæm þ hi mægen henan
ða yflan 7 fyrðran ða goodan. Forðæm se gooda bið sȳle
arwyrðe, ægþer ge on þîs andweardan ˏlife ge on þæm
5 *[*toweardan; 7 se yfela þe mon his yfel*[1]] gestioran ne mæg * 107b C.
bið sȳle wites wyrþe, ge on þisse woruldè ge on þære
toweardan. Ac ic wundrie swiðe swiðlice forhwi hit swa
went swa hit (*nu*) oft deð, þ is þte[2] mislicu witu 7 mænigfeald earfoðu cumað to þæm gôdū swa hi to ðæm yflum
10 sceoldon, 7 þa good þe sc[*e*]oldon beon edlean godū
monnū goðra weorca cumað to yflum monnum. Forðæm
ic wolde witan nu æt þe hu ðe licode þ gewrixle. Ic his
wundrode micle þy læs, gif ic wisse þ hit weas gebyrede
buton Godes willan 7 buton his gewitnesse ; ac se ælmehtega
15 God hæfð geeced mȋnne ege 7 mine wafunga mid ðisū
þingum. Forðæm he hwilū selð þa gesælða þæm goodū, 7
þæm yflum unsælða, swa hit riht wære þ he sȳle dyde ;
hwilum he eft geþafað þ þa goodan habbað unsælða 7
ungelimp on mænegum þingum, 7 þa yflan[3] habbað
20 gesælða, 7 him limpð[4] oft æfter hiora agnum willan. Þy
ic ne mæg nan oþer geþencan buton hit weas swa gebyrige,
buton þu me get þy *gesceadlicor*[5] oðer gerecce. Ða and- * 108a C.
swarode he ymbe long 7 cwæð: Nis hit nan wundor þeah
hwa wene þ swelces gehwæt[6] nu[7] unmyndlinga geberige,
25 ðonne he ne con ongitan 7 gereccan forhwy swylc God[8]
geþafað. Ac ðu ne scealt no[9] twiogan þ swa good sceppend
7 waldend eallra gesceafta rihtlice gesceop[10] eall þ he
gesceop[10], 7 rihte demð 7 welt[11] ealles, þeah þu nyte forhwy
he swa 7 swa do.

30 § iii[1]. Ða he ða þis spell areaht hæfde, þa ongan he
singan, 7 cwæð: (*Hwa unlæredra ne wundrað þæs roderes
færeldes 7 his swiftnesse, hu he ælce dæg uton ymbhwyrfð*[12]

---

1 Boeth. iv. met. 5. 'Si quis Arcturi,' &c. Cott. Metr. xxviii.

[1] *yfles* J.   [2] *te* om. B.   [3] *yflaðn* C.   [4] *gelimpð* B.   [5] em.
gesceadlior B.   [6] *hwæt* B.   [7] *nu* om. B.   [8] B has *god swylc*
for *swylc God*.   [9] From B, *on* C.   [10] *sceop* B.   [11] *wealt* B.   [12] em.
ymbhwyrð B.

ealne þisne middangeard[1]*? oððe hwa ne wundrað þte sume
tunglu habbað scyrtran hwyrft þōn sume habban, swa swa
tunglu habbað þe we hatað wænes ðisla ? Forþy hi habbað
swa sceortne ymbhwyrft*[2] *forþi hi sint swa neah þā norðende
þære eaxe þe eall þes rodor on hwerfð*[3]. *Oððe hwa ne wafað* 5
*þæs, buton þa ane þe hit witon, þæt sume tunglu habbað
lengran ymbhwyrft þōn sume habban, 7 þa lengestne þe ymb
ða eaxe middewearde hwearfað, swa nu Boeties deð, 7
Saturnus*[4] *se steorra ne cymð þær ær ymb ðritig wintra þær
he ær wæs ? Oððe hwa ne wundrað ðæs þ sume steorran* 10
*gewitað under þa sæ, swa swa sume men wenaþ þ sio sunne do
þōn hio to setle gæð ? Ac hio ne bið þeah þy near þære sæ ðe
hio bið on midne dæg. Hwa ne wafað þæs þōn se fulla mona
wyrð ofertogen mid þiostrum, oððe eft þæt þa steorran scinað
beforan þā monan, 7 ne scinað beforan þære sunnan ? Þises* 15
*hi wundriað 7 manies þyllices, 7 ne wundriað na þte men 7
ealle cwuca wuhta habbað singalne 7 unnytne andan betwuh
him. Oððe hwy ne wundriað hi þæs þ hit hwilū þunrað,
hwilū na ne onginð, oððe eft gewinnes sæ 7 winda 7 yþa
7 landes, oððe hwy þ is weorðe 7 eft for þære sunnan*[5] *sciman* 20
to his agnum gecynde weorðe ? Ac þ ungestæððige[6] *folc
wundrað*[7] *þæs þe hit seldost*[8] *gesiehð, þeah hit læsse wundor sie,
7 wenað þ þ ne*[9] *sie eald gesceaft, ac se*[10] *weas geworden
niwane. Ac þa ðe firwetgeorne weorþað*[11] *7 onginnað þōn
leornian, gif him God abrit of þā mode þ dysig þ hit ær mid* 25
*oferwrigen was, þōn ne wundriað hi no fela þæs þe hi nu
wundriað.)*

§ iv[k]. Ða se Wisdom þa þis leoð asungen hæfde, þa
geswugode he ane lytle hwile. Ða cwæð ic: Swa hit is swa
þu sægst ; ac ic[12] wolde get þ þu me hwæthwugu openlicor 30
gereahte be ðære wisan þe min mod swiðost gedrefed hæfð ;
þ is þ ic ðe ær ymb acsode ; forðæm hit wæs syle giet þin

---

[k] Boeth. iv. pr. 6. 'Ita est, inquam,' &c.

[1] *middanēard* B.　　[2] em. *ymbhwyft* B.　　[3] em. *hwefð* B.
[4] em. *satusnus* B.　[5] em. *sunna* B.　[6] em. *ungesæððige* B.　[7] em.
ne wundrað no B.　[8] em. *seldos* B.　[9] *ne* conject. om. B.　[10] em.
sæ B.　[11] em. *weorþaðað* B.　[12] *ic* om. B.

gewuna þ þu woldest ælcū mode deglu ðing tæcan 7 selð-
cuð [1].   Ða ongon he smearcian 7 cwæð to me : Ðu spænst
me on ða mæstan spræce 7 on þa earfoðestan to ge*reccanne. * 110a C.
Þa race sohton ealle uðwiotan, 7 swiðe swiðlice ymb swuncon,
5 7 uneaðe ænig com to ende þære spræce ; forðæm hit is
þeaw þære spræce 7 þære ascungæ þte symle þonne ðær
an tweo of adon bið, þonne bið þær unrim astyred ; swa
swa mon on ealdspellum sægð þ an nædre wære þe hæfde
nigon heafdu, 7 sȳle gif mon anra hwelc of aslog, þonne
10 weoxon þær siofon on [2] ðæm anum heafde. Þa geberede
hit þ þær com se foremæra Erculus to, se wæs Iobes sunu ;
þa ne [3] meahte he geþencan hu he hi mid ænige cræfte
ofercuman sceolde, ær he hi bewæg mid wuda utan 7 forbærnde þa mid fyre.   Swa is ðisse spræce þe þu me
15 æfī acsast [4] ; uneaðe hire cymð ænig mon of, gif he ærest
an cemð [5] ; ne cymð he næfre to openum ende, buton he
hæbbe swa scearp andgit swaðær [6] fyr.   Forðæm se ðe
ȳb þ acsian wile, he sceal ærest wi*t*an hwæt sie sio anfealde
foresceawung Godes, 7 hwæt wyrd sie, 7 hwæt weas ge*b*ergie [7],
20 7 hwæt sie godcund andgit 7 [go]dcund foretiohhun[g]. 7
hwæt monna *freodom sie. [Nu ðu] mihi ongitan hu hefig * 110b C.
7 hu earfoðe [8] þis is eall to gerecanne [9] ; ac ic sceal þeah
hwæthwugu his onginnan þe to tæcanne, forðæm ic hæbbe
ongiten þ hit is swiðe micel læcedom þinre sorge, gif þu
25 þises auht ongitst, þeah hit me lange to læranne sie.
Forðæm hit is neah þære tide þe ic getiohhod hæfde on oðer
weorc to fonne, 7 get næbbe þis gedon ; 7 me þincð eac þ
þu sadige hwæthwugununges, 7 þe ðyncen to ælenge [10] þas
langan spell, swelce þe nu lyste lioða.   Ic wat eac þ þe
30 hiora lyst, ac ðu scealt þeah geþolian sume hwile ; ic ne
mæg hit nu swa hraðe asingan, ne æmettan næbbe, forðæm
hit is swiðe long spe*ll*. Ða cwæð ic: Do swæðer ðu wolde [11].
     § v [1]. Þa ongan he sprecan swiðe fiorran ymbutan, swelce

---

[1] Boeth. iv. pr. 6.   L 20 P.   ' Tum uelut ab alio orsa principio,' &c.
   [1] *sedcuðe* B.   [2] *of* B.   [3] *ne* om. B.   [4] *æfī âsast* C, *æfter ascast* B.
[5] *on cymð* B.   [6] *swa þ* B.   [7] *gebyrige* B.   [8] *gearfoðe* B.
[9] *gereccanne* B.   [10] *ælengo* B.   [11] *wille* B.

he na þa spræce ne mænde, 7 tiohhode hit[1] ðeah þiderweardes
7 cwæð: Ealla gesceafta, gesewenlica 7 ungesewenlica, stillu
7 unstillu, onfoð æt þæm stillan 7 æt þæm gestæððegan 7 æt
þǣ anfealdan God[*e*] endeberdnesse 7 an[*dwlitan*] *7 gemetgung*e*; [*7 forþæm*[2] *hit swa*] *gescea*pen wæs, forðæm he wat 5
hwy he gesceop eall þ he gesceop. Nis him nanwiht unnyt
þæs þe he gesceop. Se God wunað sȳle on þære hean
ceastre his anfaldnesse 7 bilewitnesse; þonan he dælð manega
7 misleca gemetgunga eallum his gesceaftū, 7 þonan he welt
eallra. Ac ðæt ðætte we hatað Godes foreþonc 7 his 10
foresceawung, þ bið þa hwile þe hit ðær mid him[3] bið on
his mode, ærðǣ þe hit gefremed weorðe, þa hwile ðe hit
geþoht bið; ac siððan hit fullfremed bið, þonne hatað we
hit wyrd. Be þy mæg ælc mon witan þ hit sint ægþer[4]
ge twegen naman ge twa þincg, foreþonc 7 wyrd. Se fore- 15
þonc is sio godcunde gesceadwisnes; sio is fæst on þæm
hean sceppende[5] þe eall fore wat hu hit geweorðan sceall ær
ær hit geweorðe. Ac þ þ we wyrd hatað, þ bið Godes
weorc þ[6] he ælce dæg wyrcð, ægþer ge þæs (*ðe*) we gesioð
ge þæs þe us[7] ungesewenlic bið. Ac se godcunda foreþonc 20
heaðerað ealle *[gesceafta, þ hi ne moton loslupan of]* hiora
endebyrdnesse[8]. Sio wyrd þonne dælð eallum gesceaftum
anwlitan 7 stowa 7 tida 7 gemetgunga; ac sio wyrd cȳð of
ðæm gewitte 7 of ðæm foreþonce þæs ælmehtigan Godes.
Se wyrcð æfter his unasecgendlicum foreþonce (*þōn*) swa 25
hwæt swa he[9] wile.

§ vi[m]. Swa swa ælc cræftega[10] ðencð 7 mearcað his weorc
on his mode ær ær he hit wyrce, 7 wyrcð siððan eall, þios
wandriende wyrd þe we wyrd hatað færð æfter his forþonce
7[11] æft his geþeahte, swa swa he tiohhað þ hit sie. Þeah hit 30
us manigfaldlic ðince, sū good, sum yfel, hit is ðeah him
anfeald good; forðæm he hit eall to gódum ende brengð, 7

---

[m] Boeth. iv. pr. 6. l. 42 P. 'Sicut enim artifex,' &c.

[1] *hit* om. B. [2] em. *fohwam* B. [3] *him* om. B. [4] *ǽþer* C.
[5] *séppende* C. [6] *þe* B. [7] *us* om. B. [8] *wyrdnesse* B. [9] *he* from B,
hwa C. [10] *cræftga* C. [11] 7 om. B.

for goode deð eall þ þ he deð.   Siððan we hit hatað wyrd
siððan hit geworht bið; ær hit wæs Godes[1] foreþanc 7 his
foretiohhung.   Ða wyrd he þonne wyrcð oððe þurh ða
goodan e[*ng*]las oððe þurh monna sawla, oððe þurh oðerra
5 gesceafta lif, oððe þurh heofones tungl, oððe ðurh þara
scuccena[2] mislice lotwrencas; hwilū þurh an ðara, hwilū
þurh eall *ða.   Ac þ is openlice cuð þ sio godcunde fore-   * 112a C.
tiohhung is anfeald 7 unandwendlic[3], 7 welt ælces þinges
endebyrdlice, 7 eall þing gehiwað.   Sumu þing þonne on
10 þisse weorulde sint underðied þære wyrde, sume hire nanwuht
underðied[4] ne sint; ac sio wyrd 7 eall ða þing þe hire
underðied sint, sint underðied ðæm godcundan foreþonce.
Be ðæm ic ðe mæg sum bispell secgan, þ þu meaht þy
sweotolor ongitan hwilce men bioð underðied þære wyrde,
15 hwylce[5] ne bioð.   Eall ðios unstille gesceaft 7 þios hwearfiende hwearfað on ðæm stillan Gode, 7 on ðæm gestæððegan, 7 on ðæm anfealdan; 7 he welt eallra gesceafta swa
swa he æt fruman getiohhod hæfde 7 get hæfð.

§ vii[n].   Swa swa on wænes eaxe hwearfiað þa hweol 7 sio
20 eax stint stille 7 byrð þeah[6] ealne þone wæn, (7) welt
ealles þæs færeltes; þ hw[*eo*]l hwerfð ymbutan 7 sio nafu
nex[*t þæ*]re eaxe sio færð micle fæ[*stlicor*] 7 orsorglicor
þonne ða fe[*lgan* 7 *don*], swelce sio eax sie þ hehste g[*od þe
we*] *nemnað God, 7 [*þa selestan men fa*]ren nehste[8] Gode,   * 112b C.
25 swa swa sio[9] nafu færð neahst þære eaxe, 7 þa midmestan
swa swa ða[10] spacan; forðæmþe ælces spa(*ca*)n bið oðer
ende fæst on ðære nafe, oðer on þære felge.   Swa bið þæm
midlestan monnum; oðre hwile he smeað on his mode ȳb
þis eorðlice (*lif*), oðre hwile ymb ðæt godcundlice, swilce
30 he locie mid oðre eagan to heofonum, mid oðre to eorþan.
Swa swa þa[11] spacan sticiað oðer ende on þære felge oþer
on þære nafe, middeweard se spaca[12] bið ægðrum emnneah,

---

[n] Boeth. iv. pr. 6. l. 61 P. ' Nam ut orbium circa eundem cardinem,' &c.

[1] From B, *goodes* C.   [2] From B, *scnccena* C.   [3] *unawendendlic* B.
[4] *underþiede* B.   [5] *hwylce* om. B.   [6] *eal* B.   [7] *felga* J.   [8] *nehst* B.
[9] *sio* om. B.   [10] *ða* om. B.   [11] *þæs* B.   [12] *middeweardre spaca* B.

ðeah oðer ende bio fæst on þære nafe, oðer on þære felge ; swa
bioð þa midmestan [1] men onmiddan þam spacan, 7 þa
betran near þære nafe, 7 þa [2] mætran near ðæm felgum ;
bioð þeah fæste on ðære n*afe* [3], 7 se nafa [4] on ðære eaxe.
Hwæt, þa [*fe*]lga þeah hongiað on þæm spacan, [*þ*]eah hi 5
eallunga wealowigen on þær[*e e*]orðan ; swa doð þa mætestan [5] [*men o*]n þæm midmestum [6], 7 þa mid[*mestan*] on þæm
betstan, 7 þa betstan [*on God*]e. Þeah þa mætestan [5] ealle

* 113a C. hio[*ra luf*]e wenden to ðisse weorulde, *[hi' ne magon]* þæron wunigan, ne to nauhte ne weorðað, gif hi be nanum dæle 10
ne beoð gefæstnode to Gode ; þon ma þe þæs hweoles felga
magon bion on [7] ðæm færelte, gif hi ne bioð fæste on þæm
spacum, 7 þa spacan on þære eaxe.   Þa felgea bioð fyrrest
ðære eaxe ; forðæm hi farað ungeredelicost.   Sio nafu
færð neaxst þære eaxe ; forðy hio færð gesundlicost [8].   Swa 15
doð ða selestan men ; swa hi [9] hiora lufe near Gode lætað,
(7 *swiðor þas eorðlicon þing forsioð* [10]), swa hi beoð orsorgran,
7 læs reccað hu sio wyrd wandrige, oððe hwæt hio [11] brenge.
Swa swa sio nafu bið s̄yle swa [12] gesund, hnæppen þa felga
on ꝥ ðe hi hnæppen, 7 þeah bið sio nafu hwæthwugu 20
todæled from þære eaxe.   Be þy þu mealt ongitan ꝥ se [13] wæn
bið mi*c*le leng gesund þe læs bið todæled f[*rom*] þære eaxe ;
swa bioð þa men eallra orsorgestæ ægðer ge þisses
andwea(*r*)dan lifes earfoða [14], ge þæs tow[*ear*]dan, þa þe
fæste bioð on Gode ; ac swa hi swiður bioð asyndrede [15] frō 25
Gode, swa hi swiður bioð gedrefde 7 geswencte, ægþer ge

* 113b C. on mode ge *on lichoman.

    § viii [o]. Swylc *is þæt ꝥ we* wyrd *hatað* be þæm godcundan
foreþonce, swylce (*sio*) smeaung 7 sio gesceadwisnes is to
metanne wið þone gearowitan [16], 7 [17] swylce þas lænan þing 30
bioð to metanne wið ða ecan [17], 7 swilce ꝥ hweol bið to

---

[o] Boeth. iv. pr. 6. l. 74 P. 'Igitur uti est ad intellectnm,' &c.
[1] For *midmestan* B has *mæstan*.   [2] *þa* om. B.   [3] From B, *næfe* J.
[4] So also B. [5] *mæstan* B. [6] *midmestăm* C. [7] *on* om. B. [8] *gesund-*
fullicost B. [9] *hi* om. B. [10] *forséoð* B. [11] From B, *hi* C. [12] *swa* om. B.
[13] From B, *þe* C. [14] From B, *earfoðe* C. [15] From J, *asyndrode bioð* B.
[16] *gearewiton* B.   [17] 7 *swylce . . . ecan* om. B.

metanne wið ða eaxe ; forðæm sio eax welt ealles þæs wænes.
Swa deð se godcunda foreðonc ; he astereð[1] þone rodor 7
þa tunglu, 7 þa eorðan gedeð stille, 7 gemetgað þa feower
gesceafta ; þ is wæter 7 eorðe 7 fyr 7 lyft. Ða he geðwærað 7
5 wlitegað[2], hwilum eft unwlitegað, 7 on oðrū hiwe gebrengð,
7 eft geedniwað, 7 tidreð ælc tudor, 7 hi eft gehyt 7
gehelt þonne hit forealdod bið 7 forsearod, 7 eft geewð 7
geedniw[að] þonne þonne (*he wile*). Sume uðwiotan [þe]ah
secgað þ sio wyrd[3] wealde[4] ægþer ge gesælða ge ungesælða
10 ælces monnes. Ic þonne secge, swa swa ealle [*cris*]tene men
secgað, þ sio godcunde foretiohhung his walde, næs sio
wyrd ; 7 ic wat þ hio demð eall þing swiðe rihte, þeah
ungesceadwisum men[5] [*swa*] ne þince. Hi wenað þ þa[*ra*]
æl[*c*]*sie go[d þe hiora will]*an fulgæð ; nis hit nan wundor, * 114a C.
15 forðæm hi beoð ablende mid ðæm þiostrum heora scylda.
Ac se godcunda foreþonc hit understent eall swiðe rihte,
þeah us þince for urum dysige þ hit on woh fare ; forðæm we
ne cunnon þ riht understandan. He demð þeah eall swiðe
rihte, þeah us hwilum swa ne ðince.

20 § ix[p]. Ealle men spiriað æft þæm hehstan goode, ge
goode ge yfle ; ac forðy ne magon þ(*a*) yflan cuman to
ðæm hean hrofe eallra gooda, forðæm hi ne spyriað on riht
æft. Ic nat[6] þeah þu cwæðe[7] nu hwonne to me : hwylc
unriht mæg beon mare þonne geþafige[8] þ hit geweorðe,
25 swa hit hwilum gewyrð, þ þæm goodum becymð anfeald yfel
on þisse weorulde, 7 þæm yflum anfeald *god*, 7 oðre[9]
hwile ægðer gemenged, ægþer ge ðæ goodum ge þæm yflum ?
Ac ic þe acsige hwæðer þu wene þ ænig *mon* sie swa
andgitfull þ he mæg*e* ongitan ælcne mon on ryht hwylc he
30 sie, þ he nawðer ne sie ne betra ne wyrsa þonne he his wene.
Ic wat *[*þeah þ hi ne magan. Ac wyrð*[10] *swiðe*] oft on * 114b C.
won se sido þe sume men secgað þ sie mede wyrðe, sume

---

[p] Boeth. iv. pr. 6.   l. 92 P.   'Nihil est enim quod mali causa,' &c.

[1] *styreð* B.   [2] *þrarað 7 gewlitegað* B.   [3] From B, *wyrð* C.
[4] From B, *wold* C.   [5] *monnum* B.   [6] *wat* B.   [7] *cweðe* B.
[8] *he geðafige* B.   [9] *oððre* C.   [10] em. *weorðað* B.

men secgað þ he[1] sie wites wyrðe. Þeah hwa mæge ongitan
hwæt oðer do, he ne mæg witan hwæt he þencð; þeah he
mæge sume his willan ongitan, þonne ne (*mæg*) he eallne.
Ic þe mæg eac reccan sum bispell be þæm þ þu hit[2] meaht
þe sweotolor ongitan, ðeah h[*it*] ungesceadwise men ongitan 5
n*e mægen*; þ is forhwi se gooda læce selle *þam* halū men
seftne drenc 7 swetne, 7 oðrū halum biterne 7 strangne;
7 hwilū eft *þam* unhalum, sumū liðne, (*sumū*) strangne,
sumum swetne, sumum bitcrne. Ic wat þ ælc þara þe þone
cræft ne can wile þæs wundrian for*hwy hi* swa don. Ac his 10
ne wundriað þa læcas[3] nauht, forðæm hi wi[*ton*] þ ða oðre
nyton; forðæm hi *cunnon* ælces hiora medtrym*nesse ongiton*
7 *onc*nawan[4], 7 eac ða cræftas þe þærwið sculon. Hwæt is
sawla hælo but*e* rihtwisnes? oððe hwæ*t* is hiora u*ntry*mnes
 bu*te* un*þeawas? [*Hwa is þōn betera læce þære sawle*] 15
þonne se þe hi gesceop, þ is God? He arað þæm[5] goodan,
7 witnað ða yflan; he wat hwæs ælc wyrðe bið. Nis
hit nan wundor, forðæm he of þæm hean hrofe hit eall
gesihð, 7 þonan miscað 7 metgað ælcum be his gewyrhtum.

   § x[q]. Þ we þonne hatað[6] wyrd, þonne se gesceadwisa 20
God, þe ælces monnes ðearfe wat, hwæt wyrcð oððe geþafað
þæs þe we (*ne we*)nað. 7 git ic þe mæg sume bisne feaum
wordum secgan be þæm dæle þe sio mennisce gesceadwisnes
mæg ongitan þa godcundnesse. Þ is þonne þ[7] we ongitað
hwilū (*mon*) on oðre wisan, on oðre hine God ongit[8]. 25
Hwilum we tiohhiað þ he sie se betra[9], 7 þonne wat God þ
hit swa ne bið. Þonne hwæm hwæt cymð oððe goodes
oððe yfles mare þonne ðe þincð þ he wyrðe sie, ne bið sio
unrihtwisnes no on Gode, ac sio ungleawnes bið on ðe selfum,
þ þu hit ne canst on riht gecnawan. Oft gebyreð þeah þte 30
men ongitað man on[10] ða *ilcan* wisan þe hine God ongit. Oft
 hit[11] ge*by*reð þte manige [*men* **bioð swa ungetrume*[12] *ægþer*

---

[q] Boeth. iv. pr. 6. L. 117 P. 'Hic iam fit illud fatalis ordinis,' &c.

[1] *hi* B. [2] *hit* om. B. [3] From B, *læces* C. [4] From J, *tocnawan* B.
[5] *þa* B. [6] From B, *hætað* C. [7] *þ* om. B. [8] From B, *andgit* C.
[9] *betsta* B. [10] *on* om. B. [11] *hit* om. B. [12] *untrume* J.

ge on mode] ge on lichoman þ hi ne magon nan good don,
ne nan yfel nyllað unnedige, 7 bioð eac swa ungeþyldige[1] þ
hi ne magon nan earfoðu geþyldelice aberan.   Forðæm hit
gebyreð oft þ God nylle for his mildheortnesse nan unabe-
5 rendlice broc him an settan, þy læs hi forlæten hiora unsceðfulnesse 7 weorðen wyrsan, gif hi asterede[2] bioð 7 geswencte[3].
Sume men beoð ælces cræftes full cræftige, 7 full halige weras
7 rihtwise.   Þonne þincð þ Gode unriht þ he swylce swence ;
ge furðum þone deað þe eallum monnum[4] is gecynde[5] to
10 þolianne, he him gedeð seftran þonne oðrum monnum ; swa
swa gio (*sum*) wis mon cwæð þ se godcunda anwald gefrioðode his deorlingas under (*his*) fiðra sceate[6], 7 hi scilde
swa geornlice swa (*swa*) man deð þone æppel on his eagan.
Manige tiliað Gode to cwemanne to þon georne þ hi wilniað
15 hiora agnum willum manigfeald earfoðu to þrowïanne, forðæm hi w*illni*að maran are 7 ma[*ran*] hlisan 7 (*maran*)
weorðscipe mid Gode to *[*habbanne þōn þa habbað*[7] *þe softor*] * 116a C.
libbað.

§ xi[r].   Oft eac becymð se anwald þisse worulde to swiðe
20 goodum monnum, forðæm þ se anwald þara yfelana weorðe
toworpen.   Sumū monnum God seleð ægðer ge good ge
yfel gemenged, forðæm hi ægþres earniað ; sume he bereafað
hiora welan swiðe hraðe, þæs þe hi[8] ærest gesælige weorðað,
þy læs hi for longum gesælðum hi[9] to up ahæbben, 7 þonan
25 on ofermettum weorðen ; sume he[9] læt þreagan mid heardum
broce, þ hi leornigen þone cræft geþyldelice[10] on ðæm langan
geswince.   Sume him ondrædað earfoðu swiðor þonne hi
þyrfen, þeah hi hi[11] eaðe adreogan mægen ; sume hi gebycgað
weorðlicne hlisan þisses andweardan lifes mid hiora agnum
30 deaðe, forðæm hi wenað þ hi næbben nan oðer fioh þæs
hlisan[12] wyrðe buton hiora agnum fiore.   Sume men wæron
gio unoferswiðedlic*e*, swa þ hi nan ne meahte mid nanum

[r] Boeth. iv. pr. 6.   l. 138 P.   'Fit autem saepe uti bonis,' &c.

[1] *unþyldige* B.   [2] *astyred* B.   [3] *geswenced* B.   [4] *monnum* om. B.
[5] *gecynde is* B.   [6] *sceade* B.   [7] *hæbben* J.   [8] *hi* om. B.   [9] *hi* . . .
sume he om. B.   [10] *geþylde* B.   [11] *hi* once, B.   [12] *hliosan* B.

wite oferswiþan; þa bisnodon hiora æftergeng*um* þ hi næren

* 116b C. mid witum oferswiðde. On þæm wæs sweotol *[þ hi for heora godum weorcum hæf]*den ðone cræft þ hi[1] mon ne meahte oferswiðan. Ac þa yflan for hiora yflum weorcum wæron gewitnode 7[2] oferswiðde, forðæm þ ða witu gestirden 5 oðrum þ (*hi*) swa gedon[3] ne dorsten, 7 eac þa gebetan þe hi þonne brociað. þ is swiðe sweotol tacn þæm wisan þ he ne sceal lufian to ungemetlice ðas woruldgesælða, forðæm hie oft cumað to ðæm wyrrestum[4] monnum. Ac hwæt wille we cweðan be þæm andweardan welan þe oft cȳð to ðæm 10 goodū, hwæt he[5] elles sie buton tacn þæs toweardan welan, 7 þæs edleanes angin þe him God tiohhod[6] hæfð for his goodan willan? Ic wene eac þte[7] God selle mænegum yfelū men[8] gesælða forðæmþe he wat hiora gecynd 7 hiora willan swa geradne þ hi for nanum ermðum ne byoð no þy 15 betran ac þy[9] wyrsan. Ac se gooda læce, þ is God, lacnað hiora mod mid ðæm welan; wile þ (*hi*) ongiten hwonon him se wela come 7 olecce þæm þe[10] læs he him þone welan afyrre, oððe hine (*þā*) welan, 7 wende his

* 117a C. *[þeawas to gode, 7 forlæte ða unþeawas]* 7 þa yfel þe he ær 20 (*for*) his ermðum dyde. Sume bioð þeah þy wyrson gif hi welan habbað, forðæm hi[11] ofermodigað[12] for ðæm welan 7 his ungemetlice brucað.

§ xii[a]. Manegū men bioð eac forgifene forðæm þas weoruldgesælða þ he scile þæm goodum leania*n* hiora good, 25 7 þæm yflum hiora yfel. Forðæm sȳle bioð þa goodan 7 þa yflan ungeþwere[13] betwuh him, ge eac hwilum þa yflan bioð ungerade betwuh him selfū; ge furðum an yfel man bið simle[14] ungeþwære him selfum, forðæm þe[15] he wat þ he untela deð, 7 wenð him þara[16] leana, 7 nyle þeah þæs 30 geswican, ne hi[t] furðum him ne læt hreowan; 7 þonne for ðæm singalū ege ne mæg no weorðan geþwære on him

---

[a] Boeth. iv. pr. 6. 1. 168 P. ‘ Alios in cladem meritam,’ &c.

[1] From B, *him* C. [2] 7 om. B. [3] *don* B. [4] *wyrstan* B. [5] *he* om. B. [6] *getihhod* B. [7] *te* om. B. [8] *monnum* B. [9] B has *ne na þy* for *ac þy*. [10] *þy* B. [11] *hi* om. B. [12] *ofermodgian* B. [13] *ungeþwære* B. [14] *hwilum* B. [15] *þe* om. B. [16] *maran* B.

selfū.   Oft hit (*eac*) ge[*by*]reð þ se yfla forlæt his yfel [*for*]
sumes oðres yfles mannes andan, [*for*]ðæm he wolde mid
þy tælan[1] þo[*ne oðer*]ne þ he onscunode his þeawas;
[*swincð*] þonne ymb þ swa he swiðost mæg [*þ he*] tiolað
5 ungelic to bionne þæm oð[*rum*], forðæm hit is þæs godcundan
anw[*eal*]des gewuna þ he wircð of yfle good.   *[*Ac hit nis* * 117b C.
nanum men alefed þæt he mæge] witan eall þ God[2] getiohhod
hæfð, ne eac areccan þ þ he geworht hæfð.   Ac on þæm hi
habbað genoh to ongitanne þ se scippend 7 se waldend
10 eallra gesceafta welt, 7 rehte gesceop eall þ he gesceop,
7 nan yfel ne worhte ne get ne wyrcð, ac ælc yfel he
adrifð of eallū his rice.   Ac gif þu æst þæm hean[3] anwalde
spyrian wilt þæs ælmehtigan Godes, þonne ne[4] ongitst þu
nan yfel on nanum þinge, þeah þe[5] nu ðince þ her micel on
15 þys middangearde sie; forðæm hit is riht þ ða goodan
hæbben good edlean hiora gôdes, 7 þa yflan hæb[*ban*][6] wite
hiora yfles; ne bið þ nan yfel [*þ*]te riht bið, ac bið good.
Ac ic ongite ðæt ic þe hæbbe aðretne[7] (*nu*) mid þy[8] langan
[*spe*]lle[9], forðæm þe lyst nu leoða; ac on[*foh*] hiora nu,
20 forðæm hit is se læce[*dom*] 7 se drenc þe þu lange wilnodest,
[*þæt*[10] *ðu þy*] eð mæge (*þære*) lare onfon.

  § xiii[t]. Ða se [*Wisdo*]m þa þis spell areaht hæfde, [*þa
o*]ngon he eft[11] singan 7 þus cwæð: (*Gif þu willnige*[12] *mid
hlutrum mode ongitan þone hean anweald, beheald þa tunglu
25 þæs hean heofnes.   Healdað þa tunglu þa ealdan sibbe þe hi on
gesceapne wæron, swa þ sio fyrene sunne ne onhrinð no þæs
dæles þæs heofenes þe se mona on irnð, ne se mona no ne
onhrinð þæs dæles þe sio sunne on irnð, þa hwile ðe hio þæron
bið.   Ne se steorra þe we hatað Ursa ne cymð næfre on þam
30 westdæle, þeah ealle oðre steorran faren mid þā rodore æfter
þære sunnan on þa eorþan.   Nis hit nan wundor, forþā he is
swiðe neah þam upende þære eaxe.   Ac se steorra þe we hatað*

---

[a] Boeth. iv. met. 6.   ‘ Si uis celsi iura tonantis,’ &c.   Cott. Metr. xxix.

[1] *lætan* B.   [2] From B, *good* C.   [3] *hean* om. B.   [4] *ne* om. B.
[5] *þe* om. B.   [6] So J, *habban* B.   [7] em. *aretne* C, *apriet* B.   [8] *þis* B.
[9] From B, *spell* C.   [10] em. *þæ* B.   [11] *eft* om. B.   [12] em. *willnig* B.

*æfensteorra, þōn he biǧ west gesewen, þōn tacnnað he æfen.
Færð þōn æfter þære sunnan on ðære eorðan sceade oð he
ofirnð þa sunnan hindan; cymð wiðforan þa sunnan úp.
Þōn hate we hine morgensteorra, forþā he cymð eastan úp;
bodað þære sunnan cyme.   Sio sunne 7 se mona habbað* 5
*todæled betwuht him þone dæg 7 þa niht swiðe emne, 7 swiðe
geþwærlice* [1] *ricsiað þurh godcundan foresceawunga, 7 unaþ-
rotenlice þiowiað þā ælmihtigan Gode oð domes dæg.   Forþi
hi ne læt God on ane healfe þæs heofones bion, þy læs hi
fordon oðra gesceafta.   Ac gesibsuma God gemetgað ealla* 10
*gesceafta 7 geþwærað þa ðe betwuh him wuniað.   Hwilū
stihð se wæta þ dryge; hwilū* [2] *he gemengeð þ fyr wið þam
cile* [3] *; hwilū þ leohte fyr 7 þæt beorhte úp gewit, 7 sio hefige
eorðe sit þær niðere.   Be þæs cyninges gebode brengð eorðe
ælcne* [4] *westm 7 ælc tudor ælce geare, 7 se hata sumor drygð 7* 15
gearwað sæd 7 bleda, 7 westmbæra hærfest bryngð [5] *ripa
bleda.   Hæglas 7 snawas 7 se oftræda ren leccaꝺ þa eorðan on
wintra; forþā underfehð sio eorðe þæt sæd 7 gedeð þæt hit
grewð* [6] *on lengten.   Ac se metod eallra gesceafta fet on eorðan
ealle growende westmas 7 ealle forðbrengð; 7 gehyt þōn he* 20
*wyle, 7 eowað þōn he wile, 7 nimð þōn he wile.   Þa hwile þe
ða gesceafta þiowiað, sit se hehsta sceoppend on his heahsetle;
þanon he welt þā gewealdleðerū ealle gesceaftu.   Nis nan
wundor, forþæðe he is cyning 7 dryhten 7 æwelm 7 fruma
7 æ 7 wisdom 7 rihtwis dema.   He sent ealla gesceafta* [7] *on his* 25
*ærendo, 7 he het ealle eft cuman.   Þær se an gestæþþega
cyning gif he* [8] *ne staþelode ealla gesceafta* [9] *, þōn wurdon hi ealle
toslopene 7 tostencte, 7 to nauhte wurdon ealle gesceafta* [9] *.   Þeah
habbað gemænelice þa ane lufe þ hi þeowian swilcū hlaforde, 7
fægniað þæs þæt he hiora wealt.   Nis þ nan wundor, forþam* [10] 30
hi ne mihton elles bion, gif hi ne ðiowedon hiora fruman.)
Ða forlet se Wisdom þ leoð, 7 cwæð to me :

---

[1] Orig. *geðwærelice*, but middle *e* erased.   [2] em. *hylū* B.   [3] em.
lice B.   [4] em. *ælne* B.   [5] em. *brynꝺ* B.   [6] em. *grewað* B.   [7] em.
gesceaftu B.   [8] *gif he* ab. 1.   [9] em. *gesceafa* B.   [10] em. *foþan* B.

XL [u].

§ i. Hwæðer ðu nu ongite hwider þios spræce wille? Da cwæð ic: Sege me hwider sio wille. Da cwæð he: Ic wille secgan þ ælc wyrd bio good, sam hio monnū good þince, sam hio him yfel þince. Da cwæð ic: Ic wene þ hit
5 eaðe swa bion mæge, þeah us hwilū oðer þynce. Da cwæð he: Nis þæs nan tweo ðæt ælc wyrd bið good þara ðe[1] riht 7 nytwyrðe bið; forðæm ælc wyrd, sā hio bio[2] wynsū sam hio sie unwynsū, forðy cȳþ to ðæm goodan þ hio oðer twega do, oððe hine þreatige to ðon þ he bet do þonne he ær dyde,
10 oððe him leanige þ he ær tela dyde. 7 eft ælc wyrd þara þe to ðæm yflū cȳð, cymð for þæm twæm þingū, sam hio sie reðe, sam hio sy wynsū. Gif to ðæm *yflum* cymð reðu wyrd, þonne *cymð* he to edleane his yfla, oððe *to* þreunge[3] 7 to lære þ he eft[4] swa ne *do*. Þa *ongann* ic wundrian,
15 7 cwæð: Is þ *forinweardli*ce rihtracu[5] þ þu ðær *recst*. *Þa*   * 120a C. *cwæð* he: Swa hit is swa ðu sægst; ac ic wolde, gif ðu wolde, ðæt wit[6] unc wenden sume hwile to þises folces spræce, þylæs hi cweþan[7] þ wit sprecan[8] ofer monnes gemet[9]. Da cwæð ic: Sprec þ ðu wille.
20 § ii [v]. Da cwæð he: Wenst þu ðæt þ ne sie good þ nit bið? Da cwæð ic: Ic wene þ hit sie. Da cwæð he: Ælc (*wyrd*) is nyt þara þe auðer deð[10], oððe lærð, oððe wyrcð[11]. Da cwæð ic: Þ is soð. Da cwæð he[12]: Sio wiðerwearde wyrd is ðæm[13] good þe winnað wið unðeawas 7 wendað hi to goode.
25 Da cwæð ic: Ne mæg ic þæs oðsacan. Da cwæð he: Hwæt wenst þu bi þære goodan wyrde ðe oft cymð to goodū monnū on ðisse weorulde, swylce hit sie foretacn ecra[14] gooda? hwæþer þis folc mæge cweðan þ hit sie yfel wyrd? Da smear-code (*ic*) 7 cwæð: Ne cwið þ nan mon, ac cwið þ hio sie swiðe

---

[u] Boeth. iv. pr. 7. 'Iamne igitur uides,' &c.

[v] Boeth. iv. pr. 7. l. 17 P. 'Nonne igitur bonum censes,' &c.

[1] *ðe* above line in C.   [2] *sie* B.   [3] *þreatunge* B.   [4] *got* B. [5] *racu* B.   [6] *wit* om. B.   [7] So C, *cwæðon* B.   [8] So C, *spræcon* B. [9] *andget* B.   [10] B has *awerdeð* for *auðer deð*.   [11] *wricð* B.   [12] For words here omitted in text see p. 149 note.   [13] From B, *is ðæm is ðæt good* C.   [14] From B, *ælcra* C.

good, swa *hio* eac bið. Ða cwæð he : Hwæt wenst þu be þære
unwenlicran[1] wyrde þe oft þreatað þa yflan to witnianne ?
hwæðer þis folc wene þ þ good wyrd sie? Ða cwæð ic :
Ne wenað hi no þ þ gód *[wyrd sie, ac wenað þ hio sie earm]*-
lico. Ða cwæð he : Uton healdan unc þ wit ne wenen swa 5
swa þis folc wenð ; gif wit þæs wenað ðe þis folc wenð,
þonne forlæte wit ælce gesceadwisnesse 7 ælce rihtwisnesse.
Ða cwæð ic : Hwy forlæte[2] wit hi (*a*) þa[3] ma? Ða [*cwæð
he :*] Forðy þe[4] folcisce men secgað þ ælc reðu wyrd 7
unwynsumu sie yfel; ac we ne sculon þæs gelefan, forðæm 10
þe[5] ælc wyrd bið good, swa we ær spræcon, sam hio sy
reðe, sam hio sie[6] wynsum. Ða wearð ic afæred 7 cwæð :
þ is soð þ þu sægst; ic nat þeah hwa hit dyrre secgan
dysegū monnū, forðæm his ne mæg[7] nan dysi man gelefan[8].

  § iii[w]. Ða onsac se Wisdom sarlice, 7 cwæð : Forðy ne 15
scyle nan wis mon (*forhigan ne*) to swiðe ȳb þ[9] gnornian,
to hwæm his wise weorðe[10], oððe[11] hwæðer him cume þe reðu
w[*y*]rd þe liðu, ðon ma þe se hwata esne scyle ymb þ
gnornian, hu oft he fiohtan scyle. Ne bið (*his*) lof na ðy[12]
læsse, ac is wen þ hit sie þy[12] mare ; swa bið eac þæs wisan 20
med þe mare, þe him wraðre wyrd 7 reðre to becȳð. *þi* ne
[*sceolde*[13] *nan*] wis man wilnian seftes lifes, gif he ænigra
cræfta recð oððe æniges weorðscipes her for weorulde oððe
eces lifes æfter þisse weorulde. Ac ælc wis man scyle
a winnan ægðer ge wið þa reðan wyrd[*e*] ge wið þa wyn- 25
suman, þy læs he hine for ðære wynsuman wyrde fortruwige,
oððe for[14] ðære reðan forðence. Ac him is ðearf þ he aredie
þone midmestan weg betweoh[15] þære reðan wyrde 7 ðære
liðan, þ he ne wilnige wynsūran wyrde 7 maran orsorgnesse
ðonne hit gemetlic sie, ne[16] eft (*to*) reðre[17], forðæm he ne 30
mæg nauþres ungemet adriogan. Ac hit is on hiora agnum
anwealde hwæðre þara hi geciosen. Gif hi þonne þone mid-

* 120b C. (line 4)

* 121a C. (line 21)

---

[w] Boeth. iv. pr. 7. l. 37 P. 'Quare, inquit, ita uir sapiens,' &c.

[1] *unsewenlican* B.   [2] *forlete* B.   [3] *þy* B.   [4] *þe* om. B.   [5] *ð* B.
[6] *hio sie* om. B.   [7] B has *nele* for *ne mæg*.   [8] *gelefan* om. B.   [9] *to swiðe
ȳb þ* om. B.   [10] *wyrþan scyle* B.   [11] *oððe* om. B.   [12] *þe* B.   [13] *scyle* J.
[14] *for* om. B.   [15] *betwyhs* B.   [16] *ne* om. B.   [17] From B, *hreðre* C.

mestan weg aredian willaᶁ, þonne sculon hi selfe him selfū
gemetgian [1] þa wynsuman wyrde 7 þa [2] orsorgan; þonne
gemetgaᶁ [3] him God þa reᶁan wyrde ge on þisse weorulde
ge on þære toweardan, swa swa hi eaᶁe [4] adreogan [5] magan.

5 § iv [x]. Wella, wisan men, wel; gaᶁ ealle on þone weg
*ᶁe eow [*læraᶁ*] þa f[*oremæran bisna*] þara godena gumena 7 * 121b C.
þara weorᶁgeornena wera þe ær eow wæron. Eala, ge [6]
eargan 7 idelgeornan; hwy ge swa unnytte sien 7 swa
aswundne? Hwy ge nyllen ascian æfter þæm wisum
10 monnū 7 æfꞇ þæm weorᶁgeornum, hwylce hi wæron þa þe
ær eow wæron? 7 hwy ge þonne nyllen, siᶁᶁan ge hiora
þeawas geascod hæbben, him onhirian, swa ge swiᶁost
mægen? forᶁæm hi wunnon æfꞇ weorᶁscipe on þisse
worulde, 7 tiolodon goodes hlisan mid goodum weorcū,
15 7 worhton goode bisne þæm þe æfter him wæron. Forᶁæm
hi wuniaᶁ nu ofer ᶁæm tunglum on ecre eadignesse for
hiora gódum weorcum. Her endaᶁ sio fiorᶁe boc Boeties,
7 onginᶁ sio fifte.

§ v [y]. Da se Wisdom þa þis spell areaht hæfde, þa cwæᶁ
20 ic: Swiᶁe riht is þin lar; ac ic wolde þe nu myndgian þære
mænigfealdan lare þe þu me ær gehete be þære Godes foretiohhunge. Ac ic wolde ærest witan æt þe hwæᶁer *þ auht * 122a C.
sie þ we oft geheraᶁ þ men *cweᶁaᶁ* be sumum þingum þ hit
scyle weas gebyrian. Da cwæᶁ he: Me wære leofre þ ic
25 onette wiᶁ þæs þ ic þe [7] moste gelæstan þ ic þe [7] ær gehet,
7 þe mos[*le*] getæcan swa scortne weg swa ic scyrtestne
findan meahte to ᶁinre cyᶁᶁe. Ac hit is swiᶁe [8] feor [9] of
uncrum wege, of þæm wege þe wit getiohhod habbaᶁ on to
farenne; þ þ þu me ær bæde (*hit*) wære þeah nyttre to
30 gecerranne 7 (*lo*) ongitanᵽe. Ac ic ondræde þ ic þe læde
hidres þidres on ᶁa paᶁas of þinū wege, þ þu ne mæge
eft þinne weg aredian. Nis hit nan wundor þeah þu getiorie,
gif ic þe læde bi ᶁæm wege. Da cwæᶁ ic: Ne þearft (*þu*) no

---

[x] Boeth. iv. met. 7. 'Bella bis quinis operatus annis,' &c.
[y] Boeth. v. pr. 1. l. 2 P. 'Tum ego, Recta quidem, inquam,' &c.
[1] *gemetgan* C. [2] *þa* om. B. [3] *gemeᵹaᶁ* C. [4] *hi eaᶁe* om. B.
[5] *ge adrygan* B. [6] *ge* om. B. [7] *be* om. B. [8] *swa* B. [9] *fyr* B.

þ ondrædan; ac ic bio swiðe swiðe gefægen [1] gif þu me lædst
þider ic ðe bidde.   Da cwæð he: Ic þe wille læran bispellum,
swa ic þe ealne weg dyde, 7 þe þeah secgan wille [2] þæt hit nis
nauht þ mon cwið, þ ænig þing weas gebyrige.   Forðæ ælc
þing cimð of sumū þingū, forðæ [3] hit ne bið weas gebyred; 5
ac ðær hit of [4] nauhte ne come þonne wære hit weas gebyred [5].

§ vi [z]. Da cwæð ic: Ac hwonan com se (*nama*) ærest?
Da cwæð he: Aristoteles min diorlıng hit *gerehte on þære
bec þe Fisica hatte. Þa cwæð ic: Hu *rehte* he hit? Da
cwæð he: Men cwædon gio þonne him hwæt unwenunga [6] 10
geb[*irede*], þ þ wære weas gebyred; swylc[*e hwa*] nu [7] delfe
eorðan, 7 finde ðær þonne goldhord, ond secge ðonne þ þ
sie weas gebered.   Ic wat þeah gif se delfere þa eorðan n[*o*]
ne delfe, ne nan mon ær þ gold þær ne hydde, þonne *ne* [8]
funde he hit no. Forðy hit næs *na* weas funden; ac sio 15
godcunde *foretio*hhung lærde þone þe he *wolde* þ *he* [9] gold
hydde, 7 eft ðone þe he wolde þ hit funde.

§ vii [a]. Da cwæð ic: Ðæt *ic* ongite þ hit is swa swa *þu*
sægst; ac ic þe wolde [10] acsian hwæðer we ænigne freodom
hæbben oððe *ænigne anwe*ald, hwæt we don, *hwæt we ne ne* 20
don, þe sio godcunde foretiohhung oððe sio wyrd us nede to þā
þe we willan. Þa cwæð he: We habbað micelne anwald; nis
nan g*esceadwis* g*escea*ſt þ næbbe friodom. Se þe gesceadwisnes*se* hæfð, se mæg *deman* 7 tosceadan hwæs [11] he wilnigan
[*sceal*] 7 hwæt he on*scunian* sceal.   7 ælc *mon hæfð* [12] *þone* 25
freodom þ he wat hwæt h[*e*] wile, *hwæt he nele; 7 þeah
nabbað [13] ealla gescea[*d*]wisa gesceafta gelicne friodom.
Englas habbað rihte domas 7 goodne willan, 7 eall þ [14] hi
wilniað hi begitað swiðe eaðe, forðæmþe hi nanes wos [15] ne
wilniað. Nis nan [16] þe hæbbe friodom 7 gesceadwisnesse 30
buton englum 7 monnum; þa men habbað simle freodom

<hr>

[z] Boeth. v. pr. 1. l. 32 P. 'An est aliquid, tametsi uulgus lateat,' &c.
[a] Boeth. v. pr. 2. 'Animaduerto, inquam,' &c.

[1] *fægn* B.   [2] *wille* om. B.   [3] *forþi* B.   [4] *of* om. B.   [5] From B,
gebe C.   [6] *hwegnunga* B.   [7] *nu* om. B.   [8] *ne* conject., om. B.
[9] em. *ðe* B.   [10] *wolde þe* B.   [11] *hwæt* B.   [12] em. *hæf* B.   [13] *habbað* B.
[14] *hwæt* B.   [15] *woges* B.   [16] Read *nan gesceaft, nan* om. B.

þy maran þe hi heora mod near godcundum ðingum lætað,
7 habbað þæs þy læssan frio[*do*]m þe hi hiora modes
willan[1] near þisse weoruldare lætað. Nabbað hi nænne
freodom þonne hi heora agnum willum hi selfe unðeawum
5 underðiodað; ac sona swa hi hiora mod onwend[*að*][2] from
gode, swa weorðað hi ablende mid unwisdome. Swaþeah
is an ælmihtig God on his þære hean ceastre; se gesihð
ælces monnes geþoht[3], 7 his word 7 his dæda toscead[4], 7
gilt ælcū æfter his gewyrhtum. Da se Wisdom þa þis spell
10 asæd hæfde, þa ongon he singan 7 þus cwæð:

XLI[b].

§ i. (*Þeah Omerus se goda sceop, þe mid Crecū selest was:
se was Firgilies[5] lareow; se Frigilius wæs mid Lædenwa-
rum selest: þeah Omerus on his leoðū swiðe herede þære sunnan
gecynd 7 hiore cræftas 7 hiore biorhto, ne mæg heo þeah ealle
15 gesceafta gescinan, ne þa gesceafta þe heo gescinan mæg ne
mæg hio ealle endemest gescinan, ne ealle innan geondscinan.
Ac nis þū ælmihtigan[6] Gode swa, þe is scyppend ealra
gesceafta; he geseohð 7 þurhseohð ealle his[7] gesceafta ændemest. Þone mon mæg hatan buton lease soþe sunne.*)

20 § ii[c]. [*Ða s*]e Wisdom þa þis leoð asungen hæfde, ða
geswugode he ane lytle hwile. Da cwæð ic: Sum tweo
me[8] hæfð swiðe gedrefed. Da cwæð he: Hwæt is se? Da
cwæð ic: Hit is ꝥ ꝥ ðu sægst ꝥ God selle ælcū men
freodom swa good to donne swa yfel, swæðer he wille; 7 þu
25 sægst (*eac*) ꝥ (*God*) wite ælc þing ær[9] hit geweorðe; 7 þu
sægst eac ꝥ nan þing ne geweorðe bute hit God wille oððe
geðafie; 7 þu sægst *ꝥ h[*it s*]cyle eall faran swa he getiohhod * 124a C.
hæbbe. Nu wundrie ic þæs hwy he geþafige ꝥ þa yflan men
hæbben þone freodom ꝥ hi mægen d[*on swa g*]od swa yfel,
30 swæðer swa hi will[*an, þoñ*] he ær wat ꝥ hi yfel don willað.

[b] Boeth. v. met. 2. 'Puro clarum lumine Phoebum,' &c. Cott. Metr. xxx.
[c] Boeth. v. pr. 3. 'Tum ego, En, inquam,' &c.

[1] From B, *willa* C.   [2] *awendað* B.   [3] *geþanc* B.   [4] *toscæt* B.
[5] em. *firgies* B.   [6] em. *ælmiht* B.   [7] em. *hi* B.   [8] B has *tima*
for *tweo me*.   [9] *ærer* B.

Đa cwæð he : Ic þe mæg swiðe eaðe geandwyrdan þæs
spelles.   Hu wolde þe nu lician[1] gif hwilc swiðe [*rice
cyni*]ng wære 7 næfde nænne freon[*e mon*] on eallū his rice,
ac wæren eall[*e þ*]iowe ?   Đa cwæð ic : Ne þuhte me [*hit*][2]
no[3] [*r*]ihtlic, ne eac nauht[4] gerisenlic, gif him sceolden 5
þiowe men þenian.   Đa cwæð he : þ[5] wære uncynlicre[6],
gif God næfde on eallum his rice nane frige gesceaft[7] under
his anwalde.   Forðæm he gesceop twa gesceadwisa[8] gesceafta freo, englas 7 men ; þæ he geaf micle gife freodomes,
þ hi mosten don swa god swa yfel, swæðer[9] swa hi wolden. 10
He sealde swiðe fæste gife 7 swiðe fæste æ mid ðære gife
ælcum men oð[10] his ende ; ðæt is se freodom ðæt se[11] mon
mot don þ he wile, 7 þ is sio æ þ he[12] gilt ælcū be his gewyrhtum ægðer ge on þisse worulde ge on þære toweardan swa
good swa yfel, *swæðer he deð.   7 men magon be[*gitan*] 15
þurh þone freodom swa hwæt swa hi willað, *buton* deað hi ne
magon forcerran ; [*æc hi hine*] magon mid goodū weorcum
[*gelettan,*]þ he þe[13] lator cymð ; ge fur[*þū*] oð oreldo hi hine
hwilū gelettað[14].   Gif men[15] to goodum weorce ne onhagie,
hæbbe[16] goodne willan ; þ is emngood[17].   Đ[*a cwæð ic :*] 20
Wel ðu me [*hæfst aretne on þā l*]weon, 7 on þære gedrefednesse [*þe ic*] ær (*on*) wæs be ðæm freodome.   [*Ac ic eom*]
nu giet on micle maran gedrefednesse geunrotsod, fulneah
oð ormodnesse.   Đa cwæð he : [18]Hwæt is sio micle unrotnes[18] ?   Đa cwæð ic : Hit is ym ða Godes foretiohhunge ; 25
forðæm we geherað hwilum secgan þ hit scyle eall swa
geweorðan swa swa God æt fruman getiohhad hæfde, þ hit
ne mæge nan mon onwendan[19].   Nu ðincð me þ he do woh[20],
þonne he arað þa goodan, 7 eac þonne he[21] witnað þa
yflan, gif þ soð is þ (*hit*) him swa gesceapen wæs þ hi ne 30
mosten elle[*s*] don.   Unnytlice we swincað þonne we us

---

[1] *he nu locian* B.   [2] *hit me* B.   [3] *nauht* B.   [4] *nauht* om. B.
[5] *Hwæt* B.   [6] *ungecyndlicre* B.   [7] *sceaft* B.   [8] *gescedwisan* B.
[9] *swæðer* om. B.   [10] *on* B.   [11] *ðe* B.   [12] *he* om. B.   [13] *þi* B.   [14] *lettað* B.
[15] *mon* B.   [16] *habbe* B.   [17] *emn* om. B.   [18] *Hwæt . . . unrotnes*
om. B.   [19] *awendan* B.   ·   [20] The *h* of *woh* written over *n* C.
[21] From B, *he hit* C.

gebiddað, 7 ðonne we fæstað, *oððe ælmessan sellað, gif we his   * 125a C.
nabbað ðy maran þanc þe þa þe on eallum þingum wadað on
hiora (*agenne willan, 7 æfter hiora*) lichoman luste irnað.

§ iii [d]. Ða cwæð he : Þis is sio ealde siofung þe þu longe
5 siofodes, 7 manige eac ær ðe ; þara wæs sum Marcus, oðre
naman Tullius, þriddan naman he was gehaten Cicero ; se [1]
wæs Romana heretoga ; se wæs uðwita. Se wæs swiðe abisgod
mid þære ilcan spræce, ac he hi ne meahte brengan to
nanum ende.   [2] Forðy he ne meahte, ne nan mon on þone
10 timan, þa spræce to nanum ende bringan [2], forðy hiora mod [3]
wæs abisgod on ðisse weorulde wilnunga.   Ac ic þe secge,
gif þ soð is þ ge [4] secgað, þ hit wæs unnet gebod on godcundum bocum þ God bebead [5] þ mon sceolde forlætan yfel
7 don good ; 7 eft se cwide þe he cwæð: swa mon ma
15 swincð, swa mon [6] maran mede onfehð.   7 ic wundrige hwy
þu hæbbe forgiten eall þ þ wit ær spræcon.   Ða cwæð ic [7] :
[8] Hwæt hæbbe ic forgiten þæs þe wit ær spræcon ?   Ða
cwð *he [8]: Wit sædon ær þ sio godcunde f[o]retiohhung ælc   * 125b C.
gód worhte 7 nan yfel, (*ne nan*) ne tiohhode to wyrcanne,
20 ne næfre ne worhte.   Ge furðum þ wi[t] gereahton to
goodum [9] þæt folciscū monnū yfel þuhte ; þ wæs þ mon
wræce 7 witnode hwone for his yfle.   Hu ne sædon [10] wit eac
ær [11] on þisse ilcan bec þ God hæfde getiohhod freodom to sellanne monnum, 7 swa dyde ; 7 gif hi [12] þone freodom tela ge-
25 healdon [13], þ he hi wolde swiðe weorðian mid ece life [14] ; 7
gif hi [15] ðone freodom forheolden, þ he hi þonne wolde witnian
mid deaðe.   He tiohhode, gif hi hwæt gesyngoden on ðæm
freodome, þ hi hit eft on ðæm freodome mid hreowsunga
gebeten ; 7 gif hiora hwylc swa heardheort wære þ he nane
30 hreowsunge ne dyde, þ he þonne hæfde rihtlic wite.   Ealla
gesceafta he hæfde getiohhod þeowu [16], buton englum 7

[d] Boeth. v. pr. 4.   'Tum illa, Vetus, inquit,' &c.

[1] *þe* B.   [2] For *forþy . . . bringan* B has only *on þone timan.*   [3] From
B, *med* C.   [4] *ge* om. B.   [5] *bead* B   [6] *mon* om. B.   [7] *he* B.   [8] *Hwæt . . .
he* om. B.   [9] *gode* B.   [10] *sæde* B.   [11] *ær* om. B.   [12] From B,
he C.   [13] From B, *to lange heoldon* C.   [14] *rice* B.   [15] *hi* om. B.
[16] *þeowe* B.

monnum. Forðyþe þa oðra gesceafta þeowe sint, hi healdað[1] hiora þegnunga oð domes dæg; ac þa men 7 þa englas, þe freo[2] sint, forlætað hiora þegnunga. *Hwæt magon men cweðan þ sio godcunde foretiohhung getiohhod hæfde þæs ðe hio ne þurhtuge ? oððe hu magon hi hi aladian þ hi[5] ne mægen good don, nu hit awriten is þ God gelde ælcum men be[3] his gewyrhtum ? Hwy sceall þonne ænig mon bion idel, ðæt he ne wyrce ? Ða cwæð ic : Genoh þu me hæfst gefreolsod þære tweounge mines modes be þære ascunga þe ic þe ahsade[4]. Ac ic þe wolde giet acsian sumre[5] spræce[10] ðe me ymbe tweoð. Ða cwæð he : Hwæt is þæt ? Ða cwæð ic : Genog cuð me is[6] þ God hit wat eall beforan, ge good ge yfel, ær hit geweorðe[7]; ac ic nat hwæðer hit eall geweorðan sceal unanwendendlice[8] þ he wat 7 getiohhod hæfð. Ða cwæð he : (*Ne*) ðearf hit no eall geweorðan unanwen-[15] dendlice[8]; ac sum hit sceal geweorðan[9] unanwendendlice[8]; þ bið þte ure nedþearf bið, 7 his willa bið. Ac hit is sum swa gerad þ his nis nan nedþearf, 7 þeah ne dereð no þeah hit geweorðe; ne nan hearm ne bið, þeah (*hit*) no (*ne*) geweorðe. Geþenc nu be ðe selfū hwæðer þu ænig þing[20] swa fæst[10] getiohhod hæbbe *þæt þe þince þ hit næfre þinū willū onwend ne weorðe[11], ne þu butan bion ne mæge; oððe hwæðer þu eft on ængum geþeahte swa twioræde sie þ þe helpe hwæðer hit geweorðe, ðe hit no ne geweorðe. Fela is þara þinga þe God ær wat[12] ær hit geweorðe, 7 wat[25] eac þ hit dereð his gesceaftum gif hit gewyrð. Nat he hit no forðyþe he wille þ hit geweorðe, ac forðy[13] þe he wile forwernan þ hit ne[14] geweorðe, swa swa good scipstiora ongit micelne wind on hreore sæ[15] ær ær hit geweorðe[16], 7 hæt fealdan þ segl 7 eac hwilum lecgan þone mæst, 7 lætan þa[30] bætinge; gif he ær þweores windes[17] bætte, warenað[18] (*he hine*) wið ðæt weder.

---

[1] *habbað* B.   [2] *frige* B.   [3] *æfter* B.   [4] *acsode* B.   [5] *sume* B.
[6] *me is cuð* B.   [7] *gewyrðe* B.   [8] *unawendendlice* B.   [9] *wyrþan* B.
[10] *fæste* B.   [11] *onwended weorðe* B.   [12] *ær wat* om. B, but space left instead.   [13] *forþe* B.   [14] *ne* om. B.   [15] For *on hreore sæ* B has 7 *hreose.*   [16] *wiorðe* B.   [17] *winde* B.   [18] *warnað* B.

§ iv [e]. Đa cwæð ic : Swiðe wel þu min hæfst geholpen æt
þære spræce, (7) ic wundrige hwy swa mænige wise men
swa swiðe swuncen[1] mid þære spræce, 7 swa lytel gewis
funden. Đa cwæð he : Hwæs wundrast þu þær swa swiðe,
swa eðe swa hit is to ongitanne? Hu ne wast þu þ manig
þing ne bið no ongiten swa swa hit bið, *ac swa swa þæs   * 127aC.
andgites mæð bið þe þæræft spyreð? Swilc[a] is se wisdom
þ hine[3] ne mæg nan mon of þisse weorulde ongitan swilcne
swylce he is ; ac ælc winð be his andgites mæðe þ he hine
wolde ongitan gif he meahte. Ac se wisdom mæg us eallunga
ongitan swylce swylce we sint, þeah we hine ne mægen
ongitan eallunga swylcne swylce he is; forðæm se wisdom
is God. He gesihð (*eall*) ure weorc ge good ge yfel, ær hi
gewordene[4] sien, oððe furðum geþoht; ac he us ne ned no
þy hraðor to þæm þ we nede scylen[5] good don, ne us ne
wernð þ we yfel don, forðæmþe he us sealde freodom. Ic
þe mæg eac tæcan sume bisne þ þu þe yð ongitan meah[te][6]
ða spræce. Hwæt[7], þu wast [*þæt gesihð*] 7 gehernes 7
gefrednes on[*gitað þo*]ne lichoman þæs monnes, [7 *þ*]eah ne
ongitað (*hi hine no gelicne ; þa earan ongitað*) þ hi gehe<ð,
(7) ne ongitað hi þeah þone lichoman eallunga swylcne[8]
swylce he bið; sio gefrednes hine mæg[9] gegrapian 7 gefredan
þæt hit lichoma bið, ac hio ne mæg gefredan hwæðer he bið
þe blæc[9] þe hwit, *ðc fæger ðe unfæger. Ac sio gesihð æt * 127b C.
frumcerre[10], swa þa eagan on besioð, hi ongitað ealle þone
andwlitan ðæs lichoman. Ac ic wolde get reccan *su*me race,
þ ðu wisse hwæs þu wundrode.

   § v [f]. Đa cwæð ic : Hwæt is þæt? Đa cwæð he : Hit is
þ se an man ongit þ þ he (*on*) oðrū ongit synderlice ; he hine
ongit þurh þa eagan synderlice[11], þurh þa earan synderlice,
þurh his rædelsan synderlice, þurh gesceadwisnesse synderlice, þurh gewis and[*g*]it. Manige sint cwucera gesceafta

[e] Boeth. v. pr. 4. l. 69 P. ‘Cuius erroris causa est,’ &c.
[f] Boeth. v. remainder of pr. 4 and whole of 5.   ·

[1] *geswuncen* B.   [2] *hwilc* B.   [3] *þ hine* om. B.   [4] *geworden* B.
[5] *scylen* om. B.   [6] From J, B *miht*.   [7] *þ* B.   [8] *swylcne . . .
mæg* omit B.   [9] *blac* B.   [10] *fruman cerre* B.   [11] *synderlč* C.

unstirende, swa swa nu scylfiscas [1] sint, 7 habbað þeah sumne
dæl andgites, forðæm hi ne meahton elles libban, gif hi nan
grot andgites næf[*d*]en.   Sume magon gesion, sume [*magon*]
geheran, sume gefredan, sume [*g*]estincan [2].   Ac þa [3]
styriendan neten[*u s*]int monnū gelicran, forðæm [*hy*] 5
habbað eall þ ða unstyriendan ha*bb*að, 7 eac mare to; þ is
þ hi onhyriað [4] monnū; lufiað þ hi lufiað 7 hatiað þ hi hatiað,
7 flioð þ hi hatiað 7 secað þ hi lufiað.   Ða men ðonne habbað

* 127b C ends; next folio missing.

eall þ we ær ymbe* [*spræcon, 7 eac to eacan þā micle gife
gesceadwisnesse.   Englas þōn habbað gewiss andgit.   For-* 10
þam sint ðas sceafta [5] *þus gesceapene þ ða unstyriendan hi ne
ahebben ofer þa styriendan, ne him wið ne winnan, ne þa
styriendan ofer þa men, ne þa men ofer þa englas, ne þa englas
wið God.   Ac þæt is earmlic þ se mæsta dæl monna ne secð no
þ þ him forgifen is, þ is gesceadwisness; ne þ ne secð* [6] *þæt him* 15
*ofer is, þ is þæt englas habbað 7 wise men; þ is gewis andget.
Ac mest monna nu* [7] *onhyreð* [8] *nu neatū on þā þæt hi willniað
woruldlusta swa swa netenu.   Ac gif we nu hæfdon ænigne
dæl untwiogendes andgites swa swa englas habbað, þōn mihte
we ongiton þ þ andget bið micle betere þōn ure gesceadwisnes se* [9]. 20
Þeah we fela smean [10], *we habbað litellne gearowitan buton
tweon; ac þā englum nis nan tweo nanes þæra þinga þe hi
witon; forþi is hiora gearowito swa micle betra þōn ure
gesceadwisnes se, swa ure gesceadwisnes* [11] *is betere þōn nytena* [12]
andgit sie, oððe þæs gewiltes ænig dæl þe him forgifen is auþer 25
oððe hrorum neatū oððe unhrorum [13]. *Ac uton nu habban ure
mod up swa swa we yfemest mægen wið þæs hean hrofes þæs
hehstan andgites, þ ðu mæge hrædlicost cumon 7 eðelicost to
þinre agenre cyððe þonan þe ðu ær come.   Þær mæg þin
mod 7 þin gesceadwisnes geseon* [14] *openlice þ þ hit nu ymb tweoð* 30
*ælces þinges, ægþer ge be þære godcundan foresceawunge þe we
nu oft ymb spræcon, ge be urum frydome* [15], *ge swa be eallū þingū.*

---

[1] *fiscas* B.   [2] For *gestincan* B has *ge* foll. by space.   [3] *þa* om. B.
[4] *hyrigað* B.   [5] *gesceafta* J.   [6] *secað* J.   [7] *nu* from J, om. B.
[8] From J, *onstyræð* B.   [9] *gesceadwisnes sie* J.   [10] *smeagen* J.
[11] em. *gesceadwisnesse* B.   [12] *netan* J.   [13] em. *unrorum* B.
[14] em. *gesceon* B.   [15] *freodome* J.

§ vi [fa]. *Đa se Wisdom þa þis spell asæd hæfde, þa ongan he singan 7 þus cwæð:]* (*Hwæt, þu miht ongitan þ manig wyht is mistlice ferende geond[1] eorþan, 7 sint swiðe ungelices hiwes, 7 ungelice fara ð. Sume licgað mid eallon lichoman on* 5 *eorþan, 7 swa smuhende[2] faraðþ him nauþer ne fêt ne fiðeras ne fultumað; 7 sume bið twiofete, sume fiowerfete, sume fleogende, 7 ealle þeah bioð ofdune healde wið þære eorðan, 7 þider willniað, oððe þæs þe hi lyst oððe þæs þe hi beþurfon. Ac se mann ana gæþ uprihte; þ tacnað þ he sceal ma þencan* 10 *úp þôn nyðer, þi læs þ mod sie nioðoror þôn ðe lichoma.*) Đa se Wisdom ða[3] ðis leoð asungen hæfde, ða cwæð he:

XLII [G].

Forðy we scoldon ealle mægene[4] spyrian æfter Gode, þ we wissen hwæt he wære. Đeah hit ure mæð ne sie þ we witen hwylc[5] he sie, we sculon þeah be þæs andgites mæðe 15 þe he us gifð fandian[6]; swa swa we ær cwædon þ mon scolde ælc þing ongitan be his andgites mæþe, forðæm we ne magon ælc þing ongitan swylc swylce hit bið. Ælc gesceaft ðeah ægðer ge gesceadwis ge ungesceadwis þ sweotolað þ God ece is, forðæm næfre swa *manega   * 128b C. 20 gesceafta 7 swa micla 7 sw[a][7] fægra hi ne underðiodden læssan g[e]sceafte 7 læssan [an]walde þonne (*hi*) ea[lle] sindon, ne furðum emnmiclum. Đa cwæð ic: Hwæt is ecnes? Đa cwæð he: Þu me ahsast micles (7) earfoðes to ongitanne; gif þu hit witan[8] wilt, ðu scealt habban ær þines 25 modes eagan c/æne 7 hlutor[9]. Ne mæg ic ðe nauht helan ·ðæs ðe ic wat. Wast þu þ þreo ðing sindon on þis mid- dangearde? An is hwilendlic, ðæt hæfð[10] ægðer ge fruman ge ende; 7 (*ic*) nat ðeah nanwuht ðæs ðe hwilendlic is, nauðer ne his fruman ne his ende. Oðer ðing is ece, þ hæfð

---

[a] Boeth. v. met. 5. 'Quam uariis terras,' &c. Cott. Metr. xxxi.
[G] Boeth. v. pr. 6. '.Quoniam igitur,' &c.

[1] em. *geon* B.   [2] orig. *snicende, c* erased, *ni* turned into *m,* and *uh* written ab. l.   [3] *ða* om. B.   [4] *eallon mægne* B.   [5] *hwylc* om. B. [6] *fundigan* B.   [7] Conject. B has *swægra* for *swa fægra.*   [8] *ongitan* B. [9] *hlutre* B.   [10] *þæs ðe* for *ðæt hæfð* B.

fruman 7 næfð nænne ende; 7 (*ic*) wat hwonne hit onginð, 7 wat ꝥ hit næfre ne geendað; ꝥ sint englas 7 monna saula. Þridde ðing is ece buton ende 7 buton anginne; ꝥ is God. Betweoh þæm þrim is swiðe micel toscead.   Gif wit ꝥ eall sculon tosmeagan[1], þonne cume wit late to ende þisse bec, 5 oððe næfre.   Ac an þing ðu scealt nede þæran[2] witan: forhwy God is gehaten sio hehste ecnes.   Ða cwæð ic: *129a C. Hwy? Ða cwæð he: *Forðon þe[3] we witon swiðe lytel ðæs þe ær us wæs buton be gemynde 7 be geæscum[4], 7 get læsse þæs ðe æft us bið. ꝥ an us is[5] gewislice andweard 10 ꝥ þe[6] þonne bið; ac him is eall andweard, ge ꝥte ær wæs, ge ꝥte nu is, ge ꝥte æfter us bið; eall ꝥ[7] is him andweard. Ne wexð[8] his wela na, ne eac næfre ne wanað. Ne ofman he næfre nane wuht, forðæm he[9] næfre nauht ne[10] forgeat. Ne secð he nanwuht, ne ne smeað, forðæmþe he hit wat eall. 15 Ne secð he nanwuht, forðy[11] he nanwuht ne forleas. Ne eht[12] he nanre wuhte, forðy hine nanwuht ne mæg flion; ne ondræt he him[13] nane wuht, forðæm he næfð nænne ricran ne furðum nænne gelican. Simle he bið gifende, 7 ne wanað his næfre nauht. Symle he bið ælmihtig, forðæm he 20 symle wile good 7 næfre nan yfel. Nis him nanes þinges nedþearf. Sýle he bið lociende, ne slæpð he næfre. Sýle he bið *129b C. gelice manþwære. Sýle he bið ece, *forþæm næfre sio tid næs ꝥ he nære, *ne* næfre ne wyrð. Simle he *bið* freoh, ne bið he to nanum weorce geneded. For his godcundlicum 25 anwalde he is æghwær andweard. His miceln*esse* ne mæg nan man ametan; nis ꝥ ðeah no licūlice[14] to wenanne, ac gastlice, swa swa nu wisdom is 7 rihtwisnes, forðæm he ꝥ is self. Ac hwæt ofermodie ge þonne, oððe hwy ahebbe ge eow wið swa heane anwald? *forðæm* ge[15] nauht wið 30 hine don ne magon; forðæm se eca 7 se ælmehtga sýle sit on þæ heahsetle his anwaldes; þonan he mæg eall gesion, 7 gilt ælcū (*be þam*) swiðe[16] rihte æft his gewyrhtū. Forðæ

---

[1] *asmeagan* B.   [2] *þær ær* B.   [3] *þe* om. B.   [4] *geascunge* B.
[5] *is* om. B.   [6] *te* B.   [7] *hit* B.   [8] From B, *sceaxð* C.   [9] *he* om. B.
[10] *he ne* B.   [11] *forþā* B.   [12] *eft* B, with *s* above line after *f*.
[13] *him* om. B.   [14] *lichomlice* B.   [15] *ðe hi* B.   [16] *swiðe* om. B.

hit nis no unnet þ we hopien to *Gode*, forðæ he ne went [1]
no swa swa we doð.   Ac biddað [2] hine eadmodlice, forðæm
he is swiðe rūmod 7 *swiðe* mildheort. ̄ Hebbað eower mod
to him mid eowrū hondū, 7 biddað þæs þe riht sie 7 eower
5 þearf sie, forðæm he eow nele wyr[*nan*].   Hatiað yfel
7 fleoð swa ge swiðost m[*æ*]gen [3]; lufiað cræftas, 7 folgiað
þæ.   Ge habbað micle nedðearfe [4] þ ge sȳle wel do*n*,
forðæm ge sȳle beforan þā *ecan* 7 þæm ælmihtgan [5] Gode doð
eall þ þ ge doð ; *eall he hit* [*gesihð, 7 eall he*] hit forgilt.
10 FINIT [6].

DRIHTEN ælmihtiga God, wyrhta 7 wealdend ealra
gesceafta, ic bidde þe for þinre micelan mildheortnesse [7] *7 for·*
þære halegan rode tacne, 7 for Scā Marian mægðhade, 7
for Scē Michaeles gehyrsūnesse, 7 for ealra þinra halgana
15 *lufan 7 heora earnungū, þ þu me gewissige bet þonne ic*
awyrhte to þe ; 7 gewissa me to þinū willan 7 to minre [8] *sawle*
þearfe bet þonne ic sylf cunne ; 7 gestaþela min mod to þinū
willan 7 to minre sawle þearfe ; 7 gestranga me wið þæs
deofles costnungū ; 7 afyrra frā me þa fulan galnysse 7 ælce
20 *unrihtwisnysse ; 7 gescylde me wið minū wiðerwinnū gese-*
wenlicū 7 ungesewenlicū ; 7 tæc me þinne willan to wyrcenne,
þ ic mæge þe inweardlice lufian toforon eallū þingum mid
clænū geþance 7 mid clænū lichaman ; forþon [9] *þe þu eart*
min sceoppend, 7 min alesend, min fultū, min frofer, min
25 *trewnes, 7 min tohopa ; si þe lof 7 wylder nu 7 a a a to*
worulde buton æghwilcū ende.   Amen [a].

    [a] This prayer is only in B.   See Introduction.

[1] *welt* B.   [2] *abiddað* B.   [3] Conject. *magon* B.   [4] *þearfe* B.
[5] em. *ælmihgan* C, *ælmehtigan* B.   [6] *Amen Finit* B.   [7] em. *mild-*
heortnessan B.   [8] em. *mire* B.   [9] em. *foþon* B.

NOTE (i) After *ða cwæð he* : p. 137, l. 23, read : *eall bið good þte nyt*
bið. Ða cwæð ic : þ is soð. Ða cwæð he : This passage om. B.
(ii) Before *wæter* : p. 80, l. 24, read : *þæt.*

THE OLD ENGLISH VERSION OF THE LAYS OF BOETHIUS

PROEM[1]

ÐUS Ælfred us ealdspell reahte,
cyning Westsexna, cræft meldode,
leoðwyrhta list. him wæs lust micel
ðæt he ðiossum leodum leoð spellode,
monnum myrgen, mislice cwidas, 5
þy læs ælinge ut adrife
selflicne secg, þonne he swelces lyt
gymð for his gilpe. ic sceal giet sprecan,
fón on fitte, folccuðne ræd
hæleðum secgean ; hliste se þe wille. 10

METRA

I[a].

Hit wæs geara iu ðætte Gotan eastan
of Sciððia sceldas læddon,
þreate geþrungon þeodlond monig.
setton suðweardes sigeþeoda twa ;
Gotene rice gearmælum weox. 5
hæfdan him gecynde cyningas twegen,
Rædgod 7 Aleric ; rice geþungon.
Þa wæs ofer Muntgiop monig atyhted
Gota gylpes full, guðe gelysted
folcgewinnes. fana hwearfode 10

ᵃ Cf. p. 7.   ¹ The proem and first four metra are from J.

scir on sceafte; sceolend þohton
Italia ealle[1] gegongan,
lindwigende; hi gelæstan swua
efne from Muntgiop oð þone mæran wearoð
þær Sicilia sæstreamum in   15
eglond micel eðel mærsað.
ða wæs Romana rice gewunnen,
abrocen burga cyst. beadurincum wæs
Rom gerymed. Rædgot 7 Aleric
foron on ðæt fæsten. fleah casere   20
mid þam æþelingum ut on Crecas.
ne meahte þa seo wealaf wige forstandan
Gotan mid guðe. giomonna gestrion
sealdon unwillum eþelweardas,
halige aðas; wæs gehwæðeres waa.   25
þeah wæs magorinca mod mid Crecum,
gif hi leodfruman læstan dorsten.
stod þrage on ðam; þeod wæs gewunnen
wintra mænigo, oðþæt wyrd gescraf
þ þe Þeodrice þegnas 7 eorlas   30
heran sceoldan. wæs se heretema
Criste gecnoden; cyning selfa   ,
onfeng fulluhtþeawum. fægnodon ealle
Romwara bearn, 7 him recene to
friðes wilnedon. he him fæste gehet   35
þ hy ealdrihta ælces mosten
wyrðe gewunigen on þære welegan byrig
ðenden God wuolde þæt he Gotena[2] geweald
agan moste. he þ eall aleag;
wæs þæm æþelinge Arrianes   40
gedwola leofre þonne Drihtnes æ.   ,
het Iohannes godne papan
heafde beheawon; næs ðæt hærlic dæd.
eac þam wæs unrim oðres manes
þ se Gota fremede godra gehwilcum.   •   45

[1] em. *ealla* J.   [2] em. *Godena* J.

ða wæs ricra sum on Rome byrig
ahefen heretoga, hlaforde leof,
þenden cynestole Creacas wioldon.
þæt wæs rihtwis rinc; wæs mid Romwarum
sincgeofa sella, siððan longe.   50
he wæs for weorulde wis, weorðmynða georn,
beorn boca gleaw. Boitius
se hæle hatte; se þone hlisan geþah.
wæs him on gemynde mæla gehwilce
yfel 7 edwit þ him elðeodge   55
kyningas cyðdon. wæs on Creacas hold;
gemunde þara ara 7 ealdrihta
þe his eldran mid him ahton longe,
lufan 7 lissa. angan þa listum ymbe
ðencean þearflice, hu he ðider meahte   60
Crecas oncerran, þæt se casere eft
anwald ofer hi agan moste.
sende ærendgewrit ealdhlafordum
degelice, 7 hi for Drihtne bæd,
ealdum treowum, ðæt hi æft to him   65
comen on þa ceastre, lete Creca witan
rædan Romwarum, rihtes wyrðe
lete þone leodscipe. ða þa lare ongeat
Ðeodric Amuling, 7 þone þegn oferfeng,
heht fæstlice folcgesiðas   70
healdon þone hererinc. wæs him hreoh sefa,
ege from ðam eorle. he hine inne heht
on carcerne cluster belucan.
þa wæs modsefa miclum gedrefed
Boetius. breac longe ær   75
wlencea under wolcnum; he þy wyrs meahte
þolian þa þrage, þa hio swa þearl becom.
wæs þa ormod eorl, are ne wende,
ne on þam fæstene frofre gemunde;
ac he neowol astreaht niðer ofdune   80
feol on þa flore. fela worda spræc,

forþoht ðearle ; ne wende þonan æfre
cuman of ðæm clammum. cleopode to Drihtne
geomran stemne, gyddode þus.

II ᵇ.

Boeth. i. met. 1.   'Carmina qui quondam studio florente peregi.'

Hwæt, ic lioða fela lustlice geo
sanc on sælum.   nu sceal siofigende,
wope gewæged, wrecca giomor,
singan sarcwidas.   me þios siccetung hafað
agæled, ðes geocsa, þ ic þa ged ne mæg   5
gefegean swa fægre, þeah ic fela gio þa
sette soðcwida, þonne ic on sælum wæs.
oft ic nu miscyrre cuðe spræce,
7 þeah uncuðre ær hwilum fond.
me þas woruldsælða welhwæs blindne   10
on ðis dimme hol dysine forlæddon,
7 me þa berypton rædes 7 frofre
for heora untreowum, þe ic him æfre betst
truwian sceolde.   hi me to wendon
heora bacu bitere, 7 heora blisse from.   15
forhwam wolde ge, weoruldfrynd mine,
secgan oððe singan þ ic gesællic mon
wære on weorulde? ne synt þa word soð,
nu þa gesælða ne magon simle gewunigan.

III ᶜ.

Boeth. i. met. 2.   'Heu quam praecipiti mersa profundo.'

Æala, on hu grimmum 7 hu grundleasum
seaðe swinceð þæt sweorcende mod,
þonne hit þa strongan stormas beatað
weoruldbisgunga.   þonne hit winnende
his agen leoht anforlæteð,   5
7 mid uua forgit þone ecan gefean,

ᵇ Cf. p. 8.   ᶜ Cf. p. 9.

ðringð on þa ðiostro ðisse worulde,
sorgum geswenced. swa is þissum nu
mode gelumpen ; nu hit mare ne wat
for Gode godes buton gnornunge
fremdre worulde. him is frofre ðearf.

IV d.

Boeth. i. met. 5. 'O stelliferi conditor orbis.'

Æala, ðu scippend scirra tungla,
hefones 7 eorðan ; ðu on heahsetle
ecum ricsast, 7 ðu ealne hræðe
hefon ymbhwearfest, 7 ðurh ðine halige miht
tunglu genedest þ hi ðe to herað.
swylce seo sunne sweartra nihta
ðiostro adwæsceð, þurh ðine meht,
blacum leohte, beorhte steorran
mona gemetgað ; ðurh ðinra meahta sped
hwilum eac þa sunnan sines bereafað
beorhtan leohtes, þonne hit gebyrigan mæg
þæt swa geneahsne nede weorðað.
swelce þone mæran morgensteorran
þe we oðre naman æfensteorra
nemnan hera ð, ðu genedest þone
þ he þære sunnan sið bewitige ;
geara gehwelce he gongan sceal,
beforan feran. hwæt ðu, fæder, wercest
sumurlange dagas swiðe hate ;
þæm winterdagum wundrum sceorta
tida getiohhast. ðu þæm treowum selest
suðan 7 westan, þa ær se swearta storm
norðan 7 eastan benumen hæfde
leafa gehwelces ðurh þone laðran wind.
eala hwæt, on eorðan ealla gesceafta
hyrað ðinre hæse ; doð on heofonum swa some
mode- 7 mægne, butan men anum ;

ᵈ Cf. p. 10.

se wið ðinum willan wyrceð oftost.
wella, ðu eca 7 þu ælmihtiga
ealra gesceafta sceppend 7 reccend; 30
ara ðinum earmum eorðan tudre,
monna cynne, ðurh ðinra mehta sped.
hwi ðu ece God æfre wolde
þ sio wyrd on gewill wendan sceolde
yflum monnum ealles swa swiðe? 35
hio ful oft dereð unscyldegum.
sittað yfele men giond eorðricu
on heahsetlum, halige þriccað
under heora fotum. firum uncuð
hwi sio wyrd swa wô wendan sceolde. 40
swa sint gehydde her on worulde
geond burga fela beorhte cræftas.
unrihtwise eallum tidum
habbað on hospe ða þe him sindon
rihtes wisran, rices wyrðran. 45
bið þ lease lot lange hwile
bewrigen mid wrencum. nu on worulde her
monnum ne deriað máne aðas.
gif ðu nu, waldend, ne wilt wirde steoran,
ac on selfwille sigan lætest, 50
þonne ic wat þte wile woruldmen tweogan
geond foldan sceat, buton fea ane.
eala, min Dryhten, ðu þe ealle ofersihst
worulde gesceafta, wlit nu on moncyn
mildum eagum, nu hi on monegum her 55
worulde yðum wynnað 7 swincað,
earme eorðwaran; ara him nu ða.

V e.

Boeth. i. met. 7. 'Nubibus atris.'

*Ðu meaht be ðære sunnan sweotole geþencean,
7 be æghwelcum oðrum steorran

• Cf. p. 14.

þara þe æfter burgum beort*ost* scin*eð;*
gif him wan fore ·wolcen hangað,
ne mægen hi swa leoh*tne* leoman ansendan   5
ær se þicca mist þynra weorðe.
swa oft smylte sæ suðerne wind,
græge glashlutre, grimme gedrefeð,
þonne hie gemengað micla[1] ysta,
onhrerað hronmere; hrioh bið þonne   10
seo þe ær gladu onsiene wæs.
swa oft æspringe ut awealleð
of clife harū col 7 hlutor,
7 gereclice rihte floweð;
irneð wið his eardes, oð hī oninnan *[felð   15   * 3b C.
muntes mægenstan, 7 him on]* midda[*n gelig*]eð,'
atrendlod[2] of ðæm [*torre. he on*] tu siððan
tosceaden wyrð; scir bið gedrefed
burna geblonden; broc bið onwended
of his rihtryne, ryðum toflowen.   20
swa nu þa þiostro þinre *h*eortan
willað minre leohtan lare *wið*stondan,
7 ðin *m*odgeþonc miclū *g*edrefan.
ac gif ðu nu wilnast, þ ðu wel mæge,
þæt soðe *leoht sweot*ole oncnawan,   25
leohte gel[*eafan, þ*]u forlætan scealt
idle ofers*ælða,* unnytne gefe*an.*
þu scealt eac yfelne ege anforl*ætan*
woruldearfoða. ne most ðu wesan for þæm
ealles to ormod, ne ðu ðe æfre ne læt   30
wlenca *g*ewæcan, þe læs þu weorðe for him
mid o*f*ermettū eft ge*f*cended,
7 to upahaf*en* for orsor*gum*
woruldgesælðum. ne eft to waclice
geortreowe æniges godes,   35
þonne þe for worulde wiðerweardra[3] mæsð
þinga þreage, 7 þ[*u*] ðe selfum

---

[1] *mila* C.   [2] *atrendlod* C.   [3] em. *wiðerwearda* C.

swiðost onsitte. forðæm simle bið
se modsefa miclum gebunden
mid gedrefnesse, gif hine dreccean mot   40
þissa yfla hwæðer, innan swencan.
forðæm þa twegen tregan teoð tosomne*
[*wið þ mod for*]an mis[*tes*] dwolema[*n,*
þ hit seo ece ne mot] innan geondscinan
[*sunne for ðam sw*]eartum mistum, ær ðæ[*m hi ge-*]
       swiðrad weorðen.

* 4a C.

VI ͟f.

Boeth. ii. met. 3. ‘ Cum polo Phoebus roseis quadrigis.’

Ða se Wisdom eft *wordhord onleac,*
sang soðcwidas, 7 þus *selfa cwæð:*
ðonne sio sunne sweotolost *scineð,*
hadrost *of* hefone, *hræðe* bioð *aðistrod*
ealle ofir [*eorþan oðre steorra*]n ;   5
forðæm hiora b[*irhtu ne bið*] *auht*
to gesettane wið þære *sunnan* leoht.
ðonne smolte blæwð suðan 7 westan
wind under wolcnum, þon[*ne weax*]að[1] hraðe
feldes blostma[*n, fægen þ*] hi moton.   10
ac se stearca sto[*rm, þonne h*]e strong cymð
norðan 7 eas[*tan, he*] genimeð hraðe
þære rosan wlite ; 7 eac þa ruman sæ
norþerne yst [*nede gebæ*]deð[2]
þ hio *strange geondstyred* [*on staðu*] beateð.*   15
eala þ on eorðan auht [*fæstlices*
weorces on] *worulde ne wunað æfre.*

* 10a C.

VII ͟g.

Boeth. ii. met. 4. ‘ Quisquis uolet perennem.’

[*Ða ongon se Wisdom his gewunan*] fylgan ;
gliowordum gol, gyd *æf l*[3] spelle.
song soðcw[*id*]a sumne þa geta ;

[1] Cf. p. 21. [8] Cf. p. 26. [1] em. *weaxeð* J. [2] em. *-ded* C. [3] em. *æsl* J.

cwæð þæt he ne herde þ on heane munt
monna ænig mea*hte* *a*settan   5
[*healle hroff*]æste. ne þ[*earf eac hæleða nan
wenan*] þæs [*weorces þ he wisdom mæge
wið*] oferme[*tta æfre gemengan.
herdes*] þu æfr[*e þte ænig mon
on sondbe*]org[*as settan meahte   10
fæste healle ?*] ne mæg eac fira *nan
wisdom timbran þær ðær woruldgitsung
beorg*] oferbrædeð. *baru sond* [*willað*]
ren forswelgan ; *sw*[*a*] deð [*ricra nu*]
grund*leas* gitsung gilpes [*7 æhta ;*   15
gedri*]nceð to dryg*gum* dreos[*endne welan,*]
7 þeah þæs þearfan *ne bið* [*þurst ace*]led.
ne mæg hæleþa geh[*wæm hus on*] munte
lange gelæsta[*n, forðæm*] him lungre on
swift [*wind swapeð.*] ne bið sond. þon m[*a*   20
wið micelne ren*] manna ængum,
h[*uses hirde ; ac hit hreo*]san wile,
sigan [*sond æfter rene. swa bioð anra gehwæs
monna modsefan miclum awegede**,
of hiora stede styrede, þonne hi*[1] *strong dreceð*   25
wind under wolcnum woruldea]rfoða,
oþþe hi[2] eft se reða ren onhrereð
[*su*]mes ymbhogan, ungemetgemen.
ac se ðe þa ecan agan wille
s[*oðan*] gesælða, h[*e sc*]eal swiðe fl[*ion*   30
þisse worulde wlite ; wy]rce him [*siðþan
his modes hus, þær he*] mæge [*findan
eaðmetta stan unigme*]t[3] fæst[*ne,
grundweal gearone ; se to*]glidan [*ne þearf,
þeah hit wecge wind*] woruld[*earfoþa*[4]   35
oððe ymbhogena orme]te [*ren ;
forþæm on þære dene Drihten selfa*

* 14b C
about here.

---

[1] em. *he* J.   [2] em. *hit* C.   [3] *unig metfæstne* J.
[4] From here to *lædað*(l. 40) C much damaged.

þara eadmetta eardfæst wunigað,
þær se wisdom â wunað on gemyndum.]
forðon *orsorg* lif [*ealnig læda*]ð   40
woruldmen *wise buton* [*wendinge;*]
þonne he eall forsihð [*eorðlicu goo*]d
7 eac *þara* yfela or[*sorh wunað,*]
hopað to þæm ecum [*þe þæræfter*] *cu*mað,
hine þonne [*æghwonan ælmi*]htig God [1]   45
*sing*allice [*simle gehealdeð*]
*an*wunigendne his [*agenum*
modes gesælþ]um, þurh me[*todes gife,*
þeah hine se] *wi*nd [*woruldearfoða*
swiðe swence, 7 *hine singale*   50
gemen gæle, þonne him *grimme on
woruldsælþa wind wraðe blaweð,]
þeah þe [*hine ealneg se ymbhoga ðyssa*]
woruldsælða wraðe [*d*]recce.

VIII [h].

Boeth. ii. met. 5.   'Felix nimium prior aetas.'

**Sona swa se Wisdom þas word hæfde*
swetole areahte, he þa siðþan ongan
singan [*s*]oðcwidas 7 þus selfa cwæð:
hwæt, [*sio*] forme eld foldbuendum
geond [*eorð*]an sceat æghwam dohte,   5
þa þa anra gehwæm on eorðwæstmum
genoh [*ðuh*]te; nis hit nu ða swelc.
næron þa [*geo*]nd weorulde welige hamas,
ne mis[*lice*] mettas ne dri*n*cas,
ne hi þara [*hræ*]gla huru ne gemdon   10
þe nu driht[*gum*]an diorost lætað;
forðæm hiora [*næn*]ig næs þa gieta,
ne hi ne gesawon [*sun*]dbuende,
ne ymbutan hi awer ne [*h*]erdon.
hwæt, hi *firen*lusta frece ne wæron,   15

[h] Cf. p. 33.   [1] em. *good* C.

buton swa hi meahton gemet[*li*]cost
ða gecynd began þe him Crist [*g*]esceop ;
7 hi æne on dæge æton sym[*le*]
on æfentid eorþan wæstmas,
[*wu*]des 7 wyrta ; nalles win druncon   20
scir [*of*] steape.   næ[*s*] þa s[*ce*]alca nan
þe mete [*o*]ððe drin[*c*] mængan cuðe,
wæter wið [*hu*]nige, ne h[*e*]ora wæda þon ma
sioloce siowian[1] ; ne hi siarocræftum
godweb giredon, ne hi gimreced   25
setto[*n searolice,*] ac hi simle him
eallū [*tidum*] ute slepon
under beamscead[*e.   drunc*]on burnan wæter,
calde wel[*lan*[2].   *nænig*]* cepa ne seah   * end of
*ofer earge*blond *ellend*ne *wearod,*   30   20b C.
ne huru ymbe sci*p*hergas *sætilcas* ne herdon,
ne furðum *fira* nan ymb ge*feoht* sprecan.
næs ðeos *eorðe. besmiten awer* þa geta
beornes *blode, þe hi ne billrude*
ne *furð*um *wundne wer weoruldbuende*   35
gesawan under *sunnan. nænig siððan wæs*
weorð on weorulde, gif mon his willan ongeat
yfelne mid eldum ; he wæs *æghwæm lað.*
eala þær hit wurde, *oððe wolde God,*
þæt on eorð*an nu ussa tida*   40
geond þas widan *weoruld wæren æghwæs*
swelce under sunnan. ac hit is sæmre nu
þ ðeos *gitsunc hafað gumena gehwelces*
mod amerred, þ *he maran ne recð,*
ac hit on witte weallende byrnð.   45
efne sio gitsung þe *nænne grund hafað*
swearte swæfeð sumes onlice
efne þam *munte* þe *nu monna bearn*
Etne hatað ; se on iglonde

---

[1] *siwian* C.   [2] So J, C apparently has *wyl-*.   Folio 21a is almost
illegible, the words being blurred.

<table>
<tr><td>* 21b C
about here.</td><td>

Sicilia swefte byrneð;
þæt mon helle fyr hateð wide,*
forþæm hit symle [*b*]ið sinbyrnen*de*,
7 ymbutan [*h*]it oðra stowa
blate forbærnð biteran lege.
eala, hwæt *se forma* feohgitsere
wære *on* w[*o*]rulde, se þas wongstedas
grof æfter golde 7 æfter gimcynnū?
hwæt, he *frecnu* gestreon fun*de* mænegum
bewrigen on weorulde, wætere oððe eorþan.

</td><td>50

55</td></tr>
</table>

IX[i].

Boeth. ii. met. 6.   'Nouimus quantas dederit ruinas.'

<table>
<tr><td>* 27a C.</td><td>

[Hwæt[1], *we ealle witon hwelce ærleste*
ge neah ge feor Neron worhte,
Romwara cyning, þa his rice wæs
hehst under heofonum, to hryre monegum.
wælhreowes gewed wæs ful wide cuↄ,
unrihthæmed, arleasta fela,
man 7 *morðor,*] *misdæda worn,*
unrihtwi*ses* [*inwidþoncas.*
he] het him to ga*mene* [*geara for*]bærnan
Ro[*mana burig; sio his*] rices wæs
ealles e*ð*elstol. *he for* unsnyttrum
wolde fandian gif ꝥ fyr meahte
lixan swa leohte, 7 *swa* longe *eac*
read rasettan, swæ he Rom*ane*
secgan geherde ꝥ on sume [*tide*
Troia] burg ofertogen hæfde
*lega le*ohtost, lengest bur*ne*
*hama un*der hefonum. næs þæt her*lic dæd*
ꝥ hine swelces gamenes gilpan lyste,
þa he ne earnade elles wuhte

</td><td>

5

10

15

20</td></tr>
</table>

---

[1] Cf. p. 39.   [1] Top of folio 27a gone.

buton ꝥ he wolde ofer [*w*]erðiode
his anes huru *anwald* [*cyþan.*
eac hit] gesælde *æt sumum cierre*
þæt *se ilca het* ealle acwellan
**[þa¹ ricostan Romana witan*   25 * 27b C
7 *þa æþelestan eorlgebyrdum*   about here.
þe he on þæm folce gefrigen hæfde,
and² onuppan agene broðor
7 *his modor mid meca ecgum,*
billum ofbeatan. he *his bryde ofslog*   30
self mid sweorde, 7 *he symle wæs*
micle þe bliðra on breostcofan
þonne he swylces] morðres³ mæst [*gefremede.*
nal]les sorgode hwæ[*þer siðþan* á
m]ihtig Drihten *ametan wolde*   35
wrece *be gewyrhtum wohfremmendum,*
ac he on ferðe fægn facnes 7 searuwa
wælriow⁴ wunode. wiold emn*e* swa*þeah*
ealles þisses mæran middangeardes,
swa swa lyft 7 *lagu* land *ymb*clyppað,   40
garsecg embegyrt gumena rice,
secggea⁵ sitlu, suð east 7 west
oð ða norðmestan næssan on eorðan;
eall ꝥ Nerone nede [*oð*]ðe l[*ustum,*
heaðo]rinca gehw[*ilc, heran sceolde.*   45
he] hæfde *him* [*to⁶ gamene, þonne he on gylp astag,*
hu he eorðcyningas yrmde 7 *cwelmde.*
*wenst ðu ꝥ se anwald eaðe ne meahte**   * 28a C
Godes ælmihtiges þone gelpscaðan   about here.
rice berædan, 7 *bereafian*   50
his anwaldes ðurh þa ecan meaht,
oððe him his yfeles elles] *gestioran?*
eala gif he wolde, ðæt he wel meahte,

---

¹ Top of folio 27b gone.   ² So J.   ³ J's em. *moðres* C.
⁴ Top of final *w* vis.   ⁵ em. *secgge* C.   ⁶ Folio 28a much damaged.

þæt unriht him eaðe forbiodan.
eawla þ se hlaford hefig gioc slepte   55
sware on þa swyran sinra ðeg*ena*,
ealra ðara hæleða *þe on his tidum*
geond *þas* lænan *wor*old liban sce*oldon.*
he on unscyldgum eorla *b*lode
his sweord s*e*lede swiðe *gelome.*   60
ðær *wæs* swiðe sweotol, þæt we *sæ*don oft,
þæt se anwald ne deð awiht godes,
gif se wel nele þe *his* geweald hafað.

XI.

Boeth. ii. met. 7.   ' Quicumque solam mente praecipiti.'

[*Gif nu hæleða hwon*]e hlisa[*n lyste,*
unnytne gelp agan wille,
þonn[*e ic hine wolde wordum*] biddan
[*þ he hine æghwonon*] utan ym[*beþohte,*
sweotole ymb]sawe suð [*east 7 west*   5
hu widgil s]int wolcnum [*ymbutan*
heofones hwealfe.]   higesnotrum
mæg [*eaðe ðincan þ*] þeos eorðe sie
eall [*for ðæt oðer unig*]met[1] lytel,
þeah [*hio unwisum wid*]gel þince,   10
on stede [*stronglic, steo*]rleasum men.
þe[*ah mæg þone*] wisan *on gewillocan*
[*þære gitsun*]ge gelpes scamian,
ðon[*ne*] hine þæs hlisan heardost lysteð,
[*7 he*] þeah ne mæg þone tobredan   15
ofer ðas nearowan, nænige ðinga,
eorðan sceatas; is ðæt unnet *gelp.*
eala, ofermodan, hwi eow a lys*te*
mid eowrum swiran selfra *willum*
þæt swære gioc symle *underlutan ?*   20
hwy ge ymb ðæt unn*et* ealnig sw*i*ncen,

[1] Cf. p. 46.   [1] So J, cf. vii. 33.

þ ge þone hlisan *habban tiliað*
ofer ðioda ma *þonne* eow þearf [*sie*]?
þeah eow nu gesæle þ eow suð [*oððe norð*
þa] ytmestan eorðbu[*ende*   25
on monig ðiodisc] miclum herien,
[*ðeah hwa æðele sie*] eorlgebyrdū,*   * 34b C.
[*welum*] geweorð[*ad*[1], 7 *on wlencum ðio*
du]guðum d[*iore, deað þæs ne scri*]feð,
þonne [*him rum forlæt rodo*]ra wald[*end ;*   30
ac he þone welegan wæ]dlum *gelice*
[*efnmærne gedeð, æl*]ces þinges.
[*hwær sint nu þæs wisan*] Welandes [*ban*
þæs goldsmiðes, þe] wæs [*geo mærost ?*]
forþy *ic cwæð þæs wisan* Welandes *ban,*   35
forðy ængum ne mæg eorðbuendra
se cræft losian þe him Crist onlænð.
ne mæg mon æfre þy eð ænne wræccan
his cræftes beniman, þe mon oncerran mæg
sunnan onswifan, 7 ðisne swiftan rodor   40
of his rihtryne rinca ænig.
hwa wat nu þæs wisan Welandes *ban,*
on hwelcum *hi*[2] hlæwa *hrusan þeccen ?*
hwær is nu se rica Roma*n*a *wita*
7 se aroda, þe we *ymb sprecað,*   45
hiora heretoga, se gehaten wæs
mid þæm burgwarum, Brutus *nemned ?*
hwær is eac se wisa 7 se weorðgeorna
7 *se fæstræda* fol*ces hyrde,*
se wæs uðwita ælces þinges   50
cene 7 cræftig, þæm wæs Caton *nama ?*
[*hi wæron gefyrn forðge*]witene,
[*nat nænig mon hwær hi nu*] sindon.
[*hwæt is hiora here buton*]* se hlisa an ?   * 35a C.
se is *eac* to lytel swel*cra* lariowa,   55

---

[1] em. *geweorðað* J.   [2] Grein's em. *in* J.

forðæm þa magorincas maran *wyrðe*
wæron on worulde. ac hit is *wyrse nu*
þæt geond þas eorþan *æghwær sindon*
hiora gelican hwon *ymb* spræce,
sume openlice, ealle forgitene,   60
þ hi se hlisa hiwcuðe ne mæg
fore*mære* weras forð gebrengan.
þea*h* ge *nu wenen* 7 wilnigen
þ ge lange *tid libban moten,*
hwæt iow *æfre þy bet bio* oððe þince?   65
forð*æmþe nane forlet,* þeah hit lang *ðince,*
deað æfter dogorrime, þonne *he hæfð* Drihtnes leafe.
hwæt þonne *hæbbe* hæleþa ænig
guma æt *þæm gilpe,* gif hine gegripan *mot*
[*se eca*] deað æfter þissum [*worulde?*]   70

XI [k].

Boeth. ii. met. 8.   'Quod mundus stabili fide.'

[*An sceppend is but*]an ælcū tweon ;
[*se is eac wea*]ldend woruldge[*sceafta*]
heofones 7 eorðan [7 *heah*]sæ
7 ealra ðara þe ðær[*in wuniað,*
u]ngesæwenlicra, 7 eac swa [*same*   5
ðara] ðe we eagum on lociað,
[*ealra gesceaf*]ta. se is ælmihtig ;
þæ[*m*] oleccað ealle gesceafte
þe þæs ambehtes awuht cunnon,
ge eac swa same þa ðæs auht nyton   10
þ [*hi þæs ðe*]odnes þeowas sindon.
se [*us geselle*] sido 7 þeawas,
eallum [*gesceaftum una*]wendendre [1]
s[*ingallice sibbe gecyn*]de,
þa þa* [*he wolde þ þ he wolde;*   15
swa lange swa he wolde þ hit wesan sceolde,

[k] Cf. p. 48.   [1] em. *-wendendne* C.

swa hit eac to worulde sceal wunian[1] *forð;*
forþæm æfre ne magon þa unst]ill[*an*]
woruldgesceafta weorð[*an gestilde,*]
of ðæm ryne onwend, ðe [*him rodera*] weard   20
ende[by]rdes eallum [*gesette.*]
hæfð se alwealda ealle [*gesceafta*
gebæt] mid his bridle; hafað butu gedon,
ealle [*gema*]node, 7 eac getogen,
þ hi ne moten ofer metodes est   25
æfre *gestillan,* ne eft eallunga
swiðor *stirian,* ðonne him[2] sigora weard
his gewealdleþer wille onlætan[3].
he *hafað þe bridle* butu befangen
heofon 7 *eor*þan, 7 eall *holma begong.*   30
swa hæfð geheaðærod hefonrices weard
mid his anwealde ealle gescea*f*ta,
þ hiora æghwilc wið oðer winð,
7 *þeah winn*ende wreþiað fæste,
æghwilc oðer utan ymbclyppeð,   35
*þy læs hi tos*wifen. forðæm hi sy*mle sculon*
þone ilcan ryne *eft gec*yrran
þe æt frymðe fæder *getiode,*
7 swa edniwe eft gewiorðan;
swa hit nu fagað, frean eald*geweorc,*   40
*þ*te winnende wiðerweard ge*sceaft*
fæste sibbe forð anhealdað.
swa nu fyr 7 wæter, folde 7 lagustream,
manigu[4] oðru gesceaft* [*efnswiðe him*   * 37b C.
giond þas widan[5] *worulde*] winnað betweox him,   45
7 swa *þeah* magon hiora þegnunga
7 *geferscipe* fæste gehealdan.
nis hit *no þæt* an *þ* swa eaðe mæg
wiðerweard gesceaft wesan ætgædere
symbel geferan, *ac hit* is sellicre   50

<hr>

[1] em. *wuniað* J.   [2] em. *hi* C.   [3] em. *onlæten* C.   [4] So J; not
clear in C, but apparently either *mænigu* or *manugu.*   [5] em. *widas* J.

þ hiora ænig ne mæg butan oþrum bion.
ac sceal *wuhta* gehwilc wiðerweardes hwæt*hwugu*
habban under *heofo*num, þ his *hige*
*du*rre gemetgian ær *hit to micel* weorðe.
hæfð se ælmihtiga *eallum* gesceaſt*um*   55
ðæt gewrixle *geset þe nu* wun*ian sceal,*
wyrta growan, *leaf grenian,*
þ on hærfest eſt h*res*t 7 wealuwað.
winter bringeð *weder ungemet* cald,
swiſte windas. *sumor æfter* cymeð,   60
wearm gewid*eru.* [*hwæt, þa*] wonnan niht
mona [*onlihteð, oð*]ðæt monnum dæg
sunne *bringeð* giond þas sidan gesceaft.
hæfð se ilca God eorðan 7 wætere
*m*earce gesette ; merestream ne dear   65
ofer eorðan sceat *eard* gebrædan
fisca cynne butan frean leaſe ;
ne hio æfre *ne* mot eorðan þyrscwold
up o*f*ersteppan, ne ða ebban þon ma
foldes *mearce oferfaran moton.*   70
*þa gesetnes*sa sigora wealdend,
lifes leohtfruma, læt *þenden he* wile,
geond þas mæran [*gesceaft mea*]rce healden.
ac þonne [*se eca* 7] se *ælmihtiga*
þa geweald*leðeru wile onlætan,*   75
efne þara br*idla þe he gebætte* mid
his agen weorc eall *æt frymðe,*
þ is wiðerweardnes wuhte *gehwelcre*
þe we mid þæm bridle *becnan tiliað* :
gif se ðioden læt *þa toslupan,*   80
sona hi forlætað lufan 7 sibbe,
ðæs geferscipes ſreondræd*enne* ;
tilaþ anra gehwilc agnes *willan* ;
woruldgesceaſta winnað betweox him,
oðþæt *ðios* eorðe eall *forweorðeð,*   85
7 eac swa same oðra gesceaſta

[*weor*]það him selfe sióðan to na*uhte*.
ac se ilca God, se þ eall *metgað*,
se gefehð fela folca tosom*ne*,
7 *mid* freondscipe fæste gega*drað* ;   90
gesamnað¹ sinscipas, sibbe *gemenged*,
clænlice lufe. swa se *cræftga* eac
*ge*ferscipas fæste gesamnað,
þ *hi* hiora freondscipe forð on sym[*bel*]
untweofealde treowa gehealdað,   95
[*s*]ibbe samrade. eala, sigora God,
wære þis moncyn miclum gesælig*   * 38b C.
[*gif hiora modsefa meahte weorðan*
st]aðolfæst gereaht þurh þa strongan meaht,
7 geendebyrd swa swa oðra sint   100
woruld*gesceafta*. *wære* hit la þonne
murge mid monnum gif hit *meahte swa.*

XII ¹.

Boeth. iii. met. 1. 'Qui serere ingenuum nolet agrum.'

*Se þe wille wyrcan wæstm*bære lond,
atio of *ðæm æcere* ærest sona
fearn and þor*nas* 7 fyrsas swa same,
wiod þa þe w*illað* welhwær derian
clæ[*num hwæ*]te, þy læs he ciða [*leas*   5
licge on ðæm] lande. is leoda gehw[*æm*
ðios oðru] bysen efnbe*hefu* ;
þ is þætte [*ðynceð*] þegna gehwelcum
huniges [*bibre*]ad healfe þy swetre
gif [*he hwene*] ær huniges teare   10
bitres *onbyrgeð*. bið eac swa same
monna æghwilc micle þy fægenra
li*ð*es *weð*res, gif hine lytle ær
stormas [*ge*]stondað 7 se stearca wind,
*norð*an 7 eastan. nænegum þuht   15
[*d*]æg on þonce gif sio dimme ni[*ht*]

¹ em. *gesamniað* C.   ¹ Cf. p. 51.

* 40b C.

ær [*ofe*]r eldum egesan ne brohte.
swa þincð anra gehwæm eorðbuendra
sio soðe gesælð symle ðe betere*
7 þy wynsumre [1] [*þe he wita ma,*]   20
heardra he]nða, her adreogeð.
þu meaht [*ea*]c mycle þy eð on modsefan
soða gesælða sweotolor gecnawan,
7 *to* heora cyððe be[*cuman siððan,*]
gif þu [*up aty*]hsð ær[*est* [2] *sona,*   25
7 ðu *awyrtwalast of gewitlocan*
leasa gesælða, swa swa londes ceorl
of his æcere lycð yfe]l weod monig.
siððan *ic ðe* secge þ þu sweotole m*eaht*
soða gesælða sona oncnawan,   30
7 þu æfre ne recst æniges *ðinges*
ofer þa ane, gif þu hi *cal*[*les ongitst.*]

XIII [m].

Boeth. iii. met. 2. 'Quantas rerum flectat habenas.'

[*Ic wille*] mid giddum get gecyðan
[*hu se æl*]mihtga ealra gesceafta
[*bryrð*] mid his bridlum, begð ðider he w[*ile*]
mid his anwalde, ge endebyrd
[*w*]undorlice wel gemetgað.   5
hafað swa gehcaðorad heofona wealdend,
ut*an* befangen calla gesce*afta*,
geræped mid his racentan, [þ] hi aredian ne magon
þ h[*i hi æfre*] him of aslepen.
7 þeah [*wuhta ge*]hwilc wrigað [*toheald*   10

* 45a C.

sidra gesceafta] *swiðe on*helded*
wið þæs [*gecyndes þe him* [3]] cyning [*engla*],
fæder æ[*t frymðe, fæste*] getiode.
swa nu þin[*ga gehwilc ðider*]weard fundað,

[m] Cf. p. 57.

[1] 7 *þy wynsumre* written in a modern hand, apparently that of
Junius, at bottom of folio 40a.   [2] From -*est* to *yfe*- (l. 28) part
gone, rest illegible in C.   [3] em. *hi* J.

sidra [*gesceafta, buton*] sumum englum   15
7 *mon*[*cynne; þara*] micles to feola,
wor[*oldwuniendra,*] winð wið gecynde.
þeah [*nu on londe leon*] gemete
wynsume w[*iht wel atemede,*]
hire magister miclum [*lufige,*   20
7 *eac*] ondræde dogora geh[*welce,*
gif hit] æfre gesælð þ hio [*æniges*
blodes] onbyrgeð, ne ðearf [*beorna nan*]
wenan þære wyrde [*þ hio wel siððan*]
hire taman healde; [*ac ic tiohhie*   25
þ] hio ðæs niwan taman nau[*ht ne ge*]hicgge,
ac ðone wildan gew[*unan wille*] geþencan
hire eldrena; o[*ngind eor*]neste
racentan slitan, ryn, [*grymet*]igan,
7 ærest abit hire agenes   30
huses hirde, 7 hraðe siððan
hæleð[*a*] gehwilcne þe hio gehentan mæg.
nele hio forlætan libbendes wuh[*t,*
n]eata ne monna; nimð eall þ hio fint.
swa doð wudufuglas; þeah hi wel s*ien*   35
[*te*]la atemede, gif hi on treowum [*weor*]það
holt[*e*] tomiddes, hræðe bioð *forsewene*
heora lareowas þe hi lange *ær*
tydon 7 temedon. hi on treowum* [*wilde*   * 45b C.
ealdgecynde ā forð siððan   40
willum wuniað, þeah him] wolde hwi[*lc*
h]eora [*lareowa listum*] beodan
þone ilcan [*mete þe he hi*] *ær*or mid
tame gete[*de. him þa twigu*] þincað
emne swa me[*rge þ hi þæs metes*] ne recð;   45
ðincð[1] him [*to ðon wynsu*]m þ him se weald on[*cwyð;*
þonne hi] geherað hleoðrum [*brægdan*
oðre] fugelas, hi heora ag[*ne*
stefne sty]riað; *stunað* eal geado[*r*

[1] *ðihð* C.

welwinsum s]anc ; wudu eallum on[*cwyð*.   50
swa bið e]allum treowum þe [*him on æðele*] bið
þ hit on holte hy[*hst geweaxe ;*
þ]eah þu hwilcne boh [*byge wið e*]orþan,
he bið upweardes [*swa ðu an*]*forlætst
widu on willan ; [*went on ge*]cynde.   55
swa deð eac sio [*sunne,*] *þonne* hio on sige weorðeð
ofer midne dæg ; merecondel
scyfð on *ofdæle*, uncuðne weg
nihtes gene*ðeð, norð* eft 7 east ;
eldum oteweð, bren*cð* eorðwarum   60
morgen meretorhtne ; hio ofer moncyn stihð
â upweardes, oð hio eft cymeð
þær hire yfemesð bið eard gecynde.
swa swa ælc gescea*ft* calle [*mægene*]
geond ðas widan woruld wri[*gað* 7] higað   65
ealle mægene, eft symle on*[*lyt
wið his gecyndes, cymð to ðonne hit mæg.
nis nu ofer eorðan ænegu gesceaft
þe ne wilnie þ hio wolde cuman
to þam earde þe hio of becom ;   70
þ is orsorgnes 7 ecu] rest[1] ;
þ is openlice [*ælmihti God.
nis*] nu ofer eorðan æne[*gu gesceaft
þe*] ne hwearfige swa [*swa hweol deð
on*] hire selfre, for[*ðon hio swa hwearfað*]   75
þ hio eft cume [*þær hio æror wæs ;
þon*]ne hio ærest sie u[*tan behwerfed,
þon*]ne hio ealles wyrð [*utan becerred ;*]
hio sceal eft don þ hio [*ær dyde,
7 eac*] wesan þ hio æror wæs.   80

---

[1] Above *rest* can be made out *si- weoroda g* in C.

XIV [n].

Boeth. iii. met. 3.   'Quamuis fluente diues auri gurgite.'

*_H_wæt bið [1] þæm welegan woruld[_gitse_]re   * 48b C
on his mode ðe bet, [_þeah_] he micel age   near top.
goldes 7 gimma [7 _gooda ge_] hwæs,
æhta unrim, [7 _him mon erigen sc_]yle
æghwelce dæg [_æcera ðusend,_   5
ðeah] þes middangeard [7 _þis manna cyn_
_sy u_]nder sunnan [_suð west 7 east_
his] anwalde eall un[_derðieded?_
ne mot] he þara hyrsta [_hionane lædan_
_of_] ðisse worulde [_wuhte þon ma_]re   10
hordgestreona [_ðonne he hiðe_]r brohte.

•

XV [o].

Boeth. iii. met. 4.   'Quamuis se tyrio superbus ostro.'

*_Ð_eah hine [_nu se yfela unriht_]wisa   * top of
Nero[_n cynincg niwan ge_]scerpte   52a C.
wlitegum [_wædum, wund_]orlice
golde gegle[_ngd_]e [7 _gimcynn_]um,
þeah he wæs on woru[_lde wite_]na gehwelcum   5
on his lifdag[_um lað_] 7 unweorð,
fierenfull.   hwæt, s[_e feond_] swaðeah
his diorlingas dugu[_þum_] stepte ;
ne mæg ic þeah gehy[_cgan hwy_] him on hige þorfte
a ðy [_sæl wesan ;_] þeah hi sume hwile   10
gecure [_butan_] cræftum cyninga dysegast,
[_næron_] hy þy weorðran witena ænegu[_m._
ðeah] hine se dysega do to cynin[_ge,_
_hu_] mæg þ gesceadwis scealc gere[_ccan_
_þ_] he him ðy selra sie oððe þince?   15

[n] Cf. p. 60.   [o] Cf. p. 64.
[1] _bið_ above line in C.

XVI P.

Boeth. iii. met. 5.   'Qui se uolet esse potentem.'

Se þe wille anwald agon, ðonne scea[*l*] he ærest tilian
Ꝥ he his [*sel*]fes on sefan age
anwald [*i*]nnan, þy læs he æfre sie
his unþeaw[*um*] eall underðyded;
ado of his mode mi[*sli*]cra fela   5
þara ymbhogona þe him [*u*]nnet sie ;
læte sume hwile siofun[*ga*]
and[1] ermða þinra.   þeah him eall sie
þes middangeard swa swa merestreamas
utan b*elicgað* on æht gifen,   10
efne swa wid[*e*] swa swa westmest nu
an *[*iglond ligð ut on garsecg,
þær nængu bið nih*]t on sumera
ne wuhte þon ma o[*n wi*]ntra dæg
toteled tidum, Ꝥ is Tile ha[*ten*]:   15
þeah nu anra hwa ealles wealde
þæs [*igla*]ndes, 7 eac þonan
oð Indeas eastewe[*ard*]e,
þeah he nu Ꝥ eall agan mote,
hwy [*bið*] his anwald auhte ðy mara   20
gif he siððan nah his selfes geweald
ingeðances, 7 hine eorneste
wel ne bewarenað wordum 7 dædum
wið ða unþeawas þe we ymb sprecað?

XVII q.

Boeth. iii. met. 6.   'Omne hominum genus in terris.'

Ð*æt*[2] eorðwaran ealle h[*æfden,*]
foldbuende, fruma[*n gelicne ;*]
hi of anum twæm ea[*lle comon,*]

---

p Cf. p. 67.   q Cf. p. 69.
[1] Conject. 7 J.   [2] J's conject., -*ÆT* C, with large space for initial.

were 7 wife, on woruld [*innan,*]
7 hi eac nu get ealle gelice   5
[*on woruld*] cumað, wlance 7 heane.
[*nis þ nan wund*]or, forðæm witan eal[*le
þ an God is*] ealra gesceafta,
fre[*a moncynnes, fæde*]r 7 scippend.
se ðære [*sunnan leoht* seleð of heofonum,*]   10 * 56b C
monan 7 þys mærum steorrum. se gesceop men on eorðan, about here.
7 gesamnade sawle to lice
æt fruman ærest, folc under wolcnum
emnæðele gesceop, æghwilcne mon.
hwy ge þonne æfre ofer oðre men   15
ofermodigen buton andweorce,
nu ge unæðel]ne nænigne [1] [*metað ?*]
hwy ge eow for] æþelum up [*ahebben nu ?*
On þæm m]ode bið mon[*na gehwilcum*
þa ri]htæþelo þe [*ic ðe recce ymb,*   20
nales o]n ðæm flæ[*sce foldbuendra.*
ac] nu æghwilc [*mon þe mid e*]alle bið
his unþea[*wum unde*]rðieded,
he forlæt ærest [*lifes fru*]msceaft
7 his agene æþe[*lo swa s*]elfe,   25
7 eac þone fæder þe [*hine æt*] fruman gesceop.
forðæ [*hine an*]æþelað ælmihtig God,
þ he [*una*]eþele â forð þanan
wyrð [*on weoru*]lde, to wuldre ne cymð.

XVIII [r].

Boeth. iii. met. 7. ' Habet omnis hoc uoluptas.'

[*Eala*] ðæt se yfla unrihta ge[*deð*]
wraða willa wohhæmetes,
þ [*he*] mid ealle gedræfð anra ge[*hwy*]lces
monna cynnes mod [*fulneah þ*]on.
hwæt, sio wilde beo, þeah [*wis sie,*]   5
anunga sceal eall forweo[*r*]þan

[r] Cf. p. 71.   [1] em. *ænigne* C.

gif hio yrringa awuht stin[*geð ;*]
swa sceal sawla gehwilc siðð an lo[*sian*]
gif se lichoma forlegen weorþ[*eð*]
un]rihthæmede, bute him ær *cum*[*e*]   10

** 58a C.*   hreow *to heortan, [*ær he hionan wende.*]

XIX[s].

Boeth. iii. met. 8.   ' Eheu, quae miseros tramite deuios.'

*E*ala, þ is hefig dysig, hygeð [*ym*]be se ðe wile,
7 f[*re*]cenlic *fira* gehwilcum,
þ ða ea[*rman men mid*] ealle ged[*wæ*]leð

** 60a C.*   of ðæm [*rihtan wege* recene alæded.
hwæðer ge willen on wuda*] secan   5
gold ðæt reade [*on*] grenū triowu[*m*]?
Ic wat swaðeah þ hit [*wite*]na nan
þider [*ne seceð,*] forðæm [*hit þ*]ær ne wexð,
ne [*on wi*]ngeardum [*wlitige*] gimmas.
hwy [*ge*] nu ne settan [*on su*]me dune   10
fisc[*net*] eowru, þonne eo[*w*] fon lysteð
leax [*oð*]ðe cyperan? me gelicost ðincð
þte ealle witen eorðbuende
þoncolmode ðæt hi þær ne sint.
h[*wæ*]þer ge nu willen wæþan mid hundu[*m*]   15
on sealtne sæ, ðonne eow secan lyst
heorotas [7] hinda? þu gehicgan meaht
þ ge will[*a*]ð ða on wuda secan
oftor micl[*e þo*]nne ut on sæ.
is ðæt wundorlic, þ we w[*it*]an ealle,   20
þ mon secan sceal be sæwaroðe
7 be eaofrum æþele gimmas
hwite 7 reade 7 hiwa gehwæs.
hwæt, hi. eac witon hwær hi eafiscas
secan þurfa[*n, 7*] swylcra fela   25
weoruldwelena; hi þ wel [*doð,*]

* Cf. p. 73.

geornfulle men, geara gehwilc[.
ac] ðæt is earmlicost ealra þing[*a*
þ þa] dysegan sint on gedwolan word[*ene*
efne sw]a blinde ꝥ hi on breostum n[*e magon*
eaðe] gecnawan hwær þa ec[*an good,*
soða gesæl]ða, sindon gehydda;
[*forþæm hi æfre ne lyst*] æfter spyri[*an,*
secan þa gesælða. wena]ð sam[*wise*
þæt hi on* ðis lænan mægen life findan
soða gesælða, þ is] selfa God.
[*ic nat*] hu ic mæge *nænige* ðinga
ealles swa swiðe on sefan minum
hiora dysig [*tælan*] swa hit me don lysteð;
ne ic þ[*e swa*] sweotole [*gesec*]gan ne mæg,
fo[*rþæm*] hig[1] sint earm[*ran*] 7 eac dysegran
ungesæligran, [*þon*]ne ic þe secgan mæge.
hi wiln*ia*ð [*we*]lan 7 æhta
7 weorðscipes to gewinnanne;
þonne hi habbað ꝥ hiora *hige* seceð,
wenað *þon*ne swa gewitlease
ðæt hi þa soðan gesælða hæbben.

30

35 * 6ob C.
about here.

40

45

XX t.

Boeth. iii. met. 9.   ‘O qui perpetua mundum ratione gubernas.’

*Æ*ala, min Drihten, ꝥ þu eart ælmih[*tig,*
m]icel, modilic, mærþum gefræ[*ge,*]
7 wundorlic witena gehwylcum.
[*hwæt, ðu*] ece God ealra gesceafta
wun[*dorlice w*]el gesceope
ungesewenlica, [*7 eac swa s*]ame
gesewenlicra softe wealdest,
scirra gesceafta, mid gesceadwisum
mægne 7 cræfte. þu þysne middangear[*d*]
from fruman ærest forð oð ende

5

10

* Cf. p. 79.   [1] em. *hit* C.

tidum totældes, swa hit getæsos[t] wæs,
 endebyrdes, þ hi æghwæðer
ge ær farað ge eft cumað.

* 65a C.   þu þe unstilla* agna g[*esceafta*
to ðinum willan wislice] astyrest,   15
7 þe self wunæst swiðe stille
unanwendendlic a forð simle.
nis nan mihtigra ne nan mærra,
ne geond ealle þa gesceaft efnlica þín,
ne þe ænig nedþearf næs æfre giet   20
ealra þara weorca þe þu geworht hafast;
ac mid þinum willan þu hit worhtes eall,
7 mid anwalde þinum agenum
weorulde geworhtest 7 wuhta gehwæt,
þeah ðe nænegu nedðearf wære   25
eallra þara mærþa. is ðæt micel gecynd
þines goodes, þencð ymb se ðe wile,
forðon hit is eall an ælces þincges,
þu 7 þ ðin good. hit is þin agen,
forðæm hit nis [1] utan, ne com auht to ðe.   30
ac ic georne wat þ ðin goodnes .is
ælmihtig good, eall mid ðe selfum.
hit is ungelic urum gecynde;
us is utan cymen eall þa we habbað
gooda on grundū from Gode selfum.   35
næfst þu *to* ænegū andan genumenne,
forðamþe nan þing nis þin gelica,
ne huru ænig ælcræftigre;
forðæm þu eal good anes geþeahte
þines geþohtest, 7 hi þa worhtest.   40
næs æror ðe [2] ænegu gesceaft
þe auht oððe nauht auðer worhte.
ac ðu butan bysne, brego moncynnes,
ælmihtig [3] God, eall geworhtest

* 65b C.   þing þearle good; eart þe* [*selfa*   45

<hr>

[1] em. *his* C.   [2] em. *aworðe* C.   [3] *al ælmihtig* C.

þæt hehste good. hwæt ðu, halig] fæder,
æfter þinum willan woruld gesceope,
ðisne middangeard meahtū þinū,
weorada Drihten, swa þu woldest self,
⁊ mid ðinum willan wealdest ealles ;   50
forðæm þu, soða God, selfa dælest
gooda æghwilc. forðæm þu geara ær
ealla gesceafta ærest gesceope
swiðe gelice, sumes hwæðre þeah
ungelice ; nemdest eall swaðeah   55
mid ane noman, ealle togædre
woruld under wolcnum. hwæt þu, wuldres God,
þone anne naman eft todældes,
fæder, on feower ; wæs þara folde an
⁊ wæter oðer worulde dæles,   60
⁊ fyr is þridde, ⁊ feowerðe lyft ;
þæt is eall weoruld eft togædere.
habbað þeah þa feower frumstol hiora,
æghwilc hiora agenne stede,
þeah anra hwi*lc* wið oðer sie   65
miclum gemenged, ⁊ mid mægne eac
fæder ælmihtiges fæste gebunden
gesiblice softe togædre
*mi*d bebode þine, bilewit fæder,
þte heora ænig oðres ne dorste   70
mearce ofergangan for metodes ege.
ac geþweorod sint ðegnas togædre,
cyninges cēpan, cele wið hæto,
wæt wið drygum ; winn[*að*] hwæðre.
wæter ⁊ eorðe wæstmas brengað.   75
þa sint on gecynde cealda batwa,
wæter wæt ⁊ ceald. wangas ymbelicgað,
eorðe æl*greno, eac hw[*æðre ceald.*   * 66a C.
lyft is gemenged, for]þæm hio on middum wunað ;
nis þ nan wundor þ hio sie wearm ⁊ ceald,   80
wæt wolcnes tier [*win*]de geblonden,

N 2

forðæm hio is on midle, [*min*]e gefræge,
fyres 7 eorþan.   fel[*a*] mon[*na*] wat
þte yfemest is eallra gesceafta
fyr ofer eorðan, folde neoðemest.   85
is þ wundorlic, weroda Drihten,
þ ðu mid geþeahte þinum wyrcest
þæt ðu [*þæm gesce*]aftum swa gesceadlice
mearce [*geset*]test, 7 hi ne mengdest eac.
hwæt, þu þæm wættere wætu[*m 7 cea*]ldum   90
foldan to flore fæste gesettest,
forðæm hit unstille æghwider wolde
wide toscriðan wac 7 hnesce.
ne meahte hit on him selfum, soð ic geare wat.
æfre gestandan; ac hit sio eorðe hylt   95
7 swelgeð eac be sumum dæle,
þ hio siðþan mæg for ðæm sype weorðan
geleht lyftum.   forðæm leaf 7 gærs
bræd geond Bretene, bloweð 7 groweð
eldum to are.   eorðe sio cealde   100
brengð wæstma fela wundorlicra[1],
forðæm hio mid þæm wætere weorðeð[2] geþawened.
gif þ nære, þonne hio wære
fordrugod to duste, 7 todrifen siððan
wide mid winde, swa nu weorðeð[2] oft   105
axe giond eorðan eall toblawen.
ne meahte on ðære eorðan [*aw*]uht libban,
ne wuhte [*þ*]on ma [*wa*]etre[*s *brucan*,
on e]*ardian* ænige cræfte
for cele anum, gif þu, cyning engla,   110
wið fyre hwæthwugu foldan 7 lagustream
ne[3] mengdest[4] *togædre*, 7 gemetgodest
cele 7 hæto cræf[*te*] þine,
þ þ fyr ne mæg foldan 7 me[*re*]stream
blate forbærnan, þeah hit wið batwa sie   115
[*fæ*]ste gefeged, fæder ealdgeweorc.

[1] *wundorlica* C.   [2] em. *weorðað* C.   [3] *ne* conject. om. C.   [4] *mendest* C.

ne þincð me þ wundur wuhte þe læsse
þ ðios eorðe mæg 7 egorstream,
swa ceald [*ge*]sceaft, cræfta nane
ealles *ad*wæscan þ þ him oninnan sticað   120
fyres, gefeged mid frean cr[*æfte.*]
þæt is agen cræft eagorstreames[1],
wætres 7 eorþan 7 on wolcnum eac,
7 efne swa same uppe ofer rodere.
þonne is þæs fyres frumstol on riht   125
eard ofer eallum oðrum gesceaftum
gesewenlicum geond þisne sidan grund;
þeah hit wið ealla sie eft gemenged
weoruldgesceafta, þeah waldan ne mot
þ hit ænig[*e*][2] eallunga fordó   130
buton þæs leafe þe us þis lif tiode,
þ is se eca 7 se ælmihtga.
eorðe is hefigre oðrum gesceaftum,
þicre geþruen[3], forðæm[4] hio þrage stod
ealra gesceafta under niðemæst,   135
buton þæm rodere, þe þas ruman gesceaft
æghwylce dæge *ulan* ymbh[*wy*]rfeð,
7 þeah þære eorþ[*an*]* æfre ne oðrin[*eð*,   * 67a C.
ne hire on nanre ne] mot near þonne on oðre
stowe gestæppan; striceð ymbutan   140
[*ufan*]e 7 neoða*ne*, efenneah gehwæþer.
[*æghwi*]lc gesceaft þe we ymb sprecað
[*hæfð hi*]s agenne eard onsundran,
[*bið þeah wi*]ð þæm oðrū eac gemenged;
ne mæg [*hira æn*]ig butan oðrum bion.   145
þeah hi [*un*]sweotole somod eardien,
swa nu eorðe 7 wæter, earfoðtæcne
unwisra gehwæm, wuniað on fyre,
þeah hi sindan[5] sweotole þæm wisum.
is þ fyr swa same fæst on þæm wætre   150

<hr>

[1] em. *eagorstreamas* C.   [2] So J, *ænig* C, at extreme edge of folio.
[3] *geþruen* C.   [4] em. *forðæm þæm* C.   [5] Grein's em. *sint an* C.

7 on stanum eac stille geheded
earfoðhawe, is hwæðre þær.
hafað fæder engla fyr gebunden
efne to þon fæste ꝥ hit fiolan ne mæg
eft æt his eðle, þær ꝥ oðer fyr   155
úp ofer eall þis eardfæst wunað.
sona hit forlæteð þas lænan gesceaft
mid cele ofercumen, gif hit on cyððe gewit;
7 þeah wuhta gehwilc wilnað þiderweard
þær his mægðe bið mæst ætgædre.   160
ðu gestaðoladest þurh þa strongan meaht,
weroda wuldorcyning, wundorlice
eorðan swa fæste ꝥ hio ón ænige
healfe ne heldeð; ne mæg hio hider ne þider
sigan þe swiðor þe hio symle dyde.   165
hwæt, hi þeah eorðlices auht ne haldeð,*
[*is þeah efneðe up 7 ofdune*
to feall]anne foldan ðisse,
þæm anlicost þe on æge b[*ið*
g]ioleca onmiddan, glideð hwæðre   170
æg [*.ymbut*]an; swa stent eall weoruld
stille on til[*le, stream*]as ymbutan,
lag*u*floda gel[*ac, lyfte*] 7 tungla,
7 sio scire scell scriðeð [*ymbut*]an
dogora gehwilce; dyde lange swa.   175
[*hwæt*] þu, ðioda God, ðriefalde on us
sawle gesettest, 7 hi siððan eac
styrest 7 stihtest þurh ða strongan meaht,
ꝥ hire þy læsse on ðæm lytlan ne bið
anum fingre þe hire ón eallum bið   180
þæm lichoman. forðæm ic lytle ær
sweotole sæde ꝥ sio s*aul*[1] wære
þriefald gesceaft þegna gehwilces,
forðæm uðwitan ealle seggað
ðætte an gecynd ælcre saule   185

* 67b C.

____
[1] *sawl* J, but there is no sign of *w* in C.

irsung sie, oðer wilnung;
is sio þridde gecynd þæm twæm betere,
sio gesceadwisnes.   nis ðæt scandlic cræft,
forðæm hit nænig hafað neat buton monnum.
hæfð þa oðra twa unrim .wuhta;   190
hæfð þa wilnunga welhwilc neten,
7 þa yrsunga eac swa selfe;
forðy men habbæð geond middangeard
eorðgesceafta ealla oferþungen,
forðæmðe hi habbað, þæs ðe hi nabbað,   195
þone ænne cræft þe we ær nemdon.
sio gesceadwisnes* sceal on ge[*hwelcum*   * 68a C.
þære wilnunge waldan] semle,
7 irsunge eac swa selfe;
hio sceal mid geþeahte þegnes mode,   200
mid an*dgite*, ealles waldan.
hio is þ mæste mægen monnes saule,
7 se selesta sun[*dor*]cræfta.
hwæt, þu ða saule, sigora [*waldend*,]
þeoda þrymcyning, þus gesceop[*e*]   205
þ [*hio*] hwearfode on hire selfre
hire utan ymb, swa swa eal deð
rineswifte rodor, recene[1] ymbscriðeð
dogora gehwilce Drihtnes meahtum
þisne middangeard.   swa deð monnes saul,   210
hweole geli[*c*]ost; hwærfeð ymbe hy selfe,
oft smeagende ymb ðas eorðlican
drihtnes gesceafta dagum 7 nihtum;
hwilum hi selfe secende smeað,
hwilum eft smeað ymb þone ecan God,   215
sceppend hire.   scriðende færð
hweole gelicost, hwærfð ymb hi selfe.
þonne hio ymb hire scyppend mid gescead smeað,
hio bið upahæfen[2] ofer hi selfe;
ac hio bið eallunga an hire selfre   220

---

[1] *reche* C.   [2] Faint mark over the *u* resembling accent.

þonne hio ymb hi selfe secende smeað;
hio bið swiðe fior hire selfre beneoðan,
þonne hio þæs lænan lufað 7 wundrað
eorðlicu þing ofer ecne ræd.
hwæt þu, ece God, eard forgeafe   225
saulū on heofonum, selest weorðlica
ginfæsta gifa, God ælmihtig,
be geearnunga anra gehwelcre.*
[*ealle hi scinað ðurh þa sciran neaht*]
hadre on heofonum, na hwæðre þeah   230
e[*alle*] efenbeorhte. hwæt, we oft gesioð
hadrum nihtum þte heofonsteorran
ealle efenbeorhte æfre ne scinað.
[*hwæt*] þu, ece God, eac gemengest
[*þa*] heofoncundan hider wið eorðan,   235
saula wið lice; siððan wuniað
þis eorðlice 7 þ ece samod,
saul in flæsce. hwæt, hi simle to ðe
hion fundiað, forðæm hi hider of ðe
æror comon; sculon eft *to* ðe.   240
sceal se lic*hama last* weardigan
eft on eorðan, forðæm he ær of hire
weox on weorulde. wunedon ætsomne
efen swa lange swa him lyfed wæs
from þæm ælmihtigan þe hi æror gio   245
gesomnade; þ is soð cining,
se þas foldan gesceop, 7 hi gefylde þa
swiðe mislicum, mine gefræge,
neata cynnum, nergend user.
he hi siððan asiow sæda monegum   250
wuda 7 wyrta weorulde sceatum.
forgif nu, ece God, urum modum
þæt hi moten to þe, metod alwuhta,
þurg þas earfoðu up astigan,
7 of þisum bysegum, bilewit fæder,   255
þeoda waldend, to þe cuman,

7 þonne mid openum eagum moten
modes ures ðurh ðinra[1]* mægna [*sped*   * 69a C.
æwelm gesion eallra gooda,
þ] þu eart selfa, sigedrihten God,   260
ge þa eagan hal ures modes,
þ we hi on ðe selfum siððan moten
afæstnian, fæder engla.
todrif þone þiccan [*mist*] þe þrage nu
wið ða eagan foran usses modes   265
hangode hwyle hef*ig* 7 þystre.
onliht nu þa eagan usses modes
mid þinum leohte, lifes waldend ;
forðæm þu eart sio birhtu, bilewit fæder,
soðes leohtes, 7 þu selfa eart   270
sio fæste ræst, fæder ælmihtig,
eallra soðfæstra. hwæt, þu softe gedest
þ hi ðe selfne gesion moten.
ðu eart eallra þinga, þeoda waldend,
fruma 7 ende. hwæt þu, fæder engla,   275
eall þing birest eðelice   .
buton geswince. þu eart *s*elfa weg
7 *latteow* eac lifgendra gehwæs,
7 sio wlitige *stow* þe se weg to ligð,
þe ealle to a fundiað   280
men of moldan on þa mæran gesceaf*t*.

XXI [u].

Boeth. iii. met. 10. 'Huc omnes pariter nenite capti.'

[Wella, monna bearn geond mid]dangeard,   * 75a C.
friora æghwilc fundie to
þæm ecum gode þe *we ymb* sprecað,
7 to þæm gesælðum *þe we* secgað ymb.
se ðe *þ*onne nu *sie* nearwe gehefted   5

[u] Cf. p. 89.

[1] At the bottom of folio 68b are some words no longer legible in
a very small modern handwriting, apparently by J.

mid þisses mæra*n* middangeardes
unnyttre lufe, sece him eft hræðe
fulne friodom, ꝥ he forð *cume*
to þæm gesælðum saula rædes.
forðæm ꝥ is sio an *rest* eallra geswinca,   10
hyhtlicu hyð *heaum* ceolum
modes usses, meresmylt*a wic*.
ꝥ is sio an hyð þe æfre bið
æfter þam yðum *ura* geswinca,
ysta gehwelcre, ealnig smylte.   15
ꝥ is sio friðst*ow* 7 sio frofor an
eallra yrminga æfꞇ þissum
weoruldgeswincum. *ꝥ is wynsum* stów
æfꞇ þyssum *yrmðum to* aganne.
ac ic georne wat ꝥ*te gylden* maðm,   20
sylofren sincstan, *searogim*ma nan,
middangeardes wela *modes* eagan
æfre ne onlyhtað, auh*t ne ge*betað
hiora scearpnesse to *þære scea*wunga
soðra gesælða; ac hi *swiðor* get   25
monna gehwelces modes *eagan*
ablendað on breostum, þon[*ne hi hi beor*]htran ged[*on.*]

forðæm æg[*hwilc ðing *þe on þys andweardan*
life licað lænu] sindon,
eorðlicu þing a fleondu.   30
ac ꝥ is wundorlic wlite 7 beorhtnes
þe wuhta gehwæs wlite geberhteð,
7 æfꞇ þæm eallum wealdeð.
nele se waldend ðæt forweorðan scylen
saula *usse*, ac he hi selfa wile   35
leoman *on*lihtan, lifes wealdend.
gif þonne hæleða hwilc hlutrum eagum
modes sines mæg æfre ofsion
hiofones leohtes hlutre beor*hto*,
þonne wile he secgan ꝥ ðære sunnan sie   40
beorhtnes þiostro beor*na* gehwylcum

to metanne wið þ micle leoht
Godes ælmihtiges; þ is gasta gehwæm
ece butan *ende*, eade*gum* saulum.

XXII^v.

Boeth. iii. met. 11. ' Quisquis profunda mente uestigat uerum.'

**Se þe æfter rihte mid gerece wille*
inweardlice æfterspyrian
swa deoplice þæt hit todrifan ne mæg
monna ænig, ne amerran huru
ænig eorðlic ðincg, he ærest sceal
secan on him selfum þ he sume hwile
ymbutan hine æror sohte.
sece þæt siððan on his sefan innan,
7 forlæte an swa he oftost mæge
ælcne[1] *ymbhogan ðy him unnet sie,*
7 gesamnige swa he swiðost mæge
ealle to þæm anum his ingeðonc ;
geseige his mode[2] *þ hit mæg findan*
eall on him innan þ hit oftost nu
ymbutan hit ealneg seceð,
gooda æghwylc. he ongit siððan
yfel 7 unnet eal þ he hæfde
on his incofan æror lange,
efne swa sweotole swa he on þa sunnan mæg
eagum andweardum on locian ;
7 he[3] *eac ongit his ingeþonc*
leohtre 7 berhtre þonne se leoma sie
sunnan on sumera, þonne swegles gim,
hador heofontungol, hlutrost scineð.
forðæm þæs lichoman leahtras 7 hefignes
7 þa unþeawas eallunga ne magon
of mode ation monna ænegum
rihtwisnesse. ðeah nu rinca hwæm
þæs lichoman leahtras 7 hefignes

* From J,
two fols.
missing in
C after
79b.

5

10

15

20

25

^v Cf. p. 94.   [1] em. *ælcre* J.   [2] em. *mod* J.   [3] em. *hi* J.

7 unþeawas oft bysigen   30
monna modsefan mæst 7 swiðost
mid þære yflan oforgiotolnesse,
mid gedwolmiste dreorigne sefan
fortihð mod foran monna gehwelces
þ hit swa beorhte ne mot blican 7 scinan   35
swa hit wolde gif hit geweald ahte,
þeah bið sum corn sædes gehealden
symle on þære saule soðfæstnesse,
þenden gadertang wunað gast on lice.
ðæs sædes corn bið symle aweaht   40
mid ascunga, eac siððan
mid goodre lare, gif hit growan sceal.
hu mæg ænig man andsware findan
ðinga æniges, þegen mid gesceade,
þeah hine rinca hwilc rihtwislice   45
æfter frigne, gif he awuht nafað
on his modsefan mycles ne lytles
rihtwisnesse¹ ne geradscipes?
nis þeah ænig man þte ealles swa
þæs geradscipes swa bereafod sie   50
þ he andsware ænige ne cunne
findan on ferhðe, gif he frugnen bið.
forðæm hit is riht spell þ us reahte gio
ald uðwita, ure Platon;
he cwæð þte æghwilc ungemyndig   55
rihtwisnesse hine hræðe sceolde
eft gewendan into sinum
modes gemynde; he mæg siððan
on his runcofan rihtwisnesse
findan on ferhte fæste gehydde   60
mid gedræfnesse dogora gehwilce
modes sines mæst 7 swiðost,
7 mid hefinesse his lichoman,
7 mid þæm bisgum þe on breostum styreð
mon on mode mæla gehwylce.   65

¹ em. rihtwisnesses J.

XXIII [w].

Boeth. iii. met. 12.   'Felix qui potuit boni.'

*Si*e* ðæt la on eorðan ælces ðinges
*ges*ælig mon, gif he gesion mæge
þone hlutrestan heofontorhtan stream,
æþelne æwelm ælces goodes,
7 of him selfum ðone sweartan mist,   5
modes þiostro, mæg aweorpan.
w[e] sculon ðeah gita mid Godes [*fylste*
ealdu]m 7 leasum ðinne ingeþonc
be[*tan bi*]spellum, ꝥ ðu ðe bet mæge
ar[*edi*]an to rodorum rihte stige   10
on ðone ecan eard ussa saula.

* top of
84b C.

XXIV [x].

Boeth. iv. met. 1.   'Sunt etenim pennae uolucres mihi.'

*I*c hæbbe fiðru fugle swiftran,
mid ðæm ic fleogan mæg feor frā eorðan
ofer heane hrof heofones þisses;
ac ðær ic nu moste mod gefeðran,
ðinne ferðlocan, feðrum minum,   5
oððæt ðu meahte þisne middan[*g*]eard,
ælc eorðlic ðing, eallu[*nga fo*]rsion.
meahtes ofer rodorum gereclice
feðerū lacan[1], feor *up* ofer
wolcnu windan; wlitan siððan   10
ufan ofer ealle. meahtes eac faran
ofer þæm fyre ðe fela geara for
*lange be*tweox lyfte 7 rodere,
swa[2] him æt frymðe fæder getiode.
ðu meahtest ðe siððan mid *ðære* sunnan*   15 * 88a C

<hr>

[w] Cf. p. 101.   [x] Cf. p. 105.

[1] *onlacan* C, but the *on* prefixed to *lacan* seems in a different hand-writing and ink.   [2] So J, but in C looks more like *swæ*, though faint.

faran betweox oðrum tunglum;
meahtest ðe full recen on ðæm rodere ufan
siððan weorðan, 7 ðonne samtenges
æt ðæm ælcealdan anum steorran,
se yfmest is eallra tungla;   20
ðone Saturnus sundbuende
hatað under heofonum; he is se cealda
eallisig tungl, yfemest wandrað
ofer eallum ufan oðrū steorrum.
siððan ðu ðonne ðone up a hafast   25
forð oferfarenne, ðu meaht feorsian;
ðonne bist ðu siððan sona ofer uppan [1]
rodere ryneswiftum. gif ðu on riht færest,
þe þone hehstan heofon behindan lætst;
ðonne meaht ðu siðða soðes leohtes   30
habban þinne dæl, ðonan an cyning [2]
rume ricsað ofer roderum up,
7 under swa same, eallra gesceafta,
weorulde waldeð; þ is wis cyning;
þ is se ðe waldeð gio[*nd*] werðioda   35
ealra oðra eorðan cyninga;
se mid his bridle ymbebæted [*hæ*]fð
ymbhwyrft ealne eorðan 7 heofones.
he his *gewaldleð*er wel gemetgað;
se stioreð *a* ðurg ða strongan meaht   40
ðæm h*rædwæ*ne heofones 7 eorðan;
se [*an*] dema is gestæð*þig*,
unawendendlic, [*wlitig*] 7 *mære*.
gif ðu wyrst [3] on wege rih*tum*
   *up to ðæm earde, þ is æðele stow,   45
ðeah ðu hi nu geta forgiten hæbbe:
gif ðu æfre eft þæran cymest,
ðonne wilt þu *s*ecgan 7 sona cweðan:
ðis is eallunga min agen cyð,

---

[1] *ǫ̈ppan* C.   [2] *cyniᵹ* C.   [3] Conject. *wyr̠st* J.

eard 7 eþel; ic wæs ær hionan 50
cumen 7 acenned ðurh ðisses cræftgan meaht;
nylle ic æfre hionan ut witan,
ac ic symle her softe wille
mid fæder willan fæste stondan.
gif ðe ðonne æfre est geweorðeð 55
þ ðu wilt oððe most weorolde ðiostro
eft fandian, ðu meaht eaðe gesion
unrihtwise eorðan cyningas
7 þa ofermodan oðre rican
ðe þis werige folc wyrst tuciað, 60
þ hi symle bioð swiðe earme,
unmehtige ælces ðinges,
emne ða ilcan þe þis earme folc
sume hwile nu swiðost ondrædæð.

XXV ɣ.

Boeth. iv. met. 2.   'Quos uides sedere celsos.'

*G*eher nu an spell be ðæm ofermodum
unrihtwisum eorðan cyningum
ða her nu manegum 7 mislicum
wædum wlitebeorhtum wundrum scinað
on heahsetlum [*hrofe*] getenge, 5
golde gegerede 7 gimcynnum,
utan ymbestandne mid unrime
ðegna 7 eorla. þa bioð gehyrste
mid herege[*a*]twum hildetorhtum,
sweordum 7 fetel[*u*]m swiðe geglengde,* 10 * 94a C.
7 þegniað ðrymme micle
ælc oþ*rum*, 7 hi ealle him
ðonan mid þy þry*mme* þreatiað gehwider
ymbsittenda oðra ðeoda;
7 se hlaford ne *scrif*ð, ðe ðæm here waldeð, 15
freonde ne feonde, feore ne æhtum;

ɣ Cf. p. 111.

ac he reðig*mod* ræst on gehwilcne,
wedehunde *wuhta ge*licost;
bið to up áhæfen inne *on mode*
for ðæm anwalde þe him anra gehwilc   20
his tirwina to fultemað.
gif mon ðonne wolde him áwindan of
þæs cynegerelan claða gehwilcne,
7 him ðonne oftion *ðara ðegnunga*
7 þæs anwaldes þe he her hæfde,   25
ðonne meaht ðu gesion þ he bið swiðe gelic
sumum ðara gumena þe him geornost nú
mid ðegnungū ðringað ymbeutan;
gif he wyrsa ne bið, ne wene ic his na beteran.
gif him þonne æfre unmendlinga   30
weas geberede þ him wurde oftogen
þrymmes 7 wæda 7 þegnunga
7 ðæs anwaldes þe we ymbe sprecað,
gif him ænig þara ofhende wyrð,
ic wat þ him þynceð þ he þonne sie   35
becropen on carcern, oððe coðlice
racentan geræped. ic gereccan mæg
þ of ungemete ælces ðinges,
wiste* 7 wæda, wingedrinces,
7 of swetmettum, swiðost weaxað   40
þære wrænnesse wodðrag micel;
sio swiðe gedræfð sefan ingehygd
monna gehwelces; þonan mæst cymeð
yfla ofermetta, unnetta saca.
þonne hi gebolgene[1] weorþað, him wyrð on breostū inne
beswungen sefa on hreðre[2] mid ðæm swiðan welme 46
hatheortnesse, 7 hraðe[3] siððan
unrotnesse eac geræped[4],
hearde gehæfted. him siððan onginð
sū tohopa swiðe leogan   50
þæs gewinnes wræce; wilnað þ irre

* 94b C.

---

[1] em. *gebogene* C.   [2] em. *hraðre* C.   [3] em. *hreðe* C.   [4] em. *geræpeð* C.

anes 7 oðres; him þ eall gehæt
his recelest, rihtes ne scrifeð.
ic ðe sæde ær on ðisse selfan bec
þ sumes goodes sidra gesceafta
anlepra ælc á wilnode
for his agenum ealdgecynde.
unrihtwise eorðan cyningas
ne magon æfre þurhtion awuht goodes
for ðæm yfle þe ic ðe ær sæde.
nis ðæt nan wundor, forðæm hi willað hi
þæm unðeawū þe ic ðe ær nemde
anra gehwelcū á underðeodan.
sceal ðonne nede nearwe gebugan
to ðara hlaforda hæftedome[1],
þe he hine eallunga ær underþiodde.
ðæt is wyrse get, þ he winnan nyle*
wið ðæm anwalde ænige stunde.
þær he wolde á winnan onginnan,
7 þonne on ðæm gewinne þurhwunian forð,
þonne næfde he nane scylde,
ðeah he oferwunnen weorðan sceolde.

55

6o

6₅

* 95a C.

7o

XXVI[z].

Boeth. iv. met. 3.   ' Vela Neritii ducis.'

*I*c þe mæg eaðe ealdum 7 leasū
spellū reccan[2] spræce gelice
efne ðisse ilcan þe wit ymb sprecað.
hit gesælde gio on sume tide
þæt Aulixes under hæfde
þǣ casere cynericu twa;
he wæs Þracia ðioda aldor
7 Retie rices hirde.
wæs his freadrihtnes folccuð nama
Agamemnon, se ealles weold

5

10

---

[z] Cf. p. 115.   [1] em. *hæfdedome* C.   [2] *7reccan* C.

Creca rices. cuð wæs wide
þ [*on*] þa tide Troia[1] gewin
wearð under wolcnu[*m*. *fo*]r wiges heard
Creca drihten campsted secan;
Aulixes mid an hund scipa   15
lædde ofer lagustream; sæt longe ðær
tyn winter full. ða[2] sio tid gelomp
þ hi ðæt rice geræht hæfdon;
diore gecepte drihten Creca
Troia burg *h*lū gesiþū.   20

    * 98a C.

ða ða[3] Aulixes le[*a*]fe hæfde,*
Ðracia cining, þ he þonan moste,
he let him behindan hyrnde ciolas
nigon 7 hundnigontig; nænigne þonan
merehengesta ma þonne ænne   25
ferede on fifelstream, famigbor[*do*]n,
ðrireðre ceol; þ bið ðæt mæste
[*c*]reciscra scipa. þa wearð ceald weder,
stearc storma gelac; stunede sio brune
yð wið oðre, ut feor adraf   30
on Wendelsæ wigendra scola
up on þ igland þær Apolines
dohtor wunode dægrimes worn.
wæs se Apollinus æðeles cynnes,
Iobes eafora; se wæs gio cyning.   35
se licette litlum 7 miclum
gumena gehwylcū þ he god[4] wære,
hehst 7 halgost. swa se hlaford þa
þ dysige folc on gedwolan lædde,
oððæt him gelyfde leoda unrim,   40
forðæm he wæs mid rihte rices hirde
hiora cynecynnes[5]. cuð is wid[*e*]
þ on ða tide þeoda æghwilc
hæfdon heora hlaford for þone hehstan [*god*],

---

[1] *trioia* C.   [2] em. *ðe* C.   [3] em. *ðu* C.   [4] em. *good* C.
[5] *cynecyñes* C.

7 weorðodon swa swa wuldres cin*ing*,   45
gif he to ðæm rice wæs on rihte boren.
wæs þæs Iobes fæder god eac swa he;
Saturnus ðone sundbuende
heton, hæleþa bearn. hæfdon ða mægða
ælcne æfter oðrum for ecne God[1].   50
sceolde eac wesa[*n*]* Apollines   * 98b C.
dohtor diorboren, dysiges folces
gumrinca gyden ; cuðe galdra fela
drifan drycræftas. hio gedwolan fylgde
manna swiðost manegra þioda,   55
cyning[*es*] dohtor, sio Circe wæs
haten for [*he*]rigum. hio ricsode
on ðæ iglonde þe Aulixes
cining Þracia cō ane to
ceole liðan. cuð wæs sona   60
eallre þære mænige þe hire mid wunode
æþ[*eli*]nges sið. hio mid ungemete
lissū lufode liðmonna frean[2],
7 he eac swa same ealle mægne
efne swa swiðe hi on sefan lufode,   65
þ he to his earde ænige nyste
modes mynlan ofer mægð giunge ;
ac he mid þæm wife wunode siððan,
oððæt him ne meahte monna ænig
þegna[3] sinra þær mid wesan ;   70
ac hi for ðæm yrmðum eardes lyste,
[*my*]nton forlætan leofne hlaford.
[*ða*] ongunnon wercan werðeoda spell ;
[*sædon*] þ hio sceolde mid hire scinlace
beornas *for*bredan, 7 mid balo[*c*]ræftum   75
wra*þ*um weorpan on wildra [*l*]ic
cyninges *þegnas*, cyspan siððan
7 mid racentan eac ræpan mænigne.

<hr>

[1] *gōd* C.   [2] em. *frea* C.   [3] em. *þegnra* C.

sume hi *to* wulfum wurdon, ne meahton þonne word
    forðbringan,

* 99a C.   ac* hio þragmælum ðioton ongunnon.   80
sume wæron eaforas; â grym*ete*don[1]
ðonne hi sares hwæt siofian scioldon.
þa ðe leon wæron ongunnon laðlice
yrrenga ryn a þonne hi sceoldon
clipian for corþre. cnihtas wurdon,   85
ealde ge giunge, ealle forhwerfde
to sumum diore swelcum he æror
on his lifdagum gelico[*st*] wæs,
butan þam cyninge þe sio c[*wen*] lufode.
nolde þara oþra ænig onbitan   90
mennisces metes, ac hi ma lufedon
diora drohtað, swa hit gedefe ne wæs.
næfdon hi mare monnum gelices
eorðbuendum ðon[*ne*] ingeþonc ;
hæfde anra gehwy[*lc*] his agen mod ;   95
þ wæs þeah swiðe so[*r*]gum gebunden
for ðæm earfoðu[*m*] þe him onsæton.
hwæt, ða dyse[*gan*] men þe ðysum drycræftum
lo[*ng*] gelyfdon, leasum spellum,
[*wisson*] hwæðre þ þ gewit ne mæg   100
mo[*d on*]wendan monna ænig
mid drycræftum, þeah hio gedon meahte
þ ða lichoman lange þrage
onwend wurdon. is þ wundorlic
mægencræft micel moda [*gehwilces*]   105
* 99b C.   ofer lichoman* lænne 7 sænne.
swylcum 7 swylcū þu meaht sweotole ongitan
þ ðæs lichoman listas 7 cræftas
of ðæm mode cumað monna gehwylcum,
ænlepra ælc. þu meaht eaðe ongitan   110
þte ma dereð monna gehwelcū
modes unþeaw þonne mettrymnes

        [1] *gým . . . don* C.

lænes lichom[*an*]. ne þearf leoda nan
wenan þæ[*re*] wyrde þ þ werige flæsc
þ mod mon[*na*] æniges mæge [1]   115
eallunga to him æfre onwendan;
ac þa unðeawas ælces modes
7 þ ingeþonc ælces monnes
þone lichoman lit þider hit wile.

XXVII ª.

Boeth. iv. met. 4.   ' Quid tantos iuuat excitare motus.'

*H*wy ge æfre scylen unrihtfioungum
eower mod drefan, swa swa mereflodes
yþa hrera×* iscalde sæ,   * 106b C.
wecgga× for winde? hwy o×wite ge
wyrde eowre þ hio geweald nafa× ?
hwy ge þæs dea×es, þe eow Drihten gesceop,
gebidan ne magon bitres gecyndes,
nu he eow ælce dæg onet toweard ?
ne magon ge gesion þ he sȳle spyre×
æft̃ æghwelcum eor×an tudre,   10
diorum 7 fuglum? dea× eac swa same
æft̃ moncynne geond ×isne middangeard,
egeslic hunta, a bi× on wa×e;
nyle he ænig swæ× æfre forlætan
ær he gehede þ he hwile ær   15
æft̃ spyrede. is þ earmlic þing
þ his gebidan ne magon burgsittende,
ungesælige men hine ær willa×
foran tosciotan [2], swa swa fugla cyn,
o××e wildu dior; þa winna× betwuh,   20
æghwylc wolde o×er acwellan.
ac þ is unriht æghwelcum men
þæt he o×erne inwitþoncum
fioge on fær×e, swa swa fugl o××e dior.   ·

ª Cf. p. 124.   [1] Conject. om. C.   [2] *toscĩan* C.

ac þ wære rihtost þte rinca gehwylc   25
oðrū gulde edlean on riht,
weorc be geweorhtū weoruldbuendū
þinga gehwilces; þ is þ he lufige
gōdra gehwilcne swa he geornost mæge,
mildsige yflum, swa we spræcon.   30

* 107a C.   he sceal þone monnan* mode *lufian*,
7 *his unþeawas ealle* hatian
7 ofsniðan swa he swiðost mæge.

XXVIII [b].

Boeth. iv. met. 5.   'Si quis Arcturi sidera nescit.'

Hwa is on eorðan nu unlærdra
þe ne wundrige wolcna færeldes,
rodres swifto, ryne tungla[1],
hu hy ælce dæge utan ymbhwerfað[2]
eallne middangeard? hwa is moncynnes   5
þ ne wundrie ymb þas wlitegan tungl,
hu hy sume habbað swiðe micle
scyrtran ymbehwerft, sume scriðað leng
utan ymb eall ðis? an þara tungla
woruldmen hatað wænes þisla;   10
þa habbað scyrtran scride 7 færelt,
ymbhwerft læssan, ðonne oðru tungl,
forðæm hi þære eaxe utan ymbhweorfað

* 108b C.   þone norð*ende, *nean [ymbcerrað;*
on ðære ilcan] eaxe hwerfeð   15
eall ruma rodor, recene scriðeð,
suðheald swifeð swift untiorig.
hwa is on weorulde þæt ne wafige,
buton þa ane þe hit ær wisson,
þte mænig tungul maran ymbhwyrft   20
hafað on heofonum, sume hwile eft
læsse geliðað, þa þe lacað ymb eaxe ende,
oððe micle mare geferað þa hire middre[3] ȳbe

<hr>

[b] Cf. p. 125.   [1] em. *tunglo* C.   [2] em. *ymbhwerfeð* C.   [3] em. *midore* C.

þearle þrægað¹?   þara is gehaten
Saturnus sum, se hæfð ymb þritig   25
wiñ gerime[s *w*]eoruld ymbcirred.
Boetes eac beorhte scineð,
oðer steorra; cymeð efne swa same
on þone ilcan stede eft ymb þritig
gear gerimes ðær he gio ða wæs.   30
hwa is weoruldmonna þ ne wafige
hu sume steorran oð ða sæ farað
under merestreamas, þæs ðe monnum ðincð?
swa eac sume wenað þ sio sunne do,
ac se wena n[*i*]s wuhte þe soðra.   35
ne bið hio on æfe[*n*] ne on ærmorgen
merestreame þe near ðe on midne dæg,
7 þeah monnum þyncð þ hio on mere gange,
under sæ swife, þonne hio on setl glideð.
hwa is on weorulde þ ne* wundrige   40 * 109a C.
[*fulles monan, þonne he fæ*]ringa
wyrð under wolcnū wlites bereafad,
beþeaht mid þiostrum? hwa þegna ne mæge
eac wafian ælces stiorran,
hwy hi ne scinen scirum wederū   45
beforan ðære sunnan swa hi sȳle doð
middelnihtum wið þone monan foran,
hadrum heofone? hwæt, nu hæleða fela
swelces 7 swelces swiðe wundrað,
7 ne wundriað þte wuhta gehwilc,   50
men 7 netenu, micelne habbað
7 unnetne andan betweoh him,
swiðe singalne. is þ sellic þincg
þ hi ne wundriað hu hit on wolcnū oft
þearle þunrað, þragmælū eft   55
anforlæteð; 7 eac swa same
yð wið lande ealneg winneð,
wind² wið wæge. hwa wundrað þæs,

---

¹ em. *þrægeð* C.   ² em. *winð* C.

oððe oþres eft, hwi þæt ís mæge
weorðan of wætere; wlitetorht[1] scineð　　　　60
sunna swegle hat; sona gecerreð
ísmere ænlic on his agen gecynd,
weorðeð to wætre. ne þincð þ wundor micel
monna ænegum þ he mægge gesion
dogora gehwilce, ac ðæt dysie folc　　　　65
þæs hit seldnor gesihð swiðor wundrað,
þeah hit wisra gehwæm wundor ðince

* 10ᵧb C.　　on his* [*modsefan micle læsse.*
un]staðolfæste[2] ealneg wenað
þ þ ealdgesceaft æfre ne wære　　　　70
þ hi seldon gesioð; ac swiþor giet
weoruldmen wenað þæt hit weas come,
niwan gesælde, gif hiora nængum hwylc
ær ne oðcowde; is þ earmlic þinc.
ac gif hiora ænig æfre weorðeð　　　　75
to ðon firwetgeorn þ he fela onginð
leornian lista, 7 him lifes weard
of mode abrit þ micle dysig
ðæt hit oferwrigen mid wunode lange,
þonne ic wat[3] gearc þ hi ne wundriað　　　　80
mæniges þinges þe monnū nu
wæfðo[4] 7 wunder welhwær þynceð.

XXIX ᶜ.

Boeth. iv. met. 6. ‘Si uis celsi iura tonantis.’

*G*if ðu nu wilnige weorulddrihtnes[5]
heane anwald hlutre mode
on[*gi*t]an *giorne*[6], gem almægene
* 118a C.　　heofones* [*tunglu, hu hi him healdað betwuh*
sibbe] singale; dydon swa lange　　　　5
swa hi gewenede wuldres aldor
æt frumsceafte, þ sio fyrene mot

ᶜ Cf. p. 135.　　¹ em. *wlitetorh* C.　　² em. *understaðolfæste* J.　　³ em.
wæt C.　　⁴ em. *wærðo* C.　　⁵ *weorulddrihnes* C.　　⁶ em. *gionne* J.

sunne gesecan snawcealdes weg,
monna gemæro. hwæt, ða mæran tungl
auðer oðres rene â ne gehrineð　　　　　　　　10
ærþæm þ oðer of gewiteð.
ne huru se stiorra gestigan wile
westdæl wolcna, þone wise men
Ursa nemnað. ealle stiorran
sigað æfter sunnan samod mid rodere　　　　15
under eorðan grund; he ana stent.
nis þ nan wundor; he is wundrum fæst [1]
upende neah eaxe ðæs roderes.
ðonne is an steorra ofer oðre beorht,
cymeð eastan up ær þonne sunne;　　　　　20
þone [2] monna bearn morgenstiorra
hatað under heofonum, forðæm he hæleþum dæg
bodað æft burgum; brengeð æft
swegeltorht sunne samad eallum dæg.
is se forrynel fæger 7 sciene;　　　　　　　25
cymeð eastan up ær for sunnan,
7 eft æfter sunnan on setl glideð,
west under weorulde. werþioda
his noman onwendað þonne niht cymeð,
hatað hine ealle æfenstiorra;　　　　　　　30
se bið þære sunnan swiftra; siððan hi on setl gewitað,
ofirneð, *þæt is* æþele tungol,*　　　　　　　　* 118b C.
[*oðþ he be eastan eft* [3] *weorðeð*
eldum oðewed] ær þonne sunne.
habbað æþele tungol emne gedæled　　　　　35
dæg 7 nihte Drihtnes meahtum,
sunna 7 mone, swiðe geþwære,
swa him æt fryðe fæder getiohhode.
ne þearft þu no wenan þ ða wlitegan tungl
ðæs þeowdomes aþroten weorðe　　　　　　40
ær domes dæg[*e*]. deð siððan ȳbe
moncynnes fruma swa him gemet þinceð,

---

[1] em. by J, *east* C.　　　[2] em. *þonne* C.　　　[3] Grein's conject. om. J.

forðon hi be healfe heofones þisses
on ane ne læt ælmihtig God,
þy læs hi oðra fordyden æþela gesceafta;   45
ac se eca God ealla gemetgað
sida gesceafta, softa geþwerað.
hwilum ðæt drige drifð ðone wætan,
hwylum hi gemengeð metodes cræfte,
cile wið hæto; hwilum cerreð   50
eft on uprodor ælbeorhta leg,
leoht lyfte; ligeð him behindan
hefig hrusan dæl, þeah hit hwilan[1] ær
eorðe sio cealde oninnan hire
heold 7 hydde haliges meahtū.   55
be þæs cyninges gebode cymeð geara gehwæm,
eorðe bringeð æghwylc tudor,
7 se hata sumor hæleða bearnum
geara gehwilce giereð 7 drigeð
geond sidne grund sæd 7 bleda,   60
hærfest to honda herbuendū
* 119a C. ripa receð. ren æftī* þæm
sw[*ylce hagal*] 7 snaw hrusan leccað
on wintres tid, weder unhiore;
forðæm eorðe onfehð eallum sædū,   65
gedeð þ hi growað geara gehwilce;
on lenctentid leaf up spryttað.
ac se milda metod monna bearnū
on eorþan fet eall þte groweð,
waestmas on weorolde; wel forðbrengeð hit   70
þonne he wile, heofona waldend,
7 eowað eft eorðbuendū;
nimð þonn he wile, nergende God;
þ þ hehste good on heahsetle
siteð self cyning, 7 þios side gesceaft   75
þenað 7 þiowað; he þonan waldeð[2]
þæm geweltleþrum weoruldgesceafta.

[1] *hwilǎn* C.   [2] Grein's em. *þone anwald deð* C.

nis þ nan wundor; he is weroda God,
cyning 7 Drihten cwucera gehwelces,
æwelm 7 fruma eallra gesceafta,   80
wyrhta 7 sceppend weorulde þisse,
wisdom 7 ǽ woruldbuendra.
ealla gesceafta on hærendo
hionane he sendeð, hæt eft cuman[1].
gif he swa gestæððig ne staðolade   85
ealla gesceafta, æghwylc hiora
wraðe tostencte weorðan sceolden,
æghwilc hiora, ealle to nauhte;
weorðan sceoldon wraðe toslopena,
þeah þa ane lufe ealla gesceafta   90
heofones 7 eorðan hæbb*en* g*e*mæne,
þ hi þiowien swilcū þiodfrum*an*,
7 fægniað þ hiora fæder wa[*ld*]eð.
nis þ nan wundor,* for[*ðæm wuhta nan*   * 119b C.
æfre ne meahte elles] wunian,   95
gif hi eallmægene hiora ordfruman
ne þiowoden, þeodne mærum.

XXX[d].

Boeth. v. met. 2.   'Puro clarum lumine Phoebum.'

*O*merus wæs east mid Crecum
on ðæm leodscipe leoða cræftgast,*   * 123b C.
Firgilies freond 7 lareow,
þæm mæran sceope magistra betst.
hwæt, se Omerus oft 7 gelome   5
þære sunnan wlite swiðe herede,
æðelo cræftas oft 7 gelome
leoðum 7 spellum leodum reahte.
ne mæg hio þeah gescinan, þeah hio sie scir 7 beorht,
ahwærgen neah ealla gesceafta;   10
ne furðum þa gesceafta ðe hio gescinan mæg,

---

[d] Cf. p. 141.   [1] Line emended; C has *hio nane ne sendað þæt
eft cumað*. See p. 136, l. 25. The þ of þæt was orig. an *h*.

endemes ne mæg ealla geondlihtan
innan 7 utan. ac se ælmihtega
waldend [7 *wy*]rhta weorulde gesceafta
his agen weorc eall geondwliteð, 15
endemes þurhsyhð ealla gesceafta.
ðæt is sio soðe sunne mid rihte,
be ðæm we magon singan swylc butan lease.

XXXI [e].

Boeth. v. met. 5. 'Quam uariis terras animalia permeant figuris.'

[*Hwæt*[1], *þu meaht ongitan, gif his ðe geman lyst,*
þte mislice manega wuhta
geond eorðan farað ungelice;
habbað blioh 7 fær, bu ungelice,
7 mrgwlitas manegra cynna[2] 5
cuð 7 uncuð. creopað 7 snicað,
eall lichoma eorðan getenge.
nabbað hi æt fiðrum fultum, ne magon hi mid fotū
 gangan,
eorðan brucan, swa him eaden wæs.
sume fotum twam foldan peððað, 10
sume fierfete, sume fleogende

windað[3] *under** *wo*]lcnum. bi ð ðeah wuhta gehwylc
onhnigen to hrusan, hnipað ofdune,
on weoruld wlit[*eð;*] wilnað to eorðan,
sume nedþearfe, sume neodfræce; 15
man ana gæð metodes gesceafta
mid his andwlitan up on gerihte.
mid ðy is getacnod þ his treowa sceal,
7 his modgeþonc, ma up þonne niðer
habban to heofonum, þy læs he his hige wende 20
niðer swaðær nyten. nis[4] þ gedafenlic
þ se modsefa monna æniges
niðerheald wese, 7 þ neb upweard.

---

[e] Cf. p. 147. [1] From here to line 12 is part of the missing folio.
[2] em. *cynnu* C. [3] em. *windeð* J. [4] em. *is* C.

APPENDIX

——◆——

THE NAPIER FRAGMENT (N).

*For description see Introduction. The corresponding part
of the Text begins on p. 32, l. 18.*

[   ]nniscan lifes [32

[   ] ðy hi hi selfe ongiten hwæt hī
sīn, 7 hwonan hi sīen, 7 ðy hi sint wyrsan ðoñ nie[   ]nu 20
ðy hi nyllað witan hwæt hī sint, oððe hwanon hi sint. Ðæm
neatū īs gecynde ðæt hi nyten hwæt hī sīen; ac ðæt īs
ðara monna unðeaw þæt hi nyten hwæt hi sīen. N[ ] ðe
īs swiðe sweotol þ ge bioð on gedwolan, þoñ ge wenað þ
ænig ðing mæg mid f[   ]g[ ]weorðod. Gif hwa nu 25
bið mid hwelcū welū geweorðod [ ] mid h[   ]
æhtū gearad, hu ne belimpð se weorðscipe ðoñ [ ]o
þǣ ðe hine geweo[   ]anne hwene ryhtlicor.
Ne ðæt ne bið no ðy fægerre þ mid elles hwā gerenod
bið, ðeah ða gerenu fægru sīn ðe hit midgerenod bið. Gif 30
hit ær sceondlic wæs, ne b[ ] h[   ] ðy fægerre. Wite
ðu for soð þ nán god ne dereð þǣ ðe hit ah; hwæt ðu
wast nu þ ic ðe ne [ ]ge, 7 [   ] ða welan oft deriað 33
þǣ ðe hi ágon on monegū ðingū, 7 on ðǣ swiðost þ
[ ] men w[   ]ð swa upahafene for ðǣ welan þ oft se
ealra wyrresta 7 se ealra unweorðusta mon wenð þ he sī
ealles ðæs welan wyrðe þe on weorolde īs, gif he 5
wisse hu he hī tocuman meahte. Se ðe micelne welan

hæfð, he hī ondræt monigne feond; gif he nane æhta
næfde ne ðorſte he hī nanne ondrædan.   Gif ðu nu
wære wegferend[ ] 7 h[ ]de micel gold on þe 7 þu þoñ
10 become on ðeofscole, þoñ ne wendes ðu ðe ðines

(Other side of fragment.)

34   [   ]gan
be ðæm weorðscip[   ]m anwalde ðisse weorolde.
For ðæm anwalde ge eow woldon ahebban up oð ðone
[   ]ſon, gif ge meahten, ðæt is forðæm þe ge ne gemunon ne
eac ne ongitað þone heofoncundan anweald 7 þone weorðscipe
20 se īs eower āgen, 7 þonan ge comon. Hwæt, se eowe[   ]a
þoñ 7 se eower anweald ðe ge nu weorðscipe hatað, gif he
becymð to þǣ ealra wyrrestan men, 7 to þǣ ðe his ealra
unweorðost bið, swa he nu dyde to ðys ilcan Điodrice, 7 gio ær
to Nerone þæm caserc, 7 oft eac to manegū hira gelicū
25 hu ne wile he ðoñ don swa^{swa} hī dydon 7 git doð, eal ða
ricu ðe hī underbioð, oððe awer on neaweste forslean 7
forheregian swa swa fyres lig deð drygne hæðfeld, oððe eft
se birnenda sweſl þone munt bærnð ðe we hatað Etne; se
is on Sicilia þǣ ealonde. Swiðe onlice ðǣ miclan flode ðe
30 gio on Noes dagū wæs. Ic wene þ ðu mæḡ gemunan
þ te eowre ildran gio Romana witan on Torcwines
35 dagū ðæs ofermodan cyninges for his oſmetton[1] þone
cynelican naman of Romebyrg ærest adydon 7 eft
swa ilce þ͞e heretogan ðe hine ær utadriſon; hie woldon eft
utadrifan for hira ōſmettū, ac hi ne meahton; forðǣ ðe
5 se æftr͞e anweald þara heretogena ðæm romaniscū
witū git wirs licode þoñ se ærra þara cyninga, gif hit
ðoñ æfre gewyrð swa hit swiðe seldon ḡwyrð

---

[1] The *on* indistinct.

GLOSSARY

EXPLANATION OF GLOSSARY.

The order is strictly alphabetical; ð is used for both ð and þ of the text. The main-words are normalised on an early West Saxon basis.

Ordinary figures refer to page and line, Roman numerals to the Cott. Metra. Pr. = Proem; MPr. = Metrical Proem, preceding the Metra. N. = Napier Fragment.

Many of the references to the Bodleian MS. text are marked with an asterisk where attention is called to the forms.

The Headings of Chapters, pp. 3–6, and the prayer on p. 149 are not considered in the Glossary.

Verbs marked *sv*1, *sv*2 &c. belong to the strong conjugation according to the classification given in Sievers' *Angelsächsische Grammatik*, thus: āberan, *sv*4. bear. All parts and forms of the verb ' to be ' will be found under *beon*.

Verbs with preteritive presents are entered under the present indicative, e.g. *mæg, deah*. When no examples of, but only the references to, a particular case of a noun or adjective are given, the form is identical with that last given. Words compounded with the prefix *ge-* will be found under the simple forms. In adjectives the masculine of each case, being given first, is not marked as such; weak forms in *-an* have not usually the gender indicated.

In text *e* as root-vowel often = *ie* in Glossary, *io* often = *eo*, *o* before nasal = *a*.

a. = accusative.	*m. immediately follow-ing a main word =* strong masculine ; *otherwise* = masculine.	*ptcp.* = participle.
ab. = about.		*q.v.* = quod vide.
absol. = used absolutely.		*rflx.* = reflexive.
anv. = anomalous verb.		*rv.* = reduplicating verb.
comp. = comparative.	*n. immediately follow-ing a main word =* strong neuter; *follow-ing a reference* = see footnote; *otherwise =* neuter *or* nominative.	*s.* = singular.
conj. = conjunction.		*sv.* = strong verb.
d. = dative.		*sbj.* = subjunctive.
esp. = especially.		*sbst.* = substantive.
f. immediately following a main word = strong feminine ; *otherwise* = feminine.		*sup.* = superlative.
		swv. = strong-weak verb.
	perh. = perhaps.	
fq. = frequently.	*pl.* = plural.	*t.* = times.
g. = genitive.	*pp.* = past participle.	*v.* = vide, *or* verb.
gen. = generally.	*pred.* = predicate.	*vb.* = verb.
imp. = imperative.	*prep.* = preposition.	*w.* = with, *or* weak.
ind. = indicative.	*prs.* = present.	*wk.* = weak.
inst. = instrumental.	*prs.p.* = present participle.	*wm.* = weak masculine substantive.
interj. = interjection.	*pst.* = past.	*wv.* = weak verb.

A.

ā, *adv.* ever, always; *fq.* 21. 8
&c.; *w. comp.* a ðy betera 27.
27, *cf.* 31. 10, 63. 2, 64. 29, 69.
6 &c.; *without* ðy 85. 11, 101. 18.
ā, 92. 14, 93. 22, 23, 94. 4, 110. 25,
vii. 39 (J), ix. 34, xiii. 40 (J), 62,
xxv. 69, xxvi. 81, xxix. 10.

ābedecian, *wv.* get by begging;
prs. sbj. abeðecige 71. 12.

ābelgan, *sv3.* make angry, offend;
ind. pst. pl. abulgon 19. 13.

āberan, *sv4.* bear, endure; 133. 3.

ābītan, *sv1.* bite, devour; *ind. prs.*
3. *s.* abit 57. 13*, xiii. 30.

āblendan, *wv.* blind; *ind. prs.* 3. *s.*
ablent 109. 5; *pl.* ablendað 89.
16, xxi. 27; *pst. pl.* ablendan 8.
9*; *pp.* ablend 121. 13; *n. pl. m.*
ablende 131. 15, 141. 6; *n.*
122. 6; *wk.* ablendan 121. 18.

ābrecan, *sv4.* break down, take by
storm; *ind. pst. pl.* abræcon 7.
3; *pp.* abrocen i. 18.

ābregdan, *sv3.* remove; *ind. prs.*
3. *s.* abrit 126. 25*, xxviii. 78;
pp. abrogden 45. 30; pull open,
ða duru abroden (anbroden B)
97. 24.

ābysgian, *wv.* occupy, trouble;
sbj. prs. pl. abisegien 95. 11*;
pp. abisgod 51. 15, 143. 7, 11.

ac, *conj.* but; *fq.* 7. 8, i. 80 &c.

acēlan, *wv.* cool; *pp.* aceled vii.
17.

ācennan, *wv.* bring forth, give birth
to; *ind. prs.* 3. *s.* acenð 70. 12*;
pp. acenned 105. 23, xxiv. 51;
n. pl. acennede 69. 19.

ācennednes, *f.* birth; *a.* acennednesse 69. 28.

ācwelan, *sv4.* die; 102. 1; *ind.*
prs. 3. *s.* acwylð 28. 18.

ācwellan, *wv.* kill; 66. 24, ix. 24,
xxvii. 21; to acwellenne 124.
11*.

ācȳðan, *wv.* make known, reveal;
sbj. pst. 3. *s.* acyðde 39. 3*.

ādǣlan, *wv.* separate; *pp.* adæled
85. 1.

ādimmian, *wv.* grow dim; *pp.*
adimmad 55. 16.

adl, *f.* disease, infirmity; *a. pl.*
adla 70. 8.

ādōn, *anv.* remove, banish; 60. 24;
ind. prs. 3. *s.* adeð 46. 32; *pst.*
pl. adydon 35. 2; *sbj. prs.* ado
67. 28, xvi. 5; *pp.* of adon
127. 7.

ādrencan, *wv. trans.* drown; 37.
2; *ind. pst.* 3. *s.* adrencte 37. 3.

ādrēogan, *sv2.* bear, endure; 23.
21, 133. 28, 139. 4 (adrygan
B); adriogan 138. 31; *ind. prs.*
3. *s.* adreogeð xii. 21.

ādrīfan, *sv1.* drive away, banish;
35. 4, 60. 8; *ind. prs.* 3. *s.* adrifð
135. 12; *pst.* adraf xxvi. 30;
pl. adrifon 35. 3; *imp.* adrif
16. 6; *pp.* adrifen 11. 4, 10,
19, 62. 12, 63. 15.

ādrȳgan, *wv.* wipe dry; *ind. pst.*
adrigde 8. 25*.

ādwǣscan, *wv.* extinguish,
quench; xx. 120; *ind. prs.* 3. *s.*
adwæsceð 80. 24*; ðiostro adwæsceð iv. 7; adwæsceð 10. 4*.

ǣ, *f.* law; 136. 25, i. 41; ǣ 142.
11, 13, xxix. 82.

æcer, *m.* field; *d.* æcere xii. 2, 28;
pl. g. æcera xiv. 5; *d.* æcerum
52. 1.

ǣdr, *f.* vein, sinew; *d.* ædre 93. 4.

ǣfen, *m.* evening; *g.* to æfennes
33. 28*; *a.* æfen 136. 1; on
æfen xxviii. 36.

ǣfensteorra, *wm.* evening star;
10. 9, 136. 1; æfenstiorra xxix.
30.

ǣfentīd, *f.* eventide; *a.* on æfentid
viii. 19.

ǣfre, *adv.* ever; *used in interrog.*
neg. and hypoth. sentences, 8.
11, i. 82, vii. 9, xiii. 22 &c.

æfter, 1) *prep. w.d.*; *fq. written*
æft. *in* C. *a)* *place,* behind,
along; æfter burgum v. 3, xxix.
23; *motion along,* æfter ðæm
bogum 92. 1. *b)* *time,* after,
about 36 *times,* 7. 5, vii. 2 &c.;
efter 52. 8; *adv.* æfter ðam, afterwards 21. 18; *conj.* æfter ðam

ðe 70. 12.   *c) following, accompaniment,* 103. 12, 135. 30, 136.
2.   *d) pursuit, aim, obj. of verb*;
34. 11, 12, 35. 22, 32, 60. 5, 77.
5, 143. 3, viii. 57, xxii. 1, xxvii.
12;   *used with* ascian 127.
15, 139. 9, 10; higian 56. 4,
112. 31; murcnian 31. 3; swincan 76. 26, 27, 113. 12; wilnian
53. 16; winnan 76. 28, 139. 13;
w. spyrian *about* 25 *times,* 27. 21
&c.   *e)* according to, 16. 15, 19.
22, 32. 13, 39. 20, 41. 26,
49. 31, 125. 20, 128. 25; æfter
ðinum willan 58. 28, *cf.* 123. 27,
xx. .47; æfter his gewyrhtum
124. 14, 141. 9, 148. 33.   2)
adv. atterwards, after Pr. 9 (J).

æftergenga, *wm.* successor; *d. pl.*
æftergengum 134. 1.

æfterra, *comp. adj.* following,
second 47. 2; æftera 35. 5; *f.*
æfterre, æftre* 50. 5; æftere
38. 6.

æfweardnes, *f.* absence; *d.*
æfweardnesse 22. 20.

æg, *n.* egg; xx. 171; *d.* æge xx.
169.

æghwä, *pron.* each one; *g.*
æghwæs 98. 1; *used as adv.*
in every respect viii. 41; *a. n.*
æghwæt 57. 14; *pl. d.* æghwæm
viii. 38; æghwam viii. 5.

æghwær, *adv.* everywhere; 148.
26, x. 58.

æghwæðer, *pron.* either, each;
xx. 12; ægðer *the prose form*
38. 13 &c.; ægðer ge . . . . ge
Pr. 5, 11. 31 &c.; *g.* ægðres 93.
13; *d.* ægðrum 129. 32.

æghwanon, *adv.* from all sides,
everywhere; æghwonan 19. 26,
27. 11, vii. 45; æghwonon
x. 4.

æghwelc, *pron.* each (one); 53.
11*, 54. 28*; æghwilc 55. 2, xi.
33, 35, xii. 12, xvii. 22, xxi. 2,
xxii. 55; *f. (pl. vb. in each case)*
æghwilc xxvi. 43, xxix. 88;
æghwylc xxix. 86; *n.* æghwilc
xx. 64, 142, xxi. 28; æghwylc
xxvii. 21; *d.* æghwelcum v. 2,

xxvii. 10, 22; æghwilcum 149.
26*; *a. m.* æghwilcne xvii. 14;
n. æghwilc xx. 52; æghwylc
xxii. 16, xxix. 57; *inst.* æghwelce
dæg xiv. 5; æghwylce dæge
xx. 137; æghwelcra 74. 3
=hwelcra?

æghwider, *adv.* in every direction,
everywhere; xx. 92.

ægðer, *v.* æghwæðer.

æht, *f.* possession, property;
power; *a.* on æht gifen; *pl. n.*
æhta 55. 7, 72. 23; *g.* æhta vii.
15, xiv. 4, xix. 43; *d.* æhtum
32. 27, 38. 1, xxv. 16; *a.* æhta
33. 7, 66. 26; æhte 32. 14*.

ælbeorht, *adj.* very bright; *wk.*
ælbeorhta xxix. 51.

ælc, *pron. adj.* Pr. 13 &c.; xxv.
12, 56, xxvi. 110; *f.* ælc, *fq. w.*
gesceaft 92. 20 &c. *and* xiii. 64;
g. ælces 13. 18 &c., i. 36; *f.*
ælcere 8. 11*, 84. 9; ælcre 66. 21
&c. *and* xx. 185; *d.* ælcum 24. 24
&c. *and* xi. 1; ælcum anum, to
each separately; *f.* ælcere 80.
33*, 81. 34*; ælcre 67. 4 &c.; *a.*
ælcne Pr. 11 &c., xxii. 10, xxvi.
50; *n.* ælc xxiv. 7; *inst.* ælce
dæg 59. 23, 60. 15, 17, 80. 32,
124. 6, 125. 32, 128. 19. xxvii.
8; ælce dæge xxviii. 4; ælce
gearc 92. 14, 136. 15.

ælceald, *adj.* very cold; *d. wk.*
ælcealdan xxiv. 19.

ælcræftig, *adj.* all-powerful; *comp.
n. s. n.* ælcræftigre xx. 38.

ælenge, 1) *adj.* tedious; *n. pl. n.*
ælengo*, ælenge 127. 28.   2)
sbst. tediousness; ælinge MPr.
6.

ælgrēne, *adj.* all-green; *f.* ælgreno
xx. 78.

ælmesse, *wf.* alms; *a.* ælmessan
143. 1.

ælmihtig, *adj.* almighty, *only
used of God*; 48. 24, vii. 45 &c.;
ælmihti xiii. 72 (J); *wk.* ælmihtiga *about* 8 *times,* 49. 6 &c.;
ðu ælmihtiga scippend 10. 16,
iv. 29; ælmihtega 49. 16*, 101.
4, 117. 5*; ælmehtega 125. 14;

ælmehtga 148. 31; ælmihtga xiii. 2; *n.* ælmihtig xx. 32; *g.* ælmihtiges ix. 49, xx. 67, xxi. 43; *wk.* ælmihtigan 80. 29; ælmihtgan 104. 12; ælmehtigan 128. 24, 135. 13; *d. wk.* ælmihtigan 136. 8*, 141. 17*, xx. 245.

æltæwe, *adj.* perfect, sound; 74. 22; *n.* 122. 2; *a.* æltæwne 12. 6; *comp. n. s. n.* æltæwre 83. 29, 31.

ælðeod, *v.* elðeod.

ælðeodig, *v.* elðeodig.

æmetta, *wm.* leisure; *d.* æmettan Pr. 14; *a.* 117. 10, 120. 19, 127. 31.

æne, *adv.* once (semel); æne on dæg 33. 27, *cf.* viii. 18 ane xxvi. 59.

ænig, *pron. adj.* any (one); 32. 25, vii. 5 &c.; æni 110. 12; *f.* ænegu 32. 5*, 82. 25, 98. 14, xiii. 68, 73, xx. 41; *elsewhere* ænig; *g.* æniges 83. 14, xxvi. 115 &c.; ænies 23. 23*; *d.* ænegum 20. 20*, 22, 67. 16, 22, 83. 13, 123. 22, xv. 12, xx. 36, xxii. 27, xxviii. 64; ængum 144. 23, vii. 21, x. 36; *f.* ænigre 60. 6, 99. 22; *a.* ænigne 24. 29 &c.; *f.* ænige 20. 22, xx. 130 &c.; ænig 37. 19*; *n.* ænig xxvii. 14 &c.; *inst.* ænige 127. 12, xx. 109; *pl. g.* ænigra 138. 22; *d.* ænegum 44. 29*, 97. 3.

ænlic, unique, matchless; xxviii. 62; *a. n.* 101. 25.

æppel, *m.* apple of eye, eyeball; 121. 12; *a.* 133. 13.

ær, 1) *adv.* before, formerly; *fq.* 8. 2 &c.; *comp.* æror 87. 6, xiii. 43, 76, 80, xx. 41 *n.*, 240, 245, xxii. 7, 18, xxvi. 87; ær 20. 9, 83. 30; *sup.* ærest 11. 2, xii. 2 &c.; æresð 35. 2; 36. 31; ærast 51. 3*; æræst 14. 7. 2) *conj.* before, *w. sbj. or occasionally ind.* 25. 2, 11. 8, iv. 22 &c.; ær ær 128. 17, 28, 144. 29; ðon ær ðe, as soon as ever 25. 18, cf. 49. 27. 3) *prep. w.d.; time,*

before; *w. pers. prons.* 20. 19, 45. 20, 65. 9, 13, 79. 27, 139. 7, 11, 143. 5, 148. 9; ær tide 67. 11, *cf.* xii. 10, xxix. 41; *forming conjunctions,* ærðæm ðe 84. 1, 128. 12, v. 45, xxix. 11; ærðon 12. 5, 104. 31; ærðon ðe 20. 9.

ærende, *n.* errand; *d.* on his hlafordes ærende 63. 15; *a. pl.* ærendo 136. 26*; hærendo xxix. 83.

ærendgewrit, *n.* letter; *a. i.* 63; *a. pl.* ærendgewritu 7. 19.

ærmorgen, *m.* early morning; *a.* on ærmorgen xxviii. 36.

ærneweg, *m.* race-course; *g.* ærneweges 112. 23.

ærning, *f.* running, racing; *d.* ærninge 112. 24.

ærra, *comp. adj.* former; 35. 6; *d.* ærran 86. 15; *a. pl.* 103. 21.

gcæsce, *f.* inquiry, investigation; *d. pl.* be geæscum 148. 9.

æspringe, *m.* spring, fountain; v. 12.

æt, *prep. w.d. a) place,* near, at, 86. 20, 112. 22, xxiv. 19. *b) 'circumstance,* in; æt ðære spræce 145. 1. *c) motion,* to; xx. 155; *w.* bringan 18. 8, 10, 23. 19, 71. 13. *d) source, origin of gain or loss,* from; 26. 3, 27. 22, 27. 21, 31. 14, 15, 45. 2, 24, 96. 8, 125. 12, 128. 3, 139. 22, x. 69, xxxi. 8. *e) point of time;* æt sumum cyrre 39. 19, ix. 23; æt oðrum cerre 95. 28; æt fruman 129. 18, 142. 27, xvii. 13, 26; æt frymðe xi. 38, 77, xxiv. 14, xxix. 38; æt frumsceafte xxix. 7; æt frumcerre 145. 24; æt nihstan 15. 6.

ætgædere, *adv.* together; 37. 21, 76. 20, 90. 15, 93. 32, xi. 49; ætgædre 77. 24, 84. 25, 29, 90. 16, 92. 28, xx. 160.

ætsamne, *adv.* together; ætsomne 85. 13, 114. 3, 5, xx. 243.

ætwītan, *sv1.* reproach; *ind. prs. 2, pl.* ætwite ge 124. 4; *pst. 2. s.* ætwit(*e*) 17. 4.

æ'ðelcundnes, *f.* nobility; *d.*
æðelcundnesse 46. 13.

æðele, *adj.* noble by birth or
nature; x. 27; *f.* xxiv. 45; *n.*
xxix. 32; *g.* æðeles xxvi. 34; *a.*
æðelne xxiii. 4; *wk.* æðelan 82.
9; *n. pl.* æðele 24. 3, 4, 7,
xxix. 35; *f.* æðela xxix. 45; *a.*
æðele xix. 22; *sup. a. pl. wk.*
æðelestan ix. 26.

æðeling, *m.* prince, nobleman;
æðelincg 72. 30; *g.* æðelinges
xxvi. 62; *d.* æðelinge 36. 17,
40; *d. pl.* æðelingum i. 21.

æðelu, *f. a)* noble birth; *b)*
nobility of nature; *c)* habit,
nature; 92. 21 *n.* (*c?*), æðelo
69. 11 (*b*), 91. 20 (*c*); *g.* æðelo
69. 9 (*b*); *d.* æðele xiii. 51 (*c*);
a. æðelo 46. 15 (*a*), 69. 12 (*a*),
69. 31 (*b*), xvii. 25 (*b*), xxx. 7
(*c*); *d. pl.* æðelum xvii. 18 (*a*).

æwielm, *m.* spring of water;
source; æwelm 82. 28, 83. 3,
32, 136. 24, xxix. 80; æwylm
53. 5; *d.* æwelme 53. 8, 83. 4;
a. æwelm 47. 9, 82. 9, xx. 259,
xxiii. 4; æwellm 101. 20*.

āfǣran, *wv.* terrify; *pp.* afæred
138. 12; áfæred 86. 10.

āfæstnian, *wv.* make firm, fix;
82. 11, xx. 263.

āfandian, *wv.* experience; *pp.*
afandad 70. 29.

āfaran, *rv.* go away; *pp.* afaren
11. 4.

āfēdan, *wv.* feed, nourish; *pp.*
afeded, afed* 8. 18.

āferian, *wv.* carry away; *pp.*
aferod 105. 14.

āferscian, *wv.* become fresh; *ind.*
prs. 3.*s.* áfer(*s*)cað 86. 20.

āfierran, *wv.* remove; aferran 7.
18*; afýrran 39. 29*; *ind. prs.*
3.*s.* aferreð 20. 23; *imp.* aferre
20. 25; afyr 14. 19*; *sbj. prs.*
afyrre 134. 19; *pp.* afyrred 73.
13.

āfindan, *sv3.* experience; *pp.*
afunden 70. 29*.

āfrēfrian, *wv.* comfort; *pp. a. s.*
m. afrefredne 50. 13.

āfyllan, *a)* *wv.* fill; *b)* satisfy;
38. 29 (*b*); *pp. n. pl.* afylde
113. 31 (*a*).

āgǣlan, *wv.* hinder; *pp.* agæled
ii. 5.

āgǣlwan, *wv.* astonish, dismay;
pp. agælwed 86. 10.

āgan, *anv.* possess; 31. 19, 21,
67. 26, i. 39, 62, vii. 29, x.
2, xvi. 19; to aganne xxi. 19;
agon xvi. 1; *ind. prs.* 3.*s.* ah 32.
32, 63. 9, 123. 13, 14; *neg.* nah
124. 5, xvi. 21; *pl.* agon 33. 2;
pst. pl. ahton 38. 22, 123. 8; *sbj.*
prs. age 27. 20, 30. 1, xiv. 2, xvi.
2; *pst.* ahte 17. 10, 63. 22.

āgen, *adj.* own; 34. 20, xx. 122
&c.; *f.* agnu 29. 29, 80. 25;
agen xxiv. 49; *n.* agen iii. 5 &c.;
g. agenes 11. 6*, 12. 20, 37.
11, xiii. 31; agnes 16. 10
&c.; *f.* agenre 27. 26, 47. 27;
d. agenum xx. 23, xxv. 57;
agnum 11. 21 &c.; *f.* agenre 37.
29, 146. 29; ægenre 31. 32*;
a. agenne 66. 24, 80. 34, 143. 3,
xx. 64, 143; agene 39. 23*, ix.
28; *f.* agene 11. 12, 39. 23, 80.
2, iv. 30; agne 9. 1*; *n.* agen
15. 26, xi. 77 &c.; ahgen 9. 12*;
pl. agene 63. 24*; agne 17.
20; *f.* agna 23. 8; *n.* agnu
29. 27, 28; agene 31. 8*; *g.*
agenra; *d.* agenum vii. 47; agnum 11. 22*; *a. f.* agna 32. 14,
xx. 14.

āgiefan, *sv5.* give up, restore;
agifan 103. 5; *ind. prs.* 1.*s.*
agife 17. 10*; *sbj. pst. pl.*
ageafan*, agefan 102. 12.

āgnian, *wv.* appropriate, claim;
30. 29.

āhebban, *sv6.* raise; exalt; *gen-*
erally w. up; 46. 11, 104. 31;
ahebban 34. 17; *ind. prs.* 3.*s.*
ahefð 114. 19; *pl.* ahebbe ge;
pst. ahof 45. 6; *pl.* gewin up
ahofon 7. 2; *sbj. prs. pl.* ahebben
146. 12, xvii. 18; ahæbhen 133.
24; *pst.* ahofe 23. 18; *pp.* ahafen
111. 19*, v. 33; ahæfen 24.
29, xx. 219; āhæfen xxv. 19;

āhefen i. 47; *n. pl.* ahafene 9. 26*; ahæfene 33. 3.

āhefīgian, *wv.* weigh down, oppress; *pp.* ahefīgad 55. 20*.

āhwǣr, *adv.* anywhere, in any way; awer 17. 17, 34. 26*, viii. 14, 33.

āhwæðer, *pron.* either; auðer 14. 25*, xx. 42; awðer ... oððe ... oððe (ægðer B) 108. 13; auðer oððe ... oððe 146. 25*.

āhwanon, *adv.* from anywhere, on any side; ahwonan 84. 16; āhwonan 84. 13.

āhweorfan, *sv3.* remove, alter; *pp.* ahworfen 15. 19.

āhwergen, *adv.* anywhere; ahwærgen neah xxx. 10.

āhwierfan, *wv.* turn aside; *pp.* ahwerfed 114. 23.

ālādian, *wv.* excuse; 144. 5.

ālǣdan, *wv.* lead away; *ind. prs.* 3. s. alæt of ðam rihtan wege 73. 24*; *pp.* alǣded xix. 4.

ālǣtan, *rv.* let go, give up; 25. 23, 26. 6; ælætan 67. 10; *ind. prs.* 2. s. alætst 57. 23*.

āléogan, *sv2.* belie, disappoint; 3. pl. aleogað 58. 23; *pst.* ðæt eall aleag i. 39.

ālicgan, *sv5.* diminish; *pp.* alegen 43. 31.

āliefan, *wv.* allow, permit; *pp.* alefed 117. 7, 121. 18, 135. 7; alyfed 23. 20.

āliesan, *wv.* release, rescue; *ind. pst.* alysde 18. 20.

ambiht, *n.* service; *g.* ambehtes xi. 9.

āmerian, *wv.* purify; *pp.* amered 120. 15.

āmetan, *sv5.* measure; 148. 27, ix. 35.

āmierran, *wv.* hinder; amerran 94. 29, xxii. 4; *pp.* amerred 53. 13, viii. 44; *a.* amerredne 103. 30.

ān, *num. and adj.* one; only, alone, 11. 16, x. 54 &c.; on 42. 9; se an man 145. 29; *wk.* ana, alone 17. 28, 55. 12, 81. 21, 97. 11, 101. 5, 121. 29, 147. 9,

xxix. 16, xxxi. 16; *f.* an 41. 25, xxi. 10, 13, 16; *w. art.* 89. 9, 11; *n.* an 100. 13, xi. 48 &c.; no ðæt an ðæt . . . ac, not only . . . but 13. 27 &c.; *g.* anes 22. 20, xxv. 52; ðines anes geðeahte, of thee alone 79. 25, xx. 39; his anes, of himself alone ix. 22; *d.* anum 10. 15, iv. 27 &c. = one 97. 13; on anum untodæled, single 87. 31; *wk.* ðy anan, in this one respect; *f.* anre 41. 28, 68. 30, 107. 12; *a.* anne 39. 19*, 79. 34*, 86. 30, xx. 58; ænne 22. 19, 59. 18, 87. 25, 92. 25, x. 38; xx. 196, xxvi. 25; *f.* ane 14. 26 &c.; *n.* an 69. 12, xxv. 1 &c.; *inst.* ane 79. 33, xx. 56; *pl. n.* ni. ane 110. 31, xxviii. 19; *f.* ana 16. 19; *g.* anra, *w.* hwelc, gehwelc, gehwa 77. 18, 23, vii. 23, viii. 6 &c.; *d.* of anum twæm, from two only xvii. 3; *a.* ane iv. 52, xii. 32.

anbid, *n.* waiting, expectation; 120. 2* (andbid C); *d.* andbide 120. 3.

geanbīdian, *wv.* wait, await; *ind. prs.* 1. pl. (*w. g.*) geanbidiað 19. 24; *pst.* 1. s. geanbidode 50. 28.

ancor, *m.* anchor; ancer 23. 5; *n. pl.* ancras 23. 10*; oncras 23. 14.

and, *conj.* and; *passim, always written* 7, *except* and 30. 8, 72. 8, 84. 13; ond 35. 2, 36. 33, 39. 25*, 54. 5*, 140. 12.

anda, *wm.* malice, anger; *d.* andan 135. 2; *a.* 79. 24, 102. 8, 114. 30, 126. 17, xx. 36, xxviii. 52.

andefn, *f.* proportion, amount; *d.* be hire andefne 72. 26; be ðæs gyltes andefne 123. 20.

andettan, *wv.* confess; *ind. prs.* 1. s. andette; *pl.* andettað 83. 26* (andetteð C).

andgiet, *n.* intellect, reason; andgit 32. 2*, 127. 20, 146. 25*; andget 146. 20*; gewis andget

146. 16*; *g.* andgietes 45. 1;
andgites Pr. 13 &c.; *d.* andgite
Pr. 3, 58. 11, 12*, 81. 23*, 94.
18*, xx. 201; *a.* andgit Pr. 3,
127. 17; gewis andgit 145. 32,
146. 10*; andget 137. 19*;
ondgit 27. 18*.
andgietfull, *adj.* intelligent;
andgitfull 131. 29.
andgietfullíce, *adv.* intelligibly;
sup. andgitfullicast Pr. 4.
andlang, *prep. w.g.* along; 86.
21, 91. 32.
andleofen, *f.* sustenance, support;
d. andlifene 30. 4.
andrysne, *adj.* awe-inspiring; 61.
6 *n.*; *a.* 61. 4.
andsacian, *wv.* deny; *w.g.* and-
sacigan 21. 11*.
andswarian, *wv.* answer; *ind.*
pst. andswarode 23. 17 &c.;
andswarede 74. 27*; andsworode 9. 20*, 23. 9, 29. 11, 58.
29, 59. 4, 74. 29; andsworede
21. 18, 65. 5, 74. 25, 75. 3, 76.
10, 77. 20, 24, 83. 15.
andswaru, *f.* answer; *g.* ondswore
19. 25*; *a.* andsware xxii. 43,
51.
andweard, *adj., often with* lif,
wela, actual, present; 148. 26;
wk. andwearda 58. 16 &c.;
n. wk. andwearde 26. 15 &c.;
g. d. and a. wk. andweardan 33.
16 &c. *and* xxi. 28; *d.* andweardum 89. 17; *a. n. wk.* andwearde
68. 9; *pl. n. wk.* andweardan
47. 25 &c.; *g. wk.* andweardena 30. 11; andweardana 78.
21; *d.* andweardum 88. 29:
eagum andweardum, bodily eyes
xxii. 20; *a. wk.* andweardan 73.
18.
andweorc, *n.* material; 40. 15,
16; ondweorc 40. 20; *g.* andweorces 40. 10, 25; *d.* andweorce
40. 14; *d.* buton andweorce,
cause 23. 2; xvii. 16; anweorce
69. 26*.
andwlita *wm.* form, shape; *a.*
andwlitan 128. 4, 145. 26,
xxxi. 17; anwlitan 128. 23.

andwyrdan, *wv.* answer, *rarer*
than andswarian, 12. 31, 19. 11;
geandwyrdan 12. 5, 19. 28,
142. 1; *ind. pst.* andwyrde 9. 4
&c.; andwirde 13. 3; *imp.*
andwyrde 19. 23*.
andwyrde, *n.* answer; *d.* 45. 19;
a. 95. 18.
ānfeald, *adj.* single, undivided;
74. 30, 76. 9, 12; *f.* anfeald
129. 8; *wk.* anfealde 127. 18;
n. anfeald 128. 32, 131. 25, 26;
g. anfealdes 16. 18; *d. wk.* anfealdan 128. 4, 129. 17; *a. f.*
anfealde 54. 27.
ānfealdnes, *f.* singleness, unity;
g. anfaldnesse 128. 8; *a.* anfealdnesse 100. 11*.
ānforlǣtan, *rv.* forsake, abandon;
v. 28; *ind. prs.* 2.*s.* anforlætst
xiii. 54; 3.*s.* anforlæteð iii. 5,
xxviii. 56; *pst.* 2.*s.* anforlete
17. 14; *sbj. prs.* forlæte an
xxii. 9.
angel, *m.* fish-hook; *d.* angle
48. 5.
anginn, *n.* beginning; angin 13.
2, 20, 134. 12; *d.* anginne 148.
3; *a.* angin 13. 7.
anlíc, *adj. w. d.* similar; 72. 29,
111. 22; *f.* 123. 5; *n.* 49. 25,
63. 12; onlic 34. 29; *g.* anlices
44. 18, 24; onlices 44. 15; *a. n.*
anlic 115. 13; *sup.* anlicost 115.
6, xx. 169; anlicost ðe 122. 1.
anlíce, *adv.* similarly; 92. 14;
onlice viii. 47.
anlícnes, *f.* likeness, portrait; illustration; 55. 6, 82. 26, 114.
14; *a.* anlicnesse 51. 20, 67.
24, 74. 18, 114. 18, 116. 24; on-
licnesse 32. 4, 6, 117. 4; *pl.*
n. anlicnessa 78. 24; *a.* 74. 17.
ānlíepe, *adj.* single, individual;
an anlepe cræft 72. 13; *g. pl.*
used as sbst. ænlepra ælc xxvi.
110; anlepra ælc xxv. 56.
ānmodlíce, *adv.* unanimously;
83. 22.
ann, *swv.* grant; *inf.* geunnan
66. 27.
ānnes, *f.* oneness, unity; 90. 11,

21 ; *d.* annesse 90. 11 ; *a.* annesse 114. 2.

ansĭen, *f.* face, appearance, aspect ; *d.* ansene 51. 16 ; onsienc
v. 11.

anweald, *m.* authority, power;
fq; B *has forms with* ea ; C
with a, *but the foll. have* ea :
35. 5, 12, 55. 7, 65. 19; *g.*
anwealdes 37. 23 (J), 53. 29,
62. 17, 76. 25; *d.* anwealde
138. 32, xi. 32 ; *a.* his fota anweald 107. 13 ; ânwcald 39. 29*;
g. pl. anwalda 12. 1.

anwealda, *wm.* ruler; 49. 2*.

anwealdig, *adj.* powerful ; *sup.*
anwaldegost 108. 18.

ânwillĭce, *adv.* obstinately; 47. 4.

ãr, *f.* honour, dignity; 22. 29 ;
g. are 66. 22, i. 78 ; *d.* 120. 17,
xx. 100 ; *a.* 44. 9, 102. 23, 133.
16 ; *g. pl.* ara i. 57.

aræda, *v.* ârod.

ãrǣdan, *wv.* utter, deliver (a
speech) ; *pp.* arǣd 51. 27.

ãrǣfnan, *wv.* endure, bear ; 50.
17 ; *ind. prs.* 3.*s.* arǣfneð 25. 5.

ãrǣran, *wv.* lift up, raise; *ind. pst.*
arǣrde 8. 25.

ãreccan, *wv.* tell, relate, explain ;
22. 15, 47. 12, 92. 10, 74. 10,
135. 8 ; arecan 74. 12*; *ind. pst.*
areahte viii. 2 ; *pp.* areaht 39.
15, 46. 1 ; archt 51. 27*, 71. 3*.

ãredian, *wv.* find the way, go ; *w.*
weg 51. 14, 139. 1, 32 ; *ind. prs.*
3.*s.* aredað 79. 7 ; *sbj. prs.* arc-
die 138. 27 ; *without* weg : *inf.*
55. 19, 96. 28, 97. 17, 100. 6,
xiii. 8, xxiii. 10.

ãrētan, *wv.* cheer, comfort ; *ind.*
prs. 3.*s.* aret 54. 25 ; *pp. a. s. m.*
aretne 50. 15, 142. 21.

ãrian, *wv. w. d. ora.* honour; spare,
pity ; to arianne 72. 25 ; *ind.*
prs. 3.*s.* arað 132. 16, 142. 29;
imp. ara iv. 31, 57 ; *pp.* gearod
32. 27.

ãrianisc, *adj.* Arian; *d. wk.*
arrianiscan 7. 7.

ãrlēasnes, *f.* wickedness; *a.* arleasnesse 39. 18.

ãrlēast, *f.* wickedness, cruelty ; *a.*
ærleste ix. 1 ; *g. pl.* arleasta ix. 6.

ãrlĭce, *adv.* honourably ; 36. 30.

ãrod, *adj.* energetic, bold ; *wk.*
se aroda x. 45; *miswritten*
aræda? 46. 22*.

ãrweorðnes, *f.* honour, dignity ;
pl. g. arwyrðnessa 20. 2 ; *a.*
20. 14.

ãrwierðe, *adj.* honourable, vener-
able ; arwyrðe 125. 4; *wk.* arwyrða 7. 25*.

ãsãwan, *rv.* sow ; *ind. pst.* 2.*s.*
aseowe 82. 6*; 3.*s.* asiow xx.
250.

asce, *f.* ashes ; axe 80. 19*, xx. 106.

ãscian, *wv.* ask, inquire ; 82. 23,
86. 22, 139. 9; acsian 127. 18,
140. 19, 144. 10; acsigan 95.
17*; *ind. prs.* 2.*s.* acsast 127.
15 ; ahsast 147. 23 ; 3.*s.* acsað
95. 19*; *pst.* ascode 87. 21 ;
acsode 126. 32; ahsode 45. 14*;
absade 144. 10 ; *sbj. prs.* ascige
62. 2, 82. 25 ; acsige 131. 28.

geascian, *wv.* learn by inquiry,
ascertain ; *pp.* geascod 139. 12.

ãscierpan, *wv.* sharpen (sight) ;
sbj. prs. pl. ascirpan 89. 16* ;
pp. ascerped 47. 27.

ãscortian, *wv.* fall short, fail ;
ind. prs. 3.*s.* ascortað 44. 19.

ãscûfan, *sv2.* push away, repel ;
sbj. prs. ascufe 38. 18.

ãscung, *f.* inquiry, investigation ;
g. ascungæ 127. 6 ; *d.* ascunga
95. 15*, 144. 9, xxii. 41 ; geascunge 148. 9 ; *a.* acsunga 12. 30.

ãsecgan, *wv.* say, deliver (a discourse), *used w.* spell ; *pp.* asǣd
33. 20, 48. 21, 57. 1, 60. 26, 89.
4, 94. 26.

ãsettan, *wv.* place ; vii. 5.

ãsĭgan, *sv1.* sink down ; *pp.* asigen
55. 16.

ãsingan, *sv3.* sing, recite; *used*
w. leoð; 127. 31 ; *pp.* asungen
8. 15 &c. ; *w.* gebed 82. 18 ;
ãsungen 61. 1, 70. 1, 103. 24 ;
asuncgen 58. 4.

ãslēan, *sv6.* cut off (head); *ind.*
pst. of aslog 127. 9.

āslūpan, *sv2.* slip away ; *sbj. pst.
rflx.* hi hi of aslepen xiii. 9.
āsmēagan, *wv.* examine, investigate ; 148. 5*.
āspringan, *sv3.* spring up ; *ind.
prs.* 3.*s.* aspringeð 92. 2 ; *sbj.
pst.* āsprunge 99. 24.
āspylian, *wv.* wash oneself ; 115.
7.
assa, *wm.* ass ; 114. 31.
āstīeran, *wv.* rule, govern ; *ind.
prs.* 2.*s.* astyrest xx. 15 ; astyrast
79. 15* ; 3.*s.* astereð 131. 2.
āstīgan, *sv1.* ascend ; 82. 7, xx.
254 ; *ind. pst.* astag ix. 46.
āstreccan, *wv.* stretch out ; *ind.
pst.* astrehte 8. 4* ; *pp.* astreaht
i. 80.
āstȳfician, *wv.* extirpate ; *sbj.
prs.* astyfecige 61. 7* (astificige
C).
āstyrian, *wv.* move, agitate,
rouse ; astyrigan 13. 9 ; *ind.
prs.* 3.*s.* astyroð 27. 3* ; *pp.*
astyred 127. 7 ; astered 36. 2 ;
n. pl. asterede 133. 6.
āswindan, *sv3.* languish, grow
enervated ; *ind. prs. pl.* aswindað 81. 9 ; *pp. n. pl. m.* aswundne 139. 9.
āsyndran, *wv.* separate ; *pp.* asyndred 93. 6 ; *n. pl. m.* asyndrede
130. 25.
ātellan, *wv.* reckon up ; 20. 4.
ātemian, *wv.* tame ; *pp. a. s. f.*
atemede xiii. 19 ; *n. pl. m.*
57. 15, xiii. 36.
ātēon, *sv2.* pluck away, remove ;
ation 95. 8*, xxii. 27 ; *ind. prs.*
2.*s.* atyhsð xii. 25 ; 3.*s.* atiht
52. 11* ; *sbj. prs.* ateo xii. 2 ;
atio 51. 29*.
ātrendlian, *wv. trans.* roll ; *pp.*
atrendlod v. 17.
ātyhtan, *wv.* entice ; *pp.* atyhted
i. 8 ; *n. pl. m.* ntehte 71. 11.
āð, *m.* oath ; *pl.* aðas 10. 22, iv.
48 ; *a.* i. 25.
āðenian, *wv.* stretch, make intent (of the mind) ; *pp.* aðenod
70. 18.
āðēostrian, *wv.* grow dim ; *ind.*

prs. pl. aðeostriað 21. 2* ; *pp.*
aðistrod vi. 4.
āðrēotan, *sv2.* be weary ; 72. 19 ;
pp. aðroten xxix. 40.
āðrīetan, *wv. trans.* weary ; *pp.
a. s. m.* aðretne 135. 18 *n.*
āweallan, *rv.* well up ; *ind. prs.*
3.*s.* awealleð v. 12.
āweccan, *wv.* arouse, awaken ;
85. 25 ; *pp.* aweaht xxii. 40 ;
aweht 95. 15*.
āwecgan, *wv.* move, remove ; *pp.*
aweged 27. 2 ; *n. pl. m.* awegede vii. 24.
āwendan, *wv.* turn away, avert ;
46. 20 ; = onwendan 142. 28* ;
ind. prs. pl. awendað 141. 5.
āweorpan, *sv3.* cast away, expel ;
101. 21, xxiii. 6 ; *ind. prs.* 3.*s.*
awirpð 114. 21.
āwiergan, *wv.* curse ; *pp. n. pl. f.*
awirgede 8. 22*.
āwiht, 1) *pron.* anything ; ix. 62 ;
awuht xi. 9, xviii. 7, xx. 107,
xxii. 46, xxv. 59 ; auht vi. 6,
16, xi. 10, xx. 30, 166, xxi. 23 ;
so always in the prose, 12. 16
&c. ; *d. used as adv.* auhte ðy
mara xvi. 20. 2) *adv.* at all, in
any degree ; auht 22. 7 &c.
āwindan, *sv3.* strip off ; xxv. 22 ;
ind. prs. 3.*s.* awint of 111. 20*.
āwrītan, *sv1.* write, compose ;
pp. awriten 44. 5, 46. 27, 144.
6 ; *g. pl.* awritenra 11. 28.
āwyrcan, *wv.* do ; *ind. pst.*
awyrhte 149. 16.
āwyrtwalian, *wv.* root up ; *ind.
prs.* 2.*s.* awyrtwalast 52. 11, xii.
26 ; *sbj. prs.* awyrtwalige 61. 8.

B.

bæc, *n.* back ; *a.* 8. 12 ; *a. pl.*
bacu ii. 15.
bædan, *wv.* compel ; *ind. prs.* 3.*s.*
nede gebædeð vi. 14 *n.*
bæftan, *adv.* behind ; her beæftan
24. 1*.
bær, *adj.* bare ; *n. pl. n.* baru sond
vii. 13 ; *d.* barum sondum 91. 18.

gebǣran, *wv.* behave; 36. 31; gebæron 72. 3.

bærnan, *wv. trans.* burn; 123. 15; *ind. prs.* 3.*s.* bærnð 34. 28.

bǣtan, *wv.* bridle; *ind. pst.* 3.*s.* gebælte xi. 76; *of a ship*, make fast *pst. sbj.* 3.*s.* bætte 144. 31; *pp.* gebæt xi. 23.

bǣting, *f.* cable of a ship; *a.* bætinge 144. 31.

balca, *wm.* heap; *a.* balcan 37. 8.

bān, *n.* bone; *n. pl.* 46. 17, 20, x. 33, 35, 42.

be, *prep. w. d.* 1) *actual juxtaposition*, by, near; 19. 2, 74. 1, xix. 21; be healfe xxix. 43; along, læde bi ðæm wege 139. 33. 2) *mental juxtaposition*; *a*) compared with. 39. 21. *b*) *manner*, by; hangað be smale ðræde 65. 30; be nanum dæle, in no degree 130. 10; be ænegum dæle 123. 22; be sumum dæle 15. 18 &c.; be ðæm dæle 109. 21; be ðæm dæle ðe, in so far as 93. 23; be him selfum bion, by himself 101. 3. *c*) *standard, means*, judging by, by reference to, by; Pr. 3, 26. 10, 51. 19, 22, 54. 20, 56. 26, 63. 11, 92. 32, 96. 1, 108. 27, 116. 30, 148. 9; be ðæm, thereby 38. 20 &c.; be ðy 83. 1 &c. *d*) in connexion with, in the case of 36. 16, 28, 64. 17, 70. 29, 113. 32, 114. 7, 130. 28, 146. 31, 32, v. 1; be hwæm, in what connexion 96. 12, 119. 29; be ðæm ðe, by reference to the fact that 88. 14; in order that 108. 2, 132. 4. *e*) *forming obj. of vb.* concerning, nearly = ymb, *fq.* 23. 7 &c. *and* xxv. 1, xxx. 17; bi 13. 14, 137. 26. *f*) in proportion to, according to; be his æmettan Pr. 14; be Godes dome 37. 4; be ðæs cyninges gebode 136. 14; be hire andefne 72. 25; be ðæs gyltes andefne 123. 20; be hire gearnunge 81. 34; *cf.* 82. 1; be his andgites mæðe Pr. 13, 145. 9; *cf.* 147. 14, 16; be his ge-

wyrhtum 68. 27 &c.; *cf.* 119. 22, 123. 31, ix. 36, xx. 96, 228, xxvii. 27, xxix. 56.

bēacnian, *v.* bīecnan.

beadorinc, *m.* warrior; *d. pl.* beadurincum i. 18.

bēag, *m.* crown; 113. 3; *d.* beage 112. 26.

bealcettan, *wv.* belch, bring up; to bealcetenne 51. 5 *n.*

bealocræft, *m.* evil art, sorcery; *d. pl.* balocræftum xxvi. 75.

bēam, *m.* tree; 117. 29.

bēamsceadu, *f.* tree-shade; *d.* beamsceade viii. 28.

bearn, *n.* child; *d.* bearne 20. 7, 70. 21; *a.* bearn 70. 12; *pl.* bearn 70. 20, 23, 98. 32, i. 34, viii. 48, xxi. 1, xxvi. 49, xxix. 21; *g.* bearna 54. 8, 70. 28, 30; *d.* bearnum xxix. 58, 68; *a.* bearn 23. 1, 24. 12, 70. 19, 71. 2.

bearnēacen, *adj.* pregnant; *n.s.n.* 70. 12.

bearnlīest, *f.* childlessness; *d.* bearnleste 24. 10*.

bēatan, *rv. wv.* beat; *ind. prs.* 3.*s. intrans.* beateð on staðu vi. 15; *pl. trans.* beatað, belabour, attack iii. 3.

bebēodan, *sv2.* enjoin, command; *ind. prs.* 1.*s.* bebiode 89. 32; *pst.* 3.*s.* bebead 103. 6, 143. 13; *pp.* beboden 40. 10, 24.

bebod, *n.* command; *d.* bebode 80. 3, xx. 69; *pl. g.* beboda 10. 15; *d.* bebodum 19. 22.

becierran, *wv. trans.* turn; *pp.* becerred xiii. 78.

becrēopan, *sv2.* creep; *pp.* he sie becropen xxv. 36.

becuman, *sv4.* come; arrive, happen, befall; 18. 23 &c. *and* xii. 24; *ind. prs.* 3.*s.* becymð 34. 22, 61. 3, 131. 25, 133. 19; *pl.* becumað 23. 28, 30. 6, 38. 2; *pst.* 2.*s.* to monnum become, came into the world, became a man 17. 12; 3.*s.* becom 8. 1, i. 77, xiii. 70; *pl.* becoman Pr. 7; *sbj. prs.* becume 20. 18, 35. 8, 50. 18; *pst.* 2.*s.* become on ðiofscole,

fall among 33. 10 ; 3.*s.* 20. 19,
23. 13, 123. 23 ; *pp.* becumen
15. 22, 50. 18.
gebed, *n.* prayer ; *a.* 82. 18.
bedǣlan, *wv.* deprive ; *w. a. & g.*
pp. bedæled 41. 19, 95. 18,
112. 32, 113. 1, 11 ; *n. pl. m.*
bedælde 108. 29, 112. 18, 113. 30.
gebedmann, *m.* priest ; *a. pl.*
gebedmen 40. 17.
befǣstan, *wv.* entrust, commit ;
pp. befæst 40. 12*.
befōn, *rv.* surround, encompass ;
ind. prs. 3.*s.* befehð 52. 25 ; *pp.*
befangen xi. 29, xiii. 7 ; *a. pl.f.*
befangene 49. 3.
beforan, 1) *prep. a)* w.d. before,
in front of, in the presence of ;
14. 10, 17. 8, 32. 19, 82. 12,
103. 3, 117. 17, 126. 15, 149.
8, xxviii. 46. *b) w.a.* to the
presence of 36. 20. 2) *adv.*
before, in front iv. 18 ; *time,*
beforehand 144. 12.
begān, *anv.* observe, fulfil ; ða
gecynd b. viii. 17 ; *ind. pst. pl.*
ða gecynd beeodan 33. 27*.
begang, *m.* circuit ; *a.* holma begong xi. 30.
bēgen, *adj.* both ; 65. 18, 67. 5 ;
n. ba twa xx. 76, 115 ; buta
38. 11 ; buto 85. 13 ; butu xi.
23, 29 ; *d.* bæm 121. 27, 122.
5 ; *a. n.* bu xxxi. 4.
begietan, *sv5.* get, obtain ; begitan, 12 *times,* 55. 5 &c. ; beget,
engender 54. 8 ; to begitanne 53.
10, 12, 55. 23, 56. 5, 56. 19 ;
ind. prs. 2.*s.* begitst 71. 26 *n.* ;
3.*s.* begit 76. 27 ; beget 76. 30 ;
pl. begitað 107. 1, 140. 29 ; *pst.*
2.*s.* begeate 17. 14 ; *sbj. prs.*
begite 60. 29, 77. 24, 27, 88.
17 ; begete 76. 29 ; *pp.* begiten
54. 30.
behealdan, *rv. a)* keep, observe ;
b) behold, look at ; *ind. prs.* 3.*s.*
behealt 16. 20 (*b*) ; *pl.* behealdað
72. 16 (*b*) ; *pst. pl.* beheoldon
15. 26 (*a*) ; *imp.* beheald 108. 6 ;
135. 24 (*b*) ; *sbj. prs.* behealde
46. 3 (*b*).

behēawan, *rv.* behead ; heafde
beheawon i. 43.
behēfe, *adj.* suitable, becoming ;
n. s. f. behefu xii. 7.
behelian, *wv.* cover, conceal ;
17. 24 ; *pp.* behelod 34. 13 ; *n.*
pl. f. behelede 16. 1*.
behindan, 1) *prep. w. d.* behind ;
105. 15, xxvi. 23, xxix. 52. 2)
adv. behind xxiv. 29.
behōfian, *wv.* need, require ; *ind.*
prs. pl. behofiað 40. 23* ; *sbj.*
prs. pl. behofigen 40. 23 *n.*
behwierfan, *wv.* turn round ; behwerfan utan, to encompass 85.
23 ; *pp.* behwerfed 58. 2, xiii. 77.
behȳdan, *wv.* hide, conceal ; *pp.*
behyd 34. 12*.
belgan, *sv3.* swell with anger,
grow angry ; *ind. pst.* 3.*s. rflx.*
hine gebealg 61. 17 ; *pp.* gebolgen
111. 30 ; *n. pl. m.* gebolgene
xxv. 45 *n.*
belicgan, *sv5.* surround ; *ind. prs.*
pl. belicgað xvi. 10.
belimpan, *sv3. w. prep.* to ; con-
cern, pertain, belong ; *ind. prs.*
3.*s.* belimpet 16. 24 ; belimpð
32. 27, 118. 8 ; *w.* to *and g.*
29. 17, 31. 7 ; *pl.* belimpað 87.
2, 11, 88. 2.
belūcan, *sv2.* lock up ; 7. 24, i.
73 ; *pp. a. pl. f.* belocena 28. 15.
beneah, *swv. w. g.* enjoy ; *pl.*
benugon 57. 19.
beneoðan, *prep. w. d.* beneath ;
xx. 222 ; benyðan 108. 20.
beniman, *sv4.* deprive ; *w. a. &*
g. 113. 4, 6, x. 39 ; *sbj. prs. pl.*
benimen 20. 26 ; *pp.* benumen
13. 4, 17. 6, 17, 28, 30, iv. 23.
bēo, *wf.* bee ; 71. 6, xviii. 5.
bēobrēad, *n.* honeycomb ; biobread 52. 3 ; bibread xii. 9.
bēodan, *sv2.* offer ; xiii. 42 ; *ind.*
pst. 3.*s.* bead 66. 26, 143. 13* ;
sbj. prs. pl. biodan 57. 17*.
bēon, *anv.* be ; *usual form in* B,
fq. 16. 3 &c. ; *but* bion *occurs also* ;
bion *is the usual form in* C,
12. 26 &c. ; *but* beon 93. 31,
120. 14, 125. 10, 131. 24 ;

wesan v. 29, xi. 16, 49, xiii. 80, xv. 10, xxvi. 51, 70; bion xi. 51, xx. 145; to bionne, to beonne 92. 17 &c.; *ind. prs. 1.s. usual form* eom 13. 12 &c.; beo 18. 31*; *w. fut. meaning* bio 105. 1, 140. 1; *2.s. usual form* eart 8. 18 &c., xx. 1, 45. &c.; *neg.* neart 20. 15 &c.; bist 28. 23, 105. 14, xxiv. 27; *3.s.* is *and* biðᵒ *indifferently*: is Pr. 2 &c.; *neg.* nis 14. 1 &c.; biðᵒ 11. 24 &c.; beoðᵒ 10. 22*, 19. 6*, 21. 3*, 32. 29*, 35. 16*, 36. 6*, 39. 6*, 70. 28*; bioðᵒ 111. 22*; byðᵒ 60. 27*; *pl.* bioðᵒ & sint *equally often*; beoðᵒ *about* 15 *times in* C, 15. 10 &c.; *in* B beoðᵒ *most common*, 11. 17 &c.; *but* bioðᵒ *about* 7 *times*, 39. 7 &c.; byoðᵒ 134. 15; sint *usual form*, 9. 20 &c.; *but* sind 8. 22*, 9. 13*, 28*, 65. 12; sient 37. 24; sent 31. 8*; send 32. 15*, 20*, 22*; synt ii. 18; sindon *about* 15 *times in* C, 14. 7, iv. 44 &c.; *in* B, 16. 1*, 19*; sindan 17. 18*; siendon 9. 26; sendan 30. 2; seondan 9. 26*; syndon 20. 23*; *pst. 1 and 3.s.* wæs 10. 28 &c.: *often* was *in* B, 7. 6 &c.; *neg.* næs 11. 2 &c.; ne wæs 40. 3, xxvi. 92; *2.s.* wære 11. 3 &c.; *pl.* wæron 7. 3 &c.: næron 33. 23; *sbj. prs. s. usually* sie 11. 9 &c.; se 15. 24*, 31. 27*, 35. 29*, 57. 9*, 126. 23* *n.*, 146. 20*; sy 12. 25, 15. 18, 21. 17, 23. 20*, 137. 12, 138. 11, xiv. 7; si 33. 4 N, 122. 10*; seo 11. 9*, 24. 27*, 27. 24*, 39. 11*, 53. 14*, 56. 10*, 23*, 58. 14*; beo 17. 19, 69. 6*, 58. 1*; bio 63. 2, 78. 10, 85. 30, 130. 1, 137. 3, 7, x. 65; wese xxxi. 23; *pl.* sien 22. 29 &c.; sin 28. 19*, 32. 20, 30 N; sen 29. 27*, 29*, 31. 18*, 32. 23*; seon 31. 11*, 32. 16*, 46. 9*, 70. 16*; beon 57. 15*; bion 28. 2, 37. 18*, 92. 14, 101. 3, 113. 30, 117. 14; *pst.* wære

11. 19 &c.; *pl.* wæren 13. 21 &c.; wæran 23. 10*, 24. 6*.

beorg, *m.* hill; *a.* vii. 13.

beorht, *adj.* bright; 86. 9, 105. 19, xxix. 19; *f. pred.* beorht xxx. 9; *n. wk.* beorhte 136. 13; *g.* beortes, beorhtes* 121. 11; *wk.* beorhtan 121. 14, iv. 11; *d. wk.* 10. 4; *a. wk.* 10. 8; *pl. n. m.* beorhte, beorte* 10. 20, iv. 42; *wk.* beorhtan 10. 6; *a. m.* beorhte iv. 8; *comp. n. s. n.* beortre 95. 7*; *a.s.n.* berhtre xxii. 22; *a. pl. m.* beorhtran xxi. 27.

beorhte, *adv.* 81. 35, 95. 12, xxii. 35, xxviii. 27; *comp.* beorhtor 82. 1, 86. 7, 112. 17; *sup.* beorhtost 21. 2, v. 3; beortost 121. 10 (berrhtost B).

beorhtnes, *f.* brightness; 21. 3*, 89. 18*, xxi. 31, 41.

beorn, *m.* warrior, (brave) man; i. 52; *g.* beornes viii. 34; *pl. g.* beorna xiii. 23, xxi. 41; *a.* beornas xxvi. 75.

beprïewan, *wv.* wink; eage beprewan 44. 14* *n.*

berædan, *wv.* deprive; rice b. ix. 50.

beran, *sv4.* bear, support; *ind. 2.s.* birest xx. 276; brist 82. 15*; *3.s.* byrðᵒ 129. 20; *pp.* boren = natus xxvi. 46; geboren 20. 3*, 122. 2; *n. pl. m.* geborene 25. 1.

berēafian, *wv.* rob, deprive; 13. 10, ix. 50; *ind. prs. 2.s.* bereafast 10. 12; *3.s.* bereafaðᵒ 10. 7, 133. 22, iv. 10; *pst. pl.* bereafodon 8. 10; *pp.* bereafod 13. 18, xxii. 50; bereafad xxviii. 42; *n. pl. m.* bereafode 66. 21.

berïepan, *wv.* rob, deprive; *ind. pst. pl.* berypton ii. 12.

bescïelan, *wv.* look, gaze; *ind. prs. 2.s.* bescylst ... on 121. 30.

besēon, *sv5.* look, gaze; *ind. prs. pl.* on besioðᵒ 145. 25; *pst. s. rflx.* beseah he hine, looked round 103. 12; *sbj. prs.* hine besio to ... 103. 16; *pst. s.* hine underbæc besawe 103. 7, 8.

beslïepan, *wv.* slip, place; *ind.*

pst. 3.*s.* hu hefig geoc he beslepte 40. 1*.

besmītan, *sv*1. defile; *pp.* besmiten 34. 3, viii. 33.

besorg, *adj.* deserving care, dear, precious; *sup.* besorgost 66. 31; *a. s. n.* 22. 2.

bestyrman, *wv.* assail, disturb; *ind. prs. pl.* bestyrmað 9. 11.

beswemman, *wv.* make swim; *pp. n. pl. m.* beswemde 115. 8.

beswic, *m.* deceit, deception; *d.* biswice 30. 5.

beswīcan, *sv*1. deceive; 15. 6; *ind. prs.* 3.*s.* beswicð 41. 10, 47. 18; *sbj. prs.* beswice 82. 25; *pp. a. s. m.* beswicenne 19. 16; *a. pl. m.* beswicene 19. 17.

beswingan, *sv*3. beat, scourge; *pp.* beswungen 111. 30, xxv. 46.

besylian, *wv.* soil, stain; *pp.* besyled on blode 40. 2*.

bet, *v.* wel.

bētan, *wv.* improve; xxiii. 9; gebetan 60. 13, 14, 123. 23, 134. 6; *ind. prs.* 3.*s.* gebet 47. 20; *pl.* gebetað 89. 14, xxi. 23; *sbj. prs.* gebete 103. 21; *pl.* gebeten, atone for 143. 29.

betera, *v.* gōd.

betrung, *f.* improvement; 123. 25.

betst, betsta, *v.* gōd, wel.

betweox, *prep. w. d.* between, among; xi. 45, 84, xxiv. 13, 16; betwux 7. 4*, 10. 7*, 49. 10*, 11*, 13*, 80. 9*, 12*, 105. 10*; betweox 113. 26; betwyx 105. 11*; betwuh 38. 19*, 39. 25*, 70. 24*, 126. 17*, 134. 27, 28, 136. 11*, xxix. 4; *adv.* xxvii. 20; betweoh 138. 28, 148. 4, xxviii. 52; betwuht 136. 6*.

beðearf, *swv. w. g.* need; *ind. prs. s.* 31. 19, 59. 28, 75. 7, 32, 96. 32; *pl.* beðurfon 31. 21, 60. 5, 147. 8; *pst.* 3.*s.* beðorfte 97. 3; *sbj. prs.* 3.*s.* beðurfe 31. 30; *pst.* 2.*s.* beðorfte 79. 20.

beðeccan, *wv.* cover; *pp.* beðeaht xxviii. 43.

bewǣfan, *wv.* wrap up; *pp.* bewǣfed 92. 5.

bewarenian, *wv.* beware, guard; *ind. prs.* 3.*s. rflx.* hine bewarenað xvi. 23.

bewealwian, *wv.* wallow; *ind. prs. pl. rflx.* bewealwiað hi 115. 9.

bewegan, *sv*5. cover; *ind. pst.* 3.*s.* bewæg 127. 13.

bewendan, *sv*3. *intrans.* turn; *ind. pst.* 3.*s.* bewende 9. 1.

beweorpan, *sv*3. throw, plunge; *ind. pst.* 3.*s.* hwæt bewearp ðe on ðas care 15. 20.

bewerian, *wv.* defend; *pp.* beweroð 92. 5*.

bewitian, *wv.* observe, perform; bewitigan 17. 27; *sbj. prs.* 3.*s.* sið bewitige iv. 16.

bewrēon, *sv*1.2. wrap up, conceal; *pp.* bewrigen 10. 22, iv. 47, viii. 59.

bīdan, *sv*1. *w. g.* wait, await; gebidan 124. 6, xxvii. 7, 17; gebidon 124. 10; *ind. prs.* 3.*s.* gebit 119. 32; *sbj. prs.* gebide 20. 31.

biddan, *sv*5. pray, pray for; 79. 3, 5, 6, 102. 12, 18, 25, 28, x. 3; *ind. prs.* 1.*s.* bidde 140. 2; 2.*s.* bitst 51. 2; 3.*s.* bit Pr. 10, 59. 26; *pl. rflx.* we us gebiddað 143. 1; *pst.* 2.*s.* bæde 139. 29; 3.*s.* bæd 102. 29, i. 64; *pl.* bædon 7. 22; ðe wit unc to gebædon 100. 29; *sbj. prs.* bidde 50. 25; gebidde Pr. 12; *pst.* bæde 123. 11.

bīecnan, *wv.* denote, signify; becnan xi. 79; gebecnan 24. 24, 101. 12; gebeacnian 101. 12*.

bīegan, *wv. trans.* bend; began 57. 22*; *ind. prs.* 3.*s.* begð xiii. 3; *sbj. prs.* byge xiii. 53.

gebierhtan, *wv.* make bright; *ind. prs.* 3.*s.* gerberhteð xxi. 32; gebirht 89. 19*; *pp. n. pl. m.* gebirhte 86. 6.

bierhto, *f.* brightness; birhtu 81. 35, 82. 13, vi. 6, xx. 269; *a.* 89. 20*, 23*; beorhto xxi. 39; biorhto 141. 14*.

biernan, *sv*3. burn, be on fire; *ind. pres.* 3.*s.* byrneð viii. 50;

byrnð viii. 45; *pst.* 3.*s.* barn 39. 20; *sbj.* 3.*s.* burne 39. 21, ix. 17; *prs. p.* birnende 34. 9*, 28 N; byrnende 34. 7*; *used as adj. wk. m.* byrnenda 34. 28.

biflan, *wv.* tremble; *ind. pst.* 3.*pl.* bifedon 102. 6.

bilewit, *adj.* gentle, kind; xx. 69, 255, 269.

bilewitnes, *f.* gentleness, kindness; *g.* bilewitnesse 128. 8.

bill, *n.* sword; *d. pl.* billum ix. 30.

billrudu,*f.* red sword-dye, blood? *a.* billrude viii. 34.

bindan, *sv3.* bind, fetter, 37. 8; gebindan 28. 17, 66. 32; *ind. prs.* 3.*s.* gebinð 47. 21; *pl.* gebindað 38. 31; *pst.* 2.*s.* gebunde 81. 6; *sbj. pst.* 3.*s.* gebunde 96. 17; *pp.* gebunden 14. 24, 37. 9, 80. 3, 102. 30, v. 39, xx. 67, 153, xxvi. 96; *a. s. m.* gebundenne, captivated 50. 9; *n. pl. m.* gebundene 108. 7.

binnan, *prep. w. d.* within; 31. 32, 108. 21; beinnan 8. 3.

bisgian,*wv.* occupy, trouble; *ind. pst.* 3.*pl.* bisgodan Pr. 6*; *sbj. prs.* 3.*pl.* bysigen xxii. 30.

bisgo, *f.* occupation, trouble; *pl. n.* bisgu Pr. 6*; *d.* bisgum Pr. 5*, xxii. 64; bisegum 82. 8*; bysegum xx. 255.

bisgung, *f.* affliction; *d.* bisgunga 95. 23*.

bismerian, *wv.* revile, mock; *w. g.* bismrian 33. 16; *ind. pst.* 3.*s. w. a.* bismrode 45. 6.

bisn, *f.* example; bisen 52. 2*; bysen 53. 9, xii. 7; *g.* bisne 63. 11*; bisene 39. 20*; *d.* bisne 85. 23*; bysne 118. 27, xx. 43; bysene 51. 19; *a.* bisne 51. 21, 85. 12, 132. 22, 139. 15, 145. 17; bysne 97. 28; *pl.* bisna 139. 6*; *g.* biesena 65. 12; *a.* bisna 101. 9, 10, 108. 2; bisena 104. 25.

bisnian, *wv.* set an example; *ind. pst.* 3.*s.* bisnode 79. 26; *pl.* bisnodon 134. 1.

bispell, *n.* example, parable; *a.* 101. 15, 22, 114. 1, 126. 13; *pl.*

d. bispellum 140. 2, xxiii. 9; *a.* bispell 101. 9; bispel 101. 11.

biter, *adj.* bitter; 51. 2; *g.* biteres 52. 3*; bitres xii. 11, xxvii. 7; *d. wk.* biteran viii. 54; *a. m.* biterne 132. 7, 9; *pl. n. f.* bitere 50. 22.

bitere, *adv.* bitterly; ii. 15.

biternes, *f.* bitterness; *a.* biternesse 25. 7.

biwist, *f.* sustenance, food; 40. 21; *a.* biwiste 40. 21.

blac, *adj.* bright; *d.* blacum iv. 8; *wk.* blacan 10. 5.

blæc, *adj.* black; 145. 24.

blandan, *rv.* mix, blend; *pp.* geblonden v. 19, xx. 81.

blate, *adv.* lividly, with livid flame; blate forbærnð; viii. 54; b. forbærnan xx. 115.

blawan, *rv. intrans.* blow (of the wind); *ind. prs.* 3.*s.* blaweð 21. 4*, vii. 52; blæwð vi. 8; *sbj. prs.* 3.*s.* blawe 27. 13.

blêd,*f.* shoot, branch, fruit; *pl. d.* bledum 92. 2; *a.* bleda 136. 16, 17, xxix. 60.

blendan, *wv.* blind; *ind. prs.* 3.*s.* blent 121. 16.

bleo, *n.* colour, appearance; *a.* blioh xxxi. 4; *d. pl.* bleowum 33. 30.

blican, *sv1.* shine; xxii. 35.

blind, *adj.* blind; 121. 32, 122. 6; *g. wk.* blindan 15. 30; *a.* blindne 8. 10, ii. 10; *pl. n. m.* blinde xix. 30; ælces domes swa blinde 74. 6.

bliss, *f.* joy; blis 74. 24*, 75. 31, 76. 4, 86. 25, 87. 15; *g.* blisse 56. 24; *a.* blisse, favour 102. 26, ii. 15; *n. pl.* blissa, joys 20. 17.

blissian, *wv.* gladden; *ind. prs.* 3.*s.* geblissað 54. 25.

bliðe, *adj.* joyful, glad; 53. 24, 75. 30, 94. 18; *d. pl.* bliðum wordum 8. 26; bliðum eagum 10. 29; *comp.* bliðra 39. 25, ix. 32.

bliðnes, *f.* joy; *a. pl.* bliðnessa 20. 4, 15.

blōd, *n.* blood ; *g.* blodes 57.
11, xiii. 23 ; oflete blodes, let
blood 66. 29 ; *d.* blode 34. 4,
40. 3, viii. 34, ix. 59.

blōstma, *wm.* blossom, flower ;
pl. n. blostman vi. 10 ; blosman 21. 5* ; *g.* blostmæna 29.
21* ; *d.* blostmum 72. 29, 92.
2 ; *a.* blostman 12. 10, 17. 25.

blōwan, *rv.* bloom ; *ind. prs.* 3.*s.*
bloweð xx. 99 ; blewð 80.
17*.

bōc, *f.* book ; 38. 6, 103. 22, 139.
17 ; *d.* bec *about* 15 *times*,
Pr. 1. &c. *and* xxv. 54 ; bēc
41. 28* ; *a.* boc Pr. 8, 11 ; *pl.*
bec 65. 12 ; *g.* boca 11. 28,
43. 8, i. 52 ; *d.* bocum 41. 27,
143. 13 ; *a.* bec 11. 29, 30.

bōccræft, *m.* book learning, literature ; *d. pl.* boccræftum 7. 12.

bōclæden, *n.* written Latin ; *d.* of
boclædene Pr. 2.

gebod, *n.* command ; 143. 12 ; *d.*
gebode 136. 14, xxix. 56.

boda, *wm.* messenger, herald ;
103. 26.

bodian, *wv.* proclaim, herald ;
ind. prs. 3.*s.* bodað 136. 5 ; he
dæg bodað xxix. 23 ; *pst.* 3.*s.*
bodode *w. g.* 45. 6.

bōg, *m.* bough, branch ; *a.* boh
57. 22*, xiii. 53 ; *d. pl.* bogum
92. 1.

bōt, *f.* improvement, cure ; *d.* bote
9. 8.

brād, *adj.* broad 87. 4 ; widely
known 68. 21 ; *d.* bradum 41.
25 ; *wk.* brādan 41. 25*.

brǣdan, *wv.* extend ; gebrædan
49. 24, xi. 66 ; to brædanne 42.
12 ; to gebrædanne 43. 15 ; *ind.
prs.* 3.*s. intrans.* bræd xx. 99 ;
sbj. prs. 3.*pl.* bræden 68. 20 ;
gebrædan 53. 31*.

brǣding, *f.* widening, extension ;
g. brædinge 46. 6*.

brecan, *sv4.* break ; 57. 13.

bred, *n.* board ; *d.* brede 41. 25
(brēde B).

bregdan, *sv3.* hleoðrum brægdan,
modulate their song xiii. 47.

brego, *m.* chief, king ; xx. 43.

brēost, *n.* breast, heart, mind ;
d. pl. breostum xix. 30, xxi.
27, xxii. 64, xxv. 45.

brēostcofa, *wm.* mind, heart ; *d.*
breostcofan ix. 32.

brīdel, *m.* bridle ; *d.* bridle 49. 3,
xi. 29, 79, xxiv. 37 ; *a.* bridel
105. 18 ; *pl. g.* bridla 49. 28, xi.
76 : *d.* bridlum 57. 3, xiii. 3.

brīdlian, *wv.* bridle, curb ; *pp.
a. pl. f.* gebridlode 49. 28*.

bringan, *wv.* bring, lead ; 71. 12,
143. 10 ; *for* forðbringan 41. 1 ;
gebringan 7. 19, 24, 14. 8, 16.
17, 71. 12* ; brengan 17. 23*,
25, 143. 8 ; give birth to 70. 22 ;
ind. prs. 1.*s.* bringe 9. 19 ;
gebringe 18. 8, 9 ; 3.*s.* bringeð
xi. 59, 63, xxix. 57 ; bringð 48.
7, 49. 21 ; = forðbringð 80. 17 ;
brengeð xxix. 23 ; brengð 37.
31, 39. 10, 61. 28, 128. 32, 136.
14, xx. 101 ; gebrengð 131. 5 ;
brencð xiii. 60 ; bryngð 136.
16* ; *pl.* bringað 70. 14 ; brengað xx. 75 ; *pst.* brohte 60. 32 ;
gebrohte 11. 11, 17. 13 ; *sbj.
prs.* brenge 130. 18 ; *pst.*
brohte 23. 19, 102. 20, xii. 17,
xiv. 11 ; *pp.* gebroht 111. 25.

brōc, *m.* brook ; 14. 15, v. 19 ; *d.*
broce 86. 21 ; *n. pl.* brocas 82.
28.

brōc, *n.* affliction, evil ; 23. 5 ;
d. broce 133. 26 ; *a.* broc 133. 5.

brōcian, *wv.* afflict, harm ; *ind.
prs.* 3.*pl.* brociað 134. 7.

brōga, *wm.* terror ; 104. 15.

brosnian, *wv.* decay, perish ; *prs.
p. used as adj.* ðes brosnienda
wela 35. 26.

brōðor, *m.* brother ; *a.* 39. 23, ix.
28.

brūcan, *sv2. w. g.* enjoy, use ; 17.
26, 45. 30, 53. 28, 71. 30, 80.
20, xx. 108, xxxi. 9 ; to brucanne
19. 22, 24. 11 ; *ind. prs.* 3.*s.*
brycð 24. 18, 47. 22 ; *pl.* brucað 134. 23 ; *pst.* 2.*s.* bruce 15.
15 ; 3.*s.* breac* i. 75 ; *sbj. prs.*
bruce.

brūn, *adj.* brown; *n. s. f.* brune
xxvi. 29.

brȳd, *f.* bride, wife; *a.* bryde ix. 30.

bryrdan, *wv.* incite, urge on ;
ind. prs. 3.*s.* bryrð xiii. 3.

bufan, *prep.* above, 1) *w. d.* 80.
25, 105. 15 : be ufan 108. 20 *n.*
2) *w. a. motion*, 18. 13.

būgan, *sv2. intrans.* bow down,
stoop; gebugan xxv. 64.

būgian, *wv.* dwell, inhabit ; ge-
bugian 42. 3 : to bugianne 40.
21, 42. 9 ; *ind. prs. pl.* bugiað
42. 13, 22, 43. 10; bogiað 42.
15*.

burg, *f.* fortified town, town ; *g.*
burge 43. 2, 11, 43. 18; *d.*
byrig 99. 10, 104. 28, i. 37 ;
Rome byrig i. 46 ; *a.* Troia
burg xxvi. 20 ; burig 7. 3*, ix.
10 (J) ; *pl. g.* burga i. 18, iv.
42 ; *d.* burgum v. 3 ; xxix. 23.

burgsittend, *m.* town-dweller,
citizen ; *n. pl.* burgsittende
xxvii. 17.

burgware, *m. pl.* town-dwellers;
11. 18 ; *g.* burgwara 11. 14 ;
d. burgwarum 11. 22, x. 47.

burna, *wm.* brook; v. 19; *g.*
burnan viii. 28.

buton, 1) *adv.* outside, 67. 3.
2) *prep. w.d.*; *a)* outside, 113.
5 ; butan 31. 26, 55. 25. *b)*
without (sine); buton *about*
38 *times*, 11. 6 &c. ; butan
about 20 *times*, 12. 17 &c. ;
used as adv. butan 82. 30,
144. 22. *c)* except, buton 10
times, 28. 10 &c. *and* xiii. 15,
xx. 136, 189 : butan 5 *times*,
9. 24 &c. *and* iv. 27, xxvi. 89.
3) *conj. w. no construction*, except, *fq.* buton *about* 40 *times*,
18. 29 x. 54 &c.; butan *about* 10
times, 16. 18 &c. ; bute 132. 15.
4) *adversative conj.* but; buton
8. 20, 33. 26, 40. 9. 70. 26;
bute 91. 9. 5) *conj. w. sbj.*
unless ; buton *about* 18 *times*,
23. 20 &c. ; butan 9. 7, 31.
23 ; bute 141. 26, xviii. 10;
buta 11. 18*.

bycgan, *wv.* acquire by purchase,
acquire the power ; gebycgan þ
ic mote 89. 30; gebycggan 48.
12* ; *ind. prs. pl.* gebycgað
133. 28 ; *pp.* geboht ðæt ðu . . .
48. 14, 16, 18, 54. 6, 89. 27.

gebyrd, *f.* birth, descent; *pl. g.*
gebyrda 11. 14, 46. 13 ; *d.* gebyrdum 24. 3, 4, 68. 28, 69. 25.

gebyrde, *adj.* natural; *n. s. n.* ne
him nis gehyrde þ . . . 30. 2*.

gebyrian, *wv.* happen ; 139. 24;
gebyrigan iv. 11 ; *ind. prs.* 3.*s.*
gebyreð 47. 6, 57. 10, 66. 21,
77. 8, 99. 17, 111. 23, 121. 2,
132. 30, 32, 133. 4, 135. 1 ;
falls to, belongs 112. 28; gebereð 114. 11 ; *pst.* gebyrede
37. 9*, 44. 1*, 71. 1*, 99. 14, 115.
13*, 125. 13 ; geberede 36. 33,
70. 22, 127. 10, xxv. 31 ; ge-
birede 140. 11*; *sbj. prs.* gebyrige 46. 11, 125. 21, 127. 19*,
140. 4 ; geberige 125. 24 ; ge-
bergie 127. 19 ; *pp.* bið weas
gebyred 140. 5, 6 *n.*; wære weas
gebyred 140. 11 ; sie weas gebered 140. 13.

C.

cāf, *adj.* active, vigorous; *comp.*
n. pl. cafran 88. 22.

cafortūn, *m.* courtyard, enclosure;
cafertun 42. 10*; cauertun *ib.*;
a. cafertun 42. 12*; cauertun
ib.

calan, *sv6.* be cold; *impers. w. a.*
sbj. prs. cale*, kale 60. 11.

campstede, *m.* battlefield; *a.*
campsted xxvi. 14.

cann, *swv. a)* w. a. recognize,
know ; *b)* w. *inf.* know how,
be able; *ind. prs.* 2.*s.* canst
132. 30 (*b*); 3.*s.* can 63. 16,
17 (*a*), 132. 10 (*a*); con 60.
20 (*a*), 125. 25 (*b*); *pl.* cunnon
55. 17 (*a*), 61. 13 (*a*), 131. 18
(*b*), 132. 12 (*b*), xi. 9 (*a*); *con-*
trasted w. witon 48. 25 (*a*): *pst.*
2.*s.* cuðest 48. 16 (*b*); 3.*s.* cuðe
viii. 22 (*b*); xxvi. 53 (*b*); *pl.*

cuðon 33. 29 (*b*); *sbj. prs.* cunne
xxii. 51 (*b*); ðu cunne þ ... 30. 9;
pl. cunnen 108. 31 (*b*); *pst.*
cuðe 75. 22, 20. 9 (*a*), 15. 14
(*b*); *pl.* cuðen 56. 28 (*b*).

capitula, *wm.* chapter; *g.* capi-
tulan 73. 15.

carcern, *n.* prison, dungeon; *d.*
carcerne 8. 3, 45. 28, i. 73; *a.*
carcerne 7. 24, 111. 25; carcern
xxv. 36.

caru, *f.* sorrow, grief; *a.* care 15. 20.

cāsere, *m.* emperor; i. 20, 61;
kasere 7. 21; *g.* kaseres 115.
16*; *d.* casere 34. 24, 66. 31,
xxvi. 6; kasere 66. 31*, 115.
15*, 17*, 19*; kāsere 39. 18*,
30*; *d. pl.* caserum 7. 16.

ceahhettung, *f.* laughter; *a.*
cehhettunge 36. 1.

ceald, *adj.* cold; xx. 78; *wk.*
cealda xxiv. 22; ceald 80. 6*,
7*, xx. 80; ceald gesceaft xx.
119; *f. wk.* cealde xx. 100, xxix.
54; *n.* ceald 49. 20, 80. 6, xx.
77, xxvi. 28; *d.* cealdum xx.
90; *wk.* cealdan 80. 9. 13, 105.
12; *a. f.* calde viii. 29; *wk.*
cealdan 80. 13; *n.* cald xi. 59;
pl. n. f. cealda xx. 76.

ceaster, *f.* city; *d.* ceastre 128.
8, 141. 7; *a.* 96. 27, i. 66.

cempa, *wm.* soldier; *n. pl.* cem-
pan xx. 73.

cēne, *adj.* bold; x. 51.

cēol, *m.* ship; *d.* ceole xxvi. 60;
a. ðriereðre ceol xxvi. 27; *pl.*
d. ceolum xxi. 11; *a.* ciolas
xxvi. 23.

ceorfan, *sv3.* cut; *sbj. prs.* 3.*s.*
ceorfe him of 124. 16.

ceorl, *m.* free man, man; xii. 27;
n. pl. ceorlas 108. 9.

cēosan, *sv2.* choose; *ind. pst.*
2.*s.* gecure 16. 27; 3.*s.* geceas
20. 13, 66. 28; *sbj. prs.* 3.*pl.*
geciosen 138. 32; *pst.* gecure
xv. 11; *pp n. pl. m.* gecorene,
chosen, distinguished 41. 11,
64. 1* (gecorenne J).

ciele, *m.* cold; cile 80. 4; cele
xx. 73; *d.* cile 42. 3, 80. 21*,

81. 9*, 136. 13*; cele xx. 110,
158; cyle 42. 3*; *a.* cile xxix.
50; cele xx. 113.

cīepa, *wm.* trader; cepa 34. 1,
viii. 29.

cīepan, *wv.* buy; *ind. pst.* 3.*s.*
diore gecepte xxvi. 19.

cīepemann, *m.* merchant, trader;
n. pl. cepemen 42. 31.

cierr, *m.* time, occasion; *d.* æt
sumum cierre ix. 23; æt sumum
cyrre 39. 19*; æt oðrum cerre
95. 28*.

cierran, *wv. intrans.* turn, return;
gecyrran xi. 37; to gecerranne
139. 30; *ind. prs.* 3.*s.* cerreð
xxix. 50; gecerreð xxviii. 61;
pl. gecierrað, gecyrrað* 119.
33; *pst.* 3.*s.* cerde 36. 32; ham
cerde 115. 19*; *sbj. prs.* gecirre
9. 8*; gecerre hine 95. 21.

cild, *n.* child; 94. 17, 122. 2; *a.*
100. 5; *n. pl.* cild 108. 8, 10.

cine, *wf.* chink, crack; *a.* cinan
97. 14.

cīð, *m.* sprout, shoot; *pl. g.* ciða
xii. 5; *d.* ciðum 91. 26.

clǣne, *adj.* clean, pure; *d.* clænum
149. 23, xii. 5; *a. m.* clænne
109. 27; *pl. a. n.* clæne 147. 25.

clǣnlic, *adj.* pure; *d. s. f.*
clænlicre 50. 1; *a. s. f.* clænlice
xi. 92.

clǣnnes, *f.* purity; *d.* clænnesse
22. 14.

clǣnsian, *wv.* purify; *pp.* geclænsod*, geclæsnod 120. 14.

clǣnsung, *f.* purifying; 123. 25.

clamm, *m.* bond, chain; *d. pl.*
clammum i. 83.

clāðas, *pl. m.* clothes; 30. 9, 40.
22; *g.* claða 30. 17, 111. 24,
xxv. 23.

clif, *n.* cliff; *d.* clife v. 13.

clifian, *wv.* adhere, cleave; *w.*
on 37. 25, 38. 23; cleofian
38. 23 (J); cliofian 37. 25 (J).

clipian, *wv.* call; xxvi. 85; to
Gode cleopian 9. 29*; *ind.*
pst. clipode 8. 21*, 12. 12;
cleopode 8. 21, 103. 4, i. 83;
cleopode to him 50. 10.

clūd, *n.* rock ; *d. pl.* cludum 91. 18.

clŭstor, *n.* lock, bar, prison ; *a.* cluster i. 73.

gecnāwan, *rv.* know, recognize, understand ; 52. 10, 12, 56. 28, 74. 18, 132. 30, xii. 23, xix. 31 ; *ind. pst.* 3.*s.* gecneow 9. 1.

·cniht, *m.* boy, young man ; 78. 18 ; *a.* 73. 4 ; *n. pl.* cnihtas, retainers, followers xxvi. 85.

cnihthād, *m.* youth ; *d.* on cnihthade 122. 3.

cnōdan, *rv.* assign, attribute ; *pp.* gecnoden i. 32.

cnoll, *m.* hillock, hill ; *a.* 26. 24.

cōl, *adj.* cool ; *n.* v. 13.

consul, *m.* consul ; 7. 11.

gecōplīce, *adv.* fittingly, well; 8. 8.

corn, *n.* grain, seed ; 95. 13, 15, xxii. 37, 40.

corðer, *n.* troop, company ; *d.* corðre xxvi. 85.

cosp, *m.* fetter ; *a. pl.* cospas 116. 15.

coðlīce, *adv.* foully, miserably ; xxv. 36.

cræft, *m.* skill, faculty, virtue, power ; 38. 9, x. 37 &c. ; *g.* cræftes 108. 29 &c. *and* x. 39 ; art, 37. 11, 40. 14 ; *d.* cræfte 30. 9, xx. 9 &c. ; *a.* cræft 30. 22 &c. *and* xx. 196 ; *pl. gen.* = virtues, *n.* cræftas 10. 20, iv. 42 &c. ; *g.* cræfta 22. 9 &c. *and* xx. 119 ; *d.* cræftum 35. 14 &c. *and* xv. 11 ; *a.* cræftas 44. 31 &c. *and* xxx. 7.

cræftig, *adj.* skilful, powerful ; 109. 18 ; ælces ðinges c. x. 51 ; *wk.* ælc cræftega 128. 27 ; cræftga xi. 92 ; *g. wk.* cræftgan xxiv. 51 ; *d. wk.* cræftegan 46. 18* ; *pl. n.* cræftes full cræftige 133. 7 ; *comp.* cræftigra 79. 24 ; *sup.* cræftigast xxx. 2.

crēcisc, *adj.* Greek ; *g. pl.* creciscra xxvi. 28.

crēopan, *sv*2. creep ; 107. 16 ; *ind. prs.* 3.*s.* criepð 107. 18 ; *pl.* creopað xxxi. 6 ; *sbj. prs.* creope 91. 26.

crīsten, *adj.* Christian ; 7. 6 ; *n. pl. m.* cristene 131. 10.

cristendōm, *m.* Christianity ; *d.* cristendome 7. 22* ; cristenandome 7. 14*.

culpian, *wv.* cringe, fawn ; *w.* to 71. 24.

cuma, *wm.* new arrival, stranger ; *a.* cuman 36. 30, 37. 2.

cuman, *sv*4. come ; 33. 6, i. 83 &c. ; to cumanne 53. 11 &c. ; *ind. prs.* 2.*s.* cymest xxiv. 47 ; cymst 105. 20* ; 3.*s.* cymeð xi. 60, xiii. 62, xxv. 43, xxviii. 28, xxix. 20, 29, 56 ; *usual form in the prose* cymð 20. 25 &c. *and* vi. 11, xvii. 29 ; gecymð 93. 4 ; cimð 140. 5 ; ccmð 127. 16 ; *pl.* cumað 15. 8, vii. 44 &c. ; cume wit 148. 5 ; *pst.* 2.*s.* come 104. 28, 146. 29 ; 3.*s.* com 13. 6, xx. 30 &c. ; com ðær gan 8. 16 ; *pl.* comon 17. 18 ; xvii. 3 &c. ; coman 23. 29*, 69. 18* ; *sbj. prs.* cume 13. 5, xiii. 76 &c. ; *pst.* come 43. 9, 84. 14, 16, 18, 140. 6, xxviii. 72 ; *pl.* comen i. 66 ; *pp.* cumen 41. 12, xxiv. 51 &c. ; cymen xx. 34.

cunnian, *wv.* examine, test ; *w. g.* 12. 12 ; *imp.* cunna 12. 15.

cūð, *adj.* known, evident, famous ; 20. 9, xxvi. 60 ; *f.* cuðe xxvi. 53 ; *n.* cuð 54. 21, 84. 5, 129. 7, 144. 12, ix. 5, xxvi. 11, 42 ; *a. f.* cuðe ii. 8 ; *n. pl. n.* cuð xxxi. 6 ; *a. m.* cuðe 46. 30 ; *comp. n. s. n.* cuðre 51. 20.

cwēman, *wv. w.d.* please ; to cwemanne 133. 14.

cwēn, *f.* queen ; xxvi. 89.

cweðan, *sv*5. say, speak ; 20. 5, 8, 22. 23, xxiv. 48 ; cwæðan 109. 7 ; *ind. prs.* 1.*s.* cweðe 78. 13, 123. 15, 17 ; cwiðe 50. 18* ; 2.*s.* cwist 12. 27, 19. 16, 20. 13, 17, 24. 31, 77. 21 ; cwyst 12. 30, 27. 22 ; cwest 119. 29* ; 3.*s.* cwið 70. 15, 82. 29, 137. 29, 140. 4 ; *pl.* cweðað 19. 12, 58. 14, 85. 30, 32, 88. 11, 107. 28, 114. 22 ; *pst.* 1.*s.* cwæð 46. 17, x. 35 &c.

cwæt 65. 5*; 2.*s.* cwæde 12. 22
&c.; 3.*s.* cwæð, *very fq. esp. in
phrases,* ða cwæð he, ðus cwæð
&c., 8. 5, vi. 2 &c.; *in* C. *fq.
contr. to* cwð 77. 24 &c.; *pl.*
cwædon 76. 8, 124. 16, 140. 10;
sbf. prs. cweðe 47. 11; cwæðe
perh. confused w. cwæde 62. 19,
131. 23; *pl.* cweðan, cwæðon*
137. 18; *pst.* cwæde 9. 23; *prs.
p.* cweðende 10. 28.

cwic, *adj.* living, alive; *wk.*
cwuca 109. 29; *f.* cwuco 91. 9;
g. cwuces 92. 3; *a.* cwucone,
cwucene* 109. 28; *f.* cwuce 91.
6; *pl. n. f.* cwuca 126. 17; *g.*
cwucera 145. 32, xxix. 79.

cwiddung, *f.* saying, report; *d.*
cwiddunge 45. 3.

cwide, *m.* saying; 9. 22, 31. 20,
110. 30, 143. 14; principle, 78.
16; *a.* 33. 13; *a. pl.* cwidas 15.
16, MPr. 5.

cwielman, *wv.* kill; *sbj. pst.*
cwelmde ix. 47.

cyme, *m.* coming, advent; *a.* 136. 5.

gecynd, *f. n.* nature, kind; *f.* 30.
13. 37. 19, 58. 10, xx. 187; *n.
about* 8 *times,* 38. 12 &c.;
uncert. about 7 *times,* 32. 18
&c.; *g.* gecyndes 57. 24, 28,
xiii. 12, 67, xxvii. 7; natural
function 93. 17; gecynde 27. 26,
32. 6, 92. 23; *d.* gecynde *f. about*
6 *times,* 27. 24 &c.; *n. about*
5 *times,* 31. 5 &c. *and* xx. 33;
uncert. about 13 *times,* 41. 11
&c. *and* xx. 76; *a.* gecynd *f.*
33. 27; natural desire 114. 20,
21, viii. 17; *n.* 15. 26, 92. 31,
93. 21, xxviii. 62; *uncert. about*
6 *times,* 16. 28 &c.; cynd
98. 11; gecynde 57. 25, 93. 24,
108. 6, xiii. 55; *n. pl. n.* gecynd
29. 29; *g.* gecynda 81. 18, 19.
a. ? 81. 17.

gecynde, *adj.* natural, suitable;
30. 10, 63. 19, 133. 9; *wk.*
gecynda 38. 9; *f.* gecynde 93.
16; *n. about* 7 *times,* 30. 1 &c.;
a. f. xi. 14; *pl. n.* gecynde 30.
3; *a.* i. 6.

gecyndelic, *adj.* natural, fitting;
n. 32. 1; *g.* gecyndelices 39. 12,
64. 3, 124. 6; *a. f.* gecyndelice
48. 28; *n.* gecyndelic 31. 25,
53. 11, 63. 25, 64. 17; *wk.*
gecyndelice 64. 5, 95. 29, 114.
17; ðæt gecyndelic god 95. 26.

gecyndelice, *adv.* naturally, suitably; 54. 12, 98. 3.

cynecynn, *n.* royal family; *g.*
cynecynnes 115. 25, xxvi. 42.

cynegierela, *wm.* royal robe; *g.*
cynegerelan xxv. 23.

cynelic, *adj.* royal; *a. wk.* cynelican 35. 2.

cynerîce, *n.* kingdom; *a. pl.*
cynericu xxvi. 6.

cynestôl, *m.* royal seat, throne;
7. 21; *d.* cynestole i. 48.

cyning, *m.* king; 7. 14, M.Pr. 2
&c.; cyninc 66. 3; cynincg xv.
2; cining xxvi. 22; kuning Pr. 1;
g. cyninges 35. 1, xx. 73 &c.;
d. cyninge 7. 18, xv. 13 &c.;
cininge 66. 15, 102. 28; *a.* cining xxvi. 45; *pl. n.* cyningas
65. 22, 66. 17, xxv. 58; kyningas i. 56; cyngas 112. 6*; *g.*
cyninga 35. 6, xv. 11 &c.; *d.*
cyningum 7. 2, 5, 111. 13, xxv.
2; *a.* cyningas 105. 26, 115. 26,
i. 6, xxiv. 58.

cynn, *n.* kind, species; cyn xiv. 6,
xxvii. 19; *g.* ælces cynnes 64. 25,
89. 13, 74. 2, xviii. 4, xxvi. 34;
d. cynne iv. 32, xi. 67; = kin
11. 21; *pl. g.* cynna 111. 14,
xxxi. 5 *n.*; *d.* cynnum xx. 249.

cynn, *adj.* natural, fitting; *n.* cyn
56. 11, 75. 30, 99. 14 (cynn B).

cynren, *n.* kind, kin; *a.* 116. 10;
d. pl. cynrenum 82. 5.

cypera, *wm.* spawning salmon;
a. cyperan xix. 12.

cyspan, *wv.* fetter; xxvi. 77.

cyst, *f.* choice, pick, best; burga
cyst i. 18; *pl.* virtues, good
qualities, *n.* cysta 28. 4; *d.*
cystum 122. 3.

cyðan, *wv.* make known, declare;
40. 13, 19, ix. 22; gecyðan 57. 2,
xiii. 1; *ind. prs.* 3.*s.* gecyð 47.

8, 19; *pl.* gecyðað 39. 7; *pst.*
2.*s.* cyðdest 13. 22*; cyddest
13. 19, 22; 3.*s.* cyðde 43. 8,
45. 7; *pl.* cyðdon i. 56; gecyðdon 15. 27; *pp.* gecyðed 30. 31,
32. 13, 37. 22.

cyðð, *f.* native place, home; cyð
80. 25, xxiv. 49; *d.* cyððe 52.
10, 63. 30, 64. 10, 139. 27, 146.
29, xii. 24; *a.* xx. 158.

D.

dǣd, *f.* deed; 70. 27, 121. 19, i.
43, ix. 18; *pl. d.* dǣdum xvi.
23; *a.* dǣda 44. 3, 5, 141. 8.

dæg, *m.* day; 68. 2, xii. 16; *g.*
dæges 52. 6; *adv.* by day 102.
5; *d.* dæge viii. 18, xxix. 41;
used in adverbial phrases, ælce
dæge xxviii. 4; ælce dæg, 10
times, 59. 23 &c.; æghwylce
dæge xx. 137; æghwelce dæg
xiv. 5; *a.* dæg 20. 3, xi. 62 &c.;
on dæg 33. 27, 121. 16; midne
dæg 57. 24, 126. 13; *pl. g.*
daga 73. 13; *d.* dagum Pr. 7,
34. 30, 35. 1, 44. 11, xx. 213;
on ... dagum 43. 6, 44. 4; gio
dagum 45. 4; dahum 10. 10; *a.*
dagas 17. 24, 49. 21, iv. 19.

dægrīm, *n.* number of days; *g.*
dægrimes xxvi. 33.

dǣl, *m.* part, portion, share; 29.
13 &c. *and* xxix. 53; *g.* dæles 42.
1, 135. 28, xx. 60; *d.* dæle 42.
5, 16; *w.* be, extent, degree; be
sumum dæle, in some degree,
partly 15. 18 &c. *and* xx. 96;
be ðæm dæle ðe, to the extent
that, so far as 93. 23, 109. 22,
132. 23; be nanum dæle, in no
respect 130. 10; be ænegum
dæle, in any degree 123. 22;
a. dæl 13. 30 &c. *and* xxiv. 31;
a. pl. dælas 76. 17.

dǣlan, *wv.* divide, distribute,
assign; 120. 12; *ind. prs.* 2.*s.*
dælest xx. 51; dælst 79. 30; 3.*s.*
dælð 128. 8, 22; *pp.* gedæled
90. 5*, xxix. 35; *pl. m.* ge-

dælede 92. 25*; *a.* gedælde 28.
23*.

gedafenlic, *adj.* proper, fitting; is
þ *g.* xxxi. 21.

gedāl, *n.* separation; *d.* gedale
45. 25.

daru, *f.* harm, injury; 67. 23.

dēad, *adj.* dead; *d.* bion, to die
66. 25; *wk.* deada 109. 29, 110.
1; *f. pred.* dead 22. 22; *a.*
deadne 36. 10, 11, 109. 28; *pl.*
deade 46. 29; wurden deade,
died 118. 1.

dēadlic, *adj.* subject to death,
mortal; deaðlic 17. 9*, 52. 16;
d. deadlicum 13. 13; *a. n. wk.*
deaðlice 46. 9; *pl. n.* deaðlice 53. 10*; *g.* deaðlicra 22.
29; *wk.* deadlicena 29. 1*; *d.*
deadlicum 74. 8*.

dēah, *swv.* be of use, be good,
avail; *ind. prs.* 3.*s.* 63. 9; *pst.*
3.*s.* dohte 63. 8, 67. 10, viii. 5;
pl. dohton 44. 6; *sbj. prs.* dyge
123. 18.

dearr, *swv.* dare, venture; *prs.*
ind. 3.*s.* dear xi. 65; *pst.* 3.*s.*
dorste xx. 70; *sbj. prs.* dyrre.
29. 18, 138. 13; durre xi. 54;
pst. pl. dorsten 134. 6, i. 27.

dēað, *m.* death; 20. 22, x. 29 &c.;
g. deaðes 20. 24 &c. *and* xxvii.
6; *d.* deaðe 26. 13 &c.; *a.* deað
66. 28 &c.

gedēfe, *adj.* fitting, seemly; *n. s.*
n. xxvi. 92.

delfan, *sv3.* dig; 34. 11; *sbj. prs.*
delfe 140. 11, 14.

delfere, *m.* digger; 140. 13

dēma, *wm.* judge; 105. 19, 119.
28, 136. 25, xxiv. 42; *g.* deman
120. 2; *d.* 17. 9.

dēman, *wv.* judge, deem; 122.
28, 140. 24; *ind. prs.* 3.*s.* demð
125. 28, 131. 12, 18; *sbj. prs.*
3.*pl.* demen 121. 26.

demm, *m.* harm, loss; *a.* dem 13.
1, 47. 7.

denu, *f.* valley; *d.* dene 27. 7,
vii. 37.

dēofol, *m.* devil; *a.* dioful, deofel* 38. 28.

dĕop, *adj.* deep; diop 82. 28;
d. diopum 112. 15.
dĕoplīce, *adv.* deeply; xxii. 3;
dioplice 94. 27*; *comp.* dioplicor 12. 26.
dĕor, *n.* wild animal; 72. 8;
wilde *d.* 124. 11; dior 73. 1,
xxvii. 24; *d.* diore 116. 22,
xxvi. 87; *a.* dior 73. 3; *pl.*
deor 116. 23; dior 101. 28,
xxvii. 20; *g.* diora xxvi. 92;
d. diorum 121. 15, 124. 8, xxvii.
11.
dĕorboren, *adj.* of noble birth;
f. diorboren xxvi. 52.
dĕorcynn, *n.* species of animal;
d. deorcynne 116. 20; *d. pl.*
deorcynnum 116. 21*.
dĕorwierðe, *adj.* precious; *a. n.*
deorwyrðe 48. 17*; *d. pl.*
deorwyrðum 32. 26*; *comp.*
deorwyrðra 72. 23; *f.* deorwyrðre 72. 24 *n.*; *n.* 28. 8;
diorwyrðre 22. 31, 83. 31;
a. n. deorwyrðre 25. 20, 21;
diorwyrðre 48. 18*; *g. pl.* diorwyrðra 33. 24*; *sup. wk.*
deorwyrðesta 35. 25; *n. wk.*
deorwyrðeste 54. 9; deorweorðoste 48. 20; *a. n. wk.* deorwyrðoste 22. 1; *g. pl. wk.*
deorwyrðestena 55. 27.
dĕorwierðnes, *f.* precious thing,
treasure; *pl. d.* deorwyrðnessum
19. 6; *a.* deorwyrðnessa 34. 12.
derian, *wv. w. d.* harm, injure;
36. 7, 13, xii. 4; gederian 36.
15; derigan 18. 14, 117. 6;
ind. prs. 3.*s.* derað 30. 15;
dereð 32. 32, 144. 18, 26, iv.
36; xxvi. 111; *pl.* deriað 33. 1,
36. 8, 116. 31, iv. 48; derigað
36. 11; deregað 10. 21*; *sbj.*
prs. pl. derigen 52. 1*.
dīegellīce, *adv.* secretly; digellice
7. 19*; degelice i. 64.
dīegelnes, *f.* secret; *a.* diegelnesse
28. 14.
dīegle, *adj.* secret, hidden; *pl. a.*
wk. dæglan 57. 26; *n.* deglu
127. 1; *comp. d. pl.* diogolran
27. 16*.

dīere, 1) *adj.* dear, precious;
diore 27. 24, x. 29; *n.* 27. 29;
pl. deore 31. 13; *n.* diore, dyre*
16. 12; *comp.* diorra, deorra*
28. 12; *pl.* dierran 32. 16*;
deorran 31. 11; *sup.* diorust,
deorast* 27. 28. 2) *adv.* dearly,
at a dear price: diore gecepte
xxvi. 19; *sup.* diorost viii. 11.
dīerling, *m.* favourite; diorling
140. 8; *pl. g.* dyrlinga, deorlinga*
66. 31; *d.* deorlingum 62. 14;
65. 4*, 67. 15*; diorlingum
67. 15; *a.* deorlingas 64. 28*,
133. 12; diorlingas xv. 8.
dimm, *adj.* dark, dim; *f. w.*
dimme xii. 16; *a. n. wk.* dimme
8. 10, ii. 11.
dōgor, *n.* day; *g. pl.* dogora
xiii. 21, xx. 175, 209, xxii. 61,
xxviii. 65.
dōgorrim, *n.* number of days; *d.*
dogorrime x. 67.
dohtor, *f.* daughter; 22. 12, 115.
23, 116. 2, xxvi. 33, 52.
dōm, *m. a)* free will; *b)* judgement,
opinion; *c)* authority, power;
d) reputation, glory; *g.* domes
22. 9 (*d*), 74. 6 (*b*); domes
dæg, doomsday 144. 2, xxix.
41; *d.* dome 16. 30 (*c*). 22.
13 (*b*), 37. 4 (*c*), 41. 26 (*b*),
112. 9 (*c*), 121. 6 (*b*), 121. 26
(*b*); *pl. n.* domas, decrees 59.
25, 35. 32 (*a*), 140. 28.
dōmere, = demere, *m.* judge; *d.*
20. 13; *n. pl.* domeras 64. 12.
dōn, *anv. a)* do, perform; *b)* act;
c) make, render; *d)* cause; *e)*
put, set; *f) used to avoid re-*
peating another vb. = do. *a)* Pr.
14 &c. *b)* 37. 1 &c. *c)* 26. 15 &c
d) 47. 7 &c. *e)* don ðær weorðscipe to 75. 16, *cf.* 75 28 *et inf.*
f) 9. 14 &c.; dōn 117. 14, 24;
gedon, effect, bring to pass,
render 24. 25, 36. 15, xxvi.
102 &c. = do 134. 6; to donne
110. 29 &c.; *ind. prs.* 2.*s.* dest
30. 16; gedest 10. 3 &c. *and* xx.
272; 3.*s.* deð Pr. 15; vii. 14
&c.; gedeð 28. 3 &c.; *pl.* doð 14.

17, iv. 26 &c. ; gedoð 28. 4 &c. ;
pst. dyde 7. 15, xiii. 79 &c. ; *pl.*
dydon 20. 17 &c. *and* xxix. 5 ;
ðærof dydon, took away 76. 21
(c) ; gedydon 16. 7, 29. 29 ;
imp. do 29. 23, 99. 25 ; do nu
of, take away 42. 4 *(e)* ; do . . .
to, add 113. 14 *(e)* ; *sbj. prs.*
do 58. 2, xv. 13 &c. ; *pl.* don 44.
28 &c. ; don ealne ætgædere 76.
19 *(e)* ; dón 113. 2 ; gedon 28.
26, xxi. 27 ; *pst. pl.* dyden 110.
3 ; *pp.* gedon Pr. 2 &c. *and* xi.
23 ; *n. pl. m.* gedone 113. 32.
drēamcræft, *m.* music ; 38. 7.
drēamere, *m.* musician ; 38. 7.
dreccan, *wv.* vex, torment ;
   dreccean v. 40 ; *ind. prs.* 3.*s.*
   dreceð vii. 25 ; *sbj. prs.* 3.*s.*
   drecce vii. 54.
drēfan, *wv.* stir up, confuse,
   trouble ; xxvii. 2 ; gedrefan v.
   23 ; *ind. prs.* 3.*s.* gedrefeð 14.
   11, v. 8 ; gedrefð 71. 5, 111.
   28 ; gedræfð xviii. 3, xxv. 42 ;
   pl. drefe ge 124. 3 ; gedrefað
   14. 5 ; *pp.* gedrefed 9 *times*,
   8. 1 &c. *and* i. 74, v. 18 ; *n.*
   pl. m. gedrefde 130. 26.
gedrēfednes, *f.* confusion, trouble ;
   13. 8 ; *g.* gedrefednesse 14. 18 ;
   gedræfednesse 13. 1 ; *d.* gedrefednesse 14. 24, 95. 23, 142. 21,
   23 ; *a.* 59. 2 ; *g. pl.* gedrefednessa
   104. 33.
gedrēfnes, *f.* confusion, trouble ;
   d. gedrefnesse v. 40 ; gedræfnesse
   xxii. 61.
drenc, *m.* drink ; 135. 20 ; *a.*
   132. 7.
drēogan, *sv2.* suffer, endure ; *ind.*
   prs. 3.*s.* drigð 9. 11* ; *pst.* 3.*pl.*
   drogan 116. 26*.
drēorig, *adj.* sad, sorrowful ; *a.*
   dreorigne xxii. 33.
drēosan, *sv2.* fall, perish ; *prs. p.*
   perishable, *a.* dreosendne vii. 16 ;
   a. pl. wk. dreosendan 26. 29.
drīfan, *sv1. a)* drive away, expel ;
   b) practise ; drifan drycræftas
   xxvi. 54 *(b)* ; *ind. prs.* 3.*s.*
   drifð xxix. 48 *(a)*.

drincan, *sv3.* drink ; *ind. prs.* 2.*s.*
   drincst 30. 17 ; 3.*s.* gedrinceð
   vii. 16 ; *pst. pl.* druncon 34. 1,
   viii. 20, 28 ; druncan 33. 29*.
drohtað, *m.* manner of life ; *a.*
   xxvi. 92.
drūgian, *wv. intrans.* dry up ;
   sbj. pst. 3.*s.* drugode 80. 18.
drȳcræft, *m.* magic, sorcery ; *d.*
   drycræfte 116. 27 ; *a.* drycræft
   116. 14 ; *pl. d.* drycræftum xxvi.
   98. 102 ; *a.* drycræftas xxvi. 54.
drȳcræftig, *adj.* skilled in sorcery ;
   f. drycræftigu 116. 3.
drȳgan, *wv. trans.* dry ; *ind. prs.*
   3.*s.* drygð 136. 15 ; drigeð xxix.
   59.
drȳge, *adj.* dry ; *f. pred.* 80. 6* ;
   n. absol. ðæt drige, dryness
   xxix. 48 ; *d. absol.* drygum,
   dryness xx. 74 ; drinceð to
   dryggum, drinks to dryness vii.
   16 ; *wk.* drygan 80. 9 ; *a.*
   drygne N. ; drigne 34. 27 ; *f wk.*
   drigan 80. 12 ; *n.* dryge 136.
   12 ; *d. pl.* drygum 12. 9.
dryhten, *m.* lord ; *always used*
   of God except Creca drihten xxvi.
   14, 19 ; dryhten 79. 10, 136.
   24, iv. 53 ; drihten 12 *times*,
   10. 17, vii. 37 &c. ; *g.* drihtnes
   i. 41, x. 67, xx. 209, 213, xxix.
   36 ; *a.* drihten 29. 8.
dryhtguma, *wm.* retainer, soldier ;
   n. pl. drihtguman viii. 11.
drync, *m.* drink, potion ; 30. 8 ;
   g. drynces 60. 18 ; *a.* drinc viii.
   22 ; *pl.* drincas 33. 24, viii. 9 ;
   d. dryncum 111. 27.
duguð, *f. a)* flower, best ; *b)* excellence, virtue ; *c)* benefit,
   favour ; 22. 4 *(a)*, 28. 28 *(b)* ;
   pl. duguða *(b)* ; *d.* duguðum
   x. 29 *(b)*, xv. 8 *(c)*.
dūn, *f.* hill ; *d.* dune, *in adv.* ofdune *(q.v.)* ; *a.* dune 73. 28, xix.
   10 ; *d. pl.* dunum 73. 31, 91. 17.
dunnian, *wv. intrans.* obscure ;
   ind. prs. 3.*pl.* dunniað 10. 6.
duru, *f.* door ; *a.* 97. 14, 17, 24.
dūst, *n.* dust ; 80. 19 ; *d.* duste
   xx. 104 ; *a.* dust 28. 22.

dwelian, *wv.* lead astray; ge-
dweligan 78. 17*; *ind. prs. 3.s.*
gedwelað 73. 23*; *pst.* dwelode
100. 27*; *sbj. prs.* dwelige 100.
5*; *pp.* gedwelod 55. 21*.

dwellan, *wv.* lead astray; gedwellan 78. 17; *prs. ind. 3.s.*
gedwæleð xix. 3; *sbj. prs.* dwelle
105. 5, 27; *pst.* dwealde 100.
26; *pp.* gedweald 55. 21. B
has dwelian *in all these cases.*

gedwola, *wm.* error, heresy; 58.
12, 76. 13, i. 41; *g.* gedwolan
9. 18, 19. 31; *d.* 7. 7 &c. *and*
xix. 29; *a.* xxvi. 39.

dwolian, *wv.* stray, err; *ind.*
prs. pl. dwoliað 88. 27; *sbj. pst.*
2.s. gedwolode 11. 11; *prs. p.*
dwoliende 74. 31; dwoligende
108. 14.

dwolma, *wm.* confusion, chaos;
a. pl. mistes dwoleman v. 43.

gedwolmist, *m.* mist of error; *d.*
gedwolmiste 95. 11, xxii. 33.

dyderian, *wv.* deceive, mislead;
sbj. prs. 2.s. dyderie*, dydre
100. 5.

dynt, *m.* blow, crash; *a.* 117.
30.

dysig, (i) *adj.* foolish, unthinking;
26. 4, 63. 4, 98. 12, 122. 11;
dysi 138. 14; *wk.* dysega xxv. 13;
n. wk. dysige 115. 25; dysie
xxviii. 65; *g.* dysiges 68. 13, xxvi.
52; dysges 64. 2*; *d. wk.* dysegan
61. 6; dysgan 61. 3*; *a.* dysinc
17. 11, ii. 11; *n. wk.* dysige
xxvi. 39; *pl. n.* dysige 31. 12,
68. 10, 74. 30, 78. 7, 109. 2, 23,
117. 15; *wk.* dysegan 74. 5, 78.
7, 108. 12, 16, 121. 32, xix. 29,
xxvi. 98; *g.* dysigra 9. 3; dysegra
118. 12; *wk.* dysigena 63. 27;
d. dysegum 61. 4, 62. 14*, 118.
7, 9, 18, 121. 22, 138. 14; dysgum
81. 3*; *a.* dysige 41. 2; *comp.*
n. pl. dysigran 74. 11*; dysegran
xix. 41; *sup.* dysegast xv. 11;
wk. dysgosta 123. 29. (ii) *sbst.*
n. folly; 62. 13, 73. 23, 104. 6,
xix. 1; dysi 122. 1; *g.* dysiges
108. 7; *d.* dysige 39. 4* &c.;

a. dysig 9. 7 &c. *and* xix. 39,
xxviii. 78.

dysigian, *wv.* be foolish; *ind.*
prs. pl. dysegað 12. 8; *sbj. prs.*
3.pl. dysegian* 56. 1 *n.*

dysilic, *adj.* foolish; *n.* dyslic 42.
10, 84. 18.

E.

ēa, *f.* river; 83. 3, 4; *g.* 86. 21;
d. 37. 3, 83. 4, 86. 21; *pl. n.*
102. 6; *g.* 74. 3.

ēa, *interj.* oh! ah! 65. 15, 68. 10,
94. 17.

ēac, *adv.* also, besides *fq.*; *w.* ge
10. 6 &c.; eac swa same xi. 5
&c.; geac 16. 31*.

ēaca, *wm.* increase; 48. 6; *g.*
eacan 55. 29, 75. 5; *d.* to eacan,
used as prep. w. d. in addition
to 22. 30, 31. 32, 59. 29, 60.
19, 146. 9; *a.* eacan 119. 7.

ēaden, *ptcp.* granted; xxxi. 9.

ēadig, *adj.* fortunate, happy; 59.
11 &c.; *d. pl.* eadegum xxi. 44;
comp. n. pl. eadigran 60. 3.

ēadiglic, *adj.* prosperous, happy;
98. 6.

ēadignes, *f.* prosperity, happiness;
55. 1, 87. 15; *d.* eadignesse 52.
20, 139. 16; *a.* 54. 27.

ēaflsc, *m.* river-fish; *a. pl.* eafiscas
xix. 24.

eafora, *wm.* son; xxvi. 35.

ēage, *wn.* eye; *d.* eagan 121. 30,
129. 30, 133. 13; *a.* eage 44.
14; *pl. n.* eagan 122. 6, 145.
25; *g.* eagena 73. 7; *d.* eagum
11. 1, iv. 55 &c.; eahum 11. 1*;
a. eagan 8. 26, xx. 261 &c.

ēagorstrēam, *m.* sea, ocean;
egorstream xx. 118; *g.* eagorstreames xx. 122 *n.*

ēalā, *interj.* oh! alas! 9. 10, iv.
25 &c.; e. ea 65. 15; e. eaw 39.
31, 70. 7; e. wa 73. 22; æala
34. 10*, 46. 7*, iii. 1, iv. 1;
eawla ix. 55.

ēaland, *n.* island; *d.* ealonde 7.
4*, 34. 29; *a.* ealand 34. 1*.

eald, *adj.* old; ald xxii. 54; *wk.* ealda 31. 20; *n.* eald 126. 23, xxviii. 70; *a. wk.* ealdan 33. 13, 135. 25; *pl. n.* ealde xxvi. 86; *wk.* ealdan 108. 9; *d.* ealdum 22. 26, i. 65 &c.; *wk.* ealdan 103. 16; *comp. g.* eldran fæder, grandfather 22. 25; *d. pl.* eldran 20. 11; *v.* also ieldran.

ealdgecynd, *n.* original nature; *d.* ealdgecynde xiii. 40, xxv. 57.

ealdhlāford, *m.* lord from old time; *d. pl.* ealdhlafordum 7. 16, i. 63.

ealdhlāfordcynn, *n.* hereditary lordship; *g.* ealdhlafordcynnes 7. 21.

ealdor, *m.* chief, prince; aldor xxvi. 7, xxix. 6.

ealdormann, *m.* magistrate, dignitary; *n. pl.* ealdormen 22. 24, 23. 6.

ealdriht, *n.* ancient right; *pl. g.* ealdrihta 7. 8, 16, i. 36. 57; *d.* ealdrihtum 7. 22.

ealdspell, *n.* old story; *a.* M. Pr. 1; *d. pl.* ealdspellum 127. 8.

ealdgeweorc, *n.* ancient work; xi. 40, xx. 116.

eall, 1) *adj.* all; *fq.* xvi. 8 &c.; eal 41. 24, xx. 207; *f.* eall 93. 18, xx. 171 &c.; *n.* eall, eal ix. 44 &c.; *g.* ealles 33. 5 &c.; *n.* ealles *used as adv.* altogether, entirely 11. 10, 40. 8, iv. 35, v. 30 &c.; *f.* ealre *fq.*; ealræ 41. 20; *a.* eallne 9. 6, 24. 10, 104. 6, xxviii. 5; *commoner form* ealne 18. 7, iv. 3 &c.; ealne weg *adv.* always, *fq.* 9. 21 &c.; eallne weg 120. 25; eallneg 120. 24, 25; ealneg xxii. 15, xxviii. 57, 69; ealnig vii. 40, 53, x. 21, xxi. 15; *f.* ealle 76. 28 &c.; æalle 39. 19; *n.* eall 79. 31, xi. 88 &c.; eal 76. 23, 77. 1, 111. 17, xxii. 17; *inst.* ealle 69. 14, xiii. 64 &c.; eall xxix. 96; eallon 53. 18*, 67. 5*, 69. 14*,

147. 4*, 12*; mid ealle *adv.* altogether, quite 8. 12, xvii. 22 &c.; *pl. n.* ealle vi. 5 &c.; eall 23. 13*, 121. 27; *f. usual form* ealla 18. 4, iv. 25 &c.; ealle 10. 14, iv. 53 &c.; *n.* ealle *about* 10 *times*, 41. 28 &c.; *commoner form* eall 32. 15 &c.; *g.* eallra 10. 16, xx. 259 &c.; ealra 24. 25, xix. 28 &c. (*both used about equally*); eal ðinra godena weorca 18. 24; *d.* eallum xi. 21 &c.; ealum 22. 15*; *a.* ealle ix. 24 &c.; *f.* ealla *and* ealle 52. 31, xi. 32, xiii. 7 &c. (*about equally*); *n.* ealle 90. 32, xx. 56 &c.; eall 29. 9 &c.; eal 42. 6 &c. 2) *adv.* altogether, entirely; *fq. in Cott. Metra, often difficult to distinguish from* (1), x. 9, xi. 77 &c.

eallisig, *adj.* all icy, very cold; xxiv. 23.

eallmæegen, *n.* all one's power; *d.* eallmæegene xxix. 96; almæegene xxix. 3.

eallneg, *v.* eall.

eallunga, *adv.* entirely; *fq.* 21. 27, xi. 26 &c.; allunga 69. 30*; ellunga 60. 14.

eallwealda, *wm.* Almighty; alwealda xi. 22.

eallwihta, *f. pl.* all things; *g.* alwuhta xx. 253.

ealo, *n.* ale; 40. 22* (ealu J).

ēaōfer, *m.* river-bank; *d. pl.* eaofrum xix. 22; æaofrum 74. 1*.

ēargebland, *n.* surge of the sea; *a.* eargeblond viii. 30.

eard, *m.* native place, home; 91. 17, xiii. 63 &c.: *g.* eardes 116. 12, v. 15, xxvi. 71; *d.* earde 11. 10, xiii. 70 &c.; earda 83. 12; *a.* eard 80. 35, xi. 66 &c.

eardfæst, *adj.* settled, abiding; vii. 38; *n.* xx. 156.

eardian, *wv.* dwell; xx. 109; eardigan 80. 21; *ind. prs.* 3.*s.* eardað 27. 7; *pl.* eardiað 25. 2; *sbj. prs.* 3.*pl.* eardien xx. 146.

ēare, *wn.* ear; *pl. n.* earan 145. 20; *a.* 28. 13, 145. 30.

earſoðe, 1) *adj.* troublesome, difficult; *n.* earſoðe 127. 22; *g.* earſoðes 147. 23; *n. pl.* earſoðe 81. 3, 92. 24; *sup. a. f. w.* earſoðestan 127. 3. 2) *sbst. n.* hardship, trouble; *d.* earſoðe 130. 24; earefoðe 18. 28 *n.*; *pl. n.* earſoðu 56. 13, 125. 9; *g.* earſoða 27. 12; *d.* earſoðum 22. 8, 11, 66. 2, 120. 17, xxvi. 97; *a.* earſoðu 70. 12, 82. 7, 133. 3, 15, 27, xx. 254; gearſoðu 70. 5.

earfoðhāwe, *adj.* hard to be seen; *n.* 81. 5, xx. 152.

earfoðlic, *adj.* difficult; *n.* 118. 6.

earfoðnes, *f.* hardship, trouble; *g. pl.* earſoðnessa 23. 13.

earfoðrīme, *adj.* hard to count, very numerous; *n. pl. n.* earſoðrimu Pr. 7.

earfoðtǣcne, *adj.* hard to be shown; *n.* xx. 147.

earg, *adj.* a) timid; b) inert, lazy; c) depraved; *a. wk.* eargan 115. 1 (a); *n. pl. wk.* ge eargan 139. 8 (b); *comp. n. pl.* eargran 60. 4 (c).

earm, *m.* arm; *d.* earme 66. 29.

earm, *adj.* wretched, miserable; 20. 5 &c.; poor 77. 10, 124. 25; *n. wk.* earme 105. 28, xxiv. 63; *d.* earmum 10. 17; *a.* earmne 26. 17, 123. 4; *wk.* earman 10. 26, 25. 11; *pl. n.* earme 24. 6, iv. 57 &c.; *wk.* earman xix. 3; *d.* earmum iv. 31; *a.* earme 105. 27, 117. 31; *wk.* earman 73. 23; *comp.* earmra, 123. 1; *n. pl.* earmran 60. 4, 74. 11, xix. 41; *sup. n. pl. m.* earmoste 118. 2.

earmlic, *adj.* miserable, wretched; *f.* earmlico 138. 4; *n.* earmlic 74. 5, 146. 14, xxvii. 16, xxviii. 74; *sup.* earmlicost xix. 28.

earmlīce, *adv.* miserably; 71. 20; *comp.* earmlicor 72. 2.

earn, *m.* eagle; 18. 12.

earnian, *wv. w. g. a. or* ðæt *clause,* deserve, earn; geearnigan 29. 3, 44. 10; *ind. prs. 3.s.* earnað 88. 16, 20; *pl.* earniað 44. 31, 133. 22; geearnigað 112. 19; earnað þ hie sien ðy halran, gain, effect 88. 21*; *pst. 3.s.* earnade ix. 20; *pl.* geearnodon 120. 14; *sbj. prs. 3.s.* earnige* 106. 26; *pl.* earnien 106. 26; *pp.* geearnad 103. 5.

earnung, *f.* merit; *d.* geearnunga 82. 1, 124. 20, 21, xx. 228; geearnunge 81. 34; *a.* earnunga, advantage 88. 20; geearnungæ 120. 16; *pl. n.* earnunga, geearnunga* 70. 11; *a.* earnunga 52. 20.

ēast, *adv.* east; ix. 42, x. 5, xiii. 59, xiv. 7, xxx. 1; *error for* læst? xxix. 17.

ēastan, *adv.* from, in the east; 10. 12, 136. 4, i. 1, iv. 23, vi. 12, xii. 15, xxix. 20, 26; be eastan xxix. 33.

ēasteweard, *adj.* east, *used in adverbial phrases;* from easteweardum 39. 27, 67. 30; from easteweardan 41. 21*.

ēastewearde, *adv.* eastward; xvi. 18.

ēastre, *f.* Easter, spring; *d. or a.* on eastran 29. 21.

ēaðe, *adv.* easily; *fq.* 26. 9, ix. 48 &c.; *comp.* ieð 23. 12; eð 9. 27, 14. 8, 46. 19*, 52. 9*, 107. 19, 108. 2, 135. 21, x. 38, xii. 22; yð 104. 30, 124. 27, 145. 17.

ēaðmētto, *n. pl.* humility; 67. 8; *g.* eaðmetta 27. 6, vii. 33; eadmetta vii. 38.

ēaðmōd, *adj.* humble; *d. pl.* eaðmodum 18. 11.

ēaðmōdlīce, *adv.* humbly; 97. 32; eadmodlice 71. 20, 149. 2.

ēaðmōdnes, *f.* humility; *g.* eadmodnesse 27. 7*; *a.* eadmodnesse 18. 10.

eax, *f.* axle-tree, axis; 129. 20, 23, 131. 1; *g.* eaxe 126. 5, xxviii. 22; *d.* 129. 19 &c. *and* xxviii. 13, 15, xxix. 18; *a.* 126. 8, 131. 1.

ebba, *wm.* ebb, low tide; *g.* ebban 49. 26; *n. pl.* xi. 69.

ēce, *adj.* eternal; 9. 12, iv. 33 &c.; *wk.* eca 148. 31, iv. 29 &c.; *f.* ecu 120. 1, xiii. 71; *wk.* ece v. 44; *n.* ece 113. 22, xx. 237 &c.; *g.* eces 138. 24; *wk.* ecan 78. 25; *d.* ecum iv. 3; to ðæm ecum gode xxi. 3; *f.* ecre 120. 17, 139. 16; *wk.* ecan 10. 1, 23. 9, 149. 8; *a.* ecne 78. 12, xx. 224, xxvi. 50; *wk.* ecan 89. 23, iii. 6 &c.; *f.* ece 44. 9; *n.* ece 44. 17, 120. 13; *inst.* ece 143. 25; *pl.* ece 27. 23; *f.* eca 26. 11; ece 51. 25, 77. 29; *wk.* ecan 27. 11, xix. 31; *g.* ecra 137. 27*; *d.* to ðæm ecum vii. 44; *a. f.* ece 78. 12; *wk.* ecan 26. 18, 130. 31, vii. 29; *n.* ecu 113. 19, 22.

ecg, *f.* edge; *d. pl.* ecgum ix. 29.

ēcnes, *f.* eternity; 147. 23, 148. 7; *d.* on ecnesse, for ever, eternally 47. 2, 90. 12, 92. 17, 113, 4, 120. 10, 11.

edlēan, *n.* reward, retribution; 9. 21, 113. 13, 28, 125. 10; *g.* edleanes 113. 3, 13, 119. 18, 134. 12; *d.* edleane 104. 22, 137. 13; *a.* edlean 70. 11, 112. 20, 113. 9, 24, 120. 8, 9, 11, 124. 13; 135. 16, xxvii. 26; *pl. g.* edleana 112. 18; *d.* edleanum 113. 2; *a.* edlean 113. 20, 22.

ednīwe, *adj.* renewed; *n. pl. m.* edniwe xi. 39.

ednīwian, *wv.* renew, restore; *ind. prs.* 3.*s.* gecdniwað 131. 6, 8; *pp. n. pl. f.* geedniwode 92. 12; geedniwade 49. 9*.

edsceaft, *f.* new creation; *d.* edsceafte 92. 13, 15.

edwīt, *n.* reproach, disgrace; i. 55.

efen, 1) *adj.* even, level; *g. n.* emnes 58. 30*. 2) *adv.* equally, just; xx. 244.

efenæðele, *adj.* equally noble; *pl. n.* emnæðele 69. 27*; *a.* 69. 24*.

efenbehēfe, *adj.* equally necessary; *f.* efnbehefu xii. 7.

efenbeorht, *adj.* equally bright; *n. pl.* efenbeorhte xx. 233; *f.* xx. 231.

efengōd, *adj.* equally good; *n.* emngod *w.d.* 85. 2; emngood 142. 20; *g.* emngoodes 83. 25.

efenīeðe, *adj.* equally easy; *n.* efneðe xx. 167.

efenlīca, *wm.* equal; efnlica xx. 19.

efenlīce, *adv.* equally, alike; emnlice 28. 23.

efenmǣre, *adj.* equally famous; *a. s. m.* efnmærne x. 32.

efenmicel, *adj.* equally great; *d.* emnmiclum 147. 22; *a.* emnmicelne 107. 12.

efennēah, equally near; 1) *adv.* xx. 141. 2) *prep. w. d.* emnneah 80. 33*, 129. 32.

efenswīðe, *adv.* equally, to an equal degree; efnswiðe xi. 44.

efne, *adv.* equally; i. 14, viii. 46, 48, xi. 76, xvi. 11, xix. 30, xx. 124, 154, xxii. 19, xxvi. 65, xxviii. 28; emne 136. 6*, ix. 38, xxiv. 63, xxix. 35.

eft, *adv.* a second time, again; Pr. 9, i. 61 &c.; æft i. 65 (J).

ege, *m.* fear; 26. 6, i. 72; *g.* eges 22. 10; *d.* ege 66. 2, 67. 13, 117. 30, 118. 28, 134. 32, xx. 71; *a.* 14. 21, 102. 8, 125. 15, v. 28.

egefull, *adj.* terrible; egeful 43. 13.

egesa, *wm.* fear; *a.* egesan xii. 17.

egeslic, *adj.* terrible; 102. 16, xxvii. 13; *f. wk.* egeslice 48. 7; *d. wk.* egeslican 52. 6; *comp. n.* egeslicre 104. 15.

eglan, *wv. w. d.* trouble, ail; *ind. pst.* 3.*s.* eglede 15. 23.

ehtan, *wv. w. g.* pursue; *ind. prs.* 3.*s.* eht 148. 16.

elcung, *f.* delay; eldcung 120. 2 *n.*

ellen, *n.* courage; 62. 26.

ellende, 1) *adj.* foreign; *a.* ellendne viii. 30. 2) *sbst.* on ellende, abroad 63. 30, 64. 9.

elles, *adv.* otherwise, else; *often w. pronouns* nanwuht, nauht &c.

9. 14, ix. 20 &c. ; elles hwæt,
something else 76. 16, 107. 25 ;
d. elles hwam 32. 29.

elleshwǽr, *adv.* elsewhere ; 111.
6.

elpend, *m.* elephant ; 72. 5, 7.

elðeod, *f.* foreign nation ; *d.* on
ælðeode 63. 30*.

elðeodig, *adj.* foreign ; elðiodig
124. 25 ; *d. wk.* ælðeodegan
63. 31* ; *a. n.* ælðeodig 63. 16* ;
pl. n. elðeodge i. 55 ; *d.* ælðeo-
degum 71. 26.

emn-, emne, *v.* efen-, efne.

emnettan, *wv.* level ; *ind. prs.*
3.*s.* geemnet 46. 16*.

ende, *m.* end, goal ; 44. 20 &c.
and xx. 275 ; *g.* endes 13. 2, 20 ;
d. ende 52. 19, xxi. 44 &c. ; *a.*
12. 6 &c. *and* xx. 10, xxviii. 22.

endebyrd, *f.* order ; *a.?* xiii. 4.

endebyrdan, *wv.* arrange, order ;
pp. geendebyrd 50. 4, xi. 100.

endebyrdes, *adv.* in order ; xi.
21, xx. 12 ; *by error* endebyrd
xiii. 4 ?

endebyrdlice, *adv.* in due order ;
12. 19, 79. 13, 96. 19, 129. 9.

endebyrdnes, *f.* order ; *d.* endebyrdnesse 49. 2, 57. 4, 128. 22 ;
a. 94. 10 ; endeberdnesse 128. 4.

endeléas, *adj.* endless ; *n.* 104.
15 ; *n. pl. f.* endelease 118. 5.

endemes, *adv.* equally, uniformly ;
112. 23, xxx. 12, 16 ; endemest
141. 16* ; ændemest 141. 18*.

endian, *wv. intrans.* end ; *ind.
prs.* 3.*s.* endað 38. 6, 50. 5, 103.
21, 139. 17 ; geendað 44. 27,
148. 2 ; *pl.* endiað 39. 7 ;
geendiað 26. 13 ; *pst.* 3.*s.* geendode 7. 9 ; *pp. trans.* geendod
100. 8.

geendodlic, *adj.* finite ; *n. wk.
absol.* ðæt geendodlice, finite-
ness 44. 21.

endung, *f.* ending, end ; *d.* endunge 39. 7.

engel, *m.* angel ; *pl. n.* englas
98. 13, 140. 28, 144. 3, 146. 10,
13, 16, 19, 148. 2 ; *g.* engla
xiii. 12, xx. 110, 153, 263, 275 ;

d. englum 57. 8, 140. 31, 143.
31, 146. 22, xiii. 15 ; *a.* englas
129. 4, 142. 9, 146. 13.

englisc, 1) *adj.* English ; *d.* engliscum spelle Pr. 9. 2) *sbst. n.* English language ; on e. wende Pr. 2.

eofor, *m.* wild boar ; *n. pl.* eforas
116. 17* ; eaforas xxvi. 81.

eorl, *m.* nobleman, eminent man ;
i. 78 ; *d.* eorle i. 72 ; *pl.* eorlas
i. 30 ; *g.* eorla ix. 59, xxv. 8.

eorlgebyrd, *f.* noble birth ; *d.
pl.* eorlgebyrdum ix. 26, x. 27.

eorneste, *adv.* earnestly, xvi. 22 ;
fiercely, xiii. 28.

eorðbüend, *m.* earth-dweller ;
n. pl. eorðbuende x. 25, xix. 13 ;
g. eorðbuendra x. 36, xii. 18 ;
d. eorðbuendum xxvi. 94, xxix.
72.

eorðcyning, *m.* king ; *a. pl.* eorðcyningas ix. 47.

eorðe, *w. f.* earth, world ; *fq.* 49.
12, viii. 33 &c. ; *g.* eorðan 10.
1, x. 17 &c. ; *d.* 23. 6, iv. 25 &c. ;
a. 10. 26, vi. 5 &c.

eorðlic, *adj.* earthly ; *wk.* eorðlica 61. 9, 72. 20 ; *n.* eorðlic
xxii. 5 ; *wk.* eorðlice xx. 237 ;
g. eorðlices 22. 10, 81. 12, xx.
166 ; *wk.* eorðlican 40. 8, 9 ;
d. eorðlicum 81. 11 ; *wk.* eorðlican 45. 31 ; *a. n.* eorðlic xxiv.
7 ; *wk.* eorðlice 129. 29 : *n. pl.
n.* eorðlicu xxi. 30 ; eorðlice 89.
17 ; *wk.* eorðlican 30. 3, 45. 29,
58. 5 ; *g. wk.* eorðlicena 83. 13 ;
a. n. eorðlicu vii. 42, xx. 224 :
wk. eorðlican 27. 10 &c. *and*
xx. 212.

eorðrice, *n.* kingdom of the
earth ; *a. pl.* eorðricu iv. 37.

eorðgesceaft, *f.* earthly creature ;
a. pl. eorðgesceafta xx. 194.

eorðwæstm, *m.* fruit of the earth ;
d. pl. eorðwæstmum viii. 6.

eorðwaran, *m. pl.* dwellers on
earth, mankind ; iv. 57, xvii. 1 ;
d. eorðwarum xiii. 60.

eow, *pron. d. and a.* of ge, you ;
usual form 25. 14, x. 18 &c. ;
iow 25. 15, x. 65.

ēower, *poss. adj.* your; *fq.* se
eower 34. 20, 43. 14; *f.* sio
eowru 65. 18; eower 28. 30,
149. 4; *n.* 28. 32; *g.* eoweres
44. 31; eoweres ælces, of each
of you 69. 28; eowres 45. 1; *f.*
eowre 45. 1; *d.* eowrum 32. 9,
13, 44. 11, x. 19; *f.* eowerre
32. 2, 44. 9, 124. 5; eowre
xxvii. 5; *a.* eowerne 42. 11, 18,
25, 43. 4, 46. 10; *f.* eowre 32.
11; *n.* eower 16. 30, xxvii. 2;
inst. eowre 58. 6; *pl.* eowere
35. 29, 30; eowre 28. 18, 34.
31; *f.* eowra 31. 18; eowre 32.
15; *n.* 32. 15; *g.* eowerra 45.
2; *d.* eowrum x. 19; *a.* eower
73. 29*; *f.* eowra 32. 14; *n.*
eowru xix. 11; eowre 28. 27.

ēowian, *v.* īewan.

erian, *wv.* plough; *inf.* erigen
xiv. 4 (J); *sbj. prs.* 3.*s.* erige
60. 29.

esne, *m.* retainer, soldier, man;
138. 18; *d.* 103. 5.

ēst, *m.* grace, permission; *a.* ofer
metodes est xi. 25.

etan, *sv5.* eat; *ind. prs.* 2.*s.* itst
30. 17; 3.*pl.* etað 116. 23; *pst.*
3.*pl.* æton 33. 27, 28, viii. 18.

ēðel, *m. n.* native land, home;
25. 1, 105. 22, xxiv. 50; *d.*
eðele 11. 4; eðle xx. 155; *a.*
eðel i. 16.

ēðelstōl, *m.* seat of government,
capital; ix. 11.

ēðelweard, *m.* defender of country,
chief man; *n. pl.* eðelweardas
i. 24.

F.

fācen, *n.* fraud, deceit; *g.* facnes
ix. 37.

fæder, *m.* father; 69. 20, iv. 18
&c.; *g.* 11. 4, 22. 25, xx. 67,
116, xxiv. 54; *d.* 22. 15, 68.
30, 69. 18; *a.* 69. 8 &c. *and*
xvii. 26, 116.

fægen, *adj.* glad; gefægen, fægn*
140. 1; fægn ix. 37; gefagen

57. 28; *n. pl. m.* ? fægen vi. 10;
comp. fægenra xii. 12.

fægenian, *wv. absol. or w. g.*
rejoice; 102. 15; fægnian 68. 16,
18, 19, 89. 29; *ind. prs.* 2.*s.*
fægnast 31. 6; fagnast 31. 4*;
3.*s.* fægnað, fagenað* 45. 29; *pl.*
fægeniað 29. 14; fægniað 39. 4,
69. 1, 136. 30, xxix. 93; *pst.*
3.*s.* fagenode 39. 25*; *pl.*
fægnodon i. 33; *sbj. prs.* 3.*s.*
fægenige 69. 9; fægnige 29. 21,
68. 20.

fæger, 1) *adj.* beautiful; 72. 30,
73. 5, 6, 87. 3, 145. 24, xxix.
25; *n.* 29. 12, 31. 5; *g. wk.*
fægran 113. 13; *pl. n. f.* fægra
147. 20; *n.* fægru 29. 9, 32.
30; fægere 31. 9*; *g.* fægerra
29. 20; *a. n.* fægere 79. 28;
comp. fægerra 69. 6, 72. 21; *n.*
fægerre 32. 29, 31; *sup.* fægrost
72. 9; *wk.* fægeresta 29. 13;
n. wk. fægereste 79. 29. 2)
sbst. n. beauty 31. 6, 73. 12;
g. fægres 31. 7; *d.* fægere 69. 7*.

fægere, *adv.* beautifully, well;
fægre ii. 6.

fægernes, *f.* beauty; 29. 18, 54.
24; *g. pl.* fægernessa 29. 17.

fær, *n.* aspect? *a.* xxxi. 4.

færeld, *n.* motion, course, journey;
g. færeldes 125. 32*, xxviii. 2;
færeltes 129. 21; *d.* færelde 10.
2*, 28. 16; færelte 130. 12; *a.*
færeld 16. 30; færelt xxviii. 11.

færinga, *adv.* quickly, suddenly;
xxviii. 41.

færlīce, *adv.* suddenly; 117. 29.

fæst, *adj.* firm, fixed; 23. 6 &c.;
f. fæst 128. 16; *wk.* fæste xx.
271; *n.* fæst 110. 24, xx. 150;
g. fæstes 20. 29; *d. wk.* fæstan
27. 6, 80. 14; *a.* fæstne vii. 33;
f. fæste 49. 10, 142. 11, xi.
42; *n.* fæst 26. 23, 26, 144.
21; *pl.* fæste 23. 14, 110. 22,
130. 4, 25; *f.* fæste 100. 14,
130. 12; *a.* fæste racentan,
strong 57. 9; *f.* fæste vii. 11.

fæstan, *wv.* go without food, fast;
ind. prs. 1.*pl.* fæstað 143. 1.

fæste, *adv.* firmly; 21. 8, i. 35
&c.; *comp.* fæstor 91. 28.

fæsten, *n.* fortress; *a.* i. 20; *d.*
fæstene i. 79.

fæstlic, *adj.* firm, fixed; *g.*
fæstlices vi. 16.

fæstlíce, *adv.* firmly, steadily;
20. 22, 23. 28, 81. 11, i. 70;
comp. fæstlicor 129. 22.

fæstnes, *f.* firmness, solidity; *a.*
fæstnesse 72. 16.

fæstnian, *wv.* fasten; *pp. n. pl.*
m. gefæstnode 130. 11.

fæstrǽd, *adj.* steadfast; *wk.*
fæstrǽda 46. 23, x. 49; *f. pred.*
fæstrǽd 47. 17.

fæstrǽdlic, *adj.* steadfast; *g. n.*
fæstrǽdlices 20. 21.

fæstrǽdnes, *f.* steadfastness; *d.*
fæstrǽdnesse 12. 13; *a.* 11. 5.

fæt, *n.* vessel, cup; *n. pl.* fatu
104. 17.

fǽtt, *adj.* fat; *d. pl.* fettum 115. 6.

fágian, *wv.* vary, change; *ind.*
prs. 3.s. fagað xi. 40; *pl.* fagiað
49. 9.

fámigborda, *wm.* ship with foamy
sides or deck; *a.* famigbordon
xxvi. 26.

fana, *wm.* banner; i. 10.

fandian, *wv. w. g.* examine, test;
45. 9, 105. 25 *n.*, 147. 15, ix.
12, xxiv. 57; *ind. prs. 2.s.*
fandast 51. 3.

fangian, *wv.* join, fasten; *pp.* ge-
fangod 96. 14.

faran, *sv6.* go, travel; 141. 27,
xxiv. 11; *rflx.* ðe faran xxiv.
16; to farenne 107. 16, 139.
29; *ind. prs. 2.s.* færest xxiv.
28; *3.s.* færð 45. 27 &c. *and*
xx. 216; *pl.* farað 79. 14, 130.
14, 147. 4, 5, xxviii. 32,
xxxi. 3; gefarað *trans.* journey
through 42. 31; die 24. 13;
pst. 2.s. fore 11. 5; *3.s.* for 115.
18, xxiv. 12, xxvi. 13; *pl.*
foron i. 20; *sbj. prs.* fare 131.
17; *pl.* faren 129. 24, 135. 30;
pst. rflx. fore 18. 14; *prs. p.*
farende*, færende 93. 7.

geféa, *wm.* joy; 9. 12; *d.* gefean

27. 9, 29. 26, 89. 30; *a.* iii.
6, v. 27.

fealdan, *rv.* fold, furl; 144. 30.

fealg, *f.* felly of a wheel; *d.* felge
129. 27, 31, 130. 1; *pl. n.* felgea
130. 13; felga 129. 23, 130. 5,
11, 19; *d.* felgum 130. 3.

feallan, *rv.* fall; to feallanne 81.
13, xx. 168; *ind. prs. 3.s.* fealð
14. 16*; felð v. 15; *pst. 3.s.*
feol i. 81; gefeoll 8. 3.

fearn, *n.* fern; *a.* 51. 29, xii. 3.

fearr, *m.* bull; fear 72. 6, 7.

féawe, *pl. adj.* few; 25. 5; feawa
67. 18; feawa manna ongit 46.
28*; fea iv. 52; *wk.* ða feawan
67. 20*; *d.* feawum 25. 17*;
feaum 46. 27*, 71. 14, 132. 22;
feam 22. 14; *a.* feawan 48. 11.

fédan, *wv.* feed; *ind. prs. 3.s.* fet
70. 5*, 136. 19*, xxix. 69.

fefer, *m.* fever; *d.* fefre 73. 13.

fégan, *wv.* put together, join; ða
ged gefegean ii. 6; *ind. prs. 3.s.*
gefegð 49. 33; gefægð, gefehð*
54. 17; *pp.* gefeged 38. 20, xx.
116, 121.

fela, *adj. indecl.* many, much; 19.
1, 44. 25, 126. 26, 146. 21, i. 81,
ii. 1, 6, iv. 42, ix. 6, xi. 89, xvi.
5, xix. 25, xx. 101, xxiv. 12,
xxvi. 53, xxviii. 48, 76; *w. sing.*
vb. 144. 25, xx. 83; feola xiii.
16.

félan, *wv.* feel; *ind. pst. 2.s.* gefeldest 18. 27 *n.*

feld, *m.* field; *g.* feldes 21. 5, vi.
10; *d.* felda 99. 9.

feltun, *n.* privy; *d.* feltune 104. 9.

fenn, *m.* fen, swamp; *d.* fænne
42. 16*, 19*; *pl. n.* fennas 42.
6; *d.* fennum 42. 29.

feoh, *n.* property, money; 25. 27,
28. 6*, 8*, 58. 15*; fioh 48. 20;
g. feos 71. 16*; feos*, fios 31.
31; *d.* feo 48. 14*, 16*, 89. 27,
30*; fio 48. 16, 89. 30; *a.* feoh
48. 17*, 53. 29*; fioh 48. 17,
53. 29, 64. 13, 133. 30.

feohgítsere, *m.* miser; viii. 55;
d. feohgitsere 19. 1.

feoht, *n.* fight, war; *d.* gefiohte

115. 17*; *a.* gefeoht 34. 3*, viii. 32.

feohtan, *sv3.* fight; fiohtan 138. 19; *ind. pst.* 3.*s.* feaht 37. 6.

fēolan, *sv3.* enter; fiolan æt his eðle xx. 154.

fēon. *wv.* hate; *ind. pst.* 3.*s.* fiode 124. 13*; *sbj. prs.* 3.*s.* fioge xxvii. 24.

fēond, *m.* enemy; xv. 7; *d.* feonde xxv. 16; *a.* feond 67. 24; fiend 111. 18*; *pl. n.* fiend 30. 27*; *g.* fionda 48. 9; *d.* feondum 67. 20; *a.* feond 33. 7*; fiond 54. 20; fiend 48. 15; fynd 33. 7, 48. 15*.

feorh, *n.* life; *g.* feores 33. 10, 66. 22, 27; *d.* feore 66. 26, xxv. 16; fiore 133. 31; *a.* feorh 22. 7, 67. 10.

feorr, *adv.* far; feor 11. 8, 139. 27, ix. 2, xxiv. 2, 9, xxvi. 30; fior xx. 222; fyrr 139. 27*; *comp.* fier, fyr* 11. 9; *sup.* fyrrest 130. 13.

feorran, *adv.* from afar; fiorran ymbutan 127. 33.

fēorða, *num. adj.* fourth; *n.* feorðe 62. 26; feowerðe xx. 61; *f.* 80. 1; fiorðe 103. 22, 139. 17; *g.* feorðan, feorðan* 42. 1; *d.* 42. 5.

fēoung, *f.* hatred; *d.* fiounge 124. 3*.

fēower, *num.* four; 46. 4, 62. 25, 75. 29, 31, 79. 34, 86. 29, 131. 3, xx. 59, 63.

fēowerfēte, *adj.* fourfooted; *n. pl. n.* fiowerfete 147. 6*; fierfete xxxi. 11.

gefēra, *wm.* companion, associate; *pl. n.* geferan 36. 22, 49. 14; *g.* geferena 53. 17; *d.* geferum 53. 17; *a.* geferan 36. 19, 47. 18, 50. 2.

fēran, *wv.* go, proceed; iv. 18; *rflx.* ðe f. 105. 10; geferan xi. 50; *trans.* travel over 42. 2; to feranne 107. 16; *ind. prs.* 1.*s.* gefere 18. 11; 3.*pl.* geferað xxviii. 23; *prs. p.* ferende 147. 3.

ferhð, *m.n.* mind, spirit; *d.* ferhðe xxii. 52; ferhte xxii. 60 (J); ferðe ix. 37; færðe xxvii. 24.

ferhðloca, *wm.* breast, heart; *a.* ferðlocan xxiv. 5.

ferian, *wv.* carry, transport; *ind. pst.* 3.*s.* ferede xxvi. 26.

gefērrǣden, *f. a)* companionship, intercourse; *b)* retinue; 65. 3 (*b*); *d.* geferrædenne 67. 23 (*b*); *a.* 37. 19 (*a*); 49. 31 (*a*).

gefērscipe, *m. a)* association, companionship; *b)* class of people; *c)* company, retinue; 116. 21 (*c*); *g.* geferscipes 11. 15 (*a*), xi. 82 (*a*); *d.* geferscipe 111. 15 (*c*); *a.* 111. 10 (*a*), xi. 47 (*a*); *pl. n.* geferscipas 40. 23 (*b*); *d.* geferscipum 40. 20 (*b*); *a.* geferscipas xi. 93 (*a*).

fetel, *m.* belt; *d. pl.* fetelum xxv. 10; fetlum 111. 15*.

fēðe, *n.* walking, locomotion; *d.* 108. 22.

feðer, *f.* feather; *pl.* wings; *d.* feðerum xxiv. 9; feðrum xxiv. 5; *a.* feðera 105. 4.

flerdmann, *m.* soldier; *pl. d.* ferdmonnum 64. 13; *a.* ferdmen, fyrdmen* 40. 18.

flersian, *wv.* pass beyond; feorsian xxiv. 26.

fīf, *num.* five; 76. 2, 5, 6, 7, 77. 13, 20, 23, 25, 27, 86. 23; *g.* ðara fif goda 86. 28; ðissa fifa 78. 14.

fīfelstrēam, *m.* ocean; *a.* xxvi. 26.

fīfta, *num. adj.* fifth; *f.* fifte 75. 31, 139. 18; *d.* fiftan 42. 16.

findan, *sv3.* find; 74. 9, vii. 32 &c.; *ind. prs.* 2.*s.* finst 44. 18*; 3.*s.* fint 76. 21, 95. 21*, xiii. 34; *pl.* finde ge 73. 26; *pst.* 1.*s.* fond ii. 9; funde 8. 8*; 3.*s.* 34. 12*; *sbj. prs.* finde 140. 12; *pst.* funde 140. 15, 17. viii. 58; *pl.* funden 145. 4; *pp.* funden 96. 20, 97. 14, 99. 22, 140. 15.

finger, *m.* finger; *d.* fingre 81. 15, xx. 180.

fīras, *m. pl.* men; *g.* fira vii. 11, viii. 32, xix. 2; *d.* firum iv. 39.

firenfull, *adj.* sinful; fierenfull
xv. 7.

firenlust, *m.* sinful desire; *g.*
firenlustes 64. 27*; fyrenlustes
33. 26*; *g. pl.* firenlusta viii. 15.

gefirn, *adv.* long ago; gefyrn
31. 21, 33. 13, 46. 25, x. 52;
w. ær 78. 31, 80. 34, 97. 19,
101. 17, 110. 5, 112. 5.

first, *m.* space of time; fyrst 120.
28, 31; *a.* first 116. 11; fyrst
120. 27.

firwitgeorn, *adj.* inquisitive;
firwetgeorn xxviii. 76; *n. pl.*
m. firwetgeorne 126. 24.

fisc, *m.* fish; 48. 5; *pl. g.* fisca
xi. 67; *a.* fiscas 74. 3.

fiscian, *wv.* fish; 73. 28.

fiscnett, *n.* fishing-net; *a. pl.*
fiscnet xix. 11.

fitt, *f.* song, poem; *a.* fitte 68. 6.

fiðere, *m. n.* wing; *pl. n.* fiðeras
147. 5*; *g.* fiðra 133. 12; *d.*
fiðerum 105. 6; fiðrum xxxi.
8; *a.* fiðru xxiv. 1.

gefiðerian, *wv.* provide with
wings; 104. 30*; gefiðerigan
105. 6*; gefeðeran 104. 30;
gefeðran xxiv. 4.

flæsc, *n.* flesh; 72. 1, xxvi. 114;
d. flæsce 69. 11, 29, 72. 4, 109.
11, xvii. 21, xx. 238.

flæsclic, *adj.* fleshly, carnal; *pl.*
n. wk. flæsclican 73. 10; *d.*
flæsclicum 74. 25; *a. wk.*
flæsclican 70. 3.

fleogan, *sv2.* fly; 36. 7, 104. 31,
xxiv. 2; fliogan 105. 5*, 7*;
rflx. ðe fliogan 105. 9*; ðe
fligon 105. 8*; *prs. p.* fleogende
147. 7*, xxxi. 11.

fleon, *sv2.* fly from, avoid; 27.
5; flion 25. 9, 148. 17, vii. 30;
to flionne 31. 16*, 103. 15; *ind.*
prs. 3.*s.* flihð 76. 25, 92. 21,
136. 12; *pst.* 3.*s.* fleah i. 20;
imp. pl. fleoð 149. 6; *prs. p.*
fleeting, transitory; flionde 72.
29; *n. pl. n.* fleondu xxi. 30;
fleonde 89. 18*.

geflit, *n.* strife; *n. pl.* geflitu 59.
25.

flitan, *sv1.* struggle, contend;
sbj. prs. 3.*s.* flite 107. 30.

flod, *m. n.* flood, flood-tide; *g.*
flodes 49. 26; *d.* flode 34. 29.

flor, *f.* floor, base; 52. 30, 110.
25; *d.* flore 110. 23, xx. 91;
a. flore i. 81; flor 8. 4, 80. 14.

flowan, *rv.* flow; *ind. prs.* floweð
v. 14; *pst.* 3.*s.* fleow 53. 8; *prs.*
p. flowende 72. 29*, 80. 14.

fodor, *n.* food, fodder; *d.* fodre
32. 1.

folc, *n.* people; 105. 28 &c. *and*
xxiv. 63, xxviii. 65; *often w.*
ðis, *or uncomplimentary epithet,*
ungestæððig, dysig &c. 126. 21,
64. 2 &c.; *g.* folces 43. 11 &c.
and x. 49, xxvi. 52; *d.* folce
43. 13, 123. 6, ix. 27; *a.* folc
41. 14 &c. *and* xvii. 13, xxiv.
60; *g. pl.* folca xi. 89.

folccuð, *adj.* well known, cele-
brated; xxvi. 9; *a.* folccuðne
MPr. 9.

folcisc, *adj.* of the people, common, *w.* men; *pl. n.* folcisce
69. 2, 102. 22, 138. 9; *d.*
folciscum 143. 21.

folcgesið, *m.* chief, noble; *a. pl.*
folcgesiðas i. 70.

folcgewinn, *n.* battle, war; *g.*
folcgewinnes i. 10.

foldbuend, *m.* earth-dweller,
man; *pl. n.* foldbuende xvii. 2;
g. foldbuendra xvii. 21; *d.*
foldbuendum viii. 4.

folde, *wf.* earth; xi. 43, xx. 59,
85; *g.* foldan iv. 52, xx. 91;
d. foldan xx. 168; *a.* xx. 111,
247, xxxi. 10.

foldes, *error for flodes* ? xi. 70 *n.*

folgað, *m.* service (as a courtier);
65. 7.

folgere, *m.* follower; *pl. g.*
folgera 78. 11; *d.* folgerum
66. 15, 78. 26.

folgian, *wv. w. d.* follow; 35. 23,
37. 16; *ind. prs.* 3.*s.* folgað 14.
4; *imp. pl.* folgiað 149. 6; *sbj.*
prs. pl. folgien 30. 2, 108. 30.

fon, *rv.* seize, take, receive; 101.
15, MPr. 9, xix. 11; gefon

57. 14, 69. 15; on oðer weorc to fonne, take up, begin 127. 27; *ind. prs. 2.s.* fehst on . . . 100. 7, 9; *3.s.* gefehð 124. 9, xi. 89; *pl.* fo we . . . on 101. 10; *pst. 2.s.* gefenge 14. 1; *3.s.* feng to rice 7. 5, 65. 28; *pp.* gefangen 18. 19, 48. 5, 83. 17.

for, *prep.*; 1) *w. d.*: *a) place,* before, in front of: for sunnan xxix. 26; for herigum xxvi. 57; clipian for corðre xxvi. 85. *b)* in the sight of, as regards: for Drihtne i. 64; for Gode iii. 10; for worulde 11. 14, 20. 2, 23. 11, 15, 113. 23, 138. 23. *c) cause,* owing to, on account of: *fq.* Pr. 4 &c.; fore, *foll. c.* 88. 13. *d) purpose*: for goode deð 129. 1. *e* = from, 45. 28 (of, B). 2) *w.a.*; *a*) *w. vbs. of reckoning, esteeming* &c., for, as: for nauht to tellenne 56. 10 &c. and xxvi. 44, 50; wite ðu for soð 17. 20, 32. 32. *b)* instead of, 82. 26. *c)* compared with, 29. 5, 42. 14, 116. 29, x. 9. *d) benefit,* on behalf of: for hine gebidde Pr. 12, *cf.* 22. 8. 3) *Forming advs. and conjs. w. d. & inst. a interrog.* forhwy, why? 62. 4 &c.; forhwi 124. 3*, 125. 7, 132. 6; *w. sbj.* 68. 15, 91. 25, 125. 28; forhwam ii. 16. *b) adv.* therefore, forðæm, 12. 24, v. 29 &c.; forðon vii. 40, xxix. 43; forðy 23. 21 &c. *c) conj.* because, forðæm 13. 8, v. 38 &c.; forðæm ðe 13. 33, x. 16 &c.; forðæm þ 18. 32; forðon 12. 5, xiii. 75 &c.; forðon ðe 12. 3 &c. *d) w. sbj.* forðæm, in order that 134. 5. *e) combinations,* forðæm . . forðæm, for this reason . . . because or because . . . therefore: forðæm . . . forðy 63. 24, 78. 15, 89. 16; forðæm . . . forðon 13. 17; forðy . forðy 76. 21 &c. *and* x. 35; orðy . . . forðæm (ðe) 82. 28 &c. *and* xx. 193; forðy . . . ðe 88. 19 &c.;

forðy . . . þ 40. 25, 43. 27, 147. 12.

foran, *adv.* in front, before; on ðæt neb foran, in the face 36. 24; wið ðæt mod foran v. 43; wið ða eagan foran xx. 265; wið ðone monan foran xxviii. 47; fortihð mod foran, draws in front of; forsceotað hine foran, anticipate him 124, 11, *cf.* xxvii. 19.

forbærnan, *wv. trans.* burn up: 18. 20, 39. 19, ix. 9, xx. 115; *ind. prs. 3.s.* forbærnð 34. 10, 80. 23, viii. 54; *pst. 3.s.* forbærnde 127. 13.

forbēodan, *sv2.* forbid; 103. 10; forbiodan ix. 54.

forberan, *sv4.* forbear, refrain from; forberan þ he ne . . . 104. 11; *pp.* forboren, borne with, forgiven 121. 1.

forberstan, *sv3.* collapse; *ind. pst. 3.s.* forbærst 45. 19.

forbregdan, *sv3.* transform; forbredan 116. 14, xxvi. 75.

forbūgan, *sv2.* avoid, prevent; 37. 12.

forcēowan, *sv2.* bite off; *ind. pst. 3.s.* forceaw 36. 23.

forcierran, *wv.* avoid, escape; forcerran 142. 17.

forcuman, *sv4.* destroy; 80. 28 *n.*

forcūð, *adj.* depraved, wicked, bad; *comp.* forcuðra 63. 10, 111. 23; *n.* forcuðre 109. 1; *n. pl.* forcuðran 54. 22; *sup. wk.* forcuðesta 41. 16; *a. wk.* forcuðestan 114. 16 *pl. n. wk.* 37. 27; *d.* forcuðestum 37. 16, 38. 2.

forcweðan, *sv5.* rebuke; *ind. pst. 3.s.* forcwæð 61. 17.

fordōn, *anv.* destroy; *ind. prs. 3.pl.* fordoð 49. 32; *sbj. prs. 3.s.* fordo xx. 130; *pl.* fordon 136. 10; *pst. pl.* fordyden xxix. 45; *pp. n. pl. m.* fordone 67. 4.

fordrīfan, *sv1.* drive out of course; *pp.* fordrifen 115. 22, 116. 4; *a. wk.* fordrifenan 116. 7.

fordrūgian, *wv. intrans.* dry up;
pp. fordrugod xx. 104.

fordwylman, *wv.* confuse, obscure; *ind. prs.* 3.*pl.* fordwilmaÐ Ða soÐan gesihÐe 14. 5.

fordysilio, *adj.* very foolish; fordyslic 42. 10.

fore, *prep. w. d.* before, in front
of; him . . . fore . . . hangaÐ v.
4.

forealdian, *wv.* grow old, become obsolete; *ind. pst.* 3.*pl.*
forealdodon 44. 6; *pp.* forealdod
40. 27, 131. 7.

foremǣre, *adj.* eminent, famous;
53. 21 &c.; *wk.* foremæra 37.
5, 46. 21; *g. wk.* foremeran 46.
16*; *pl. n.* foremære 69. 1; *f.
wk.* foremæran 139. 6; *g. wk.*
foremærena 44. 25* (formæra
J); *a.* foremære 46. 28, x. 62;
comp. n. pl. foremærran 69. 2;
sup. foremærost 76. 26; *n. pl.*
formæroste 44. 4.

foremǣrlic, *adj.* eminent; 75. 24.

foremǣrnes, *f.* eminence, dignity;
56. 10, 76. 4, 77. 17, 86. 24,
87. 14; formæmes 77. 14; *g.*
foremæmesse 56. 24.

forerynel, *m.* forerunner, harbinger; 103. 26; forrynel xxix. 25.

forescēawung, *f.* providence;
127. 19, 128. 11; *d.* foresceawunge 146. 31; *a.* foresceawunga 136. 7*.

forescēotan, *sv2.* anticipate, forestall; *ind. prs.* 3.*pl.* forsceotaÐ
hine foran 124. 11.

foresprǣc, *f.* pleading, defence;
123. 18.

foresprecen, *adj.* above mentioned; *d. pl. wk.* foresprecenan 7. 5*, 113. 14.

foretācn, *n.* foretoken, presage;
137. 27.

foreteohhung, *f.* predestination;
foretiohhung 127. 20, 129. 3, 7,
131. 11, 140. 16, 21, 143. 18,
144. 4; *d.* foretiohhunge 139.
21; *a.* 142. 25.

foreÐanc, *m.* forethought, providence; 129. 2; foreÐonc 128.

10, 15, 20, 131. 2, 16; *d.*
foreÐonce 128. 24, 25, 29, 129.
12, 130. 29.

foreÐingian, *wv. w. d.* plead for,
defend; *ind.* 3.*s.* foreÐingaÐ
123. 19; *sbj. prs.* 3.*s.* foreÐingie
123. 17.

forewāt, *swv.* know beforehand;
ind. prs. 3.*s.* 128. 17.

forgiefan, *sv5.* give, grant; forgifan 19. 9, 62. 30, 78. 14, 26,
82. 24, 119. 28; *ind. prs.* 3.*s.*
forgifÐ 62. 23; *pst.* 2.*s.* forgeafe
81. 33, xx. 225; 3.*s.* forgeaf 29.
9; *imp.* forgif 82. 6, 10, xx.
252; *pp.* forgifen 93. 21, 146.
15, 25; = forgiven 119. 21; *n. pl.
f.* forgifene 134. 24.

forgieldan, *sv3.* repay, requite;
ind. prs. 3.*s.* forgilt 149. 9.

forgietan, *sv5.* forget; *ind. prs.*
1.*s.* forgite 90. 2; 3.*s.* forgit 57.
11, iii. 6; forget 9. 12; *pst.* 3.*s.*
forgeat 148. 14; *sbj. prs.* forgite
90. 1; *pp.* forgiten 8. 20 &c.
and xxiv. 46; *n. pl. m.* forgitene
40. 26, 46. 29, x. 60.

forhealdan, *rv.* illtreat, misuse;
sbj. pst. 3.*pl.* forheolden 143. 26;
pp. n. pl. m. forhealden 65. 18.

forhelan, *sv4.* conceal; 66. 17;
pp. n. pl. m. forholene 40. 27.

forhergian, *wv.* lay waste; forheregian 34. 27.

forhogian, *wv.* despise, neglect;
imp. pl. forhogiaÐ 35. 19*.

forhwierfan, *wv.* transform; *pp.*
forhwerfed 116. 21*; *n. pl. m.*
forhwerfde xxvi. 86.

forhycgan, *wv.* despise, neglect;
forhigan 138. 16*; *imp. pl.*
forhycgaÐ 35. 19.

forinlīce, *adv.* thoroughly, exceedingly; 94. 6.

forinweardlīce, *adv.* thoroughly,
genuinely; 137. 15.

forlǣdan, *wv.* mislead; *ind. pst.*
3.*pl.* forlæddon ii. 11.

forlǣtan, *rv.* leave, forsake; 16.
15, v. 26 &c.; forfeit 103. 9;
forlætan Þ he ne, desist from
102. 33; to forlætanne 16. 13;

to forlætenne 116. 13*; *ind.
prs. 2.s.* forlætest 100. 8; 3.s.
forlæteð xx. 157; forlæt 14. 3 &c.
and x. 30, xvii. 24; let go, relax
49. 28; allow 49. 5; *pl.* forlætað 15. 7 &c. *and* xi. 81;
forlæte wit 138. 7; *pst. 1.s.*
forlet 13. 29; 2.s. forlete 11. 5,
20. 31, 62. 5; 3.s. forlet 52. 14
&c. *and* x. 66; *pl.* forleton 44.
3; forletan 8. 10*; *sbj. prs.*
forlæte 67. 29 &c.; *pl.* forlæten
20. 32, 108. 29, 133. 5; *pst. pl.*
forleten 64. 4; *pp.* forlæten 16.
10 *n.*; *d. wk.* forlætenan 95. 31.
forlēosan, *sv2.* lose; 17. 21, 59.
31; *ind. prs. 3.s.* forlyst 90. 32,
103. 20; *w. d.* 113. 8; forlist *w.
d.* 111. 3; *pl.* forleosað 111. 5;
pst. 2.s. forlure 15. 13 &c.; 3.s.
forleas 148. 16; *sbj. prs.* forleose 87. 6; *pst.* forlure 17. 21;
pp. forloren 15. 2 &c.; *n. pl. f.*
forlorena 24. 27.
forliogan, *sv5.* commit fornication;
pp. forlegen, adulterous, impure
xviii. 9.
forlustlīce, *adv.* very cheerfully,
willingly; 51. 18.
forlytel, *adj.* very little; *n.* 29.
5; *n. pl. f.* forlytla 26. 8; *each
written as one word in* C.
forma, *wk. adj.* first; 34. 10, viii.
55; *f.* forme 33. 21, viii. 4, 38.
6; *d.* forman 95. 32.
formicel, *adj.* very much, very
great; *n.* 93. 1.
fornēah, *adv.* very nearly, almost;
113. 32.
forscieppan, *sv6.* transform; for-
sceoppan to leon 116. 16*.
forsēarian, *wv. intrans.* wither;
ind. prs. 3.s. forscarað 91. 22;
pp. forsearod 131. 7.
forsēon, *sv5.* despise, neglect;
forsion 71. 30, xxiv. 7; to for-
seonne 56. 3, 75. 12; *ind. prs.
3.s.* forsiehð 46. 14; forsihð 27.
9, 45. 29, vii. 42; forscoð
45. 29*; *pl.* forseoð 57. 16*,
61. 15*; forsioð 44. 31, 63. 3,
130. 17*; forseo we 18. 12; *pst.*

3.s. forseah 61. 21, 68. 9; *sbj.
prs. 2.s.* forseo 20. 30*; *pst.*
forsawe 61. 25, 62. 13; *pp.* forsewen 104. 17, 120. 4, 124. 25,
forsawen 22. 18; *n. pl. m.*
forsewene 104. 8, xiii. 37.
forsewennes, *f.* contempt; *d.*
forsewennesse 12. 1.
forslāwian, *wv.* hesitate, be loth;
sbj. pst. 2.s. forslawode 22. 7.
forslēan, *sv6.* kill; 34. 26; *pp.*
forslagen 37. 8*.
forstandan, *sv6. a)* understand;
b) avail; 12. 30 (*a*); 50. 30 (*a*);
67. 8 (*b*); *ind. prs. 3.s.* forstent
11. 30 (*a*), 45. 22 (*b*), 47. 1 (*b*),
67. 16 (*b*), *pst. 3.s.* forstod 45.
20 (*b*), 67. 14 (*b*), *sbj. prs.* forstande 47. 10 (*a*).
forstelan, *sv4.* steal; *sbj. prs. 2.s.*
forstele 71. 17.
forswelgan, *sv3.* swallow, absorb;
vii. 14.
forsweltan, *sv3.* die; *ind. prs. 3.s.*
forswilt 70. 21.
forswīgian, *wv. trans.* pass over
in silence, ignore; *pp.* forsugod,
forswugod* 40. 28.
forswīðe, *adv.* very strongly;
excessively 40. 8.
fortēon, *sv2. a)* cover; *b)* lead
astray; *ind. prs. 3.s.* fortihð
xxii. 34 (*a*); *sbj. prs. 3.s.* fortio
95. 12 (*b*).
fortrūwian, *wv.* be over-confident; -
ind. pst. rflx. ðu ðe fortruwudest
18. 21*; *sbj. prs. 3.s.* fortruwige
138. 26.
fortrūwung, *f.* presumption; *d.*
fortruwunga 9. 7*.
forð, *adv.* 1) *motion*, forth,
forward; 79. 14, 103. 12, 105.
14, xxiv. 26. 2) *time*, hence-
forth; xi. 17, 42, xxi. 8, xxv.
70; a forð xiii. 40, xvii. 28,
xx. 17; forð on symbel, for
ever xi. 94; 7 swa forð, sub-
sequently 122. 4. 3) swa forð
swa swa ... as far as ... 32.
4; swa forð ðæt ... to such
an extent that ... 75, 23.
forðbringan, *wv.* bring forth,

produce, accomplish; 9. 27*,
43. 21, 29; word f. utter xxvi.
79; forðbrengan 66. 18, 110.
34; forðgebrengan x. 62; *ind.
prs.* 3.*s.* forð ne bringð 54.
12*; forðbrengeð xxix. 70;
forðbrengð 136. 20*; *pl.* bringað
symle forð 110. 34.

forðencan, *wv. rflx.* despair;
ind. prs. 3.*s.* hine forðencð 19.
31; *sbj. prs.* 3.*s.* hine forðence
138. 27; *pst.* ðu ðe forðohte 19.
30; *pp.* forðoht, in despair 19.
29, i. 82.

forðforlætennes, *f.* licence; *d.*
forðforlætnesse 12. 2.

forðryccan, *wv.* oppress, afflict;
pp. n. pl. m. forðrycte 9. 25.

forðgewītan, *sv1.* depart, die;
pp. m. pl. n. forðgewitene 46.
25, x. 52; *a.* 46. 28.

forwel, *adv.* very well; 40. 8.

forweorðan, *sv3.* perish; 71. 7
&c. *and* xviii. 6, xxi. 34; *ind.
prs.* 3.*s.* forweorðeð xi. 85; *pst.*
2.*s.* forwurde 13. 28; *sbj. prs.*
3.*pl.* forweorðan 89. 19.

forweorðfullic, *adj.* very distinguished; 65. 15.

forwiernan, *wv. w. d. and g.*
prevent, restrain; forwernan 144.
28; *ind. prs.* 3.*s.* forwyrnð 49.
22*; *pp.* hire bið forwerned
hire gecyndes 93. 17.

forwyrd, *f.* destruction; *d.* forwirde 70. 20.

fōstorfæder, *m.* foster-father; *a.*
66. 24.

fōstormōdor, *f.* foster-mother;
a. fostermodor*, fæstermodor
8. 27.

fōt, *m.* foot; *pl. n.* fet 147. 5; *g.*
fota 107. 13, 15; *d.* fotum 10.
20, iv. 39, xxxi. 8, 10.

fox, *m.* fox; 114. 28.

gefrǣge, 1) *n.* inquiry, information; *d.* mine gefræge, as I
have heard xx. 82, 248. 2) *adj.*
famous; xx. 2.

fram, 1) *prep. w.d.*; *a) motion*,
from, 14. 19*, 16. 6*, 17*, 20.
28*, xxiv. 2; from, *sq.* 17. 7

&c. *b) separation from*, 38. 18,
60. 24, 78. 5, ii. 15; *w.* tosceadan, todælan &c. 84. 28;
&c. *c) source*, from Gode wisse
12. 22, *cf.* 13. 6, 79. 23, i. 72,
xx. 35. *d)* from . . . oð: *place*,
39. 27 &c. *and* i. 14; *time*, 44.
22, 79. 12, xx. 10. *e) agent*,
by, 62. 12, 66. 22; xx. 245. 2)
adv. away; 8. 12, 81. 10, 114.
11.

framweard, *adj.* ready to depart;
n. pl. f. fromwearde 26. 2*.

frēa, *wm.* lord; xvii. 9; *g.* frean
xi. 40, 67; *a.* xxvi. 63 *n.*

frēadryhten, *m.* lord; *g.* freadrihtnes xxvi. 9.

frec, *adj.* greedy, covetous; *n. pl.
w.g.* hi firenlusta frece ne wæron
viii. 15.

frēcenlic, *adj.* dangerous; *n.* 30.
16, xix. 2; frecendlic 73. 23*;
comp. a. n. frecenlicre 119. 15.

frēcennes, *f.* danger, hardship;
frecenes, frecennes* 50. 17; *g.*
frecennesse 48. 1, 93. 12.

frēcne, *adj.* dangerous, wicked;
a. wk. frecnan 27. 5; *pl. a. wk.*
frecnan 34. 12; *n.* frecnu viii.
58.

gefrēdan, *wv.* feel, perceive; 145.
22, 23, 146. 4; *ind. prs.* 3.*s.*
gefret 91. 15.

gefrēdnes, *f.* feeling, perception;
145. 19, 22.

fremde, *adj.* strange, foreign; *g.
f.* fremdre iii. 11; *pl. g.* fremdra
45. 2; *d.* fremdum 17. 28, 31.
26, 31. 25; fræmdum 24. 11*;
a. n. fremde 29. 29*; *wk.*
fremdan 9. 13, 29. 27.

fremman, *wv.* perform, accomplish; 106. 13; *ind. pst.* 3.*s.*
fremede i. 45; gefremede ix. 33;
pp. gefremed 128. 12.

fremu, *f.* advantage; 30. 10, 60.
27.

frēo, *adj.* free; 89. 6 *n.*; freoh
148. 24; *a.* freone 142. 3; *f.*
frige 142. 7; *pl.* freo, frige*
144. 3; *g.* friora xxi. 2; *a.* freo
142. 9.

R

frēodōm, *m.* freedom; 127. 21, 142. 12; *g.* freodomes 142. 9; *d.* freodome 11. 25, 142. 22, 143. 28, 146. 32; frydome 146. 32*; *a.* freodom 89. 8 &c.; friodom 140. 23, 27, 30, 141. 2, xxi. 8.

frēogan, *wv.* set free; *ind. prs.* 3.*s.* gefreoð 47. 23.

frēolīce, *adv.* freely; friolice 45. 27.

frēolsian, *wv.* deliver; *pp.* gefreolsod 144. 9.

frēond, *m.* friend; xxx. 3; *g.* freondes 54. 15, 67. 24; *d.* freonde xxv. 16; *a.* friend 111. 18*; *pl. n.* friend 8. 13*, 48. 19*, 54. 9; frend 67. 16, 18; *g.* freonda 48. 8, 67. 15*; *a.* freond 54. 20*; friend 54. 17*; frend 48. 15; frind 48. 15*, 50. 2*.

frēondrǣden, *f.* friendship; *d.* freondrædenne 49. 33, 50. 3; *a.* xi. 82.

frēondscipe, *m.* friendship; *d.* 53. 20; *a.* 7. 8, xi. 90, 94.

fricgan, *sv5.* inquire, learn; *pp.* gefrigen ix. 27.

frignan, *sv3.* ask, inquire; *ind. pst.* 3.*s.* frægn, fran* 8. 26, 9. 4; *sbj. prs.* 3.*s.* æfter frigne xxii. 46 (*or take as compound ?*); *pp.* frugnen xxii. 52.

frið, *m.n.*; *a)* protection; *b)* peace; *g.* friðes i. 35 (*b*); *d.* friðe 60. 6 *n.* (*a*).

friðian, *wv.* protect; *ind. prs.* 3.*s.* friðað 91. 24; *pst.* 3.*s.* gefrioðode 133. 11.

friðstōw, *f.* refuge; 89. 11, xxi. 16.

frōfor, *f.* consolation; xxi. 16; frofer 50. 12, 89. 11*; frofr (*error for* hrof) 52. 24; *g.* frofre 8. 3, i. 79, ii. 12, iii. 11; *masc.* frofres 9. 17*.

frōforbōc, *f.* book of consolation, *translation of the Latin title* De Consolatione; froferboc*, frofrboc 50. 6.

fruma, 1) *wm.* beginning, origin; 52. 21, xx. 275 &c.; *d.* fruman

79. 13, 136. 31; æt fruman 129. 18, 142. 27, xvii. 13, 26; from fruman xx. 10; *a.* 58. 9, 69. 18, 147. 27, 29, 148. 1, xvii. 2. 2) *adj.* = forma, first; *d.* ðære fruman gecynde 69. 24*; *a.* fruman sceaft = frumsceaft 69. 27*, 31*.

frumcierr, *m.* first time; *d.* æt frumcerre, at once 145. 25.

frumsceaft, *f.* creation, origin; *d.* frumsceafte 58. 8, xxix. 7; *a.* frumsceaft xvii. 24.

frumstōl, *m.* original seat, home; xx. 125; *a.* xx. 63.

frymð, *f.* origin, beginning; *d.* æt frymðe xi. 38, 77, xiii. 13, xxix. 38.

fugol, *m.* bird; fugl xxvii. 24; *d.* fugle xxiv. 1; *pl. g.* fugla 57. 20, xxvii. 19; *d.* fugelum 115. 4*; fuglum 121. 15*, 124. 8, xxvii. 11; *a.* fugelas xiii. 48.

fūl, *adj.* dirty, foul; *d. pl.* fulum 115. 7.

full, 1) *adj.* full, complete; 22. 9 &c. *and* i. 9; full man, perfect 114. 8; ful 23. 20*, iv. 36, ix. 5; *wk.* fulla 110. 19, 126. 13; *f. wk.* fulle 83. 21, 85. 17; *n.* full 83. 8 &c.; *wk.* fulle 83. 5, 84. 1, 90. 15; *g.* fulles xxviii. 41; *a.* fullne 39. 3, 111. 2; fulne 25. 22, 110. 18, xxi. 8; *f.* fulle 78. 13; *n.* full 88. 28; *inst.* fulle 103. 18, 109. 14; *pl. n.* fulle 113. 31; *f.* fulla 65. 12; *wk.* fullan 88. 29, 78. 8; *a. f.* fulla 77. 19, 82. 24, 88. 28; fulle 78. 22, 88. 18; *wk.* fullan 77. 23; *sup.* fullast 84. 2; *n.* fullost 83. 12. 2) *adv.* fully, quite; *fq.* 24. 7 &c. *and* xxiv. 17, xxvi. 17; ful 12. 26 &c. (*equally common*).

fullfremman, *wv.* accomplish, complete; 106. 13, 111. 1; to fulfremmanne 19. 23; *ind. prs.* 3.*s.* fullfremeð 103. 19; *sbj. prs.* 3.*s.* fullfremme 103. 17; *pp.* fullfremed, complete, perfect 111. 3, 128. 13; *n. wk.* fullfremede 83. 6; *f. wk.* fulfremede

78. 10; *a. n.* fulfremed 73. 19;
g. pl. fulfremedra 41. 12.

fullfremednes, *f.* perfection; *g.*
fullfremednesse 84. 9.

fullgān, *anv. w. d.* accomplish,
perform; fulgan 19. 21, 124. 28;
fulgān 9. 25*; fulgangan 18. 4;
ind. prs. 3.*s.* fulgæð 70. 16,
109. 14, 131. 14; *pst.* 3.*s.* fuleode
12. 23; *sbj. prs.* 2.*s.* fulgonge,
observe 16. 32; 3.*s.* fulga 53.
25*.

fullīce, *adv.* fully, perfectly; *fq.*
28. 25 &c.; *comp.* fullicor 74. 28.

fullmannod, *adj.* fully populated;
a. n. fullmonnad 40. 17.

fullnēah, *adv.* very nearly, almost; 58. 14*; fulneah *fq.* 10.
23 &c. *and* xviii. 4.

fulltrūwian, *wv. w. d.* trust; *ind.
prs.* 2.*pl.* fultruwiað 60. 23.

fulluhtðēawas, *m. pl.* baptismal
rite; *d.* fulluhtðeawum i. 33.

fullwyrcan, *wv.* complete; 99. 15.

fultum, *m.* help, support; *g.* fultumes 31. 20, 59. 29, 65. 17,
75. 8; fultomes 59. 32, 96. 32,
97. 2; *d.* fultume 66. 19, 104.
19; fultome 101. 1; *a.* fultum
47. 7, 79. 3, xxxi. 8.

fultumian, fulteman, *wv. w. d.*
help; gefulteman 71. 21 *n.*; *ind.
prs.* 3.*s.* fultumað 147. 6; fultemað xxv. 21; *pst.* 3.*s.* gefultu-
made 13. 28; gefultumede 7. 23*.

fundian, *wv.* move (towards), tend
to go; 51. 7; *ind. prs.* 3.*s.*
fundað 106. 10, xiii. 14; *pl.*
fundiað *fq.* 82. 5 &c. *and* xx.
239, 280; *sbj. prs.* 3.*s.* fundie
xxi. 2; fundige 89. 6, 92. 18.

furh, *f.* furrow; *d. pl.* furum 12. 9.

furðor, *adv.* further, more; 49.
14*; furður 50. 30, 99. 22, 102.
21, 27.

furðum, *adv. a) time,* first, just,
.103. 12, 108. 8. *b)* even, so
much as, 42. 31 &c.; *fq. w.* ne
34. 4, viii. 32 &c.; ne furðon
34. 2; ge furðum, aye, and even,
fq. 24. 30 &c.; ge furðon 39.
22*, 23*, 70. 24*.

fylgan, *wv. w. d.* follow; vii. 1;
fylgean 64. 5*; *ind. pst.* 3.*s.*
fylgde xxvi. 54; filgde, fyligde*
102. 32.

gefyllan, *wv.* fill, satisfy; 25. 11,
28. 21, 31. 24, 38. 15; *ind. prs.*
3.*s.* gefylð 28. 12; gefyllð 62.
28*; *pst.* 2.*s.* fyldest 82. 5*;
3.*s.* gefylde xx. 247; *sbj. prs.*
3.*s.* gefylle 19. 4; *pp.* gefylled
19. 6, 60. 17; *n. pl. m.* gefylde
71. 15.

fylst, *f.* help; *d.* fylste xxiii. 7.

fȳr, *n.* fire; 34. 7, ix. 12 &c.; *g.*
fyres 34. 27, 80. 26, xx. 83, 121,
125; *d.* fyre 80. 10 &c. *and* xx.
111, 148, xxiv. 12; *a.* fyr 18. 20
&c. *and* xx. 153; fir 80. 21*.

fȳren, *adj.* fiery; *f. wk.* fyrene
135. 26, xxix. 7.

fyrmest, *adv.* chiefly, most; 32. 5
(furemest B).

fyrs, *m.* furze, furze-bush; *a. pl.*
fyrsas 51. 29, xii. 3.

fyrðran, *wv.* advance, help on;
125. 3; *ind. prs.* 3.*s.* fyrðrað
91. 24; *pst.* 1.*s.* gefyrðrede 20.
12; *pp. n. pl. m.* gefyrðrode 9.
28*.

G.

gadertang, *adj.* united; xxii. 39.

gadrian, *wv.* bring together,
collect, unite; gegadrian 55.
25; gegaderian 53. 29, 108. 1;
to gadrianne 19. 8; *ind. prs.*
2.*s.* gaderast 31. 13*; gæderast
31. 16*; gegæderast 82. 2;
3.*s.* gadrað 28. 3, 61. 10;
gegadrað xi. 90; gaderað 27.
30*; gegaderað 53. 1, 84. 24 *n.*;
gegæderað 50. 2*; *pl.* gegaderiað 9. 6*; gegaderigað 24.
10*; *pst.* 3.*s.* gegaderode 69.
23*; *sbj. prs.* gegaderige 31.
29, 60. 28*; gegæderige, *absol.
or w. obj. omitted,* concentrate
(himself, his thoughts) 95. 2*;
pl. gegaderien 73. 17; *pp.*
gegadrod 92. 26; gegadrad 61.
11, 90. 10; gegaderod, com-

pacted 96. 14*; *n. pl. n.*
gegadrade 90. 7; gegaderode
96. 15; gegaderade 76. 5;
gegaderudu 113. 16; gega-
derede 76. 3; gederode 95. 14*;
gegaderod 96. 17.

gadrung, *f.* bringing together,
collecting; gegaderunc 75. 19;
a. gegadrunga 55. 27.

gǣlan, *wv.* hinder, impede; *sbj.
prs. 3.s.* gǣle vii. 51.

gærs, *n.* grass; xx. 98.

gafol, *n.* tribute, tax; *d.* gafole
35. 32.

gāl, *adj.* wanton, frivolous; *d. wk.*
galan 115. 3.

galan, *svб.* sing; *ind. pst. 3.s.*
gol vii. 2.

gamen, *n.* amusement, sport; *g.*
gamenes ix. 19; *d.* him to
gamene ix. 9, 46.

gān, gangan. *anv.* go, walk; 8. 16,
107. 13, 15, 108. 8. 9, 23; *rflx.*
ðe gan 33. 12; gangan xxxi. 8;
gongan iv. 17; *ind. prs. 3 s.*
gǣð 27. 17, 47. 25, 126. 12,
147. 9, xxxi. 16; walks 107.
18; *pl.* gað 14. 10; *pst. 3.s.*
eode 8. 24, 102. 21, 26, 103.
11; *imp. pl.* gað 139. 5; *sbj.
prs. 3.s.* gange xxviii. 38; *pst.
pl.* eoden 101. 30.

gegangan, *anv.* overrun, invade;
gegongan i. 12.

gārsecg, *m.* ocean; ix. 41; *d. ?* ligð
ut on garsecg xvi. 12.

gāst, *m.* spirit, soul; 93. 6, xxii.
39; *g. pl.* gasta xxi. 43.

gāstlic, *adj.* spiritual; *n. pl. n.*
gastlicu 87. 2.

gāstlīce, *adv.* spiritually; 11. 15,
148. 28.

ge, *conj.* and (atque), *sq.*; *often w.*
eac 10. 6, xi. 10 &c.; ge ... ge
12. 4, ix. 2 &c.; ægðer ge ...
ge 11. 31 &c.

gē, *pron. n. pl.* you; 8. 22, x. 63
&c. *See also* ēow.

geador, *adv.* together; xiii. 49.

gealdor, *n.* incantation; *g. pl.*
galdra xxvi. 53.

gēar, *n.* year; 17. 24; *d.* geare

17. 25, 92. 15; 136. 15; on
geare, yearly 64. 14; *a.* ger 65.
23; *pl. g.* geara 44. 17, 19, 25,
iv. 17, xix. 27, xxiv. 12, xxix. 56,
59, 66; geo geara 70. 25; *a.*
gear 44. 23, 115. 19, xxviii. 30.

gēara, *adv.* long ago; i. 1, ix. 9,
xx. 52.

gēarmǣlum, *adv.* year by year;
i. 5.

gearo, *adj.* ready; 107. 32; *a.*
gearone vii. 34.

gearowita, *wm.* full, perfect
understanding; gearowito 146.
23*; *a.* gearowitan, *superior to*
gesceadwisnes 130. 30.

gearwe, *adv.* completely, thoroughly; *gen. w.* witan; geare 12.
26, 98. 20, 103. 6, 122. 28, xx.
94, xxviii. 80; geara 26. 5, 31.
17*; geare, geara*, *once w.*
geman 96. 6.

gearwian, *wv.* make ready, fur-
nish; *ind. prs. 3.s.* gearwað 136.
16*; *pp.* gearod, gegyrewod* 32.
27.

geat, *n.* gate; *a. pl.* gatu 102. 11*.

geatweard, *m.* janitor; 102. 16.

gēo, *adv.* formerly, of old; 8. 6*,
7*, 9. 22*, 15. 13; geo geara
70. 25*, ii. 1, x. 34; *usual form*
gio 13. 3, ii. 6 &c.; gio dagum
45. 4; giu 34. 30*; iu 34. 23,
i. 1.

geoc, *n.* yoke; *a.* 46. 9; gēoc
40. 1*; gioc ix. 55, x. 20.

geocsa, *wm.* sobbing; ii. 5.

geogoðhād, *m.* (period of) youth;
a. giogoðhad 122. 4.

geoloca, *wm.* yolk of egg; gioleca
xx. 170.

gēomann, *m.* man of old; *g. pl.*
giomonna i. 23.

gēomerian, *wv.* mourn, lament;
ind. prs. 2.s. geomrast 15. 3;
prs. p. geomriende.

gēomerung, *f.* mourning, lamentation; *d.* geomerunge*, geomrunga 11. 1.

gēomor, *adj.* sad, sorrowful;
giomor ii. 3; *d. wk.* geomran i.
84.

geond, *prep. w. a.* throughout, over; *w.* eorðan x. 58, xxxi. 3, 43. 4, 53. 7, 68. 22. 147. 3 *n.*; g. burga sela iv. 42 ; g. foldan sceat iv. 52 ; g. eorðan sceat viii. 5 ; g. weorulde viii. 8, *cf.* viii. 41, ix. 58, xiii. 65 ; g. ðas mæran gesceaft xi. 73, *cf.* xx. 19; g. Bretene xx. 99; g. ðisne sidan grund xx. 127, *cf.* xxix. 60 ; g. middangeard xx. 193, *cf.* xxi. 1, xxvii. 12 ; giond : g. ealle Romana mearce 64. 12 ; g. eorðricu iv. 37 ; g. worulde xi. 45; g. gesceaft xi. 63; g. eorðan xx. 106; g. werðioda xxiv. 35.

geondliehtan, *wv.* shine over, illuminate ; geondlihtan xxx. 12.

geondscīnan, *sv*1. illuminate ; 141. 16, v. 44; *ind. prs.* 3.*s.* geondscinð 86. 9*.

geondstyrian, *wv.* stir up, agitate ; *pp.* geondstyred vi. 15.

geondwlītan, *sv*1. see through, look over ; *ind. prs.* 3.*s.* geondwliteð xxx. 15.

geong, *adj.* young; *a.* geongne, giungne* 20. 6 *n.* ; giongne 20. 10 ; *f.* giunge xxvi. 67 ; *n. pl.* geonge 22. 26*; giunge 22. 26, xxvi. 86.

geongra, *wm.* young follower, disciple ; *n. pl.* gingran 9. 5*.

georn, *adj.* desirous, eager ; i. 51.

georne, *adv.* eagerly, earnestly ; 11 *times*, 16. 22 *and* xx. 31, xxi. 20 ; carefully 91. 24 ; gionne xxix. 3 ; *sup.* geornost xxv. 27, xxvii. 29.

geornfull, *adj.* desirous, eager, earnest ; 51. 9; *d. wk.* geornfullan 51. 24 ; *n. pl.* geornfulle 73. 32, xix. 27.

geornfullīce, *adv.* earnestly ; 50. 31.

geornfullnes, *f.* desire, eagerness ; *d.* geornfulnesse 54. 3, 7.

geornlīce, *adv.* earnestly, carefully ; 7 *times*, 9. 29 &c.

gēotan, *sv*2. pour, cast (metal) ; *pp.* to anum wegge gegoten 90. 8.

giedd, *n.* song, poem ; *a.* gyd vii. 2 ; *pl.* ged ii. 5 ; *d.* giddum 57. 2, xiii. 1.

gieddian, *wv.* sing, recite ; 64. 24 ; gieddigan 73. 22 ; giddian 9. 10*, 39. 16, 48. 22, 51. 28*, 60. 27*, 71. 4 ; giddigan 48. 22*, 60. 27, 64. 24* ; gyddian 46. 2 ; giddien 9. 29* ; *ind. pst.* 2.*s.* giddodest 12. 22 ; 3.*s.* giddode, *used in formula*, 21. 1 &c. ; gyddode i. 84; geoddode 26. 22*.

giefan, *sv*5. give; gifan 71. 24, 78. 23 ; *ind. prs.* 2.*s.* gifst 81. 34 ; 3.*s.* gifð 65. 3, 113. 9, 119. 32, 120. 1, 147. 15 ; *pst.* 3.*s.* geaf 142. 9; *sbj. prs.* 3.*s.* gife 27. 22 ; *prs. p.* gifende 148. 19 ; *pp.* gifen xvi. 10.

giefol, *adj.* freely giving, liberal ; giful 119. 31.

giefu, *f.* gift, grace; gifu 22. 24, 120. 1 ; gifo 119. 32 ; *d.* gife 142. 11 ; *a.* 62. 22, 119. 28, 142. 9, 11, 146. 9 ; *pl. n.* gifa, gifta* 40. 21 ; *g.* 17. 15 ; gifena 17. 17* ; *d.* gifum 27. 21 ; *a.* gifa 81. 34, xx. 227.

gieldan, *sv*3. pay, reward, requite; *ind. prs.* 3.*s.* gilt 141. 9, 142. 13, 148. 33 ; *sbj. prs.* 3.*s.* gelde 144. 6 ; *pst.* 3.*s.* gulde 124. 13, xxvii. 26.

gielp, *m.* boasting, glory, fame ; 55. 7 ; gilp 42. 15*, 47. 1*, 56. 21* ; gelp x. 17 ; gylp 68. 29 ; *g.* gilpes 41. 12*, 45. 21*, 71. 27, vii. 15 ; gelpes 45. 21, x. 13 ; gylpes i. 9 ; *d.* gilpe 9. 7*, 45. 8, MPr. 8, x. 69 ; gelpe 45. 8 ; *a.* gielp 68. 12 ; gilp 46. 3* ; gelp x. 2 ; gylp ix. 46.

gielpan, *sv*3. *w. g.* boast ; gilpan 29. 18, 20, ix. 19 ; *ind. prs.* 2.*s.* gilpst 30. 29 ; 3.*s.* gilpð 68. 29 ; *imp.* gilp 29. 20 ; *sbj. prs.* 3.*pl.* gilpen 66. 5.

gielpsceaða, *wm.* boastful enemy

or criminal ; *a.* gelpscaðan ix. 49.

gīeman, *wv. w. g.* heed, care for ; geman xxxi. 1 ; *ind. prs.* 3.*s.* gymð MPr. 8 ; 3.*pl.* gimdon 33. 31* ; gemdon 33. 26*, viii. 10 ; *imp.* gem, observe xxix. 3.

gīemelēast. *f.* carelessness, negligence ; *d.* gimeleste 44. 2 ; *a.* giemelieste, gemeleste* 11. 12.

gīemen, *f.* care, heed ; gemen 27. 13*, 70. 28, vii. 51 ; *d.* gemenne 70. 30*.

gierela, *wm.* dress, clothing ; gegerela 30. 20 *n.* ; *d.* gegerelan 111. 26.

giernan, *wv. w. g.* desire, long for ; to girnanne 90. 13 ; *ind. prs.* 2.*s.* girnst 71. 27 ; *pl.* girnað 35. 25, 43. 3 ; geornað 43. 3* ; *pst.* 1.*s.* girnde 40. 9* ; *pl.* girndan 33. 24*.

gierwan, *wv.* get ready, adorn ; *ind. prs.* 3.*s.* giereð xxix. 59 ; *pst.* 3.*pl.* giredon viii. 25 ; *pp. n. pl. m.* gegerede xxv. 6.

giese, *adv.* yes ; gise la gese 39. 30* ; gyse 87. 12.

gīet, *adv.* yet, still ; *often w. comp.* 12. 26 &c. ; *w.* nu, ða, 43. 8 &c. ; giet *usual form in* C, 12. 26 ; xx. 20 &c., *but hardly occurs in* B ; git *about 6 times* in C *and about 12 times in* B ; get *about 20 times* in C *and about 8 times in* B ; gyt 51. 14* ; geot 105. 21* ; gieta viii. 12 ; gita xxiii. 7 ; geta vii. 3, viii. 33, xxiv. 46.

gif, *conj.* if ; *fq.* ; *gen. w. subj.* Pr. 12, i. 27 &c. ; *w. ind.* 9. 18, iv. 49 &c.

gifernes, f. greed ; *g.* gifernesse 102. 32 ; *d.* 70. 18.

gifre, *adj. a)* greedy ; *b)* desirous, eager ; 50. 23 (*b*), 102. 32 (*a*).

gift, *v.* **giefu.**

gigant, *m.* giant ; 99. 7 ; *pl. n.* gigantes, gigantas* 98. 30 ; *d.* gigantum 98. 33.

gimm, *m.* gem, jewel ; gim xxii. 23 ; *pl. n.* gimmas 73. 27, 89.

13 ; *g.* gimma 28. 27, 29. 1, xiv. 3 ; *d.* gimmum 11. 27, 28. 29, 34. 12, 64. 26 ; *a.* gimmas 74. 1, xix. 9, 22.

gimmcynn, *n.* kind of jewel ; *g.* gimcynnes 60. 29 ; *a.* gimcyn 74. 2 ; *d. pl.* gimcynnum viii. 57, xv. 4, xxv. 6.

gimmreced, *n.* jewelled hall, palace ; *a.* gimreced viii. 25.

ginfæst, *adj.* abundant, liberal ; *a. pl. f.* ginfæsta gifa xx. 227.

giscian, *wv.* sob ; *prs. p.* gisciende 8. 8.

git, *pron.* you two ; *d.* inc 19. 28.

gītsere, *m.* covetous person, miser ; 34. 11, 38. 14, 65. 26, 114. 26 ; *g.* gitseres 38. 29 ; *d.* gitsere 60. 28 ; gietsere 19. 9 ; *a. pl.* gitseras 28. 3.

gītsian, *wv. w. g.* covet ; *ind.* 3.*s.* gitsað 59. 26.

gītsung, *f.* covetousness, greed ; 26. 29, 28. 3, 34. 7, 40. 7, 60. 20, 109. 5, vii. 15, viii. 46 ; gitsunc viii. 43 ; *g.* gitsunge x. 13 ; *d.* 51. 8 ; gidsunge 71. 16 ; *a.* gitsunga 17. 29, 19. 18, 26. 28 ; gitsunge 17. 29*, 28. 21* ; gidsunga 17. 30 ; *pl. g.* gitsunga 19. 7 ; *a.* 31. 23, 38. 15, 29.

glæd, *adj.* bright, pleasant ; *f.* gladu 14. 14, v. 11.

glæs, *n.* glass ; *d.* glase 11. 26.

glæshluttor, *adj.* clear as glass ; *f.* glæshlutru 14. 12* ; *a. f.* glashlutre v. 8.

glēaw, *adj.* shrewd, wise ; boca gleaw i. 52 ; *n.* 16. 20.

glengan, *wv.* adorn ; *ind. pst.* 3.*s.* geglengde 64. 26, xv. 4 ; *pp.* geglengde xxv. 10.

glīdan, *sv1.* glide ; *ind. prs.* 3.*s.* glideð xx. 170, xxviii. 39, xxix. 27.

glīwian, *wv.* sing ; gliowian 26. 22*.

glīwword, *n.* song, poem ; *d. pl.* gliowordum vii. 2.

gnætt, *m.* gnat ; *n. pl.* gnættas 36. 8.

gnornian, *wv.* grieve ; 138. 16,

19; *ind. prs.* 3.*pl.* gnorniað
24. 13.

gnornung, *f.* grief, lamentation;
13. 4; *d.* gnornunga 12. 4;
gnornunge iii. 10; *a.* gnornunga
9. 14, 15. 21; *n. pl.* 16. 8.

gōd, 1) *adj.* good; *v. fq.*; good
is usual form in C, god *in* B;
exx. of god *in* C *are given;*
god 35. 13; *wk.* gooda, goda
104. 2 &c.; *f.* good, god 47.
22; gōd 138. 4; *n.* good, god 28.
11; *g.* goodes, godes 38. 28, ix.
49, 62; gōdes 119. 12; *wk.*
goodan, godan 35. 10*; gōdan
113. 27; *d.* goodum, gōdum
128. 32; *f.* goodre xxii. 42 &c.;
wk. goodan, godan 18. 22; *a.*
goodne, godne 38. 33, 53. 22, i.
42; *wk.* gōdan 123. 28; *pl. m.*
f. n. goode, gode 35. 23; gōde
106. 33; *wk.* goodan, gōdan
104. 20; *g.* goodra, godra 18.
16, 45. 23, 124. 20, 125. 11,
i. 45; gōdra xxvii. 29; *wk.*
godena 45. 2, 139. 6; *d.* goodum,
godum 41. 6, 125. 10; gōdum
113. 32, 118. 27, 125. 9, 139.
17; *a.* goode, gode 39. 14; *wk.*
goodan, godan 37. 30; *f.* gooda
62. 15; *n.* goode, gode 79.
28*; good xx. 45; *comp.* betera
27. 27, 35. 16, 72. 14, 21, 23,
132. 15; betra 28. 12, 131. 30,
132. 26, 146. 23; *f.* betere 18.
32, 72. 24, 146. 24, xii. 19, xx.
187; *n.* betere *about* 10 *times,*
20. 28 &c.; betre *about* 4 *times,*
84. 17 &c.; *g.* beteran xxv. 29;
a. 71. 22; *n.* betere 83. 25, 85.
21; betre 18. 33; *n. pl.* betran
130. 3, 134. 16; *sup.* betst xxx.
4; *wk.* betsta 110. 26, 132. 26;
n. betst 53. 21 &c.; *a. wk.*
betstan 114. 15; *pl. n. wk.* 130.
8; *g. wk.* betstena 69. 14; *d.*
betstum 45. 20; *wk.* betstan 130.
8. 2) *sbst. n.* good; good *usual*
form in C, 37. 21 &c.; god
about 12 *times,* 29. 6 &c.; gōd
29. 5, 83. 6, 98. 21; *g.* goodes
52. 21 &c.; godes 13. 18 &c.;

gōdes 76. 19, 110. 25, 135. 16; *d.*
goode 71. 13, 89. 6* &c.; gode
44. 28, 114. 9, 141. 6, iii. 10; *a.*
good; god 22. 14, 56. 27, 88.
25; gōd 106. 34, 107. 8, 143.
19; *pl. n.* good; *g.* gooda; goda
56. 7; *d.* goodum, godum 39. 13,
88. 29; *a.* good, god 18. 10, 29.
9, 31. 25; gōd 27. 10*.

god, *m.* 1) god; 98. 28, 109. 21,
115. 24, 28; *a.* 115. 26, 116. 1;
pl. n. godas 113. 19, 114. 20;
g. goda 109. 17; *a.* godas 115.
27; godu 98. 28, 102. 11. 2)
God; 12. 19 &c., *often difficult*
to distinguish from gōd (2); *in*
C *the two are occasionally*
confused, God *-being written*
good, *or* gōd 83. 27, 84. 2, 13,
26, 87. 30, 94. 4, 109. 16, 17;
occurs about 170–175 *times in*
all; g. Godes 11. 7 &c.; *d.* Gode
9. 29 &c.; *a.* God 38. 26 &c.

godcund, *adj.* Godlike, divine;
wk. godcunda 39. 29 &c.; *f.*
godcund 127. 20; *wk.* godcunde
128. 16 &c.; *n.* godcund 127.
20; *g. wk.* godcundan 135. 5;
d. wk. 99. 18 &c.; *a.* godcundne
26. 25; *wk.* godcundan 25. 15;
gōdcundan 79. 3; *without arti-*
cle, 136. 7; *d. pl.* godcundum 54.
11, 141. 1, 143. 12.

godcundlic, *adj.* divine; *g.* godcundlices 32. 2; *d.* godcundlicum
148. 25; *a. n. wk.* godcundlice
129. 29.

godcundlīce, *adv.* divinely; 31. 27.

godcundnes, *f.* divine quality,
Godhead; 85. 28; *g.* godcundnesse 100. 11, 31; *a.* 85. 32,
132. 24.

gōdnes, *f.* goodness; goodnes 100.
16, 114. 19, xx. 31; godnes 79.
21*, 84. 24, 90. 21; gōdnes
113. 27; *g.* goodnesse 98. 2,
100. 21.

godwebb, *n.* fine cloth; godweb
28. 31; *a.* viii. 25.

gold, *n.* gold; 27. 28, 29; *g.*
goldes xiv. 3; *d.* golde 11. 27,
28, 19. 5, 34. 11, viii. 57, xv. 4,

xxv. 6; *a.* gold 33. 9, 73. 25, 140. 14, 16, xix. 6.

goldhord, *mn.* hoard of gold, treasure ; *a.* 140. 12.

goldsmiðð, *m.* goldsmith (Weland); *g.* goldsmiðes 46. 17, x. 34.

græg, *adj.* grey ; *a. f.* græge v. 8.

grafan, *sv6.* dig ; *ind. pst.* 3.*s.* grof viii. 57.

gram, *adj.* fierce, cruel ; *a. wk.* graman 36. 21 ; *pl. a. wk.* 102. 22.

grāpian, *wv.* handle, touch ; gegrapian 145. 22 ; *ind. pst.* 1.*s.* grapode, felt, groped 97. 18.

grēat, *adj.* stout, thick ; 117. 29.

grēne, *adj.* green ; *d. pl.* grenum xix. 6.

grēnian, *wv.* become green ; xi. 57.

grētan, *wv.* salute, greet ; *ind. pst.* 3.*s.* gegrette 8. 17*.

grimm, *adj.* terrible, grim ; *d.* grimmum iii. 1.

grimme, *adv.* fiercely ; v. 8, vii. 51.

grīpan, *sv1.* seize ; gegripan x. 69 ; *ind. prs.* 3.*s.* gegripð 47. 2.

grot, *n.* grain, particle ; *a.* 95. 17, 146. 3.

grōwan, *rv.* grow ; 91. 25, 95. 16, xi. 57, xxii. 42 ; *ind. prs.* 3.*s.* groweð xx. 99, xxix. 69 ; grewð 49. 19*, 80. 17*, 91. 31, 136. 19* ; gegrewð 91. 21 ; *pl.* growað xxix. 66 ; *sbj. pst.* 3.*s.* greowe 91. 26 ; *prs. p.* growende 136. 20.

grund, *m.* bottom, ground, land ; *a.* viii. 46, xx. 127, xxix. 16, 60 ; oð ðone grund, thoroughly 52. 12 ; *d. pl.* grundum xx. 35.

grundlēas, *adj.* bottomless ; *f.* vii. 15 ; *f. wk.* grundlease 19. 7 ; *d.* grundleasum 9. 10, iii. 1 ; *a. pl. wk.* grundleasan, insatiable 38. 15, 29.

grundweall, *m.* foundation ; *a.* grundweal vii. 34.

grymettan, grymetian ; *wv.* roar, grunt ; grymetigan xiii. 29 ; *ind.*

pst. 3.*pl.* grymetodan 116. 18* ; grymetedon xxvi. 81.

guma, *wm.* man ; x. 69 ; *g. pl.* gumena 139. 6, ix. 41, xxv. 27, xxvi. 37.

gumrinc, *m.* man ; *g. pl.* gumrinca xxvi. 53.

gūð, *f.* war, battle ; *d.* guðe i. 23.

gyden, *f.* goddess ; xxvi. 53 ; gydene 116. 2* ; *a. pl.* gydena 102. 22.

gylden, *adj.* golden xxi. 20 ; *a.* heafodbeag gyldenne 112. 23 ; *n. pl. n.* gyldenu 104. 17 ; *m. wk.* gyldenan 89. 12 ; *d.* gyldenum 111. 16.

gylt, *m.* guilt ; *g.* gyltes 123. 20.

H.

habban, *wv. a)* have ; *b)* hold, regard ; 17. 31, x. 22 &c., 109. 8 (*b*) ; gehabban, hold, retain 25. 9 ; to habbanne 16. 13 &c., 68. 26 (*b*) ; to habbenne 30. 10* &c. ; *ind. prs.* 1.*s.* hæbbe 13. 16 &c. ; habbe 17. 17* ; *neg.* nabbe 127. 27 ; 2.*s.* hafast xx. 21, xxiv. 25 ; hæfst 12. 25 &c. ; hafst 105. 21* ; *neg.* næfst 31. 15 &c. ; xx. 36 ; 3.*s.* hafað 72. 2*, ii. 4, viii. 43, 46, ix. 63, xi. 23, 29, xiii. 6, xx. 153, 189, xxviii. 21 ; *neg.* nafað xxii. 46, xxvii. 5 ; hæfð x. 67, xi. 22, 31, 55, 64, xx. 143, 190, xxiv. 37, xxviii. 25 ; *usual form in prose* 16. 20 &c. ; *neg.* næfð 53. 3 &c. ; gehæfð, holds, possesses 47. 2* ; *pl.* habbað 13. 29, iv. 44 &c. ; habbæð xx. 193 ; *neg.* nabbað 37. 25 &c. *and* xx. 195, xxxi. 8 ; hæbbe we 77. 14 ; *pst.* 2.*s.* hæfdest 15. 2 &c. ; hæfdes 22. 2, 23. 20* ; *neg.* næfdest 15. 12 ; 3.*s.* hæfde Pr. 8, iv. 23 &c. ; = sceolde 52. 27 ; *pl.* hæfdon 7. 16, xxvi. 18 &c., 116. 1 (*b*) ; *neg.* næfdon xxvi. 93 ; hæfdan i. 6 (J) ; *sbj. prs.* hæbbe 19. 17, x. 68 &c. ; habbe *occas. in* B, 29. 23* &c. ; *neg.* næbbe

25. 21 &c.; *pl.* hæbben 35. 19
&c. *and* xix. 47, xxix. 91 ;
habben 77. 20; habban *occas.*
in B, 62. 12* &c. *and* 120. 7;
neg. næbben 31. 26; *pst.* hæfde
25. 22 ; *neg.* næfde 33. 11, xxv.
71 ; *pl.* hæfden 64. 4, 67. 6,
xvii. 1; *neg.* næfden 117. 11, 118.
32 ; *pp.* hæfd, gehæfd* 30. 25 ;
neg. næfd, genæfd* 30. 26.

hādor, *adj.* bright, clear; xxii. 24 ;
d. hadrum 21. 2*, xxviii. 48 ;
pl. n. f. hadre xx. 230 ; *d.*
hadrum xx. 232.

hādre, *adv.* brightly, clearly; *sup.*
hadrost vi. 4.

hæftan, *wv.* bind, imprison ; *pp.*
gehæfted xxv. 49 ; gehefted xxi.
5 ; gehæft 24. 31, 89. 7 ; hæft
24. 31*; *pl. n.* gehæfte 112. 2 ;
a. f. gehæfte 57. 5*.

hæftedōm, *m.* captivity; *d.*
hæftedome xxv. 65.

hæle, *m.* man (vir) ; i. 53.

hæleð, *m.* man; *g. pl.* hæleða vii.
6, 18, ix. 57, x. 1, 68, xiii. 32,
xxi. 37, xxvi. 49, xxviii. 48,
xxix. 58; *d.* hæleðum MPr. 10,
xxix. 22.

hælig, *adj.* inconstant, variable;
d. wk. hælgan 115. 3*.

hælo, *f.* health, prosperity ; 54.
25, 92. 31* *n.*, 132. 14 ; *g.* hæle
13. 30 ; hælo 107. 28.

hæmedðing, *n.* sexual intercourse;
g. hæmedðinges 93. 18.

hærfest, *m.* autumn ; 29. 24, 49.
18, 136. 16, xxix. 61 ; *a.* on
hærfest 49. 19, xi. 58.

hærfesttīd, *f.* autumn ; *a.* on
hærfæsttīd 10. 12.

hæs, *f.* command ; *d.* hæse iv.
26.

hæto, *f.* heat ; *d.* hæto xx. 73 ; *a.*
80. 5, 92. 7, xx. 113, xxix. 50;
hæto 42. 3*.

hæðfeld, *m.* heathland ; *a.* 34. 27.

hagol, *m.* hail ; hagal xxix. 63 ;
n. pl. hæglas 136. 17*.

hāl, *adj.* unimpaired, sound, healthy;
22. 6, 28 ; *n.* 91. 9, 94. 1, 104.
32, 122. 2 ; gehal 93. 32, 94. 1*;

d. halum 132. 7 ; ðam halum
men 132. 6 ; *pl. n.* hale 22. 29 ;
a. n. 82. 10 ; hal xx. 261 ; *comp.*
n. pl. halran 88. 21.

hālig, *adj.* holy; xx. 46 ; *f.* halige
iv. 4 ; *g.* haliges xxix. 55 ; *pl.*
n. halige 133. 7 ; *wk.* halgan
26. 21 ; *a.* halige 10. 19, i. 25,
iv. 38 ; *sup.* halgost xxvi. 38.

hām, 1) *m.* home, dwelling ; *pl. n.*
hamas 33. 23, viii. 8; *g.* hama ix.
18. 2) *adv.* homewards, ham
cerde 115. 19.

hāmfæst, *adj.* resident, dwelling ;
43. 3, 32.

hand, *f.* hand ; *d.* honda xxix. 61 ;
d. pl. hondum 9. 3*, 149. 4.

hangian, *wv. intrans.* hang;
hongian on ðam anwealde, cling
to, 35. 22 ; *ind. prs.* 3.*s.* hangað
65. 29, 82. 11*, v. 4 ; h. on ðæm,
depends on, 101. 9 ; 3.*pl.* hongiað 130. 5 ; *pst.* 3.*s.* hangode
xx. 266.

hār, *adj.* grey, hoar ; *d.* harum
v. 13.

hara, *wm.* hare ; 102. 7, 115. 2.

hāt, *adj.* hot ; *wk.* hata 136. 15,
xxix. 58 ; *n.* hat xxviii. 61 ; *d.*
wk. hatan 80. 9 ; *a. pl.* hate iv. 19.

gehāt *n.* promise ; *a. pl.* 7. 9*.

hātan, *rv.* call, name (*w. the*
name in the nom. case) ; command ; *fq.* 39. 5 &c. ; command
66. 23 ; *ind. prs.* 1.*s.* hate 96. 22 ;
3.*s.* hateð viii. 51 ; hæt 99. 10*;
commands 144. 29; hat 116. 20*;
pl. hatað *fq.* 7. 12, viii. 49 &c. ;
hætað 132. 20; hate we 136. 4 ;
pst. 2.*s.* hete 79. 33 ; 3.*s.* het,
commanded 7. 11 &c. *and* i. 42,
ix. 9, 24 ; heht i. 70, 72 ; *pl.*
heton, named xxvi. 49; *relic of*
pass. voice 3.*s.* hatte, is *or* was
called i. 53, 34. 8*, 9, 37. 3,
41. 23, 99. 9, 10*, 101. 23, 140.
9 ; *sbj. prs.* 3.*pl.* haten 68. 10 ;
pst. 3.*s.* hete 117. 3 ; *pp.* haten
36. 17, 43. 7, 46. 22, 101. 26,
xvi. 15, xxvi. 57 ; gehaten 7.
12*, 50. 7*, 83. 29*, 143. 6,
148. 7, x. 46, xxviii. 24 ; *n. pl.*

hatene 115. 16; hatne 7. 3*;
gehatene 114. 22.

gehātan, *rv.* promise; *ind. prs.*
2.*s.* gehætst 105. 30; 3.*s.* gehæt
47. 17, xxv. 52; *pl.* gehataðꝺ 58.
21, 22, 59. 19, 73. 16, 17; *pst.*
1.*s.* gehet 78. 6, 139. 25; *2.s.*
gehete 9. 21, 50. 26, 78. 9, 31*,
139. 21; 3.*s.* gehet 7. 7, 71. 13,
102. 20, 112. 4, i. 35.

hāte, *adv.* hotly; *sup.* hatost 12. 8.

hātheortnes, *f.* violent temper,
anger; *g.* hatheortnesse 112. 1,
xxv. 47.

hatian, *wv.* hate; 123. 28, xxvii
32; *ind. prs.* 3.*s.* hataðꝺ 123. 28;
pl. hatiaðꝺ 146. 7, 8; *imp. pl.*
149. 5; *sbj. prs.* 3.*s.* hatige 123.
30, 124. 16.

hāwian, *wv.* look upon, survey;
imp. hawa 10. 26.

hē, *pron.* he; Pr. 3 &c. *Oblique
cases often reflx.*; *g.* his, *gen. used
as a poss. adj.* his, Pr. 7 &c.;
w. article: his sio hea goodnes
84. 14; sio his gesælðꝺ 89. 1;
his ðꝺære hean ceastre 141. 7;
his ðꝺam anwealde 69. 23; ðꝺara
his ðꝺegna 111. 22; *w. wk. adj.*
103. 16; *d.* him Pr. 12 &c.; *a.*
hine Pr. 12 &c.; *for pl. v.* **hīe**.

hēafod, *n.* head; *d.* heafde 65. 30,
127. 10, i. 43; *a. pl.* heafdu
102. 14, 17, 127. 9.

hēafodbēag, *m.* crown; *a.* 112.
23.

hēah, 1) *adj.* high, deep; sublime;
f. wk. hea 84. 14, 85. 20; *n.*
heah 99. 12; h. weder, rough,
stormy 115. 21; *g. wk.* hean
32. 6, 135. 25, 146. 27; *d.* heaum
98. 18; *wk.* hean 26. 31 &c.;
heohan 14. 16*; *a.* heane 148. 30,
vii. 4, xxiv. 3, xxix. 2; *wk.* hean
105. 5, 135. 24; *pl. d.* heaum xxi.
11; *comp. a. s. n.* herre 55. 26 *n.*;
sup. hehst xxvi. 38; *wk.* hehsta
62. 24 &c.; *f. wk.* hehste 50.
12 &c.; *n.* hyhst xiii. 52; hehst
ix. 4; *wk.* hehste 52. 22 &c.
and xx. 46, xxix. 74; hehstæ
90. 7; *g. wk.* hehstan 55. 17 *n.*

&c.; *d. wk.* 18. 8 &c. *and* xxiv.
29, xxvi. 44; *inst.* on ðꝺæm
hehste goode 100. 14; *pl. g.
wk.* hehstena 56. 6, 77. 25; *a.
wk.* hehstan 18. 9. 2) *adv.* on
high 57. 21.

hēahburg, *f.* chief town; 7. 20.

hēahsǣ, *f.* deep sea; *g.* xi. 3.

hēahsetl, *n.* high seat, throne; *d.*
heahsetle 136. 22, 148. 32, iv. 2,
xxix. 74; *pl. g.* heahsetla 11. 27;
d. heahsetlum 10. 19, 111. 13,
iv. 38, xxv. 5.

heald, *adj.* leaning, inclined; *f.
pred.* 57. 6*; *pl. n.* healde 55.
16*, 147. 7*.

healdan, *rv.* hold, keep; observe;
perform; 93. 24, 98. 11; restrain
109. 31, 138. 5; healdon i. 71
(J); healden xi. 73 ?; gehealdan
40. 23, 59. 29, 65. 16, 76. 33,
124. 28, xi. 47; support, satisfy
28. 23; to gehealdenne 50. 24;
ind. prs. 2.*s.* helst 31. 13; 3.*s.*
haldeðꝺ xx. 166; gehealdeðꝺ vii.
46; healt 81. 12*; helt 80. 16*;
gehelt 27. 11*, 53. 2, 84. 25,
131. 6; hilt 28. 3; hylt xx. 95;
pl. healdaðꝺ 10. 15 &c. *and* xxix.
4; gehealdaðꝺ xi. 95; *pst.* 3.*s.*
heold xxix. 55; *pl.* hioldon 64.
13; *imp.* gehcald 114. 2; *sbj.
prs.* 3.*s.* healde xiii. 25; gehealde
76. 29; *pst.* 3.*pl.* heolden 94.
10; geheoldon 143. 25; *pp.*
gehealden 22. 1 &c.; contented
43. 27, 60. 21; healdon 57. 6*.

healf, *f. a)* half; *b)* side; *d.* healfe
43. 10 (*b*); be healfe heofones
ðꝺisses, in one part xxix. 43;
adv. healfe ðꝺy swetre, by half
xii. 9; *a.* healfe 81. 11 (*b*), 136.
9 (*b*), xx. 164 (*b*); *pl. d. used as
adv.* healfum, half 42. 16; *a.* on
feower healfe his, all round him
46. 4* (*b*).

hēalic, *adj.* high, exalted; *a. n.*
54. 4; *comp.* healicra 72. 21.

hēalīce, *adv.* in a high degree;
comp. healicor onbryrdan 14. 2.

heall, *f.* hall; *a.* healle vii. 6; *a.
pl.* vii. 11.

healsian, *wv.* entreat, implore;
ind. prs. 1.*s.* healsige 51. 17,
84. 8, 120. 6; halsige 105. 31;
3.*s.* healsað, halsað* Pr. 11.

hēan, *adj.* lowly, humble; *a. wk.*
heanan 46. 15; *pl. n.* heane
xvii. 6; *a. wk.* heanan 46. 16.

hēanes, *f.* height, high region; *d.*
heanesse 12. 1; *a.* 104. 31.

hēanlio, *adj.* abject, vile; *n. pl. f.*
heanlica 23. 27.

heard, *adj. a)* hard; *b)* severe,
ruthless; *c)* hard to bear; wiges
heard, bold xxvi. 13; *f.* heard
67. 8 (*b*); *g. f.* heardre (*a*); *pl.*
g. heardra henða xii. 21 (*c*); *d.*
heardum broce 133. 25 (*c*).

hearde, *adv.* firmly, excessively;
xxv. 49; *sup.* heardost 105. 28,
x. 14.

heardheort, *adj.* hard-hearted;
143. 29.

heardsǣlig, *adj.* unfortunate; *d.*
wk. heardsælgan 71. 1.

heardsǣlð, *f.* misfortune; *a. pl.*
heardsælða 117. 24; bad conduct,
wickedness 44. 1.

hearm, *m.* injury, harm; 144. 19.

hearmcwidian, *wv.* revile, abuse;
45. 10; hearmcwiddigan *ib.**

hearpe, *w. f.* harp; *d.* hearpan
102. 11.

hearpere, *m.* harp-player; 101. 23,
24, 102. 2, 18; *g.* hearperes
102. 1; *d.* hearpere 101. 27,
102. 9.

hearpian, *wv.* play on the harp;
101. 27; *ind. pst.* 3.*s.* hearpode
102. 5, 103. 3, 4.

hearpung, *f.* playing on the harp;
d. hearpunga 102. 16, 102. 31,
103. 6.

heaðorian, *wv.* restrain, confine;
ind. prs. 3.*s.* heaðerað 128. 21;
pp. geheaðorad xiii. 6; geheaðærod xi. 31; *a. pl. f.* geheaðorade 49. 6, 57. 5.

heaðorino, *m.* warrior; *g. pl.*
heaðorinca ix. 45.

hebban, *sv*6. raise; habban 146.
26, xxxi. 18; *imp. pl.* hebbað
149. 3.

hēdan, *wv.* catch up, seize; *sbj.*
prs. 3.*s.* gehede xxvii. 15.

hefig, *adj.* heavy; grievous; 70.
27, xx. 266, xxix. 53; *n.* 25. 3,
73. 23, xix. 1; difficult 127. 21;
f. wk. hefige 136. 13; *d. f.*
hefigre 108. 7; *wk.* hefegan 70.
30; *a. n.* hefig 40. 1, ix. 55;
comp. f. hefigre 80. 30, xx. 133;
g. hefigran 50. 20; *a. n.* hefigre
119. 15.

hefiglīce, *adv.* grievously; 41.
10.

hefignes, *f.* heaviness, sluggishness;
xxii. 25, 29; melancholy 56. 14;
hæfignes 95. 7*; *d.* hefignesse
95. 27; hefinesse xxii. 63; hæfignesse 95. 22*.

helan, *sv*4. conceal; 147. 25; *ind.*
prs. 3.*s.* hilð 61. 12.

hell, *f.* Hades, hell; *g.* helle 102.
11, 13, 103. 14, viii. 51; *d.* 34.
8, 102. 2.

hellware, *pl. m.* inhabitants of
hell; *wk.* hellwaran 102. 27;
g. hellwara 103. 2, 4; *wk.*
hellwarana 103. 4*.

helm, *m.* tree-top; 91. 28; *a.* 92. 1.

helma, *wm.* helm of ship; 97. 11;
d. helman 98. 2.

helpan, *sv*3. *w. g. or d.* 122. 31;
gehelpan 30. 12; *imp.* help 10.
16; *sbj. prs.* 3.*s.* helpe 123. 16;
impers. help, avail 144. 24; *pp.*
geholpen 145. 1.

hentan, *wv.* catch, seize; gehentan xiii. 32.

hēo, *pron.* she; *usual form in* B,
Pr. 10 &c.; hio *usual form in*
C, 13. 9, i. 77 &c.; *about* 20
times in B, Pr. 2 &c.; hi 130.
18; hie 49. 24*, 57. 26*; *g.* and
d. hire; *g. often used as a possess.*
adj., her, its 22. 20, xiii. 20
&c.; *often* hiere *in* B, 22. 15*
&c.; heore 10. 4*, 7*, 24*, 11.
6*, 49. 24*; hiore 47. 10*, 141.
14; hyre 9. 8*; *a.* hie, *usual*
form Pr. 1*, 13. 31, v. 9 &c.;
hi Pr. 9*, 25. 8 &c. *and* xx. 166,
214, 217, 219, xxvi. 65; *for pl.*
v. hīe.

hēofian, *wv. intrans.* lament; *prs. p.* heofiende 8. 6.

heofon, *m.* sky, heaven; 72. 21·; heofen 17. 23*; hefon 99. 13*; *g.* heofones 10. 1, x. 7 &c.; hiofones xxi. 39; beofenes 72. 17, 98. 29, 135. 27; hiofenes 105. 19; heofnes 135. 25; hefones iv. 2; *d.* heofone 10. 6, 21. 2, 99. 12, xxviii. 48; hefone vi. 4; *a.* heofon 10. 2, 41. 24, 99. 1, 105. 16, xi. 30, xxiv. 29; hefon 18. 7, iv. 4; *pl. g.* heofona xiii. 6, xxix. 71; *d.* heofonum 9. 19, 18. 10, 129. 30, iv. 26 &c.; heofenum 98. 29; hiofonum 81. 33; hefonum 24. 29, 45. 27, ix. 18.

heofoncund, *adj.* heavenly; heofencund 8. 16; *g. wk.* heofencundan 11. 17; *a. wk.* heofoncundan 34. 19; *pl. n. wk.* hefoncundan 30. 2; *a. wk.* heofoncundan xx. 235.

heofonlic, *adj.* heavenly, celestial; *g. wk.* heofonlican 45. 30; heofenlican 89. 21; *d. wk.* heofonlican 104. 27, 120. 15; heofonlicon 18. 21*; *a. pl. wk.* heofonlican 121. 30; hiofonlican 82. 2; hefonlican 18. 10.

heofonrīce, *n.* kingdom of heaven; *g.* hefonrices xi. 31.

heofonsteorra, *wm.* star; *n. pl.* heofonsteorran xx. 232.

heofontorht, *adj.* heavenly bright; *a. wk.* heofontorhtan xxiii. 3.

heofontungol, *n.* heavenly body, sun; xxii. 24.

heonon, *adv.* hence; hionon 105. 24; hionan 82. 4, 105. 22, 23, xviii. 11, xxiv. 50, 52; hion xx. 239; hionane xiv. 9, xxix. 84 *n.*

heor, *f.* hinge; hior 88. 12 *n.*

heorot, *m.* stag; heort 102. 6; *a. pl.* heorotas xix. 17.

heorte, *wf.* heart; *g.* heortan 28. 14, 15, v. 21; *d.* xviii. 11.

hēr, *adv.* here; 11. 29, iv. 41 &c.; her on worulde 24. 25, 46. 31, 118. 4, 123. 23; *cf.* iv. 47; her for

worulde 23. 15, 24. 25, 113. 23, 138. 23.

hērbūende, *m.* dweller on earth; *d. pl.* herbuendum xxix. 61.

here, *m.* host, multitude: x. 54 (?); *d.* here xxv. 15; *d. pl.* herigum xxvi. 57.

heregeat, *n.* military dress; *d. pl.* heregeatwum 111. 16, xxv. 9.

hererinc, *m.* soldier, hero; *a.* i. 71.

heretīema, *wm.* commander, general; heretema i. 31.

heretoga, *wm.* general, leader, chief man 37. 5, 46. 22, 24, 50. 7, 61. 24, 143. 7, i. 47, x. 46; heretoha, consul 7. 12; *g.* heretogan 43. 6; *pl. n.* heretogan 35. 3, 64. 12; *g.* heretogena 35. 5.

herian, *wv.* praise; 118. 26; to herianne 32. 28, 69. 3; to heriganne 64. 19; *ind. prs. 3. pl.* heriað 69. 2; *pst. 3. s.* herede 141. 13, xxx. 6; *sbj. prs.* herige 30. 22, 68. 17; *pl.* herien x. 26; herigen 46. 12, 72. 20; *pp. used as adj.* geherod*, gehered 68. 23; *comp.* geheredra*, heredra 69. 5.

herlic, *adj.* martial, soldierly; *f.* ix. 18; hærlic i. 43.

herung, *f.* praise; *d.* heringe 64. 2*, 68. 31, 104. 22.

hider, *adv.* hither; 60. 32, 82. 4, xiv. 11, xx. 164, 235, 239.

hidres, *adv.* hidres ðidres, hither and thither 108. 14 (hider 7 ðider B), 139. 31; hidres 7 ðidres 100. 5.

hīe, *pron.* they; *n. & a. pl. of* he, heo, hit; *usual form in* C *and* B *is* hi; hie *is fq. in* B, *rarer in* C, 15. 5, 15. 12* &c.; hy *ab.* 15 *times in* C, 15. 27, i. 36 &c.; *in* B, 15. 6*, 8*, 16. 16*, 146. 5*; hio 33. 25*, 114. 22; *g.* hira 44. 5, 99. 3, xx. 145; 35. 4 N.; hiera 30. 13*, 99. 1; *usual form in* C *is* hiora, *but* heora *is fq.,* 28. 21, ii. 13 &c.; heora *is usual form in* B, *but* hiora *also occurs* *several times* 26. 30 &c. ; heore 28. 3*, 32. 7* ; *d.* him.

hieldan, *wv.* lean, incline ; *ind. prs.* 3.*s.* heldeð xx. 164 ; helt 81. 11*.

hienan, *wv.* bring low, humiliate; henan 122. 32, 125. 2.

hienð, *f.* ignominy, humiliation ; *d.* hænðe 24. 5 ; *g. pl.* henða xii. 21.

hieran, *wv. w. a.* hear; *w. d.* obey ; heran i. 31, ix. 45 ; geheran 50. 21, 78. 32, 96. 8, 118. 11, 121. 8, 146. 4 ; to geheranne 50. 10, 24 ; to gehyranne 51. 10* ; *ind. prs.* 1.*s.* gehere 121. 6 ; 3.*s.* geherð 28. 13, 43. 2 ; *pl.* herað iv. 5, 15 ; geherað 68. 16, 139. 23, 145. 20, xiii. 47 ; *w. inf.* 142. 26 ; hyrað iv. 26 ; *pst.* 1.*s.* geherde 51. 9, 124. 24 ; 2.*s.* geherdest 50. 26, 98. 26 (*w. inf.*); gehyrdest 45. 4*, 65. 9* ; herdes vii. 9 ; 3.*s.* geherde 34. 2, 43. 18, 45. 11, 122. 8, ix. 15 ; *pl.* herdon 70. 25, viii. 14, 31 ; geherdon 33. 26, 43. 11, 66. 30 ; geheordon 70. 25* ; *imp.* gehere 114. 1 *n.* ; geher 101. 16, 111. 12, 114. 1*, xxv. 1 ; *sbj. prs.* 3.*s.* here *w. d.* 66. 14 ; *pl.* gehiran 57. 20* ; *pst.* 3.*s.* herde vii. 4 ; *pl.* herden *w. d.* 98. 7, 9 ; *prs. p. used as noun* : *pl. g.* geherendra, hearers 85. 26 ; *d.* geherendum 101. 13 ; *pp.* gehered 45. 12, 67. 12.

hierde, *m.* shepherd, guardian ; hirde xxvi. 8, 41 ; hyrde x. 49 ; *d.* hirde vii. 22 ; *a.* xiii. 31.

gehiernes, *f.* sense of hearing; gehernes 145. 18.

hiersum, *adj.* obedient ; *a. pl. n.* gehyrsume 10. 3*.

hiersumian, *wv.* obey ; heorsumian 9. 22* ; *ind. prs.* 3.*pl.* heorsumiað 10. 14*.

hierwan, *wv.* despise, value lightly ; *ind. prs.* 1.*pl.* herwað, herewiað* 29. 6.

higian, *wv.* hasten, strive to go, tend ; 25. 18 ; *ind. prs.* 3.*s.*

higað 56. 4, 69. 14, xiii. 65 ; *sbj. prs.* 3.*s.* higie 51. 25*, 112. 30 ; higige 51. 25.

hildetorht, *adj.* shining in battle ; *d. pl.* hildetorhtum xxv. 9.

hiltsweord, *n.* hilted sword ; *d. pl.* hyltsweordum 111. 16.

hind, *f.* female hart ; *a. pl.* hinda xix. 17.

hindan, *adv.* from behind ; 136. 3.

hired, *m.* body of retainers, court ; *d.* hirede 67. 3, 104. 16.

hirgedon, B's *reading for* C's styredon 101. 28.

hit, *pron.* it ; 7. 25 &c. ; *g.* his ; *d.* him ; *a.* hit ; *for pl. v.* hie.

hiw, *n.* appearance, form, shape ; *g.* hiwes 147. 3 ; *d.* hiwe 131. 5 ; *g. pl.* hiwa xix. 23.

hiwcuð, *adj.* familiar ; *a. pl. m.* hiwcuðe x. 61.

hiwian, *wv.* shape, form ; *ind. prs.* 3.*s.* gehiwað 129. 9.

hiwung, *f.* (false) appearance, dissimulation ; *d.* hiwunga 47. 22.

hlæw, *m.* mound, barrow ; *g. pl.* hlæwa x. 43.

hlaford, *m.* lord ; 35. 31, ix. 55, xxv. 15, xxvi. 38 ; *g.* hlafordes 30. 26, 63. 15 ; *d.* hlaforde 98. 9, 136. 29, i. 47 ; *a.* hlaford 65. 17, xxvi. 44, 72 ; *pl. n.* hlafordas 35. 30, 37. 26, 67. 5 ; *g.* hlaforda xxv. 65.

hlafordhold, *adj.* loyal, faithful ; *n. pl. m.* hlafordholde 30. 27.

hlafordscipe, *m.* authority, supremacy ; *d.* 16. 27.

hleahtor, *m.* laughter ; *d.* hleahtre 36. 2.

hleoðor, *n.* melody, song ; *d. pl.* hleoðrum xiii. 47.

hlisa, *wm.* report, reputation ; 28. 11 &c. *and* x. 54, 61 ; *g.* hlisan 41. 13 &c. *and* x. 1, 14 ; hliosan 133. 31* ; *d.* hlisan 41. 17 &c. ; *a.* 41. 15 &c. *and* i. 53, x. 22.

hliseadig, *adj.* of good repute, renowned 75. 25 ; *a. pl. m.* hliseadige 28. 5 ; *comp.* hliseadigra 27. 29 ; *n. pl.* hliseadigran 28. 1.

hlīsēadignes, *f.* renown ; *a.* hliseadignesse 75. 28.

hlūd, *adj.* loud ; *a.* hludne 117. 29.

hlūtor, *adj.* clear, pure ; *n. v.* 13; *d.* hlutrum 135. 24 ; *a. f.* hlutre xxi. 39 ; *wk.* hluttran 101. 20 ; *inst.* hlutre xxix. 2; *pl. g.* hluterra 33. 31 ; *d.* hlutrum xxi. 37 ; hluttrum eagum 89. 21, 115. 8 ; *a. n.* hlutor, hlutre* 147. 25; *sup. a. s. wk.* hlutrestan xxiii. 3.

hlūtre, *adv.* clearly, brightly; *sup.* hlutrost xxii. 24.

hlystan, *ww.* listen ; *sbj.* 3.*s.* hliste MPr. 10.

hnæppan, *ww. intrans.* strike, collide ; *sbj. prs.* 3.*pl.* hnæppen 130. 19, 20.

hnesce, *adj.* soft, delicate ; *n.* h. wæter, fluid, yielding 80. 14, xx. 93 ; *compl. n. pl.* hnescran, *opposed to* heard 92. 27 ; *sup.* hnescost 92. 4.

hnipian, *ww.* droop ; *ind. prs.* 3.*s.* hnipað xxxi. 13.

hogian, *ww.* think (about), be intent ; 35. 22.

hol, *n.* hole, cave ; dungeon ; *a.* 8. 10, ii. 11 ; *a. pl.* holu 19. 8.

hold, *adj.* gracious, friendly ; i. 56.

holm, *m.* ocean, sea ; *g. pl.* holma xi. 30.

holt, *nm.* thicket, copse ; *d.* holte xiii. 37, 52.

hōn, *rv. trans.* hang, hang up ; *ind. prs.* 2.*s.* hehst 30. 18 ; 3.*s.* hehð 112. 23.

hopian, *ww.* (*w.* to) ; hope, trust ; *ind. prs.* 3.*s.* hopað 27. 10, vii. 44 ; *sbj. prs. pl.* hopien 149. 1.

hord, *n.* hoard ; *d.* horde 31. 13.

hordgestrēon, *n.* hoarded wealth; *g. pl.* hordgestreona xiv. 11.

horusēað, *m.* pit, abyss ; *d.* horoseaðe 112. 15.

hosp, *m.* insult, contumely ; *d.* hospe iv. 44.

hræd, *adj.* swift ; *d.* hrædum 10. 2.

hrædfērnes, *f.* swiftness ; *a.* hrædfernesse 72. 17.

hrædlīce, *adv.* swiftly, speedily 117. 8 ; rædlice 21. 14* ; *sup.* hrædlicost 146. 28.

hrædwǣn, *m.* swift car, chariot ; *d.* hrædwæne 105. 1, 20, xxiv. 41.

hrægl, *n.* dress ; *g.* hrægles 60. 18; *pl. g.* hrægla 33. 24, 30, viii. 10 ; *d.* hræglum 111. 14.

hranmere, *m.* 'whale pool,' ocean; *a.* hronmere v. 10.

hraðe, *adv.* quickly, soon ; *usual form in* B, 8. 20* &c., 48. 8, 127. 31, 133. 23, vi. 9, 12, xiii. 31 ; raðe 95. 4* ; hræðe 41. 18, 62. 23, 78. 6, iv. 3, vi. 4, xiii. 37, xxi. 7, xxii. 56 ; ful hræðe ðæs, immediately afterwards 50. 10 ; hreðe xxv. 47 ; *sup.* hraðor 28. 19, 145. 15 ; hræðor 68. 18, 21 ; ðy hræðor, rather, more 73. 7, 18 *n.*, 77. 19 ; *sup.* hraðost 39. 9 *n.*, 41. 3, 91. 15.

hrēoh, *adj.* stormy, fierce ; i. 71 ; *f. pred.* hrioh v. 10 ; *d. f.* hreore 144. 29.

hrēosan, *sv2.* fall ; decay, perish ; vii. 22 ; *ind. prs.* 3.*s.* hrest xi. 58; gehrist 117. 28 ; *prs. p.* perishable, *d. wk.* hreosendan 60. 23 ; *pl. n. f.* hreosende 25. 31* ; *d.* hreosendum 54. 1 *n.* ; *by error*, hreorendum 32. 8*.

hrēosendlic, *adj.* perishable ; *d. pl.* hreosendlicum 32. 8.

hrēowan, *sv2.* repent : *impers. w. d. and g.* 134. 31 ; *ind. prs.* 3.*s.* hreowð 109. 30.

hrēowsian, *ww.* sorrow, be sorry; 9. 9 ; *prs. p. d.* hreowsiendum 8. 24.

hrēowsung, *f.* repentance : 70. 7 ; *g.* hreowsunga 70. 6* ; *d.* 20. 1, 143. 28 ; *a.* hreowsunge 143. 30.

hrēran, *ww.* stir up, agitate ; *ind. prs.* 3.*pl.* hrerað 124. 4, xxvii. 3.

hreðer, *m.* breast, heart ; *d.* hraðre xxv. 46 *n.*

hrīnan, *sv1.* touch ; *ind. prs.* 3.*s.* gehrineð xxix. 10.

hrōf, *m.* roof, summit, *gen. used metaphorically*, 25. 17 &c. ; *g.*

hrofes 146. 27; *d.* hrofe 41. 11
&c. *and* xxv. 5; *a.* hrof 105. 5,
xxiv. 3.
hrŏffæst, *adj.* with firm roof; *a. f.*
hroffæste vii. 6.
hrŏr, *adj.* moving, active, *d. pl.*
hrorum neatum 146. 26.
hrūse, *wf.* earth, ground; *g.*
brusan xxix. 53; *d.* x. 43, xxix.
63; xxxi. 13.
hryre, *m.* fall, ruin, destruction; *d.*
ix. 4; *a. pl.* hryras 39. 17.
hŭ, *adv. interrog. direct and indirect,* how? 8. 17 &c.; *often w.*
ne = *Lat.* nonne 18. 16 &c.
hūmeta, *adv.* how? 70. 26*,
96. 5*.
hund, *m.* dog; 102. 13, 111. 18,
114, 27; *a.* hund 102. 7; *pl. n.*
hundas 101. 30; *d.* hundum
xix. 15; *a.* hundas 73. 29.
hund, *n.* hundred; mid an h.
scipa xxvi. 15.
hundnigontig, *num.* ninety;
xxvi. 24.
hundred, *n.* hundred; sume h.
scipa 115. 18.
hundseofontig, *num.* seventy;
42. 27, 99. 17.
hunig, *n.* honey; *g.* huniges 52.
3, xii. 9, 10; *d.* hunige 33. 29,
viii. 23.
hunta, *wm.* hunter; xxvii. 13.
huntian, *wv.* hunt; 73. 30.
hŭru, *adv.* at least, at any rate;
20. 22, 47. 1, 92. 8, ix. 22; ne
huru, nor indeed, nor even 67.
9, 68. 27, 77. 23, viii. 10, 31,
xx. 38, xxii. 4, xxix. 12.
hŭs, *n.* house; 26. 30, vii. 18; *g.*
huses 110. 23, vii. 22, xiii. 31;
d. huse 55. 18; *a.* hus 26. 23,
26, 27. 6, vii. 32.
hwā, *pron.* 1) *interrog.* who? 60.
8, x. 42 &c.; *w. sbj.* xxviii. 43;
n. hwæt, what? 34. 10 &c. =
who 36. 22, = hwy 17. 16, 31.
3, 6, 104. 26, 148. 29, *used as
an interj.* ah! well! why! *fq.* 10.
14, ii. 1 &c.; hwæt la 9. 20; *g.*
hwæs 90. 19, 140. 24, 145. 4,
27; *d.* hwæm 16. 17; *inst.* to

hwon, why? 8. 12*, 16. 4*, 31.
4*, 42. 17*. 2) *indef.* any one,
some one, *fq.* 26. 7 &c. *and* x. 27,
xvi. 16; *neut. n. and a.* hwæt,
anything, something 15. 21 &c.;
often w. part. g. swelces hwæt,
something of the sort 17. 10;
lytles hwæt, a little 23. 24, 60.
5; *d.* hwæm 16. 14 &c.; *a.*
hwone 68. 17 &c. *and* x. 1;
hwæne 106. 19*; *a. n.* hwæt;
gif hi hwæt gesyngoden, in any
way 143. 27. 3) swa hwa swa,
whoever 11. 23 &c. *v.* swa.
gehwā, *pron.* 1) *distributive;* each,
every, every one; *g.* gehwæs
xiv. 3, xix. 23, xx. 278, xxi. 32;
anra gehwæs monna, of each
individual man vii. 23; *d.*
gehwæm vii. 18, xii. 6, 18, xx.
148, xxi. 43, xxviii. 67, xxix. 56;
anra gehwæm, to each one viii.
6; *a. n.* gehwæt 16. 23, 40. 22.
2) *indef.* swelces gehwæt, anything of the sort 125. 24.
hwær, *interrog. adv.* where? 46.
20, x. 33 &c.
hwæt, *adj.* active, bold; *wk.*
hwata 138. 18.
hwǣte, *m.* wheat; 52. 1; *d.*
xii. 5.
hwæthwegu, 1) *pron.* something,
a little; *always* hwæthwugu
in C, 15. 22 &c. *and* xi. 52, xx.
111; hwæthwega *usual form in*
B, 32. 1* &c.; hwæthwegu 87.
24*, 95. 9*; hwæthweg 60. 17*,
71. 29*; *g.* hwæshwugu 25. 12,
60. 17, 82. 30, 88. 8. 2) *adv.*
somewhat, a little, *fq.* 8. 25 &c.
hwæthweguningas, *adv.* somewhat, a little; hwæthwugununges 23. 18, 127. 28; hwæt-
hweganunges 23. 18*; hwæthwegununga 80. 21*.
hwætnes, *f.* activity; 54. 24.
hwæðer, 1) *pron.* which (of two);
87. 17 &c. *and* v. 41; *g.* hwæðres 106. 12; *a.* hwæðerne 122.
28; *f.* hwæðre 138. 32; *n.*
hwæðer 107. 11. 2) *interrog.
adv. direct and ind.; gen. w. sbj.*

13. 10 &c. ; *alternative question* hwæðer ðe . . . ðe 20. 30 &c.; hweðer *sometimes in* B, 65. 2* &c. ; hwæðer . . . ðeah, nevertheless 27. 24.

gehwæðer, *pron.* each of two, both ; *g.* gehwæðeres i. 25.

hwæðre, *adv.* nevertheless; xx. 54, 74, 78, 152, 170, 230, xxvi. 100.

hwanon, *adv.* whence ; 32. 21 N. ; hwonon 8. 19*, 12. 14, 134. 18 ; hwonan 13. 5, 15. 8, 32. 20*, 32. 21*, 75. 34, 140. 7.

hwealf, *f.* vault, arch ; 46. 4 ; *pl.* hwealfa 46. 4 ; hwealfe x. 7 (J).

hwearflan, *wv. intrans. a)* turn, revolve ; *b)* change, vary ; 81. 26 (*a*) ; *ind. prs.* 2.*s.* hwearfost 16. 5 (*b*) ; 3.*s.* hwearfað 57. 32 (*a*), 58. 1 (*a*), 88. 12 (*a*), 126. 8 (*a*), 129. 16 (*a*), xiii. 75 (*a*) ; *pl.* hwearfiað 16. 3 (*b*), 129. 19 (*a*) ; *pst.* 3.*s.* hwearfode i. 10, xx. 206 ; *sbj. prs.* hwearfie 18. 30 (*b*); hwearfige xiii. 74 ; *pl.* hwearfigen 18. 31 (*b*) ; *pst.* hwearfode 18. 28 (*b*) ; *prs. p.* hwearfiende 129. 15 (*a*).

hwearfung, *f.* change ; 18. 31, 20. 18 ; *d.* hwearfunga 18. 27, 20. 21 ; *a. pl.* 18. 29 ; motions 17. 1.

hwelc, *pron.* (hwylc *usual form in* C, *but sq.* hwilc, *more rarely* hwelc ; *most usual forms in* B *are* hwelc *and* hwilc, *occas.* hwylc) ; 1) *interrog. direct and indirect,* which, of what kind. 2) *indef.* any (one), some (one). *forms* : *m. f. and n.* hwelc 9. 8* (2), 30. 20 (2), 43. 19 (2), 60. 27* (1), 63. 14 (2), 64. 29* (1), 77. 23* (2), 89. 20 (2) ; hwilc 30. 10 (1), 35. 28 (1), 51. 1 (1), 85. 2* (1), 92. 9 (1), 142. 2 (2), xiii. 41 (1), xx. 65 (2), xxi. 37 (2), xxii. 45 (2) ; hwylc *in* C *ab.* 6 *times* (1), 67. 22 &c., *and ab.* 7 *times* (2), 84. 30 &c. *in* B, 82. 21* ; *g.* hwelces 13. 2* (1), 20 (1) ; hwilces 11. 15* (1) ; *d.* hwelcum x. 43 (1) ;

hwilcum 114. 25 (2) ; hwylcum 77. 18 (2), 77. 22 (2) ; hwilcon 43. 3* (1) ; *f.* hwelcere 13. 23 (1) ; hwilcere 57. 4* (1) ; *a.* hwelcne 16. 20* (1), 57. 22* (2); hwilcne xiii. 53 (1) ; hwylcne 119. 2 (2) ; *f.* hwelce 35. 31 (2), ix. 1 (1) ; hwilce 39. 18* (1) ; *n.* hwelc 12. 8 (2), 127. 9 (2) ; hwilc 90. 32 (2), 90. 32 (2), 107. 29 (2), 39. 17* (1) ; hwylc 87. 6 (2) ; *inst.* hwelce 36. 2 (1) ; *pl. m.* ; hwilce 129. 14 (1) ; hwylce 129. 15 (1), 139. 10 (1) ; *f.* hwylce 38. 18 (1) ; *n.* hwelc 73. 10* (1) ; *g.* hwylcra 11. 14* (1) ; *d.* hwelcum 22. 8 (2), 32. 26* (2), 74. 2* (1) ; hwylcum 118. 29 (1) ; *a.* hwelce 16. 2* (1) ; hwilce 39. 17* (1) ; *f.* hwelce 26. 3* (1), 39. 17* (1) ; *n.* hwelc 64. 29* (1).

gehwelc, *pron. w. g.* each (one), every (one), *only in* Metr. *except* 103. 14 ; gehwilc 9 *times* ix. 45 &c. ; gehwylc xxvi. 95, xxxi. 12 ; *g.* gehwelces 6 *times,* iv. 24 &c. ; gehwilces xx. 183, xxvi. 105, xxvii. 28 ; gehwylces xviii. 3 ; *f.* gehwelcre xx. 228 ; *d.* gehwelcum 5 *times,* xii. 8 &c. ; gehwilcum i. 45, xvii. 19, xix. 2 ; gehwylcum 4 *times,* xx. 3 &c. ; *f.* gehwelcre xi. 78, xxi. 15 ; *a.* gehwilcne 4 *times,* xiii. 32 &c. ; gehwylcne, *not w. g.* 103. 14 ; *inst.* gehwelce iv. 17, xiii. 21 ; gehwilce 6 *times,* i. 54 &c. ; gehwylce xxii. 65.

hwelchwegu, *pron.* some ; hwilchwugu 120. 2 ; hwylchwugu 103. 24.

hwēne, *adv.* somewhat, a little, *w. comp.* 32. 28, 50. 20, 92. 27 ; hwene ær 5 *times,* 12. 22 &c. *and* xii. 10.

hwēol, *n.* wheel ; 16. 33, 57. 32, 81. 27, 102. 29, 129. 21, 130. 31, xiii. 74 ; *g.* hweoles 130. 11 ; *d.* hweole xx. 211, 217 ; *n. pl.* hweol 129. 19.

hweorfan, *sv*3. *intrans. a*) turn,
move ; *b*) return ; 8. 23* (*b*), 10.
24* (*a*); *ind.* 3.*pl.* hweorfaᵭ 16.
17* (*a*); *sbj. prs.* hweorfe 71. 8*
(*b*); *prs. p.* hweorfende 16. 14
(*a*).

hwider, *adv.* whither ; 51. 6 &c.

hwierfan, *wv. intrans. a*) revolve;
b) change; hwyrfan 10. 18*
(*b*) ; *ind. prs.* 3.*s.* hwerfeᵭ xxviii.
15 (*a*); hwærfeᵭ xx. 211 (*a*);
hwerfᵭ 81. 27* (*a*), 126. 5 (*a*),
129. 21 (*a*); hwærfᵭ xx. 217
(*a*); *sbj. prs.* hwerfe 100. 10
(*a*); *prs. p.* hwerfende 16. 33*
(*a*).

gehwierfan, *wv.* bring back, restore ; *pp. n. pl. f.* gehwerfde
49. 8*.

hwierflic, *adj.* changing, transitory ; *n. pl. f.* hwerflice 25. 10*.

hwil, *f.* space of time, time ; *g.*
hwile 44. 14 ; *a. fq. in adv.
phrases* : hwile ær, some time
before xxvii. 15 ; hwyle xx. 266;
sume hwile *fq.* 45. 12, xv. 10
&c. ; ane hwile, for a while,
for a time 52. 15, 124. 19, *cf.*
14. 26, 120. 29, 126. 29, 141.
21 ; ænige h. 20. 22 ; nane h.
58. 30 ; oᵭre hwile . . . oᵭre
hwile, at one time . . . at another
64. 18 &c. ; ᵭa hwile ᵭe, *conj.*
while, *fq.* 23. 14 &c. ; *pl. g.*
hwila 44. 15 ; *d.* hwilum, *used
as adv.* at times, occasionally,
fq. 10. 8, ii. 9 &c. ; hwylum
xxix. 49; hwilan xxix. 53 ; nu
hwilum 123. 8 ; hwilum eft 132.
8 &c. ; hwilum . . . hwilum,
sometimes . . . at other times
Pr. 2, 3 &c. ; *a.* hwila, moments
44. 11, 13.

hwilwendlic, *adj.* temporary,
transitory ; *n.* 147. 27, 28 ; *g.
wk.* hwilwendlican*, hwilendlican 44. 12 ; *a. pl. wk.* hwilendlican 20. 14.

hwit, *adj.* white ; 145. 24 ; *a.
pl. m.* hwite 74. 1, xix. 23.

hwon, *adv.* somewhat, a little ;
12. 13, x. 59.

hwonne, 1) *interrog.* when ? 60.
8, 148. 1.   2) *conj. w. sbj.* until,
20. 31, 124. 10.   3) *gives indef.
meaning to advv. of time,* nu
hwonne 109. 23, 131. 23; seldum
hwonne 115. 8.

hwurfolnes, *f.* fickleness; *d.* hwur-
fulnesse 47. 19.

hwȳ, *inst. of* hwæt ; *used as
interrog. adv. w. sbj. or ind.*
why ? 10. 17, x. 21 &c. ; *fq.* hwi
in B *and* C, 17. 5 iv. 33 &c.

hwyrft, *m.* revolution, orbit ; *a.*
126. 2*.

hycgan, *wv.* think, imagine; ge-
hycgan xv. 9 ; gehicgan xix.
17 ; *ind. prs.* 3.*s.* ; hygeᵭ xix.
1 ; *sbj. prs.* 3.*s.* gehicgge xiii.
26.

hȳd, *f.* skin, hide ; *d.* hyde 31.
32.

hȳdan, *wv.* hide, conceal ; *ind.
prs.* 3.*s.* gehyt 131. 6, 136. 20;
pst. 3.*s.* hydde xxix. 55 ; *sbj. pst.*
hydde 140. 14, 17 ; *pp.* geheded
xx. 151 ; *a. f.* gehydde 95. 22,
xxii. 60 ; *n. pl. m.* iv. 41 ; *f.*
gehydda xix. 32 ; gehydde 74.
7*.

hyge, *m.* mind, heart ; hige xi. 53,
xix. 45 ; *d.* xv. 9 ; *a.* xxxi. 20.

hygesnottor, *adj.* wise ; *d. pl.*
higesnotrum x. 7.

hyhtlic, *adj.* hoped for, pleasant ;
f. hyhtlicu xxi. 11.

hyngran, *wv.* be hungry ; *impers.
sbj. prs.* hingre, hingrige* 60. 11.

hyrian, *wv. w. d.* imitate ; *ind.
prs. pl.* hyriaᵭ 108. 11 *n.* ; hyri-
gaᵭ 146. 7*.

hyrnede, *adj.* horned, beaked ; *a.
pl. m.* hyrnde xxvi. 23.

hyrst, *f.* ornament, trappings ; *g.
pl.* hyrsta xiv. 9.

hyrstan, *wv.* dress, adorn ; *pp.
n. pl. m.* gehyrste 111. 16, xxv.
8.

hyspan, *wv.* revile ; 45. 10.

hysping, *f.* reviling ; *a.* hispinge
45. 12.

hȳᵭ, *f.* port, haven ; 89. 9, xxi. 11,
13.

I.

ic, *pron.* I ; 8. 6, MPr. 8. &c. ; îc
39. 31* ; *g.* min 41. 6 &c. ; *d.* me
8. 12 &c. ; *a.* 8. 9 &c.

īdel, *adj.* useless, vain ; 68. 29 ;
idle, lazy 144. 8 ; *g. wk.* idelan
45, 21 ; *d. wk.* 46. 9 ; *a. wk.*
46. 3 ; *inst.* idele 29. 26 ; *a.pl.f.*
idle v. 27.

īdelgeorn, *adj.* lazy, ease-loving ;
n. pl. m. wk. ge idelgeornan
139. 8.

īecan, *wv.* increase, add to ; ecan,
ᵹeecan* 75. 15 ; ycan 60. 15 ;
ind.prs. 3.*s.* ecð 65. 21 ; *pl.* ecað
60. 24* ; *pst.* 3.*s.* ecte 26. 22* ;
pp. geecced 125. 15.

īegland, *n.* island ; iglond xvi.
12 ; eglond i. 16 ; *g.* iglandes
xvi. 17 ; *d.* ieglande 34. 8* ;
iglande 116. 4* ; iglonde viii.
49, xxvi. 58 ; *a.* igland xxvi. 32 ;
iglond 115. 22* ; iland 67. 32*.

ield, *f.* age, period ; eld 33. 21*,
viii. 4.

ielde, *pl.* men ; *d.* eldum viii. 38,
xii. 17, xiii. 60, xx. 100, xxix.
34.

ielding, *f.* delay ; eldung 120. 2*.

ieldran, *pl.* parents, ancestors ;
ildran 34. 21 N. ; eldran 24. 13*,
34. 31, 69. 13*, i. 58 ; *g.* eldrena
70. 20*, xiii. 28 ; eldrana 57.
12*.

ierman, *wv.* ill-treat ; *ind.pst.* 3.*s.*
yrmde ix. 47.

ierming, *m.* wretched person ; *g.
pl.* erminga 89. 11 ; yrminga
xxi. 17.

iermð, *f.* misery ; *a.* ermðe 60. 24*,
65. 27 ; yrmðe, earmðe* 59. 14 ;
pl. n. yrmða 118. 3, 5 ; *g.*
ermða xvi. 8 ; yrmða 71. 23 ;
eormða 67. 29* ; *d.* ermðum
89. 11*, 116. 26*, 134. 15*,
134. 21 ; yrmðum xxi. 19, xxvi.
71 ; eormðum 52. 8* ; *a.* ermða
19. 4, 65. 21, 117. 21 ; yrmða
60. 9.

iernan, *sv3.* run ; irnan 101. 29 ;

ind. prs. 3.*s.* irneð v. 15 ; irnð
135. 27*, 28* ; *pl.* irnað 108.
14, 112. 29, 143. 3 ; yrnað 112.
24 ; *pst. pl.* urnon 49. 8, 102.
27 ; *sbj. prs.* ierne, irne* 24. 24 ;
pl. irnen 82. 28.

ierre, *n.* anger ; irre xxv. 51 ; *g.*
yrres 81. 24* ; *d.* irre 12. 4.

ierringa, *adv.* angrily ; irringa
71. 6* ; yrringa xviii. 7 ; yrrenga
xxvi. 84.

iersian, *wv.* be angry ; *ind. prs.*
2.*s.* yrsast 19. 12 ; *prs.p.* irsiende
81. 18* ; *a. wk.* yrsiendan 114.
29.

iersung, *f.* anger ; irsung 81. 20*,
112. 4*, xx. 186 ; *g.* irsunge xx.
199 ; *a.* yrsunga xx. 192.

īeðe, *adj.* easy ; *n.* eðe 145. 5 ;
pl. n. ieðe 16. 13 ; eðe 92. 27 ;
comp. n. eðre 81. 13*.

īeðelīce, *adv.* easily ; eðelice 98.
23, xx. 276 ; *sup.* eðelicost 146.
28*.

īeðnes, *f.* ease, comfort ; *g. pl.*
eðnessa 7. 15*.

īewan, *wv.* show, reveal ; eowian
78. 7, 85. 25, 97. 28, 104. 25 ;
ind. prs. 3.*s.* geewð 131. 7 ;
eowað 61. 11*, 136. 21*, xxix.
72 ; *pp.* geeowad 55. 6.

ilca, *pron. adj.* same ; 48. 27, ix.
24 &c. ; *n.* ilce 15. 23 &c. ; *g.d.a.*
ilcan 7. 5, 10. 9, xi. 37 &c. ; *a. n.*
ilce 12. 22 &c. ; *pl.* ilcan 16. 7
&c. *and* xxiv. 63.

ilce, *adv.* swa ilce, in the same way ;
35. 3 &c.

in, *prep. a)* w. *d.* in, 7. 12*, xx.
238 ; *foll. case,* i. 15. *b) w. a.*
into, 7. 4*.

inc, *v.* git.

incofa, *wm.* breast, mind ; *d.* incofan xxii. 18.

ingehygd, *f. n.* mind, thoughts ; *a.*
xxv. 42.

inierfe, *n.* household goods,
valuables ; *a.* 31. 19.

inn, *adv.* in ; in to 8. 16*, xxii.
57 ; in gæð on, enters 27. 17* ;
in on, into 53. 6*, 91. 26, 96.
26.

innan, 1) *prep. a) w. d.* in,
within; innon 73. 31*. *b) w. a.*
into; innon 86. 19, 91. 26*, 96.
26*. 2) *adv.* within, inside; 36.
9*, 12, 51. 4, 73. 5, 8*, 141.
16*, v. 41, 44; innon 73. 5*; inne
43. 31*, i. 72, xxv. 19, 45. *v.
also* oninnan.

innanweard, 1) *adj.* inward, in-
ternal; *inst.* mid innewearde
mode 50. 11, 28. 119. 11; inneweardan 94. 28*, 119. 11*. 2)
adv. within; 92. 3.

innian, *wv.* enter; *prs. ind.* 3.*s.*
innað 51. 4 *n.*

innoð, *m.* interior, inside (of
body); *d.* innoðe 51. 4.

innung, *f.* contents; 72. 22.

ingeðanc, *m.* thoughts, mind; 54.
2*, 56. 4*, 106. 25; ingeðonc
106. 10, xxvi. 118; *g.* ingeðances 68. 3*, xvi. 22; ingeðonces
44. 31; *d.* ingeðance 52. 16*;
ingeðonce 51. 25; *a.* ingeðanc
95. 6*; ingeðonc 78. 5, xxii. 12,
21, xxiii. 8, xxvi. 94; *a. pl.*
ingeðoncas 14. 27.

inweardlic, *adj., v.* forinweard-
lic.

inweardlice, *adv.* inwardly, earnestly; xxii. 2.

inwitðanc, *m.* evil thought; *pl. n.*
inwidðoncas ix. 8; *d.* inwitðon-
cum xxvii. 23.

is, *n.* ice; 126. 20, xxviii. 59.

isceald, *adj.* icy-cold; *a. f.* iscalde
xxvii. 3.

isig, *adj.* icy; 105. 13.

ismere, *m.* frozen pool; xxviii.
62.

L.

la, *interj.* oh! ah! why! 8. 13,
xi. 101 &c.; nese, la, nese 58.
29, 62. 19.

gelác, *n.* rapid movement, com-
motion; laguflóda g. xx. 173;
storma g. xxvi. 29.

lácan, *rv. a) intrans.* move quickly,
fly; xxiv. 9; *ind. prs. pl.* lacað
xxviii. 22. *b) trans.* entice; *sbj.*

pst. pl. ðe liolcen (oleccan B)
15. 29.

lácnian, *wv.* treat (a disease),
cure; *ind. prs.* 3.*s.* lacnað 134.
17.

lǽce, *m.* physician; 38. 8, 132. 6,
15, 134. 16; *d.* 123. 13, 33; *pl.
n.* lǽcas 132. 11 *n.*; *g.* lǽca 107.
28.

lǽcecræft, *m.* (art of) medicine;
remedy; 38. 8, 51. 1.

lǽcedom, *m.* remedy, medicine;
127. 24, 135. 20; *a.* 50. 20.

lǽdan, *wv.* lead; 51. 11, 102. 2,
123. 33, xiv. 9; to lædanne 51.
7; *ind. prs.* 2.*s.* lædst 100. 5,
140. 1; 3.*s.* lǽt 27. 8*, 60. 31*;
gelǽt 104. 27; *pl.* lædað 48. 11,
vii. 40; *pst.* 3.*s.* lædde 103. 10,
xxvi. 16, 39; *pl.* læddon 102. 27,
i. 2; *sbj. prs.* læde 51. 13, 123.
13, 14, 139. 30, 33; *pl.* læden
73. 30*; *pp.* gelæd 36. 21.

læden, *n.* Latin language; *d.* of
lædene Pr. 9. *v. also* bóclæden.

lǽfan, *wv.* leave; bequeath; to
læfanne 41. 5; *ind. prs. pl.* læfað
24. 10; læfed 23. 20, 42. 9.

lǽnan, *wv.* lend, grant; *pp. n. pl.*
gelænde 31. 11.

lǽne, *adj.* transitory, precarious;
41. 18; *g.* lænes xxvi. 113; *d.
wk.* lænan xix. 35; *a.* lænne xxvi.
106; *wk.* lænan ix. 58, xx. 157;
pl. n. lænu xxi. 29; *d.* lænum 53.
13, 54. 1; *wk.* lænan 74. 8*; *a.*
xx. 223.

lǽran, *wv.* teach; 140. 2; to læranne
127. 25; *ind. prs.* 3.*s.* lærð 137.
22; gelæreð 47. 20; *pl.* lærað
103. 14, 139. 6; *pst.* 1.*s.* gelærde
17. 13, 20. 10; 3.*s.* lærde 9. 2,
79. 17, 140. 16; *sbj. prs.* lære
69. 8; *pp.* gelæred 8. 18, 15. 14.

lǽstan, *wv. w. d.* follow; i. 27.

gelǽstan, *wv. a) trans.* perform,
carry out; 58. 21, 73. 16, 105. 31,
139. 25; *ind. pst.* gelæste 7.
9 *n.*; *pl.* gelæstan, followed,
marched i. 13; *sbj. prs.* gelæste
50. 24; *pl.* gelæsten 58. 23. *b)
intrans.* last, endure; *inf.* vii. 19.

lǣtan, *rv. a*) allow; *b*) leave; leave behind; *c*) think, deem; *d*) cause; 38. 12 (*a*), 71. 22 (*c*), 123. 26 (*a*); l. ða bǣtinge, let go 144. 30; l. bion, let alone, drop 88. 32; *ind. prs.* 1.*s.* ic lǣte nu to . . . set store by 121. 26; 2.*s.* lǣtest iv. 50 (*a*); lǣtǣst 16. 30 (*b*); lǣtst 105. 15*(*b*), xxiv. 29 (*b*); 3.*s.* lǣt 26. 6 (*a*), xi. 72 (*a*) &c., 133. 25 (*d*.): *pl.* lǣtað 23. 7, 9 (*a*), 24. 10 (*b*), viii. 11 (*c*); place, 130. 16, 141. 1, 3; lǣte ge 72. 19 (*a*); *pst.* 3.*s.* let xxvi. 23 (*b*); *imp.* lǣt v. 30 (*a*); *pl.* lǣtað 8. 23 (*a*); *shj. prs.* lǣte 119. 23 (*b*), xvi. 7 (*b*); lǣte 104. 2 (*a*); *pl.* lǣten 67. 6 (*a*); *pst.* lete 117. 5 (*a*), 119. 30 (*b*), i. 66 (*a*), 68 (*b*?); *pl.* leten 67. 6 (*a*).

lāf, *f.* remnant; *d.* to lafe, remaining, left over 46. 26.

lagu, *m.* sea, flood; ix. 40.

lagufiōd, *m.* sea; *g. pl.* lagufloda xx. 173.

lagustrēam, *m.* sea; xi. 43; *a.* xx. 111, xxvi. 16.

land, *n.* land; country; 40. 21; lond 29. 12; *g.* landes 91. 22, 126. 20*; londes 42. 16*, xii. 27; *d.* lande *about* 9 *times*, 43. 17 &c. *and* xii. 6, xxviii. 57; londe 43. 25, 26, xiii. 18; *a.* land 51. 29*, 60. 29*, 115. 20*, ix. 40; lond 40. 17, xii. 1; *pl.* lond 29. 10; *d.* londum 42. 30.

lang, *adj.; gen. of time,* long; 44. 25; *n.* 44. 19, x. 66; *of body,* tall 87. 4; long 117. 28, 127. 32; *n. wk.* lange 117. 32; *d. wk.* langan 133. 26; *a.* longne 120. 27; *f.* lange iv. 46, x. 64, xxvi. 103; *n.* lang 100. 28; ymbe long, at great length 125. 23; *pl. wk.* langan 127. 29; *d.* longum 133. 24; *comp.* lengra 120. 29; *a.* lengran 126. 7; *pl. a.* langran 10. 11*; *sup. a.* lengestne 126. 7.

gelang, *adj.* dependent on, owing to; *n.* on ðe gelong 15. 24.

lange, *adv. of time,* long, for a long time; *about* 19 *times*, 9. 2, vii.

19 &c.; longe *about* 10 *times*, 103. 3, i. 50 &c.; long xxvi. 99; *comp.* leng 84. 3 &c. *and* xxviii. 8; *sup.* lengest ix. 17.

langfǣre, *adj.* lasting, enduring; *g.* longfǣres 117. 26.

langsum, *adj.* prolonged, tedious; 45. 17.

lār, *f.* teaching, doctrine; 27. 17, 139. 20; *g.* lare 51. 2, 135. 21, 139. 21; *d.* 95. 15, v. 22, xxii. 42; lǣre, lesson 137. 14; *a.* lare 9. 3, 104. 29, i. 68; *pl. d.* larum 8. 23, 11. 4, 14. 18, 20. 12; *a.* lara 50. 26, 101. 14, 108. 1.

lārēow, *m.* teacher; 141. 12, xxx. 3; *pl.* lareowas 57. 17, xiii. 38; *g.* lareowa xiii. 42; lariowa x. 55; *a.* lareowas 57. 16.

lāst, *m.* footprint, track; *a.* last weardigan, remain behind xx. 241; on last, in the end, at last 15. 5, 48. 1, 100. 23.

late, *adv.* slowly, late; 46. 32, 148. 5; *comp.* lator 142. 18; *sup.* latost 91. 16.

lāttēow, *m.* guide; leader; xx. 278; ladðeow 82. 16, 105. 2; *a.* ladteow 57. 13.

lāð, 1) *adj.* hostile; hateful; 64. 26, viii. 38, xv. 6; *pl.* laðe 9. 24; *a.* 28. 4; *comp. a.* laðran iv. 24; *a. n. wk.* laðre 22. 3. 2) *sbst. n.* offence; *g.* laðes 19. 27.

lāðlīce, *adv.* hatefully, horribly; xxvi. 83.

lēaf, *f.* permission; *d.* leafe xi. 67, xx. 131; *a.* 80. 29, 120. 27, x. 67, xxvi. 21.

lēaf, *n.* leaf; xx. 98; *pl.* xxix. 67; *g.* leafa 10. 12, iv. 24; *d.* leafum 92. 2; *a.* leaf 10. 13, xi. 57.

gelēafa, *wm.* belief, faith; *d.* geleafan 12. 21 *n.,* 14. 19, v. 26; *a.* 12. 25.

leahtor, *m.* vice, sin; *pl.* leahtras xxii. 25, 29.

lēan, *n.* reward; *a.* 113. 14; *pl. g.* leana 54. 17, 108. 13, 134. 30; lǣna 54. 17*; *d.* leanum 111. 4, 113. 8; *a.* lean 18. 24, 113. 14.

lēanian, *wv. w. d.* reward ; 134.
25 ; *sbj. prs.* leanige 137. 10 ;
pp. geleanod 119. 22.

lēas, 1) *adj. a) w. g.* devoid of ;
ciða leas xii. 5. *b)* false, feigned ;
wk. leasa 63. 27 ; *f.* leas 47. 18.
82. 25 ; *wk. f.* lease 47. 6, 48.
1 ; *n.* leas 68. 8 ; *wk.* lease 10.
22, iv. 46 ; *g.* leases 41. 12, 45.
24 ; *d.* leasum 45. 8, xxiii. 8 ;
f. leasre 68. 10, 100. 25 ; *wk.*
hiora leasan cyninge 66. 22 ;
a. wk. 114. 28 ; *pl.* lease, un-
truthful 116. 13 ; *wk.* leasan 48.
10, 51. 24, 103. 14 ; *g. wk.*
leasena 51. 16, 55. 6, 101. 11 ;
d. leasum 18. 3 &c. *and* xxvi.
1, 99 ; *a. f.* leasa xii. 27 ; *wk.*
leasan 15. 29 &c. 2) *sbst. n.*
falsehood ; *d.* lease 141. 19, xxx.
18 ; *a.* leas 118. 14.

lēaslic, *adj.* false, unreal ; *a. f.*
leaslice 54. 6.

lēasspellung, *f.* false speech,
falsehood ; *d.* leasspellunga 14.
4.

lēasung, *f.* falsehood, false story ;
21. 21 ; *pl. n.* leasunga 99. 5 ;
leasungum 45. 18, 116. 27 ; *a.*
leasunga 99. 4.

leax, *m.* salmon ; *a.* xix. 12.

leccan, *wv.* wet, moisten ; *ind.
prs. pl.* leccað 136. 17, xxix. 63 ;
pp. geleht 80. 17*, xx. 98.

lecgan, *wv.* place, lay ; 37. 8 ; l.
ðone mæst, lower 144. 30.

lēf, *adj.* diseased, weak ; 121. 12.

lencten, *m.* spring (season) ; 49.
18 ; *a.* on lencten 10. 12*, 49.
18* ; on lengten 136. 19*.

lenctentīd, *f.* springtime ; *a.* on
l. xxix. 67.

lendan, *wv.* arrive ; *ind. prs. 3.s.*
gelent 53. 6.

lengo, *f.* length (of time) ; *a.* lengu,
lenge* 44. 13.

lēo, *wmf.* lion, lioness ; 57. 9 (*f.*),
72. 6, 7, 114. 30 ; lio 114. 30* ;
d. leon 116. 16 ; *a.* 102. 7 (*m.*),
xiii. 18 (*f.*) ; *pl. n.* leon xxvi.
83 (*m.?*).

lēode, *pl. m.* people ; *g.* leoda

xii. 6, xxvi. 40, 113 ; *d.* leodum
MPr. 4, xxx. 8.

lēodfruma, *wm.* chief, leader ; *d.*
leodfruman i. 27.

lēodhata, *wm.* tyrant ; *g.* leodhatan 36. 29.

lēodscipe, *m.* nation ; *d.* xxx. 2 ;
a. i. 68.

lēof, *adj.* dear ; acceptable ; 20. 9,
i. 47 ; *a.* leofne xxvi. 72 ; *n. pl.*
n. leofe 16. 12 ; *comp. n.* leofre
22. 32, 24. 5, 139. 24, i. 41 ; *a.*
n. 22. 3 ; *sup. n.* leofast 20. 27 ;
n. pl. wk. leofostan 67. 2.

lēoftǣle, *adj.* acceptable, pleasant ; *a. pl. m.* 28. 5 ; *comp. n.*
pl. leoftælran 28. 1.

lēofwende, *adj.* amiable, popular ;
comp. leofwendra 27. 30.

lēogan, *sv2.* tell a lie, make an
erroneous statement ; 112. 3,
xxv. 50 ; *ind. prs. 1.s.* leoge 33.
1 ; *3.s.* lihð 47. 15 ; him on
lihð, misrepresent him 68. 16.

leoht, 1) *sbst. n.* light ; 14. 1, 52.
6 ; *g.* leohtes 10. 7, iv. 11 &c. ;
d. leohte 10. 5, iv. 8 &c. ; liohte
103. 15 ; *a.* leoht 9. 12, iii. 5
&c. 2) *adj.* bright ; xxix. 52 ;
n. wk. leohte 136. 13 ; *d. wk.*
leohtan v. 22 ; *a.* leohtne v. 5 ;
inst. leohte v. 26 ; *pl. d.*
leohtum larum, *metaph.* 14. 18 ;
a. leohte 17. 24, 49. 21 ; *comp.*
n. leohtre 95. 7 ; *a. n.* xxii. 22 ;
sup. leohtost ix. 17.

leoht, *adj.* light (not heavy) ;
comp. pl. metaph. leohtran 23.
14.

leohte, *adv.* brightly, brilliantly ;
39. 21, ix. 13.

leohtfruma, *wm.* creator of light ;
xi. 72.

lēoma, *wm.* ray of light, radiance ;
xxii. 22 ; *d.* leoman xxi. 36 ; *a.*
v. 5.

leornian, *wv.* learn, study ; 126.
25, xxviii. 77 ; leornigan 7. 17,
ind. pst. 2.s. ; leornodest 41.
27, 78. 30 ; liornodest 41.
23 ; *pl.* leornodon 36. 28, 70.
22 ; *imp. pl.* leorniað 35. 18 ;

sbj. prs. pl. leornigen 133. 26;
pp. geleornod 35. 19; *a. f.* geleornode Pr. 8.

lēoð, *n.* song, poem; *d.* leoðe Pr.
10, 26. 23; *a.* leoð *about* 8 *times*
B *and* C, 8. 15 &c. *and* MPr.
4; lioð 50. 7, 70. 1, 124. 18;
pl. g. leoða 135. 19, xxx. 2;
lioða 127. 29, ii. 1; *d.* leoðum
141. 13, xxx. 8; *a.* lioð 8. 6.

lēoðwyrhta, *wm.* song maker,
poet; MPr.; 3.*pl.* leoðwyrhtan
18. 28.

lesan, *sv5.* gather; *ind. prs. 3.s.*
lisð 61. 10.

lettan, *wv.* hinder; gelettan 142.
18; *ind. prs. 3.s.* let 71. 11;
pl. gelettað 142. 19; *sbj. prs.*
lette 105. 32.

libban, *wv.* live, be alive; 46. 31
&c. *and* x. 64, xx. 107; liban
ix. 58 (J); to libbanne 41. 4; *ind.
prs. 2.s.* liofost 22. 28*; *3.s.*
leofað 22. 5, 26. 16*, 65. 13;
liofað 22. 11, 16; liofað 109.
30*; *pl.* libbað 114. 18, 133.
18; *pst.* lifde 41. 4; *sbj. prs. pl.*
libban 22. 29*; *prs. p.* libbende
45. 26; *g.* libbendes 71. 5, 80.
20, xiii. 33; *d.* libbendum 13.
12; *pl.* libbende 40. 1; *g.* lifgendra xx. 278.

līc, *n.* body; *d.* lice viii. 47, xvii.
12, xx. 236, xxii. 39; *a.* lic 116.
15*, xxvi. 76.

gelīc, *adj. w. d.* similar; relevant,
pertinent; xxv. 26; *f. præd.* 22.
15; *n.* 84. 21 &c.; *g.* gelices
88. 10, xxvi. 93; *a.* gelicne 69.
18, 91. 23, 140. 27, 145. 20,
xvii. 2; *f.* gelice 79. 32, xxvi.
2; *n.* gelic 43. 25, 99. 6; *wk.*
gelican 148. 19; *pl.* gelice 30.
5, xvii. 5; *n.* 87. 25; *a. f.* gelica 91. 23; gelice xx. 54; *comp.*
gelicra 115. 4; *n. pl.* gelicran
122. 14, 146. 5; *sup.* gelicost
xxv. 18, xxvi. 88; *n.* xix. 12;
n. pl. m. gelicoste 22. 26.

gelīca, *wm.* equal; ðin gelica 79.
17, 25, xx. 37; *pl.* hiora gelican
x. 59; *d.* gelicum 34. 24.

gelīce, *adv.* similarly, in the same
way (as); alike; 46. 15, 58. 6,
69. 19, 148. 23, x. 31; swa gelice 107. 21*; *sup.* gelicost 104.
16, xx. 211, 217 (*or adj.?*).

līcettan, *wv.* pretend; *ind. prs.*
3.s. licet 47. 15, 22; *pl.* licettað
58. 21; *pst. 3.s.* licette 45. 13,
115. 24, xxvi. 36.

licgan, *sv5.* lie, be placed; 115. 6;
ind. prs. 3.s. ligeð 42. 8; ligð
82. 16, 115. 5, xvi. 12, xx. 279,
xxix. 52; geligeð v. 16; *pl.*
licgað 104. 8, 147. 4; licggað
46. 29; *sbj. prs.* licge xii. 6.

līchama, *wm.* body; 114. 5, xx.
241; lichoma *fg.* 36. 3 &c. *and*
xviii. 9, xxxi. 7; *g.* lichoman 45.
25, xxii. 25 &c.; *d.* Pr. 6 &c. *and*
xx. 181; *a.* 69. 23 &c. *and*
xxvi. 106, 119; *pl.* xxvi. 103;
a. 82. 3, 116. 28.

līchamlic, *adj.* of the body, carnal;
g. wk. lichomlican 26. 19; *pl. n.*
lichomlicu 87. 3; *wk.* lichamlican*, licumlican 54. 22; *d.* licamlicum*, licumlicum 54. 26.

līchamlīce, *adv.* in the body,
corporeally; lichomlice 45. 26,
148. 27*; licumlice *ib.*

līcian, *wv. w. d.* please; 29. 12,
101. 18, 142. 2; *ind. prs. 3.s.*
licað 43. 26 &c.; *pl.* liciað 16.
4 &c.; *pst.* licode 35. 6 &c.;
sbj. prs. licige 66. 2; *pl.* licien
29. 9; *pst.* licode 43. 28, 62. 13.

gelīcnes, *f.* similarity; *d.* gelicnesse 31. 14.

līcwierðe, *adj.* pleasing, praise-
worthy; *g.* licwyrðes 35. 9.

lidmann, *m.* sailor; *g. pl.* liðmonna xxvi. 63.

līefan, *wv.* allow; *pp.* lyfed xx.
244.

gelīefan, *wv. w. g. d. or a., or
clause,* believe; gelefan 84. 26,
106. 8, 121. 7 (*d.*), 138. 10 (*g.*),
14 (*g.*); ðe . . . swelces to gelefan,
believe such a thing of you 11.
13; gelyfan 90. 21, 122. 18 (*g.*);
to gelefanne 84. 2; *ind. prs. 1.s.*
gelefe 123. 2 (*g.*), gelyfe 12. 18;

2.*s.* geliefæst 13. 31 ; gelefst 12.
16, 84. 25 ; gelyfst 84. 22 ; 3.*s.*
gelyfð 107. 10 (*g.*) ; *pst.* 1.*s.* gelifde 12. 18* ; 3.*s.* gelyfde 115.
25*(*d.*),xxvi. 40(*d.*);*pl.*gelesdon
116. 27 (*d.*) ; gelyfdon xxvi. 99
(*d.*) ; *imp.* gelief, gelef* 31. 14 ;
sbj. prs. gelefe 118. 16 ; *pl.*
gelesen 109. 26 (*g.*),117. 15 (*g.*) ;
pst. gelesde 18. 33 (*a.*).
lieg, *mn.* flame ; lig 34. 27 N. ; leg
34. 27, xxix. 51 ; *d.* lege viii.
54 ; *g. pl.* lega ix. 17.
liegetu, *f.* lightning ; *a.* lygetu
99. 2* ; *a. pl.* ligeta 99. 2.
liehtan, *wv.* shine ; *ind. prs.* 3.*s.*
lyht 86. 8.
lietan, *wv. trans.* bend, incline ;
ind. prs. 3.*s.* lit xxvi. 119.
liexan, *wv.* shine ; lixan ix. 13.
lif, *n.* life ; 22. 31 &c. ; *g.* lifes
14. 1, xi. 72 &c. ; *d.* life, *esp. in
phrase* on ðys andweardan life
21. 17, xxi. 29 &c.; *a.* lif 20. 25,
vii. 40 &c. ; *a. pl.* (*or s.?*) lif
awriten 44. 5.
lifdæg, *m.* day of life ; *d. pl.*
lifdagum xv. 6, xxvi. 88.
lifer, *f.* liver ; *a.* lifre 103. 1.
lim, *n.* limb, member ; *a.* 86. 30,
90. 32 ; *pl.* limu 86. 26, 87. 18,
22, 23 *n.* ; *g.* lima 87. 24, 114.
8 ; *d.* limum 81. 14, 114. 8 ; *a.*
limu 90. 32.
limian, *wv.* cement, join ; *ind.
prs.* 3.*s.* gelimð 54. 17 ; *pp.*
gelimed 96. 14.
limpan, *sv*3. happen ; *ind. prs.*
3.*s.* limpð, gelimpð* 125. 20 ;
pst. 3.*s.* gelamp 101. 22; gelomp
7. 25*, xxvi. 17, 45. 4 ; *pp.* gelumpen iii. 9.
limplice, *adv.* suitably, fittingly ;
49. 17.
lindwigend, *m.* warrior ; *n. pl.*
lindwigende i. 13.
liss, *f.* kindness, favour ; *pl. g.*
lissa i. 59 ; *d.* lissum xxvi. 63.
list, *m.* cunning, skill ; art ; *a.*
MPr. 3 ; *pl.* listas xxvi. 108 ; *g.*
lista xxviii. 77 ; *d.* listum i. 59,
xiii. 42.

lið, *n.* strong drink ; *g.* liðes 111.
27.
liðan, *sv*1, journey, sail ; xxvi. 60;
ind. prs. pl. geliðað xxviii. 22.
liðe, *adj.* mild, pleasant ; 51. 4 ;
f. liðu 138. 18 ; *g.* liðes xii. 13 ;
d. wk. liðan 138. 29 ; *a.* liðne
132. 8 ; *d. pl.* liðum 8. 26.
locian, *wv.* (*gen. w.* on) look; xxii.
20 ; l. ongean 121. 10 ; see, 121.
15 ; to locienne 14. 14 ; *ind. prs.*
2.*s.*locast 121. 31;*pl.* lociað 121.
27, xi. 6 ; *pst.* lucude 11. 1 ; *pl.*
locodon 11. 1* ; *imp.* loca 14. 9,
99. 21 ; *sbj. prs.* locie to ... 129.
30 ; *prs. p.* lociende 148. 22.
lof, *n.* praise ; 43. 31, 138. 19 ; *g.*
lofes 47. 8, 108. 13 ; *d.* lofe 36.
25, 44. 29 ; *a.* lof 104. 7 ; renown 43. 25.
gelome, *adv.* frequently ; ix. 60,
xxx. 5, 7.
loppe, *wf.* flea ; 36. 11.
losian, *wv.* be lost ; perish ; 25.
27, 28, 71. 6, x. 37, xviii. 8 ;
losigan 46. 18 ; *ind. prs. pl.*
losiað 63. 26 ; *pst.* 3.*s.* losade
103. 13 ; *pl.* losodon 44. 7 ; *sbj.
prs.* losige 117. 25 ; *pl.* losien
26. 5.
lot, *n.* wile, deceit ; 10. 22, iv. 46.
lotwrenc, *m.* wile, deceit ; *a. pl.*
lotwrencas 129. 6.
lox, *m.* lynx ; 73. 3.
lucan, *sv*2. *a*) lock, fasten ; *b*)
pluck, pull up ; *ind. prs.* 3.*s.*
lycð xii, 28 (*b*) ; *pp.* locen wið
hire gecynde 57. 6 (*a*).
lufian, *wv.* love ; 58. 22 &c. *and*
xxvii. 31 ; to lufianne 108. 21,
113. 14 ; *ind. prs.* 2.*s.* lufast 29.
26 ; 3.*s.* lufað 22. 17 &c. *and*
xx. 223 ; *pl.* lufiað 28. 6 &c. ;
pst. 3.*s.* lufode 124. 14, xxvi. 63,
65, 89 ; lufude 34. 6 ; *pl.* lufedon
67. 21, xxvi. 91 ; *sbj. prs.* lufie
124. 16 ; lufige 57. 10, xiii. 20,
xxvii. 28.
lufigend, *m.* lover ; *pl. d.* lufigen-
dum 70. 14 ; lufiendum 73. 16 ;
a. lufiendas 62. 27, 73. 20.
lufu, *swf.* love ; 23. 8, 93. 18 ; *g.*

lufan i. 59 ; *d.* lufe 50. 1, 54.
18, 89. 7, xxi. 7 ; lufan 101. 11,
116. 9, 12 ; *a.* lufe 103. 9, 130.
9, 16, 136. 29, xxix. 90 : lufan
xi. 81 ; *d. pl.* lufum, sake 22.
22, 51. 19, 54. 16, 67. 20.

lungre, *adv.* quickly, suddenly;
vii. 19.

lust, *m.* desire, pleasure ; 55. 10,
12, MPr. 3 ; *g.* lustes 15. 30 ; *d.*
luste 143. 3 ; *a.* lust 88. 17, 93.
21 ; *pl. d.* lustum 53. 25, 74. 25,
115. 6, ix. 44.

lustbǣre, *adj.* pleased, glad ; 50.
10 ; *a.* lusðbærne 54. 26.

lustbǣrlīce, *adv.* pleasantly ; 8. 6,
103. 23.

lustbǣrnes, *f.* desire ; pleasure ;
g. lustbærnesse 8. 11 ; *a.* 74. 7.

lustlīce, *adv.* gladly, willingly; 25.
4, 50. 27, 123. 26, ii. 1.

lūtan, *sv2.* incline, sink (of the sun);
sbj. prs. lute 57. 25.

lyft, *f.* air, atmosphere ; 80. 1, ix.
40 &c. ; *g.* lyfte xx. 173 ; *d.* 80.
25, 105. 10, xxiv. 13, xxix. 52 ;
d. pl. lyftum, clouds xx. 98.

lystan, *wv. impers. w. a. and g.*
19. 14 ; *ind. prs.* 3.*s.* lysteð x.
14, xix. 11, 39 ; lyst 11. 26, xix.
16, 33, xxxi. 1 ; *pst.* lyste 18. 15
&c. *and* ix. 19, xxvi. 71 ; *sbj.*
prs. lyste Pr. 11 &c. *and* x. 1.

gelystan, *wv.* fill with desire,
make glad ; *pp.* guðe gelysted
i. 9.

lȳtel, *adj.* little, small ; 41. 18,
x. 55 ; *wk.* lytla 46. 26 ; *f.*
lytlu 41. 25 ; *wk.* lytle 36. 11 ;
n. lytel 124. 22 &c. *and* x. 9 ;
g. lytles 31. 22, xxii. 47 ; lytles
hwæt 23. 23, 24. 23 ; *d.* litlum
xxvi. 36 ; *wk.* lytlan 13. 33 &c.
and xx. 179 ; lytlon 30. 13* ; *a.*
lytelne 97. 15 ; litellne 146. 21* ;
f. lytle 14. 26 &c.; *n.* lytel 148. 8;
wk. lytle 97. 18 ; *pl. f.* lytla 26.
9; *d.* lytlum 24. 21 &c.; *comp. f.?*
læsse xxviii. 22 ; *n.* 28. 14, xx.
117 &c. ; *d.* læssan 77. 6 &c.; *a.*
123. 8, 141. 2, xxviii. 12 ; *n.*
læsse 148. 10; *pl.* læssan 83. 2 ;

d. 110. 27 ; *sup. d. wk.* læstan
81. 15 ; *n. pl.* 36. 7.

lytelīce, *adv.* craftily ; 15. 5.

lytig, *adj.* cunning, sly ; *a. wk.*
lytegan 114. 28 ; *n. pl.* lytige
30. 24.

lȳtle, *adv.* a little ; 50. 26 &c.
and xii. 13, xx. 181 ; *comp.* læs,
less 101. 7, 130. 18, 22 (*v.* also
ðylæs) ; *sup.* læst, least 15. 6,
117 30.

lȳtlian, *wv. trans.* diminish ; *ind.*
prs. 3.*s.* lytlað 65. 20.

M.

macian, *wv.* arrange, manage ;
ind. prs. 3.*s.* macað 98. 21.

gemæc, *adj.* well matched, suitable ; *a. n.* 24. 8.

mæg, *swv.* be able ; avail ; *ind.*
prs. 1 *and* 3.*s.* mæg 13. 7, xv.
9 &c. ; mag 42. 31 ; mæg þ
he ne wundrie, can help 92. 7 ;
to nauhte ne m., is good for
nothing 69. 8 ; m. ðæt, enables
38. 7 ; m. to sorge, may be
a care 24. 16 ; 2.*s.* meaht,
miht* 12. 10 &c. ; meht 92. 4 ;
pl. magon 22. 26, ii. 19 &c. :
magan 131. 31*, 139. 4 ; mahon
14. 10* ; *pst.* 1 *and* 3.*s.* meahte
12. 19 &c. ; mihte Pr. 4 ; 2.*s.*
meahtest 17. 21, 18. 25, xxiv.
15, 17 ; meahtes 18. 26, 33. 12,
16, 51. 14, 72. 11, xxiv. 8, 11 ;
mihtest 48. 15* ; *pl.* meahton
35. 4 &c. ; mihtan 34. 6*; mihte
we 23. 12*, 146. 19* ; *sbj. prs.*
mæge 12. 13 ; mægge xxviii.
64 ; mage 94. 29* ; *pl.* mægen
9. 27 &c. ; magen 28. 26* ;
mægon 59. 17*, 74. 8 ; mahan
18. 14* ; *pst.* meahte 45. 17 &c. ;
absol. xi. 102 ; *pl.* meahten 34.
18 &c.

mǣg, *m.* kinsman ; *d. pl.* mægum
71. 27 ; gemagum 54. 12.

mǣgden, *n.* maiden ; *g. pl.*
mædena 116. 6.

mǣgen, *m.* strength ; 93. 2, xx.

202 ; *g.* mægnes 108. 28 ; *d.*
mægene 38. 4 ; mægne iv. 27,
xx. 9, 66 ; *adv.* ealle mægene,
with might and main 112. 31,
147. 12, xiii. 64, 66, *cf.* 69. 14,
xxvi. 64, xxix. 96 ; eallon
mægene 53. 18*, 67. 5* ; *pl. n.*
mægno 72. 11 ; *g.* mægena,
powers 21. 11, 41. 12 ; mægna
xx. 258.

mægencræft, *m.* strength, power ;
xxvi. 105.

mægenstān, *m.* great rock ; v.
16.

mægð, *f.* maiden ; *a.* xxvi. 67.

mǣgð, *f.* family ; tribe, nation ;
mægðe xx. 160 ; *d.* 7. 1 ; *n. pl.*
mægða xxvi. 49.

gemægð, *f.* power, grandeur ; 40.
7*.

mægwlite, *m.* appearance, aspect ; *a. pl.* mægwlitas xxxi. 5.

mǣl, *n.* time, occasion; *g. pl.*
mæla i. 54, xxii. 65.

mǣnan, *wv. a)* mean, allude to ;
b) complain (of); 22. 2 (*b*) ;
ind. prs. 2.*s.* mænst 23. 23 (*b*) ;
3.*s.* mænð 118. 17 (*a*) ; *pst.* 2.*s.*
mændest 17. 20 (*b*) ; 3.*s.* mænde
128. 1 (*a*) ; *sbj. prs.* mæne 12.
25 (*a*) ; 71. 15 (*a*).

gemǣne, *adj.* common ; *d.* gemæ-
num 18. 25 ; *a. f.* gemæne xxix.
91 ; *wk.* gemænan 109. 16.

gemǣnelīce, *adv.* in common ;
136. 29.

mǣre *n.* boundary, borderland ;
a. gemære 103. 11 ; *a. pl.* gemæro xxix. 9 ; mæru 49. 23 *n.*

mǣre, *adj.* renowned, famous ; 68.
25, xxiv. 43 ; *g. wk.* mæran ix.
39, xxi. 6 ; *d.* mærum xxix. 97 ;
wk. mæran xxx. 4 ; *a. wk.* i. 14,
iv. 13, xi. 73, xx. 281 ; *pl. wk.*
xxix. 9 ; *d.* mærum xvii. 11 ;
comp. mærra 69. 5, xx. 18 ;
sup. mærost x. 34.

mǣrlic, *adj.* renowned, glorious ;
sup. mærlicost 75. 21.

mǣrsian, *wv.* proclaim, cele-
brate ; *ind. prs.* 3.*s.* mærsað i.
16 ; *pp. a. pl.* gemærsode,

marked out, distinguished ? 80.
12.

mǣrð, *f.* fame, glory ; *g.* mærðe
108. 10 ; *a.* 54. 6 ; *pl.* mærða
74. 24 ; *g.* 77. 3, xx. 26 ; *d.*
mærðum xx. 2 ; *a.* mærða 78.
13.

mǣst, *m.* ship's mast ; *a.* 144. 30.

mǣtan, *wv. impers.* dream ; *ind.
prs.* mæt 51. 13 ; *sbj. prs.* mæte
58. 8.

mǣte, *adj.* unimportant ; *comp.
n. pl.* mætran 130. 3 ; *sup. pl.
wk.* mætestan 130. 6, 8 ; mæstan 130. 8*.

mǣð, *f.* measure, capacity ; 145.
7, 147. 13 ; *d.* Pr. 14, 145. 9,
147. 14, 16.

magister, *m.* master ; teacher ;
70. 30 ; *a.* 57. 10, 66. 24, xiii.
20 ; *g. pl.* magistra xxx. 4.

magurinc, *m.* man, warrior ; *pl.*
magorincas x. 56 ; *g.* magorinca i. 26.

geman, *swv. w. a. or g.* remember ;
inf. gemunan 11. 13, 20. 2, 34.
30, 58. 30, 104. 18, 106. 24 ;
ind. prs. 1.*s.* geman 96. 6, 97. 8,
100. 11, 106. 27, 119. 1 ; 2.*s.*
gemanst 118. 30 ; gemunst 106.
28 ; 3.*s.* gemonð 57. 12* ; *pl.*
gemunon 34. 18 ; *pst.* 1.*s.* gemunde ; *w. a.* 13. 3, 101. 13 ;
2.*s.* gemyndest 95. 32 ; 3.*s. w. g.*
gemunde 7. 15, 8. 3, i. 57, 79 ;
imp. gemun 113. 12 ; *sbj. prs.*
gemune 122. 7.

mān, 1) *sbst. n.* wickedness,
crime ; ix. 7 ; *g.* manes i. 44 ;
d. mane 7. 10 ; *a.* man 39. 18.
2) *adj.* false ; wicked ; *n. pl.*
mane aðas 10. 22 ; māne iv.
48.

gemāna, *wm.* intercourse, society ;
d. gemanan 11. 23.

mānfull, *adj.* sinful, wicked ; *pl.*
manfulle 10. 19 ; *g.* manfulra
12. 2.

gemang, *n.* on gemong *prep. w.
d.* among 102. 3, 119. 12.

manian, *wv.* warn, restrain ; *pp.
a. pl.* gemanode xi. 24 ; *f.* 49. 3.

manig, *adj*. many a, many; monig
i. 8; *f.* manigu xi. 44; manig
147. 2; *n.* 70. 21, 145. 5; mænig
86. 5, 93. 12; *g.* maniges 88. 9;
manies 126. 16*; *d.* manegum
7. 10*, 43. 13, 65. 14*, 66. 12*,
134. 24; monegum 24. 28;
mænegum 22. 31, 134. 13; *f.*
monigre 15. 4; *a.* manigne 37.
2*, 4; monigne 99. 16; mænigne
66. 13, 69. 12, 76. 28, xxvi. 78;
f. monige 25. 7; *n.* manig 46.
12*; mænig 65. 23, 74. 31, 86.
30; *pl.* manige 24. 9*, 46. 29*,
61. 12*, 13*, 63. 2, 70. 20*, 82.
28*, 132. 32, 133. 14, 143. 5;
manege 24. 7*, 53. 23*, 61.
13*, 87. 8*; monige 24. 1*, 41.
14*; mænige 17. 22, 145. 2;
mænege 82. 28; *f.* manega 42.
22*, 49. 12*, 147. 19; manige
145. 32; *n.* manegu 87. 4;
monegu 86. 26; *g.* manegra 26.
19*, 65. 23*, 71. 14, 22, 111.
14*; monegra 60. 19; *d.* manegum 16. 1*, 20. 11*, 33. 2, 36.
18, 42. 29, 92. 32, 96. 13*, 112.
22; monegum 26. 10, 43. 30;
mænegum 34. 24, 54. 20, 125.
19; *a.* manige 46. 27*; monige
33. 7, 76. 17; *f.* manega 42. 28,
46. 10*, 70. 8*, 101. 9, 104. 25,
108. 2, 128. 8; *n.* manigu 108.
1; mænegu 19. 8; mænig 76.
10, 13.

manigfeald, *adj*. manifold, various;
58. 11; *g. wk.* mænigfealdan
139. 21; *a.n.* manigfeald 62. 3,
90. 4; monifeald 9. 7 *n.**; *pl. n.*
mænigfeald 125. 8; *pl.* manigfealdum Pr. 5*, 111. 16*; mænigfealdum 52. 17; *a.* manigfealde
108. 11; *n.* manigfeald 104. 10,
118. 23, 133. 15; *wk.* manig-
fealdan 7. 13*.

manigfealdlic, *adj.* various; *n.*
manigfaldlic 128. 31.

mann, *m.* man, person; mankind;
55. 2*, 147. 9*; man *about* 24
times, chiefly in B, 11. 11 &c. *and*
xxii. 43, 49, xxxi. 16; monn
34. 4*; mon *usual form* Pr. 13

&c. *and* ii. 17, vii. 9, *often used
as indef. pron.* one, they 13. 17*,
18. 20, viii. 37 &c.; *g.* mannes
69. 7*, 114. 18, 135. 2; monnes
usual form 38. 25 &c.; *d.* men
10. 15 &c.; *a.* mann 24. 19*;
man 62. 15*, 66. 13, 114. 25,
31, 124. 16*; *indef.* 132. 31;
mon 36. 9 &c.; *pl.* menn 53.
14*, 116. 26*, 124. 10*; men
13. 21 &c.; *g.* manna *fq.* in B,
10. 24* &c. *and* 68. 11, vii. 21,
xiv. 6, xxvi. 55; monna *usual
form in* B *and* C, 11. 7, iv. 32
&c.; mona 41. 26*; *d.* monnum
9. 21, iv. 35 &c.; *a.* menn 69.
24*; men xvii. 11.

manna, *wm.* man; *a.* mannan
123. 28; monnan 26. 15, 123.
32, xxvii. 31.

manncynn, *n.* mankind; moncynn
41. 28*; moncyn 10. 23*, 50.
3*, 83. 22, 112. 27, xi. 97;
moncynnes 22. 4, xvii. 9 &c.;
moncynne 10. 17, xiii. 16, xxvii.
12; *a.* moncynn 111. 17*;
moncyn 10. 26, iv. 54, xiii. 61.

mannðwǣre, *adj.* gentle, kind;
148. 23.

martyr, *m.* martyr; *n. pl.* martiras
26. 21.

māðm, *m.* treasure; xxi. 20.

māðmhierde, *m.* treasurer; *n. pl.*
maðmhirdas 64. 13.

mearc, *f.* boundary, limit; *a.*
mearce 49. 24, 64. 12, 80. 4, xi.
65, 70, 73, xx. 71, 89.

mearcian, *wv.* mark out, design;
ind. prs. 3.s. mearcað 128. 27.

mearrian, *wv.* go astray, err; *sbj.
prs. 3.pl.* mearrigen 55. 23.

mēce, *m.* sword; *g. pl.* meca ix.
29.

mēd, *f.* reward; *g.* mede 45. 3,
112. 32, 131. 32; *d.* 112. 32;
a. 45. 2, 143. 15.

gemēde, *adj.* acceptable, agree-
able; *a. n.* 24. 9.

medeme, *adj.*; *a)* perfect, excellent;
b) w. g. capable (of); 122. 5 *(b)*,
9 *(b)*; *n. wk.* 82. 21 *(a)*; *a.*
medomne, medumne* 38. 33 *(a)*;

comp. a. n. medemre, more excellent 85. 21 ; *sup.* medomest, medemast* 122. 9 ; *a. n.* medemast 56. 2*.

medemlīce, *adv.* suitably, satisfactorily ; 92. 10.

medemnes, *f.* excellence ; medomnes, medumnes* 39. 6 ; *d.* medemnesse 35. 14* ; medumnesse 35. 15* ; *a.* medemnesse, dignity, high estate 32. 11.

meldian, *wv. a)* declare, proclaim ; *b) w.* on, inform against ; 36. 18 (*b*) ; *ind. pst.* 3.*s.* meldode MPr. 2 (*a*).

melu, *n.* meal, flour ; meolo 93. 5 ; *a.* 93. 5.

mengan, *wv.* (*oftcn w.* wiÞ) mix ; 33. 30* ; gemengan 38. 12, vii. 8 ; mængan viii. 22 ; *ind. prs.* 2.*s.* gemengest 82. 3, xx. 234 ; 3.*s.* gemengeÞ 136. 12, xi. 91, xxix. 49 ; *pl.* gemengaÞ v. 9 ; *pst.* 2.*s.* mengdest xx. 89, 112 ; gemengdest 80. 22 ; *sbj. prs. pl.* gemengen, join, connect 86. 14 ; *pp.* gemenged *fq.* 14. 13 &c. *and* xx. 66, 79, 128, 144 ; *a. f.* gemengde 80. 12 ; *n. pl.* 81. 4.

menigo, *f.* multitude, host ; 30. 23 ; menigu 67. 15 ; mænigo i. 29 ; *d.* mænige xxvi. 61.

mennisc, *adj.* human ; mennisc man, human being 76. 6 ; *wk.* mennisca 76. 13 ; *f. wk.* mennisce 60. 16, 132. 23 ; *n. wk.* 27. 2 ; *g.* mennisces xxvi. 91 ; *n.* 54. 2 ; Þæs m. human nature, humanity 114. 15 ; *wk.* menniscan 32. 18 ; *d.* menniscum 20. 20 ; *f. wk.* menniscan 114. 20, 21 ; *pl. wk.* 23. 27.

mennisclic, *adj.* human ; *n. pl.* mennisclice 114. 17.

meox, *n.* dung ; miox 104. 8.

mere, *m.* lake ; *a.* xxviii. 38.

merecandel, *f.* sun ; merecondel xiii. 57.

mereflōd, *m.* ocean ; *g.* mereflodes xxvii. 2.

merehengest, *m.* 'sea-horse,' ship ; *g. pl.* merehengesta xxvi. 25.

meresmylte, *adj.* calm, undisturbed ; *f.* ? meresmylta wic xxi. 12.

merestrēam, *m.* sea ; xi. 65 ; *d.* merestreame xxviii. 37 ; *pl.* merestreamas xvi. 9 ; *a.* xxviii. 33.

meretorht, *adj.* (rising) bright from the sea ; *a.* meretorhtne xiii. 61.

mersc, *m.* marsh ; *d. pl.* merscum 91. 17.

gemet, 1) *sbst. n.* measure ; limit, moderation ; *a.* 30. 7, 11, 16, 17, 60. 21, 137. 19 ; Þises middangeardes gemēt, measurement 41. 28*. 2) *adj.* fit, proper, *n.* xxix. 42.

metan, *sv*5. measure, compare ; to metanne wiÞ, compared with 29. 4 &c. *and* xxi. 42 ; to metane 29. 6 ; *sbj. prs.* mete 44. 23.

mētan, *wv.* meet with, find ; 69. 26 ; to metanne xxi. 42 ; *ind. prs.* 2.*s.* metst 114. 23 ; 3.*s.* gemet 79. 6 ; *pl.* metaÞ 76. 18, 107. 4, 5, xvii. 17 ; gemetaÞ 63. 10, 106. 34, 107. 4*, 5* ; *pst.* 3.*s.* mette, gemette* 102. 22 ; gemette hine sittan, found him sitting 61. 18 ; *sbj. prs.* gemete 11. 26, 62. 19, xiii. 18 ? *pst.* mette 62. 19 ; *pl.* gemetten 107. 3.

mete, *m.* food ; 30. 8, 40. 22, 93. 3 ; *g.* metes 60. 18, xiii. 45, xxvi. 91 ; *d.* mete 93. 2 ; *a.* 116. 22, viii. 22, xiii. 43 ; *pl.* mettas, kinds of food viii. 9 ; *g.* metta 57. 18 ; *a.* mettas 57. 17.

gemetfæst, *adj.* temperate ; modest ; *f.* 22. 13 ; *pl. d.* gemetfæstum 115. 4 ; *a.* gemetfæste 62. 27.

gemetgian, *wv.* measure out, assign ; regulate, control ; 49, 16, 139. 2, xi. 54 ; *ind. prs.* 3.*s.* metgaÞ 132. 19, xi. 88 ; gemetgaÞ 57. 4, iv. 9 &c. ; *pst.* 2.*s.* gemetgodest xx. 112.

gemetgung, *f. a)* moderation, temperance ; *b)* regulation, ordinance ; 60. 7 (*b*) ; 62. 26 (*a*),

87. 7 (*a*); *a.* gemetgunge 12ᵃ.
4* (*b*); *a. pl.* gemetgunga 128.
23 (*b*), 128. 9 (*b*).

gemetlic, *adj.* fitting, suitable; *n.*
31. 30*, 138. 30; *comp. n.*
gemetlicre 31. 30.

gemetlice, *adv.* moderately, regu-
larly; 33. 27, 96. 19; *sup.*
gemetlicost viii. 16.

metod, *m.* Lord of destiny, God;
136. 19, xx. 253, xxix. 68; *g.*
metodes vii. 48, xi. 25, xx. 71,
xxix. 49, xxxi. 16.

metten, *f.* Fate; *a. pl.* ða graman
metena ðe folcisce men hatað
Parcas 102. 22.

mettrumnes, *f.* ill-health, sickli-
ness; 116. 33; mettrymnes xxvi.
112; *a.* medtrymnesse 132.
12.

micel, *adj.* large; much; 14. 15,
xx. 2 &c.; *wk.* micla 117. 28;
f. micel 12. 3 &c.; *n.* 13. 26, i.
16 &c.; *wk.* micle xxviii. 78; *g.*
micceles 23. 26, 31. 20; micles
31. 21, 147. 23; *adv.* xiii. 16;
mycles xxii. 47; *d.* miclum 14.
11 &c.; *used as adv.* greatly,
much, 86. 7, *and* 8 *times in* Metr.
i. 74 &c.; miclon 111. 15; *f.*
micelre 7. 25 &c.; *wk.* miclan
34. 29 &c.; *a.* micelne 33. 6,
vii. 21 &c.; *f.* micele 62. 3;
micle 116. 5, 142. 9; *n.* micel
xiv. 2 &c.; *inst.* micle xxv. 11;
after mid, 48. 14, 16, 66. 9,
89. 27; *pl. f.* micla 147. 20, v.
9; *d.* miclum xxvi. 36 &c.; *a.*
f. micla, micele* 70. 8; *comp.*
mara 72. 7, 84. 27, xvi. 20; *f.*
mare 9. 17 &c.; *n.* 36. 3 &c.; *g.*
maran 31. 22, viii. 44 &c.; *d.*
79. 4 &c.; *a.* 53. 27 &c. *and* xxviii.
20; *f.* maran*, maron 65. 27; *n.*
mare 19. 9, iii. 9 &c.; *pl.* maran
72. 5; *d.* 110. 28; *sup. wk.*
mæsta 22. 4; *f.* mæst 120. 30;
wk. mæste 21. 16, 121. 18;
meste 22. 29*; *n. used as sbst.*
w. gen. most; mæst xxv. 43;
mæsð v. 36; mest 146. 17; *wk.*
mæste 83. 2, xx. 202, xxvi. 27;

g. wk. mæstan 119. 17; *d.*
mæstum 53. 23; *f.* mæstere 53.
24; *wk.* mæstan 15. 7 &c.; *a.*
mæstne 58. 27 &c.; *wk.* mæstan
13. 30 &c.; *n.* mæst, = *sbst.* 54.
8, ix. 33; *pl. wk.* mæstan 8. 23,
74. 23.

micellic, *adj.* great, grand; *g.*
micellices 42. 14.

micelnes, *f.* greatness; *a.* micel-
nesse 148. 26.

micle, *adv.* much; *fq. w. comp.*
8. 1, ix. 32 &c.; mycle xii. 22;
micele 72. 24*, 95. 7*, *comp.*
ma 17. 3, xxvi. 91 &c.; *w. g.*
fq. = *sbst.* a greater number,
more, 30. 17, x. 23 &c.; ðon
ma ðe, (not) any more than 24.
17 &c.; *sup.* mæst 15. 28, xx.
160 &c.

mid, i) *prep.* 1) *w.d.*; *a*) accompaniment, co-existence, together with, with, 7. 2, i. 21
&c.; among, 61. 20, 141. 11, 12,
viii. 38, x. 47, xxx. 1; in the
case of 16. 1, 28. 14. *b*) instrument, means, with, by, 8. 7, iv.
47 &c.; *fq. foll. case* 32. 30 &c.
and xi. 77, xiii. 43, xxviii. 79;
swuncen mid ðære spræce, at,
over 145. 3. *c*) manner, with,
7. 9 &c.; mid rihte, rightly,
rightfully 17. 31 &c. *and*
xxvi. 41, xxx. 17; mid unrihte
36. 20; mid nanum ryhte 29.
2; mid ungemete, exceedingly
xxvi. 62; mid ðæm, thereby,
therewith 32. 13 &c.; mid
hwæm hi mægen . . . the where-
withal to 60. 13; *conj.* mid
ðæm þ, in that, inasmuch as 17.
22, 47. 24, 60. 24; mid ðæm
ðe ða, as soon as 8. 27. 2) *w.*
inst.; *same meanings as* (1); mid
ane noman xx. 56; mid bebode
ðine xx. 69; mid ðy ðrymme
xxv. 13; *adv.* mid ðy, thereby,
therewith 85. 25, 103. 1, 135.
2, xxxi. 18; mid ealle, *v.* ealle.
3) *w.a.*; *a*) accompaniment; mid
an hund scipa xxvi. 15. *b*)
manner; mid gescead xx. 218.

ii) *adv.* together, 18, 27; therewith, 28. 23, 99. 3, 101. 12.

middangeard, *m.* earth, world;
39. 26, 96. 13, xiv. 6, xvi. 9;
middaneard 60. 30*; *g.* middangeardes 26. 29*, 41. 21*, 27*,
96. 4*, 10, ix. 39, xxi. 6, 22;
midangeardes 33. 22*; middaneardes *fq.* in B, 27. 5* &c.; *d.*
middangearde 135. 15, 147. 26;
middanearde 60. 31; *a.* middangeard 67. 30*, 79. 30*, 104. 6,
126. 1*, *and* 8 *times in* Metr.
xx. 9 &c.; middaneard 49. 32*.

midde, *wf.* middle; *d.* on middan, in the middle 130. 2, v.
16, xx. 170.

midde, *adj.* middle; *d.* middum
18. 25, xx. 79; *f.* middre xxviii.
23 *n.*; midre 18. 27; *a.* midne
12. 11; midne dæg, midday 57.
24, 126. 13, xiii. 57, xxviii.
37; *sup. a. wk.* midmestan
138. 28, 32; *pl. wk.* average,
medium 129. 25, 130. 2, 7; *d.*
midmestum 130. 7.

middel, 1) *adj.* intermediate;
sup. d. pl. wk. midlestan 129.
28. 2) *sbst. m.* middle, midst;
d. on ðam midle 80. 9; on midle
xx. 82.

middelniht, *f.* midnight; *d. pl.*
middelnihtum xxviii. 47.

middeweard, 1) *adj.* middle;
d. f. on ðære nafe middeweardre 129. 32*; *a. f.* middewearde 126. 8*. 2) *adv.* in the
middle; 129. 32.

middewinter, *m.* midwinter; *a.*
midewinter 12. 11*.

midferhð, *m.* middle age; *d.*
midferhðe 122. 5.

mierran, *wv.* hinder; *ind. prs.*
myrð 71. 11, 73. 7.

miht, *f.* might, power; *a.* 49. 22*,
iv. 4; mieht 25. 15; meaht ix.
51, xi. 99, xx. 161, 178, xxiv.
40. 51; meht iv. 7; *pl.* mehta
110. 4; *g.* meahta iv. 9; mehta
iv. 32; meahtum xx. 48, 209,
xxix. 36, 55.

mihtig, *adj.* powerful, mighty;

99. 27, 110. 12*, ix. 35; meahtig
110. 12; *a.* mihtigne 98. 15;
n. pl. mihtige 108. 28; *comp.*
mihtigra 79. 16, xx. 18; mehtigra
107. 17, 18, 110. 9; *sup.* mihtigost 108. 22*; meahtegost 108.
25.

mihtiglīce, *adv.* mightily; 98. 21.

milde, *adj.* gentle, kind, merciful;
wk. milda xxix. 68; *d.* mildum
iv. 55.

mildelīce, *adv.* kindly, mercifully;
10. 26 *n.*

mildheort, *adj.* gentle, merciful;
149. 3.

mildheortnes, *f.* mercy; *g.* mildheortnesse 120. 16; *d.* 133. 4;
a. 120. 13.

milts, *f.* kindness; *a.* miltse 102.
26*.

miltsian, *wv. w. d.* pity, have
mercy on; *sbj. prs.* miltsige
123. 30; mildsige 124. 15*,
xxvii. 30.

miltsung, *f.* pity, mercy; mildsung 123. 31.

mīn, *poss. adj.* my; iv. 53 &c.;
se min 23. 15; *f.* 27. 17, xxiv.
49; *n.* 18. 7; *g.* mines 8. 22;
f. minre 51. 2; *d.* minum xix.
38; *f.* minre 8. 18, v. 22; *a.*
minne 105. 1, 125. 15; *f.* mine
125. 15; minne 20. 10*; *n.* ðæt
min mod 8. 16; *inst.* mine
gefræge xx. 82, 248; *pl.* mine 8.
13 &c. *and* ii. 16; ða mine 18.
5, 21. 13; *f.* ða mina 23. 15;
g. minra 17. 15, 18. 4; *d.* minum
8. 23; *a. f.* mina 50. 26, 108. 1.

miscian, *wv.* mix, apportion;
ind. prs. 3. *s.* miscað 132. 19.

miscierran, *wv.* pervert, misuse;
ind. prs. 1. *s.* miscyrre ii. 8.

misdǣd, *f.* misdeed, crime; *g. pl.*
misdæda ix. 7.

misfōn, *rv. w. g.* fail to find; *ind.*
prs. 1. *s.* misfo 8. 9.

mishwierfed, *adj.* perverted, perverse; *n.* mishweorfed 31. 27.

missenlic, *adj.* different, various;
n. mislic 90. 4; *d.* mistlicum
82. 6*; *a. n.* mislic 31. 19; *pl.*

mislice viii. 9; mistlice 33. 23*;
f. mislica 42. 22, 43. 22; mistlice
42. 22*, 81. 35*; mistle 43. 22*;
n. mislicu 125. 8; *g.* mislicra xvi.
5; *d.* mislicum l'r. 5 &c. *and*
xx. 248, xxv. 3; mistlicum l'r.
5 &c.; *a.* mislice 52. 18, 53.
10*, 129. 6, MPr. 5; mistlice
52. 18*; *f.* mislica 18. 29, 101.
9; misleca 128. 9.
missenlice, *adv.* variously; mislice
56. 25, 106. 32, xxxi. 2; mistlice
147. 3*.
mist, *m.* mist; v. 6; *g.* mistes v.
43; *a.* mist 82. 11, xx. 264,
xxiii. 5; *pl.* mistas 14. 5, 6; *d.*
mistum v. 45.
miðan, *sv1.* conceal; *sbj. prs.* 1.*s.*
ðeah ic his miðe, conceal the
fact 59. 3.
mōd, *n.* mind, heart; *sq.*; i. 26, iii.
2 &c.; *used for* Boethius *in the
dialogue, where it is printed with
a capital M,* 8. 27 &c.; *g.* modes
9. 9, vii. 32 &c.; *d.* mode Pr.
6, iii. 9 &c.: *a.* mod 41. 10,
v. 43 &c.; *pl. g.* moda 47. 21,
50. 12, xxvi. 105; *d.* modum
15. 5, 82. 7, xx. 252; *a.* mod
48. 8.
mōdig, *adj.* headstrong, proud;
a. wk. modgan 114. 29.
mōdiglic, *adj.* high-minded; modilic xx. 2.
mōdor, *f.* mother; 21. 10; modur
21. 10*; *d.* meder 68. 31, 69.
19; *a.* modor 9. 1, 39. 23, ix.
29.
mōdsefa, *wm.* mind, heart; i. 74,
v. 39, xi. 98, xxxi. 22; *d.* modsefan xii. 22, xxii. 47, xxviii.
68; *a.* xxii. 31; *n. pl.* vii. 24.
mōdgeðanc, *m.* thoughts, mind;
a. modgeðonc v. 23, xxxi. 19.
molde, *wf.* earth; *d.* moldan xx.
281.
mōna, *wm.* moon; 10. 5, 49. 21,
86. 7, 135. 27, 136. 5, iv. 9, xi.
62, xxix. 37 *n.*; se fulla m. 126.
13; *g.* monan 29. 15, xxviii. 41;
d. 69. 22, 126. 15, xvii. 11; *a.*
xxviii. 47.

mōnað, *m.* month; *d.* monðe 12.
7; *d. pl.* monðum 91. 30.
mōr, *m.* moor, mountain; *pl.*
moras 42. 7; *d.* morum 91. 18.
morgen, *m.* dawn, morning; *a.*
xiii. 61.
morgensteorra, *wm.* morning-
star 10. 9*, 136. 4*; morgenstiorra xxix. 21; *a.* morgensteorran iv. 13.
morðor, *n.* murder, crime; ix. 7;
g. morðres ix. 33.
gemōt, *n.* meeting, debate; *n. pl.*
59. 25.
mōt, *swv.* be allowed, may; *ind.
prs.* 1.*s.* 12. 12 &c.; 2.*s.* most
105. 25, v. 29, xxiv. 56; 3.*s.* mot
8. 14, v. 40 &c.; *pl.* moton 18.
5 &c. *and* vi. 10, xi. 70; motan
17. 26; *pst.* moste 105. 6, 139.
25, 26; *pl.* mostan 7. 8*; *subj.
prs.* mote 91. 28, xvi. 19; *pl.*
moten 82. 9, x. 64 &c.; *pst.*
moste 89. 31, i. 39 &c.; *pl.*
mosten 99. 15, i. 36.
gemundbyrdan, *wv.* protect; *sbj.
pst.* 3.*s.* gemundbyrde 102. 19.
munt, *m.* mountain, hill; 34. 9; *g.*
muntes v. 16; *d.* munte 14. 16,
26. 31, 34. 8, vii. 18, viii. 48;
a. munt 34. 28, vii. 4; *pl. g.*
munta 43. 10; *d.* muntum 7. 4,
42. 29, 102. 4; *a.* muntas 43. 9.
murcian, murcnian, *wv.* complain, lament; *ind. prs.* 2.*s.*
murcas 17. 5*; murcnast 17.
5, 31. 3; *prs. p.* murciende*,
murcniende 11. 3.
murcung, *f.* complaint, lament;
a. murcunga 16. 17.
murnan, *sv3. a)* be anxious; *b)*
care about, heed; *ind. prs.* 2.*s.*
myrnst 16. 4 (*a*); 3.*s.* myrnð
111. 18* (*b*); *prs. p. a. n. wk.*
murnende 8. 17 (*a*).
mūs, *f.* mouse; 36. 4; *a.* 35. 31;
a. pl. mys 35. 31.
must, *m.* grape-juice, must; *g.*
mustes 12. 11.
mūð, *m.* mouth; *d.* muðe 51. 2;
d. pl. ea muðum 74. 3.
gemynd, *f. n.* memory, recollec-

tion ; 32. 2 ; *g.* gemynde 13. 4 ;
d. 27. 8, 95. 21, 106. 30, 148. 9,
i. 54, xxii. 58 ; *a.* gemynd 103.
25 ; *d. pl.* gemyndum vii. 39.

myndgian, *wv. w. a. and g.* re-
mind ; 139. 20 ; *ind. prs.* 1.*s.*
mindgige 25. 25 ; *pst.* 1.*s.* mynd-
gode 97. 26 ; 2.*s.* myndgodest,
mynegodest 95. 25.

gemyndig, *adj.* mindful, remem-
bering ; *n.pl. pred.* min gemyndig
41. 6.

gemyndwierðe, *adj.* ; *a. pl.* ge-
myndwyrðe 46. 28*.

mynle, *wf.* desire ; *a.* mynlan
xxvi. 67.

myntan, *wv.* intend ; *ind. pst. pl.*
mynton 96. 28, xxvi. 72.

myrige, *adj.* pleasant, delightful ;
n. murge xi. 102 ; *g.* myrges 70.
14 ; *n. pl. n.* merge xiii. 45.

myrigen, *n.* pleasure, joy ; *a.*
myrgen MPr. 5.

myrigð, *f.* pleasure, delight ; *d.*
mergðe, mirhðe* 102. 8 ; *a.*
myrhðe 15. 12.

N.

nā, *adv.* not; *about* 9 *times in* C, 17.
21 &c. *and* xx. 230, xxv. 29 ; no
usual form in B *and* C, 11. 29
&c. *and* xi. 48.

nacod, *adj.* naked ; *wk.* nacoda
33. 14 ; *n.* nacod sweord 65.
29.

nǣdre, *wf.* serpent ; 127. 8.

nǣfre, *adv.* never ; 11. 18 &c.

nǣnig, *adj.* no, none ; viii. 12, 29,
36, x. 53 ; *f.* nænegu xx. 25 ;
nængu xvi. 13 ; *n.* nænig xx.
189 ; *d.* nænegum xii. 15 ; nængum xxviii. 73 ; *a.* nænigne xxvi.
24 ; *adv.* nænige ðinga, in no
way, not at all x. 16, xix. 37.

nǣs, *adv.* not ; *fq.* 27. 25 &c. ;
nas 27. 26*, 31. 6*.

nǣssa, *wm.* headland, promontory ;
a. pl. næssan ix. 43.

nafa, *wm.* nave of wheel ; 130. 4.

nafu, *f.* nave of wheel ; 129. 21,

25, 130. 14, 19, 20 ; *d.* nafe 129.
27, 32, 130. 1, 3, 4.

nāhū, *adv.* in no way ; nahu elles,
in no other way 71. 16.

nāhwǣr, *adv.* nowhere ; nawer
80. 32 ; nawer neah, nowhere
near, nothing like 42. 1, 43. 5.

nāhwæðer, 1) *pron.* neither ;
nawðer 67. 10 ; *usually* nauðer
39. 7*, 85. 15 &c.; *g.* nauðres
138. 31 ; *d.* nauðrum 80. 20.
2) *disjunct.* nauðer ne . . . ne,
neither . . . nor 47. 6 &c.; nawðer 5 *times in* C, 16. 12 &c.

nāhwanon, *adv.* from nowhere ;
nahwonan 89. 2.

nāhwider, *adv.* to no place ; nohwider 108. 26.

nama, *wm.* name ; 43. 1 &c. *and*
x. 51, xxvi. 9 ; *g.* naman 17. 30
&c.; *d.* Pr. 11 &c. *and* iv. 14 ;
noman xx. 56 ; *a.* 17. 31 &c.
and xx. 58 ; noman xxix. 29.

nān, *adj.* no, none ; 9. 23, vii. 6
&c.; non 34. 2*, 5*; *f. always*
nan 25. 25 &c.; *n.* xvii. 7 &c. ;
nān 29. 5 ; *g.* nanes 47. 8 &c.;
f. nanre 8. 3 &c.; *d.* nanum ; *f.*
nanre 14. 23 &c. *and* xx. 139; *a.*
nanne *usual in* B, 28. 25* &c.;
nænne *in* C, 26. 12 &c. *and* viii.
46 ; nonne 26. 6*; *f.* nane 37. 11
&c. *and* xxv. 71 ; *inst.* xx. 119 ;
pl. nane. 61. 20 ; *f.* 26. 9 &c.;
g. nanra 54. 16 ; *d.* nænum 45.
7 ; *a.* nane x. 66 ; *f.* 25. 29, 33. 7.

nānwiht, 1) *pron.* nothing ; 128.
6 ; nanwuht *fq.* 18. 23 &c. 2)
adv. not at all ; nanwuht 39. 24
&c.

nāwiht, 1) *pron.* nothing, nought ;
n. and a. nauht 9. 14, 44. 24 &c.
and xx. 42 ; ne bið se nauht, of
no account, worthless 109. 31 ;
cf. 109. 16, 17, 110. 18 ; for
nauht telle 56. 11 &c.; noht 15.
1, 22. 21 ; *used as indecl. adj.,*
nauht welan, worthless wealth
32. 15 ; *g.* nauhtes 75. 2, 4 ; *d.*
nauhte *about* 11 *times*, 23. 4 &c.
and xi. 87, xxix. 88 ; *pl.* nauhtas
114. 13 ; of no account, worth-

less 109. 24. 2) *adv.* not, not
at all; 13. 32 &c. *and* xiii. 26;
naht 26. 30*; noht 12. 27.

ne, *adv. and conj.* not, nor; 8. 14
&c.; *superfluous,* þonne we ne
ðyrfen 84. 3.

nēadinga, *v.* **nīedinga.**

nēah, near. 1) *adv.* ix. 2; closely
94. 18; nawer neah, not nearly
42. 1, 43. 5; ahwærgen neah,
(not) anywhere near, (not) nearly
xxx. 10; *comp.* near 8. 24. 2)
used as prep. w. d. 99. 10 &c.
and xxix. 18; *comp.* near 126. 12
&c. *and* xx. 139, xxviii. 37; *sup.*
next 129. 22; neahst 129. 25.
3) *adj. sup. n. pl.* nehste 129.
24; æt nihstan, finally 15. 6.

genēahsen, *adj.* near, close together; *pl.* geneahsne iv. 12.

nēahstōw, *f.* neighbouring place;
pl. neahstowa 34. 10.

nēalǣcan, *wv. w.d.* approach;
sbj. prs. 3.s. genealæce 80. 32.

nealles, *adv.* not; 30. 22; nalles
26. 18, 33. 28*, 38. 24, 81. 21*,
93. 8, 113. 31, 114. 27, viii. 20,
ix. 34; nallas 19. 22*, 61. 12*,
93. 19*; nalæs 38. 24*; nales
16. 10*, 19. 14, 22, 72. 2, 93.
19, xvii. 21.

nēan, *adv.* from near, near; xxviii.
14.

nearo, *adj.* narrow; limited,
cramped; 43. 14; neara 46. 5;
a. wk. nearwan 46. 7; *pl. f.*
nearwa, nearewe* 23. 26; *a.
wk.* nearowan x. 16.

nearones, *f.* strait, distress; 56.
13 (nearanes B); *d.* nearonesse
70. 7; nearanesse 7. 25; *a.*
70. 5.

nearwe, *adv.* tightly, closely;
xxi. 5, xxv. 64.

nearwian, *wv.* narrow, limit;
pp. generwed 42. 17*.

nēat, *n.* ox; animal; 102. 7,
114. 25, xx. 189; *pl.* 31. 31;
g. neata 57. 14*, xiii. 34, xx.
249; *d.* neatum 30. 5, 32. 22,
58. 6, 146. 17*, 26*.

nēawist, *f.* neighbourhood, pre-

sence; neawest 65. 7; *d.* on
neaweste 34. 26, 67. 24, 125. 2.

nebb, *n.* face; neb xxxi. 23; *a.*
36. 24.

nemnan, *wv.* name; mention;
114. 24, iv. 15; *ind. prs. pl.*
nemnað 129. 24, xxix. 14; *pst.*
1.s. nemde 112. 8, xxv. 62; 2.s.
nemdest 79. 33, 94. 23, xx. 55;
pl. nemdon 55. 10, 11, 77. 18,
110. 22, xx. 196; *sbj. prs.* to
twæm ðingum nemne, reckon as
75. 10; *pst.* genemde 79. 33;
pp. nemned x. 47; genemned,
defined 80. 3, 7; *pl.* genemde
114. 20.

nēodfracu, *f.* greed; *d.* neodfræce xxxi. 15.

neoðan, *adv.* beneath, below;
neoðon 80. 33.

neowol, *adj.* prostrate; i. 80;
niwol 8. 4*; *a. n.* niowul 8.
25 n.

nergend, *m.* preserver, saviour;
xx. 249.

nerian, *wv.* save, protect; *prs. p.*
nergende God xxix. 73.

nese, *adv.* no; 90. 2; nese nese *fq.*
29. 18 &c.; nese la nese, why,
no! oh no! 58. 29, 62. 18.

nett, *n.* net; *a.* 73. 28; *a. pl.*
net 73. 30.

nēðan, *wv.* venture on; *ind. prs.*
3.s. geneðeð xiii. 59.

nīedan, *wv.* compel; *ind. prs.*
2.s. genedest iv. 5, 15; 3.s. ned
145. 14; *sbj. prs.* nede 140. 21;
pst. nedde, oppressed 35. 32;
pp. geneded 148. 25; gened 93.
13.

nīede, *adv.* of necessity, compul-
sorily; nede iv. 12, vi. 14, ix.
44; *w.* sceal, needs must 94.
15 &c. *and* xxv. 64.

nīedinga, *adv.* by force; neadinga
48. 1, 4.

nīedðearf, *f.* necessity; need;
(what is) necessary; nedðearf
144. 17 &c. *and* xx. 20, 25;
neodðearf 79. 17; *d.* nedðearfe
60. 21, xxxi. 15; *a.* 53. 2, 77.
11, 149. 7; nydðearfe 30. 8*.

nīeten, *n.* animal ; neten xx. 191, nyten xxxi. 21 ; *pl.* netenu 42. 1*, 70. 16, 81. 19*, 117. 3, 146. 5, 18*, xxviii. 51 ; nytenu 32. 20, 93. 9 ; neotena 31. 31* ; nytena 32. 20* ; *g.* netena 82. 5* ; nytena 146. 24* *n.* ; *d.* netenum*, nytenum 30. 4 ; neatenum 30. 5*.

nīetenlic, *adj.* beast-like ; *pl.* ge netenlican men 35. 28 (netelican B).

nigon, *num.* nine ; 127. 9, xxvi. 24.

niht, *f.* night ; 52. 7, xii. 16 &c. ; *g.* nihte 10. 5 &c. ; *a.* xxix. 36 ; niht 136. 6*, xi. 61 ; on niht, by night 49. 21*, 121. 16 ; neaht xx. 229 ; *pl. g.* nihta iv. 6 ; *d.* nihtum 19. 3, xx. 213, 232.

nihtes, *adv.* at night ; 102. 5, xiii. 59.

niman, *sv4.* take, take away ; receive ; geniman 17. 25 ; *w.* on 25. 24, 46. 19 ; *ind. prs.* 3.*s.* genimeð vi. 12 ; nimð 28. 7 *n.*, 136. 21, xiii. 34, xxix. 73 ; *pl.* nimað 48. 11, 59. 24 ; *pst.* 1.*s.* genom 20. 7 ; *pl.* noman 34. 20* ; *imp.* nim 91. 19 ; *sbj. prs. pl.* nimen 16. 25 ; *pst. pl.* naman 67. 5* ; *pp.* genumen 18. 2, 42. 6, 7, 54. 5, 59. 26 ; *a.* genumenne xx. 36.

niðer, *adv.* downwards, down ; i. 80, xxxi. 19, 21 ; nyðer, below 147. 10*.

niðerheald, *adj.* bent downwards ; xxxi. 23.

niðerlic, *adj.* lowly, inferior ; *d. pl.* niðerlicum 32. 7 *n.*

hiðerra, *comp. adj.* lower ; *f.* niðerc 136. 14* ; *g.* neoðeran 11. 25* ; *sup.* niðemæst xx. 135 ; neoðemest xx. 85 ; *d. wk.* niðemæstan 18. 9 ; *a. pl. wk.* niðemystan 18. 8 ; nyðemestan 32. 12.

niðor, *adv.* lower ; nioðor 80. 30* ; nioðoror 147. 10*.

nīwan, *adv.* recently ; xv. 2, xxviii. 73 ; niwane 126. 24*.

nīwe, *adj.* new ; 43. 12 ; *g.* niwes 15. 21, 85. 25 ; *wk.* niwan xiii. 26 ; *a. wk.* 57. 11.

genōg, 1) *adj.* enough, sufficient ; *g.* genoges 31. 23 ; *a. pl.* genoge 24. 12*, 31. 28*. 2) *adv.* enough, sufficiently, *usual form* genog 22. 6 &c. ; genoh *about* 16 *times*, 15. 4 &c. *and* viii. 7.

norð, *adv.* in the north ; x. 24, xiii. 59.

norðan, *adv.* from the north ; norðan 7 eastan 10. 11, iv. 23, vi. 12, xii. 15.

norðanēastan, *adv.* from the north-east ; 21. 6.

norðanwind, *m.* north wind ; *g.* norðanwindes 21. 7 ; *n. pl.* norðanwindas 52. 5.

norðemest, *sup. adj.* most northern ; *a. pl. wk.* norðmestan ix. 43.

norðende, *m.* north end ; *d.* 126. 4 ; *a.* xxviii. 14.

norðerne, *adj.* from the north, northern ; *f.* vi. 14.

norðeweard, *adj.* north ; *used as sbst.* ; *d.* norðeweardum 41. 22 ; *a.* norðeweardne 39. 28*, 41. 22*.

norðwestende, *m.* north-west end or part ; *d.* 67. 32.

notian, *wv. w. g.* make use of, enjoy ; *ind. prs.* 3.*pl.* notiað, notigað* 42. 1.

notu, *f.* use, profit ; *d.* note 31. 11.

nū, 1) *adv. a) time*, now, at present ; Pr. 10, xi. 40 &c. ; nu ryhte, just now 101. 13 ; nu hwene ær 12. 22. *b) inference*, therefore, then ; *fq. w.* gif 15. 8 &c. ; *w.* ðeah 24. 23, x. 63 &c. ; *w. imperat.* 8. 21 &c. ; *w. interrog.* 9. 21, xxviii. 48 &c. ; nu ðonne 64. 15. 2) *conj.* since ; *fq.* 22. 3, ii. 19 &c.

genyht, *nf.* sufficiency, abundance ; 75. 14, 76. 4, 86. 24, 87. 15, 96. 30 ; geniht 75. 12 (*n.*) ; *a.* genyht 75. 10 ; geniht 75. 16 (*n.*), 78. 13 (*f.*).

nytt, 1) *sbst. f.* profit, advantage ;

d. nytte 101. 13.   2) *adj.* useful,
profitable ; *f.* nyt 137. 22 ; *n.*
111. 5 ; nit 137. 20 ; *a. n.* nyt
121. 22 ; *comp.* nyttra 109. 29 ;
n. nyttre 139. 29.

nytwierðe, *adj.* profitable ; *f.* nyt-
wyrðc 137. 7 ; *g.* nytwyrðes 64.
20 ; *comp. f.* nytwyrðre 47. 14 ;
sup. n. nytwyrðost 56. 8.

O.

of, 1) *prep. w. d.* ; *often foll. c.* ;
a) motion, from, away from ; *fq.*
8. 22, i. 2 &c. *b) starting-point,*
from, at ; he onginð of ðæm
wyrtrumum 91. 31, *cf.* vi. 4.
c) distance ; hit is swiðc feor of
uncrum wege 139. 27, 28. *d)*
removal, from ; 91. 20, xii. 2 &c. ;
foll. c. him awint of ða claðas
111. 19, *cf.* xxv. 22 ; ceorfe him
of 124. 17, *cf.* xiii. 9 ; of
(boc:lædene on englisc (ge)-
wende Pr. 1, 9 ; sette andgit of
andgite Pr. 3. *e) source, origin,*
from ; *fq.* 62. 31, xvii. 3 &c. ;
Gotan of Sciððiu 7. 1 ; þe is
micel unrotnes getenge of þinum
irre 12. 4 ; ðæt ís mæge weorðan
of wætere xxviii. 60 ; wyrcð of
yfle good, out of 135. 6 ; of
ealdum leasum spellum, (taken)
from 115. 12. *f) opposition,*
opposed to ; 12. 20, 57. 8. *g)*
cause ; of his agenre gecynde 27.
25, *cf.* 31. 5. *h)* concerning,
about ; ne ðincð me nauht oðres
of ðinum spellum 107. 26. 2)
adv. a) motion ; irnen mænege
brocas 7 riða of, therefrom 82.
28. *b) deprivation,* off, away ;
of atihð 52. 11, *cf.* 51. 29 ; do
nu of 42. 4, *cf.* 127. 7 ; of aslog
127. 9. *c)* absent, missing ; gif
ðara lima hwylc of bið 114. 8.

ofbēatan. *rv.* slay ; ix. 30.

ofdæl, *adj.* prone, inclined ; *comp.*
hit bið ofdælre ðærto 53. 14 *n.*

ofdæle, *n.* downward course,
descent ; *a.* on ðæt ofdæle asigen
55. 16, *cf.* xiii. 58.

ofdūne, *adv.* down ; 8. 4, 57. 22,
81. 13, 92. 19, 20, 147. 7, i. 80,
xx. 167, xxxi. 13.

ofer, (ofir vi. 5) i) *prep.* 1) *w. d.*
a) position, over, above ; 65. 30,
xx. 124 &c. *b) motion,* over,
across; 105. 8, 9, 13, xii. 17, xxiv.
8. 12, 24, 27. 2) *w. a. a)*
position, above ; ofer eall ðis
wunað xx. 156. *b) extension,*
throughout, over ; 42. 12, 18, 43.
20, 49. 24, 67. 30, 104. 6, viii.
30, ix. 21, x. 16, 23, xi. 66, xiii.
68, 73, xx. 85, xxiv. 11 ; *foll. c.*
42. 25. *c) motion,* above, beyond ;
43. 9, i. 8 &c. *d) superiority,*
authority, over ; he hæfde sige
ofer ða Africanas 37. 7 ; hlaford
ofer 35. 31, *cf.* 98. 28, 124. 28,
125. 1 ; ricsað ofer hi 97. 31, *cf.*
98. 31, i. 62, xxvi. 67, 106. *e)*
distance, beyond, farther than ;
108. 24. *f) excess,* beyond, more
than ; 41. 13, xii. 32 &c. ; ofer
gemet 30. 11, 16, 17, *cf.* 137.
18 ; *time,* past, ofer midne dæg
57. 24, xiii. 57 ; besides, 52. 13,
23. *g)* beside, in comparison
with ; heo hit hæfð eall forsawen
ofer ðe anne 22. 18. *h)* contrary
to, ofer metodes est xi. 25. ii)
adv. over, beyond ; nænne weg
findan ofer 85. 24.

oferbrǣdan, *wv.* cover ; *ind. prs.*
3.*s.* oferbrædcð vii. 13.

ofercuman, *sv4.* overcome ; 127.
13 ; *ind. prs.* 3.*s.* ofercymð 93.
15, 109. 4 ; *pp.* ofercumen 83.
17, xx. 158 ; *a. m.* ofercumene
50. 15.

oferdrencan, *wv.* intoxicate ; *pp.*
oferdrenced 55. 21.

oferdruncen, *adj.* intoxicated ; 55.
18.

oferfaran, *sv6.* pass over, beyond ;
xi. 70 ; *pp. a.* oferfarenne xxiv.
26.

oferfōn, *rv.* seize ; *ind. pst.* 3.*s.*
oferfeng i. 69.

oferfyllo, *f.* superfluity, excess ;
oferfyll 70. 5*.

ofergān, *anv. a)* overstep ; *b)* pass

away, come to an end; ofergangan
xx. 71 (*a*); *ind. prs.* 3.*pl.* ofergað
20. 16 (*b*); *pst.* 3.*s.* ofereode 80.
4 (*a*).

ofergietolnes, *f.* forgetfulness; *d.*
ofergiotulnesse 95. 11; oforgiotolnesse xxii. 32 (J).

oferhīeran, *wv.* not listen to, dis-
regard; *ind. prs.* 3.*s.* oferheorð
10. 15*.

oferhogian, *wv.* despise; *imp.*
oferhoga 16. 6*.

oferhycgan, *wv.* despise; *imp.*
oferhige 16. 6.

oferhygd, *f.* pride; *a. pl.* oferhyda
62. 16.

ofering, *f.* excess; 30. 18* (oferinc
C); *d.* oferinge 31. 23.

ofermētto, *f.* pride; *a.* 14. 21;
pl. ofermetta 111. 29; ofermetto
67. 9; *g.* ofermetta xxv. 44; *d.*
ofermettum 35. 1, 4, 133. 25, v.
32; *a.* ofermetta 26. 25, vii. 8.

ofermōd, *adj.* proud, over-confident; *g. wk.* ofermodan 35. 1; *pl.*
n.wk. 46. 8, x. 18; *d.* ofermodum
111. 12, xxv. 1; *a. wk.* ofermodan 105. 26, xxiv. 59.

ofermōdian, *wv.* be proud, arro-
gant; *ind. prs.* 2.*pl.* ofermodige
ge 69. 25; ofermodie 148. 29;
3.*pl.* ofermodigað 134. 22; *sbj.*
prs. pl. ofermodigen xvii. 16.

ofermōdlic, *adj.* proud; *d.* ofer-
modlicum 45. 8.

ofermōdnes, *f.* pride, arrogance;
d. ofermodnesse 15. 7.

oferreccan, *wv.* confute; *pp. a.*
oferreahtne 85. 5.

ofersǣlð, *f.* excessive enjoyment;
a. pl. ofersælða v. 27.

ofersēon, *sv5.* look upon, survey;
ofersion 105. 7; *ind. prs.* 2.*s.*
ofersihst 10. 25, iv. 53.

ofersittan, *sv5.* spread over,
occupy; *pp.* oferseten 42. 4
(ofseten B).

oferstæppan, *sv6.* overstep; 49. 23;
ofersteppan xi. 69.

oferswīðan, *wv.* overcome; 134. 1,
4; *pp.* oferswīðed 109. 11; *pl.*
n. oferswiðde 134. 2, 5.

ofertēon, *sv2.* cover; *pp.* ofertogen
126. 14, ix. 16.

oferðearf, *f.* great need; *a.* oferðearfe 70. 6.

oferðēon, *sv1,3.* surpass; *pp.* oferðungen 22. 13, 81. 22, xx.
194.

oferwinnan, *sv3.* overcome; *pp.*
oferwunnen xxv. 72.

oferwrēon, *sv1,2.* cover up; *pp.*
oferwrigen 126. 26, xxviii. 79.

ofhende, *adj.* out of one's possession, absent; *n.* xxv. 34.

ofiernan, *sv3.* overtake; *ind. prs.*
3.*s.* ofirneð xxix. 32; ofirnð
136. 3.

oflǣtan, *rv.* let (blood); *sbj. pst.*
3.*s.* hine (him B) oflete blodes
66. 29.

oflyst, *adj.* desirous; he wæs oflyst
ðæs seldcuðan sones 102. 21.

ofman, *swv.* recollect; *ind. prs.*
3.*s.* 148. 13.

ofgerād, *adj.* straightforward, simple; *pl. g.* ofgeradra worda misfo
8. 8.

ofscamian, *wv. reflx. w. a. and g.*
ofsceamian 9. 18.

ofsēon, *sv5.* gaze on; ofsion xxi.
38.

ofsittan, *sv5.* beset, assail; *ind.*
prs. 3.*s.* ofsit 109. 4; *sbj. prs.*
3.*s.* ofsitte 109. 9; *pp.* ofseten =
oferseten 42. 4.

ofslēan, *sv6.* kill; 7. 11, 28. 17,
39. 22, 67. 1, 99. 3; *ind. prs.*
3.*s.* ofslog 39. 24, 99. 16, ix. 30;
sbj. pst. ofsloge 70. 25; *pp.*
ofslægen 36. 32; *g.* ofslægenes
34. 3.

ofsnīðan, *sv1.* cut off; xxvii. 33.

ofswelgan, *sv3.* swallow up; *ind.*
prs. 3.*s.* ofswelgð 46. 15 *n.*

oft, *adv.* often; Pr. 5, ii. 8 &c.;
comp. oftor 54. 20, xix. 19; *sup.*
oftost 30. 7, iv. 28, xxii. 9, 14;
oftosð 39. 14.

oftēon, *sv2.* take away; oftion
xxv. 24; *ind. prs.* oftihð *w. d.*
and g. 111. 21; *pp.* oftogen xxv.
31; withheld 20. 11; him wyrð
ðara ðenunga oftohen 111. 24*.

oftrǣde, *adj.* frequent ; *wk.* se oftrœda ren 136. 17.

ofðryccan, *wv.* oppress, overwhelm ; *pp.* ofðrycced 19. 27 ; *pl. n.* ofðrycte 24. 5.

ofðyncan, *wv. impers. w. d.* be displeased ; ofðincan 98. 33.

ofwundrian, *wv.* be astonished ; *pp.* ofwundrod 28. 30.

ōleccan, *wv. w. d.* propitiate, flatter ; 60. 10, 71. 20, 102. 11 ; *ind. prs.* 3. *s.* olecð 55. 12 ; *pl.* oleccað 15. 5, 55. 11, xi. 8 ; *pst. pl.* geolectan 15. 28 ; *sbj. prs.* olecce 134. 18 ; *pl.* oleccen 60. 5.

ōlecoung, *f.* flattery ; *d.* olecunga 16. 21* ; olecunge*, oliccunga 48. 3 ; *a.* olecunga 54. 5.

on (an 42. 5, 61. 20, 68. 17, 19, 116. 15, 127. 16, 133. 5 ; ōn 90. 12), i) *prep. fq. foll. c.* 1) *w. d.* a) *place*, in ; 10. 27, i. 37 &c. ; *metaph. fq.* 20. 1, i. 54 &c. ; on, upon, 10. 19, i. 11 &c. ; *metaph.* 35. 22 &c. ; on ðe, on your person 33. 9 ; among ix. 27. *b) time*, during, in ; *fq.* Pr. 7, viii. 18 &c. ; on wintra 68. 2 &c. ; on sumera 49. 20 &c. ; on geare 64. 14 ; on gewinne 53. 23 ; on sibbe 53. 23 ; on wite, undergoing punishment 120. 25 ; on ðæm ende, at the end 73. 14. *c) connexion*, in respect of ; 24. 3, xx. 76 &c. ; fægrest on wlite 72. 9, *cf.* 54. 24 ; on hwæm, in what respect 19. 13, 36. 12 ; on ðy ... forðam ðe 58. 19 ; *conj.* on ðæm ðe, in that 88. 27 ; on ðam þ 146. 17 ; *w.* genog : ðincð him genog on ðam ðe hi, think it sufficient that they 31. 32, *cf.* 33. 22, 55. 30 ; on ðæm wel gehealden, satisfied with 43. 27 ; mon him on lihð, concerning 68. 16, *cf.* 64. 19 ; him soð an seggað 68. 19, *cf.* 68. 17, 70. 3. *d)* in the shape of ; on crœftum 38. 1 ; on leafum 92. 2. *e) deprivation*, from ; *w.* niman 18. 2, 42. 6, 46. 19, 59. 24, 26 ; *w.* reafian 27. 30. *f) motion*, into,

to ; 11. 11, 18. 10 ; *w.* gebrengan 131. 5 ; on ; him spigettan on 61. 24 ; *adv. phrases* : on sige, setting xiii. 56 ; on ryne, in motion 16. 33 ; on him selfum, by himself xx. 94 ; on ðonce, satisfactory xii. 16 ; on rihte, rightly xxvi. 46 ; on gerihte, upright xxxi. 17 ; habbað on hospe, insult, revile iv. 44. 2) *w. a. a) motion*, into, to ; 7. 24, i. 20 &c. ; upon, on to, 19. 14, i. 81 &c. ; *w.* weg 56. 29, 57. 25, 107. 16, 139. 28 ; *metaph. fq.* 14. 21, ix. 46 &c. *b) direction* ; on feower healfe 46. 3, *cf.* 43. 10, 81. 11, 136. 9, xx. 163. *c) disposition*, towards ; on Crecas hold i. 56. *d) change of state*, into ; weorpan hi an wilde deora lic 116. 15, *cf.* xxvi. 76 ; on englisc wende Pr. 2. *e)* against ; winð ælc on oðer 49. 31. *f) partition*, into ; *w.* todælan 42. 27, xx. 59 &c. ; on mænig tonemned 76. 10, *cf.* v. 17 ; willað on tu, diversely 92. 32, 113. 26. *g) purpose*, sent on his ærendo 136. 25, *cf.* 63. 15, xxix. 83 ; on æht gifen xvi. 10. *h) place*, in ; 8. 10, 51. 3, 75. 1, xvi. 12. *i)* in the case of, in ; 69. 12 ; in respect to 12. 2. *k)* in conformity with, in accordance with ; on yfelra manna gewill 10. 24, *cf.* 24. 24, 48. 13, iv. 34, xiii. 55. *l)* concerning ; 70. 3. *m) w.* fon, take up, take in hand ; 100. 7 &c. *and* MPr. 9. *n) adv. phrases*, on last, at last, in the end ; 15. 5, 48. 1, 100. 23 ; on ecnesse, for ever 47. 2 &c. ; on ða gerad þ, on condition that 18. 15 ; on riht, rightly 14. 28, 56. 28 ; on woh, wrongly 131. 17, *cf.* 131. 31 ; on ane, continuously xxix. 44 ; on nane wisan, in no wise 37. 11, *cf.* 132. 25, 31 ; on symbel, always xi. 94 ; on manig ðeodisc, in many tongues 46. 12. *o) point of time*, in, at ; 39. 19, ix. 15 &c. ; on midne winter 12. 11, *cf.* 126.

13, xxviii. 37; on dæg 121. 16;
on niht 49. 21; on ærmorgen
xxviii. 36; on æſen *ib.*, *cf.* viii.
19; on lencten 10. 12, 49. 18,
136. 19, *cf.* xxix. 67; on hærfest 49. 19, xi. 58, *cf.* 10. 12,
on eastran 29. 21; on tid, when
the time comes 67. 11. ii) *adv.*
w. similar sense to (i); 14. 14 &c.
onǣlan, *wv.* inflame, inspire; *pp.*
onæled 29. 26, 51. 8.
onbindan, *sv3.* unbind; *ind.*
prs. 3.*s.* onbinð, anbint* 47. 23.
onbītan, *sv1. w. g.* taste, eat;
xxvi. 90.
onbregdan, *sv3.* pull open; *pp.*
ða duru anbroden 97. 24.
onbryrdan, *wv.* inspire, incite;
14. 2.
onbyrigan, *wv. w. g.* taste; *ind.*
prs. 3.*s.* onbyrgeð xii. 11, xiii.
23; onbirigð 52. 4*, 57. 11*.
oncierran, *wv.* turn, change;
oncerran 17. 1, i. 61, x. 39;
pp. oncerred 23. 16.
oncnāwan, *rv.* recognize, know;
understand; 14. 19, 15. 14, 132.
13, v. 25, xii. 30; *sbj. prs. pl.*
oncnawen 58. 10; *pst.* oncneowe
8. 27.
oncweðan, *sv5.* answer, re-echo;
ind. prs. 3.*s.*; oncwyð xiii. 46,
50; *sbj. prs.* oncweðe 57. 20.
ondrǣdan, *rv. rflx.* dread, fear;
13. 33, 33. 8, 12, 140. 1; *ind.*
prs. 1.*s.* ondræde 47. 5, 50.
23 *n.*, 118. 19, 139. 30; 3.*s.*
ondrædæð xxiv. 64; ondræt 7
times, 24. 18 &c.; ondræd 66.
9; *pl.* ondrædað 133. 27; *sbj.*
prs. (not reflx.) ondræde 57. 10;
xiii. 21; *pst.* ondrede 33. 14,
59. 31.
ōnettan, *wv.* hasten; *ind. prs.*
3.*s.* onet 124. 7, xxvii. 8; *pl.*
onettað 112. 29; *sbj. pst.* onette
139. 25.
onfægnian, *wv.* show pleasure,
greet; o. mid his steorte 102.
15.
onfindan, *sv3.* discover; *ind. pst.*
3.*s.* onfunde 66. 25.

onfōn, *rv.* receive, accept; *w. g.*
66. 27; *ind. prs.* 3.*s.* onfehð
143. 15, xxix. 65; *pl.* onfoð 128.
3; *pst.* onfeng i. 33; *imp. w. g.*
onſoh 135. 19.
ongean, 1) *prep. a)* *w. d.* towards;
102. 27. *b)* *w. a.* towards, 102.
13, 121. 10; against, contrary to,
83. 18. 2) *adv.* in reply 45.
13.
ongietan, *sv5.* perceive, understand; 12. 13, 15. 8, 10, 11, 22.
27; *usual form* ongitan 23. 15,
xxvi. 107 &c.; ongiton 50. 28*;
ongetan 41. 24; ongeotan 73.
11*; to ongitanne 36. 16 &c.;
to ongitonne 81. 3*; *ind. prs.*
1.*s.* ongiete 15. 3; ongite 19.
26 &c.; 2.*s.* ongitest 25. 18;
ongitst 24. 21 &c. *and* xii. 32;
ongitsð 21. 24; 3.*s.* ongit 41.
18 &c. *and* xxii. 16, 21; andgit 132. 25; *pl.* ongitað 32. 8
&c.; ongite ge 43. 14; *pst.* 1
and 3.*s.* ongeat 11. 3 &c. *and*
7. 13, i. 68, viii. 37; 2.*s.* ongeate 62. 8 &c.; *imp.* ongit
108. 2, 113. 9, 22, 119. 10;
ongite 118. 15; *sbj. prs.* ongite
Pr. 12 &c.; *pl.* ongiten 35. 28,
134. 17; ongiton 32. 19*; *pst.*
ongeate 51. 6 &c.; *pl.* ongeaten
123. 22; *pp.* ongiten 13. 16 &c.;
ongieten 14. 27, 15. 1.
onginnan, *sv3.* begin; 102. 11
&c. *and* xxv. 69; *ind. prs.* 1.*s.*
onginne 9. 19; 3.*s.* onginneð
38. 6, 103. 22; onginð *usual*
form 25. 9, xiii. 28 &c.; ongynð 12. 6; *pl.* onginnað 14. 4,
126. 24; *pst.* 3.*s.* ongan *usual*
form in B *and* C, 7. 17 &c. *and*
viii. 2; angan i. 59; ongann
52. 15*, 137. 14*; ongon *about*
16 *times in* C, 27. 15 &c. *and*
vii. 1; *pl.* ongunnon 101. 7,
xxvi. 73 &c.; *sbj. prs.* onginne
94. 29; *pl.* onginnen 110. 33.
onhagian, *wv. impers. w. d.* be
convenient; *sbj. prs.* gif men to
goodum weorce ne onhagie, if
a man do not find it convenient,

in his power, to do a good work 142. 19.

onhealdan, *rv.* keep; *ind. prs. pl.* sibbe anhealdað xi. 42.

onhebban, *sv6.* raise, exalt; *sbj. prs.* anhebbe 14. 21*.

onhieldan, *wv.* bend down, incline; *pp.* onhelded xiii. 11.

onhnīgan, *sv1.* bend down, bow; *pp.* onhnigen xxxi. 13.

onhrēran, *wv.* stir up, agitate; *ind. prs.* 3.*s.* onhrereð vii. 27; *pl.* onhrerað v. 10.

onhrīnan, *sv1.* touch, interfere with; *ind. prs.* 3.*s.* onhrinð 135. 26, 28.

onhweorfan, *sv3. intrans.* change; *ind. pst.* 3.*s.* onhwearf 65. 14.

onhwierfan, *wv. ind. prs.* 3.*s.* onhwerfð, revolves; 81. 27; *pp.* onhwyrfed, changed 15. 3.

onhyrian, *wv. w. d.* imitate; onhirian 139. 12; *ind. prs.* 3.*s.* onhyreð 146. 17*; *pl.* onhyriað 146. 7.

oninnan, 1) *prep. w. d.* inside, within; 25. 15 &c. *and* xxix. 54; *foll. c.* v. 15, xx. 120; on . . . innan xvi. 3, xvii. 4, xxii. 8, 14, xxx. 13. 2) *adv.* 14. 16.

onlǣnan, *wv.* lend, grant; *ind. prs.* 3.*s.* onlænð x. 37; *pst.* 3.*s. w. d. and g.* onlænde 19. 22; *pp. n. pl.* onlænde 17. 8* *n.*

onlǣtan, *rv.* relax; xi. 75; onlæten xi. 28.

onliehtan, *wv.* illuminate; onlihtan 89. 20, xxi. 36; *ind. prs. pl.* onlihtað 89. 13; onlyhtað 121. 17, xxi. 23; *pst.* 3.*s.* onlyhte, onlichte* 14. 1; *imp.* onliht ða eagan, give sight to 82. 12, xx. 267; *pp.* onlihted xi. 62; *n. pl.* onlihte 86. 6.

onlīesan, *wv.* unloosen, deliver; *pp.* onlesed 45. 28.

onlūcan, *sv2.* unlock; *ind. pst.* 3.*s.* onleac vi. 1.

onlūtan, *sv2. intrans.* bend down; *ind. prs.* 3.*s.* onlyt xiii. 66.

onsacan, *sv6.* deny; *ind. prs.* 1.*s.* onsace 54. 31; *pst.* 3.*s.* onsac,

expressed his disapproval 59. 33, 138. 15.

onscamian, *wv. impers.* be ashamed; onsceamian 9. 18.

onscunian, *wv.* avoid, shun; 19. 18, 140. 25; to anscunianne 41. 9; *ind. prs.* 1.*s.* onscunige 11. 25; 3.*s.* onscunað 22. 19, 37. 20, 38. 13, 17; *pst.* 2.*s.* onscunedest 15. 15; 3.*s.* onscunode 102. 6, 135. 3; *pl.* onscunedon 101. 30, 116. 22; *sbj. prs.* onscunige 16. 6.

onsendan, *wv.* send; ansendan v. 5.

onsīgan, *sv1.* sink; *sbj. prs.* onsige 57. 25.

onsittan, *sv5.* fear; *sbj. prs.* onsitte v. 38.

onstyrian, *wv.* disturb, affect; 13. 9; *ind. prs.* 3.*s.* onstyreð 21. 7*; *pp.* onstyred 15. 18.

onsundran, *adv.* apart, separately; 38. 11, xx. 143; onsundron 80. 35*.

onswīfan, *sv1. trans.* turn aside; x. 40.

ontēon, *sv2.* untie; *pp.* ontiged 45. 27.

onuppan, 1) *prep. w. d.* upon; 26. 27. 2) *adv.* besides; ix. 28.

onwæcnian, *wv. intrans.* awake; *ind. prs.* 3.*s.* onwæcnað 111. 27.

onwendan, *wv. trans.* change; 16. 28, 17. 2, 116. 28, 142. 28, xxvi. 101, 116; *ind. prs. pl.* onwendað 141. 5, xxix. 29; *pst.* 3.*s.* onwende 116. 29; *pp.* onwended 15. 18*, 144. 22*, v. 19; onwend 144. 22, xi. 20, xxvi. 104; diverted 49. 1; *pl. f.* onwenda 15. 24; onwende 25. 6.

onwendedlic, *adj.* changeable; *g. pl.* anwendendlicra 101. 5.

onwrēon, *sv1,2.* unfold, reveal; *ind. prs.* 3.*s.* onwrihð 47. 9.

onwunian, *wv.* dwell, abide; *prs. p. a.* anwunigendne vii. 47.

open, *adj.* open; clear, evident; *n.* 106. 34; *pl. f.* opene 16. 1;

d. openum 82. 8, 127. 16, xx. 257 ; *comp. n.* openre 62. 1.

openian, *wv.* make clear, reveal ; *ind. prs.* 3.*s.* openað* 28. 15 ; geopenað 28. 15, 39. 1, 47. 9, 24, 48. 8.

openlīce, *adv.* clearly, evidently ; *fq.* 21. 24 &c. *and* x. 60, xiii. 72 ; *comp.* openlicor 74. 28, 126. 30.

ordfruma, *wm.* origin, originator ; *d.* ordfruman xxix. 96.

oreald, *adj.* very old, ancient ; 102. 18.

orgellīce, *adv.* proudly, presumptuously ; 45. 6.

orieldo, *f.* extreme old age ; *a.* oreldo 142. 18.

ormǣte, *adj.* excessive ; ormete vii. 36 ; *a. n.* ormæte 53. 29.

ormōd, *adj.* despondent, sad ; 8. 4, 19. 31, i. 78, v. 30 ; *f.* 22. 22.

ormōdnes, *f.* despondency ; despair ; *d.* ormodnesse 15. 7 ; *a.* 13. 16, 142. 24.

orsorg, *adj.* free from care, untroubled ; prosperous ; 27. 9, 33. 15, 18, 59. 1 ; orsorg ælces eorðlices eges, secure from 22. 9 ; ðara yfela orsorh vii. 43 ; *f. wk.* orsorge 47. 14, 15 ; *n.* orsorh 104. 32 ; *a.* orsorgne 71. 25, 28 ; *f. wk.* orsorgan 139. 2 ; *n.* orsorg vii. 40 ; *pl. wk.* orsorgan 121. 3 ; *d.* orsorgum v. 33 ; *a.* ðæs orsorge 88. 33 ; *comp. n. pl.* orsorgran 130. 17 ; *sup. n. pl.* orsorgestæ 130. 23.

orsorglīce, *adv.* securely ; *comp.* orsorglicor 53. 27, 129. 22.

orsorgnes, *f.* security, prosperity ; 21. 13, xiii. 71 ; orsorhnes 47. 25 *n.* ; *g.* orsorgnesse 117. 9, 138. 29 ; *d.* 14. 22, 57. 31.

geortrīewan, *wv. w. g.* despair ; geortrewan 23. 7, 9 ; geortreowan 23. 7* ; *imp.* geortreowe v. 35 ; *sbj. prs.* geortrywe 14. 23*.

oð, 1) *prep. w. a.* ; *a) extension and motion,* up to, as far as, 34. 17, i. 14 &c. ; *metaph.* oð ormod-

nesse 142. 24. *b) time,* until, 20. 3 &c. *and* xx. 10. 2) *conj.* until ; *about* 11 *times,* 50. 29 &c. *and* v. 15, xiii. 62 ; oððe 57. 27, 65. 17 ; oððæt *about* 14 *times,* 14. 26, i. 29 &c.

ōðer, *pron. adj.* second ; other ; 11. 11, xx. 60 &c. ; *f.* oðru 47. 18 &c. *and* xi. 44, xii. 7 ; oðer 80. 1* ; *n.* 63. 29, xx. 155 &c. ; oðer twega oððe ... oððe, either ... or 23. 27 &c. ; *g.* oðres 13. 14, i. 44 &c. ; *pl.* oðra 88. 6 ; *f.* oðre 32. 12 ; *d* oðrum 20. 19, v. 2 &c. ; *f.* oðre 43. 10, xx. 139 &c. ; oðerre 39. 21*, 81. 2* ; *a.* oðerne 28. 26 &c. *and* xxvii. 23 ; *f.* oðre 32. 14 ; *n.* oðer 38. 13, xx. 65 &c. ; *inst.* oðre naman 10. 9 &c. *and* iv. 14 ; *w.* mid 121. 30, 129. 30 ; *pl.* oðre 61. 20 &c. *and* vi. 5 ; *f.* oðra 18. 5, viii. 53 &c. ; oðre 81. 8* ; *n.* oðru 55. 11 &c. *and* xxviii. 12 ; *g.* oðerra 32. 10 &c. ; oðra 88. 6, xxiv. 36, xxvi. 90 ; *d.* oðrum 20. 25, xx. 126 &c. ; *a.* oðre 16. 25, xiii. 48 &c. ; *f.* oðra 52. 31 &c. *and* xxv. 14 ; oðre 35. 31* ; *n.* oðru 10. 13 &c. ; oðre 54. 29* &c. ; oðer ... oðer, different 16. 25 &c.

oðfæstan, *wv.* entrust, commit ; 12. 9.

oðhrīnan, *sv1. w. g.* touch ; *ind. prs.* 3.*s.* oðrineð xx. 138.

oðīewan, *wv.* show ; appear ; *ind. prs.* 3.*s.* oteweð xiii. 60 ; *pst.* 3.*s.* oðeowde xxviii. 74 ; *sbj. prs.* oðewe 51. 17 ; *pp.* oðewed xxix. 34.

oðsacan, *sv6. w. g. or clause,* deny ; 12 *times,* 66. 17 &c. ; *ind. prs.* 3.*s.* oðsæcð 59. 30, 119. 24.

oðstandan, *sv6.* stand still, stop ; *ind. pst.* 3.*s.* oðstod 102. 30.

cððe, *conj.* or ; 11. 15, ii. 17 &c. ; oðer twegra oððe . . . oððe, either . . . or 23. 27 &c.

oðwītan, *sv1. w. d.* reproach, taunt ; 23. 3 ; *ind. prs.* 2.*pl.* oðwite ge xxvii. 4.

P.

pæð, *m.* path ; *a. pl.* paðas 52. 18, 139. 31.

pæððan, *wv.* walk over, traverse ; *ind. prs.* 3.*pl.* peððað xxxi. 10.

pâpa, *wm.* pope ; *a.* papan 7. 11, i. 42.

pearroc, *m.* enclosed space, tract ; *d.* pearroce 42. 21.

piða, *wm.* pith, core ; *g.* piðan 91. 32.

plantian, *wv.* plant ; *sbj. prs.* plantige 61. 9.

plega, *wm.* game, sport ; 18. 7 ; *a. pl.* plegan 108. 11.

plegian, *wv.* play, frolic ; plegian wið hine 102. 15 ; *ind. prs. pl.* plegiað 108. 11.

pleoh, *n.* danger, risk ; 13. 26 ; *d.* plio 30. 19.

plēolic, *adj.* dangerous ; *comp. n. pl.* pliolicran 30. 25.

prica, *wm.* point ; 42. 14*.

price, *wf.* point ; 41. 25 (pricu B), 42. 14.

pyff, *m.?* puff (of wind), gust ; 47. 26 *n.*

R.

racente, *wf.* chain, fetter ; *d.* racentan 108. 7, xiii. 8, xxv. 37, xxvi. 78 ; *a.* xiii. 29 ; *d. pl.* racentum 37. 10 &c. ; *a.* racentan 57. 9 &c. *and* xxvi. 78.

racian, *wv. w. d.* govern, rule ; *ind. prs.* 3.*s.* racað 98. 22 ; *pst.* 3.*s.* racode 94. 13.

racu, *f.* explanation, argument ; 123. 4, 137. 15 ; rhetoric 38. 8 ; *d.* race 89. 26, 121. 7 ; *a.* 122. 17*, 127. 4, 145. 26 ; *pl. d.* racum 108. 27 ; *a.* raca 122. 17.

râd, *f.* riding ; *d.* rade 88. 20, 21.

gerâd, 1) *sbst. n.* condition ; on ða gerad þ, on condition that 18. 15. 2) *adj. a) denoting condition, circumstance*; gerad beon wið, in opposition to 24. 15 ; *f.* wel gerad, of a good disposition

22. 12 ; *n.* swa gerad, of such a kind 144. 18 ; *a.* swa geradne 134. 15. *b)* wise, prudent ; *a.* geradne 11. 26.

gerâdian, *wv.* arrange ; *pp. pl. n.* geradode 96. 15.

gerâdscipe, *m.* discretion, prudence ; *g.* geradscipes xxii. 48, 50.

rēcan, *wv.* offer, present ; *ind. prs.* 3.*s.* receð xxix. 62.

gerēcan, *wv.* win, gain ; *pp.* geræht xxvi. 18.

rēd, *m.* counsel, plan ; *g.* rædes ii. 12, xxi. 9 ; *a.* ræd MPr. 9, xx. 224.

rēdan, *wv. a) w. d.* govern, control ; *b)* read ; Pr. 11 (*b*) ; i. 67 (*a*) ; *ind. prs.* 3.*s.* ræt 97. 12 (*a*) ; *pst.* 3.*s.* rædde 94. 13 (*a*) ; *sbj. pst.* 96. 9 (*a*).

rēdelse, *wf.* imagination, fancy ; 63. 27 ; *d.* rædelsan 100. 25 ; *a.* 145. 31.

rēpan, *wv.* bind, fetter ; xxvi. 78 ; *pp.* geræped xiii. 8, xxv. 37, 48 *n.* ; *n. pl.* geræpte 112. 1.

rēsan, *wv.* rush ; *ind. prs.* 3.*s.* ræst xxv. 17.

rēswan, *wv.* conjecture ; *ind. prs.* 3.*s.* ræsweð*, hræsweð 51. 13.

randbēag, *m.* boss of shield ; rondbeag 41. 25.

râp, *m.* rope ; *d.* rape 28. 17.

râsettan, *wv.* rage (*of fire*) ; ix. 14.

rēad, *adj.* red ; *a. n.* ix. 14 ; *wk.* reade xix. 6 ; *a. pl.* reade 74. 2, xix. 23.

rēafere, *m.* robber ; 114. 26.

rēafian, *wv.* rob ; *ind. prs.* 3.*s.* on oðrum reafað 28. 1 ; *sbj. prs.* gereafige 71. 17.

rēaflâc, *m.* stolen property, plunder ; *g.* reaflaces 59. 26.

rēo, *m.* smoke ; 117. 17.

gerec, *n.* rule, government ; *d.* gerece 49. 25, xxii. 1.

reccan, *wv. a)* direct, wield ; 40. 11, 13. *b)* explain ; prove ; narrate ; reckon ; *about* 11 *times,* 77. 15 &c. *and* xxvi. 2 ; gereccan

about 18 *times*, Pr. 4, xv. 14 &c.
to recenne 40. 26; to gereccanne
127. 3, 22*; to gerecanne 127.
22; *ind. prs.* 1.*s.* recce 73. 13,
106. 9, xvii. 20; gerecce 24. 20;
2.*s.* recst 103. 27, 123. 5, 137. 15;
pl. reccað 44. 28; *pst.* 1.*s.* reahte
73. 14, 106. 24; rehte 73. 14*;
2.*s.* reahtes 100. 12, 103. 28,
123. 5; gereahtes 97. 22, 100.
24; gerehtest 11. 9*, 97. 20; 3.*s.*
reahte 103. 28, MPr. 1, xxii. 53,
xxx. 8; rehte 140. 9*; gerehte
140. 8*; *pl.* reahton 109. 22,
110. 6, 8, 118. 3; gereahton,
reckoned 143. 20; in anwald
gerehton, subjugated 7. 4*; *sbj.*
prs. recce 96. 26; gerecce 82.
20, 100. 30, 118. 13, 125. 22;
pst. gereahte 122. 20, 126. 31;
pp. gereaht *about* 9 *times*, 26. 10
&c. *and* xi. 99; *a.* gereahtne
habbað 98. 16.
reccan, *wv. w. g.* care for, reck;
ind. prs. 2.*s.* recst xii. 31; recstu
18. 30; 3.*s.* recð 26. 7, 46. 14,
138. 23, viii. 44; *impers. w. a.*
xiii. 45; *pl.* reccað 57. 18, 130.
18; *sbj. prs.* recce 52. 23, 121.
26.
reccelēas, *adj.* careless, negli-
gent; *n. pl.* recelease 13. 21.
reccelīest, *f.* negligence; reccelest
112. 4; recelest xxv. 53; *d.*
recceleste 44. 2.
reccend, *m.* ruler; 101. 4, iv.
30.
reccere, *m.* reasoner, rhetorician;
38. 8.
recene, *adv.* at once, quickly; i.
34, xix. 4, xx. 208, xxviii. 16;
recen xxiv. 17.
gereclīce, *adv.* a) straight (of
direction); v. 14, xxiv. 8. b)
in an orderly manner, methodi-
cally 98. 22.
gerecu, *f.* rule, government; *d.*
gerece 13. 23.
rēn, *m.* rain; 27. 4, 136. 17, vii.
27, 36, xxix. 62; *d.* rene 18.
21, 27. 2, vii. 23; *a.* ren 26. 28,
vii. 14, 21; *n. pl.* renas 52. 5.

gerēne, *n.* ornament; *n. pl.*
gerenu 32. 30.
rēnian, *wv.* adorn, ornament;
pp. gerenod 32. · 29, 30; *d.*
gerenedum 61. 18; *g. pl.* gerenodra 11. 28.
rest, *f.* rest, resting-place; xiii.
71, xxi. 10; ræst 57. 31*, 82.
14*, 89. 9*, xx. 271; *d.* ræste 55.
19*, 57. 30*.
rētan, *wv.* cheer, comfort; *ind.*
prs. 3.*s.* ret 55. 12; *pp. a.* geretne
50. 15.
rēðe, *adj.* fierce, unpropitious;
wk. se reða ren vii. 27; *f.*
reðu; *w.* wyrd 137. 12, 138. 9,
17; *pred.* reðe 137. 12, 138. 12;
wk. 48. 7; *g. f.* reðre*, hreðre 138.
30; *d. wk.* reðan 138. 27, 28;
a. wk. absol. ðone reðan 114.
27; *w.* wyrd 138. 25, 139. 3;
comp. f. reðre 138. 21.
rēðigmōd, *adj.* fierce, raging;
xxv. 17.
rīce, 1) *adj.* powerful, influential;
45. 5, 63. 14, 124. 26, 142. 2;
wk. rica x. 44; *g.* rices 43. 1;
a. wk. rican 46. 15, 61. 18; *pl.*
wk. 62. 32, 63. 29; *g.* ricra
61. 8, 12, i. 46, vii. 14;
wk. ricena 53. 20; *d.* ricum
123. 11, 14; *a. wk.* rican 46.
16, 105. 26, 123. 26, xxiv. 59;
comp. a. ricran 148. 18; *sup. a.*
pl. wk. ricostan ix. 25. 2) *sbst.*
n. power, authority; kingdom;
37. 22, 63. 18, i. 5, 17, ix. 3;
g. rices 40. 9, iv. 45, ix. 3, 10,
xxvi. 8, 11, 41; *d.* rice 7. 1, i.
7 &c.; *a.* 7. 17, ix. 41 &c.; *a.*
pl. ricu Pr. 7, 34. 26.
ricsian, *wv.* rule, reign; · 53. 20,
98. 29, 30; to ricsianne 40. 16;
ind. prs. 2.*s.* ricsast 10. 2; 3.*s.*
ricsað 14. 25, 97. 31, 105. 17;
rixað 104. 6; *pl.* ricsiað 136. 7;
pst. 3.*s.* ricsode xxvi. 57; *sbj.*
prs. ricsige 67. 30.
rīdan, *sv*I. ride; 88. 19; *ind.*
prs. 3.*s.* rit 88. 19; *pl.* ridað
108. 10.
riht, 1) *adj.* straight; right,

proper; 9. 23 &c.; *f.* 123. 4,
137. 6, 139. 20; *n.* 16. 32
&c. *and* xxii. 52; ryht 95.
19*; *g.* rihtes 11. 29; *d.*
rihtum 14. 19, xxiv. 44; *wk.*
rihtan 73. 24, xix. 4; *f.* ryhtre
85. 3; *a.* rihtne 51. 14, 111. 9;
ryhtne 79. 7; *f.* rihte xxiii. 10;
n. ryht 95. 18; *pl. d.* rihtum 9.
24; *a.* rihte 122. 17, 140. 28;
comp. n. rihtre 123. 30; *sup.*
rihtost xxvii. 25; *a. wk.* rihtestan
56. 29. 2) *sbst. n.* right, justice;
123. 29; ryht 124. 12*, 13*;
g. rihtes i. 67, iv. 45, xxv. 53;
d. rihte 94. 28, xxii. 1; mid
rihte, rightly, properly *fq.* 17.
31, xxvi. 41 &c.; mid nanum
ryhte 29. 2; on rihte, rightfully xxvi. 46; *a.* riht 72. 10
&c.; on riht, rightly *fq.* 14.
28, xx. 125 &c.
rihtæðelo, *f.* true nobility; *n. pl.?*
xvii. 20; ryhtæðelo 69. 28*.
rihtan, *wv.* guide, control; *ind.*
prs. 3.*s.* riht 97. 12; *pp.* 50. 4.
rihte, *adv.* a) *of direction,*
straight; 55. 22, v. 14. b)
rightly; 11. 30 &c.; ryhte 59.
27*; rehte 135. 10; rihte ða,
at the moment when 15. 28.
gerihte, *n.* straight direction; up
on gerihte, upright xxxi. 17.
rihtend, *m.* ruler; 10. 16.
rihtere, *m.* director, ruler; 12.
20, 28 *n.*
rihtgeléaffull, *adj.* orthodox;
g. pl. ryhtgeleaffulra 7. 18*.
rihtlic, *adj.* just, proper; 142. 5;
a. n. 143. 30; *comp. n. pl.*
rihtlicran 69. 3.
rihtlíce, *adv.* justly, fairly;
correctly; 83. 16, 121. 1, 125.
27; *comp.* rihtlicor Pr. 12;
ryhtlicor 32. 28.
rihtracu, f. correct explanation;
137. 15.
rihtryne, *m.* right course; *g.*
rihtrynes 14. 17; *d.* rihtryne 14.
15, v. 20, x. 41.
rihtgesetnes, *f.* correct course or
function; *d.* rihtgesetnesse 12. 23.

rihttíma, *wm.* proper season; *a.*
rihttiman 12. 23.
rihtwillende, *adj.* righteous; *g.*
pl. ryhtwillendra 11. 17.
rihtwís, *adj.* righteous; 85. 31,
119. 28, 136. 25, i. 49; *pl.*
rihtwise 133. 8; *wk.* rihtwisan
9. 24; *g.* rihtwisra 7. 19; *wk.*
rihtwisena 11. 17; ryhtwisena
11. 23; *a.* rihtwise 62. 28; *wk.*
rihtwisan 10. 21; *sup. wk.*
rihtwisesta 7. 13*.
rihtwísian, *wv.* direct, rule; *sbj.*
prs. rihtwisige 12. 28.
rihtwíslíce, *adv.* righteously; xxii.
45; ryhtwislice 95. 16*.
rihtwísnes, *f.* righteousness; 62.
26, 87. 8, 148. 28; *g.* rihtwisnesse 95. 21 *n.*, xxii. 48, 56;
ryhtwisnesse 95. 17*, 18*; *d.*
rihtwisnesse 18. 22; *a.* 85. 31,
95. 9 *n.*, xxii. 28, 56; ryhtwisnesse 95. 22*.
gerím, *n.* number; *g.* ymb ðritig
winter gerimes, in number xxviii.
26; *cf.* xxviii. 30.
rinc, *m.* man; *g. pl.* rinca x. 41,
xxii. 28, 45, xxvii. 25.
rind, *f.* bark; *g.* rinde 92. 1; *d.*
92. 6.
rípe, *adj.* ripe; *a. pl. f.* ripa 136.
16, xxix. 62.
gerísan, *sv1. w. d.* suit, befit; *ind.*
prs. 3.*s.* gerist 91. 14.
gerisenlic, *adj.* suitable, fitting;
n. 142. 5.
gerisenlíce, *adv.* suitably; 40. 11.
ríð, *f.* stream, rivulet; *pl.* riða 82.
28; *d.* ryðum v. 20.
rodor, *m.* firmament; 126. 5*,
xx. 208, xxviii. 16; *g.* roderes
125. 31*, xxix. 18; rodres xxviii.
3; *d.* rodore 80. 26* &c.; rodere
in Metr. xx. 124 &c.; *a.* rodor
131. 2, x. 40; *pl. g.* rodora x.
30; rodera xi. 20; *d.* rodorum
xxiii. 10, xxiv. 8; roderum xxiv.
32.
rómánisc, *adj.* Roman; 43. 17; *d.*
romaniscum 36. 17; *d. pl.* 7. 15,
35. 5.
rose, *wf.* rose; *f.* rosan 21. 6, vi. 13.

rûm, 1) *adj.* spacious; *wk.* eall
ruma rodor xxviii. 16; *f.* rum
46. 5; *a. f. wk.* ruman vi. 13,
xx. 136. 2) *sbst. n.* opportunity,
free play; *a.* x. 30; gerum 49. 5.
rûme, *adv.* far and wide; xxiv. 32.
rûmedlic, *adj.* ample, liberal; *g.*
rumedlices 42. 14.
rûmedlîce, *adv.* liberally; 119. 32.
rûmmöd, *adj.* liberal, generous;
149. 3.
rûncofa, *wm.* mind; *d.* runcofan
xxii. 59.
rȳman, *wv.* clear, evacuate; *pp.*
gerymed i. 19.
rȳn, *wv.* roar; 57. 12, xiii. 29,
xxvi. 84; *ind. pst. 3.s.* ryde 116.
17.
ryne, *m.* course; orbit; 96. 20;
d. 49. 1, 8, xi. 20, xxiv. 28; on
ryne, in motion 16. 33; *a.* xi.
37, xxviii. 3; rene xxix. 10.
ryneswift, *adj.* swiftly moving;
rineswifte rodor xx. 208.

S.

sacu, *f.* dispute, quarrel; *g. pl.*
saca xxv. 44.
sadian, *wv.* become satiated,
weary; *sbj. prs. 2.s.* sadige 127.
28.
sæ, *f. m.* (18 *times f.*; *twice m.*;
8 *times uncert.*) sea; 17. 26 &c.;
g. 29. 14, 126. 19; *d.* 42. 16 &c.
and xix. 19; sæ 53. 5*, 86. 19;
a. 14. 12 &c. *and* xxvii. 3, xxviii.
32, 39.
sæd, *n.* seed; 91. 26, 95. 13; *g.*
sædes xxii. 37, 40; *d.* sæde 82.
6, 92. 12; *a.* sæd 12. 8, 136. 18,
xxix. 60; *pl. g.* sæda xx. 250;
d. sædum xxix. 65; *a.* sæd 136.
16.
sæl, *m.* (prosperous) time; *d. pl.*
sælum ii. 2, 7.
sælan, *wv.* happen; *ind. prs. 3.s.*
gesælð xiii. 22; *pst. 3.s.* gesælde
ix. 23, xxvi. 4; *sbj. prs.* gesæle
x. 24; *pst.* gesælde xxviii. 73.

gesælig, *adj.* happy, prosperous;
8. 13 &c. *and* xxiii. 2; *f.* 33. 21;
n. 50. 3, 94. 17, xi. 97; *a.* gesæligne 26. 6, 15. 30. 24, 58. 17;
gesælinne 26. 6*; *pl.* gesælige
113. 19, 133. 23; gesælie 13. 21,
104. 24; *n.* gesælegu 70. 17;
comp. gesæligra 119. 5; *pl.*
gesæligran 118. 22, 122. 18;
sup. gesælegost 24. 19, 48. 12,
58. 26; *wk.* gesælgosta 58. 14*;
gesælgesta 20. 8; *a. wk.* gesælgostan 24. 25.
gesæliglic, *adj.* happy; gesællic
ii. 17.
gesæliglîce, *adv.* happily; gesælilice 24. 9*; gesællice 24. 9, 18*.
gesælignes, *f.* happiness, prosperity 100. 17; *d.* gesælignesse
31. 14; *d. pl.* gesælignessum
54. 27.
gesælð, *f.* prosperity, wealth:
happiness; *fq.* 25. 4 &c. *and*
xii. 19; *g.* gesælðe 58. 9 &c.; *d.*
53. 24 &c.; *a.* 86. 28; *pl. more
fq. than sing.* 21. 13 &c. *and* ii.
19, xix. 32; sælða 6 *times*, 21. 13
&c.; *g.* gesælða *fq.* 21. 25 &c. *and*
xxi. 25; *d.* gesælðum *fq.* 8. 14
&c. *and* vii. 48, xxi. 4, 9; *a.*
gesælða *fq.* 21. 20, vii. 30 &c.;
sælða 14. 20, 15. 29.
sæmra, *comp. adj.* worse, bad; *n.*
sæmre viii. 42; *a. pl.* sæmran,
inferior 75. 1.
sæne, *adj.* sluggish; *a.* sænne
xxvi. 106; *wk.* sænan 114. 30.
sæstrêam, *m.* seaman; *d. pl.*
sæstreamum i. 15.
sætilce, *m.* seaman? *pl.* sætilcas
viii. 31 (*read* scealcas *w. Grein?*).
sæwaroð, *m.* sea-shore; *d.* sæwaroðe 74. 1, xix. 21.
sam, *conj. w. sbj.* sam . . . sam
whether . . . or; 60. 6, 94. 15,
108. 17, 137. 3, 7, 11, 138. 11.
same, *adv.* in the same way; xii.
3; eac swa same, 8 *times in*
Metr. xi. 5 &c.; efne swa same
xx. 124, xxviii. 28; some iv. 26;
swa same swa, just like 81. 20;
conj. swa some swa, as 44. 7.

gesamnian, *wv.* bring together, collect, unite; *ind. prs.* 3.*s.* gesamnað 50. 1, xi. 91 *n.*, 93; *pst.* 3.*s.* gesamnade xvii. 12; gesomnade xx. 246; *sbj. prs.* gesamnige xxii. 11; gesomnige 84. 27.

gesamnung, *f.* gathering, assemblage; *d.* gesomnunga 55. 25.

samod, *adv.* together; xx. 237, xxix. 15; samad xxix. 24; somod xx. 146.

samrād, *adj.* united, unanimous; *a. f.* samrade xi. 96.

samtinges, *adv.* forthwith, immediately; samtenges xxiv. 18.

sāmwīs, *adj.* ignorant, foolish; *pl.* samwise xix. 34.

samwrǣdnes, *f.* union; *a.* samwrædnesse 114. 4.

sand, *n.* sand; sond 26. 28, vii. 20, 23; *d.* sonde 27. 1; *pl.* sond vii. 13; *d.* sondum 91. 18.

sandbeorg, *m.* sand-hill; *a. pl.* sondbeorgas vii. 10; sondbeorhas 26. 26*.

sandcorn, *n.* grain of sand; *g. pl.* sondcorna 19. 2.

sang, *m.* song; sanc xiii. 50; *g.* sanges 50. 9, 15; *a.* sang 52. 15.

sār, *n.* pain; sorrow, grief; 56. 14; *g.* sares 16. 18, xxvi. 82; *d.* sare 15. 7 &c.; *a.* sar 10. 28 &c.

sārcwide, *m.* plaint, lament; *pl. d.* sarcwidum 11. 9; *a.* sarcwidas ii. 4.

sārgian, *wv. trans.* grieve, afflict; *pp. a.* gesargodne 123. 33.

sārig, *adj.* grieved, sorrowful; 22. 10, 102. 3.

sārlic, *adj.* painful; *g. pl.* sarlicra 26. 19.

sārlīce, *adv.* sorrowfully; 59. 33, 138. 15; lamentably 44. 1.

sāwan, *rv.* sow; 51. 28; *ind. prs.* 3.*s.* sæwð 61. 10.

sāwol, *f.* soul; sawul 81. 16*; sawl 6 *times in* C, 45. 26 &c., *twice in* B, 71. 7, 95. 14; saul 6 *times in* C, *not in* B, 86. 29 &c. *and* xx. 210, 238; *g.* sawle 4 *times in* C, 45. 25 &c., *twice in* B, 81. 15, 132. 15; saule 81. 27*, 87. 7, xx. 185, 202; *d.* sawle 95. 13*; saule 32. 2*, 72. 4*, 87. 1, xxii. 38; *a.* sawle 91. 11, 93. 26, 27*, xvii. 12, xx. 177; saule 81. 25*, 102. 2, xx. 204; *pl.* sawula 26. 11*; sawla 26. 11; saula 148. 2, xxi. 35; *g.* sawla 132. 14*, xviii. 8; saula xxi. 9, xxiii. 11; *d.* sawlum 81. 33*; saulum xx. 226, xxi. 44; *a.* sawla 81. 14, 82. 2*, 129. 4; saula 69. 23*, xx. 236.

gescād, *n.* discrimination, reason; *d.* gesccade xxii. 44; *a.* gescead xx. 218.

gescādlic, *adj.* rational, reasonable; *n.* gesceadlic 86. 11*.

gescādlīce, *adv.* with discrimination, rationally; gesceadlice 100. 28, xx. 88; *comp.* gesceadlicor 125. 22.

gescādwīs, *adj.* discriminating, intelligent; gesceadwis 31. 28, 61. 24, 64. 29, 66. 15, 109. 15 *and* xv. 14; *wk.* gesceadwisa 132. 20; *f.* gesceadwis 81. 19, *n.* 140. 23, 147. 18; *d.* gesceadwisum 13. 12, xx. 8; *wk.* gesceadwisan 36. 15, 72. 4; *pl.* gesceadwise 25. 5; *wk.* gesceadwisan 109. 7; *f.* gesceadwisa 140. 27; *d.* gesceadwisum 63. 30; *a. f.* gesceadwisa 142. 8.

gescādwīslic, *adj.* rational, reasonable; *wk.* gesceadwislica 32. 3; *n.* gesceadwislic 86. 11; *d. f.* gesceadwislicere 89. 26.

gescādwīslīce, *adv.* rationally, reasonably; gesceadwislice 27. 21 &c.; skilfully 103. 23.

gescādwīsnes, *f.* discrimination, intelligence; gesceadwisnes 10 *times*, 12. 15 &c. *and* xx. 188, 197; sceadwisnes 12. 15*; *g.* gesceadwisnesse 45. 1, 146. 10; *d.* 4 *times*, 11. 16 &c.; *a.* 5 *times*, 29. 1 &c.

scamian, *wv. impers. w. g.* be ashamed; 6ª. 15, x. 13; scamigan 46. 6*; *ind. prs.* 3.*s.*

sceamað 20. 1, 69. 12*, 98. 25;
pst. sceamode 19. 30.
scamlēas, *adj.* shameless; *a.*
sceamleasne 62. 9*.
scamu, *f.* shame; *a.* sceame 24. 2.
scandlic, *adj.* disgraceful, in-
famous; xx. 188; *n.* 32. 31.
sceaða, *wm.* worker of harm, enemy;
pl. sceaðan 8. 23*.
sceadu, *f.* shadow; 63. 26; *d.*
sceade 63. 13, 133. 12; *a.* 136.
2; *pl. d.* sceadum 33. 31; *a.*
sceaduwa 74. 17 *n.*
sceaft, *m.* pole; *d.* sceafte i. 11.
gesceaft, *f. n.* creation; creature;
very fq. 32. 5, xi. 41 &c.; *g.*
gesceafte 28. 31, 94. 22; gesceaftes
29. 3; *d.* gesceafte 147. 21; *a.*
gesceaft 142. 7; sceaft 69. 27*,
31*, 142. 7*; *pl.* gesceafta 10.
14, iv. 25 &c.; sceafta 146. 11*;
gesceafte xi. 8; *g.* gesceafta 10.
16, iv. 30 &c.; *d.* gesceaftum
31. 26 &c. *and* xi. 13, 55; *a.*
gesceafta 10. 25, xi. 32 &c.;
gescefta 49. 6*; gesceaftu 136.
23*.
sceal, *anv. denoting obligation,
necessity, reasonableness,* shall,
must, ought, is to; *w.* niede 84.
26, 85. 19, 94. 14, 106. 14, 145.
15, 148. 6; *absol.* sceal nede to
ðara hlaforda dome, is bound
by, must obey 112. 8; *denoting
second-hand statement, fq.* 98.
27 &c. *and* xxvi. 51, 74; licette
þ he sceolde bion, that he was
115. 24; *forms:* *ind. prs.* 1.*s.*
51. 19, MPr 8 &c.; 2.*s.* scealt
125. 26 &c. *and* v. 26, 28; 3.*s.*
sceal Pr. 13, vii. 30 &c.; sceall
128. 17, 144. 7; scel 123. 33;
pl. sculon 12. 26, xxiii. 7 &c.;
sceolon 94. 14*; *pst.* 1 *and* 3.*s.*
scolde 17. 31, 147. 16, ii. 14;
sceolde 115. 24, ii. 14 &c.; 2.*s.*
sceoldest 18. 26* &c.; sceoldes
13. 26, 19. 16; *pl.* scoldon 67. 10,
147. 12; sceoldon ix. 58, xxvi.
84, xxix. 89; sceoldan 8. 13*,
116. 18*, i. 31 (J); scioldon xxvi.
82; *sbj. prs.* scyle 12. 14 &c.

and xiv. 4; scile 134. 25; *pl.*
scylen 79. 5 &c. *and* xxi. 34;
scylon 42. 25*, 56. 22*, 70. 10*;
scylan 46. 31*, 60. 3*; *pst.* 1
and 3.*s. like ind.* sceolde 18. 26,
iv. 35 &c.; *pl.* sceolden 31. 2,
45. 3, 142. 5, xxix. 87; scolden
118. 4; sceoldon 9. 6* &c.
scealc, *m.* servant; man; xv. 14;
g. pl. scealca viii. 21.
sceard, *n.* indentation, inlet; *a. pl.*
42. 6.
scearp, *adj.* sharp, keen; 127. 17.
scearpnes, *f.* keenness; *a.* scearpnesse 89. 14, xxi. 24.
scearpsiene, *adj.* keen-sighted;
72. 31, 73. 3.
sceat, *m. a)* region, quarter; *b)*
spread, shelter; *d.* sceate 133.
12 (*b*); *a.* sceat iv. 52 (*a*), viii.
5 (*a*), xi. 66 (*a*); *a. pl.* sceatas
x. 17 (*a*).
sceawian, *wv.* see; *ind. prs.* 3.*pl.*
sceawiað 73. 8; *sbj. prs.* gescea-
wige 51. 21.
sceawung, *f.* seeing, contempla-
tion; *d.* sceawunga 89. 15, xxi.
24.
scendan, *wv.* put to shame; *pp.*
gescended v. 32.
scēotend, *m.* warrior; *pl.* i. 11.
scield, *m.* shield; *d.* scelde 41.
26; *a. pl.* sceldas i. 2.
scieldan, *wv.* protect; *ind. pst.*
3.*s.* scilde 133. 12; ða scylde he
ongean, defended himself 45. 13.
sciell, *f.* shell; scell xx. 174.
sciellfisc, *m.* shell-fish; *n. pl.*
scylfiscas 146. 1.
sciene, *adj.* beautiful; xxix. 25.
scieppan, *sv6.* create, make;
sceppan ðone naman 39. 5; *ind.
pst.* 2.*s.* gesceope 31. 8, xx. 5
&c.; 3.*s.* gesceop 29. 8, viii. 17
&c.; sceop 125. 27*; *sbj. pst.*
2.*s.* gescope 29. 21*; *pp.* gesceapen 57. 7 &c.; him swa
gesceapen wæs, they were so
fashioned, constituted 142. 30;
pl. gesceapene 30. 5, 31. 9; *f.*
146. 11*; *n.* 30. 4; gesceapne
135. 26.

scieppend, *m.* creator; scippend
10. 1*, 16*, 135. 9, iv. 1, xvii.
9; sceppend 19. 19, 48. 22*,
72. 18, 85. 2, 93. 20 *n.*, 125. 26,
iv. 30, xi. 1, xxix. 81; scyppend
141. 17*; sceoppend 136. 22*;
g. scippendes 98. 10, 12*; sceppendes 19. 21, 32. 5*; scyppendes 92. 8, 9, 10; sceoppendes
19. 14*, 32. 4*; *d.* scippende
32. 9; sceppende 128. 17; *a.*
scippend 69. 28*, 81. 29*;
sceppend 69. 31*, xx. 216;
scyppend xx. 218; sceoppend
81. 28*.

scierpan, *wv.* clothe, deck; *ind.*
pst. 3.*s.* gescerpte xv. 2; gescyrpte 64. 25*; *pp.* gescerped
92. 5.

scīma, *wm.* light, brightness; 12.
7; *g.* sciman 89. 22; *d.* 10. 4,
126. 20; *a.* 97. 15.

scīnan, *sv1.* shine; 95. 12, xxii.
35; *ind. prs.* 3.*s.* scineð 21. 2*,
v. 3, vi. 3, xxii. 24, xxviii. 27,
60; scinð 12. 8, 121. 11; *pl.*
scinað 19. 3, 81. 35, 111. 13,
112. 16, 126. 14, 15, xx. 229,
233, xxv. 4; *sbj. prs.* 3.*pl.*
scinen xxviii. 45.

gescīnan, *sv1.* shine on, illuminate; 141. 15, 16, xxx. 9, 11;
ind. prs. 3.*s.* gescinð 86. 8.

scinlāc, *n.* magic art; *d.* scinlace
xxvi. 74.

scip, *n.* ship; *g.* scipes 16. 29; *d.*
scipe 97. 13; *g. pl.* scipa 115.
18, 20, xxvi. 15, 28.

sciphere, *m.* fleet; *a.* sciphere 34.
2; *a. pl.* sciphergas viii. 31.

scipstīera, *wm.* steersman; scipstiora 144. 28.

scīr, *adj.* bright, clear; i. 11, v.
18; *f.* xxx. 9; *wk.* scire xx.
174; *a. f. wk.* sciran xx. 229;
n. scir win, pure 33. 29, viii.
21; *pl. g.* scirra iv. 1, xx. 8; *d.*
scirum xxviii. 45.

scolu, *f.* a) school; b) troop,
host; *d.* scole 8. 18 (a); *a. pl.*
scola xxvi. 31 (b).

scop, *m.* poet; sceop 68. 8, 141.

11*; sciop 101. 3; *d.* sccope
xxx. 4.

scort, *adj.* short; 44. 26; *n. wk.*
scorte 117. 32; *d. wk.* scortan
44. 30; *a.* scortne 126. 4, 139.
26; *a. pl. f.* scorte 10. 10*;
sceorta iv. 20 (J); *comp. a.*
scyrtran 126. 2, xxviii. 8, 11;
sup. a. scyrtestne 139. 26.

scride, *m.* course, orbit; *a.*
xxviii. 11.

scridwǣn, *n.* carriage, chariot;
d. scridwæne 61. 19.

scrīfan, *sv1.* a) decree, ordain;
b) care for, reck; *ind. prs.* 3.*s.*
w. g. scrifeð x. 29 (b), xxv. 53
(b); *w. d.* scrifð xxv. 15 (b);
pst. 3.*s.* gescraf i. 29 (a).

scrīðan, *sv1.* glide, move; *ind.*
prs. 3.*s.* scriðeð xx. 174, xxviii.
16; *pl.* scriðað xxviii. 8; *prs.*
p. scriðende xx. 216.

scucca, *wm.* evil spirit, demon;
g. pl. scuccena 129. 6.

scūfan, *sv2.* move, fall; *ind. prs.*
3.*s.* scyfð xiii. 58.

scūrmǣlum, *adv.* in gusts,
stormily; scyrmælum 47. 25.

scyld, *f.* guilt; *d.* scylde 67. 4,
102. 30; *a.* 112. 12, xxv. 71;
pl. g. scylda 131. 15; *a.* 123.
22.

scyldig, *adj.* guilty; *d. wk.*
scyldgan 123. 19; *a.* scyl-
digne 19. 26; *wk.* scyldgan 123.
18; *pl. wk.* scyldgan 123. 21;
d. scildigum 10. 19*; *comp.*
scyldigra, more to blame 19. 19.

se, *demonst. adj.* (*f.* seo; *n.* ðæt);
that, the; *passim*; *w. proper*
names, 7. 6, xxvi. 34 &c.; *fq.*
used as pers. pron. 7. 13 &c.;
as rel. 19. 31 &c.; *esp. n.* ðæt
7. 3, xix. 3 &c.; *w. masc. antec.*
xxviii. 5, 18, 31, 40; *fem.* 35. 31;
compd. that which Pr. 14, xiii. 79
&c.; eall ðæt 22. 30, xxii. 14 &c.;
ðæt ðæt 11. 30, xx. 120 &c.; *fq.*
used as conj., v. ðæt; ðæs *used*
as adv., v. ðæs; ðæm *w. strong*
adj. 134. 32; *inst.* ðon, ðy;
ðon *only used w. preps. or as*

adv. w. comp., v. ðon; ðy 17.
25, 32. 18; also as *adv., v.* ðȳ;
and w. preps.: *w.* be 83. 1; mid
135. 18, xxv. 13, xxxi. 18; for
101. 28 &c.; on 58. 19; *forms*:
f. sio *usual in* C, 12. 16, iv. 34
&c.; seo 29. 16, i. 22 &c.; seo
usual in B, 23. 8 &c.; sio *about*
12 *times*, 22. 24 &c.; sie 80.
6*; *n.* ðæt; *g. gen.* ðæs *in* B
and C, 11. 25 &c.; ðas 53. 26*,
28*, 111. 24*; *f.* ðære; *d.*
ðæm *in* C, 12. 7, i. 40 &c.;
ðam *about* 14 *times*, 12. 20, i.
44 &c.; ðam *in* B, 7. 20 &c.;
ðan 9. 16*; *f.* ðære; ðæræ 49.
22*; *a.* ðone; ðæne 115. 26*;
f. ða; *n.* ðæt; *inst.* ðon, ðy;
ðy *is usual form in* C; ði 138.
21; ðe 82. 25, 121. 22, xi. 29
and fq. as *adv., v.* ðe; ða 138.
8; ði *in* B, 35. 15 &c.; *pl.* ða;
ta *after* ðæt 107. 7; *g.* ðara;
ðæra 53. 20, 80. 1*, 146. 22*;
d. ðæm *in* C, 15. 5, iv. 20 &c.;
ðam *about* 7 *times*, 25. 1, i. 21
&c.; ðam *in* B, Pr. 4 &c.;
ðan 14. 13*; *a.* ða; ðā 40. 1.

sealt, *adj.* salt; *a.* sealtne xix.
16.

searo, *n.* device, wile; *g. pl.*?
searuwa ix. 37.

searocræft, *m.* device, artifice; *d.
pl.* siarocræftum viii. 24.

searogimm, *m.* precious stone;
g. pl. searogimma xxi. 21.

searolice, *adv.* cunningly, clever-
ly; viii. 26.

sēað, *m.* pit; *d.* scaðe 9. 11, iii. 2.

sēcan, *wv.* seek; *fq.* 12. 10, xix.
5 &c.; gesecan 102. 10, xxix.
8; to secanne 74. 8, 94. 24;
ind. prs. 1.*s.* sece 11. 29; 3.*s.*
seceð xix. 8, 45, xxii. 15; secð
56. 17 &c.; *pl.* secað 1 *fq.* 31.
26 &c.; sece ge 25. 14; *pst.*
1.*s.* sohte 97. 25; 3.*s.* 95. 1,
xxii. 7; *pl.* sohton 26. 18, 99.
23, 127. 4; *sbj. prs.* sece 89. 7,
xxi. 7, xxii. 8; gesece 53. 5;
pl. secan 73. 25*; *prs. p.*
secende xx. 214, 221.

secg, *m.* man; *a.* MPr. 7; *g. pl.*?
secgge *for* secggea (?) ix. 42.

secgan, *wv.* say, tell; *fq.* 36. 21,
ii. 17 &c.; gesecgan 71. 14, xix.
40; seggan 8. 13*, 68. 7, 70. 2,
3, 99. 4, 6; secgean 27. 15,
MPr. 10; secggean 66. 20; to
secganne 13. 14, 39. 10*, 41.
3*; *ind. prs.* 1.*s.* secge 27. 25
&c. *and* xii. 29; seccge 54. 9;
2.*s.* sægst *usual form in* C, 75.
6 &c.; segst *in* B, 23. 12 &c.;
3.*s.* sægð 83. 26, 127. 8; *pl.*
secgað 81. 17 &c. *and* xxi. 4;
seggað 68. 19, xx. 184; *pst.* 1.*s.*
sæde xxv. 54, 60; 2.*s.* sædest
usual form 9. 23 &c.; sædes 8
times in C, 98. 24 &c.; 3.*s.* sæde
9. 5 &c.; *pl.* sædon 143. 22, ix.
61, xxvi. 74; sæde wit 143. 22*;
imp. saga 21. 26, 107. 20;
sæge 13. 2, 27. 23; sege *usual
form* 27. 27 &c.; gesege 12. 27,
20. 28, 62. 2, 68. 14; *sbj. prs.*
secge 75. 3, 120. 6, 140. 12;
gesecge 95. 2, xxii. 13; *pst.*
sæde 50. 21, xx. 182; *pp.*
gesæd 5 *times*, 25. 29 &c.

sefa, *wm.* mind, heart; i. 71; xxv.
46; *g.* sefan xxv. 42; *d.* xvi. 2,
xix. 38, xxii. 8, xxvi. 65; *a.*
xxii. 33.

sēfte, *adj.* easy, mild; *f. wk.* 82.
13; *g.* seftes 138. 22; *a.* seftne
132. 7; *comp. a.* seftran 133.
10.

segl, *n.* sail; *a.* 16. 29, 144. 30.

sēl, *adv.* better; sæl xv. 10; *sup.*
selest 91. 14.

seldan, *adv.* seldom; seldon 35.
7, xxviii. 71; seldum hwonne
115. 8; *comp.* seldnor xxviii. 66;
sup. seldost 126. 22.

seldcūð, *adj.* rare, wonderful: *g.*
seldcuðes 85. 25; *wk.* seldcuðan
102. 21; *a. f.* seldcuðe 100. 10;
a. pl. n. seldcuð 127. 2.

seldhwonne, *adv.* seldom; 43. 30.

self, *pron.* self; same; ic . . . self
47. 5; ðu self 13. 11, xx. 16 &c.;
ðu ðe self 11. 8, 28. 24, 104. 4;
he self 22. 32, ix. 31 &c.; hio . . .

self 47. 19 ; sio gesælð self 87.
19 ; *n.* good self 83. 7 ; *wk.*
selfa 11 *times in* Met. i. 32 &c. ;
eart ðe selfa xx. 45 ; *g.* ðines
selfes 25. 22 ; his selfes 37. 15,
59. 32, xvi. 2, 21 ; *d.* ðe selfum
13. 14, v. 37 &c. ; ðe selfum
agnes 69. 10 ; Gode selfum xx.
35 ; him selfum *f.* selfre xiii.
75, xx. 206, 220, 222 ; *wk.* on
ðisse selfan bec, same xxv. 54 ;
a. ðe selfne 16. 26 &c. *and* xx.
273 ; hinc selfne 8. 5 &c. ; *f.* hie
selfe 13. 31, xx. 211 &c. ; *pl.* ge
selfe 32. 16 ; him selfe 49. 32,
53. 20, xi. 87 ; *g.* selfra willum,
by your own consent x. 19 ;
heora selfra 30. 12, 38. 22 ; *d.*
eow selfum 31. 25 ; *a.* us selfe
29. 6, 8 ; eow selfe 29. 5, 32.
13 ; hie selfe 32. 19, 38. 21.

selfe, *adv.* swa selfe, in the same
way, also ; xvii. 25, xx. 192, 199.

selflíce, 1) *sbst. n.* conceit, ego-
tism ; *a.* 9. 27. 2) *adj.* conceited ;
a. selflicne MPr. 7.

selfwill, *n.* one's own will ; *d.*
selfwille 24. 20, iv. 50.

sellan, *wv.* give ; 14. 10, 25. 30,
58. 20, 64. 14, 22, 78. 11, 22 ;
to sellanne 117. 21, 143. 23 ;
ind. prs. 2.*s.* selest 10. 10, 30.
14, iv. 21, xx. 226 ; sellest 10.
13* ; 3.*s.* seleð 133. 21, xvii. 10 ;
selð 19. 10, 27. 30, 28. 2, 7, 69.
21, 125. 16 ; geselð*, gesælð 77.
5 ; *pl.* sellað 143. 1 ; *pst.* 1.*s.*
sealde 8. 21 ; 2.*s.* sealdest 22. 8 ;
gesealdest 16. 31 ; 3.*s.* sealde
113. 7, 142. 11, 145. 16 ; *pl.*
sealdon i. 24 ; *sbj. prs.* selle 38.
32, 132. 6, 134. 13, 141. 23 ; *pl.*
sellen 28. 20 ; *pp.* geseald 28. 8,
77. 8 ; *a.* gesealdne 18. 2.

sellic, *adj.* rare, wonderful ; *n.*
xxviii. 53 ; *comp. n.* sellicre xi.
50.

sélra, *comp. adj.* good ; better ;
xv. 15 ; sella i. 50 ; *sup.* selest,
best 141. 11, 13 ; *wk.* selesta
xx. 203 ; *f. wk.* seleste 52. 31,
53. 15 ; *d.* selestum, gesælestum*

76. 15 ; *pl. wk.* selestan 77. 28,
30, 84. 4, 5, 129. 24, 130. 16 ;
a. wk. 56. 17.

sendan, *wv.* send ; 99. 2 ; *ind. prs.*
3.*s.* sendeð xxix. 84*n.* ; sent 136
25 ; *pst.* 3.*s.* sende 7. 19, i. 63.

séo, *v.* se.

séoc, *adj.* ill, sick ; *wk.* sioca 123.
13 ; *a.* siocne 107. 29, 123. 32.

seofian, *wv. trans. and intrans.*
lament ; siofian 21. 26, 116. 18,
120. 27, xxvi. 82 ; *ind. prs.* 2.*s.*
siofast 17. 16 ; *pl.* seofiað 61.
14* ; *pst.* 2.*s.* seofodest 11. 31 ;
siofodes 120. 24, 143. 5 ; *sbj.*
prs. scofige 19. 4 ; siofige 104.
11, 26 ; *prs. p.* siofigende ii. 2.

seofon, *num.* seven ; siofon 127.
10.

seofung, *f.* lamenting, lamentation ; 59. 25 ; siofung 143. 4 ; *a.*
seofunga 19. 3, 67. 29 ; *g. pl.*
siofunga xvi. 7.

seolfor, *n.* silver ; 120. 15 ; *d.*
seolfre 19. 5.

seolfren, *adj.* of silver ; *n.* sylofren xxi. 21 ; *pl. wk.* seolfrenan
89. 12 ; *n.* selfrenu, sylfrenu*
104. 17.

seoloc, *m.* silk ; *d.* sioloce viii. 24.

seolocen, *adj.* of silk ; *g. pl.*
seolocenra 33. 30.

geséon, *wv.* see ; *usual form in*
B, 39. 21 &c. ; gesion 89. 20*,
105. 8*, 124. 7* ; seon 122. 1* ;
gesion *in* C, 89. 31, xx. 259 &c. ;
to seonne 14. 12* ; to geseonne
81. 3* ; *ind. prs.* 1.*s.* geseo 9.
16* ; 2.*s.* gesihst 9. 24 &c. ; 3.*s.*
gesiehð 126. 22* ; gesihð 38. 4
&c. *and* xxviii. 66 ; geseohð 141.
18 ; *pl.* geseoð 61. 13* &c. ;
gesioð 107. 30 &c. *and* xx. 231,
xxviii. 71 ; *pst.* 1.*s.* geseah 11. 3
&c. ; 3.*s.* seah viii. 29 ; geseah
34. 1 &c. ; *pl.* gesawon 33. 25,
99. 25, viii. 13 ; gesawan viii.
36 (J) ; *sbj. prs.* gesio 22. 32,
52. 1* ; *pst.* gesawe 22. 8, 62.
15 ; *pl.* gesawan 35. 31* ; *pp.*
gesewen 136. 1*.

setl, *n. a)* seat, abode ; *b)* setting

(of sun); *d.* setle 10. 2 (*a*), 126.
12 (*b*); *a.* setl 19. 14 (*a*); on
setl xxviii. 39 (*b*), xxix. 27 (*b*),
31 (*b*); *a. pl.* sitlu ix. 42 (*a*).

gesetnes, *f.* institution; decree,
law; *a.* gesetennesse 49. 26 *n.*;
pl. gesetenessa 43. 22; *a.* gesetnessa 10. 14, xi. 71.

settan, *wv.* place, set; appoint,
establish; 26. 24, vii. 10; him
an settan, inflict 133. 5; gesettan, compose 8. 7; to gesettane
vi. 7 (J); *ind. prs.* 3.*s.* set 98.
23; geset 69. 22; *pl.* settað 73.
29; *pst.* 1.*s.* sette ii. 7; 2.*s.*
settest 19. 14; gesettest 79. 13,
80. 2, xx. 89, 91, 177; 3.*s.* sette
word be worde, translated Pr.
3; gesette 48. 27; *pl.* setton
viii. 26; *intrans.* set out, i. 4;
imp. sete 26. 27, 91. 21; *sbj.*
prs. sette 26. 26; sette domas
35. 31; gesette xi. 12, 21; *pl.*
settan 73. 28*, xix. 10; setton
73. 31*; *pp.* geset 25. 15, 49. 2,
49. 17, xi. 56; *a. f.* gesette 49.
24, xi. 65.

seðan, *wv.* prove; geseðan 17. 9;
pp. geseðed 89. 26.

gesewenlic, *adj.* visible; *pl. f.*
gesewenlica 128. 2; *g.* gesewenlicra 48. 24, xx. 7; *d.* gesewenlicum 80. 27, xx. 127; *a. f.* gesewenlice 79. 11*.

sibb, *f.* peace; *d.* on sibbe 53. 23;
a. 48. 28, xi. 14 &c.

gesibblice, *adv.* peacefully; gesiblice xx. 68.

gesibbsum, *adj.* peaceable, mild;
wk. gesibsuma 136. 10.

sibbsumlice, *adv.* peacefully; sib-
sumlice 80. 3.

sicettung, *f.* sighing, lamentation;
siccetung ii. 4 (J).

sid, *adj.* spacious; *f. wk.* side
xxix. 75; *a.* sidne xxix. 60;
wk. sidan xi. 63, xx. 127; *pl. g.*
sidra xiii. 11, xxv. 55; *a. f.* sida
xxix. 47.

sidu, *m.* custom, habit; sido 61.
19, 131. 32; *a.* 48. 27, xi. 12;
sidu 16. 28; *pl. d.* sidum 42. 24.

sierwan, *wv.* plot; *w.* ymbe; *ind.*
pst. pl. sieredon 36. 19*, 22*,
70. 24*; siredon 36. 19; syredon
36. 22.

sifeða, *f. pl.* siftings, bran; syfeða,
siofoða* 93. 5.

siftan, *wv.* sift; *ind. prs.* 3.*s.* seft
93. 5.

sigan, *sv*1. fall, sink; iv. 50, vii.
23, xx. 165; *ind. prs. pl.* sigað
xxix. 15; *sbj. prs.* sige 81. 12;
prs. p. sigende 26. 28; *d. wk.*
sigendan 27. 1.

sige, *m.* setting (of sun); *d.* on sige
xiii. 56; *a.* 37. 7.

sigedryhten, *m.* victorious lord,
king; sigedrihten xx. 260.

sigeðeod, *f.* victorious nation; *n.*
pl. sigeðeoda i. 4.

sigor, *m.* victory, triumph; *g. pl.*
sigora xi. 27, 71, 96, xx. 204.

gesihð, *f.* sight, sense of sight;
145. 18, 24; *a.* gesihðe 14. 6.

simbel, *adv.* always; on symbel
18. 6, xi. 50, 94.

simle, *adv.* always; *usual form*
in B, 11. 20 &c.; *about* 15 *times*
in C, 30. 26, ii. 19 &c.; symle
usual form in C, *about* 60 *times*,
18. 17, viii. 18 &c.; *sometimes*
written syle 106. 5 &c.; *not in*
B; siemle 14. 24*, 18. 31*;
semle 87. 31, 117. 32, xx. 198.

sin, *rflx. poss. adj.* his, her, its; *g.*
sines iv. 10, xxi. 38, xxii. 62; *d.*
sinum xxii. 57; *g. pl.* sinra ix.
56, xxvi. 70.

sinbiernende, *adj.* ever-burning;
n. sinbyrnende viii. 52.

sincgiefa, *wm.* giver of treasure,
lord; sincgeofa i. 50.

sincstan, *m.* jewel; xxi. 21.

singal, *adj.* continuous, lasting;
wk. singala 26. 6; *f.* singale vii.
50; *wk.* 27. 13; *d.* singalum 134.
32; *a.* singalne 78. 12, 126. 17,
xxviii. 53; *f.* singale xxix. 5.

singallice, *adv.* continually, constantly; 27. 11, 41. 9, vii. 46,
xi. 14.

singan, *sv*3. sing; recite; 8. 7, ii.
4 &c.; *ind. prs. pl.* singað 18.

28 ; *pst.* 1.*s.* sanc ii. 2 (J); song
8. 6*; 3.*s.* sang 33. 13, vi. 2 ;
song vii. 3; *prs. p.* singend 8. 5 ;
singende 9. 29 &c. ; singende
ðone ealdan cwede 33. 13 ; singinde 73. 22.

sinhīwscipe, *m.* marriage ; *a. pl.*
sinhigscipas 50. 1.

sinscipe, *m.* marriage ; *a. pl.* sinscipas xi. 91.

sittan, *sv*5. sit ; dwell ; 18. 25, 61.
18, 22, III. 13 ; *ind. prs.* 3.*s.*
siteð xxix. 75 ; sit 136. 14, 22,
148. 31 ; *pl.* sittað 10. 19, iv.
37 ; *pst.* 3.*s.* sæt 102. 4, xxvi.
16 ; *pl.* sæton 61. 20 ; on sæton,
attacked ; *sbj. prs. rflx.* sitte
him 104. 33.

sīð, *m. a*) journey ; xxvi. 62 ; *a.*
iv. 16. *b*) time ; on anne sið,
all at once 39. 19.

gesīð, *m.* companion, warrior ; *d.*
pl. gesiðum xxvi. 20.

siððan, 1) *adv.* since, afterwards ;
14. 7, v. 17 &c.; siðða xxiv. 30.
2) *conj.* after, since ; 20. 3, xxiv.
25 &c. ; *w. sbj.* 52. 24, 139. 11 ;
siððan þ 112. 2 ; siðæs 45. 30*.

sīwian, *wv.* sew ; siowian viii. 24.

slǣpan, *rv.* sleep ; *ind. prs.* 3.*s.*
slæpð 148. 22 ; *pl.* slapað 93.
9 ; *pst. pl.* slepon 33. 31 ; *rflx.*
him slepon viii. 27.

slǣwð, *f.* sloth ; *d* slæwðe 44. 2,
109. 4.

slǎw, *adj.* sluggish, slothful ; 114.
31.

slēan, *sv*6. *a*) strike ; *b*) cast ; *c*)
intrans. plunge ; 116. 15 (*b*) ;
ind. prs. pl. sleað 99. 24 (*a*),
115. 9 (*c*).

sliepan, *wv.* slip, put (on) ; *ind.*
pst. 3.*s.* hefig geoc slepte ix. 55.

slītan, *sv*I. tear, rend ; xiii. 29 ;
ind. pst. 3.*s.* slat 103. 1.

slīðen, *adj.* severe, cruel ; *f. wk.*
sliðne 13. 24.

smæl, *adj.* narrow, slender ; *inst.*
smale 65. 30 (smalan B) ; *n. pl.*
wk. smalan 36. 9.

smale, *adv.* finely ; smale todæle
swa dust 28. 22.

smēagan, *wv.* investigate, examine ; reflect ; 7. 17, 36. 5,
41. 19 ; smeagean 50. 28 ; *ind.*
prs. 3.*s.* smeað 81. 29, 30, 129.
28, 148. 15, xx. 214, 215, 221 ;
pst. 3.*s.* smeade 55. 9 ; *imp. pl.*
smeageað, smeagð* 73. 9 ; *sbj.*
prs. pl. smeagen, smean* 146.
21 ; *prs. p.* smeagende 81. 27,
xx. 212.

smēalic, *adj.* searching, profound ;
d. wk. smealican 50. 14.

smēalice, *adv.* searchingly, pro-
foundly ; 28. 22, 52. 15 ; *comp.*
smealicor 27. 16 ; *sup.* smealicost
21. 15.

smearcian, *wv.* smile ; 127. 2 ;
ind. pst. 3.*s.* smearcode 91. 11,
94. 16, 137. 28 ; smearcade 98.
20 ; smercode 94. 16*.

smēaung, *f.* meditation, reflec-
tion ; 130. 29.

smīec, *m.* smoke ; smcc 63. 27.

smolte, *adv.* gently ; vi. 8.

smūgan, *sv*2. creep ; *prs. p.*
smugende 53. 7 ; smuhende 147.
5*.

smylte, 1) *adj.* calm, mild ; *f.*
smyltu 89. 10 ; smylte xxi. 15 ;
n. 52. 4 ; *g. f.* smyltre 29. 14 ;
a. wk. smyltan 10. 13 ; smylton
21. 7 ; *f.* smylte v. 7 ; *inst.* 14.
12 ; *g. pl.* smyltra 17. 26. 2)
adv. gently, softly ; 21. 4.

snǎw, *m.* snow ; xxix. 63 ; *pl.*
snawas 52. 5, 136. 17.

snǎwceald, *adj.* cold as snow ; *g.*
snawcealdes xxix. 8.

snīcan, *sv*I. creep ; *ind. prs.* 3.*pl.*
snicað xxxi. 6 ; *prs. p.* snicende
147. 5 *n.*

snīðan, *sv*I. cut off, remove ; 123.
15.

snytro, *f.* prudence, wisdom ; *a.*
20. 11 ; snyttro 17. 13.

sōfte, 1) *adj.* quiet, gentle ; *a.*
pl. f. softa xxix. 47. 2) *adv.*
gently ; xx. 7, 68, 272, xxiv. 53 ;
comp. softor, more comfortably,
more easily 133. 17.

sol, *n.* mire ; *pl.* dirty places ; *d.*
solum 115. 7 ; *a.* solu 115. 9.

sŏn, *m.* sweet sound, music; *g.*
sones 102. 8, 21.

sōna, *adv.* immediately, at once;
9. 19, viii. 1 &c.; sona swa, as
soon as 11. 2, 14. 3, 116. 6, 141.
5.

sorg, *f.* grief; affliction; 70. 27;
g. sorges 16. 18*; sorge 127.
24; *d.* 16. 11, 24. 16, 70. 7; *d.
pl.* sorgum 66. 3, iii. 8, xxvi. 96.

sorgian, *wv.* grieve, be troubled;
to sorgienne 24. 16*; *ind. pst.*
3.*s.* sorgode ix. 34; *prs. p.* sorgiende 17. 14, 116. 26; *a.*
sorgiendne 20. 31.

sōð, 1) *adj.* true, real; 17. 18 &c.
and xx. 246; *wk.* soða xx. 51;
f. soðe 141. 19*; *wk.* 39. 9 &c.
and xxx. 17; *n.* soð 21. 12 &c.;
wk. soðe 89. 28; *g.* soðes xx.
270, xxiv. 30; *d.* soðum; to
soðum, for a truth 12. 19; *wk.*
soðan 12. 20 &c.; *a. wk.* 14. 6
&c.; *n.* soð 78. 26 &c.; *wk.*
soðe 14. 8 &c. *and* v. 25; *pl.*
soðe 18. 6 &c.; *f.* soða 118. 3
&c. *and* xii. 23, xix. 32; *n.* soð
ii. 18; *g.* soðra xxi. 25; *wk.*
soðena 51. 22 &c.; *d.* soðum
48. 2 (soðan J) &c.; *a. f.* soða
82. 26, xii. 30 &c.; *wk.* soðan
51. 23 &c. *and* vii. 30; *comp.*
soðra xxviii. 35; *n.* soðre 59.
20, 85. 21; *a. n.* 94. 8. 2)
sbst. n. truth; *d.* soðe 21. 19
&c.; *a.* soð 17. 20 &c. *and* xx.
94; for soð, for a fact 17. 20.

sōðcwide, *m.* true saying, truth;
pl. g. soðcwida ii. 7, vii. 3; *a.*
soðcwidas 14. 3, vi. 2, viii. 3.

sōðfæst, *adj.* truthful, just; *g. pl.*
soðfæstra xx. 272.

sōðfæstnes, *f.* truth; justice; *g.*
soðfæstnesse 95. 13, 99. 24, 121.
14, xxii. 38; *a.* 97. 27, 101. 12.

sōðlio, *adj.* true; *n.* 121. 5.

sōðspell, *n.* true narrative; *a.* 99.
5.

spāca, *wm.* spoke of wheel; 129.
32; *g.* spacan 129. 26 *n.*; *d.*
130. 2, 5; *pl.* 129. 26, 31, 130.
13; *d.* spacum 130. 13.

spanan, *rv.* attract, allure; *ind.
prs.* 2.*s.* spænst 127. 2; *pl.*
spanað 16. 6.

spearca, *wm.* spark; 99. 24; *d.*
spearcan 13. 33; *a.* trace, scin-
tilla 123. 21.

spēd, *f. a)* success; *b)* power,
means; *a.* iv. 9 (*b*), 32 (*b*), xx.
258 (*b*); *d. pl.* spedum 110.
27 (*a*).

spell, *n.* narrative, tale; discourse,
argument; 95. 19 &c.; *g.* spelles
142. 2; *d.* spelle 118. 20, 135.
19 *and* vii. 2; engliscum spelle,
prose Pr. 9; *a.* spell, *contrasted
with* leoð 26. 23 &c. *and* xxv.
1, xxvi. 73; spel 27. 15, 60.
26, 71. 3; *pl.* spell 103. 14 &c.;
g. spella 118. 12, 14; *d.* spellum
70. 25, xxvi. 2 &c.; *a.* spell
108. 1.

spellian, *wv.* discourse; *contrasted
with* singan; 34. 15 &c.; spelligan 65. 2*; spillian 47. 4; *ind.
pst.* 3.*s.* spellode MPr. 4.

spigettan, *wv.* spit; 61. 23.

spor, *n.* track; *d.* spore 121. 25.

sprǣc, *f.* speech; discourse,
argument; subject of dis-
cussion; 42. 26; spræce 137.
1; *g.* 97. 26, 127. 5, 6; *d.*
42. 23. &c.; *a.* 88. 32, ii. 8 &c.;
g. pl. spræca, languages 42. 27.

sprecan, *sv5.* speak; *fq.* Pr. 14
&c. *and* MPr. 8, viii. 32; *contrasted w.* singan 9. 16; *ind.
prs.* 1.*s.* sprece 31. 17 &c.; 3.*s.*
spricð 28. 14*; sprecð Pr. 14*;
pl. sprecað x. 45 &c.; *pst.* 1.*s.*
spræc 118. 28; 2.*s.* spræce 100.
8; 3.*s.* spræc i. 81; *pl.* spræcon
23. 6 &c. *and* xxvii. 30; *imp.*
sprec 137. 19; *sbj. prs. pl.*
sprecen 84. 3; sprecan 137. 18;
pst. pl. spræcen 17. 3; spræcon
137. 18*; *pp.* gesprecen 41. 7.

springan, *sv3.* spring; *ind. prs.*
3.*s.* sprincð 57. 23*.

spryttan, *wv.* sprout; *ind. prs.*
3.*pl.* spryttað xxix. 67.

spyrian, *wv.* (*usually w.* æfter)
follow up, investigate; *fq.* 72.

10 &c. *and* xix. 33, xxii. 2 ;
spirigan 94. 27* ; *ind. prs. 2.s.*
spyrast 59. 27*, 90. 27* ; spyrest
27. 21 ; *3.s.* spyreð 145. 7, xxvii.
9 ; *pl.* spyriað 121. 21 &c. ;
spiriað 131. 20 ; *pst. 3.s.* spyrede
xxvii. 16 ; *pl.* spyredon 78. 19 ;
sbj. prs. spyrie 121. 24 ; *pl.*
spyrien 101. 7 ; spyrigen 99.
21, 118. 16 ; gespyrigen 99.
21*.

stæf, *m. a*) stick ; *b*) letter of
alphabet ; *d. pl.* stafum 46. 27
(*b*), 108. 11 (*a*).

stæppan, *sv*6. step, go ; gestæppan
xx. 140.

stæð, *n.* shore ; *a. pl.* staðu vi.
15.

gestæððig, *adj.* steady, steadfast ;
gestæððig 105. 19, xxiv. 42,
xxix. 85 ; *wk.* gestæððega 136
26* ; *d. wk.* gestæððigan 128.
3 ; gestæððegan 129. 16.

stán, *m.* stone, rock ; 14. 15,
xxi. 21 ; *d.* stane 27. 6 ; *a.* stan
92. 25, vii. 33 ; *pl.* stanas 92.
23, 101. 28 ; precious stones
89. 12 ; *d.* stanum 81. 5, xx.
151 ; *a.* stanas 73. 2.

standan, *sv*6. stand ; stand fast,
abide ; 26. 31*, 48. 29*, 49.
27*, 105. 23* ; gestandan 80.
15* ; xx. 95 ; stondan 91. 28,
101. 29, xxiv. 54 ; to standanne
57. 21* ; *ind. prs. 3.s.* stent
27. 1, 81. 12, xx. 171, xxix. 16 ;
stent on, depends on 124. 20 ;
stint 129. 20 ; *pst. 3.s.* stod i. 28,
xx. 134 ; *pl.* stodon, stood still
102. 6 ; *prs. p. g.* stondendes
21. 8*.

gestandan, *sv*6. attack, assail ;
ind. prs. 3.s. gestent 27. 1 ; *pl.*
gestondað xii. 14 ; *pst. 3.s.*
gestod 115. 21.

staðol, *m.* foundation ; 86. 2, 4.

staðolfæst, *adj.* firm, fixed ; 97.
11, xi. 99.

staðolian, *wv.* fix, hold fast ;
ind. 3.s. gestaðolað 57. 4 ; *pst.*
2.s. gestaðoladest 81. 10*, xx.
161 ; *3.s.* staðolade xxix. 85 ;

staðelode 136. 27* ; *pp.* gestaðelod 50. 4*.

stéap, *m.* drinking-vessel, bowl ;
d. steape viii. 21.

stearc, *adj.* rough, violent ; *wk.*
stearca 21. 5, vi. 11, xii. 14 ;
n. stearc xxvi. 29 ; *a. wk.*
stearcan 10. 11 ; *pl.* stearce 52.
5 ; *a. wk.* stearcan 92. 6.

stede, *m.* place, position ; 80.
26, 96. 20 ; space, extent, 46.
5 ; *d.* 27. 3 ; 46. 20, vii. 25,
x. 11 ; *a.* xx. 64, xxviii. 29.

stemn, *f.* voice ; *d.* stemne 68.
11, 116. 24, i. 84 ; *a.* 57. 20 ;
stefne xiii. 49.

stemn, *m.* trunk (of tree) ; 91.
28, 32 ; foundation, base, 86. 2.

stéora, *wm.* steersman ; stiora 97.
11, 13.

stéorléas, *adj.* uncontrolled ;
misguided ; *d.* steorleasum x.
11 ; *pl.* stiorlease 13. 21.

steorra, *wm.* star ; 105. 12, xxviii.
28 &c. ; *g.* stiorran xxviii. 44 ;
d. steorran v. 2, xxiv. 19 ; stiorran 105. 12* ; *a.* steorran 10.
8 ; *pl.* 10. 6 &c. *and* vi. 5,
xxviii. 32 ; stiorran xxix. 14 ;
g. steorrena 19. 2, 29. 15 ; *d.*
steorrum 105. 13, xvii. 11,
xxiv. 24 ; *a.* steorran iv. 8.

stéorróðor, *n.* rudder ; steorroðer
97. 11 ; *d.* stiorroðre 98. 2,
100. 21.

steort, *m.* tail ; *d.* steorte 102.
15.

sticel, *m.* sting, bite ; *d. pl.*
sticelum 36. 8.

stician, *wv.* stick fast, remain ;
ind. prs. 3.s. sticað xx. 120 ; *pl.*
sticiað 112. 16, 129. 31 ; sticiað
gehydde 10. 20.

stíepan, *wv.* raise, exalt ; *ind.*
pst. 3.s. stepte xv. 8.

stíeran, *wv. w. a. or d.* guide,
wield, govern ; *w. d. or a. and g.*
restrain (from) ; stiran 10. 25*
(*d.*) ; steoran 40. 11* (*a.*), iv.
49 ; gestéoran 39. 30* (*d.* and *g.*) ;
stioran 40. 14* (*a.*) ; gestioran
125. 5 (*a. and g.*), ix. 52 (*d.*

and g.) ; *ind. prs.* 2 *s.* styrest 81.
14* (*a.*) ; xx. 178 (*a.*) ; 3 *s.*
stiore$ xxiv. 40 (*d.*) ; stior$ 105.
19* (*d.*) ; *pst.* 3 *s.* stiorde 94. 13
(*d.*) ; *sbj. pst. pl.* gestirden 134.
5 (*d.*) ; *pp.* him bi$ gestiored
hiora orsorgnessa 117. 8.

stīg, *f.* path ; *a.* stige xxiii. 10.

stīgan, *sv1.* ascend ; gestigan
xxix. 12 ; *ind. prs.* 3 *s.* stig$
57. 25* ; stih$ xiii. 61.

stihtan, *wv.* arrange, regulate ;
ind. prs. 2 *s.* stihtest xx. 178.

stillan, *wv.* cease from motion,
become still ; gestillan 49. 4,
xi. 26 ; *ind. prs.* 3 *s.* gestilde
102. 33 ; *pl.* gestildon 103. 2 ;
pp. trans. gestilled 49. 1 ; *pl.*
f. gestilde xi. 19.

stille, *adj.* (*often w.* gesceaft)
motionless, calm ; 79. 15, xx.
16 ; *f.* 129. 20, xx. 172 ; *n.*
xx. 151 ; *g.f.* stillre 92. 23 ; *wk.*
stillan 128. 3, 129. 16 ; *a. f.*
stille 131. 3 ; *wk.* stillan 49.
25 ; *n. pl.* stillu 128. 2 ; stille
101. 29.

stilnes, *f.* calmness ; *d.* stilnesse
15. 19 ; on stilnesse, at rest
16. 9.

gestincan, *sv3. trans.* smell ; 146.
4.

stingan, *sv3.* sting ; *ind. prs.* 3 *s.*
sting$ xviii. 7 ; sting$ 71. 7.

storm, *m.* storm ; iv. 22, vi. 11 ;
d. storme 14. 11 ; *pl.* stormas
18. 13, 52. 5, 92. 6, iii. 3, xii.
14 ; *g.* storma xxvi. 29.

stormsǣ, *mf.* stormy sea ; 115.
22.

stōw, *f.* place ; 24. 30, 82. 16,
xx. 279, xxi. 18, xxiv. 45 ; *d.*
stowe 80. 33, 91. 20, 105. 21,
107. 12, xx. 140 ; *a.* 11. 26, 91.
21 ; *pl.* stowa viii. 53 ; *g.* 88.
23 ; *d.* stowum 96. 20 ; *a.* stowa
128. 23.

strang, *adj.* strong ; severe ; 87.
4 ; strong 38. 3*, vi. 11, vii.
25 ; *a.* strangne 132. 7, 8 ; *f. wk.*
$a strongan meaht xi. 99, xx.
161, 178, xxiv. 40 ; *pl. wk.* iii.

3 ; *g.* strongra 27. 3* ; *comp.*
strengra 37. 3, 72. 7, 93. 14 ;
strencra, strængra* 54. 23 ; *g.*
strengran 75. 8 ; *pl.* 59. 23,
72. 5.

strange, *adv.* strongly, violently ;
vi. 15.

stranglic, *adj.* strong, firm ; *f.*
stronglic x. 11 ; *a. n.* 38. 4.

strēam, *m.* stream ; *a.* xxiii. 3 ;
a. pl. streamas xx. 172.

strengo, *f.* strength ; 73. 12.

gestrēon, *n.* property ; 48. 6* ;
gestrion i. 23 ; *pl. d.* gestreonum,
possessions 9. 28* ; *a.* gestreon
viii. 58.

strēon, *n.* procreative power ? 73.
12*.

strīcan, *sv1.* move, go ; *ind. prs.*
3 *s.* strice$ xx. 140.

strīenan, *wv. a*) acquire ; *b*)
beget ; *pp.* gestrined 70. 20 (*b*) ;
gestryned 54. 4* (*a*).

gestrod, *n.* plunder ; *d. pl.* gestrodum 9. 28.

stund, *f.* point of time, moment ;
d. stunde xxv. 68.

stunian, *wv.* resound ; *ind. prs.*
3 *s.* stuna$ xiii. 49 ; *pst.* 3 *s.*
stunede sio brune y$ wi$ o$re,
dashed with loud noise xxvi. 29.

stycce, *n.* short space (of time) ;
a. ymbe sticce, after a while
100. 7.

styrian, *wv. trans. and intrans.*
move, stir ; 49. 4 ; stirian xi.
27 ; *ind. prs.* 3 *s.* styre$ xxii.
64 ; *pl.* styria$ xiii. 49 ; *pst.*
3 *pl. rflx.* hi styredon 101. 28 ;
prs. p. n. pl. wk. styriendan,
endowed with motion 146. 5,
13 ; *a.* 146. 12 ; *pp. n. pl.*
styrede vii. 25.

styrman, *wv.* be stormy ; *prs. p.*
a. f. wk. styrmendan 18. 12 ; *d.*
pl. styrmendum 18. 13.

styrung, *f. a*) motion ; *b*) stirring,
stimulus ; styring 48. 30* (*a*) ;
d. styringe 47. 27* (*b*).

sulh, *f.* plough ; *g. pl.* sula 60.
30.

sum, *pron. adj.* some, a certain

(one); 7. 11, i. 46 &c.; *n.* 83.
10 &c. *and* xxii. 37; *g.* sumes
55. 29, vii. 28 &c.; *used as adv.*
to some extent, viii. 47, xx. 54;
d. sumum 15. 18, ix. 23 &c.; *f.*
sumere 63. 11; sumre 43. 8 &c.;
a. sumne 24. 19 &c. *and* vii.
3; *f.* sume 85. 12, ix. 15 &c.;
n. sum 54. 4 &c.; *pl.* sume 24.
11 &c.; *n.* sumu 129. 9; sume
126. 1 &c. *and* xxxi. 10; *g.*
sumra 91. 16 &c.; *d.* sumum
57. 8, xiii. 15 &c.; *a.* sume 78.
16 &c.; *f.* suma 101. 14; sume
65. 25 &c.; *n.* sume ten gear
115. 18; sume hundred scipa
ib.

sume, *adv.* to some extent, partially; 132. 3 (*or error for*
sumne?).

sumor, *m.* summer; 136. 15, xi.
60, xxix. 58; sumer 49. 19; *g.*
sumeres 10. 10; *d.* on sumera
49. 20, 68. 1, 92. 7, xvi. 13,
xxii. 23.

sumorlang, *adj. a. pl.* sumurlange
dagas, the long days of summer.
iv. 19.

gesund, *adj.* uninjured, sound;
healthy; 22. 6, 130. 22; *f.* 130.
19; *a.* gesundne 102. 20;
n. gesund 22. 1.

sundbūende, *mpl.* sea-dwellers,
men, people; viii. 13, xxiv. 21,
xxvi. 48.

gesundfullice, *adv.* safely; *sup.*
gesundfullicost 130. 15*.

gesundfulnes, *f.* prosperity; *d.*
gesundfulnesse 14. 22.

gesundlīce, *adv.* safely; *sup.*
gesundlicost 130. 15.

sundorcræft, *m.* special art or
power; *a.* 62. 33; *g. pl.* sundor-
cræfta xx. 203.

sundorgiefu, *f.* special gift or
grace; *a.* sundorgife 62. 22.

sundorstōw, *f.* special place; *a.*
sunderstowe 80. 2*.

sunna, *wm.* sun; xxviii. 61, xxix.
37.

sunne, *wf.* sun; *fq.* 21. 2, iv. 6
&c.; *g.* sunnan 12. 7, iv. 16

&c.; *d.* 14. 9, v. 1 &c.; *a.* 10.
3, iv. 10 &c.

sunu, *m.* son; 36. 33 &c.; *g.*
suna 115. 23; *pl.* suna 98. 30;
g. 115. 28; *d.* sunum 22. 23.

sūð, *adv.* southward, south; ix.
42, x. 5, 24, xiv. 7.

sūðan, *adv.* from the south; iv.
22, vi. 8.

sūðanwestan, *adv. used as adj.*
from the south-west; 21. 4.

sūðanwesterne, *adj.* south-west;
a. wk. suðanwesternan 10. 13.

sūðēastende, *m.* south-eastern
extremity; 67. 31.

sūðerne, *adj.* southern; v. 7;
wk. suðerna 14. 11.

sūðeweard, *adj.* southward; *g.*
suðweardes, *used as adv.* i. 4;
d. from suðeweardum, from
the south 39. 27, 41. 22.

sūðheald, *adj.* southward; xxviii.
17.

swā, 1) *adv.* so, thus; 12. 17,
iii. 8 &c.; swæ 90. 16; swa nu,
thus for instance xi. 43, xiii. 14;
swa selfe, in the same way xvii.
25, xx. 192, 199; swa ilce 20.
16 &c.; swa ilce swa 92. 17;
swa swa xiii. 64; swa . . . þ,
in such a way . . . that 7. 8 &c.;
swa 7 swa, in such ways 125.
29; *introducing simile*, v. 7 &c.;
comparison, like, xxvi. 47;
alternatives, swa . . . swa, either
. . . or 141. 24, 29, 142. 10, 15;
w. adj. 7. 25, i. 77 &c.; *w. adv.*
12. 19, ii. 6 &c.; swua efne
from . . . oð i. 13; swa longe
. . . swæ ix. 13; *w. comp.* swa
swa leng swa bet, the longer
the better 97. 27, *cf.* 8. 1, 19.
9, 60. 9, 130. 16; *w. sup. and
sbj.* of mæg, as . . . as 149. 6,
xxvii. 29 &c.; *w. ind.* 135. 4.
2) *conj.; often doubled, and correl.*
w. preceding swa (1); *manner*,
as, 18. 4, xi. 100 &c.; swæ ix.
14; *w. sbj.* 12. 15; swa swa 19.
24; swa swa Pr. 3 &c., *cf.* 32.
5; *time*, as soon as, xiii. 54;
sona swa 14. 3 &c. *and* viii. 1;

swa ... swa 57. 23; *place,*
swa swa, wherever ix. 40;
as rel. pron. eall swa swa,
whatsoever xvi. 9; *indef.* swa
hwa (hwæt) swa 11. 23, 23. 12
&c.; swa hwæs swa 112. 3;
swa hwelc swa 112. 24; swa
hwæðer swa 91. 19; swa hwær
swa 17. 19.

swæcc, *m.* taste, flavour; 93. 4.

swǣfan, *wv.* burn? *ind. prs.* 3. *s.*
swæfeð viii. 47.

swǣr, *adj.* heavy, burdensome;
a. n. wk. swære x. 20.

swǣre, *adv.* heavily, grievously;
sware ix. 56.

swǣrnes, *f.* sluggishness; 95. 10.

swǣslīce, *adv.* affably, kindly;
36. 31.

swǣð, *n.* footprint, track; *a.* 124.
9, xxvii. 14.

swǣðer, *pron.* whichever (of two)
w. swa ... swa 101. 8 &c.

swangornes, *f.* sluggishness, lan-
guor; swongornes 109. 4.

swāpan, *rv. intrans.* sweep, rush;
ind. prs. 3. *s.* swapeð vii. 20.

swāðǣr, *adv.* like, *used like* swa
swa; 47. 26, 117. 17, 127. 17,
xxxi. 21; swæðer 47. 26*.

swāðēah, *adv.* however, nevertheless; 16. 27, ix. 38 &c.

sweart, *adj.* black, gloomy; *wk.*
swearta iv. 22; *g. f. wk.*
sweartan 10. 5; *a. wk.* xxiii. 5;
pl. wk. 14. 9; *g.* sweartra iv. 6;
d. sweartum v. 45.

swearte, *adv.* darkly; viii. 47.

swefl, *m.* sulphur; swefel 34. 28;
d. swefle 34. 9, viii. 50.

sweg, *m.* sweet sound, melody;
d. swege 101. 28.

swegl, *n.* sky; *g.* swegles xxii.
23.

swegle, *adv.* brightly, radiantly;
xxviii. 61.

swegltorht, *adj.* heavenly bright;
f. xxix. 24.

swelc, *adj. pron.* such; *often foll.*
by swelce, *q. v.* 17. 9 &c.;
swilc 145. 7; swylc 75. 34; *f.*
swelc 20. 19, 59. 25; *n.* viii. 7;

swylc 104. 12, 130. 28; *g. m.*
and n. swelces 11. 13 &c.;
swelces 7 swelces, this and the
like xxviii. 49; swylces ix. 33;
f. swelcre 104. 11; *d. m. and n.*
swelcum 30. 9*, 63. 22 &c.; on
swelcum lande swa hi wæron,
in no matter what country 64.
6; swilcum 17. 8*, 136. 29*,
xxix. 92; swylcum 7 swylcum,
by this and the like xxvi. 107,
cf. 116. 30; *f.* swelcere 31. 14*;
a. swelcne 42. 12; swilcne 62.
19 &c.; swylcne 145. 12, 21;
f. swylce 20. 10; *n.* swelc 21.
15*; swilc 78. 23; swylc 125.
25, 147. 17, xxx. 18; *pl.* swelce
14. 6, 87. 8, viii. 42; swilce 34.
6*; swylce 15. 25, 27; *f.* swelca
23. 29; swilca 36. 11; *n.* swelce
59. 25*; swælce 31. 9*; *g.*
swelcra 92. 8, x. 55; swylcra
xix. 25; *d.* swelcum 54. 1*, 91.
10; swilcum 54. 1, 116. 30*;
swylcum *ib.*; *a.* swylce 133. 8,
145. 11.

swelce, 1) *adv. a)* like, as it
were; 42. 9 &c.; swilce 41. 25,
42. 13. *b)* also; iv. 13; swylce
iv. 6, xxix. 63. 2) *conj. a) w.*
ind. correl. w. preceding swelc
17. 9 &c.; swilce 91. 1 &c.;
swylce 145. 9 &c. *b) w. sbj.* as
if; *fq.* 15. 22 &c.; swilce 92.
14; swylce (4 *times in* C) 92.
12 &c.

swelgan, *sv*3. swallow; absorb;
ind. prs. 3. *s.* swelgeð xx. 96;
swilgð 80. 16*; swylgð 26. 28*,
29*.

swelgend, *f.* abyss; 19. 7.

sweltan, *sv*3. die; *ind.* 3. *pl.*
sweltað 45. 26; *sbj. prs.* swelte
22. 32; *prs. p.* sweltende 23. 1.

swencan, *wv.* afflict, torment; 123.
33, v. 41; *ind. prs.* 3. *s.* swencð
52. 17; *sbj. prs.* swence 133. 5*,
8, vii. 50; *pp.* geswenced 8. 19,
54. 2, iii. 8; *pl.* geswencte 130.
26, 133. 6.

swēor, *m.* father-in-law; swior
22. 5.

swēora, *wm.* neck ; *d.* swiran 46.
8*, x. 19 ; *a. pl.* swyran ix. 56.
sweorcan, *sv*3. grow dark ; *prs. p.*
sweorcende iii. 2.
sweord, *n.* sword ; 65. 30 ; *d.*
sweorde 28. 17, 39. 24. ix. 31 ;
a. sweord ix. 60 ; *n. pl.* 40. 2*.
gesweostran, *f. pl.* sisters ; *g.* ge-
swysterna (geswystrena* B`,
bearn, cousins 98. 32.
sweotol, *adj.* evident, manifest; *n.*
fq. 26. 12 &c. *and* ix. 61 ; swiotol
22. 24*, 25. 10; *sup. n. wk.*
sweotoloste 119. 17.
sweotole, *adv.* clearly, distinctly ;
21. 16, v. 1 &c. ; sweotule 15.
4* ; sweotcle 9. 1* ; swutole 21.
24* ; swetole viii. 2 (J) ; switole
48. 14* ; *comp.* sweotolor 24.
1 &c. *and* xii. 23 ; *sup.* sweotolost
Pr. 4, vi. 3.
sweotolian, *wv.* reveal, declare ;
ind. prs. 3.*s.* sweotolað 147.
19.
swēte, *adj.* sweet ; 51. 5 ; *a.* swetne
132. 7, 9 ; *comp. n.* swetre xii.
9 ; *pl.* swetran 99. 5.
swētmettas, *m. pl.* daintics, deli-
cacies ; swotmettas 33. 23* ; *d.*
swetmettum 111. 27*, xxv. 40.
swētnes, *f.* sweetness ; 25. 7 ; *d.*
swetnesse 15. 4.
sweðrian, *wv.* subside, cease ; *pp.*
geswiðrad v. 45.
geswīcan, *sv*1. *w. g.* cease ; 134.
31 ; *sbj. prs.* geswice 109. 11.
swīfan, *sv*1. *intrans.* move ; *ind.*
prs. 3.*s.* swifeð xxviii. 17 ; *sbj.*
prs. swife 14. 15 *n.,* xxviii. 39.
swift, *adj.* swift ; vii. 20, xxviii.
17 ; *d.* swiftum xxiv. 28 ; *a. wk.*
swiftan x. 40 ; *pl.* swifte xi. 60 ;
a. f. 105. 4* ; *comp.* swiftra 72.
8, xxix. 31 ; *pl.* swiftran 72. 6 ;
a. n. xxiv. 1.
swiftnes, *f.* swiftness ; *g.* swiftnesse 125. 32.
swifto, *f.* swiftness ; *g.* xxviii. 3.
swīgian, *wv.* be silent ; gesugian
45. 17 ; *ind. pst.* 2.*s.* geswugodes
50. 27 ; 3.*s.* geswigode 14. 26,
40. 5*, 41. 7 ; geswugode 52. 15,

124. 18, 126. 29, 141. 21 ; gesugode 40. 5, 41. 7.
swīn, *n.* pig ; *d. pl.* swinnm 115. 6.
geswinc, *n.* toil, effort ; 42. 10 ;
d. geswince 46. 9, 82. 15, 98.
23, 133. 27, xx. 277 ; *g. pl.*
geswinca, hardships, troubles 27.
3, 89. 9, 10, xxi. 10, 14.
swincan, *sv*3. labour, toil ; 87.
26, 96. 25 ; *ind. prs.* 2.*s.* swincst
121. 25 *n.* ; 3.*s.* swinceð iii. 2 ;
swincð 76. 26, 27, 113. 12, 135.
4, 143. 15 ; *pl.* swincað 43. 15,
142. 31, iv. 56 ; *pst. pl.* swuncon
127. 4 ; *sbj. prs. pl.* swincen x.
21 ; *pst. pl.* swuncen, geswuncen*
145. 3.
geswincfull, *adj.* laborious, troublesome ; *comp. pl.* geswincful-
ran 30. 25.
swīð, *adj.* strong ; *d. wk.* swiðan
xxv. 46 ; *comp.* swiðra 93. 15.
swīðe, *adv.* strongly, much ; 11.
28 &c. *and* iv. 35, xix. 38 ; *in-*
tensive, w. adj. or adv. very : *fq.*
Pr. 7, iv. 19 &c. ; swyðe 36. 8 ;
swiðe swiðe, exceedingly 51. 5,
140. 1 ; *comp.* swiðor, more 8.
1, xi. 27 &c. ; swiður 130. 25,
26 ; *sup.* swiðost, most, especially 15. 5, xxii. 11 &c. ; swiðust 55. 3, 5, 76. 15 ; swa he
swiðost mæge, as hard as he
can 109. 12, *cf.* 135. 4, 139. 12,
149. 6.
swīðlic, *adj.* excessive, violent ; *d.*
swiðlicum 27. 2.
swīðlīce, *adv.* strongly ; exceedingly, much ; swiðe s. 51. 8,
107. 31, 111. 28, 125. 7, 127. 4.
swīðrian, *wv.* grow stronger,
prevail ; *pp.* geswiðrad v. 45.
sylian, *wv.* stain, pollute ; *ind.*
pst. 3.*s.* selede ix. 60.
synderlic, *adj.* special, peculiar ;
81. 24.
synderlīce, *adv.* separately ; specially ; 43. 1, 145. 29, 30, 31.
syndrian, *wv.* separate ; *pp. pl.*
gesindrede 114. 6.
synfull, *adj.* sinful ; *pl. n. wk.*
synfullan 121. 12.

syngian, *wv*. sin ; *sbj. pst.* 3.*pl.*
gesyngoden 143. 27.
synn, *f.* sin ; syn 84. 19, 31.
sype, *m.* soaking, absorption ; *d.*
80. 16, xx. 97.

T.

tācn, *n.* sign, token ; 107. 28,
118. 11, 134. 7, 11 ; tacen 119.
17 ; *a.* tacn 107. 29 ; *d. pl.* tac-
num 26. 11.
tācnian, *wv.* mark, signify ; *ind.
prs.* 3.*s.* tacnað 136. 1, 147. 9 ;
pl. tacniað 83. 27.
tācnung, *f.* indication, emblem ;
20. 24 ; *d.* tacnunge 16. 18*.
tǣcan, *wv.* point out, show ; 118.
18, 127. 1, 145. 17 ; getǣcan 51.
20, 78. 10, 32, 89. 32, 104.
27, 139. 26 ; to tǣcanne 127. 23 ;
ind. prs. 2.*s.* tǣhst 121. 22 ; *pst.*
1.*s.* tǣhte 90. 1, 6 ; 2.*s.* tǣhtest
97. 16 ; *imp.* getǣc 24. 19, 105.
32 ; *sbj. prs.* getǣce 74. 20.
tǣcing, *f.* demonstration ; *d.*
tǣcinge 90. 1.
tǣcning, *f.* demonstration ; *d.*
tǣcninge 90. 1*.
tǣlan, *wv.* blame ; 118. 26, 135.
3, xix. 39 ; getǣlan 21. 19, 23.
3, 74. 10 ; to tǣlenne 64. 18* ;
ind. 3.*pl.* tǣlað 10. 21.
tǣlwierðlic, *adj.* blameworthy ;
sup. n. tǣlwyrðlicoð 43. 24.
getǣse, *adj.* fitting, convenient ;
sup. n. getǣsost xx. 11.
talian, *wv.* reckon, account ; to
talianne 56. 8.
tam, *adj.* tame ; *f.* 57. 9 ; *pl. n.*
tamu 101. 29 ; *a.* tame 57. 18,
xiii. 44.
tama, *wm.* tameness ; *g.* taman
xiii. 26 ; *a.* 57. 11, xiii. 25.
tear, *m.* tear ; drop ; *d.* teare xii.
10 ; *d. pl.* tearum 22. 22.
tela, *adv.* well, satisfactorily ;
137. 10, 143. 24, xiii. 36 ; *ex-
pression of approval,* telo ðonne
þ ðe swa ðincð 119. 10*.
tellan, *wv.* reckon, reckon up ;

account, consider ; *absol.* state
the case, 17. 8 ; to tellanne 54.
11, 56. 6, 110. 20, 111. 2 ; to
tellenne 56. 10 ; *ind. prs.* 1.*s.*
telle 30. 21 ; 2.*s.* getelest 44. 11 ;
pl. tellað 53. 23 ; *pst.* 1.*s.* tealde
22. 30, 113. 15 ; *pl.* tealdon 96.
29 ; *sbj. prs.* telle 44. 22, 56.
11 ; *imp.* tele 44. 13, 44. 16.
temian, *wv.* tame ; *ind. pst.* 3.*pl.*
temedon xiii. 39.
getenge, *adj. w.d.* *a)* close to ;
b) pressing on, afflicting ; xxxi.
7 (*a*) ; *f.* 12. 4 (*b*) ; *n.* 23. 5 (*b*) ;
pl. xxv. 5 (*a*).
teohhian, *wv.* consider ; determine
on, design, intend ; *ind. prs.*
1.*s.* tiohhie xiii. 25 ; 2.*s.* tiohhast
121. 24 ; getiohhast iv. 21 ; 3.*s.*
teohhað 54. 29* ; tiohhað 54.
29, 31, 55. 3, 4*, 76. 14, 128.
30 ; tehhað 55. 3* ; tihhað 54.
31*, 68. 21 ; *pl.* teohhiað 32.
15*, 53. 21* ; tiohhiað 60. 3,
91. 27, 132. 26 ; tiohiað 53. 21 ;
pst. 2.*s.* teohhodest*, tiohhodes
31. 1 ; 3.*s.* tiohhode 98. 14,
128. 1, 143. 19, 27 ; him tiohhode to wite. determined to
punish 36. 26 ; getiohhode
xxix. 38 ; *pl.* teohhodon 9. 6* ;
tihodon 116. 12* ; *sbj. prs.*
teohhie 51. 6* ; tiohhie 51. 12*,
98. 9, 100. 29 ; tiohhige 63.
28 ; tiohige 51. 6, 12 ; *pp.*
tiohhod 134. 12 ; getiohhod 11
times in C, 112. 30 &c. *and*
117. 21* ; getiohhad 88. 18,
142. 27 ; getehhod 18. 3* ;
getihhod 134. 12*.
tēon, *sv2.* pull ; attract, entice ;
train ; getion 116. 34* ; *ind.
prs.* 3.*s.* teohð 58. 11* ; tihð
48. 1*, 58. 11 ; getyhð 48. 4 ;
pl. teoð v. 42 ; tioð 116. 32 ;
pst. 3.*s. intrans.* teah, with-
drew 102. 4 ; *sbj. prs.* teo 57.
21 ; getio 28. 27 ; *pp.* getogen
17. 28 ; trained, instructed, xi.
24 *and a. pl. f.* getogene 49. 3*.
tēon, *wv.* make ; arrange, ordain ;
ind. pst. 3.*s.* tiode xx. 131 ;

getiode xi. 38, xiii. 13, xxiv.
14 ; getede xiii. 44.

tēona, *wm.* injury, wrong ; *a.*
teonan 32. 9.

tēorian, *wv.* grow tired ; *sbj. prs.*
2.s. getiorie 139. 32.

tēoða, *num. adj.* tenth ; *a.* teoðan
42. 19.

teran, *sv4.* lacerate, cause to
smart ; *ind. prs. 3.s.* tirð 51. 3.

tīd, *f.* time ; season ; 148. 23, x.
64, xxvi. 17 ; tiid 12. 5 ; *d.*
tide 7. 1, 127. 26 ; ær tide,
in good time 67. 11 ; *a.* tide
ix. 15, xxvi. 4, 12, 43 ; on tid,
when the time comes 67. 11 ; on
wintres tid xxix. 64 ; *pl.* tida
34. 6, viii. 40 ; *d.* tidum 40. 1,
iv. 43 &c. ; *a.* tida 10. 10, 79.
12, 128. 23.

tīdan, *wv.* happen ; *ind. prs. 3.s.*
getideð 77. 8* ; *psl. 3.s.* getydde
36. 33*.

tīedernes, *f.* frailty, delicacy ; *d.*
tydernesse 9. 9*.

tīedre, *adj.* frail, delicate ; tedre
41. 18*, 72. 29 ; *d. wk.* tedran
109. 11 ; *pl. f.* tiedre*, tedra
47. 24 ; tedre 25. 31* ; *comp.*
tederra 36. 6.

tīen, *num.* ten ; tin 44. 14* ; ten
44. 14, 115. 18* ; tyn xxvi. 17.

tier = tioro, drop? xx. 81.

tigris, *m.* tiger ; 72. 6, 8, 116.
20.

til, *adj.* good, brave ; *d. pl.* tilum
xxvi. 20.

tilian, *wv. w. g.* strive after ; attend
to ; look after ; *w. supine or*
sbj. strive, endeavour ; 12. 14,
13. 17, 55. 24, xvi. 1 ; tiligan
67. 27 ; *ind. prs. 2.s.* tilast 23.
1, 31. 15* ; tiolast *ib.* : *3.s.* tilað
xi. 83 ; tiolað 38. 18, 53. 18,
67. 11, 135. 4 ; *pl.* tiliað 53.
22, 54. 6, 133. 14, x. 22, xi.
79 ; tioliað 43. 15 ; *psl. 1.s.*
tiolode 50. 31 ; *pl.* tiolodon
139. 14 ; *sbj. prs.* tilige 69. 10,
123. 13, 124. 1.

till, *n.* point, place ; *d.* tille xx.
172.

tilung, *f.* striving, yearning ; *d.*
tiluncga, tiolunga* 54. 3 ; *a.*
tilunga 55. 15*.

tīma, *wm.* time, occasion ; 14. 2,
92. 11 ; *a.* timan 115. 26, 143.
10 ; *d. pl.* timum 121. 5.

timbrian, *wv.* build ; 26. 24,
26, 27, 27. 6, vii. 12.

tīrwine, *m.* follower, retainer ;
g. pl. tirwina xxv. 21.

tō, i) *prep.* 1) *w. g.* towards ; to
æfennes 33. 28 ; to ðæs lytel,
adv. so, 53. 5. 2) *w.d.* often
foll. *c.* a) *motion, direction,*
towards, to, 9. 19, 103. 16,
i. 65 &c. ; *metaph.* 8. 23 &c. b)
in conformity with, 79. 15, 20.
7, xx. 15. c) *bringing together,*
55. 27, xvii. 12 &c. d) *mental*
attitude, towards ; andan to
manum ðinge 79. 24, *cf.* 102.
8, xx. 36, xxvi. 66. e) *obj. of vb.*
w. hopian 27. 10, 149. 1, vii.
44 ; belimpan 118. 8 ; sellan
16. 31 ; sprecan 118. 9 ; cweðan
131. 23 ; *w.* hieran, obey iv.
5 ; clipian 9. 29, i. 83 ; fon 65.
28 ; culpian 71. 24 ; biddan
100. 29. f) *change of state,*
into, *or not transl.*: *w.* forscieppan 116. 16 ; forhwierfan
116. 21, xxvi. 87 ; *w.* gebetan
xxi. 24 ; weorðan 49. 33, xi.
87 &c. ; *w.* don 23. 4 &c.
and xv. 13 ; gewyrcan Pr. 10 ;
to engliscum spelle gewende
Pr. 9 ; hi gesceop to gemagum
54. 12 ; fordrugod to duste
xx. 104 ; gedrinceð to dryggum
vii. 16. g) *w. vbs. of reckoning,*
considering &c. = as ; *w.* reccan
41. 3 &c. ; tellan 53. 23 &c. ;
teohhian 76. 14 ; to twæm
ðingum nemnan 75. 10. h)
result, as, to ; him mæg to sorge
24. 16 ; to hiora eldrena for-
wyrde 70. 20, *cf.* 36. 25. i)
purpose, for, as, 20. 25, xxv. 21
&c. ; him to gamene ix. 9, 46 ;
tol to swelcum cræfte 30. 9 ;
w. d. of inf. 13. 14, vi. 7 &c. ;
destination, to domere geceas

20. 12, *cf.* xxvi. 46. *k*) concerning, in the case of; *w.*
geliefan 11. 13; wenan 27. 31;
l) *source*, from, 45. 3; *w.* secan
19. 15, 31. 26, 32. 7. *m*)
addition, to ðam tolum 40. 20;
to eacan 7. 10; to eac ðæm
87. 4; *w.* don 75. 16, 28; to
ðam, moreover 57. 32. *n*)
phrases: to worulde, for ever 48.
29, xi. 17; to lafe, remaining,
left 46. 26; to soðum, for
a truth 12. 19. *o*) *w. prons.*
forming advs. or conjs.; also w.
inst. a) *degree*, so, to ðæm 25.
5, 55. 21, 67. 7; to ðon 55.
21, 69. 9, 133, 14; to ðon ꝥ, to
such a degree that 42. 11, xiii. 46
&c.; to ðam ꝥ 104. 26; *β*) *pur-*
pose, to hwæm, to what end 16.
17, 17. 4; *conj. w. sbj.* in order
that, to ðam ꝥ 20. 26, 51. 21;
to ðon ꝥ 65. 17, 79. 1, 137. 9.
ii) *adv. a*) *w. meaning of* (i);
motion: 23. 29, 86. 18, 101. 29,
112. 23, 26, xiii. 67; 7 eac
mare to, besides 146. 6. *b*) *excess*,
too; 8. 20, v. 30 &c.
tōblāwan, *rv.* blow away; *pp.*
toblawen xx. 106.
tōbrǣdan, *wv. trans.* extend,
spread; 42. 25, 43. 4, 20, 46. 7,
10, 68. 22; tobredan x. 15; *ind.*
prs. 2 s. segl tobrædest 16. 29;
sbj. prs. pl. tobrædan 42. 18*.
tōbrecan, *sv4.* break to pieces,
destroy; 99. 1; *pp. a. f.* tobrocene 9. 3.
tōbregdan, *sv3.* tear asunder; *pp.*
a. f. tobrogdene 9. 3.
tōclēofan, *sv2.* cleave asunder;
ind. prs. 2 s. toclifst 92. 25.
tōcnāwan, *rv.* discern, distinguish;
48. 9, 15, 19, 108. 31, 132.
13.
tōdǣlan, *wv.* divide; distribute;
to tedælenne 92. 24, 28; *ind.*
prs. 3 s. todæleð 76. 13; to-
dælð 14. 16; *pl.* todælað 76.
18; *pst. 2 s.* todældest 79.
34; todældes xx. 58; *3 s.*
todælde 99. 16; *sbj. prs.* to-

dæle 28. 22; *pl.* todælen 74.
31; *pp.* todæled 11 *times*, 42.
26 &c.; *pl.* todælede 85. 18;
todælde 90. 31, 92. 25; *f.* todælda 42. 28.
tōdrīfan, *sv1.* disperse; xxii. 3;
imp. todrif 82. 11, xx. 264; *pp.*
todrifen 80. 18, xx. 104.
tōflōwan, *rv.* flow in different
directions; *sbj. pst.* toflowen,
tofleowon* 94. 9; *pp.* toflowen
v. 20.
tōgædere, *adv.* together; 37. 20,
50. 1, 55. 25, xx. 62, 68; togædre
xx. 56, 72, 112; togadre 54. 18;
togedere 79. 33*.
tōglīdan, *sv1.* slip away, collapse;
vii. 34.
tōheald, *adj.* leaning, inclined; *n.*
xiii. 10.
tōhopa, *wm.* hope; 23. 8, 112. 3,
xxv. 50.
tōl, *n.* tool; instrument; 40. 16;
tōl 30. 9*; *pl. g.* tola 40. 9; *d.*
tolum 40. 14, 19, 20, 24; tolan
40. 19; *a.* tol 40. 23.
tōlicgan, *sv5.* separate; *pp. pl. f.*
tolegena 42. 28.
tōmiddes, *prep. w. d.* in the midst
of; xiii. 37.
tōnemnan, *wv.* distinguish, separa-
ate verbally; *pp.* tonemned 76.
10; *pl. n.* tonemde 76. 2.
torr, *m.* tower; cliff; *d.* torre v.
17; *a.* tor 99. 9, 16.
tōsamne, *adv.* together; tosomne
38. 20, 92. 24, 96. 14, 99. 24, v.
42, xi. 89.
tōscād, *n.* distinction, difference;
toscead 148. 4.
tōscādan, *rv.* distinguish; separate;
48. 17*; tosceadan 140. 24; *ind.*
prs. 3 s. toscæt*, toscead 141.
8; *pp.* tosceaden 84. 28, 30, v.
18.
tōscēotan, *sv2.* anticipate; hine
foran tosciotan xxvii. 19.
tōscrīðan, *sv1.* flow in different
directions, disperse; xx. 93.
tōslūpan, *sv2.* be loosened, re-
laxed; 49. 8, 30, 128. 21, xi.
80; *sbj. prs. pl.* toslupen 94. 11.

96. 18; *pp. pl. f.* toslopena xxix.
89; toslopene 136. 28*.

tōsmēagan, *wv.* investigate mi-
nutely; 148. 5.

tōstencan, *wv.* disperse; destroy;
ind. pst. 3.*s.* tostencte 99. 15;
pp. tostenced 117. 17; *pl. f.*
tostencte 136. 28, xxix. 87.

tōswīfan, *sv1.* rush asunder; *sbj.
prs.* 3.*pl.* toswifen xi. 36.

tōtellan, *wv.* separate, distinguish;
ind. pst. 2.*s.* totældes xx. 11;
pp. toteled xvi. 15.

tōteran, *sv4.* tear to pieces, destroy; *pp. a.* totorenne 9. 5; *f.*
totorene 9. 3.

tōweard, 1) *adj.* approaching;
about to happen, future; *n.* 24.
17; *g. wk.* toweardan 130. 24,
134. 11; *d. wk.* 27. 10, 90. 24,
120. 23, 125. 5, 7, 139. 4, 142.
14. 2) *prep. w. d.* towards;
eow onet toweard xxvii. 8.

tōweardes, *prep. w. d.* towards;
eow toweardes onet 124. 6.

tōweorpan, *sv3.* disperse, destroy;
99. 3; *ind. prs.* 3.*s.* toweorpð
21. 6; *pst.* 3.*s.* towearp 99. 15;
pp. toworpen 133. 21.

tōwrītan, *sv1.* describe; *ind. pst.*
3.*s.* towrat 41. 27.

trega, *wm.* grief, trouble; *n. pl.*
tregan v. 42.

trēow, *n.* tree; 92. 5; *g.* treowes
91. 30; *pl. g.* treowa 33. 28*, 82.
6*; triowa 33. 31*; *d.* treowum
57. 21*, 73. 25*, 91. 10, iv. 21,
xiii. 36, 39, 51; triowum xix. 6;
a. treowa 10. 11*, 73. 2*.

trēow, *f.* faith, trust, faithfulness;
pl. treowa 23. 8, 15. 30*; *d.*
treowum 67. 21, i. 65; triowum
54. 16; *a.* treowa 15. 30, xi.
95, xxxi. 18; truwa 15. 30*.

trēowen, *adj.* wooden; *a. pl. n.*
treowenu 104. 17.

getrēowlīce, *adv.* faithfully,
loyally; 50. 2.

trīewan, *wv. w. d.* trust; *ind.
prs.* 3.*pl.* trewað 112. 25; *pst.*
3.*pl.* getreowedon betwuh him,
conspired 70. 23.

getrīewe, *adj.* faithful, trusty;
g. wk. getreowan 54. 15*; *pl.*
getreowe 15. 11, 48. 19*;
treowe 15. 11*; *wk.* getriewan
54. 9; *n.* getrewe 16. 13*; *g.*
getreowra 48. 8; *a. wk.* getreowan 48. 11; *n.* getrewe 16. 16.

trum, *adj.* firm, strong; *pl.* trume
23. 11.

trūwian, *wv. w. d.* trust, believe
in; ii. 14; *ind. pst.* 1.*s.* truwode 8. 11.

trymman, *wv.* encourage; getrymian 104. 25.

tūcian, *wv.* ill-treat, torment; 123.
27; *ind. prs.* 3.*pl.* tuciað xxiv. 60.

tūddor, *n.* offspring, fruit; *d.*
tudre iv. 31, xxvii. 10; *a.* tudor
131. 6, 136. 15, xxix. 57.

tunge, *wf.* tongue; *d.* tungan 36.
23; *a. ib.*

tungol, *n.* heavenly body, star,
constellation; 105. 14, xxix.
32, 35; tungul xxviii. 20; tungl
xxiv. 23; *a.* 129. 5; *pl.* tunglu
69. 22 *n.*, 126. 2, 3, 6, 135. 25;
tungl xxviii. 6, 12, xxix. 9, 39;
g. tungla iv. 1, xx. 173, xxiv.
20, xxviii. 9; *by error*, tunglo
xxviii. 3? *d.* tunglum 14. 9,
105. 11, 139. 16, xxiv. 16; *a.*
tunglu 10. 3, 131. 3, 135. 24,
iv. 5, xxix. 4.

twēgen, *num.* two; 107. 11, 128.
15, v. 42; *f.* twa i. 4, xx. 190;
n. 38. 18, 106. 9, 128. 15; tu
77. 17, 85. 12; *g.* twega 14. 24,
32. 3, 106. 11, 107. 17; *often
in phrase*, oðer twega oððe . . .
oððe 23. 27 &c.; twegra 107.
17*; *d.* twæm 22. 23, 75. 10,
87. 1, xvii. 3, xx. 187; twam
22. 23*, xxxi. 10; *a.* twegen i.
6; *f.* twa 42. 27, 115. 15, 142.
8; *n.* twa *in* B, 81. 19 &c.;
xxvi. 6; twua 120. 12; .tu 61.
2, 99. 16; on tu, diversely 92.
32, 113. 26; on tu tosceaden,
in two v. 17.

twelf, *num.* twelve; 91. 30.

twēo, *wm.* doubt; 37. 27 &c.;
d. tweon 35. 20 &c. *and* xi. 1.

twēogan, *wv. w.g.; pers. and impers.* doubt; 26. 12 (*i.*), 75. 14 (*i.*), 91. 12 (*p.*); 93. 25 (*p.*); 113. 21 (*i.*); iv. 51 (*i.*); twiogan 98. 5 (*i.*), 125. 26 (*p.*); twiogean 90. 14 (*p.*), 97. 30 (*i.*); *ind. prs.* 2.*s.* tweost 12. 27; 3.*s.* tweoð 9 *times imp.* 38. 3 &c.; *once pers.* 146. 30*; twioð 96. 11 (*i.*); *pst.* 1.*s.* tweode 93. 28; 2.*s.* tweodest 93. 25; 3.*s.* tweode 96. 9 (*i.*); *sbj. prs.* 1.*s.* tweoge 105. 30; 2.*s.* 12. 28; 3.*s.* 118. 12 (*i.*).

twēogung, *f.* doubt; *g.* tweounge 144. 9.

twēon, *m.* doubt; *d.* tweonne 109. 17.

twēonung, *f.* doubt; *a.* tweonunga 10. 23.

twifēte, *adj.* two-footed; *pl. n.* twiofete 147. 6*.

twig, *n.* twig, branch; *pl.* twigu xiii. 44.

twinclian, *wv.* glimmer, twinkle; 97. 18.

twirǣde, *adj.* irresolute; twiorǣde 144. 23.

twiwa, *adv.* twice; tuwa 95. 25*.

tȳdran, *wv.* bring forth, engender; *ind. prs.* 3.*s.* tidreð 131. 6; *sbj. prs.* tydre, tydrige* 91. 23.

tȳdrung, *f.* procreation; *d.* tidringe 93. 30.

tyht, *m.* training, habit; *a.* 20. 10; *d. pl.* tyhtum 20. 7.

tyhtan, *wv.* incite, persuade; 118. 27.

tȳn, *wv.* educate, train; *ind. pst.* 1.*s.* getyde 20. 7; getydde 17. 12*; 3.*s.* tyde 9. 2*; *pl.* tydon xiii. 39.

tyndre, *wf.* tinder; *g.* tyndran 13. 30; *d.* 14. 1.

Ð.

ðā, 1) *adv.* at that time, then; thereupon; 7. 5, i. 8 &c.; ða giet, up till then 43. 8 &c. 2) *conj.* then; 7. 23, viii. 6 &c.; ða ... ða ... ða 7. 24 &c.

ðǣr, 1) *adv.* in that place, there; 7. 20, vii. 39 &c.; ðær on londe, in that country 63. 18; com ðær gan 8. 16; in that instance ix. 61; ðar III. 22*; ðer 11. 19*; *often w. preps., combined or separate,* ðær æfter 145. 7; ðærbetwyx 28. 16; ðærin xi. 4; ðærmid 18. 30, xxvi. 70; ðæröf 76. 21; ðærofer 99. 13; ðæron 11. 11 &c. *and* xxiv. 47; ðærto, besides 45. 3 &c.; ðærwið 81. 4, 132. 13; ðærymbutan 34. 10, 43. 13; ðærinne 7. 24. 2) *conj.* a) where, wherever, 14. 24, vii. 32 &c.; ðær ðær 9. 5, vii. 12 &c.; ðær, at the time when 11. 4, 13. 22. b) *w. sbj.* if, if only, *about* 14 *times*, 11. 13, viii. 39 &c.

ðǣrrihte, *adv.* on the spot, immediately; 45. 19.

ðǣs, *adv.* to such a degree, so; 75. 4; *w. comp.* the xxviii. 66; ðæs ðy 141. 2; ðæs ðe, *conj.* so far as 58. 30, 78. 10, xxviii. 33; whereas xx. 195.

ðæt, 1) *conj. passim,* that; Pr. 11, i. 36 &c.; *sq. w.* te 20. 20, iv. 51 &c.; ðæt ðe i. 30. 2) *demonst. adj., v.* se.

geðafa, *wm.* (*w.* beon *and g.*) assent to, grant; *sq.* 59. 23 &c.; *pl.* geðafan 84. 21, 85. 19. 94. 15.

ðafian, *wv.* consent to, permit; endure; geðafian 104. 3; *ind. prs.* 3.*s.* ðafað 123. 1; ðafæð 123. 3; geðafað 125. 18, 26, 132. 21; *pl.* geðafiað 37. 26, 109. 2; *sbj. prs.* geðafige 37. 12, 131. 24, 141. 28; geðafie 141. 27.

ðafung, *f.* consent; *d.* geðafunga, ðafunge* 11. 7.

ðanc, *m. a)* thought; *b)* favour, grace; *c)* accord, consent; *d)* thanks; *g.* ðonces 98. 8 (*b*); ðines ðances, of your own accord 27. 24, *cf.* (ðonces) 11. 6, 16. 10, 20. 30, 37. 15, 40. 4; *d.* on ðonce, satisfactory, pleasant xii.

16; *a.* ðanc 17. 15 (*d*), 143. 2 (*d*); geðanc 141. 8* (*a*).

ðancian, *wv. w. d.* thank; *imp.* ðonca 13. 28.

ðancolmōd, *adj.* thoughtful; *pl.* ðoncolmode xix. 14.

ðancwierðe, *adj.* acceptable, pleasing; *comp. n.* ðancwyrðre 52. 4*, 6*.

ðanon, *adv.* thence; 136. 23*; ðanan xvii. 28; ðonan *fq.* 12. 13, i. 82 &c.; ðonon 105. 11*.

ðanonweard, *adj.* about to depart; ðonanweard 103. 7.

ðawenian, *wv.* moisten; *pp.* geðawened xx. 102.

ðe, 1) *indecl. rel. pron.* which, who; *generally nom. or a.* Pr. 7, MPr. 10 &c.; *g.* ðe he full is 84. 14; ðe ic, me who ii. 13; ðehim, to whom xiii. 51; te *after* ðæt, *fq.*; *v.* ðæt; *but* ðe 148. 11, i. 30. 2) *after comp.* than; 37. 21, x. 39 &c.; *v.* ðy. 3) *alternatives:* ðe . . . ðe, whether . . . or 122. 29 &c.; ðe hi ne, nor did they viii. 34.

ðeah, 1) *adv.* yet, nevertheless; Pr. 8, i. 26 &c.; *gen. foll.* ðeah (2), 25. 3, x. 12 &c. 2) *conj. w. sbj.* though; 7. 6, vii. 35 &c.; ðeah ðe 27. 12 &c.; ic nat ðeah, whether 64. 9; ge ðeah ðu ma wille, and more if you like 44. 17.

geðeaht, *n.* thought, counsel; plan; 80. 11; *d.* geðeahte 11. 7, 13. 25, 31, 79. 25, 81. 23, 128. 30, 144. 23, xx. 39, 87, 200.

geðeahtere, *m.* councillor, senator; *pl.* geðcahteras 22. 24.

ðearf, *f.* need, necessity; *about* 11 *times*, 9. 17, iii. 11 &c.; *d.* ðearfe 18. 16; *a.* 18. 17, 123. 8, 13, 132. 21, 149. 7.

ðearf, *swv. w. g. or inf.* require, need; 1.*s.* 70. 28; ðearfe 96. 25; 2.*s.* ðearft 13. 32 &c. *and* xxix. 39; 3.*s.* ðearf 26. 12, vii. 6 &c.; *pl.* ðurfon 31. 22 &c.;

ðurfan xix. 25; ðurfe we 56. 14*; *pst.* 2.*s.* ðorftes 33. 12; 3.*s.* ðorfte 75. 23, 97. 1, xv. 9; *sbj. prs.* ðyrfe 31. 16 &c.; ðurfe in B, *ib.* &c.; *pl.* ðyrfen 60. 6, 133. 28; *pst.* ðorfte 33. 8 &c.

ðearfa, *wm.* person in need, poor man; *g.* ðearfan vii. 17.

ðearflice, *adv.* profitably, with good effect; i. 60.

ðearl, *adj.* severe; *f.* i. 77.

ðearle, *adv.* excessively; i. 82, xx. 45, xxviii. 24, 55.

ðēaw, *m.* custom, habit; 112. 22 &c.; *g.* ðeawes 62. 28; *d.* ðeawe 62. 10; *a.* ðeaw 61. 7; *pl.* qualities, character, virtues, 15. 25 &c.; *g.* ðeawa 17. 23, 28; *d.* ðeawum 9. 24 &c.; ðeowum 18. 4 &c.; *a.* ðeawas 15. 9 &c. *and* xi. 12.

ðeccan, *wv.* cover; *sbj. prs. pl.* ðeccen x. 43.

ðegen, *m.* servant; follower; courtier; (*in Metr.*) man; 16. 3, xxii. 44; ðegn 16. 22; *g.* ðegenes 8. 22; ðegnes xx. 200; *a.* ðegn i. 69; *pl.* ðegnas 30. 26, 116. 11, i. 30, xx. 72; *g.* ðegena ix. 57; ðegna 66. 19, 111. 15, 116. 6, xii. 8 &c.; *d.* ðegnum 66. 20; *a.* ðegnas xxvi. 77.

ðegnian, *wv. w. d.* serve; ðenian 142. 6; *ind. prs. 3.s.* ðenað xxix. 76; *pl.* ðegniað xxv. 11; ðeniað 111. 22.

ðegnung, *f.* service*; function; *d.* ðenunga 18. 4*; *a.* ðegnunga 144. 2, 3; *pl. g.* ðegnunga xxv. 24, 32; ðenunga 111. 21*, 24*; *d.* ðegnungum xxv. 28; ðenungum 16. 23*; *a.* ðegnunga xi. 46.

ðencan, *wv.* think; think of; *w. infin.* determine, design; 52. 16, 53. 11, 83. 18, 147. 9; ðencean i. 60; to ðencenne 16. 19; *ind. prs. 1.s.* ðence 21. 16; 3.*s.* ðenceð; *w. infin.* 103. 20; ðencð 93. 31, 32, 132. 2, xx. 27; thinks out, plans 128. 27;

pst. 3.*s.* ðohte 102. 10; *pl.*
ðohton i. 11; *sbj. pst.* ðohte 83.
20, x. 4; *pp.* geðoht 128. 13,
145. 14.

geðencan, *wv.* think of, imagine;
remember; design, contrive; *sq.*
36. 5 &c. *and* xiii. 27; geðen-
cean v. 1; to geðencanne 76. 1,
84. 31; to geðencenne 52. 2;
ind. pst. 2.*s.* geðohtest 79. 26,
29, xx. 40; *imp.* geðenc 27. 18
&c.; *pl.* geðencað 42. 21 &c.

ðenden, *conj.* while, as long as;
i. 38, 48, xi. 72, xxii. 39.

ðēod, *f.* nation, race; i. 28; *g.*
ðeode 43. 2; *d.* 43. 32; ðiode
99. 9, 101. 23; *pl.* ðeoda 42.
22; ðioda 46. 11, 115. 15; *g.*
ðeoda 42. 24, 43. 21, xx. 205,
256, 274; xxvi. 43; ðioda 65.
23, x. 23, xx. 176, xxvi. 7, 55;
d. ðiodum 42. 7, 112. 23; *a.*
ðeoda 46. 10, xxv. 14; dialects,
42. 28 *n.*; ðioda 115. 15.

geðeode, *n.* dialect; *a.* 63. 17;
g. pl. geðioda 99. 17.

ðeoden, *m.* lord, king; ðioden
xi. 80; *g.* ðeodnes xi. 11;
d. ðeodne xxix. 97.

ðecdfruma, *wm.* prince, lord; *d.*
ðiodfruman xxix. 92.

ðeodisc, *n.* language; *a.* 46. 12;
ðiodisc x. 26.

ðeodland, *n.* country; *a.* ðeod-
lond i. 3.

ðeof, *m.* thief; *pl.* ðeofas 33. 15.

ðeofscolu, *f.* band of thieves; *a.*
ðiofscole 33. 10.

ðeon, *sv*1,3. thrive, flourish; *pst.*
pl. geðungon i. 7; *sbj. prs.*
ðeo 46. 13; ðio x. 28; *prs. p.*
ðionde 122. 3.

ðeosternes, *f.* darkness; ðeosternes 89. 22 *n.*

ðeostrian, *wv.* darken; *ind. prs.*
3.*s.* ðiostrað 121. 16.

ðeotan, *sv*2. howl; ðioton xxvi.
80; *ind. pst.* 3.*pl.* ðuton 116. 19.

ðeow, 1) *shst. m.* servant, slave;
pl. ðeowas 17. 19, 18. 5, xi. 11;
d. ðeowum 18. 4, 6, 11; *pl.*
ðeowas 72. 1, xi. 11. 2) *adj.*
enslaved, not free; *pl.* ðiowe
142. 4, 6; *f.* ðeowe 144. 1;
a. n. ðeowu 143. 31.

ðeowdom, *m.* servitude; *g.* ðeow-
domes xxix. 40; *d.* ðeowdome
11. 24.

ðeowian, *wv. w. d.* serve; *ind.*
prs. 3.*s.* ðiowað xxix. 76; *pl.*
ðeowiað 48. 25, 26; ðiowiað
136. 8, 22; *pst. pl.* ðiowedon
136. 31; *sbj. prs. pl.* ðeowian 136.
29*; ðiowien xxix. 92; *pst. pl.*
ðiowoden xxix. 97.

ðerscold, *m.* threshold; *a.* ðeor-
scwold 49. 23*; ðyrscwold xi. 68.

ðes, *demonst. adj.* this; 35. 26, ii.
5 &c.; *f.* ðios *in* C, 13. 4, ii. 4
&c.; ðeos viii. 33, 43, x. 8;
ðeos *in* B, 48. 6 &c.; *n.* ðis 9.
13, 26. 15, xi. 97 &c.; *g.* ðisses
in C, 37. 31, ix. 39 &c.; ðysses
60. 17; ðises *in* B, 27. 5 &c.;
f. ðisse iii. 7 &c.; *d.* ðissum iii.
8, x. 70; ðisum 42. 21*, 89. 17*,
99. 6; *f.* ðisse Pr. 1, xiv. 10
&c.; *a.* ðisne 20. 3, x. 40 &c.;
ðysne 49. 32*, xx. 9; *f.* ðas Pr.
8, viii. 41 &c.; *n.* ðis 68. 9, ii.
11 &c.; *inst.* ðys *about* 7 *times*
in C, 21. 17 &c. *and* xxi. 28; ðis
about 8 *times*, 25. 25 &c. *and*
xix. 35; ðïs 125. 4; *pl.* ðas ii.
10 &c.; ðæs 30. 3*, 48. 10, 73.
10, 86. 25; *g.* ðissa 14. 24, v.
41 &c.; ðyssa vii. 53; *d.* ðissum
8. 19, 66. 4, xxi. 17; ðisum 19.
2, 40. 18 *n.**, 74. 8*, 88. 28,
116. 27*, xx. 255; ðysum xxvi.
98; ðeossum MPr. 4; ðissan
40. 18; ðys mærum steorrum
xvii. 11; *a.* ðas 8. 9, viii. 1 &c.
? ðæs xx. 223.

ðicce, *adj.* dense, thick; 99. 12
(ðicke B); *wk.* ðicca v. 6; *a.*
ðicne 100. 6; *wk.* ðiccan xx.
264; *comp. f.* ðiccre 80. 30; ðicre
xx. 134.

ðicgan, *sv*5. take; partake of;
ind. prs. 1.*pl.* ðiggað 93. 3; *pst.*
3.*s.* geðah i. 53.

ðider, *adv.* thither; 51. 7, i. 60
&c.; *rel.* whither 140. 2 ðider

ðider 108. 4; ðider . . . ðider 92. 20.

ðiderweard, *adv.* in that direction; xiii. 14, xx. 159.

ðiderweardes, *adv.* in that direction; 128. 1.

ðidres, *adv.* thither; hidres ðidres 108. 14, 139. 31; hidres 7 ðidres 100. 6.

ðīedan, *wv.* join, associate; geðiodan 53. 20; *ind. prs.* 3.*s.* geðiet 47. 21, 24*; *pl.* ðeodað geðeodað* 39. 13; geðiodað 39. 14; geðeodað 48. 2*.

ðīestre, 1) *adj.* dark, gloomy; ðystre xx. 266; *d.* ðiostrum 112. 15; *d. pl.* 19. 3. 2) *sbst. n.* darkness; *pl.* ðeostro 14. 17*; ðiostro 121. 17, v. 21; *g.* ðiostra 105. 25*; *d.* ðeostrum 17. 24; ðiostrum 97. 16, 126. 14*, 131. 15, xxviii. 43; *a.* ðiostro 101. 21, 103. 15, iii. 7, iv. 7, xxiii. 6, xxiv. 56; ðistro 9. 13*; ðeostro 10. 4*.

ðīestro, *f.* darkness; ðiostro xxi. 41; *g.* 103. 11; *d.* 52. 6.

ðīn, *poss. adj.* thy, your; 22. 5, xx. 37 &c.; *notes on forms:* se ðin 27. 23; *f.* ðin 24. 31, xx. 31 &c.; *n.* ðæt ðin 80. 11; *g.* anes geðeahte ðines, of thee alone xx. 40; *inst.* ðine xx. 69, 113; *pl. f.* ðin agna 23. 8; *n.* ðine 121. 5; *g.* ðara ðinra 24. 29, 50. 21; *d.* ðinum lufum, love of thee 22. 21; *a. f.* ðina 21. 26, 27; ðine 79. 11*; *forms and uses otherwise normal.*

ðing, *n.* thing; *in Metr.* xx. 37 &c.; ðincg 104. 5, xxii. 5; ðinc xxviii. 74; *g.* ðinges 53. 15, x. 32 &c.; ðinces 75. 22; ðincges xx. 28; *d.* ðinge 79. 24 &c.; *a.* ðing 25. 27, xxiv. 7; *pl.* ðing 16. 12, 29. 28, 30. 2*, xxi. 30; ðincg 77. 17, 87. 18, 128. 15; *g.* ðinga 29. 1, v. 37 &c.; *d.* ðingum 32. 8 &c.; for swiðe lytlum ðingum, reasons 24. 21, *cf.* 59. 28 &c.; for ðæm ðingum ðe, because 99. 11; for ðinum

ðingum, for your sake 16. 25, *cf.* 17. 5, 6; *a.* ðing xx. 45, 224, 276; ðincg 121. 28, 30.

ðingere, *m.* advocate; *a.* 123. 26; *pl.* ðingeras 123. 7.

ðingian, *wv. w. d.* intercede, advocate; *ind. prs.* 3.*pl.* ðingiað 123. 8, 9; *pst.* 3.*s.* ðingode 123. 11.

ðixl, *f.* waggon-shaft or pole; *pl.* wænes ðisla 126. 3, xxviii. 10.

ðocerian, *wv.* run; *sbj. prs. rflx.* ðocrige him 105. 1.

geðoht, *m.* thought; *d.* geðohte 8. 25; *a.* geðoht 141. 8.

ðolian, *wv. trans. and intr.* suffer; endure, have patience; i. 77; geðolian 16. 22, 18. 26, 23. 12. 70. 4, 127. 30; to ðolianne 133. 10; *ind. pst.* 3.*s.* ðolade 122. 30.

ðon, *inst.* of se; *used fq. as adv. w. comps.*; 17. 1, vii. 20 &c.; ðon ma ðe, (not) any more than 37. 20 &c.; (*usually* ðe *in* B).

ðonēcan, *conj.* whenever; *w. sbj.* 44. 7; ðonecan ðe 58. 2; *w. ind.* 61. 5.

ðonne, (*usually* ðōn *in* B; ðonñ 25. 14, 34. 25); 1) *adv. a) time*, then, 25. 12, xiii. 78 &c. *b) sequence*, next, 14. 4, xxv. 24 &c. *c) inference*, then, therefore, 18. 30 &c.; *fq. correl. w. preceding* gif 20. 15, iv. 51 &c. *w.* ðeah 68. 24. 2) *conj. time*, when, 9.11, ii. 7 &c.; *fq. doubled*, 14. 12, 20. 27, vi. 9 &c. 3) *after comp.* than; 15. 1, i. 41 &c.; *fq. foll. by sbj.* 11. 9, x. 23 &c.

ðorn, *m.* thorny plant; *a. pl.* ðornas xii. 3.

ðræd, *m.* thread; *d.* ðræde 65. 30.

ðrægan, *wv.* run; *ind. prs.* 3.*s.* ðrægeð xxviii. 24 *n.*

ðrāg, *f. a)* space of time, interval; *b)* attack, fit; 111. 28(*b*); *a.* ðrage, for a time i. 28, xx. 134, 264, xxvi. 103; evil time i. 77.

ðrāgmǣlum, *adv.* at intervals; xxvi. 80, xxviii. 55.

ðrēan, *wv.* threaten; oppress, afflict; ðreagan 133. 25; *ind. prs.* 3.*s.* ðreað (*w. d.*) 10. 19*; ðreat 10. 18*; *sbj. prs.* ðreage v. 37.

ðrēat, *m.* crowd, throng; *d.* ðreate i. 3.

ðrēatian, urge on; threaten; oppress; ðreatigan 118. 27; *ind. prs.* 3.*s.* ðreatað 138. 2; *pl.* ðreatiað 111. 17, xxv. 13; *sbj. prs.* ðreatige 137. 9.

ðrēatung, *f.* reproof; threat; *d.* ðreatunge 137. 13*.

ðrēawung, *f.* reproof; threat; *d.* ðreunge 137. 13; *a.* ðreaunga 16. 21*.

ðrēo, *num.* three; *n.* 23. 9, 147. 26; ðrio 75. 20, 77. 17; *masc.* ðre 40. 22*; *g.* ðreora 73. 13; ðriora 75. 19; *d.* ðrim 40. 20 &c.; *a. f.* ðrio 117. 19; *n.* ðreo 32. 4*, 75. 17*, 25*; ðrio 81. 17*, 102. 14, 17.

ðridda, *num. adj.* third; *f.* ðridde 50. 6 &c. *and* xx. 187; *n.* 118. 15, 148. 3, xx. 61; *d.* ðriddan 43. 7 &c.

ðrifeald, *adj.* threefold; *f.* ðreofeald 81. 16*; *n.* ðriefald xx. 183; *a. f.* ðriefalde xx. 176; *a. pl. wk.* ðriefealdan 81. 14.

ðrirēðre, *adj.* with three banks of oars; ðrierēðre xxvi. 27; *n.* ðrerēðre 115. 21.

ðringan, *sv3. intrans.* press on, hurry; 35. 23; *ind. prs.* 3.*s.* ðringð 9. 13, iii. 7; *pl.* ðringað xxv. 28; *trans.* geðrungon, crowded into, oppressed i. 3.

ðrītig, *num.* thirty; 126. 9, xxviii. 25, 29.

ðrote, *wf.* throat; *a.* ðrotan 51. 3.

ðrowian, *wv.* endure, suffer; to ðrowianne 133. 15; *ind. prs.* 2.*s.* ðrowast 21. 21; 3.*s.* ðrowað 70. 12, 104. 33; *pst.* 3.*s.* geðrowode, was passive 80. 4.

geðruen, *v.* ðweran.

ðryccan, *wv.* trample; *ind. prs.* 3.*pl.* ðrycað 10. 20; ðriccað iv. 38.

ðrymm, *m.* grandeur, magnificence, pomp; *g.* ðrymmes xxv. 32; *d.* ðrymme 111. 17, xxv. 11, 13.

ðrymcyning, *m.* glorious king; xx. 205.

ðū, *pers. pron.* thou, you; 8. 18, iv. 1 &c.; *g.* ðin 12. 14 &c.; *d.* ðe 9. 17, v. 37 &c.; *a.* 9. 19, v. 36 &c.

ðunor, *m.* thunder, thunderbolt; *a. pl.* ðunras 99. 2.

ðunrian, *wv.* thunder; *ind. prs.* 3.*s.* ðunrað 126. 18, xxviii. 55.

ðurh, (ðurg 5 *times in* C, 97. 5 &c.) *prep. w.a. a) motion, penetration,* through, 93. 3 &c. *b) metaph.* by means of, through, 9. 26, iv. 4 &c.

ðurhcrēopan, *sv2.* creep through; *ind. prs.* 3.*s.* ðurgcrypð 93. 5.

ðurhfaran, *sv6.* pass through, penetrate; *ind. prs.* 3.*s.* ðurhfærð 28. 15.

ðurhsēon, *sv5.* see through; ðurhsion 72. 31, 73. 2, 4; *ind. prs.* 3.*s.* ðurhsyhð xxx. 16.

ðurhtēon, *sv2.* carry out, accomplish; ðurhtion xxv. 59; ðurgtion 117. 13, 18; *ind. prs.* 3.*s.* ðurhteoð 141. 18*; *pl.* ðurgtioð 117. 20; *pst.* 3.*s.* ðurhteah 70. 13; *sbj. prs.* ðurhtio 88. 17; *pst.* ðurhtuge 144. 5.

ðurhwunian, *wv.* continue, persist; 8. 14, 112. 11, xxv. 70; *ind. prs.* 2.*s.* ðurhwunast 79. 16; *pl.* ðurhwuniað 23. 29, 51. 26; *pst.* 3.*s.* ðurhwunode 7. 7, 65. 10; *sbj. prs.* ðurhwunige 44. 26; *prs. p.* enduring, abiding; *g.* ðurhwunigendes 64. 21; *a.* ðurhwunigendne 78. 11; *pl.* ðurhwuniende 23. 11.

ðurst, *m.* thirst; 19. 6, vii. 17.

ðurstig, *adj.* thirsty; *f.* ðurstegu 26. 30.

ðus, *adv.* thus, so; *refers to what precedes or follows,* 26. 22, 39. 15, i. 84 &c.

ðūsend, *n. f.* thousand; 44. 15, 17, 19, 60. 29, xiv. 5.

ðwǣnan, *wv.* moisten ; *ind. pst.*
3.*s.* geðwǣnde 80. 18.
geðwǣre, *adj.* united, reconciled,
harmonious ; 62. 7 ; geðwǣre on
him selfum, at peace 134. 32 ;
pl. xxix. 37 ; *f.* geðwǣra 49. 13 ;
d. geðwǣrum 81. 14.
geðwǣrian, *wv.* reconcile ; *ind.*
prs. 3.*s.* geðwǣrað 131. 4, 136.
11, xxix. 47.
geðwǣrlīce, *adv.* in agreement,
harmoniously ; 136. 7.
ðweorh, *adj.* adverse, contrary ;
g. ðweores 144. 31.
ðweorian, *wv.* be opposed ; *pp.*
geðweorod xx. 72.
ðwēortīeme, *adj.* contentious,
quarrelsome ; ðweorteme 114.
27.
ðweran, *sv*4. forge together, weld ;
pp. geðruen xx. 134 *n.*
ðȳ, 1) *adv. a)* therefore ; 22. 26
&c. ; ðy . . . ðy 32. 20 &c.
b) w. comp. ; *often w.* a = the ;
9. 27, i. 76 &c. ; ði *in* B, 52.
9 &c. ; *fq.* ðe *in* B *and* C, 63.
3, 104. 30, ix. 32 &c. 2) *conj.*
because ; 32. 21 &c.
ðyf, *v.* pyff.
ðȳlǣs, *conj. w. sbj.* lest, in order
that . . . not ; 39. 26, MPr. 6
&c. ; ði lǣs 147. 10* ; ðe lǣs
134. 18.
geðyld, *f.* patience ; 87. 7 ; *g.*
geðylde 133. 26 (?) ; *d.* 120. 3.
geðyldelīce, *adv.* patiently ; 25. 4,
45. 11, 101. 16, 133. 3, 26.
geðyldig, *adj.* patient ; 45. 17 ?
pl. d. geðyldegum 25. 12 ; *a.*
geðyldige 62. 28.
ðyllic, *pron. adj.* such ; *f.* ðillecu
20. 18 ; ðellecu 20. 18 ; *g.*
ðyllices 126. 16* ; *d.* ðyllecnm
39. 24 ; *a. n.* ðyllic 118. 25 ;
ðillic 10. 28 ; *pl. d.* ðyllecum
39. 25* ; ðillicum 54. 21 ; *a. f.*
ðyllica 99. 4.
ðyncan, *wv. w. d.* seem, seem
good ; ðincan 36. 1, 50. 22, 75.
25, 118. 19, x. 8 ; *ind. prs.* 3.*s.*
ðynceð xii. 8, xxv. 35, xxviii.
82 ; ðyncð 60. 1, 107. 2, 124.

22, xxviii. 38 ; ðinceð xxix. 42 ;
ðincð *usual form* 22. 21, xii.
18 &c. ; *pl.* ðyncað 16. 11*,
23. 13 ; ðincað 31. 12, 121. 5,
xiii. 44 ; *pst.* ðuhte 24. 28 &c.
and viii. 7 ; *sbj. prs.* ðynce 25.
8, 47. 17*, 117. 27, 137. 5 ;
ðince 20. 29, x. 10 &c. ; *pl.*
ðyncen 127. 28 ; *pst.* ðuhte 48.
13, xii. 15.
ðynne, *adj.* thin ; *comp.* ðynra
v. 6.
ðynnian, *wv.* make thin, dissipate ;
geðinnian 14. 7.
ðȳrel, *n.* hole, aperture ; *a.* 93. 5.
ðyrstan, *wv. impers. w. a.* be
thirsty ; *sbj. prs.* 3.*s.* ðyrste
60. 11.

U.

ufan, *adv.* from above, downwards ;
80. 33, xxiv. 11, 17, 24 ; ufane
xx. 141.
ufor, *comp. adv.* higher ; 57. 26,
94. 25, 105. 13 ; *sup.* yfemest
146. 27.
ultor, *m.* vulture ; 102. 33.
unāberendlic, *adj.* intolerable ;
n. 23. 5 ; *a. n. wk.* unaberendlice
133. 4.
unābindendlic, *adj.* indissoluble ;
d. pl. unabindendlicum 38. 31,
96. 17* ; unanbindendlicum 57.
6*, 81. 6*, 96. 17.
unæðele, *adj.* not noble, mean ;
24. 6, 69. 32, xvii. 28 ; *a.*
unæðelne 69. 26, xvii. 17.
unæðelian, *wv.* degrade, debase ;
ind. prs. 3.*s.* anæðelað xvii. 27
(J) ; *pp.* anæðelad 69. 32*.
unandergildes, *v.* unundergielde.
unāreht, *quasi ptcp.* not explained ;
77. 16* (unreht J).
unārīmed, *adj.* countless ; un-
arimedum 89. 30 ; *pl.* 7. 10.
unāsecgendlic, *adj.* ineffable ; *d.*
unasecgendlicum 128. 25 ; una-
secgendlicne 37. 7.
unāðrotenlīce, *adv.* unweariedly ;
74. 5, 136. 7.

unǎwendedlic, *adj.* unchangeable; 79. 16*.
unǎwendende, *adj.* unchangeable; *a.* unawendendne xi. 13.
unǎwendendlic, *adj.* unchangeable; xxiv. 43; *f.* 129. 8*;
unawendenlïc 101. 5*; unanwendendlic 96. 21, 101. 5, xx.
17; *a.* unawendendlicne 48.
27*.
unǎwendendlïce, *adv.* unchange-
ably, inevitably; 144. 14*, 15*,
16*; unanwendendlice *ib.* C;
unonwendendlice 27. 9*.
unǎwendlic, *adj.* unchangeable;
f. unandwendlic 129. 8.
unbeorhte, *adv.*; *comp.* unbeorhtor, less brightly 86. 7; unbyrhtor
82. 1*.
unbrocheard, *adj.* delicate,
tender; *sup. w.* unbrocheardost
92. 4.
ungebyrde, *adj.* uncongenial; *n.*
92. 22.
unc, *v.* wit.
uncer, *poss. adj.* of us two; *d.*
uncrum 139. 28; *a. pl. n.* uncru
99. 23.
unclǣne, *adj.* unclean; *g. wk.*
unclænan 11. 25.
uncǔð, *adj.* unknown, not certain;
n. iv. 39; *g.* uncuðes 87. 33,
100. 30; *d. f.* uncuðre ii. 9; *a.*
uncuðne xiii. 58; *f.* uncuðe 100.
9; *pl. n.* uncuð xxxi. 6.
uncweðende, *adj.* without speech,
dumb; *pl. wk.* uncweðendan
92. 16.
ungecynde, *adj.* not natural,
alien; *a. f.* 91. 21 (uncynde B).
ungecyndelic, *adj.* unnatural;
n. 70. 23*, 93. 11; *comp. n.*
ungecyndlicre 142. 6*.
uncynlic, *adj.* unsuitable, impro-
per; *comp. n.* uncynlicre 142. 6.
undǣled, *adj.* undivided; *n.* 93.
32*; *pl.* undælde 90. 30*.
ungedafenlïce, *adv.* unfittingly,
immoderately; 43. 19.
undēadlic, *adj.* immortal; *pl. f.*
undeadlica, undeaðlice* 26. 11.
under, i) *prep.* 1) *w.d. a) place*;

under, 10. 20, i. 76 &c. *b) subjection*, under the authority of,
under, 7. 16, 34. 26, 104. 12,
115. 15, 125. 1, 142. 7; beneath
(in position) 29. 7. 2) *w. a.*
a) motion, under, 114. 21, 126.
11, xxviii. 33, 39, xxix. 16, 28;
b) subjection, under, 32. 12. ii)
adv. underneath, below, xxiv. 33.
underbæc, *adv.* backwards, back;
103. 7, 8, 13.
underetan, *sv5.* undermine, *metaph.*; *pp.* undereten 27. 2.
underfön, *rv.* receive; underfoon
36. 30; *ind. prs.* 3.*s.* underfehð
33. 19, 62. 1, 136. 18; *pst.* 1.*s.*
underfeng 17. 12, 20. 6; *sbj. prs.*
underfenge 16. 9, 37. 30; *pp.*
underfangen Pr. 8.
underlütan, *sv2.* stoop under,
submit to; x. 20; *sbj. prs. pl.*
46. 8*.
understandan, *sv6.* understand;
50. 29, 131. 18; *ind. prs.* 2.*s.*
understenst 27. 18*; 3.*s.* understent 131. 16; *pp.* understanden
86. 22.
understaðolfæst, *v.* unstaðolfæst.
underðïedan, *wv.* subject; *ind.
prs. pl.* underðeodað 32. 11;
underðiodað 112. 8*, 141. 5;
pst. 3.*s.* underðeodde 112. 9*;
underðiodde xxv. 66; *sbj. prs.*
underðiede, underðeode* 72. 3;
pst. pl. underðiodden 147. 20;
pp. underðieded xiv. 8, xvii. 23;
underðyded xvi. 4; underðeoded
60. 30*, 69. 30*; underðied 129.
10, 11, 12, 14; underðeod 39.
26*, 67. 28*; *pl.* underðeodde
48. 4*; *f.* underðiodde 100. 23.
unēaðe, *adv.* with difficulty; 7
times, 12. 30 &c.; ungeaðe 97.
15*.
ungeendod, *adj.* unending; *g.
wk.* ungeendodan 44. 12; *a.
n. wk.* ungeendode 44. 18.
ungeendodlic, *adj.* endless, eternal; *a. n. wk.* ungeendodlice 44.
21.
unfæger, *adj.* ugly; 145. 24.

unfǣglic, *adj.* not fatal, not serious;
  a. n. 107. 29* (ungefæglic C).
unfæst, *adj.* not firm, unstable;
  n. 25. 30.
unfæstrǣdnes, *f.* instability, in-
  constancy; *a.* unfæstrædnesse
  15. 27.
ungefēre, *adj.* impassable; *d. pl.*
  ungeferum, ungefærum* 42. 30.
unfracoðlīce, *adv.* virtuously; 40.
  11 (unfracodlice B).
ungefrǣglīce, *adv.* extraordinari-
  ly; 61. 17, 101. 24, 111. 19.
ungefylled, *adj.* insatiable; *a. f.*
  wk. ungefylledan 17. 29.
unglǣd, *adj.* cheerless, unpleasant;
  f. ungladu 14. 14.
unglēawnes, *f.* obtuseness, stu-
  pidity; 132. 29.
unhāl, *adj.* unsound, diseased;
  pl. n. unhale 24. 12*; *d.* unhalum
  132. 8; *a. n.* unhale 121. 9.
unhered, *adj.* not praised; 68.
  24 (unherod B).
unhīere, *adj.* fierce, cruel; *a. n.*
  unhiore xxix. 64.
unhrōr, *adj.* without motion; *d.*
  pl. unhrorum 146. 26* *n.*
unhwearflende, *adj.* unchanging;
  g. unhwearfiendes 20. 29.
unhȳðig, *adj.* unhappy; unhydig,
  unhiðy* 59. 5.
unīeðnes, *f.* difficulty, trouble; *a.*
  uneðnesse 62. 3.
unlǣred, *adj.* untaught, ignorant;
  a. unlæredne 17. 11, 20. 6; ungelæredne 17. 11*; *g. pl.* unlæredra xxviii. 1.
unland, *n.* waste or barren land;
  g. unlondes 42. 16*.
ungelīc, *adj.* unlike, different;
  135. 5; *n.* 92. 22, xx. 33; *g.*
  ungelices 147. 3; *a. f. (or
  adv. ?)* ungelice 106. 26; *n.*
  ungelic 101. 15, 118. 14; *pl.*
  ungelice 43. 22 *n.*; *f.* xxxi. 3;
  a. f. 52. 19, 79. 32, xx. 55; *n.*
  xxxi. 4.
ungelīce, *adv.* differently; 147. 4.
ungelīefedlīc, *adj.* incredible;
  comp. n. ungelefedlicre, ungelefendlicre* 118. 19.

ungelimp, *n.* misfortune; *a.* 125.
  19.
unmǣre, *adj.* not famous, obscure;
  68. 25.
unmǣrlic, *adj.* ignoble; *f.* 75.
  19.
unmǣte, *adj.* excessive; *d. wk.*
  unmætan 111. 25 *n.*
unmedome, *adj.* imperfect, unworthy; *n. wk.* unmedeme 82.
  22*; *d. wk.* unmedeman 61.
  28*.
ungemenged, *adj.* unmixed; *f.*
  100. 31.
unmennisclic, *adj.* contrary to
  human nature, unnatural; *f.* un-
  mennisclicu 70. 26.
ungemet, 1) *sbst. n.* excess; *d.*
  ungemete xxv. 38, xxvi. 62; *a.*
  ungemet 138. 31. 2) *adv.* excessively xi. 59; unigmet vii. 33,
  x. 9.
ungemetfæst, *adj.* immoderate,
  intemperate; *a.* ungemetfæstne
  61. 23; *pl.* ungemetfæste 30. 6.
ungemetfæstnes, *f.* intemper-
  ance, incontinence; 109. 9.
ungemetgīemenn, *f.* excessive
  care; ungemetgemen vii. 28.
ungemetlic, *adj.* excessive; enor-
  mous; 26. 31; *g.* ungemetlices
  27. 4, 41. 13; *f.* ungemetlicre
  71. 30; *d.* ungemetlicum 81. 9;
  wk. ungemetlican 95. 30, 111.
  19, 26; *inst.* ungemetlice 89.
  29; *d. pl.* ungemetlicum 13.
  27.
ungemetlīce, *adv.* excessively,
  immoderately; *about* 17 *times,*
  12. 24 &c.
unmiht, *f.* feebleness; *a.* unmeahte
  66. 17; *pl.* unmihta*, unmeahta
  110. 5.
unmihtig, *adj.* weak; unmehtig
  109. 15; *pl.* unmihtige 66. 16*;
  unmehtige 108. 3, xxiv. 62; *a.*
  unmihtige 105. 27*; *comp. pl.*
  unmihtegran 108. 5.
ungemyndig, *adj.* w. *g.* unmind-
  ful; 95. 20, xxii. 55.
unmyndlinga, *adv.* undesignedly;
  125. 24; unmendlinga xxv. 30.

geunnan, *v.* ann.

ungeniedd, *adj.* uncompelled;
ungened 91. 8; *pl. f.* ungenedde
100. 22.

unniedig, *adj.* uncompelled; *pl.*
unnedige 133. 2.

unnytlice, *adv.* in vain; 142. 31.

unnytt, 1) *adj.* useless, vain;
unnet 68. 29, xxii. 10; *n.* unnytte 95. 1*; *wk.* unnettan 14.
20*; *comp. n.* unnyttre 72. 20*.
2) *sbst. n.* frivolity, folly; unnet
xvi. 6; *a.* 95. 5*, x. 21, xxii.
17.

unoferswiðedlic, *adj.* invincible;
pl. unoferswiðedlice 133. 32.

ungeräd, *adj.* discordant; *pl.* ungerade 134. 28; *d.* ungeradum
wordum, unskilful, unsuitable
8. 7.

ungerædelice, *adv.* irregularly,
unstably; *sup.* ungeredelicost
130. 14.

ungereclice, *adv.* in a disorderly
manner; intemperately; 94. 10,
109. 30.

unriht, 1) *adj.* wrong, unjust;
wk. unrihta xviii. 1; *f.* unriht
123. 2; *n.* 112. 21, 133. 8, xxvii.
22; *g.* unryhtes 41. 13*; *d. f.*
unrihtre 124. 3; *a. f.* unrihte
119. 28; *n.* unriht 9. 27. 2)
sbst. n. wrong, injustice; 131.
24; *d.* unrihte 36. 20; *a.* unriht
119. 30, ix. 54; *d. pl.* unrihtum,
acts of injustice, misdeeds 39. 26.

unrihtfēoung, *f.* wicked hatred;
d. pl. unrihtfioungum xxvii. 1.

unrihtgītsung, *f.* covetousness;
g. unrihtgitsunga 19. 23.

unrihthǣmed, *n.* fornication,
adultery; ix. 6; *g.* unrihthæmedes 71. 5; *d.* unrihthæmede
71. 7, xviii. 10; *a. pl.* unryhthæmedu 39. 17*.

unrihtlīc, *adj.* wrong, unjust; *g.*
unrihtlices 18. 23.

unrihtlice, *adv.* wrongly, wrong-
fully; 43. 15, 65. 28, 120. 32.

unrihtlust, *m.* wrongful desire;
d. pl. unrihtlustum 19. 20.

unrihtwis, *adj.* unjust, wicked;

wk. unrihtwisa 36. 25 &c. *and*
xv. 1; *g.* unrihtwises ix. 8; *wk.*
unrihtwisan 62. 7; *d. wk.* 7. 18;
unrihtwīsan 39. 29; *pl.* unrihtwise 30. 6, iv. 43, xxv. 58; *wk.*
unryhtwisan 9. 26* &c.; *g.* un-
rihtwisra 11. 31; *d.* unrihtwisum
111. 12, xxv. 2; *a.* unrihtwise
xxiv. 58; *wk.* unrihtwisan 105.
26.

unrihtwīsnes, *f.* injustice, wickedness; 62. 13, 104. 6, 132. 29;
g. unrihtwisnesse 19. 29.

unrīm, *n.* countless number; 127.
7, i. 44, xx. 190, xxvi. 40; *d.*
unrime xxv. 7; *a.* unrim 26. 17,
xiv. 4; ungerim 60. 28.

ungerisene, *n.* inconvenience; *d.*
pl. ungerisenum 30. 19.

ungerisenlic, *adj.* unsuitable, unseemly; *n.* 68. 7; *a. pl.* ungerisenlice 67. 29; *comp. n.*
ungerisenlicre 68. 14.

ungerisenlīce, *adv.* in an unseemly
manner, disgracefully; 67. 28.

unrōt, *adj.* sad, despondent; 8. 4,
58. 25; *n. wk.* unrote 9. 20, 23.
10; *pl.* 24. 8, 11.

unrōtnes, *f.* sadness, despondency;
fq. 12. 3 &c.; *g.* unrotnesse 9.
17 &c.; *d.* 11. 3 &c. *and* xxv.
48; *a.* 14. 28, 70. 9; *pl.* unrotnessa 20. 16; *d.* unrotnessum
20. 4.

unrōtsian, *wv.* make sad; *pp.*
geunrotsod 39. 24*, 142. 23;
geunrotsad 21. 23; *pl.* geunrotsode 24. 5.

ungesǣlig, *adj.* unhappy; 20. 5
&c.; *a.* ungesæligne 119. 2; *pl.*
ungesælige 104. 24, 122. 26,
xxvii. 18; *wk.* ungesæligan 124.
9; *comp.* ungesæligra 119. 8;
pl. ungesæligran 74. 11 &c. *and*
xix. 42; *sup. pl.* ungesælgoste
118. 2.

unsǣlð, *f.* unhappiness, misfortune;
21. 17, 120. 31; *pl.* unsælða 65.
22; ungesælða 65. 22*, 124.
23*; ungesalða 124. 23; *g.* ungesælða 24. 30*, 108. 7, 131. 9;
d. unsælðum 21. 21; ungesæl-

ðum 13. 27, 21. 21 ; *a.* unsælða
21. 27, 117. 19, 125. 17, 18 ;
ungesælða 14. 20*, 117. 19*.

unsamwrǣde, *adj.* not in agreement, opposed ; *pl.* 106. 6.

ungescǣdwīs, *adj.* unreasoning ;
irrational ; *n.* ungesceadwis 147.
18 ; *g. wk.* ungesceadwisan 28.
31 ; *d.* ungesceadwisum 131.
13 ; *a.* ungesceadwisne 61. 22 ;
pl. ungesceadwise 26. 14, 132.
5 ; *wk.* ungesceadwisan 31. 30 ;
g. wk. ungesceadwisene 31.
29*.

ungescǣdwīsnes, *f.* want of dis-
cernment ; 73. 7, 109. 2, 6.

unsceðfulnes, *f.* harmlessness,
innocence ; *a.* unsceðfulnesse
133. 5.

unscyldig, *adj.* innocent ; 122.
31 ; *g. wk.* unscyldgan 123. 16 ;
d. unscyldegum 40. 3* ; unscyldgum ix. 59 ; *a. wk.* unscyldigan 122. 24 ; unscyldgan
122. 30 ; *pl. d.* unscyldegum iv.
36 ; unscyldgum 123. 12 ; *a.*
unscyldige 123. 10 ; *wk.* unscildigan 10. 18*.

ungesewenlic, *adj.* invisible ; *n.*
128. 20 ; *d. wk.* unsewenlican
138. 2* ; *pl. f.* ungesewenlica
128. 2 ; *g.* ungesewenlicra 48.
24, xi. 5 ; *a. f.* ungesewenlica
xx. 6 ; ungesewenlice 79. 11*.

unsnytro, *f.* folly ; *d. pl.* unsnyt-
trum ix. 11.

ungestæðði̇g, *adj.* unsteady, fickle ;
n. wk. ungestæðði̇ge 126. 21* ;
d. wk. ungestæðði̇egan 115. 3.

unstaðolfæst, *adj.* unsteady, ill
balanced (in mind) ; *pl.* un-
staðolfæste xxviii. 69 *n.*

unstille, *adj.* endowed with
movement ; constantly moving,
restless ; *f. wk.* 129. 15 ; *n.*
102. 29, xx. 92 ; *pl. wk.* unstillan xi. 18 ; *n.* unstillu 128.
3 ; *g. wk.* unstillena 48. 30 ;
d. unstillum 115. 4 ; *a. f.* unstilla xx. 14 ; *wk.* unstillan 79.
15.

unstrenge, *adj.* weak ; *d. pl.* un-

strengum 59. 24 *n.* ; *comp.* unstrengra 75. 7, 109. 10.

unstyrigende, *adj.* motionless,
stationary ; *pl. f.* unstirende
146. 1 ; *wk.* unstyriendan 146.
6, 11.

unsweotol, *adj.* not clear, not
discernible ; *f.* 81. 1* ; *pl.* un-
sweotole xx. 146.

untǣle, *adj.* blameless ; *f.* un-
tǣlu 47. 27*.

ungetǣse, *adj.* inconvenient, unpleasant ; *n.* 30. 16 ; *g.* ungetæses 71. 29.

untela, *adv.* evilly, wrongly ;
134. 30.

unteorig, *adj.* untiring, unceasing ;
untiorig xxviii. 17.

untīdlīce, *adv.* unseasonably ;
untiidlice 12. 6.

untilod, *quasi ptcp.* ; ðonne bið
his untilad, no provision will be
made for him, no attention paid
him 67. 12.

untōdǣled, *adj.* undivided ; 76.
9 &c. ; *n.* 90. 16 &c. ; *pl.* untodælde 90. 30.

untōdǣledlic, *adj.* indivisible,
inseparable ; 89. 1* ; untodæ-
lendlic 74. 30 ; *d. f.* untodeledlicre 54. 18*.

untrēow, *f.* unfaithfulness, per-
fidy ; *pl. d.* untreowum ii. 13 ;
a. untriowa 16. 5.

untrīewe, *adj.* perfidious ; *pl.*
wk. ungetreowan 8. 9*.

untrum, *adj.* feeble, infirm ; *pl.*
untrume, ungetrume* 132. 32.

untwēogende, *adj.* unhesitating,
sure ; *g.* untwiogendes 146. 19*.

untwifeald, *adj.* united ; simple,
sincere ; *wk.* untweofealda 111.
2* ; *a.* untwifealdne 109. 27 ;
pl. untwifealde 30. 27* ; *a. f.*
untweofealde xi. 95.

untȳdd, *adj.* uninstructed, un-
trained ; *a.* untydne 20. 6.

unðearf, *f.* detriment, disadvan-
tage ; *d.* to ðinre unðearefe 16.
7*.

unðeaw, *m.* bad habit, vice ; 32.
23, 95. 8, xxvi. 112 ; *g.* un-

ðeawes 64. 27 ; *pl. fq.* unðeawas
70. 6 &c. *and* xxii. 26, 30, xxvi.
117 ; *g.* unðeawa 112. 16 ; *d.*
unðeawum 67. 28, xvi. 4 &c. ;
a. unðeawas 61. 8 &c. *and* xvi.
24, xxvii. 32.

ungeðwǽre, *adj.* at variance,
discordant 134. 29 ; *a.* unge-
ðwǽrne, turbulent 62. 10 *n.* ;
pl. f. ungeðwǽra 49. 12 ; *n.*
ungeðwǽre 113. 26.

ungeðwǽrnes, *f.* variance, dis-
cord ; 111. 29 ; *pl.* ungeðwǽr-
nessa 9. 11.

ungeðyld, *f.* impatience ; *d.* on
ungeðylde 25. 6.

ungeðyldelīce, *adv.* impatiently ;
45. 13.

ungeðyldig, *adj.* impatient ; *pl.*
ungeðyldige, unðyldige* 133. 2.

unundergielde, *adj.* not to be
replaced, (in)valuable ; *g.* unandergildes 27. 20*.

ungewealdes, *g. used as adv.*
ures ungewealdes, without our
control ; 93. 7.

unwēnlic, *adj.* unexpected; *comp.*
d. unwenlicran 138. 2.

unwēnunga, *adv.* unexpectedly ;
140. 10.

unweorðian, *wv.* dishonour ; *pro.*
ind. 2.s. unweorðast 16. 26.

unweorðscipe, *m.* dishonour ; *a.*
61. 27*.

unwierðe, *adj.* without honour ;
unworthy, ignoble ; unwyrðe 62.
17 ; unweorðe 62. 20* ; unweorð 64. 26*, xv. 6 ; *f.* 75. 19 ;
a. unwyrðne 62. 9 ; *pl.* unwyrðe
41. 15 ; *n.* unweorðe*, unweorð
24. 12 ; *comp.* unweorðra 63. 2*,
63. 3*, 4 ; *a.* unweorðran 63.
7 *n.* ; *sup.* unweorðost 34. 23* ;
wk. unweorðesta 33. 4* ; *pl.*
unweorðoste 61. 16*.

unwierðnes, *f.* disgrace ; *d.* un-
weorðnesse 12. 1.

unwilla, *wm.* ; *d. pl.* unwillum,
used as adv. unwillingly i. 24 ;
w. pers. pron. ðinum unwillum,
against your will 62. 5, *cf.* 93. 7,
98. 7, 8.

unwīs, *adj.* foolish ; 26. 4 ; *pl. g.*
unwisra xx. 148 ; *d.* unwisum
x. 10.

unwīsdom, *m.* folly, ignorance ;
d. unwisdome 141. 6.

ungewiss, *adj.* uncertain ; mys-
terious ; 26. 4 (unwis J) ; *g.*
ungewislices 15. 22.

ungewitfulle, *adv.* senselessly ;
74. 13.

unwitnod, *quasi ptcp.* unpunished;
n. 119. 16 ; *f.* 121. 19 ; *pl.* unwitnode 104. 23, 119. 14 ; ungewitnode 119. 16* ; *a.* unwitnode 119. 24 ; lete unwitnod
119. 30.

ungewittig, *adj.* unreasoning,
irrational ; *pl. wk.* ungewittigan
108. 4 ; ungewittegan 108. 15*.

unwlitigian, *wv.* deprive of form
or beauty ; *ind. prs. 3.s.* unwlitegað 131. 5.

unwreoen, *quasi ptcp.* unpunished;
n. 123. 20.

unwriten, *quasi ptcp.* unwritten ;
a. pl. forleton unwriten 44. 3.

ungewunelic, *adj.* unusual, extra-
ordinary ; *n.* 70. 23 ; *g.* ungewunelices 15. 22.

unwynsum, *adj.* unpleasant ; *f.*
unwynsumu 138. 10 ; unwynsum
137. 8 ; *n.* 30. 15.

unwyrd, *f.* misfortune ; *a.* 50. 16.

unwyrht, *n.* be hiora unwyrhtum,
without their deserving it 123.
32.

ūp, *adv.* (ub 86. 20 ; ūp 136. 4*,
13*, xx. 156) ; *a)* rest, above, on
high, 57. 21, 73. 31, 92. 20, xxiv.
32, xxxi. 19. *b)* motion, up, upwards, 18. 11, xii. 25 &c. ; up on
26. 24. *c)* direction, xxxi. 17.

ūpende, *m.* upper end ; *d.* 135.
32, xxix. 18.

uppan, *prep. w. d.* above ; ofer
uppan xxiv. 27.

uppe, *adv.* on high ; xx. 124.

ūprihte, *adv.* upright, erect ; 147.
9.

ūprodor, *m.* sky ; *a.* xxix. 51.

ūpryne, *m.* upward course ; *g.*
uprynæs 57. 26*.

ûpweard, *adv.* upwards ; xxxi. 23.
ûpweardes, *adv.* upwards ; 91.
31, xiii. 54, 62.
ûre, *poss. adj.* our, ours; 79. 4,
93. 6, xxii. 54; user xx. 249; *f.*
ure 144. 17 &c.; *n.* 101. 9; *g.*
ures 19. 21 &c. *and* xx. 258,
261; usses xx. 265, 267, xxi.
12; *d.* urum 29. 7*, 93. 2, 146.
32, xx. 33; ussum 29. 7; *a.*
ðone urne, ours 84. 28; *n.* ure
146. 26; *pl. f.* nre 34. 6*; ussa
viii. 40; ussc xxi. 35; *g.* urra
89. 9, 10; ura xxi. 14; ussa
xxiii. 11; *d.* urum 82. 7, xx.
252; *a.* ure 145. 13.
ût, *adv. a` place*, out, 115. 22. *b)*
motion, out, outside, 11. 4, i. 21
&c.
ûtan, *adv.* outside, from outside ;
fg. 36. 9, x. 4 &c.; uton 5 *times*
in B, 79. 21 &c.
ûtane, *adv.* from outside, outside ;
62. 33, 63. 1, 80. 32, 89. 2.
ûte, *adv.* outside, out of doors ;
33. 31, 95. 4, viii. 27; *comp.*
utor 94. 25.
ûtemest, *sup. adj.* outermost; *v.*
ytemest.
uton, let us; let us do; *w. inf.*
75. 15, 88. 32, 138. 5; wutun
103. 4; ute 17. 8*; *w. g.* uton
ðæs 75. 17.
ûðwita, *wm.* philosopher, sage;
45. 7 &c. *and* x. 50, xxii. 54;
g. uðwitan 45. 5; *pl.* 81. 17, xx.
184; uðwiotan 127. 4, 131. 8;
g. uðwitena 85. 24.

W.

wâ, 1) *sbst. n.* suffering, hardship;
waa i. 25 (J); *d.* mid uua iii. 6
(J). 2) *interj.* oh! alas! 73. 22.
wâc, *adj.* unstable, yielding; *n.*
xx. 93.
wâclic, *adj.* insignificant; *n.* 56.
8.
wâclîce, *adv.* weakly; v. 34.
wadan, *svb.* go, proceed; *ind.*

prs. 3. *pl.* wadað 143. 2; *sbj. pst.*
wode 48. 13.
wæcan, *wv.* weaken; gewæcan
v. 31.
wæcce, *wf.* watching, vigil; *a. pl.*
wæccan 70. 8.
wæd, *f.* dress, clothes; *pl.* wæda
77. 11; *g.* xxv. 32, 39; *d.* wædum
64. 25, xv. 3, xxv. 4; *a.* wæda
viii. 23.
wædl, *f.* poverty; 60. 16; *d.*
wædle 24. 4; *a.* 28. 21, 31. 16,
60. 24, 76. 25.
wædla, *wm.* (*gen. used as adj.*) poor
man; 28. 24, 65. 15, 76. 24; *d.*
wædlan 28. 26; *pl.* 28. 10; *d.*
wædlum x. 31.
wæfð, *f.* wonderful spectacle,
marvel; wæfðo xxviii. 82 *n.*; *g.*
wæfðe 104. 11.
wæg, *m.* wave; *d.* wæge xxviii.
58.
wægan, *wv.* afflict; *pp.* gewæged
ii. 3.
wægn, *m.* carriage, waggon;
wæn 130. 21; *g.* wænes 129.
19, 131. 1; wænes ðisla, the
Waggon-Shafts (Charles' Wain)
126. 3, xxviii. 10; *a.* wæn 129,
20.
wælhrêow, *adj.* fierce, cruel;
wælriow ix. 38; *wk.* wælhreowa
7. 23; *g.* wælhreowes ix. 5; *d.*
wk. wælreowan 36. 28.
wælhrêownes, *f.* fierceness, cruelty; 67. 7; *a. pl.* wælriownessa
39. 17*.
wæpen, *n.* weapon; *pl.* wæpnu
40. 22; *g.* wæpna 8. 20.
wær, *adj.* cautious; *f.* wæru 47.
27* *n.*; *a. pl.* wære 62. 27.
wærscipe, *m.* caution; 62. 25,
87. 7.
wærðo, *v.* wæfð.
wæstm, *m.* crop, produce; *a.*
westm 136. 15*; *pl.* wæstmas
30. 3; *g.* wæstma xx. 101; *d.*
wæstmum 29. 24, 33. 23*; *a.*
wæstmas 33. 28*, viii. 19, xx.
75, xxix. 70; westmas 80. 17*,
136. 20*.
wæstmbêre, *adj.* fertile; *wk.*

westmbæra 136. 16* ; *a.* wæstmbære 51. 28, xii. 1.
wǣt, 1) *adj.* wet, moist; *f.* 80. 7 ;
n. 80. 6, 7, xx. 77, 81 ; *d.*
wætum xx. 90 ; *wk.* wætan 80.
13. 2) *sbst. n.* wetness, moisture ; 80. 5, xx. 74.
wǣta, *wm.* moisture ; 136. 12 ; *a.*
wætan 33. 29, xxix. 48.
wæter, *n.* water ; 49. 11, xi. 43
&c. ; *g.* wæteres 80. 5, 20, 25 ;
wætres xx. 108, 123 ; *d.* wætcre
80. 13, viii. 59 &c. ; wættere
xx. 90 ; wætre xx. 150, xxviii.
63 ; *a.* wæter 34. 1, viii. 23, 28 ;
pl. wætru 53. 4 ; *d.* wæterum
74. 2* ; wætrum 115. 8.
wǣðan, *wv.* hunt ; xix. 15.
wāflan, *wv. w. g.* be astonished,
marvel at ; xxviii. 44 ; *ind. prs.*
3.*s.* wafað 126. 5, 13 ; *pl.*
wafiað 31. 12 ; *sbj. prs.* wafige
xxviii. 18, 31 ; *prs. p.* wafiende
50. 10.
wāfung, *f.* astonishment, wonder ;
a. wafunga 125. 15.
wāg, *m.* wall ; wah 110. 23 ; *g.*
pl. waga 11. 27.
wagian, *wv. intrans.* move, sway ;
ind. pst. 3.*s.* wagode 101. 27.
wālā, *interj.* alas ! oh ! iv. 29,
xxi. 1 ; wella . . . wel 89. 5,
139. 5.
wālāwā, *interj.* alas ! 124. 9*,
weilawei 103. 10.
wana, *wm.* want, deficiency ; 22.
20 &c. ; *used as adj.* deficient,
83. 9, 11, 84. 1, 85. 16.
wancol, *adj.* wavering, fickle ; *f.*
47. 20* ; *a. pl. wk.* wanclan 15.
30.
wandlung, *f.* changing, variable-
ness ; *d.* wandlunga 15. 27.
wandrian, *wv.* wander ; vary ;
ind. prs. 3.*s.* wandrað 105. 13,
xxiv. 23 ; *sbj. prs.* wandrige
130. 18 ; *prs. p.* wandriende
128. 29.
wang, *m.* plain, field ; *pl.* wangas
xx. 77.
wangstede, *m.* place ; *a. pl.*
wongstedas viii. 56.

wanian, *wv. trans. and intr.*
diminish ; 91. 2 ; *ind. prs.* 3.*s.*
wanað 60. 16, 71. 18, 148. 13,
20 ; *pl.* waniað 92. 11 ; *pp.*
gewanod 28. 16, 99. 19 ; *pl. f.*
gewanode 24. 27.
wann, *adj.* dark ; *n.* wan v. 4 ;
a. wk. wonnan xi. 61.
warnian, *wv. rflx. w.* wið ;
beware, guard ; *ind. prs.* 3.*s.*
warenað 68. 4, 144. 31 (wærnað
B) ; gewarenað 16. 21.
waroð, *n.* shore ; *a.* wearoð i.
14 ; wearod viii. 30 ; weroð
34. 1.
wāt, *swv.* know ; *inf.* witan 15.
10 &c. ; *ind. prs.* 1.*s.* wat
8. 20, iv. 51 &c. ; wæt xxviii.
80 ; *neg.* nat x. 53, xix. 37 ; 2.*s.*
wast 13. 5 &c. ; *interrog.* wastu
13. 13, 18. 16 ; wasð ðu 62. 5,
65. 11 ; wæst 66. 3 ; *neg.* nast
13. 16, 104. 26 ; 3.*s.* wat 26. 2,
iii. 9 &c. ; *neg.* nat 9. 14 &c. ;
pl. witon 24. 1 &c. *and* ix. 1,
xix. 24 ; witan 67. 1, xvii. 7, xix.
20 ; *neg.* niton 32. 23, 83. 25,
108. 16 ; nyton 25. 16 &c. *and*
xi. 10 ; *pst.* 1.*s. and* 3.*s.* wisse,
wiste* 15. 14, ll. 7*, 61. 22
&c. ; *neg.* nysse, nys(s)te* 96.
3 &c. *and* xxvi. 66 ; nesse 94.
21 *n.* ; 2.*s.* wistest 24. 17* ; *neg.*
nystes 13. 20, 22 ; nestes 13. 19 ;
pl. wisson xxvi. 100, xxviii. 19 ;
wisston 116. 27* ; *neg.* nyston
115. 25 ; *imp.* wite 17. 20 &c. ;
sbj. prs. 78. 16 &c. ; *neg.* nyte
12. 31 &c. ; *pl.* witen 121. 21,
147. 14, xix. 13 ; *pst.* wisse 13.
10 &c. ; *neg.* nysse 97. 19, 22 ;
nesse 94. 21, 96. 2 ; *pl.* wissen
147. 13.
wāð, *f.* hunting ; *d.* waðe xxvii.
13.
wē, *pers. pron.* we ; 13. 29, ix. 1
&c. ; *g.* ure 19. 14 &c. ; *d. and*
a. us 29. 9, xi. 12 &c.
wēa, *wm.* misery, misfortune ; *a.*
wean 118. 23.
wēalāf, *f.* survivors of misfortune ;
i. 22.

weald, *m.* forest; 57. 19, xiii. 46.

geweald, *n.* power, control; *g. used as adv. w. pers. prons.* ðines gewealdes, in your power 29. 24, 25; heora agnes gewealdes, of their own accord 37. 24, *cf.* 37. 29; *a.* geweald 38. 22, 107. 15, 124. 5, i. 38, xvi. 21, xxii. 36, xxvii. 5.

wealdan, *rv.* (*w. g.*; *except* 89. 19 (*d.*) *and* 136. 23 (*a.*)); wield, control; govern; 17. 23. 65. 24, 81. 23; waldan xx. 129, 198, 201; to wealdanne 97. 1; *ind. prs. 2.s.* wealdest xx. 7, 50; weltst 79. 12*, 30*; 3.*s.* wealdeð xxi. 33; waldeð xxiv. 34, 35, xxv. 15, xxix. 76 *n.*, 93; wealt 98. 1*, 125. 28, 136. 30*; wilt 13. 23, 97. 9; welt 57. 3*, 86. 3 &c.; causes 111. 7; wylt 97. 5; *pl.* wealdað 65. 23; *pst. 3.s.* weold 96. 6*, xxvi. 10; wiold ix. 38; *pl.* wioldon i. 48; *sbj. prs.* wealde 12. 16 &c. *and* xvi. 16; walde 131. 11; *pl.* wealden 65. 23; walden 102. 25; *pst.* weolde 96. 4, 5, 96. 21; wiolde 96. 10, 97. 23, 100. 20; *prs. p.* waldende 104. 21, 107. 7.

wealdend, 1) *m.* ruler, controller; 48. 23, xi. 2 &c.; waldend *more usual* 83. 23, iv. 49 &c.; *pl.* wealdendas 13. 21, 32. 11; waldendas 35. 30; *d.* wealdendum 64. 22. 2) *adj.* powerful; *a.* wealdendne 38. 16, 30*, 65. 4; waldendne 38. 30.

gewealdleðer, *n.* rein, bridle; *g.* wealdleðres 49. 5; *a.* gewealdleðer 49. 27, 105. 18, xi. 28; gewaldleðer xxiv. 39; *pl. d.* gewealdleðerum 136. 23; geweltleðrum xxix. 77; *a.* gewealdleðeru xi. 75.

wealhstod, *m.* interpreter; Pr. 1.

weallan, *rv.* boil, seethe; *prs. p.* weallende viii. 45.

wealwian, *wv. intrans.* roll; fade, wither; wealowian 91. 16; *ind.*

prs. 3.s. wealuwað xi. 58; wealwað 49. 19*; *sbj. prs. pl.* wealowigen 130. 6; *prs. p.* wealwiende 14. 16.

weard, *m.* guardian; xi. 20, 31, xxviii. 77.

weardian, *wv.* keep; last weardigan, keep its place, remain xx. 241.

wearm, *adj.* warm; *f.* 80. 8, xx. 80; *n.* 49. 20; *g.* wearmes 12. 11; *pl. n.* wearm xi. 61.

wēas, *adv.* by chance; 125. 13 &c. *and* xxv. 31, xxviii. 72.

weaxan, *rv.* grow, increase; 14. 5 &c.; to wexanne 91. 20; *ind. prs.* weaxð 73. 26*; wexð 71. 18, 148. 13*, xix. 8; geweaxð*, gewexð 91. 30; gewyxð 99. 18; *pl.* weaxað 21. 4 &c. *and* vi. 9 *n.*, xxv. 40; wexað 92. 11; *pst.* weox i. 5, xx. 243; *pl.* weoxon 127. 10; *sbj. prs.* geweaxe xiii. 52; wexe 46. 12*.

wecg, *m.* lump, ingot; *d.* wecge*, wegge 90. 8.

wecgan, *wv. trans.* move; *ind. prs. 3.pl.* wecggað xxvii. 4; *sbj. prs.* wecge vii. 35.

wēdan, *wv.* be mad; *prs. p.* wedende hund 111. 18; *d. wk.* wedendan gietsere 19. 9.

gewēde, *n.* madness, frenzy; gewed ix. 5.

wēdehund, *m.* mad dog; wedehunde xxv. 18.

weder, *n.* weather, season; 52. 4, 115. 21, xxvi. 28; *g.* weðres xii. 13 (J); *d.* wedere 14. 12; *a.* weder 144. 32, xi. 59, xxix. 64; *d. pl.* wederum 12. 10, xxviii. 45; wedrum 18. 13.

weg, *m.* way, path; 73. 24, 82. 16, xx. 277, 279; *g.* weges 106. 1; *d.* wege 73. 24, 139. 28, 31, xix. 4, xxiv. 44; *a.* weg *sq.* 51. 14 &c. *and* xiii. 58, xxix. 8; *a. pl.* wegas 53. 10, 57. 26.

wegfērend, *m.* traveller; 33. 9, 14.

wel, *adv.* well; 12. 11, v. 24

&c.; wel tam, quite 57. 9,
cf. xiii. 50; *comp.* bet 46. 32,
x. 65 &c.; *sup.* betst 8. 11
&c. *and* ii. 13.

wela, *wm.* prosperity, riches; *fq.*;
plural more usual, 17. 18 &c.
and xxi. 22; *g.* welan 24. 2 &c.
and xix. 43; *d.* 26. 3 &c.;
a. 24. 10 &c. *and* vii. 16; *pl.*
17. 20 &c.; *g.* welena 19. 1,
27. 20, 60. 28; welona 17. 7;
d. welum 18. 3 &c. *and* x. 28;
a. welan 59. 24, 60. 14.

welhwǽr, *adv.* nearly everywhere;
xii. 4, xxviii. 82.

welhwǽs, *adv.* nearly; ii. 10 (J).

welhwelc. *pron. adj.* nearly every;
n. welhwilc xx. 191.

welig, *adj.* prosperous, wealthy;
29. 24 &c.; *g. wk.* welegan
63. 20; *d. wk.* xiv. 1, i. 37;
welgan 60. 28*; *a.* weligne
59. 18, 65. 4; *wk.* welegan 77.
1*, x. 31; *pl.* welige 24. 7,
33. 23, viii. 8; *wk.* welgan 60.
12; *g.* weligra 19. 4; *d.* welegum 60. 9; *a.* welige 73. 20;
wk. welegan 60. 11; *sup.* welgost 59. 14.

weligian, *wv.* enrich; gewelegian 28. 26.

welwynsum, *adj.* very pleasant;
welwinsum xiii. 50.

wēn, *f.* hope, expectation; 138.
20.

wēna, *wm.* hope, expectation;
opinion; 63. 27, xxviii. 35; *d.*
wenan 68. 13.

wēnan, *wv. w. g. or sbj.* hope for,
expect; think, believe; 13. 26,
vii. 7 &c.; to wenanne 37. 31
&c.; *ind. prs.* 1.*s.* wene 23. 18
&c. *and* xxv. 29; 2.*s.* wenst 15.
21 &c. *and* ix. 48; ðu wensð
24. 27; *interrog.* wenstu *fq.* 12.
31 &c.; 3.*s.* wenð 107. 9, 110.
14; wenð him ðara 134. 30;
pl. wenað 15. 6, xix. 34 &c.;
pst. 1.*s.* wende 21. 13 &c.; 2.*s.*
wendest 11. 5 &c.; wendes 120.
24; wendes ðu ðe 33. 10; 3.*s.*
wende 15. 13, 45. 9, i. 78, 82;

imp. wen 47. 4; *sbj. prs.* wene
54. 17 &c.; *pl.* wenen 26. 14
&c. *and* x. 63; *pst.* 13. 24 &c.

wend, *n.* course, alternative;
oððe ðridde wend 118. 15.

wendan, *wv. trans. and intr.*
turn, direct; go; 13. 32, iv. 34,
40; gewendan xxii. 57; *ind.
prs.* 1.*s.* wende 121. 6; 3.*s.* went
10. 23, 103. 18, 149. 1, xiii.
55; turn out, come to pass, 125.
8; *pl.* wendað 97. 32 &c.; *pst.*
on englisc wende, translated
Pr. 2; gewende Pr. 9; *pl.*
wendon 8. 11, ii. 14; *sbj. prs.*
wende 78. 4 &c. *and* xviii. 11,
xxxi. 20; *pl.* wenden 130. 9,
137. 17.

wendung, *f.* alteration, change;
d. wendinge vii. 41.

wenian, *wv.* accustom, train; *ind.
pst.* 3.*s.* gewenede xxix. 6; *pl.*
gewenedon 57. 18.

wēod, *n.* weed; *a.* xii. 28; *a. pl.*
52. 1*; wiod xii. 4.

weorc, *n.* work; 128. 19; *g.*
weorces 12. 20 &c. *and* vi. 17,
vii. 7; *d.* weorce 40. 10 &c.;
a. weorc 38. 4, xi. 77 &c.; *pl.
g.* weorca 41. 13 &c. *and* xx.
. 21; *d.* weorcum 41. 6 &c.; *a.*
weorc 145. 13.

geweorc, *n.* work, structure; *a.*
99. 3.

weorcmann, *m.* workman, la-
bourer; *a. pl.* weorcmen 40. 18.

weorpan, *sv3.* cast, throw; change;
116. 14, xxvi. 76; *ind. prs.* 3.*s.*
wearp 18. 20; wearp hine mid
ðære tungan, threw the tongue
at him 36. 23.

weorðan, *sv3.* happen; become;
fq. used as auxiliary vb. 37. 20,
xi. 19 &c.; *fq. w.* to, 83. 3
&c.; *rflx.* ðe weorðan on,
arrive at 105. 11, xxiv. 18; *ind.
prs.* 2.*s.* wyrst xxiv. 44 *n.*; 3.*s.* weorðeð xiii. 56, xviii. 9, xx. 102 *n.*,
xxviii. 63, 75, xxix. 33; wyrð
usual form 10. 8 &c.; 6 *times
in Metr.* v. 18 &c.; *pl.* weorðað
33. 3, xiii. 36 &c.; arrive, 57.

16; wiorðað 92. 12; *pst. 1.s.*
wearð 12. 20 &c.; *2.s.* wurde
8. 19; *3.s.* wearð 37. 9 &c. *and*
xxvi. 13, 28; *pl.* wurdon 67. 4,
xxvi. 79 &c.; *sbj. prs.* weorðe
21. 17, v. 6 &c.; is formed, 126.
20; wiorðc 69. 13; *pl.* weorðen
25. 6 &c. *and* v. 45; weorðan
122. 6; *pst.* wurde 62. 12 &c.
and viii. 39, xxv. 31; *pl.*
wurden 40. 26 &c.; wurdon 96.
16, 136. 27*; *pp.* geworden
126. 23; *pl.* wordene xix. 29.

geweorðan, *sv3.* happen, come to
pass; 6 *times*, 12. 17 &c.;
gewiorðan xi. 39; *ind. prs. 3.s.*
geweorðeð xxiv. 55; gewyrð 5
times, 39. 4 &c.; gewirð 35. 7;
pst. 3.s. gewearð 36. 24; *sbj.*
prs. geweorðe 11 *times*, 128. 18
&c.; *pst.* gewurde 9. 4; *pp. pl.*
n. gewordene 145. 14.

weorðfullic, *adj.* honourable; *g.*
weorðfullices 42. 15.

weorðfullice, *adv.* honourably;
41. 4.

weorðgeorn, *adj.* ambitious; *wk.*
weorðgeorna x. 48; *pl. g. wk.*
weorðgeornena 139. 7; *d.*
weorðgeornum 139. 10; *sup.*
pl. weorðgeornuste 44. 4*.

weorðian, *wv.* honour; esteem;
143. 25; to weorðianne 72. 27,
75. 13, 14; *ind. prs. pl.* geweorðað 32. 28; *pst.* weorðode
64. 27, 30; *pl.* weorðodon 115.
27, xxvi. 45; *sbj. prs.* weorðige
104. 17; *pp.* geweorðod 32. 25,
26; geweorðad x. 28; *pl.* ge-
weorðode 69. 4.

weorðlic, *adj.* valuable; distinguished, glorious; 75. 24;
a. weorðlicne 133. 29; *a. pl. f.*
weorðlica xx. 226; weorðlice
81. 34*; *sup. n.* weorðlicosð
75. 21.

weorðmynd, *f.* honour, dignity;
30. 20; *a.* weorðmynde 30. 21;
g. pl. weorðmynða i. 51.

weorðscipe, *m.* dignity, honour;
fq. 17. 18 &c.; *g.* weorðscipes
17. 7 &c. *and* xix. 44; *d.*

weorðscipe 23. 19 &c.; wyrð-
scipe 36. 25*; *a.* weorðscipe
32. 7 &c.; *d. pl.* weorðscipum
54. 2.

wepan, *rv.* weep; bewail; 102.
26; *rflx.* 8. 5; to wepanne 23.
1; *ind. pst. 3.s.* weop 102. 5;
prs. p. wepende 8. 8.

wer, *m.* man; 22. 9; *d.* were xvii.
4; *a.* wer viii. 35; *pl.* weras 133.
7; *g.* wera 139. 7; *a.* weras 46.
28, x. 62.

werelic, *adj.* unsubstantial, paltry;
pl. werelice, werilice* 28. 24;
f. werelica 25. 10 *n.*

werelice, *adv.* abjectly, meanly;
71. 24 (wærelice B).

werig, *adj.* weary; *n. wk.* werie
72. 1; werige 72. 1*, xxvi. 114;
d. wk. weregan 72. 3; *a. n. wk.*
werige xxiv. 60; *g. pl.* werigra
50. 13.

werod, *n.* host, troop; *d.* werede
66. 9; *pl. g.* weroda xx. 86, 162,
xxix. 78; weorada xx. 49; *a.*
werode 116. 6.

werod, *adj.* sweet; *comp.* weorodra 52. 3.

werodan, *wv.* become sweet;
ind. prs. 3.s. werodað*, weredað
51. 4.

werðeod, *f.* nation; *a.* werðiode
ix. 21; *pl.* werðeoda xxvi. 73;
werðioda xxix. 28; *a.* xxiv. 35.

wesan, wese, *v.* beon.

west, *adv.* west, westwards; 136.
1, ix. 42, x. 5, xiv. 7, xxix. 28.

westan, *adv.* from the west; iv. 22,
vi. 8.

westdæl, *m.* west part; *d.* westdæle 135. 30; *a.* westdæl xxix.
13.

weste, *adj.* waste, uninhabited;
g. westes 42. 7; *a. pl. n.* westu
holu 19. 8.

westenn, *n.* desert; *d. pl.* weste-
num 42. 30.

westeweard, *adj.* western; *a.* oð
westeweardne 39. 27, 41. 21,
67. 31.

westmest, *adj.* westernmost; *n.*
xvi. 11.

wīo, *n.* bay, creek; xxi. 12.
wīd, *adj.* wide; *a. wk.* widan
viii. 41, xi. 45, xiii. 65.
wīdcūð, *adj.* widely known,
famous; *pl.* widcuðe 24. 4.
wīde, *adv.* widely; 93. 6, viii. 51
&c.
gewider, *n.* weather; *pl.* gewideru
xi. 61.
wīdgiell, *adj.* extensive; *f.* widgel
x. 10; *pl. f.* widgille 46. 4*;
widgil x. 6.
wīdgielnes, *f.* spaciousness; *a.*
widgielnesse 72. 16.
wīdmǣre, *adj.* far-famed; 53.
22.
wiell, *m.* spring, fountain; *g. pl.*
wella 34. 1.
wiella, *wm.* spring, fountain; *a.*
wellan viii. 29.
wielm, *m.* boiling, surging; *d.*
welme 111. 30*, xxv. 46.
wierdan, *wv.* injure; *ind. prs.*
3. *pl.* wyrdað.
wiernan, *wv. a)* prevent; *b)* re-
ject, refuse; wyrnan 149. 5 (*b*);
ind. prs. 3. *s.* wernð 145. 16 (*a*).
wiers, wiersa, wierst, *v.* yfel,
yfle.
wierðe, *adj. w. g.* worthy; hon-
oured; weorðe 35. 18*; wyrðe
usual form 11. 23*, 33. 5 &c.;
weorð 61. 6*, 124. 26, viii. 37;
f. wyrðe 47. 8; *n.* 43. 24 &c.;
a. wyrðne 63. 18*; weorðne 61.
4, 64. 9; *pl.* wyrðe 7. 8 &c. *and*
i. 37, x. 56; weorðe 104. 10;
f. wyrðe 98. 8; *a.* weorðe 28. 5,
62. 27, 64. 6; wyrðe i. 67; *comp.*
weorðra 64. 29; *a.* wyrðran 122.
29; weorðran 63. 7, 71. 22; *pl.*
xv. 12; wyrðran iv. 45; *sup.*
weorðost 53. 17; *pl. wk.* weorðestan 61. 21, 67. 2.
wīf, *n.* woman; wife; 22. 11 &c.;
g. wifes 103. 13; *d.* wife xvii.
4, xxvi. 68; *a.* wif 22. 32; *pl.*
g. wifa 54. 7; *a.* wif 22. 13.
wīfian, *wv.* marry (a wife); *pp.*
gewifod 24. 9.
wīg, *n.* war; *g.* wiges xxvi. 13;
d. wige i. 22.

wīgend, *m.* warrior; *g. pl.* wigendra xxvi. 31.
wiht, *fn.* thing; creature; xiii.
19; wuht *usual form* 12. 22
&c.; wyht 147. 2*; *g.* (*f.*)
wuhte 36. 6, 60. 6, 148. 17; *d.*
(*f.*) 93. 11, 23, xi. 78; *used as*
adv. w. comp. wuhte ðon mare
xiv. 10, *cf.* xvi. 14, xx. 108,
117, xxviii. 35; *a.* (*f.*) wiht
xiii. 19; wuht 91. 6, 148. 14, 18;
pron. anything, xiii. 33; elles
wuhte ix. 20; *pl.* wuhta 36. 11,
126. 17, xxxi. 2; *g.* 93. 31, 94.
7, xi. 52 &c.
wilde, *adj.* not tame, wild; *f.*
xviii. 5; *n.* 124. 11; *g. wk.*
wildan 57. 12; *a.* xiii. 27; *pl.*
wilde xiii. 39; *n.* wildu 101. 28,
xxvii. 20.
wilder, *n.* wild beast; *pl.* wildior
117. 3; *g.* wildra xxvi. 76;
wildedeora 116. 15*; *d.* wildiorum 122. 14.
gewill, *n.* will, wish; *a.* 9. 27,
10. 24, 19. 23, iv. 34.
willa, *wm.* will; desire; 16. 25
&c. *and* xviii. 2; *g.* willan 11.
29 &c. *and* xi. 83; *d.* 9. 25, iv.
28 &c.; *a.* 17. 27 &c. *and* viii.
37, xiii. 55; *pl. d. w. prons. fq.*
hiora willum, of their own accord 25. 2, *cf.* 25. 23, 91. 4
&c.; selfra willum x. 19; *adv.*
willum, joyfully xiii. 41.
willan, *anv.* wish, be willing; *fq.*
used as auxil. will, would; *ind.*
prs. 1. *s.* wille 9. 28 &c. *and*
xiii. 1, xxiv. 52; *neg.* nylle
xxiv. 52; *w. ellipse of inf.* nelle
105. 23; 2. *s.* wilt 9. 18 &c. *and*
iv. 49, xxiv. 48, 56; *neg.* nelt
10. 24*; 3. *s.* wille *fq. in* B, 26.
23 &c.; wile *in* C, 12. 8, iv. 51
&c.; wyle 136. 21*; *neg.* nylle
91. 7 &c.; nyle 38. 12*, 79. 6
&c. *and* xxvii. 14; nele 70. 16,
122. 18, 140. 26, 149. 5; xiii.
33, xxi. 34; *pl.* willað 15. 5, v.
22 &c.; wille we 5 *times*, 22.
23 &c.; *neg.* nyllað 109. 3 &c.;
nellað 32. 21*, 108. 12; *pst.* 1. *s.*

and 3*s.* wolde 35. 32 &c. *and* ix. 12, xi. 15; wuolde i. 38; *neg.* nolde 84. 12 &c. *and* xxvi. 90; 2*s.* woldest 10. 17 &c. *and* xx. 49; woldes 48. 12, 118. 29, 122. 29; *neg.* noldes 25. 24, 59. 6; *pl.* woldon 34. 17 &c.; woldan 9. 22*, 25, 31. 10; woldean 53. 26*; wolde ge ii. 16; *sbj. prs.* wille 12. 15, xiii. 27 &c.; wile 60. 12, xiii. 3 &c.; *neg.* nylle 91. 4 &c.; nyle xxv. 67; nelle 72. 4*; nele ix. 63; *pl.* willen 109. 23 &c. *and* xix. 5, 15; willan *in* B, 94. 15* &c.; willon 98. 17; *neg.* nyllen 122. 13, 139. 11; nyllan 94. 15*; *pst.* wolde 18. 24, iv. 33 &c.; *pl.* wolden 35. 3; woldan 36. 1*, 65. 24; woldon 88. 22, 26.

wilnian, *wv. w. g., a, sbj., or ger. inf.* 106. 16; wilnigan 140. 24; to wilnianne 39. 11 &c.; to wilnienne 31. 3*; *ind. prs.* 2.*s.* wilnast 16. 24 &c. *and* v. 24; 3.*s.* wilnað 25. 11 &c. *and* xx. 159, xxv. 51; willnað 55. 5*, 66. 7*, 109. 18; *pl.* wilniað 31. 22 &c. *and* xix. 43; *w.* æfter, yearn 53. 16; wilnigað 41. 14*, 45. 3*; willniað 74. 12*, 93. 27; *w. ellipse of inf.* ðider willniað 147. 8*; wilnige ge 42. 17; *pst.* 1.*s. and* 3.*s.* wilnode 40. 9, 13. 20 &c. *and* xxv. 56; 2.*s.* wilnodest 19. 15, 135. 20; *pl.* wilnodon 26. 19 &c.; gewilnodon 26. 20; wilnedon 67. 4, i. 35 (J); *sbj. prs.* wilnige 13. 2 &c. *and* xxix. 1; wilnie xiii. 69; willnige 135. 23*; welnige 118. 11; *pl.* welnigen 35. 24 &c. *and* x. 63; wilnien 31. 23, 106. 32; wilnigan 35. 21*; wilnian 46. 30*; *prs. p.* wilnigende 81. 18*.

wilnung, *f.* desire; 41. 12, 81. 20, xx. 186; *g.* wilnunga 81. 24; wilnunge xx. 198; *d.* wilnunga 143. 11; *a.* xx. 191; *pl.* welnunga 38. 31.

wīn, *n.* wine; *a.* 12. 10, 33. 29, viii. 20.

wind, *m.* wind; 14. 11, v. 7 &c.; *g.* windes 16. 30 &c.; *d.* winde 80. 19, xx. 81 &c.; *a.* wind 10. 11 &c. *and* iv. 24; *pl. g.* winda 126. 19; *a.* windas 99. 2, xi. 60.

windan, *sv3. intrans.* wind; fly; xxiv. 10; *ind. prs.* 3.*pl.* windað xxxi. 12 *n.*; *pst.* 1.*s.* ic gewand ymb Croeses ðearfe, looked after his interests 18. 18.

wīngedrinc, n. wine-drinking; *g.* wingedrinces xxv. 39.

wīngeard, *m.* vineyard; *d. pl.* wingeardum 73. 27, xix. 9.

gewinn, *n.* contest, war; gewin xxvi. 12; *g.* gewinnes 126. 19, xxv. 51; *d.* gewinne 53. 23 &c. *and* xxv. 70; *a.* gewin 7. 2.

gewinna, *wm.* foe; *pl.* gewinnan 106. 4.

winnan, *sv3.* strive, endeavour; struggle, contend; 98. 10 &c. *and* xxv. 67, 69; *ind. prs.* 2.*s.* winsð 16. 26; 3.*s.* winneð xxviii. 57; winð 10. 27 &c. *and* xi. 33, xiii. 17; *pl.* winnað 42. 10, xi. 45 &c.; wynnað iv. 56 (J); *pst. pl. w.* æfter wunnon 139. 13; *sbj. prs.* winne 98. 19 &c.; *pl.* winnan 146. 12*; *prs. p.* winnende iii. 4, xi. 34, 41.

gewinnan, *sv3.* attain; overcome, conquer; to gewinnanne xix. 44; *pp.* gewunnen 36. 20, 54. 5, 115. 20, i. 17, 28.

winter, *m.* winter; 49. 19, xi. 59; *g.* wintres xxix. 64; *d.* on wintra 49. 20, 68. 2, 136. 18, xvi. 14; *a.* winter 12. 11, 92. 6; *pl. g.* wintra 126. 9, i. 29, 44. 15; *a.* winter xxvi. 17, xxviii. 26.

winterdæg, *m.* winter day; *d. pl.* winterdagum 10. 10, iv. 20.

wintrig, *adj.* wintry; *d. pl.* wintregum 12. 9.

wīs, *adj.* wise; 45. 4 &c. *and* i. 51, xxiv. 34; *wk.* wisa 9. 23 &c. *and* x. 48; *f.* wis xviii. 5; *g. wk.* wisan 45. 11, x. 33 &c.; *d.*

wisum 35. 8, 63. 5; *wk.* wisan
36. 24 &c.; *a.* wisne 62. 15 &c.;
wk. wisan x. 12; *pl.* wise 35. 23
&c. *and* vii. 41, xxix. 13; *wk.*
wisan 110. 31; *abs. without art.*
139. 5; *g.* wisra 41. 26, 113. 10,
xxviii. 67; *d.* wisum 139. 9, xx.
149; *a.* wise 62. 27; *comp. pl.*
wisran iv. 45; *sup. pl. wk.*
wisestan 64. 14; *a. wk.* 39. 22.

wīsdom, *m.* wisdom, philosophy;
*fq. used as the name of one of the
two persons of the dialogue,* 8. 16,
vi. 1 &c.; *g.* wisdomes 22. 9 &c.;
d. wisdome 40. 28 &c.; *a.* wisdom 35. 18, vii. 7 &c.; *a. pl.*
wisdomas 18. 5.

wīse, *wf.* manner; state, condition; affair; 14. 3, 138. 17;
g. wisan 51. 20; *d.* 126. 31, 132.
25; *a.* 37. 11.

wīslīce, *adv.* wisely; 41. 17, xx.
15.

gewiss, 1) *adj.* certain, sure; *n.*
gewis 146. 16; *a.* 145. 32, 146.
10; *comp. n.* gewisre 86. 12. 2)
sbst. n. certainty; *a.* gewis 145.
3.

gewisslīce, *adv.* with certainty,
surely; gewislice 26. 17, 96. 19,
148. 10.

wist, *f.* provision, sustenance; 77.
11; *g.* wiste xxv. 39.

wit, *pers. pron.* we two; *about* 33
times, 12. 25 &c. *and* xxvi. 3;
wyt 78. 19; *d.* unc 19. 23, 122.
14; *a.* 82. 25, 88. 32, 100. 29,
137. 17, 138. 5.

wita, *wm.* councillor, senator; x.
44; *pl.* witan 34. 31, 64. 14; *g.*
witena xv. 5, 12, xix. 7, xx. 3;
d. witnm 35. 6, 64. 26; *a.* witan
39. 22, i. 66, ix. 25.

gewita, *wm.* witness; 45. 31.

wītan, *sv1.* blame, reproach; *ind.
prs. 2.s.* witst 19. 12; *sbj. prs.*
wite Pr. 12.

gewītan, *sv1.* depart; witan xxiv.
52; *ind. prs. 3.s.* gewiteð xxix.
11; gewit 18. 13, 114. 10, 11,
136. 13, xx. 158; *pl.* gewitað
20. 28 &c. *and* xxix. 31; *pst.*

3.*pl.* gewitan 8. 12*; *imp. pl.*
gewitað 8. 21; *sbj. prs.* gewite
81. 10, 114. 11; *pp.* gewiten 24.
20, 33. 15.

wīte, *n.* punishment, torture; *fq.*
113. 22 &c.; *g.* wites 43. 24
&c.; *d.* wite 36. 26 &c.; on wite,
undergoing punishment 120. 25;
a. 111. 6 &c.; *pl.* witu 103. 2,
125. 8, 134. 5; *g.* wita 26. 20
&c. *and* xii. 20; *d.* witum 7. 15
&c.; *a.* witu 104. 10, 117. 21,
118. 23.

gewitlēas, *adj.* senseless, foolish;
pl. gewitlease xix. 46.

gewitloca, *wm.* mind; *d.* gewitlocan x. 12, xii. 26.

gewitnes, *f.* cognizance, knowledge; *d.* gewitnesse 125. 14.

wītnian, *wv.* punish; 143. 26;
to witnianne 138. 2; *ind. prs.*
3.*s.* witnað 122. 19, 25, 132. 17,
142. 29; witniað 122. 19; *pst.*
3.*s.* witnode 103. 2, 122. 30, 143.
22; *pp. pl.* gewitnode 134. 5;
wk. gewitnodan 121. 3.

wītnung, *f.* punishment; 123. 2.

gewitt, *n.* reason, understanding;
gewit 11. 30, 116. 25; *g.* gewittes
13. 9, 146. 25; *d.* gewitte 128.
24; witte viii. 45; *a.* gewit 13.
29, 110. 14, 116. 25, xxvi. 100;
d. pl. gewittum, minds 20. 11.

gewittig, *adj.* rational; *pl. wk.*
gewittigan 108. 15.

wið, 1) *prep.* (*fq. foll. c.*) 1) *w. g.
motion, direction,* towards, *about*
14 *times,* 8. 27, v. 15 &c.; smearcode wið min 94. 16, *cf.* 17. 5;
wið ðæs þ, with a view to 139.
25. 2) *w.d. a) relation, conduct,* towards; 36. 31, 80. 5, *cf.*
17. 16, 19. 13. *b)* compared
with; 20. 4, 29. 4, 6. *c)* in exchange for; 66. 26, 77. 8. *d) aim,*
with a view to, to gain; 26. 20,
44. 29; wið ðæm ðe, in order
to 76. 29, 77. 7. *e)* contrary to;
23. 25, 24. 22, 23, 31. 17, iv.
28. *f) attack, defence,* against;
7. 1, xiii. 17 &c. *g) w.* (ge)mengan 33. 29 &c.; *w.* lucan 57. 6.

3) *w.a.*; *a*) *direction*, towards; 103. 13. *b*) *relation, attitude*, towards; 80. 3, 4; geferscipe w., with 111. 10; plegian w. 102. 15. *c*) compared with; *fq.* 36. 3, vi. 7 &c. *d*) *w.* (ge)mengan *fq.* 25. 7, vii. 8 &c. *e*) *attack, defence*, against; *fq.* 37. 6 &c. and xi. 33, xvi. 24. ii) *adv.*; *a*) towards; 9. 1, 37. 19. *b*) against; 98. 19, 109. 13. *c*) in exchange; 77. 10.

wiðcweðan, *sv5.* contradict, deny; 21. 11, 83. 17, 98. 18.

wiðerweard, *adj.* adverse; opposite; *fq.*; *f.wk.* wiðerwearde 47. 13 &c.; *n.* wiðerweard 25. 3 &c. and xi. 41, 49; *wk.* wiðerwearde 49. 15; *g.* wiðerweardes 38. 12, 71. 29, xi. 52; *a. n. wk.* wiðerwearde 49. 16; *pl. f.* wiðerwearda 96. 15; *n.* wiðerweard 37. 18; *wk.* wiðerweardan 49. 9; ða wiðerweardan englas, rebellious 98. 13; *g.* wiðerwearda v. 36; *d.* wiðerweardum 37. 18; *comp. pl.* wiðerweardran 38. 19.

wiðerweardnes, *f.* opposition; adverseness; 47. 26, 48. 3, 7, 49. 29, xi. 78; *d.* wiðerweardnesse 14. 23.

wiðforan, *prep. w. a.* before; 136. 3; wið . . . foran v. 43, xx. 265, xxviii. 47.

wiðstandan, *sv6. w.d.* resist, oppose; 14. 18; wiðstondan v. 22; *ind. prs.* 3.*s. w. d. and g.* wiðstent, prevents 14. 17.

wlætan, *wv.* debase, defile; *pp. a.* gewlætne 114. 23.

wlætta, *wm.* disgust, nausea; *d.* wlættan 30. 19.

wlanc, *adj.* proud, grand; *pl.* wlance xvii. 6.

wlātian, *wv. impers.* feel disgust; *sbj. prs.* ðe wlatige 23. 21.

wlenco,*f.* prosperity, riches; *pl. g.* wlencea i. 76; *d.* wlencum 18. 3, 46. 14, x. 28; *a.* wlenca v. 31.

wlitan, *sv1.* look; xxiv. 10; *ind.*

prs. 3.*s.* wliteð xxxi. 14; *imp.* wlit iv. 54.

wlite, *m.* brightness, beauty; 28. 27, 72. 28, xxi. 31; *g.* wlites 28. 29, 29. 14, 31. 2, 113. 5, xxviii. 42; *d.* wlite 72. 9; *a.* 21. 6, 27. 5, vi. 13, vii. 31, xxi. 32, xxx. 6.

wlitebeorht, *adj.* beautiful, splendid; *d. pl.* wlitebeorhtum xxv. 4.

wlitetorht, *adj.* splendidly bright; *n.* xxviii. 60 *n.*

wlitig, *adj.* beautiful; xxiv. 43; *f. wk.* wlitige xx. 279; *pl. wk.* wlitegan xxix. 39; *d.* wlitegum xv. 3; *a.* wlitige xix. 9; *wk.* wlitegan xxviii. 6; *sup. d. pl.* wlitegestum 64. 25.

wlitigian, *wv.* form, fashion; *ind. prs.* 3.*s.* wlitegað, gewlitegað* 131. 5.

wōd, *adj.* mad, raging; *f. wk.* wode 111. 28.

wōdðrāg, *f.* fit of madness; xxv. 41.

wōh, 1) *adj.* wrong; perverse; *f.* wō iv. 40; *n.* woh 119. 26; wog 119. 23; *g.* woges*, wos 140. 29; *a. wk.* won 70. 9; wōon 11. 31; *pl. wk.* won 38. 31; *a. wk.* 9. 26. 2) *sbst. n.* wrong; *a.* 142. 28; on woh, wrongly 107. 9, 131. 17; on wog 107. 25.

wōhfremmend, *m.* evil-doer; *d. pl.* wohfremmendum ix. 36.

wōhhǣmed, *n.* fornication, adultery; *g.* wohhæmetes xviii. 2.

wōl, *m.* pestilence, calamity; 67. 22; *a.* 13. 1 *n.*

wolcen, *n.* cloud; v. 4; *g.* wolcnes xx. 81; *pl.* wolcnu 14. 10; *g.* wolcna xxviii. 2, xxix. 13; *d.* wolcnum i. 76 &c.; *a.* wolcnu 18. 13, 105. 9, xxiv. 10.

wōp, *m.* weeping; *d.* wope 23. 22, ii. 3.

word, *n.* word; speech; report, fame; 28. 11, 12; *d.* worde Pr. 3; *a.* word Pr. 3; *pl.* ii. 18; *g.* worda 8. 9, 68. 19, i.

81 ; *d.* wordum 8. 7 &c. *and*
x. 3, xvi. 23; *a.* word 45. 11
&c. *and* viii. 1, xxvi. 79.

wordhord, *n.* store of words ; *a.*
vi. i.

worn, *m.* great number, multitude ; ix. 7 ; *a.* xxvi. 33.

woruld, *f.* (*forms w.* o *most fq.
in* C, *including compounds*),
world ; life, lifetime ; 58. 28
&c. ; weoruld xx. 62, 171 ; *g.*
worulde 9. 11, iii. 7 &c.;
weorulde 20. 27, xx. 251 &c.;
weorolde xxiv. 56 ; *d.* worulde
11. 15, iv. 41 &c.; to worulde
48. 30 ; *more usually* weorulde
20. 2, i. 51 &c.; woruld 18. 29 ;
a. worulde xi. 45 ; weorulde
viii. 8, xx. 24, xxix. 28 ;
woruld 11. 6, 13. 25, 18. 12,
24. 14, 42. 11, 53. 16, xiii. 65,
xvii. 4, 6, xx. 47, 57 ; worold
ix. 58 ; weoruld 13. 32, 18. 24,
76. 28; viii. 41, xxviii. 26, xxxi.
14. *Note: eo forms rare in* B.

woruldǽht, *f.* worldly possession;
g. pl. woruldæhta 27. 19.

woruldár, *f.* worldly honour,
good fortune ; *d.* weoruldare
141. 3 ; *a.* woruldare 17. 13.

woruldbisgo, *f.* worldly occupation ; *d. pl.* weoruldbisgum Pr.
5.

woruldbisgung, *f.* worldly trouble ; *g. pl.* weoruldbisgunga
iii. 4.

woruldbúend, *m.* human being ;
pl. weoruldbuende viii. 35 ; *g.*
woruldbuendra xxix. 82 ; *d.*
weoruldbuendum xxvii. 27.

worulddryhten, *m.* Lord ; *g.*
weorulddrihtnes xxix. 1.

woruldearfoð, *n.* worldly trouble;
g. pl. woruldearfoða v. 29, vii.
26, 35, 49.

woruldfréond, *m.* earthly friend;
pl. weoruldfrynd ii. 16.

woruldgielp, *n.* worldly boasting
or pride ; *d.* woruldgylpe 74.
24.

woruldgitsere, *m.* covetous man ;
d. xiv. 1.

woruldgitsung, *f.* covetousness ;
vii.12 ; *d.* woruldgidsunga ; 15.9.

woruldgód, *n.* worldly good ; *pl.*
32. 16 ; *d.* woruldgodum 54. 10.

woruldlic, *adj.* worldly ; *g.*
woruldlices 20. 29.

woruldlust, *m.* worldly desire or
pleasure ; 55. 8, 56. 21 ; *d.*
woruldluste 54. 15, 55. 8 ; *a.*
weoruldlust 76. 28 ; *pl.* woruld-
lustas 70. 14 ; *g.* woruldlusta
53. 28, 146. 18 ; *d.* woruldlustum 70. 15.

woruldmann, *m.* man ; *pl.*
woruldmen 41. 14, vii. 41,
xxviii. 10 ; weoruldmenn 17.
22 ; weoruldmen xxviii. 72;
g. woruldmonna 17. 29 ;
weoruldmonna xxviii. 31 ; *a.*
woruldmen iv. 51.

woruldrice, *n.* earthly kingdom ;
d. weoruldrice 74. 22.

woruldsælð, *f.* worldly prosperity; *pl.* woruldsælða 9
times, 8. 9 &c. *and* ii. 10 ;
weoruldgesælða 37. 22, 134.
25 ; *g.* woruldsælða 17. 1, 18.
32, 27. 13, vii. 52, 54 ; weoruldgesælða 54. 10 ; *d.* woruldsælðum 8. 2, 16. 31, 19. 11 ;
woruldgesælðum 39. 10, 54. 19,
v. 34 ; *a.* woruldsælða 15. 2,
17. 4 ; woruldgesælða 26. 1,
134. 8.

woruldgesceaft, *f.* earthly creature; *pl.* woruldgesceafta xi.
19, 84, 101 ; *g.* xi. 2 ; weoruldgesceafta xxix. 77 ; *d.* woruld-
gesceaftum 80. 10, 26 ; *a.*
weoruldgesceafta xx. 129.

woruldsorg, *f.* worldly care ; *pl.*
woruldsorga 8. 22, 9. 13 ; *d.*
woruldsorgum 8. 19.

woruldspéd, *f.* worldly riches;
a. pl. weoruldspeda 12. 3.

woruldgeswinc, *n.* earthly hardship; *d. pl.* weoruldgeswincum
xxi. 18.

woruldðéaw, *m.* worldly custom;
d. pl. woruldðeawum 7. 13.

woruldðing, *n.* worldly affair ;
g. pl. woruldðinga 56. 9.

woruldwela, *wm.* worldly wealth or prosperity ; *g.* woruldwelan 24. 2, 60. 18 ; *d.* 62. 32 ; *pl.* 30. 4 ; *g.* weoruldwelena xix. 26 ; *d.* woruldwelum 74. 22.

woruldwilla, *wm.* worldly desire ; *g.* woroldwillan 24. 2.

woruldwuniende, *adj.* dwelling in the world ; *g. pl.* woroldwuniendra xiii. 17.

wracu, *f.* revenge ; vengeance, punishment ; *g.* wræce 112. 3 ; xxv. 51 ; *a.* 118. 24.

wræc, *n.* exile ; *d.* wræce 116. 12.

wræcca, *wm.* exile, outcast ; wræccan 13. 18 ; wrecca 8. 6*, 124. 25, ii. 3 ; *a.* wræccan x. 38 ; wreccan 105. 27*.

wræcsið, *m.* exile, misery ; *d.* wræcsiðe 22. 11.

wræcstōw, *f.* place of exile or confinement ; 24. 31.

wrǣnnes, *f.* lewdness, lechery ; 93. 16, 109. 9 ; *g.* wrænnesse 71. 30, 111. 28, xxv. 41 ; *d.* 70. 18, 71. 30.

wræðan, *wv.* support ; *ind. prs.* 3.*s.* wræðeð 49. 7*.

wrāð, *adj.* angry, hostile ; *wk.* wraða xviii. 2 ; *d. pl.* wraðum xxvi. 76 ; *comp. n.* wraðre 138. 21.

wrāðe, *adv.* fiercely ; grievously ; 7. 9, vii. 52, 54, xxix. 87, 89.

wrecan, *sv5.* punish ; *sbj. prs.* wrece 104. 4, 123. 31, ix. 36 ; wræce 143. 22 ; *pl.* wrecen 102. 24 ; *pp.* gewrecen 121. 2.

wrēgan, *wv.* accuse ; *sbj. prs.* wrege 123. 17.

wrenc, *m.* trick, wile ; *d. pl.* wrencum 10. 22, iv. 47.

wreðian, *wv.* prop up, support ; *ind. prs.* 3.*pl.* wreðiað xi. 34.

wrīgian, *wv.* move forward, hasten, tend ; *ind. prs.* 3.*s.* wrigað 57. 23, 28, xiii. 10, 65.

wringan, *sv3.* squeeze, press out ; win wringan 12. 10.

wrītan, *sv1.* write ; *sbj. pst. pl.* writon 44. 8*.

gewrit, *n.* writing ; *pl.* gewritu 44. 6.

wrītere, *m.* writer ; *pl.* writeras 44. 8 ; *g.* writera 44. 1.

gewrixle, *n.* change, alternation ; 49. 26, 125. 12 ; *a.* 49. 17, xi. 56.

wudu, *m.* wood, forest ; timber ; 91. 13, 101. 27, xiii. 50 ; widu xiii. 55 ; *g.* wuda 57. 19 ; wudes viii. 20 ; *d.* wuda 57. 16 ; 102. 4, 117. 29, 127. 13, xix. 5, 18 ; *a.* 91. 19* ; wudu 91. 19, 23, 100. 6 ; *pl.* wudas 102. 5 ; *g.* wuda 91. 17, xx. 251 ; *d.* wudum 42. 29, 73. 31.

wudufugol, *m.* forest bird ; *pl.* wudufuglas 57. 15, xiii. 35.

wuhhung, *f.* fury, madness ; *g.* wuhhunge 39. 30*.

wuldor, *n.* glory ; 56. 21, 68. 7, 11 ; wuldur 68. 9 ; *g.* wuldres xxvi. 45, xxix. 6 ; *d.* wuldre xvii. 29 ; *a.* wuldor 68. 12.

wuldorcyning, *m.* king of glory ; xx. 162.

wulf, *m.* wolf ; 114. 26 ; *d. pl.* wulfum xxvi. 79 ; wulfan 116. 19*.

gewuna, *wm.* habit, custom ; 15. 17 &c. ; *g.* gewunan 57. 12, 60. 1 ; *d.* 24. 23, vii. 1 ; *a.* 17. 27, xiii. 27.

wund, *adj.* wounded ; *a.* wundne viii. 35.

wundian, *wv.* wound ; *pp.* gewundod 34. 4.

wundor, *n.* wonder ; 69. 20, xvii. 7 &c. ; wundur xx. 117 ; wunder 80. 8*, xxviii. 82 ; *d. pl.* wundrum *used as adv.* wonderfully, 24. 25, iv. 20, xxv. 4, xxix. 17.

wundorlic, *adj.* wonderful ; xx. 3, xxi. 31 ; wunderlic 79. 10* ; *n.* wundorlic 47. 11, xix. 20 &c. ; wunderlic 35. 32*, 79. 20* ; *a. f.* wundorlice 100. 10 ; *n.* wundorlic 100. 12, 28 ; *inst.* wundorlice 80. 22 ; *g. pl.* wundorlicra xx. 101.

wundorlice, *adv.* wonderfully ;

57. 2, xiii. 5 &c. ; wunderlice
79. 11*.

wundrian, *wv. w. g.* wonder (at),
admire ; 101. 6 &c. ; to wundriganne 28. 28 ; to wundrianne
104. 4 ; to wyndrianne 72. 27* ;
ind. prs. 1.*s.* wundrige 12. 24
&c. ; 2.*s.* wundrast 145. 4 ; 3.*s.*
wundraÞ 81. 32, xx. 223 &c. ;
pl. wundriaÞ 29. 14, xxviii. 50
&c. ; *pst.* 1.*s.* wundrode 122.
19 ; 3.*s.* 98. 17 ; *sbj. prs.*
wundrige 104. 11, 143. 15,
145. 2, xxviii. 2, 40 ; wundrie
92. 8, 119. 27, 125. 7, 141. 28,
xxviii. 6 ; *pl.* wundrigen 28. 32,
72. 20, 92. 9 ; wundrien 29. 3 ;
pst. wundrode 125. 13.

gewunelic, *adj.* customary, familiar ; *n.* 37. 17 ; gewunlic 91. 15.

wunian, *wv.* dwell ; abide, remain ;
xi. 17 *n.*, 56, xxix. 95 ; gewunian
116. 11 ; wunigan 130. 10 ;
gewunigan ii. 19 ; gewunigen
(*by error*) i. 37 (J) ; *ind. prs.*
2.*s.* wunæst xx. 16 ; 3.*s.* wunaÞ
20. 22, vi. 17 &c. ; *pl.* wuniaÞ
25. 13, xi. 4 &c. ; wunigaÞ vii.
38 ; *pst.* 3.*s.* wunode 116. 4, ix.
38 &c. ; *pl.* wunedon xx. 243 ;
prs. p. wuniende 21. 8, 27. 12 ;
wunigende 95. 14 ; *pp.* gewunod,
accustomed 8. 2.

wynsum, *adj.* pleasant ; *f.* wynsumu 25. 8 ; wynsum 137. 7,
12, 138. 12, xxi. 18 ; *n.* wynsum 33. 17, 86. 11 ; gewun-
sum 70. 19 ; *g.* wynsumes 64.
20 ; *d. wk.* wynsuman 138. 26 ;
a. f. wynsume xiii. 19 ; *wk.*
138. 25, 139. 2 ; *comp. f.* wynsumre xii. 20 ; *n.* 57. 19, 65.
6, 86. 12 ; winsumre 52. 8* ; *g.*
wynsumran 138. 29.

wynsumlice, *adv.* pleasantly ;
54. 8.

wynsumnes, *f.* delightfulness,
pleasantness ; *d.* wynsumnesse
50. 8, 13.

wyrcan, *wv.* make, construct ;
cause ; do ; 29. 22 &c. *and* xii.
1 ; wircan 111. 5 ; wercan xxvi.

73 ; to wyrcanne 40. 10 &c. ;
to wyrcenne 40. 25* ; *ind. prs.*
2.*s.* wyrcest xx. 87 ; wercest iv.
18 ; 3.*s.* wyrceÞ iv. 28 ; wyrcÞ
38. 4 &c. ; wircÞ 135. 6 ; *pl.*
wyrcaÞ 86. 30 ; gewercaÞ 87.
24 ; *pst.* 2.*s.* worhtest 29. 19,
79. 18, xx. 40 ; worhtes xx. 22 ;
geworhtest 29. 19* &c. *and* xx.
24, 44 ; 3.*s.* worhte 30. 21 &c.
and ix. 2 ; geworhte Pr. 9 ;
weorhte 39. 18* ; *pl.* worhton
99. 4, 139. 15 ; *sbj. prs.* wyrce
112. 20 &c. *and* vii. 31 ; *pp.*
geworht 129. 2, 135. 8, xx. 21 ;
to witum geworht, subjected
36. 18 ; *g.* geworhtes 29. 22 ;
pl. n. geworhte 96. 16 ; *g.* ge-
worhtra 11. 27.

wyrd, *f.* fate ; *fq.* 10. 18, i. 29
&c. ; weord 11. 6* ; *g.* wyrde
102. 25, xiii. 24 &c. ; *d.* 23. 2
&c. *and* xxvii. 5 ; *a.* 138. 25,
139. 2, 3 ; wirde iv. 49 ; wyrd
usual form 11. 31 &c.

gewyrht, *n.* desert, merit ; *only in*
d. pl. gewyrhtum 11. 7 &c. ;
butan gewyrhtum, undeservedly
50. 19 &c. ; be his gewyrhtum
68. 27 &c. ; *cf.* ix. 36 ; be
geweorhtum xxvii. 27 ; æfter
his gewyrhtum 124. 14 &c.

wyrhta, *wm.* maker, creator ;
30. 22, xxix. 81, xxx. 14 ; *d.*
wyrhtan 12. 17, 30. 21.

wyrm, *m.* reptile ; *pl.* wyrmas 36. 9.

wyrt, *f.* vegetable, plant ; 91. 13 ;
a. 91. 19 ; *pl. g.* wyrta 82. 6,
91. 16, viii. 20, xx. 251 ; *d.*
wyrtum 91. 10 ; *a.* wyrta 33.
28, 91. 23, xi. 57.

wyrtruma, *wm.* root ; *d. pl.*
wyrtrumum 91. 26, 31.

wyrtwalian, *wv.* uproot ; *sbj.*
prs. wyrtwalige 61. 8*.

gewȳscan, *wv.* wish ; 117. 23.

Y.

yfel, 1) *adj.* bad, evil ; *wk.* yfela
71. 4*, 125. 5*, xv. 1 ; yfla 107.
24 &c. *and* xviii. 1 ; *f.* yfel 137.

28; *g.* yfles 132. 28 &c.; *wk.*
yfelan 113. 28; *d.* yfelum 38.
32, 124. 15, 134. 14; *wk.* yflan
121. 13, xxii. 32; *a.* yfelne v.
28, viii. 38; *wk.* yflan 14. 20,
123. 30; *n.* yfel xii. 28; *pl.*
yfele 24. 12 &c. *and* iv. 37;
yfle *commoner form in* C,
107. 4 &c.; *wk.* yfelan 62. 11
&c.; yflan *more fq. in* C, 106.
5 &c.; *g.* yfelra 10. 24; *wk.*
yflena 110. 2 &c.; yfelana 133.
20; *d.* yflum 107. 21 &c. *and*
iv. 35, xxvii. 30; yfelum 120.
12*; *a. wk.* yfelan 14. 19 &c.;
comp. wyrsa 63. 9*, 69. 13, 131.
30, xxv. 29; wirsa 67. 22; *n.*
wyrse 46. 27 &c. *and* x. 57,
xxv. 67; *a.* wyrsan 63. 7 *n.*, 71.
23; *n.* wyrse 22. 3; *pl.* wyrsan
32. 20 &c.; wyrson 134. 21;
a. wyrsan 32. 14; *sup.* wyrresta
33. 4; *n.* wyrrest 120. 23; *g.*
wk. wyrrestan 119. 18; *d. wk.*
34. 22, 37. 25; *d. pl.* wyrrestum
61. 15, 134. 9 (wyrstan B);
wyrrestan 37. 25. 2) *sbst. n.*
evil; 37. 21 &c. *and* i. 55; *g.*
yfeles 119. 7, 17, ix. 52; yfles
113. 22, 31, 120. 11; *d.* yfle
109. 14 &c. *and* xxv. 60; *a.*
yfel 37. 12 &c. *and* xxii. 17;
eofel 18. 27* *n.*; *pl. g.* yfela 14.
25*, 71. 14, vii. 43; yfla 137.
13, v. 41, xxv. 44; *d.* yfelum
118. 23*; yflum 7. 10 &c.; *a.*
yflu 27. 10*; yfel 7. 14*, 134.
20.

yfele, *adv.* badly, wrongly; 7. 9,
17. 12; *comp.* wyrs 35. 6; *sup.*
wyrst xxiv. 60.

yfelnes, *f.* badness, wickedness;
114. 21.

yfelwillende, *adj.* evilly disposed,
wicked; 122. 21, 24; *pl. wk.*
yfelwillendan 112. 16; *a.*
yfelwillende 34. 5; *wk.* yfelwillendan 117. 2.

yfelwyrcende, *adj.* evil-doing;
122. 22, 25.

yfemest, *adj. sup. of* uferra;
xxiv. 23; yfemeſð xiii. 63;

yfmest xxiv. 20; *f.* yfemest 57.
27; *n.* 80. 10, xx. 84.

yflian, *wv.* ill-treat, injure; *ind.*
prs. 3.*s.* yflað 123. 9, 10; *pst.*
3.*s.* yflode 122. 32; *sbj. prs.*
yflige 119. 23.

ymb (ymb *more fq. in* C *than*
ymbe; ym 31. 1 *n.*, 142. 25;
emb 17. 3, 74. 17; embe 86. 13,
18, 104. 20), 1) *prep. w.a.*
a) motion, round; 126. 7, xxviii.
9, 22; ymbe xx. 211. *b)* concerning, about (*the usual meaning*); *fq.* 12. 21, viii. 32 &c.;
ymbe 18. 17 &c. *and* viii. 31.
c. time; ymb ðritig wintra, every
thirty years 126. 9, *cf.* xxviii.
25, 29; ymbe sticce, after a time,
from time to time 100. 7; ymbe
long, at great length 125. 23.
d) in connexion with, about;
swincan ymbe 87. 26 &c.; ymb
þ bion, busy, occupied with 12.
26, *cf.* 92. 31; siredon ymb,
against 36. 19, *cf.* 70. 24; don
ymbe hine, towards 37. 1. 2)
adv. same senses as (1); 16. 19,
127. 4, xx. 27, xxviii. 6; ymbe
36. 22, i. 59, xix. 1, xxviii. 24,
xxix. 41.

ymbbǣtan, *wv.* curb; *pp.* ymbe-
bræted xxiv. 37.

ymbcierran, *wv.* revolve round;
ind. prs. 3.*s.* ymbcerreð xxviii.
14; *pp.* ymbcirred xxviii. 26.

ymbclyppan, *wv.* embrace; *ind.*
prs. 3.*s* ymbclyppeð xi. 35; *pl.*
ymbclyppað ix. 40.

ymbfōn, *rv.* surround, encompass;
ind. prs. 3.*s.* ymbfehð 53. 1; *pp.*
ymbfangen 13. 1.

ymbgyrdan, *wv.* engirdle; *ind.*
prs. 3.*s.* embegyrt ix. 41.

ymbhabban, *wv.* surround; *ind.*
prs. 3.*s.* ymbhæfð 53. 1*.

ymbhoga, *wm.* care, anxiety; vii.
53; *g.* ymbhogan 27. 4; *pl. g.*
ymbhogena vii. 36; ymbhogona
xvi. 6; *d.* ymbhogum 52. 18, 55.
20; *a.* ymbhogan 67. 29, 95. 1,
vii. 28.

ymbhweorfan, *sv3.* go round,

revolve round; *ind. prs.* 2.*s.*
ymbhweorfest 10. 2*; ymb-
hweorfest iv. 4 (J); 3.*s.* ymb-
hweorfeð xxviii. 13; *prs. p.*
ymbhweorfende 18. 7.
ymbhwierfan, *wv.* revolve round;
ind. prs. 3.*s.* ymbhwerfeð xxviii.
4 *n.*; ymbhwyrfð 125. 32* *n.*
ymbhwyrft, *m.* revolution, orbit;
circuit, compass; *g.* ymbhweorftes 105. 18; *a.* ymbhwyrft 41.
20, 126. 4, 7, xxiv. 38, xxviii.
20; ymbhwerft xxviii. 12; ymbehwerft xxviii. 8.
ymblicgan, *sv*5. surround; *ind.
prs.* 3.*pl.* ymbelicgað xx. 77.
ymbscriðan, *sv*1. revolve round;
ind. prs. 3.*s.* ymbscriðeð xx. 208.
ymbsēon, *sv*5. look round; *sbj.
pst.* 3.*s.* ymbsawe x. 5.
ymbsittend, *m.* neighbour; *g. pl.*
ymbsittenda xxv. 14.
ymbstandan, *sv*6. surround; *pp.*

pl. ymbstandene 111. 14 *n.*;
ymbestandne xxv. 7.
ymbðencan, *wv.* reflect upon;
sbj. pst. 3.*s.* ymbeðohte x. 4.
ymbūtan, 1) *adv.* around, about;
129. 21, xx. 140, 171, 172, 174;
swiðe feorran ymbutan, very
circuitously 127. 33; ymbeutan
xxv. 28. 2) *prep.*; *a*) *w. d.; foll.
c.* 97. 18, 108. 20, 125. 2; utan
ymb xx. 207. *b*) *w. a.* 25. 14,
viii. 14, 53, xxii. 7, 15; ymbuton
95. 1*; ymbeutan 100. 10.
ȳst, *f.* tempest, storm; 21. 7, vi.
14; *pl.* ysta v. 9; *g* xxi. 15; *d.*
ystum 89. 10.
ȳtemest, *sup. adj.* outermost;
farthest outside; *pl. wk.* ytmestan
x. 25; utemestan 46. 11.
ȳð, *f.* wave; xxvi. 30, xxviii. 57;
pl. yða 124. 4, xxvii. 3; *g.* 17.
26, 126. 19; *d.* yðum 10. 27,
14. 13, 89. 10, iv. 56, xxi. 14.

INDEX OF PROPER NAMES

THE IND

6/10/98

Clarendon Press Series.

The English Language and Literature.

HELPS TO THE STUDY OF THE LANGUAGE.

1. DICTIONARIES.

A NEW ENGLISH DICTIONARY, ON HISTORICAL PRINCIPLES: founded mainly on the materials collected by the Philological Society. Imperial 4to.

PRESENT STATE OF THE WORK.

			£	s	d.
Vol. I. {A B} Edited by Dr. MURRAY. . . . . Half-morocco			2	12	6
Vol II. C Edited by Dr. MURRAY. . . . . Half-morocco			2	12	6
Vol III. {D E} Edited by Dr. MURRAY / Edited by HENRY BRADLEY } . . . Half-morocco			2	12	6
Vol. IV. {F G} Edited by HENRY BRADLEY	F-Field	0	7	6
	Field-Frankish	0	12	6
	Franklaw-Fyz—G-Gain-coming .	0	5	0
	Gaincope—Germanizing . .	0	5	0
Vol. V. H-K Edited by Dr. MURRAY.	H-Haversian . . .	0	5	0
	Haversine-Heel . . .	0	2	6

Bosworth and Toller. *An Anglo-Saxon Dictionary,* based on the MS. Collections of the late JOSEPH BOSWORTH, D.D. Edited and enlarged by Prof. T. N. TOLLER, M.A. Parts I-III, A-SÁR. . . . [4to, 15*s.* each.
Part IV, Section I, SÁR—SWÍÐRIAN. . . . . [4to, 8*s.* 6*d.*
„ „ II, SWÍÞ-SNEL—ÝTMEST . . . [4to, 18*s.* 6*d.*
₊ *A Supplement, which will complete the Work, is in active preparation.*

Mayhew and Skeat. *A Concise Dictionary of Middle English,* from A. D. 1150 to 1580. By A. L. MAYHEW, M.A., and W. W. SKEAT, Litt.D.
[Crown 8vo, half-roan, 7*s.* 6*d.*

Skeat. *A Concise Etymological Dictionary of the English Language.* By W. W. SKEAT, Litt.D. *Sixth Edition.* . . [Crown 8vo, 5*s.* 6*d.*

2. GRAMMARS, READING BOOKS, &c.

Earle. *The Philology of the English Tongue.* By J. EARLE, M.A., *Fifth Edition.* . . . . (Extra fcap. 8vo, 8s. 6d.

——— *A Book for the Beginner in Anglo-Saxon.* By J. EARLE, M.A., *Third Edition.* . . . . . . |Extra fcap. 8vo, 2s. 6d.

Mayhew. *Synopsis of Old-English Phonology.* By A. L. MAYHEW, M.A. . . . . . . [Extra fcap. 8vo, bevelled boards, 8s. 6d.

Morris and **Skeat.** *Specimens of Early English—*
Part I. From Old English Homilies to King Horn (A.D. 1150 to A.D. 1300). By R. MORRIS, LL.D. *Third Edition.* . . . [Extra fcap. 8vo, 9s.
Part II. From Robert of Gloucester to Gower (A.D. 1298 to A.D. 1393). By R. MORRIS, LL.D., and W. W. SKEAT, Litt.D. *Third Edition.* [7s. 6d.

Skeat. *Specimens of English Literature,* from the 'Ploughmans Crede' to the 'Shepheardes Calender.' . . |Extra fcap. 8vo, 7s. 6d.

——— *The Principles of English Etymology—*
First Series. The Native Element. *Second Edition* |Crown 8vo, 10s. 6d.
Second Series. The Foreign Element. . [Crown 8vo, 10s. 6d.

——— *A Primer of English Etymology.* [Extra fcap. 8vo, *stiff covers,* 1s. 6d.

——— *Twelve Facsimiles of Old-English Manuscripts.* [4to, 7s. 6d.

Sweet. *A New English Grammar, Logical and Historical.* Part I. Introduction, Phonology, and Accidence. . [Crown 8vo, 10s. 6d.

——— *A Short Historical English Grammar.* [Extra fcap. 8vo, 4s. 6d.

——— *A Primer of Historical English Grammar.* [Extra fcap. 8vo, 2s.

——— *History of English Sounds from the Earliest Period.* With full Word-Lists. . . . . [8vo, 14s.

——— *First Steps in Anglo-Saxon.* . . [Extra fcap. 8vo, 2s. 6d.

——— *An Anglo-Saxon Primer, with Grammar, Notes, and Glossary.* *Eighth Edition.* . . . . [Extra fcap. 8vo, 2s. 6d.

——— *An Anglo-Saxon Reader.* In Prose and Verse. With Grammatical Introduction, Notes, and Glossary. *Seventh Edition, Revised and Enlarged.* . . . . [Crown 8vo, 9s. 6d.

——— *A Second Anglo-Saxon Reader.* . . [Extra fcap. 4s. 6d.

——— *Old English Reading Primers—*
I. *Selected Homilies of Ælfric.* . . [Extra fcap. 8vo, *stiff covers,* 2s.
II. *Extracts from Alfred's Orosius.* . [Extra fcap. 8vo, *stiff covers,* 2s.

——— *First Middle English Primer, with Grammar and Glossary.* *Second Edition.* . . . . [Extra fcap. 8vo, 2s. 6d.

——— *Second Middle English Primer.* Extracts from Chaucer, with Grammar and Glossary. . . . . . [Extra fcap. 8vo, 2s. 6d.

——— *A Primer of Spoken English.* . . [Extra fcap. 8vo, 3s. 6d.

——— *A Primer of Phonetics.* . . . [Extra fcap. 8vo, 3s. 6d.

——— *A Manual of Current Shorthand, Orthographic and Phonetic.* [Crown 8vo, 4s. 6d.

Tancock. *An Elementary English Grammar and Exercise Book.* By O. W. TANCOCK, M.A. *Third Edition.* . . [Extra fcap. 8vo, 1s. 6d.

——— *An English Grammar and Reading Book,* for Lower Forms in Classical Schools. By O. W. TANCOCK, M.A. *Fourth Edition.* [3s. 6d.

A SERIES OF ENGLISH CLASSICS.

(CHRONOLOGICALLY ARRANGED.)

Chaucer. I. *The Prologue to the Canterbury Tales.* (*School Edition.*) Edited by W. W. Skeat, Litt. D. . . [Extra fcap. 8vo, *stiff covers*, 1s.

—— II. *The Prologue; The Knightes Tale; The Nonne Prestes Tale.* Edited by R. Morris, LL.D. *A New Edition, with Collations and Additional Notes,* by W. W. Skeat, Litt. D. . . [Extra fcap. 8vo, 2s. 6d.

—— III. *The Prioresses Tale; Sir Thopas; The Monkes Tale; The Clerkes Tale; The Squieres Tale, &c.* Edited by W. W. Skeat, Litt. D. *Sixth Edition.* . . . . [Extra fcap. 8vo, 4s. 6d.

—— IV. *The Tale of the Man of Lawe; The Pardoneres Tale: The Second Nonnes Tale; The Chanouns Yemannes Tale.* By the same Editor. *New Edition, Revised.* . . . . [Extra fcap. 8vo, 4s. 6a.

—— V. *Minor Poems.* By the same Editor. [Crown 8vo, 10s. 6d.

—— VI. *The Legend of Good Women.* By the same Editor.
[Crown 8vo, 6s.

—— VII. *The Hous of Fame.* By the same Editor. [Crown 8vo, 2s.

Langland. *The Vision of William concerning Piers the Plowman,* by William Langland. Edited by W. W. Skeat, Litt. D. *Sixth Edition.*
[Extra fcap. 8vo, 4s. 6d.

Gamelyn, The Tale of. Edited by W. W. Skeat, Litt. D.
[Extra fcap. 8vo, *stiff covers*, 1s. 6d.

Wycliffe. *The New Testament in English,* according to the Version by John Wycliffe, about A.D. 1380, and Revised by John Purvey, about A.D. 1388. With Introduction and Glossary by W. W. Skeat, Litt. D.
[Extra fcap. 8vo, 6s.

—— *The Books of Job, Psalms, Proverbs, Ecclesiastes, and the Song of Solomon:* according to the Wycliffite Version made by Nicholas de Hereford, about A.D. 1381, and Revised by John Purvey, about A.D. 1388. With Introduction and Glossary by W. W. Skeat, Litt. D. [Extra fcap. 8vo, 3s. 6d.

Minot. *The Poems of Laurence Minot.* Edited, with Introduction and Notes, by Joseph Hall, M.A. *Second Edition.* [Extra fcap. 8vo, 4s. 6d.

Spenser. *The Faery Queene.* Books I and II. Edited by G. W. Kitchin, D.D., with Glossary by A. L. Mayhew, M.A.
[Extra fcap. 8vo, 2s. 6d. each.

Hooker. *Ecclesiastical Polity,* Book I. Edited by R. W. Church, M.A., late Dean of St. Paul's. . . . . . . [Extra fcap. 8vo, 2s.

Marlowe and **Greene.** Marlowe's *Tragical History of Dr. Faustus,* and Greene's *Honourable History of Friar Bacon and Friar Bungay.* Edited by A. W. Ward, Litt. D. *New and Enlarged Edition.* [Crown 8vo, 6s. 6d.

Marlowe. *Edward II.* Edited by O. W. Tancock, M.A. *Second Edition.* . . . . . [Extra fcap. 8vo. *Paper covers,* 2s.; *cloth,* 3s.

Shakespeare. Select Plays. Edited by W. G. CLARK, M.A., and W. ALDIS WRIGHT, D.C.L. . . . . [Extra fcap. 8vo, *stiff covers*

The Merchant of Venice. 1s.
Richard the Second. 1s. 6d.
Macbeth. 1s. 6d.
Hamlet. 2s.

Edited by W. ALDIS WRIGHT, D.C.L.

The Tempest. 1s. 6d.
As You Like It. 1s. 6d.
A Midsummer Night's Dream. 1s. 6d.
Twelfth Night. 1s. 6d.
Julius Caesar. 2s.
Henry the Eighth. 2s.
Coriolanus. 2s. 6d.
Richard the Third. 2s. 6d.
Henry the Fifth. 2s.
King John. 1s. 6d.
King Lear. 1s. 6d.
Much Ado About Nothing. 1s. 6d.

Henry the Fourth, Part I. 2s.

Shakespeare as a Dramatic Artist; *a popular Illustration of the Principles of Scientific Criticism.* By R. G. MOULTON, M.A. [Cr. 8vo, 7s. 6d.

Bacon. *Advancement of Learning.* Edited by W. ALDIS WRIGHT, D.C.L. *Third Edition.* . . . . . . [Extra fcap. 8vo, 4s. 6d

———— *The Essays.* Edited, with Introduction and Illustrative Notes, by S. H. REYNOLDS, M.A. . . . . [Demy 8vo, *half-bound*, 12s. 6d.

Milton. I. *Areopagitica.* With Introduction and Notes. By JOHN W. HALES, M.A. *Third Edition.* . . . . [Extra fcap. 8vo, 3s.

———— II. *Poems.* Edited by R. C. BROWNE, M.A. In two Volumes. *New Edition.* . . . . . [Extra fcap. 8vo, 6s. 6d.

Sold separately, Vol. I. 4s., Vol. II. 3s.
In paper covers, *Lycidas*, 3d. *Comus*, 6d.

By OLIVER ELTON, B.A.

Lycidas, 6d. *L'Allegro*, 4d. *Il Penseroso.* 4d. *Comus*, 1s.

———— III. *Paradise Lost.* Book I. Edited with Notes, by H. C. BEECHING, M.A. . [Extra fcap. 8vo, 1s. 6d. *In Parchment*, 3s. 6d.

———— IV. *Paradise Lost.* Book II. Edited by E. K. CHAMBERS, B.A. . . . [Extra fcap. 8vo, 1s. 6d. Books I and II together, 2s. 6d.

———— V. *Samson Agonistes.* Edited, with Introduction and Notes, by JOHN CHURTON COLLINS, M.A. . . [Extra fcap. 8vo, *stiff covers*, 1s.

Milton's Prosody. By ROBERT BRIDGES. [Extra fcap. 8vo, 1s. 6d.

Bunyan. I. *The Pilgrim's Progress, Grace Abounding, Relation of the Imprisonment of Mr. John Bunyan.* Edited by E. VENABLES, M.A. [Extra fcap. 8vo, 3s. 6d. *In Parchment*, 4s. 6d.

———— II. *The Holy War, and the Heavenly Footman.* Edited by MABEL PEACOCK. . . . . [Extra fcap. 8vo, 3s. 6d.

Clarendon. I. *History of the Rebellion.* Book VI. Edited, with Introduction and Notes, by T. ARNOLD, M.A. *Second Edition.* [Crown 8vo, 5s

———— II. *Selections.* Edited by G. BOYLE, M.A., Dean of Salisbury [Crown 8vo, 7s. 6d.

Dryden. *Select Poems.* (*Stanzas on the Death of Oliver Cromwell; Astraea Redux; Annus Mirabilis; Absalom and Achitophel; Religio Laici; The Hind and the Panther.*) Edited by W. D. CHRISTIE, M.A. *Fifth Edition.* Revised by C. H. FIRTH, M.A. . . . . [Extra fcap. 8vo, 3s. 6d.

———— *Essay of Dramatic Poesy.* Edited, with Notes, by T. ARNOLD, M.A. *Second Edition.* . . . . . . [Extra fcap. 8vo, 3s. 6d.

Locke. *Conduct of the Understanding.* Edited, with Introduction, Notes, &c., by T. FOWLER, D.D. *Third Edition.* . [Extra fcap. 8vo, 2s. 6d.

Addison. *Selections from Papers in the 'Spectator.'* By T. ARNOLD, M.A. *Sixteenth Thousand.* . . . . . [Extra fcap. 8vo, 4s. 6d.

Steele. *Selections from the Tatler, Spectator, and Guardian.* By AUSTIN DOBSON. *Second Edition.* . . . . . [Crown 8vo, 7s. 6d.

Swift. *Selections from his Works.* Edited, with Life, Introductions, and Notes, by Sir HENRY CRAIK, K.C.B. Two Vols.
[Crown 8vo, cloth extra, price 15s.
Each volume may be had separately, price 7s. 6d.

Pope. I. *Essay on Man.* Edited by MARK PATTISON, B.D. *Sixth Edition.* . . . . [Extra fcap. 8vo, 1s. 6d.

———— II. *Satires and Epistles.* By the same Editor. *Fourth Edition.*
[Extra fcap. 8vo, 2s.

Thomson. *The Seasons,* and *The Castle of Indolence.* Edited by J. LOGIE ROBERTSON, M.A. . . . . . [Extra fcap. 8vo, 4s. 6a.
———— *The Castle of Indolence.* By the same Editor. [Extra fcap. 8vo, 1s. 6a.

Berkeley. *Selections.* With Introduction and Notes. By A. C. FRASER, LL.D. *Fourth Edition.* . . . . . . [Crown 8vo, 8s. 6d.

Johnson. I. *Rasselas.* Edited, with Introduction and Notes, by G. BIRKBECK HILL, D.C.L.
[Extra fcap. 8vo, *limp,* 2s.; *Bevelled boards,* 3s. 6d.; *in Parchment,* 4s. 6d.

———— II. *Rasselas ; Lives of Dryden and Pope.* Edited by ALFRED MILNES, M.A. . . . . . . [Extra fcap. 8vo, 4s. 6d.
Lives of Dryden and Pope. . . [Stiff covers, 2s. 6d.

———— III. *Life of Milton.* Edited, with Notes, &c., by C. H. FIRTH, M.A. . . . [Extra fcap. 8vo, *stiff covers,* 1s. 6d. ; *cloth,* 2s. 6d.

———— IV. *Vanity of Human Wishes.* With Notes, by E. J. PAYNE, M.A. . . . . [Paper covers, 4d.

Gray. *Selected Poems.* Edited by EDMUND GOSSE, M.A.
[In Parchment, 3s.

———— *The same,* together with Supplementary Notes for Schools. By FOSTER WATSON, M.A. . . . . [Extra fcap. 8vo, *stiff covers,* 1s. 6d.

———— *Elegy,* and *Ode on Eton College.* . . . [Paper covers, 2d.

Goldsmith. *Selected Poems.* Edited, with Introduction and Notes, by AUSTIN DOBSON. . . [Extra fcap. 8vo, 3s. 6d. In Parchment, 4s. 6d.

———— *The Traveller.* Edited by G. B. HILL, D.C.L. [Stiff covers, 1s.

———— *The Deserted Village.* . . . . . [Paper covers, 2d.

Cowper. I. *The Didactic Poems of* 1782, with Selections from the Minor Pieces, A.D. 1779-1783. Edited by H. T. GRIFFITH, B.A.
[Extra fcap. 8vo, 3s.

———— II. *The Task, with Tirocinium,* and Selections from the Minor Poems, A.D. 1784-1799. By the same Editor. [Extra fcap. 8vo, 3s.

Burke. I. *Thoughts on the Present Discontents ; the two Speeches on America.* Edited by E. J. PAYNE, M.A. . [Extra fcap. 8vo, 4s. 6d.

———— II. *Reflections on the French Revolution.* By the same Editor. *Second Edition.* . . . . . . [Extra fcap. 8vo, 5s.

———— III. *Four Letters on the Proposals for Peace with the Regicide Directory of France.* By the same Editor. [Extra fcap. 8vo, 5s.

Burns. *Selected Poems.* Edited by J. LOGIE ROBERTSON. M.A.
[Crown 8vo, 6s.

Keats. *The Odes of Keats.* With Notes and Analyses and a Memoir, by ARTHUR C. DOWNER, M.A. With Four Illustrations.
[Extra fcap. 8vo, 3s. 6d. net.

———— *Hyperion,* Book I. With Notes, by W. T. ARNOLD, B.A. 4d.

Byron. *Childe Harold.* With Introduction and Notes, by H. F. TOZER, M.A. . . . . . [Extra fcap. 8vo, 3s. 6d. *In Parchment,* 5s.

Shelley. *Adonais.* With Introduction and Notes. By W. M. ROSSETTI. . . . . Crown 8vo, 5s.

Scott. *Lady of the Lake.* Edited, with Preface and Notes, by W. MINTO, M.A. With Map. . . . . [Extra fcap. 8vo, 3s. 6d.

———— *Lay of the Last Minstrel.* Edited by W. MINTO, M.A. With Map. . . . [Extra fcap. 8vo, *stiff covers,* 2s. *In Parchment,* 3s. 6d.

———— *Lay of the Last Minstrel.* Introduction and Canto I, with Preface and Notes, by W. MINTO, M.A. . . . . . [*Paper covers,* 6d.

———— *Lord of the Isles.* Edited, with Introduction and Notes, by THOMAS BAYNE. . . . [Extra fcap. 8vo, *stiff covers,* 2s.; *cloth,* 2s. 6d.

——— *Marmion.* By the same Editor. . [Extra fcap. 8vo, 3s. 6d.

Campbell. *Gertrude of Wyoming.* Edited, with Introduction and Notes, by H. MACAULAY FITZGIBBON, M.A. *Second Edition.* [Extra fcap. 8vo, 1s.

Wordsworth. *The White Doe of Rylstone.* Edited by WILLIAM KNIGHT, LL.D., University of St. Andrews. . . [Extra fcap. 8vo, 2s. 6d.

Typical Selections *from the best English Writers. Second Edition.* In Two Volumes. . . . . . . [Extra fcap. 8vo, 3s. 6d. each.

HISTORY AND GEOGRAPHY.

Greswell. *History of the Dominion of Canada.* By W. PARR GRESWELL, M.A. . . . . [Crown 8vo, 7s. 6d.

———— *Geography of the Dominion of Canada and Newfoundland.* By the same Author. . . . . [Crown 8vo, 6s.

———— *Geography of Africa South of the Zambesi.* By the same Author. . . . . [Crown 8vo, 7s. 6d.

Hughes (Alfred). *Geography for Schools.* Part I, *Practical Geography.* With Diagrams. . . . . . [Extra fcap. 8vo, 2s. 6d.

Lucas. *Historical Geography of the British Colonies.* By C. P. LUCAS, B.A.

Introduction. With Eight Maps. . . . . [Crown 8vo, 4s. 6d.

Vol. I. *The Mediterranean and Eastern Colonies (exclusive of India).* With Eleven Maps. . . . . [5s.

Vol. II. *The West Indian Colonies.* With Twelve Maps. . . [7s. 6d.

Vol. III. *West Africa.* With Five Maps. . . . . . [7s. 6d.

Vol. IV. *South and East Africa.* Historical and Geographical With Eleven Maps. . . . . [9s. 6d.

Also Vol. IV in two Parts—
Part I. *Historical.* 6s. 6d.   Part II. *Geographical.* 3s. 6d.

MATHEMATICS AND PHYSICAL SCIENCE.

Aldis. *A Text Book of Algebra (with Answers to the Examples).* By W. STEADMAN ALDIS, M.A. . . . . . . [Crown 8vo, 7s. 6d.

Emtage. *An Introduction to the Mathematical Theory of Electricity and Magnetism.* By W. T. A. EMTAGE, M.A. . [Crown 8vo, 7s. 6a.

Fisher. *Class-Book of Chemistry.* By W. W. FISHER, M.A., F.C.S. *Fourth Edition.* . . . . [Crown 8vo, 4s. 6d.

Fock. *An Introduction to Chemical Crystallography.* By ANDREAS FOCK, Ph.D. Translated and Edited by W. J. POPE. With a Preface by N. STORY-MASKELYNE, M.A., F.R.S. . . . . . [Crown 8vo, 5s.

Hamilton and Ball. *Book-keeping.* By Sir R. G. C. HAMILTON, K.C.B., and JOHN BALL. *New and Enlarged Edition.* [Extra fcap. 8vo, 2s.
  *** *Ruled Exercise Books adapted to the above may be had,* price 1s. 6d.;
  also, *adapted to the Preliminary Course only,* price 4d.

Harcourt and Madan. *Exercises in Practical Chemistry.* By A. G. VERNON HARCOURT, M.A., and H. G. MADAN, M.A. *Fifth Edition.* Revised by H. G. MADAN, M.A. . . . . . [Crown 8vo, 10s. 6d.

Hensley. *Figures made Easy: a first Arithmetic Book.* By LEWIS HENSLEY, M.A. . . . . . . [Crown 8vo, 6d. *Answers, 1s.*

—— *The Scholar's Arithmetic.* By the same Author.
  [Crown 8vo, 2s. 6d. *Answers, 1s. 6d.*

—— *The Scholar's Algebra.* An Introductory work on Algebra. By the same Author. . . . . . [Crown 8vo, 2s. 6d.

Johnston. *An Elementary Treatise on Analytical Geometry.* By W. J. JOHNSTON, M.A. Crown 8vo, 6s.

Minchin. *Geometry for Beginners.* An easy Introduction to Geometry for Young Learners. By GEORGE M. MINCHIN, M.A., F.R.S. Extra fcap. 8vo, 1s. 6d.

Nixon. *Euclid Revised.* Containing the essentials of the Elements of Plane Geometry as given by Euclid in his First Six Books. Edited by R. C. J. NIXON. M.A. *Third Edition.* . . . . . . [Crown 8vo, 6s.
  *** May likewise be had in parts as follows—
  Book I, 1s.   Books I, II, 1s. 6d.   Books I-IV, 3s.   Books V, VI, 3s. 6d

—— *Geometry in Space.* Containing parts of Euclid's Eleventh and Twelfth Books. By the same Author. . . . [Crown 8vo, 3s. 6d.

—— *Elementary Plane Trigonometry; that is, Plane Trigonometry without Imaginaries.* By the same Author. . . . [Crown 8vo, 7s. 6d.

Russell. *An Elementary Treatise on Pure Geometry.* By J. WELLESLEY RUSSELL, M.A. . . . . [Crown 8vo, 10s. 6d.

Selby. *Elementary Mechanics of Solids and Fluids.* By A. L. SELBY, M.A. . . . . [Crown 8vo, 7s. 6d.

Williamson. *Chemistry for Students.* By A. W. WILLIAMSON, Phil. Doc., F.R.S. . . . . [Extra fcap. 8vo, 8s. 6d.

Woollcombe. *Practical Work in General Physics.* By W. G. WOOLL-COMBE, M.A., B.Sc. . . . . [Crown 8vo, 2s.

—— *Practical Work in Heat.* By the same Author.
  [Crown 8vo, 2s.

—— *Practical Work in Light and Sound.* By the same Author.
  [Crown 8vo, 2s.

—— *Practical Work in Electricity and Magnetism.* By the same Author. *In the Press.*

MISCELLANEOUS.

Cookson. *Essays on Secondary Education.* By Various Contributors. Edited by CHRISTOPHER COOKSON, M.A.   . [Crown 8vo, *paper boards, 4s. 6d.*

Balfour. *The Educational Systems of Great Britain and Ireland.* By GRAHAM BALFOUR, M.A.   [Crown 8vo, 7s. 6d.

Buckmaster. *Elementary Architecture for Schools, Art Students, and General Readers.* By MARTIN A. BUCKMASTER. With thirty-eight full-page Illustrations.   .   .   .   . [Crown 8vo, 4s. 6d.

Fowler. *The Elements of Deductive and Inductive Logic.* By T. FOWLER, D.D.   .   .   .   . [Extra fcap. 8vo, 7s. 6d.

Also, separately—

The Elements of Deductive Logic, designed mainly for the use of Junior Students in the Universities. With a Collection of Examples.   [Extra fcap. 8vo, 3s. 6d.

The Elements of Inductive Logic, designed mainly for the use of Students in the Universities. *Sixth Edition.* .   .   . [Extra fcap. 8vo, 6s.

Music.—Farmer. *Hymns and Chorales for Schools and Colleges.* Edited by JOHN FARMER, Organist of Balliol College, Oxford   .   . [5s.
☞ *Hymns without the Tunes, 2s.*

Hullah. *The Cultivation of the Speaking Voice.* By JOHN HULLAH.   [Extra fcap. 8vo, 2s. 6d.

Maclaren. *A System of Physical Education: Theoretical and Practical.* By ARCHIBALD MACLAREN. *New Edition,* re-edited and enlarged by WALLACE MACLAREN, M.A., Ph.D.   .   .   . [Crown 8vo, 8s. 6d. net.

Troutbeck and **Dale.** *A Music Primer for Schools.* By J. TROUTBECK, D.D., and R. F. DALE, M.A., B.Mus. .   .   . [Crown 8vo, 1s. 6d.

Tyrwhitt. *Handbook of Pictorial Art.* With Illustrations, and a chapter on Perspective by A. MACDONALD. By R. ST. J. TYRWHITT, M.A. *Second Edition.*   .   .   .   . [8vo, *half-morocco,* 18s.

Upcott. *An Introduction to Greek Sculpture.* By L. E. UPCOTT, M.A. .   .   .   . [Crown 8vo, 4s. 6d.

Helps to the Study of the Bible, taken from the *Oxford Bible for Teachers.* New, Enlarged and Illustrated Edition. Pearl 16mo, stiff covers, 1s. *net.* Large Paper Edition, Long Primer 8vo, cloth boards, 5s.

Helps to the Study of the Book of Common Prayer. Being a Companion to Church Worship. By W. R. W. STEPHENS, B.D. [Crown 8vo, 2s.

The Parallel Psalter, being the Prayer-Book Version of the Psalms, and a new Version arranged on opposite pages. With an Introduction and Glossaries by the Rev. S. R. DRIVER, D.D., Litt.D. Fcap. 8vo, 6s.

Old Testament History for Schools. By T. H. STOKOE, D.D.
Part   I.   From the Creation to the Settlement in Palestine. (*Second Edition.*)
Part II.   From the Settlement to the Disruption of the Kingdom.
Part III.   From the Disruption to the Return from Captivity. *Completing the work.*   [Extra fcap. 8vo, 2s. 6d. each Part.

Notes on the Gospel of St. Luke, for Junior Classes. By E. J. MOORE SMITH, Lady Principal of the Ladies' College, Durban, Natal.   [Extra fcap. 8vo, *stiff covers,* 1s. 6d.

𝖮𝗑𝖿𝗈𝗋𝖽

AT THE CLARENDON PRESS

𝔏𝔬𝔫𝔡𝔬𝔫, 𝔈𝔡𝔦𝔫𝔟𝔲𝔯𝔤𝔥, 𝔞𝔫𝔡 𝔑𝔢𝔴 𝔜𝔬𝔯𝔨

HENRY FROWDE

Clarendon Press Series.

Modern Languages.

FRENCH.

Brachet. *Etymological Dictionary of the French Language,* with a Preface on the Principles of French Etymology. Translated into English by G. W. KITCHIN, D.D., Dean of Durham. *Third Edition.*   [Crown 8vo, 7s. 6d.

———— *Historical Grammar of the French Language.* Translated into English by G. W. KITCHIN, D.D. . . . [Extra fcap. 8vo, 3s. 6d.

Brachet and **Toynbee.** *A Historical Grammar of the French Language.* From the French of AUGUSTE BRACHET. Rewritten and Enlarged by PAGET TOYNBEE, M.A. . . . . [Crown 8vo, 7s. 6d.

Saintsbury. *Primer of French Literature.* By GEORGE SAINTS-BURY, M.A. *Fourth Edition, Revised.* . . . . [Extra fcap. 8vo, 2s.

———— *Short History of French Literature.* By the same Author. *Fifth Edition, Revised, with the Section on the Nineteenth Century greatly enlarged* . . . . [Crown 8vo, 10s. 6d.

———— *Specimens of French Literature,* from Villon to Hugo. By the same Author. . . . . [Crown 8vo, 9s.

Toynbee. *Specimens of Old French (ix–xv centuries).* With Introduction, Notes, and Glossary. By PAGET TOYNBEE, M.A.   [Crown 8vo, 16s.

———◆———

Beaumarchais. *Le Barbier de Séville.* With Introduction and Notes by AUSTIN DOBSON. . . . . [Extra fcap. 8vo, 2s. 6d.

Blouët. *L'Éloquence de la Chaire et de la Tribune Françaises.* Edited by PAUL BLOUËT, B.A. (Univ. Gallic.) Vol. I. *French Sacred Oratory.*   [Extra fcap. 8vo, 2s. 6d.

Corneille. *Horace.* With Introduction and Notes by GEORGE SAINTSBURY, M.A. . . . . [Extra fcap. 8vo, 2s. 6d.

———— *Cinna.* With Notes, Glossary, &c. By GUSTAVE MASSON, B.A. . . . . . . [Extra fcap. 8vo, *stiff covers,* 1s. 6d.; *cloth,* 2s.

Gautier (Théophile). *Scenes of Travel.* Selected and Edited by G. SAINTSBURY, M.A. . . . . [Extra fcap. 8vo, 2s.

Masson. *Louis XIV and his Contemporaries;* as described in Extracts from the best Memoirs of the Seventeenth Century. With English Notes, Genealogical Tables, &c. By GUSTAVE MASSON, B.A. [Extra fcap. 8vo, 2s. 6d.

Molière. *Les Précieuses Ridicules.* With Introduction and Notes by ANDREW LANG, M.A. . . . . . [Extra fcap. 8vo, 1s. 6d.

———— *Les Femmes Savantes.* With Notes, Glossary, &c. By GUSTAVE MASSON, B.A. . [Extra fcap. 8vo, *stiff covers,* 1s. 6d.; *cloth,* 2s.

———— *Le Misanthrope.* Edited by H. W. GEGG MARKHEIM, M.A.   [Extra fcap. 8vo, 3s. 6d.

Molière. *Les Fourberies de Scapin.* With Voltaire's Life of Molière. By Gustave Masson, B.A. . . . [Extra fcap. 8vo, *stiff covers,* 1s. 6d.

Musset. *On ne badine pas avec l'Amour,* and *Fantasio.* With Introduction, Notes, &c., by Walter Herries Pollock. [Extra fcap. 8vo, 2s.

NOVELETTES—

Xavier de Maistre.	*Voyage autour de ma Chambre.*	
Madame de Duras.	*Ourika.*	By Gustave
Erckmann-Chatrian.	*Le Vieux Tailleur.*	Masson, B.A.,
Alfred de Vigny.	*La Veillée de Vincennes.*	3rd Edition. Ext. fcap. 8vo,
Edmond About.	*Les Jumeaux de l'Hôtel Corneille.*	2s. 6d.
Rodolphe Töpffer.	*Mésaventures d'un Écolier.*	

Voyage autour de ma Chambre, separately, limp, 1s. 6d.

Quinet. *Lettres à sa Mère.* Edited by G. Saintsbury, M.A. [Extra fcap. 8vo, 2s.

Racine. *Esther.* Edited by G. Saintsbury, M.A. [Extra fcap. 8vo, 2s.

Regnard. . . . *Le Joueur.* } By Gustave Masson, B.A.
Brueys and Palaprat. *Le Grondeur.* } [Extra fcap. 8vo, 2s. 6d.

Sainte-Beuve. *Selections from the Causeries du Lundi.* Edited by G. Saintsbury, M.A. . . . . [Extra fcap. 8vo, 2s.

Sévigné. *Selections from the Correspondence of* **Madame de Sévigné** and her chief Contemporaries. By Gustave Masson, B.A. [Extra fcap. 8vo, 3s.

Voltaire. *Mérope.* Edited by G. Saintsbury, M.A. [Extra fcap. 8vo, 2s.

ITALIAN AND SPANISH.

Primer of Italian Literature. By F. J. Snell, B.A.
[Extra fcap. 8vo, 3s. 6d.

Dante. *Tutte le Opere di Dante Alighieri,* nuovamente rivedute nel testo dal Dr. E. Moore: Con un Indice dei Nomi Propri e delle Cose Notevoli contenute nelle Opere di Dante, compilato da Paget Toynbee, M.A.
[Crown 8vo, 7s. 6d.
*** Also, an India Paper edition, cloth extra, 9s. 6d.; and Miniature edition, 3 vols., in case, 10s. 6d.

—— *Selections from the 'Inferno.'* With Introduction and Notes, by H. B. Cotterill, B.A. . . . . . [Extra fcap. 8vo, 4s. 6d.

Tasso. *La Gerusalemme Liberata.* Cantos i, ii. With Introduction and Notes by the same Editor. . . . . [Extra fcap. 8vo, 2s. 6d.

Cervantes. *The Adventure of the Wooden Horse, and Sancho Panza's Governorship.* Edited, with Introduction, Life and Notes, by Clovis Bévenot, M.A. . . . . [Extra fcap. 8vo, 2s. 6d.

GERMAN, &c.

Buchheim. *Modern German Reader.* A Graduated Collection of Extracts in Prose and Poetry from Modern German Writers. Edited by C. A. BUCHHEIM, Phil. Doc.

    Part I. With English Notes, a Grammatical Appendix, and a complete Vocabulary. *Seventh Edition.* . . . [Extra fcap. 8vo, 2s. 6d.

    Part II. With English Notes and an Index. . [Extra fcap. 8vo, 2s. 6d.

———— *German Poetry for Beginners.* Edited, with Notes and Vocabulary, by EMMA S. BUCHHEIM. . . . . [Extra fcap. 8vo, 2s.

———— *Short German Plays, for Reading and Acting.* With Notes and a Vocabulary. By the same Editor. . . . [Extra fcap. 8vo, 3s.

———— *Elementary German Prose Composition.* By EMMA S. BUCHHEIM. *Second Edition.* [Extra fcap. 8vo, *cloth*, 2s. ; *stiff covers*, 1s. 6d.

Lange. *The Germans at Home;* a Practical Introduction to German Conversation, with an Appendix containing the Essentials of German Grammar. By HERMANN LANGE. *Third Edition.* . . . . . [8vo, 2s. 6d.

———— *The German Manual;* a German Grammar, a Reading Book, and a Handbook of German Conversation. By the same Author. [7s. 6d.

———— *A Grammar of the German Language,* being a reprint of the Grammar contained in *The German Manual.* By the same Author. [8vo, 3s. 6d.

———— *German Composition;* a Theoretical and Practical Guide to the Art of Translating English Prose into German. By the same Author. *Third Edition.* . . . . [8vo, 4s. 6d.

      [A Key to the above, price 5s.]

———— *German Spelling:* A Synopsis of the Changes which it has undergone through the Government Regulations of 1880. . [*Paper cover,* 6d.

Becker's 'Friedrich der Grosse. With an Historical Sketch of the Rise of Prussia and of the Times of Frederick the Great. With Map. Edited by C. A. BUCHHEIM, Phil. Doc. . . . [Extra fcap. 8vo, 3s. 6d.

Chamisso. *Peter Schlemihl's Wundersame Geschichte.* With Notes and Vocabulary. By EMMA S. BUCHHEIM. *Fourth Thousand.* [Extra fcap. 8vo, 2s.

Goethe. *Egmont.* With a Life of Goethe, &c. Edited by C. A. BUCHHEIM, Phil. Doc. *Fourth Edition.* . . . [Extra fcap. 8vo, 3s.

———— *Iphigenie auf Tauris.* A Drama. With a Critical Introduction and Notes. Edited by C. A. BUCHHEIM, Phil. Doc. *Fourth Edition.* [Extra fcap. 8vo, 3s.

———— *Dichtung und Wahrheit:* (The First Four Books.) Edited by C. A. BUCHHEIM, Phil. Doc. . . . . . [Extra fcap. 8vo, 4s. 6d.

Halm's *Griseldis.* With English Notes, &c. Edited by C. A. BUCHHEIM, Phil. Doc. . . . . [Extra fcap. 8vo, 3s.

Heine's *Harzreise.* With a Life of Heine, &c. With Map. Edited by C. A. BUCHHEIM, Phil. Doc. *Second Edition.* [Extra fcap. 8vo, *cloth*, 2s. 6d.

———— *Prosa,* being Selections from his Prose Works. Edited, with English Notes, &c., by C. A. BUCHHEIM, Phil. Doc. [Extra fcap. 8vo, 4s. 6d.

Hoffmann's *Heute Mir Morgen Dir.* Edited by J. H. MAUDE, M.A. [Extra fcap. 8vo, 2s.

Lessing. *Laokoon.* With Notes, &c. By A. HAMANN, Phil. Doc.,
M.A. Revised, with an Introduction, by L. E. UPCOTT, M.A.
[Extra fcap. 8vo, 4*s*. 6*d*.

———— *Minna von Barnhelm.* A Comedy. With a Life of Lessing,
Critical Analysis, Complete Commentary, &c. Edited by C. A. BUCHHEIM,
Phil. Doc. *Seventh Edition.* . . . . [Extra fcap. 8vo, 3*s*. 6*d*.

———— *Nathan der Weise.* With English Notes, &c. Edited by
C. A. BUCHHEIM, Phil. Doc. *Second Edition.* . [Extra fcap. 8vo, 4*s*. 6*d*.

Niebuhr's *Griechische Heroen-Geschichten.* Tales of Greek Heroes.
Edited with English Notes and a Vocabulary, by EMMA S. BUCHHEIM.
Edition A. Text in German Type. ⎱ [Extra fcap. 8vo, *stiff, 1s. 6d.;*
Edition B. Text in Roman Type. ⎰ *cloth, 2s.*

Riehl's *Seines Vaters Sohn* and *Gespensterkampf.* Edited with Notes,
by H. T. GERRANS. . . . . [Extra fcap. 8vo, 2*s*.

Schiller's *Historische Skizzen:—Egmonts Leben und Tod,* and *Bela-
gerung von Antwerpen.* Edited by C. A. BUCHHEIM, Phil. Doc. *Fifth
Edition, Revised and Enlarged, with a Map.* . [Extra fcap. 8vo, 2*s*. 6*d*.

———— *Wilhelm Tell.* With a Life of Schiller; an Historical and
Critical Introduction, Arguments, a Complete Commentary, and Map. Edited
by C. A. BUCHHEIM, Phil. Doc. *Seventh Edition.* [Extra fcap. 8vo, 3*s*. 6*d*.

———— *Wilhelm Tell.* Edited by C. A. BUCHHEIM, Phil. Doc.
School Edition. With Map. . . . . . [Extra fcap. 8vo, 2*s*.

———— *Jungfrau von Orleans.* Edited by C. A. BUCHHEIM, Phil.
Doc. *Second Edition.* . . . . . [Extra fcap. 8vo, 4*s*. 6*d*.

———— *Maria Stuart.* Edited by C. A. BUCHHEIM, Phil. Doc.
[Extra fcap. 8vo, 3*s*. 6*d*.

Scherer. *A History of German Literature.* By W. SCHERER.
Translated from the Third German Edition by Mrs. F. C. CONYBEARE. Edited
by The Rt. Hon. F. MAX MÜLLER. 2 vols. . . . . . ' [8vo, 21*s*.
*** Or, separately, 10*s*. 6*d*. each volume.

———— *A History of German Literature from the Accession of Frederick
the Great to the Death of Goethe.* Reprinted from the above. [Crown 8vo, 5*s*.

Max Müller. *The German Classics from the Fourth to the Nineteenth
Century.* With Biographical Notices, Translations into Modern German, and
Notes, by The Rt. Hon. F. MAX MÜLLER, M.A. A New edition, revised,
enlarged, and adapted to WILHELM SCHERER's *History of German Literature,*
by F. LICHTENSTEIN. 2 vols. . . . . . . [Crown 8vo, 21*s*.
*** Or, separately, 10*s*. 6*d*. each volume.

Wright. *An Old High German Primer.* With Grammar, Notes,
and Glossary. By JOSEPH WRIGHT, M.A., Ph.D. . [Extra fcap. 8vo, 3*s*. 6*d*.

———— *A Middle High German Primer.* With Grammar, Notes,
and Glossary. By the same Author. . . . [Extra fcap. 8vo, 3*s*. 6*d*.

———— *A Primer of the Gothic Language.* With Grammar, Notes, and
Glossary. By the same Author. . . . . [Extra fcap. 8vo, 4*s*. 6*d*.

Oxford

AT THE CLARENDON PRESS

London, Edinburgh, and New York

HENRY FROWDE

𝔈𝔩𝔞𝔯𝔢𝔫𝔡𝔬𝔫 𝔓𝔯𝔢𝔰𝔰 𝔖𝔢𝔯𝔦𝔢𝔰.

Latin Educational Works.

GRAMMARS, LEXICONS, &c.

Allen. *Rudimenta Latina.* Comprising Accidence, and Exercises of a very Elementary Character, for the use of Beginners. By J. BARROW ALLEN, M.A. . . . . [Extra fcap. 8vo, 2s.

—— *An Elementary Latin Grammar.* By the same Author. *New Edition, Revised and Enlarged.* . . . . [Extra fcap. 8vo, 2s. 6d.

— *A First Latin Exercise Book.* By the same Author. *Eighth Edition.* . . . . [Extra fcap. 8vo, 2s. 6d.

—— *A Second Latin Exercise Book.* By the same Author. *Second Edition.* . . . . [Extra fcap. 8vo, 3s. 6d.

[A Key to First and Second Latin Exercise Books : for Teachers only, price 5s.]

Fox and **Bromley.** *Models and Exercises in Unseen Translation.* By H. F. Fox, M.A., and T. M. BROMLEY, M.A. [Extra fcap. 8vo, 5s. 6d.

[A Key to Passages quoted in the above: for Teachers only, price 6d.]

Gibson. *An Introduction to Latin Syntax.* By W. S. GIBSON, M.A. [Extra fcap. 8vo, 2s.

Jerram. *Reddenda Minora.* By C. S. JERRAM, M.A. [Extra fcap. 8vo, 1s. 6d.

—— *Anglice Reddenda.* FIRST SERIES. [Extra fcap. 8vo, 2s. 6d.

— -- *Anglice Reddenda.* SECOND SERIES. [Extra fcap. 8vo, 3s.

—— *Anglice Reddenda.* THIRD SERIES. [Extra fcap. 8vo, 3s.

Lee-Warner. *Hints and Helps for Latin Elegiacs.* By H. LEE-WARNER, M.A. . . . . [Extra fcap. 8vo, 3s. 6d.

[A Key is provided : for Teachers only, price 4s. 6d.]

Lewis. *An Elementary Latin Dictionary.* By CHARLTON T. LEWIS, Ph.D. . . . . [Square 8vo, 7s. 6d.

—— *A Latin Dictionary for Schools.* By the same Author. [Small 4to, 18s.

Lindsay. *A Short Historical Latin Grammar.* By W. M. LINDSAY, M.A. . . . . [Crown 8vo, 5s. 6d.

Nunns. *First Latin Reader.* By T. J. NUNNS, M.A. *Third Edition.* [Extra fcap. 8vo, 2s.

Ramsay. *Latin Prose Composition.* By G. G. RAMSAY, M.A., LL.D. *Fourth Edition.* Extra fcap. 8vo.

Vol. I. *Syntax, Exercises with Notes, &c., 4s. 6d.*

Or in two Parts, 2s. 6d. each, viz.

Part I. *The Simple Sentence.* Part II. *The Compound Sentence.*

. *A Key to the above, price 5s. net. Supplied to Teachers only, on application to the Secretary, Clarendon Press.*

Vol. II. *Passages of Graduated Difficulty for Translation into Latin, together with an Introduction on Continuous Prose, 4s. 6d.*

Ramsay. *Latin Prose Versions.* Contributed by various Scholars. Edited by G. G. RAMSAY, M.A., LL.D. . . . [Extra fcap. 8vo, 5s.

Owen and **Phillimore**. *Mvsa Clavda.* Translations into Latin Elegiac Verse. By S. G. OWEN and J. S. PHILLIMORE. [Crown 8vo, paper boards, 3*s.* 6*d.*

Sargent. *Easy Passages for Translation into Latin.* By J. Y. SARGENT, M.A. *Seventh Edition.* . . . . . [Extra fcap. 8vo, 2*s.* 6*d.*
    [*A Key to this Edition is provided : for Teachers only, price 5s., net.*]
—— *A Latin Prose Primer.* By the same Author. [Ex. fcap. 8vo, 2*s.* 6*d.*

King and **Cookson.** *The Principles of Sound and Inflexion, as illustrated in the Greek and Latin Languages.* By J. E. KING, M.A., and CHRISTOPHER COOKSON, M.A. . . . . [8vo, 18*s.*
—— *An Introduction to the Comparative Grammar of Greek and Latin.* By the same Authors. . . . . . [Crown 8vo, 5*s.* 6*d.*

Papillon. *A Manual of Comparative Philology.* By T. L. PAPILLON, M.A. *Third Edition.* . . . . [Crown 8vo, 6*s.*

Caesar. *The Commentaries* (for Schools). With Notes and Maps. By CHARLES E. MOBERLY, M.A.
  The Gallic War. New Edition. Extra fcap. 8vo—
    Books I and II, 2*s.* ; I-III, 2*s.* ; III-V, 2*s.* 6*d.* ; VI-VIII, 3*s.* 6*d.*
  The Civil War. Second Edition. . . . [Extra fcap. 8vo, 3*s.* 6*d.*

Catulli Veronensis *Carmina Selecta,* secundum recognitionem ROBINSON ELLIS, A.M. . . . . . [Extra fcap. 8vo, 3*s.* 6*d.*

Cicero. *Selection of Interesting and Descriptive Passages.* With Notes. By HENRY WALFORD, M.A. In three Parts. *Third Edition.*
                           [Extra fcap. 8vo, 4*s.* 6*d.*
  Part I. *Anecdotes from Grecian and Roman History.* . [*limp*, 1*s.* 6*d.*
  Part II. *Omens and Dreams; Beauties of Nature..* . [,, 1*s.* 6*d.*
  Part III. *Rome's Rule of her Provinces.* . . . . [,, 1*s.* 6*d.*
—— *De Amicitia.* With Introduction and Notes. By ST. GEORGE STOCK, M.A. . . . . [Extra fcap. 8vo, 3*s.*
—— *De Senectute.* With Introduction and Notes. By LEONARD HUXLEY, B.A. *In one or two Parts.* . . . . [Extra fcap. 8vo, 2*s.*
—— *Pro Cluentio.* With Introduction and Notes. By W. RAMSAY, M.A. Edited by G. G. RAMSAY, M.A. *Second Edition.* [Extra fcap. 8vo, 3*s.* 6*d.*
—— *Pro Marcello, pro Ligario, pro Rege Deiotaro.* With Introduction and Notes. By W. Y. FAUSSET, M.A. . . . [Extra fcap. 8vo, 2*s.* 6*d.*
—— *Pro Milone.* With Notes, &c. By A. B. POYNTON, M.A.
                           [Extra fcap. 8vo, 2*s.* 6*d.*
—— *Pro Roscio.* With Introduction and Notes. By ST. GEORGE STOCK, M.A. . . . . [Extra fcap. 8vo, 3*s.* 6*d.*
—— *Select Orations* (for Schools). *In Verrem Actio Prima. De Imperio Gn. Pompeii. Pro Archia. Philippica IX.* With Introduction and Notes. By J. R. KING, M.A. *Second Edition.* . [Extra fcap. 8vo, 2*s.* 6*d.*
—— *In Q. Caecilium Divinatio* and *In C. Verrem Actio Prima.* With Introduction and Notes. By J. R. KING, M.A. [Extra fcap. 8vo, 1*s.* 6*d.*
—— *Speeches against Catilina.* With Introduction and Notes. By E. A. UPCOTT, M.A. *Second Edition.* . . . [Extra fcap. 8vo, 2*s.* 6*d.*

Cicero. *Philippic Orations.* With Notes, &c., by J. R. KING, M.A. *Second Edition.* . . . . [8vo, 10s. 6d.

—— *Selected Letters* (for Schools). With Notes. By C. E. PRICHARD, M.A., and E. R. BERNARD, M.A. *Second Edition.*
[Extra fcap. 8vo, 3s.

—— *Select Letters.* With English Introductions, Notes, and Appendices. By ALBERT WATSON, M.A. *Fourth Edition.* . . [8vo, 18s.

—— *Select Letters.* Text. By the same Editor. *Second Edition.*
[Extra fcap. 8vo, 4s.

Early Roman Poetry. *Selected Fragments.* With Introduction and Notes. By W. W. MERRY, D.D. . . . . . [Crown 8vo, 6s. 6d.

Horace. With a Commentary. Volume I. *The Odes, Carmen Seculare,* and *Epodes.* By EDWARD C. WICKHAM, D.D. *New Edition.*
[Extra fcap. 8vo, 6s.

—— *Odes,* Book I. By the same Editor. . . [Extra fcap. 8vo, 2s.

—— *Selected Odes.* With Notes for the use of a Fifth Form. By the same Editor. . . . . [Extra fcap. 8vo, 2s.

—— *The Complete Works.* By the same Editor.
[On writing-paper, 32mo, 3s. 6d.; on India paper, 5s.

Juvenal. *XIII Satires.* Edited, with Introduction, Notes, &c., by C. H. PEARSON, M.A., and H. A. STRONG, M.A. *Second Edition.* [Crown 8vo, 9s.

Livy. *Selections* (for Schools). With Notes and Maps. By H. LEE-WARNER, M.A. . . . . [Extra fcap. 8vo.
 Part I. *The Caudine Disaster.* . . . . . *[limp,* 1s. 6d.
 Part II. *Hannibal's Campaign in Italy.* . . . . [„ 1s. 6d.
 Part III. *The Macedonian War.* . . . . . . [„ 1s. 6d.

—— *Book I.* With Introduction, Historical Examination, and Notes. By J. R. SEELEY, M.A. *Third Edition.* . . . . . . [8vo, 6s.

—— *Books V—VII.* With Introduction and Notes. By A. R. CLUER, B.A. *Second Edition.* Revised by P. E. MATHESON, M.A. [Extra fcap. 8vo, 5s. *Book V,* 2s. 6d.; *Book VII,* 2s. By the same Editors.

—— *Books XXI—XXIII.* With Introduction, Notes, and Maps. By M. T. TATHAM, M.A. *Second Edition* . . . [Extra fcap. 8vo, 5s.

—— *Book XXI.* By the same Editor. . . [Extra fcap. 8vo, 2s. 6d.

—— *Book XXII.* By the same Editor. . . [Extra fcap. 8vo, 2s. 6d.

Nepos. With Notes. By OSCAR BROWNING, M.A. *Third Edition.* Revised by W. R. INGE, M.A. . . . [Extra fcap. 8vo, 3s.

—— *Lives from.* *Miltiades, Themistocles, Pausanias.* With Notes, Maps, Vocabularies, and English Exercises. By JOHN BARROW ALLEN, M.A.
[Extra fcap. 8vo, 1s. 6d.

Ovid. *Selections* (for the use of Schools). With Introductions and Notes, and an Appendix on the Roman Calendar. By W. RAMSAY, M.A. Edited by G. G. RAMSAY, M.A. *Third Edition.* . [Extra fcap. 8vo, 5s. 6d.

—— *Tristia,* Book I. The Text revised, with an Introduction and Notes. By S. G. OWEN, B.A. *Second Edition.* . [Extra fcap. 8vo, 3s. 6d.

—— *Tristia,* Book III. With Introduction and Notes. By the same Editor. . . . . [Extra fcap. 8vo, 2s.

Persius. *The Satires.* With Translation and Commentary by J. Conington, M.A., edited by H. Nettleship, M.A. *Third Edition.* [8vo, 8s. 6d.

Plautus. *Captivi.* With Introduction and Notes. By W. M. Lindsay, M.A. . . . . [Extra fcap. 8vo, 2s. 6d.

—— *Trinummus.* With Notes and Introductions. By C. E. Freeman, M.A., and A. Sloman, M.A. . . . . . [Extra fcap. 8vo, 3s.

Pliny. *Selected Letters* (for Schools). By C. E. Prichard, M.A., and E. R. Bernard, M.A. *Third Edition.* . . . [Extra fcap. 8vo, 3s.

Quintilian. *Institutionis Oratoriae Liber X.* Edited by W. Peterson, M.A. . . . . [Extra fcap. 8vo, 3s. 6d.

Sallust. *Bellum Catilinarium* and *Jugurthinum.* With Introduction and Notes, by W. W. Capes, M.A. . . [Extra fcap. 8vo, 4s. 6d.

Tacitus. *The Annals.* Books I—IV. Edited, with Introduction and Notes for the use of Schools and Junior Students, by H. Furneaux, M.A.
[Extra fcap. 8vo, 5s.

—— *The Annals.* Book I. By the same Editor. . . [*limp*, 2s.

—— *The Annals.* (Text only). . . . . . [Crown 8vo, 6s.

Terence. *Adelphi.* With Notes and Introductions. By A. Sloman, M.A. . . . . [Extra fcap. 8vo, 3s.

—— *Andria.* With Notes and Introductions. By C. E. Freeman, M.A., and A. Sloman, M.A. *Second Edition* . . [Extra fcap. 8vo, 3s.

—— *Phormio.* With Notes and Introductions. By A. Sloman, M.A. . . . . [Extra fcap. 8vo, 3s.

Tibullus and **Propertius.** *Selections.* Edited, with Introduction and Notes, by G. G. Ramsay, M.A. *Second Edition.* . [Extra fcap. 8vo, 6s.

Virgil. With an Introduction and Notes. By T. L. Papillon, M.A., and A. E. Haigh, M.A.
[Crown 8vo, 2 vols., *cloth, price 6s. each, or in stiff covers,* 3s. 6d. each.

—— *The Text, including the Minor Works.*
[On writing-paper, 32mo, 3s. 6d.; on India paper, 5s.

—— *Aeneid.* With Introduction and Notes, by the same Editors. In Four Parts. . . . . [Crown 8vo, 2s. each.

—— *Aeneid I.* With Introduction and Notes, by C. S. Jerram, M.A.
[Extra fcap. 8vo, *limp*, 1s. 6d.

—— *Aeneid IX.* Edited, with Introduction and Notes, by A. E. Haigh, M.A. . . . [Extra fcap. 8vo, *limp*, 1s. 6d. *In two Parts*, 2s.

—— *Bucolics.* With Introduction and Notes, by C. S. Jerram, M.A.
[Extra fcap. 8vo, 2s. 6d.

—— *Bucolics and Georgics.* By T. L. Papillon, M.A., and A. E. Haigh, M.A. . . . . [Crown 8vo, 2s. 6d.

—— *Georgics.* Books I, II. By C. S. Jerram, M.A. [Extra fcap. 8vo, 2s. 6d.

—— *Georgics.* Books III, IV. By the same Editor. [Extra fcap. 8vo, 2s. 6d.

𝕺𝖝𝖋𝖔𝖗𝖉

AT THE CLARENDON PRESS

𝕷𝖔𝖓𝖉𝖔𝖓, 𝕰𝖉𝖎𝖓𝖇𝖚𝖗𝖌𝖍, 𝖆𝖓𝖉 𝕹𝖊𝖜 𝖄𝖔𝖗𝖐

HENRY FROWDE

𝕮𝖑𝖆𝖗𝖊𝖓𝖉𝖔𝖓 𝕻𝖗𝖊𝖘𝖘 𝕾𝖊𝖗𝖎𝖊𝖘.

Greek Educational Works.

GRAMMARS, LEXICONS, &c.

Chandler. *The Elements of Greek Accentuation* (for Schools). By H. W. CHANDLER, M.A. *Second Edition.* . [Extra fcap. 8vo, 2s. 6d.

Fox and **Bromley.** *Models and Exercises in Unseen Translation.* By H. F. Fox, M.A., and T. M. BROMLEY, M.A. [Extra fcap. 8vo, 5s. 6d.

[*A Key to Passages quoted in the above: for Teachers only, price 6d.*]

Jerram. *Graece Reddenda.* By C. S. JERRAM, M.A. . . [2s. 6d.

—— *Reddenda Minora.* . . . . [Extra fcap. 8vo, 1s. 6d.

—— *Anglice Reddenda.* First Series. . [Extra fcap. 8vo, 2s. 6d.

—— —— Second Series. . . . .. [Extra fcap. 8vo, 3s.

—— —— Third Series. . . . . . [Extra fcap. 8vo, 3s.

Liddell and **Scott.** *A Greek-English Lexicon.* . . [4to, 36s.

—— *An Intermediate Greek-English Lexicon.* [Small 4to, 12s. 6d.

—— *A Greek-English Lexicon,* abridged. . [Square 12mo, 7s. 6d.

Sargent. *A Primer of Greek Prose Composition.* By J. YOUNG SARGENT, M.A. . . . . . . [Extra fcap. 8vo, 3s. 6d.

₊ A Key to the above, price 5s. Supplied *to Teachers only*, on application to the Secretary, Clarendon Press.

—— *Passages for Translation into Greek Prose.* [Extra fcap. 8vo, 3s.

—— *Exemplaria Graeca*; being Greek Renderings of Selected "Passages for Translation into Greek Prose." . . . [Extra fcap. 8vo, 3s.

—— *Models and Materials for Greek Iambic Verse.* . . [4s. 6d.

Wordsworth. *A Greek Primer.* By the Right Rev. CHARLES WORDSWORTH, D.C.L. *Eighty-third Thousand.* [Extra fcap. 8vo, 1s. 6d.

—— *Graecae Grammaticae Rudimenta in usum Scholarum.* Auctore CAROLO WORDSWORTH, D.C.L. *Nineteenth Edition.* . . . [12mo, 4s.

King and **Cookson.** *An Introduction to the Comparative Grammar of Greek and Latin.* By J. E. KING, M.A., and C. COOKSON, M.A.
[Crown 8vo, 5s. 6d.

Papillon. *A Manual of Comparative Philology.* By T. L. PAPILLON, M.A. . . . . [Crown 8vo, 6s.

A COURSE OF GREEK READERS.

Easy Greek Reader. By EVELYN ABBOTT, M.A. [Extra fcap. 8vo, 3s.

First Greek Reader. By W. G. RUSHBROOKE, M.L. *Third Edition.*
[Extra fcap. 8vo, 2s. 6d.

Second Greek Reader. By A. M. BELL, M.A. [Extra fcap. 8vo, 3*s*.

Specimens of Greek Dialects; being *a Fourth Greek Reader*. With Introductions and Notes. By W. W. MERRY, D.D.   [Extra fcap. 8vo, 4*s*. 6*d*.

Selections from Homer and the Greek Dramatists; being *a Fifth Greek Reader*. By EVELYN ABBOTT, M.A. . .   [Extra fcap. 8vo, 4*s*. 6*d*.

Wright. *The Golden Treasury of Ancient Greek Poetry*. By Sir R. S. WRIGHT, M.A. *Second Edition, Revised.* . .   [Extra fcap. 8vo, 10*s*. 6*d*.

Wright and **Shadwell.** *A Golden Treasury of Greek Prose*. By Sir R. S. WRIGHT, M.A., and J. E. L. SHADWELL, M.A. [Extra fcap. 8vo, 4*s*. 6*d*.

THE GREEK TESTAMENT.

A Greek Testament Primer. An Easy Grammar and Reading Book for the use of Students beginning Greek. By E. MILLER, M.A. *Second Edition.*
[Extra fcap. 8vo, *paper covers*, 2*s*. ; *cloth*, 3*s*. 6*d*.

Evangelia Sacra Graece. . .   [Fcap. 8vo, *limp*, 1*s*. 6*d*.

Novum Testamentum Graece juxta Exemplar Millianum.   [2*s*. 6*d*.

Novum Testamentum Graece. Accedunt parallela S. Scripturae loca, &c. Edidit CAROLUS LLOYD, S.T.P.R. . . . .   [18mo, 3*s*.

—— Critical Appendices to the above. By W. SANDAY, M.A. 3*s*. 6*d*.

The Greek Testament, with the Readings adopted by the Revisers of the Authorised Version, and Marginal References. . . [Fcap. 8vo, 4*s*. 6*d*.

Outlines of Textual Criticism applied to the New Testament. By C. E. HAMMOND, M.A. *Fifth Edition.* . . .   [Crown 8vo, 4*s*. 6*d*.

GREEK CLASSICS FOR SCHOOLS.

Aeschylus. *Agamemnon.* With Introduction and Notes, by ARTHUR SIDGWICK, M.A. *Fourth Edition.* . . . . [Extra fcap. 8vo, 3*s*.

—— *Choephoroi.* By the same Editor. . . .[Extra fcap. 8vo, 3*s*.

—— *Eumenides.* By the same Editor. . . . [Extra fcap. 8vo, 3*s*.

—— *Prometheus Bound.* With Introduction and Notes, by A. O. PRICKARD, M.A. *Second Edition.* . . . . [Extra fcap. 8vo, 2*s*.

Aristophanes. *The Acharnians.* With Introduction and Notes, by W. W. MERRY, D.D. *Fourth Edition.* . . . [Extra fcap. 8vo, 3*s*.

—— *The Birds.* By the same Editor. . . [Extra fcap. 8vo, 3*s*. 6*d*.

—— *The Clouds.* By the same Editor. *Third Edition.*
[Extra fcap. 8vo, 3*s*.

—— *The Frogs.* By the same Editor . . [Extra fcap. 8vo, 3*s*.

—— *The Knights.* By the same Editor. . [Extra fcap. 8vo, 3*s*.

—— *The Wasps.* By the same Editor , . [Extra fcap. 8vo, 3*s*. 6*d*.

Cebes. *Tabula.* With Introduction and Notes, by C. S. JERRAM, M.A.
[Extra fcap. 8vo, 2*s*. 6*d*.

*** Abridged School Edition. Paper boards,* 1*s*. 6*d*.

Demosthenes. *Orations against Philip.* With Introduction and Notes. By Evelyn Abbott, M.A., and P. E. Matheson, M.A.

    Vol. I. *Philippic I* and *Olynthiacs I—III.* . . [Extra fcap. 8vo, 3s.

    Vol. II. *De Pace, Philippic II, De Chersoneso, Philippic III.* . [4s. 6d.

    Philippics only, reprinted from the above, 2s. 6d.

Euripides. *Alcestis.* By C. S. Jerram, M.A. [Extra fcap. 8vo, 2s. 6d.

—— *Bacchae.* By A. H. Cruickshank, M.A. . . [3s. 6d.

—— *Cyclops.* By W. E. Long, M.A. . [Extra fcap. 8vo, 2s. 6d.

—— *Hecuba.* By C. H. Russell, M.A. [Extra fcap. 8vo, 2s. 6d.

—— *Helena.* By C. S. Jerram, M.A. . . [Extra fcap. 8vo, 3s.

—— *Heracleidae.* By the same Editor. . . [Extra fcap. 8vo, 3s.

—— *Ion.* By the same Editor. . . . [Extra fcap. 8vo, 3s.

—— *Iphigenia in Tauris.* By the same Editor. [Extra fcap. 8vo, 3s.

—— *Medea.* With Introduction, Notes, and Appendices. By C. B. Heberden, M.A. *In one or two Parts.* . . . [Extra fcap. 8vo, 2s.

Herodotus. Book IX. Edited, with Notes, by Evelyn Abbott, M.A. *In one or two Parts.* . . . . . . [Extra fcap. 8vo, 3s.

—— *Selections.* Edited, with Introduction, Notes, and a Map, by W. W. Merry, D.D. . . . . . . [Extra fcap. 8vo, 2s. 6d.

Homer for Beginners. *Iliad,* Book III. By M. T. Tatham, M.A. [Extra fcap. 8vo, 1s. 6d.

Homer. *Iliad,* Books I–XII. With an Introduction, a brief Homeric Grammar, and Notes. By D. B. Monro, M.A. . . [Extra fcap. 8vo, 6s.

—— *Iliad,* Books XIII–XXIV. By the same Editor. . . [6s.

—— *Iliad,* Book I. By the same Editor. . [Extra fcap. 8vo, 1s. 6d.

—— *Iliad,* Book XXI. By Herbert Hailstone, M.A. [1s. 6d.

—— *Odyssey,* Books I–XII. By W. W. Merry, D.D. . . [5s.

—— *Odyssey,* Books I and II. By the same Editor. . [Each 1s. 6d.

—— *Odyssey,* Books VI and VII. By the same Editor. . [1s. 6d.

—— *Odyssey,* Books VII–XII. By the same Editor. [Extra fcap. 8vo, 3s.

—— *Odyssey,* Books XIII–XXIV. By the same Editor. *New Edition.* . . . . [Extra fcap. 8vo, 5s.

—— *Odyssey,* Books XIII–XVIII. By the same Editor. [Extra fcap. 8vo, 3s.

Lucian. *Vera Historia.* By C. S. Jerram, M.A. [Extra fcap. 8vo, 1s. 6d.

Lysias. *Epitaphios.* Edited by F. J. Snell, B.A. [Extra fcap. 8vo, 2s.

Plato. *The Apology.* With Introduction and Notes. By St. George Stock, M.A. *Second Edition.* . . . . [Extra fcap. 8vo, 2s. 6d.

—— *Crito.* With Introduction and Notes. By the same Editor. [2s.

—— *Meno.* By the same Editor. . . [Extra fcap. 8vo, 2s. 6d.

Plato. *Selections.* With Introductions and Notes. By J. PURVES, M.A., and Preface by B. JOWETT, M.A. *Second Edition.* . [Extra fcap. 8vo, 5s.

Plutarch. *Lives of the Gracchi.* Edited, with Introduction, Notes, and Indices, by G. E. UNDERHILL, M.A. . . . . [Crown 8vo, 4s. 6d.

Sophocles. Edited, with Introductions and English Notes, by LEWIS CAMPBELL, M.A., and EVELYN ABBOTT, M.A. New Edition. 2 Vols. 10s. 6d. [or, Vol. I. Text, 4s. 6d. ; Vol. II. Notes, 6s.

☞ *Also in single Plays. Extra fcap. 8vo, limp, 2s. each.*

-— *Oedipus Rex:* Dindorf's Text, with Notes by W. BASIL JONES, D.D., late Bishop of St. David's. . . . [Extra fcap. 8vo, *limp,* 1s. 6d.

Theocritus. Edited, with Notes, by H. KYNASTON, D.D. (late SNOW). *Fifth Edition.* . . . . [Extra fcap. 8vo, 4s. 6d.

Thucydides. Book I. With Introduction, Notes, and Maps. By W. H. FORBES, M.A. . . . . [8vo, 8s. 6d.

Xenophon. *Easy Selections.* By J. S. PHILLPOTTS, B.C.L., and C. S. JERRAM, M.A. With Map. *Third Edition.* . . . . . [3s. 6d.

——. *Selections* (for Schools). With Notes and Maps. By J. S. PHILLPOTTS, B.C.L. *Fourth Edition.* . . . [Extra fcap. 8vo, 3s. 6d.
A Key to Sections I-III, for Teachers only, price 2s. 6d. net.

—— *Anabasis,* Book I. With Introduction, Notes, and Map. By J. MARSHALL, M.A. . . . . [Extra fcap. 8vo, 2s. 6d.

—— *Anabasis,* Book II. With Notes and Map. By C. S. JERRAM, M.A. . . . . [Extra fcap. 8vo, 2s.

—— *Anabasis,* Book III. With Introduction, Analysis, Notes, &c. By J. MARSHALL, M.A. . . . . . . [Extra fcap. 8vo, 2s. 6d.

—— *Anabasis,* Book IV. With Introduction, Notes, &c. By the same Editor. . . . . [Extra fcap. 8vo, 2s.

———— Books III and IV. By the same Editor. [Extra fcap. 8vo, 3s.

—— *Vocabulary to the Anabasis.* By the same Editor. . [1s. 6d.

—— *Cyropaedia,* Book I. With Introduction and Notes. By C. BIGG, D.D. . . . . [Extra fcap. 8vo, 2s.

—— *Cyropaedia,* Books IV, V. With Introduction and Notes. By the same Editor. . . . . [Extra fcap. 8vo, 2s. 6d.

—— *Hellenica,* Books I, II. With Introduction and Notes. By G. E. UNDERHILL, M.A. . . . . . . [Extra fcap. 8vo, 3s.

—- *Memorabilia.* Edited for the use of Schools, with Introduction and Notes, &c. by J. MARSHALL, M.A. . . . [Extra fcap. 8vo, 4s. 6d.

𝕺𝖝𝖋𝖔𝖗𝖉
AT THE CLARENDON PRESS
𝕷𝖔𝖓𝖉𝖔𝖓, 𝕰𝖉𝖎𝖓𝖇𝖚𝖗𝖌𝖍, 𝖆𝖓𝖉 𝕹𝖊𝖜 𝖄𝖔𝖗𝖐
HENRY FROWDE